PALESTINE TO ISRAEL

Mandate to State, 1945-1948

Touro University Press Books

Series Editors

Michael A. Shmidman, PhD (Touro College, New York)
Simcha Fishbane, PhD (Touro College, New York)

PALESTINE TO ISRAEL

Mandate to State, 1945-1948

Volume II: Into the International Arena, 1947-1948

MONTY NOAM PENKOWER

New York
2019

Library of Congress Cataloging-in-Publication Data

Names: Penkower, Monty Noam, 1942- author.

Title: Palestine to Israel : mandate to state, 1945-1948 / Monty N. Penkower.

Description: New York, NY : Touro University Press, 2019. |

Series: Touro University Press books

Identifiers: LCCN 2018023261 (print) | LCCN 2018032209 (ebook) | ISBN 9781618118752 (ebook) | ISBN 9781618118738 | ISBN 9781618118738 (volume 1 : hardcover) | ISBN 9781618118745 (volume 1 : pbk.) | ISBN 9781618118769 (volume 2 : hardcover) | ISBN 9781618118776 (volume 2 : paperback)

Subjects: LCSH: Palestine—History—1929-1948. | Israel—History—1948-1967.

Classification: LCC DS126.4 (ebook) | LCC DS126.4 .P435 2018 (print) | DDC 956.94/04—dc23

LC record available at https://lccn.loc.gov/2018023261

ISBN (hardback) 9781618118738 (vol. I)
ISBN (hardback) 9781618118769 (vol. II)
ISBN (paperback) 9781618118745 (vol. I)
ISBN (paperback) 9781618118776 (vol. II)
ISBN (electronic) 9781618118752

Book design by Kryon Publishing Services (P) Ltd.
www.kryonpublishing.com
Cover design by Ivan Grave

Published by Touro University Press and Academic Studies Press.
Typeset, printed and distributed by Academic Studies Press.
Touro University Press
Michael A. Shmidman and Simcha Fishbane, Editors
320 West 31st Street, Fourth Floor,
New York, NY 10001, USA
touropress.admin@touro.edu

Academic Studies Press
28 Montfern Avenue
Brighton, MA 02135, USA
press@academicstudiespress.com
www.academicstudiespress.com

To the Cherished Memory of

Yael Goodman Penkower (1945–2016)

"Most blessed of women be Yael" (*Judges* 5:24)

Table of Contents

Volume I: Rebellion Launched, 1945–1946

Volume II: Into the International Arena, 1947–1948

6. To the United Nations

The continuing deterioration of law and order in Palestine found the Colonial Civil and War Offices at loggerheads in the Defence Committee's meeting on New Year's Day 1947. Creech Jones cautioned that the adoption of more aggressive tactics against terrorism would upset the political balance, weaken the Jewish moderates, and make achieving a settlement more difficult. Montgomery, echoing Secretary of State for War A. V. Alexander, charged *per contra* that the country was "in the grip of lawlessness," and he called for mobile columns of troops to deal swiftly with outrages. The retention of Palestine was strategically essential to HMG's position in the Middle East, Bevin argued, a region without whose oil and other resources the British domestic standard of living they were aiming for could not be achieved. Moreover, he stressed, the government had to realize that any solution it was going to impose would be met with opposition from both Jews and Arabs. "To continue the present policy placed the Armed Forces in an impossible position," Attlee concluded. Alexander received a green light to prepare a revised directive, working in conjunction with Creech Jones and Cunningham, for submission to the committee and the Cabinet. Montgomery's draft two days later authorized the High Commissioner to take "all possible steps" by the police and the military against law breakers "to ensure that the initiative lies with the forces of the Crown."[1]

In Bevin's view, Great Britain's great economic difficulties necessitated a Palestine policy that favored the Arabs. Three weeks earlier, he and the Chiefs of Staff Committee had both advised Attlee that the 84,000 troops in Egypt had to be completely evacuated by September 1949, with General Headquarters moved to the Canal Zone as soon as possible. "Nothing to bargain with—no credits, coal or goods," his memorandum to the Cabinet read on January 1, and Anglo-American negotiations were pending as to British sterling balances. The Mediterranean problem would have been easier, he asserted, if HMG had claimed Cyrenaica by conquest "and let Egypt and Palestine go." One hope lay in the protection by recent postwar treaties regarding Jewish property in Rumania and Hungary, which he thought would help the Palestine problem. Most important, he and Minister of Fuel and Power Shinwell advised the Cabinet in a joint paper on the 7th, the Middle East was likely to provide "a greater proportion of the total world increase of production than any other oil-producing region," Saudi Arabia, Bahrain, Kuwait, and Iraq becoming the world's major oil producers by 1950. Offending the Arabs, they emphasized, "by appearing to encourage Jewish settlement and to endorse the Jewish aspiration for a separate State," would entail grave risks. An analysis signed by Beeley on January 2 for Attlee, advocating a unitary state in Palestine as called for in the Arab plan, reflected Bevin's preference. Yet the Foreign Secretary also had to satisfy the primary concern of the Chiefs of Staff: might the Mandate be surrendered and at the same time allow for safeguarding Britain's strategic needs in Palestine and wider interests in the region? Any Palestine solution, the Joint Planning Staffs' memorandum of the 5th stated, "must ensure the retention of the goodwill of the Arab world."[2]

Cunningham had no desire to hand over matters to the military, he told Fishman just before leaving for consultations in London, but he worried what might happen if the terrorist outbreaks continued. (To Creech Jones, he described Zionism as a movement where "the forces of nationalism are accompanied by the psychology of the Jew, which it is important to recognize as something quite abnormal and unresponsive to rational treatment.") At a conference in the Colonial Office on the 3rd, he dissented from Montgomery's offer of the "whole strength of the British Army" if necessary to mount thorough searches throughout Palestine, "turning the place upside down," without waiting for evidence. The Army had not been unduly restricted there, he claimed, and general searches would merely disturb innocent people and mean "a general conflagration." It would probably lead to the evacuation of British women and children, as well as warfare throughout the country, thus destroying the hope of a political settlement. He agreed to Montgomery's draft that "all possible steps" would be taken to establish and maintain law and order, but he was not prepared to give the military commander in Palestine a free hand, since as High Commissioner he had to "take into account the political aspect." The decision as to how the revised directive would most effectively be carried out now rested with the Cabinet.[3]

Backing Cunningham, Creech Jones pointed out that there had recently been a stiffening of the *yishuv* moderates and the growth of a hatred of terrorism. In the Colonial Secretary's interview with Ben-Gurion the previous day, the newly reelected Agency Executive chairman had denounced terrorism and so had the recent World Zionist Congress in Basle. Explaining to Creech Jones that Weizmann had been defeated at the Congress because of his "blind trust" in Britain, Ben-Gurion had asked for free immigration to Palestine and cultivation of the soil, together with the *yishuv*'s right to shape its own life as freely as any other free people. He proposed that so long as no change occurred in British policy, informal talks with the Agency could be held instead of attendance at the resumed London Conference. The Executive was not bound to any formula, not even to the idea of a Jewish commonwealth. The Congress had ruled out a trusteeship, Ben-Gurion explained, and if HMG could not be bound by the Mandate in ruling Palestine, then "there must be a Jewish State." Martin, present along with Gater, noted that Ben-Gurion's attitude throughout was one of "marked cordiality." The Zionist leader had referred several times to the natural sympathy between the Jews and the British people, and expressed his belief that, if only the British government would trust the Jews, there would be a growth of confidence on both sides and hope of a settlement.[4]

The Foreign Secretary's initial suggestions for a long-term policy surfaced when meeting Cunningham the next day, Creech Jones also in attendance. Hearing the High Commissioner explain his differences with Montgomery and his claim that only a definitive political settlement would finally end terrorism, Bevin suggested that provincial autonomy should be carried out as an interim arrangement designed to lead to partition within a reasonably short period. The Jewish and Arab provinces, each responsible for law and order in their specific area, would have a right to "secede" after some such period as five years. HMG would have difficulty at the UN in proposing immediate partition, he explained, but if the conclusion were reached that it should be put into effect immediately, London should try to induce Washington to make the proposal in the first instance. Discussion which followed of steps to make partition more palatable to certain of the Arab states included the port of Aqaba to be ceded to Ibn

Saud; Abdullah relinquishing some of south Jordan to the Wahhabi monarch in return for getting parts of Palestine; and the cession to Syria of the northeastern corner of Palestine including the Huleh Basin, with the Jews being compensated for the loss of the Huleh by incorporating in their area parts of western Galilee. Hearing that Ben-Gurion and Executive colleagues were prepared to enter unconditionally into exploratory talks, Bevin declared that it was essential to open discussions with the Jews. He thought it of no consequence if this took place within the framework of the conference or on some other footing, and asked Creech Jones to make sure that the Jewish Agency delegation would be available in London at the time of the conference.[5]

In Palestine, British all-day curfews in Tel Aviv and Rehovot on January 1–2 and the screening there of more than 4,000 men did nothing to check the storm clouds gathering again across that troubled landscape. Concerted attacks by the Irgun and the Stern Group took place against military installations in Tel Aviv, Jerusalem, Haifa, Tiberias, and Hadera. One British officer and a Jewish constable were killed, and many people wounded. A police mobile truck and a troop-carrier were blown up by road-mines. Another whole-day search in Tel Aviv screened 3,000 people; 62 were detained. Gurney warned Fishman and Ben-Zvi that he could not hold back the Army for long, and asked Myerson and Remez on the 7th for a halt to "refugee ships." The *yishuv* understood that terror damaged its cause from a political and moral point of view, she responded, but the emotion of a "Jewish heart" after the dispatch of a boat of refugees was greater than political instinct. Those in the DP camps could not wait; their arrival posed no danger to any Palestinian Arab, but for the Jew "this is a question of life." Time worked in the Arabs' favor, Myerson added, whereas we lacked power to insure that in a short time there would truly be a good solution. Gurney repeated that he understood the Jewish needs and views, but their demands were beyond his powers.[6]

As for the death sentence passed on January 1 by the Jerusalem Military Court on Dov Gruner, a former lance corporal in the British Army's Italian campaign who had been badly wounded while taking part in the Irgun attack on the Ramat Gan police station in April 1946, the final word rested with G. O. C. Barker. The accused had refused to recognize the court's authority, and only made a brief statement, concluding thus: "There is no force in the world that can break the link between the people of Israel and its one and only country. He who attempts it—his hand will be cut off and the curse of God will fall on him for ever and ever."[7]

Remarkably, at this very moment Attlee challenged the basic assumptions of the Chiefs of Staff and the Imperial Defence College regarding HMG's Near Eastern policy. One month earlier, he had advised "my dear Ernest" that he disagreed with the Chiefs' wish to keep British forces in Greece for at least another year, and considered that the strategic importance of communications through the Mediterranean in terms of modern warfare were very much overrated by his military advisers. Continuing to maintain heavy military commitments in the region with large sums of money against a possible Russian attack, the endeavor to keep British influence over "weak, backward and reactionary states," he now deemed "a strategy of despair." This included keeping two divisions in Palestine, his TOP SECRET memorandum observed on January 5, where Britain had either to offend the Arab states and possibly Turkey and Persia as well, or offend world Jewry "with its powerful influence in the USA." He wished to explore the possibility of negotiations with Stalin, seeking to discover if it were possible to persuade the USSR that Britain had no offensive intentions against it; if an easing of Russia's internal economic situation would cause this country to be less ready to "throw away what she has gained"; and if Moscow could be convinced that war with the United States was not inevitable. If satisfactory answers could be given to these questions, Attlee concluded, perhaps HMG could secure an agreement as to oil rights in Persia, settle the Dardanelles Straits question on principles applicable to all major international waterways, and get some degree of unity and economic cooperation in Germany and elsewhere in Europe.[8]

Without dealing with the strategic side of the question, Bevin replied at length in a "top secret" response four days later after his leading officials had met to discuss the matter, asserting that the political arguments against these proposals seemed to him "overwhelming." Attlee's memorandum reversed the whole policy that the Foreign Secretary had been pursuing in the Middle East with the Cabinet's consent, a program aimed at strengthening that region's economic development on the basis of independent states and at taking the lead in any UN regional defense scheme. When London had resolved issues with Egypt and Iraq "and if we settle Palestine," very little British manpower would be involved. HMG had to be able to mount a counter-offensive against Russia if required; evacuation of the area would gift the manpower and oil of the region to Moscow, making a difference of "100 millions in the government's balance sheet" and possibly a great difference in HMG's future dollar earnings. Help to the countries in that area could make them once again economically prosperous and a valuable market for Britain. It would be as idle to place reliance on gaining British security by large-scale, one-sided concessions to Russia as it was with Hitler, while improvements in that dictatorship's internal situation would make Moscow more aggressive. Only the Americans could perhaps dissuade the Russian leaders that war with the United States was not inevitable.

Many further objections arose regarding a British withdrawal from the Middle East, Bevin went on. It would be "Munich over again, only on a world scale," with Greece, Turkey, and Persia as the first victims in place of Czechoslovakia. The United States, on which Britain was dependent economically and militarily, would "write us off entirely." India would gravitate toward Russia; the UN would be imperiled; Egypt and all of Africa might fall under Communist control; the effect on the Dominions would be "incalculable." HMG was withdrawing from Egypt, soon would be doing so in Greece, "and then we shall only have troops in Palestine." In proportion as the Americans realized the importance to them of this area, we could expect them to bear a greater part of the burden. Rather than "leading from weakness," negotiating with Stalin could take place once the British economy and that of Europe were revived, and Moscow finally realized that it could not drive a wedge between Washington and London. "There is no hurry," Bevin concluded. Everything suggested that the Russians were "drawing in their horns" and had no immediate aggressive intentions. Great Britain should focus on restoring its strength, and, with American help as necessary, meanwhile hold on to essential positions and concentrate on building up the UN organization.[9]

That very afternoon, Attlee, Bevin, and Alexander met to discuss the Middle East. No other officials were present and no minutes were taken, but the Foreign Secretary confided in his Principal Private Secretary Pierson Dixon, who had drafted the earlier reply to the Prime Minister, its conclusions. There would be no withdrawals of British forces from the Middle East in excess of the programs already contemplated, the policy regarding oil should be reviewed with particular reference to the building up of underground stocks in crude oil in Great Britain, and Alexander would examine the position in consultation with the Oil Committee. Attlee was, however, "still not satisfied" that HMG's overall defense plans required continuance of the government's policy in the Middle East, and it was agreed that the discussion would be continued with the Chiefs of Staff present. A meeting of Attlee, Bevin, and Alexander with the Chiefs on January 13 endorsed the military's view of the Middle East and its defense requirements, Chief of the Air Staff Lord Tedder again emphasizing the need not to alienate the Arab states whatever the final policy arrived at. Attlee suggested that a provisional autonomy scheme might secure British military rights if satisfactory treaties (as hoped for after India's imminent reception of independence) could be negotiated with the successor states.[10]

In Palestine, a hoped-for truce from terrorist attacks lasted but a brief time. The Hagana's warning on the 4th that the *yishuv*'s patience with the "separatist bodies" was nearly at an end, as well as Silver's strong speech in like vein after meeting with the sympathetic Inverchapel, had led to a general belief that the dissidents would again agree to await the outcome of the London negotiations. Gurney's cancelling the sentence of flogging passed by a military court on an Irgun youth of 17 indicated, according to an editorial in *HaAretz*, that "civilian flexibility and insight have smoothed military stubbornness." Returning briefly to Palestine after a second talk with Creech Jones on the 8th, Ben-Gurion declared over the mandatory's radio broadcast system in Tel Aviv that informal talks with HMG would continue, that the political struggle now included the UN, and that unity was called for in order to achieve the Basle Congress's resolutions as conducted by the nation's "elected representatives." This respite abruptly changed on January 12, when a powerful LEHI bomb concealed in an RAF van blew up in the District Police Security Compound in Haifa, killing two British and two Arab policemen and wounding more than 100. Two days later, a military court sentenced another seventeen-year-old Irgun fighter to life imprisonment and eighteen strokes for firing at employees of the Ottoman Bank the previous September; the whipping was revoked because of his poor health, and only his age saved Yehuda Katz from the death penalty.[11]

The continued assaults united a Cabinet otherwise still divided over a long-range solution for Palestine. With Montgomery leading the charge on January 15, it unanimously agreed that any terrorist convinced of capital offense would be put to death. Searches could be conducted at any time with, as the CIGS put it, "more robust action" and patrols increased in dangerous areas, although supreme control still rested in Cunningham's hands. Bevin's championing a bi-national unitary State found in Creech Jones a strong voice for partition on the grounds that otherwise illegal Jewish immigration and tension would not subside. (A recent British conference in Paris to check that traffic, Fierst confided to Epstein, had found the French in agreement, but State's George Warren insisted that the Americans' responsibility lay only in their German zone.) Dalton and Shinwell supported a Jewish state "however small it might be," while Bevan warned of "a general outbreak" of antisemitism in Great Britain if the mandatory had to resort to repressive force, and of the likely rise of extremist leadership within the *yishuv* if this opportunity for "a compromise solution" were lost. A friendly Jewish commonwealth in Palestine, he added, would give HMG a safer military base, whereas an Arab Palestine might pass to Russian influence. Alexander disagreed, repeating his department's view that "the goodwill of the Arab world" had to be retained from a defense point of view. One day later, the Colonial Secretary's memorandum argued that adoption of Bevin's plan would lead to "disorder and bloodshed on a scale which we could never contemplate"; be "a gross betrayal" of the Jews, who would be "handed over to the mercy" of an Arab state run by the former Mufti; poison relations with the United States; and betray past Labour Party pledges to the Jews. If the UN rejected what was the one solution which possessed "an element of finality," he closed, it would have the obligation to find an alternative.[12]

Since the legal advisors of the Foreign and Colonial Offices, with the approval of the Lord Chancellor and the Attorney-General, had just concluded that a discussion of Palestine would take place in the UN whatever course the government adopted, Bevin raised the question of the possible result of reference to that world organization. In his view, partition would not get the required two-thirds majority vote in the General Assembly for passage. The "whole temper" of the GA opposed creating religious states, and "Jewry is a religion," while "apart from Hitler persecution" no kinship existed between a Polish and a French Jew. A Palestine state with equal rights for Arab and Jew, save that Jews should not have uncontrolled right of immigration, could gain approval. Difficulties with the UN, Creech Jones responded, would exist no matter the solution HMG put forward. Noel-Baker thought that partition might go through, as did Shinwell, but Attlee observed that the Arabs and India would object, and probably the Slavs, too. The Slav nations would oppose partition because they wished Arab oil, Bevin opined, and, personally doubting that the United States could control the Philippines or China, he judged that the two-thirds majority could not be obtained. No conclusion was drawn, although a memorandum prepared by Beeley the next day, in consultation with the Colonial Office, observed that probable negative votes among the 55 member states for partition (17), a unitary state (16), or provisional autonomy (17), with a number of abstentions, would see any of these British proposals defeated. The calculation assumed that Washington would oppose the second proposal, but if it opposed the first or third, the number of adverse votes would be considerably larger. Conversely, if the United States were to abstain from voting against the second, the opposition to a unitary state would be appreciably reduced.[13]

The State Department did not wish to intervene at this stage, hewing to Byrnes's advice to Silver on January 6th that the Jews should attend the London Conference. The Secretary did not press HMG, as the Zionist leader had requested, to announce their inclination toward partition, but did inform a receptive Inverchapel that he supported Silver's other suggestion that Britain release a substantial number of immigrants currently in Cyprus detention camps. The Arab Office in Washington protested the mandatory's expenditures for the refugees held on that island, bringing Epstein's rejoinder that the *yishuv* was paying 75–80 percent of the total taxes in Palestine to the government. Shertok's personal appeal to Acheson on the 15th to intercede with London to reach a solution favorable to the Jews at this "critical time" and effect the immediate transfer of 100,000 Jews to Palestine met with a refusal as well. The Under Secretary, whose "decidedly reserved attitude" surprised his guest, was convinced that Britain was "sincere" in reaching a solution at this time, and so it would serve "no useful purpose" for Washington to approach the Attlee government.[14]

Told by Emir Feisal two days later that the Arab world opposed Zionism because it had certain connections with communism, was anti-democratic, aggressive, and totalitarian, and was anti-God, Byrnes replied that he knew from personal experience that by means of frank discussions it was "frequently possible" for parties with different views to find solutions for problems "which on their face appeared insoluble."

When the prince retorted that the Arabs would not sit down with the Zionists and "merely" asked that the British halt Jewish immigration, Byrnes noted that the Jews would not attend the conference unless a Jewish state was to be established in Palestine. He still felt that no matter how divergent their opposing views, it would be "helpful to talk the matter over." He concluded that because Palestine represented one of the most difficult of international problems in the world today, it should be approached "with moderation and a conciliatory spirit."[15]

On January 21, the same day that General George C. Marshall, the highly regarded former U. S. Army Chief of Staff whom Frankfurter was certain would handle every problem "on its merits," succeeded Byrnes, Inverchapel heard from Acheson how the United States would vote in the General Assembly. He was sure that Washington would consider partition the "easiest" to put into effect and therefore the easiest to back. Washington would equally support a bi-national state "looking to eventual partition" if this state failed in its dual task of satisfying Jew and Arab alike. One of these two solutions should emerge from the coming talks in London, because failure would prolong the present state of affairs, which would be "disastrous" for the entire region. The adoption of either plan would cause "commotion and violent denunciations," but eventual acquiescence "might safely be counted upon." The entry of 100,000 Jewish refugees into Palestine "in a comparatively short time," and some reasonable immigration thereafter, was essential to any possible solution. Despite Arab fears, they already had a substantial majority in the country and their birth rate was considerably higher than the Jewish. In his view, for Britain to surrender the Mandate to the Assembly without recommendations almost amounted to a confession that a solution was not possible, and presented an invitation to "a great deal of confusion." Acheson could go no further than that, confessed to ignorance of the new Secretary of State's views about Palestine, and agreed to consult his superior and Truman at once.[16]

When the Cabinet discussion resumed on January 22, Bevin and Creech Jones consented to try in their talks with the Arabs and Jews to move each side from their present "irreconcilable" positions. The Foreign Secretary expressed himself not opposed to partition on its merits, but was impressed by the difficulty of imposing any solution against the active opposition of either rival Palestinian community, envisaging "first class difficulty whichever way it goes." The Colonial

Secretary still backed a solution along the lines of partition, which Shinwell favored with the argument that recent British experiences in Egypt and India had indicated that, unlike a Jewish state, a unitary state with an Arab majority would not necessarily remain friendly to HMG or allow it to maintain a strategic base in Palestine and the vital oil port at Haifa. Attlee cautioned not to rely on the continuing friendship of Palestine's Jews, who were "mainly European and may well turn to Russia." Bevin: "These U.S. Jews are hostile and disloyal." Shinwell: "In two wars Jews were on our side. Could you rely as much on Arabs?" The Cabinet ultimately agreed that, failing an agreed settlement at the London talks, "any solution would have to come before the United Nations." Given "the internal situation" in Palestine, it was likely that the issue would call for a special session before the GA was due to meet next in September.[17]

Truman continued to believe that regardless of which group might be in the numerical majority at any given time in Palestine, "one of the most difficult problems" currently faced by the world, all living there should have similar opportunities and freedoms. Disagreeing with Ibn Saud's further accusation that the Zionists wished to use their state in Palestine as a base for aggression against the neighboring Arab countries, he replied at length on January 24 that "no people has suffered more than the Jews during recent years from aggression and intolerance" or "stands more in need of world sympathy and support at the present time." It was therefore "inconceivable" that responsible Jewish leaders would contemplate acts of aggression against Arabs, which would certainly provoke indignation throughout the world. The terrorist acts by "certain irresponsible groups" in Palestine were by no means indicative of the temper of world Jewry or symbolic of Jewish aspirations respecting Palestine. His own various statements, including that at least 100,000 European Jewish refugees should be admitted there, were not inconsistent with the U.S. Government's commitment to consult both Arabs and Jews before a change occurred in the basic situation in Palestine. Past attempts that had failed in this regard only served to emphasize the urgency of the problem, as well as the necessity for a solution without protracted delay. Truman ended with the assurance that the people of the United States desired to maintain and strengthen their feelings of friendship toward the monarch, the peoples of Saudi Arabia, and the rulers and peoples of all Arab lands.[18]

Cunningham informed Ben-Gurion that his stance in London had averted the imposition of martial law, and the Va'ad HaLeumi announced on the 20th that force would be used against those terrorizing the *yishuv*, but two kidnappings on January 25–26 brought Palestine to the brink. After Barker confirmed Gruner's death sentence on the 24th, with execution set for the 28th, the Irgun snatched retired Major H.A.I. Collins and then Judge Ralph Windham in a plan to thwart Gruner's hanging. The High Commissioner convoked Myerson, Kaplan, and Tel Aviv's Mayor Israel Rokach to deliver an ultimatum that unless the two men were returned unharmed within forty-eight hours, martial law would be introduced in Tel Aviv, Petah Tikva, and Ramat Gan, an unprecedented step in the Mandate's history. The Jewish Agency Executive and Rokach immediately issued unequivocal condemnations of the "demented desperadoes" responsible, and called for the captives' release without delay. Both men were freed after it was announced on the 27th that Barker had granted a stay of execution, intimating that Gruner could appeal to the Privy Council in London. Convinced of the Irgun's threat to "turn Palestine into a bloodbath" if Gruner were hanged, Cunningham proposed to Creech Jones on the 27th that all British women, children, and nonessential personnel be evacuated from Palestine and the remainder concentrated behind barbed-wire enclaves. The *yishuv* would derisively call these "Bevingrads." Montgomery railed in a letter to Creech Jones against Cunningham's response to the Gruner case and the kidnappings; a polite reply followed. The CIGS only agreed to retract both missives in response to Attlee's argument that they could impact adversely on the London talks and a critical debate in the House that was about to take place.[19]

The Arabs' first meeting with Bevin, Creech Jones, and Brook on January 27 yielded no results. Informed by the Foreign Secretary that HMG still suspended a final decision until it had heard the views of Palestine's Arabs and Jews, Husseini expressed his people's desire for self-government and their "inflexible" opposition to partition. Al-Khoury noted that the Arab delegation had already given its views last September, and did not wish to have further discussions until receiving the British government's response. If the "usual democratic principles" were denied to the people of Palestine and the situation deteriorated still further, he warned, the people would be compelled "to resort to their own means to defend themselves." The Arab mood was generally gloomy, Beeley reported to Gallman; Azzam and some of the other leaders had not come because they did not like the prospect of being associated with a conference which they felt was bound to fail. In private conversations, the delegates indicated that if Gruner were not executed, it would be a sign of British appeasement to Jewish terrorism and Zionist demands for partition, and the Arabs "will know what to do." Bevin's statement that the best solution lay in Morrison-Grady, but if the London talks failed HMG would transfer the Palestine problem to the UN, did not deter the delegation. They considered that possible referral to be to their advantage, al-Khoury told Sasson. The Syrian diplomat saw no prospect of a compromise between the Jews and the Arabs in Palestine, he added, and the Arabs had not given up the option of using violence and a Palestinian Arab uprising to exert pressure on the UN and on Great Britain.[20]

Ben-Gurion opened the Jews' first meeting of exploratory talks two days later with a call for 100,000 immediately and a large-scale immigration from Europe and the oriental countries of 1.2 million, Palestine's full development to benefit the entire area, and statehood for the one people whose "whole fate and existence" were bound up in that country. When told that all the lights had gone out due to a fuel shortage during Britain's coldest winter in decades, Bevin said "Except the Israelites," then fell into a paroxysm of husky laughter in which no one else joined. He countered Ben-Gurion by claiming that two viable states could not be created there; partition would never receive UN approval; the Arab states would object "intensely"; Zionist schemes to increase absorptive capacity were impractical; and the 1.2 million figure "was out of the question." He favored a variant of Morrison-Grady, and tried unsuccessfully to have the Agency submit a partition scheme "without prejudice."

Deeming the present state of affairs "intolerable," Creech Jones vehemently rejected Ben-Gurion's suggestion to return to the pre-White Paper regime, saying that HMG was no longer prepared to maintain an administration in Palestine which had no roots in the country's people and thus operate contrary to democratic principles. Reiterating that his reputation was staked on finding a solution for Palestine and his opinion that the Balfour Declaration's promising "the same thing to two peoples" was "a disastrous policy," Bevin remarked that he would have been prepared to accept the entire Anglo-American Commission report, but Washington chose to endorse only the 100,000 recommendation. What guarantees could the Jews offer, he wondered, that they would not use their wealth in America to buy up the Arabs and create a "landless proletariat"? Reporting soon thereafter to Gallman, Shertok and Neumann thought that with Bevin clearly "the boss" and HMG "apparently" planning to reject both Mandate and partition, the time might soon arrive for US intervention.[21]

At their second meeting on January 30, Bevin told the Arabs that their plan would meet with immediate Jewish resistance, similar to the Arabs' response to any Jewish expansion such as partition. HMG was therefore faced with the unwelcome prospect of imposing some solution; any decision would have to be referred to the UN. Would they consider, just as he had asked the Jews, a bi-national central government combined with a large measure of local autonomy for the two communities? Any solution would be difficult so long as the Jews were armed, Husseini responded, to which Creech Jones commented that it was almost impossible to disarm the Jews. Taking up this point, the AHC official wondered if the government was sincerely endeavoring to find a solution on the basis of the basis of right and justice, or whether it was following an appeasement policy under Jewish armed threats. The Arab representatives reserved comment on Bevin's statement, and at the meeting's end it was agreed that they would prepare a reply for early the next week. The delegates from Syria and Iraq, Beeley thought, seemed especially depressed, but all were gloomy. Until all avenues were explored, he told Gallman, the Cabinet continued to keep an open mind and suspend final judgment.[22]

Ben-Gurion detailed the Zionists' objections to the unitary state proposal when the two sides met on February 3, and reverted to his earlier criteria of large-scale immigration, development, and sovereignty. If this were not accepted, the Jews, who had a special status in Palestine, would welcome a return to the Mandate "for a few years," with full rights in the country "without exception." This was "aggression," Bevin responded, just like the white men driving out the Red Indians in the United States. (His courteous guests did not counter by noting HMG's occupying and colonizing significant parts of the globe, and particularly the British massacre of indigenous Aboriginal Australians in Tasmania.) Partition itself, which went "far beyond" the terms of the Mandate, he considered a "counsel of despair," and London would not impose a solution requiring the mandatory to take up arms against Arabs.

When Creech Jones remarked that the Jewish zone in a unitary state would have a large measure of freedom for immigration, Bevin objected that there should be specific limits just as in the present White Paper. He also quickly disagreed with the Colonial Secretary's thought that if either community wished to secede after a trial period of five to ten years this might be possible. Britain did not need Palestine strategically, Bevin declared (thereby disagreeing with the Chiefs of Staff), and was prepared to throw the problem into the UN without recommendations because that body would be entitled to re-examine the question afresh. Ben-Gurion's ending appeal as one Socialist Laborite to another failed to move the Foreign Secretary, concerned as he was with the "practical politics" of the situation. Reference to the UN might involve very serious delay, Creech Jones noted, and in the present deteriorating position HMG had been "left to carry the baby." "The trouble," Bevin added, "was the baby was twins—by different fathers."[23]

The Arabs stood their ground when replying formally to Bevin on February 4. Al-Khoury set the tone by stating that their September proposals represented the "only just and equitable settlement." Delegates from Iraq, Lebanon, Syria, and Egypt elaborated on some of his points. Husseini claimed that, even if no more immigrants were admitted, the present congestion on Arab farm land in Palestine would get worse in the next twenty years due to high Arab fertility. Did not the mandatory under a Socialist government, he asked, feel responsible for this social problem? One Arab member's stating that "partition means war" drew applause from his colleagues. Bevin appealed for a more yielding attitude on the part of the delegation, noting that British public opinion believed that further Jewish immigration should take place. He was determined to evolve a proposal for a solution which would commend itself "to all reasonable people." Within a few days and after consulting the Cabinet, he would present British proposals "in some form" to them. (To the Jews, Bevin had spoken of presenting a "personal paper" without commitment, but had now changed his mind.) Whitehall's draft, Beeley confided in Gallman the next day, envisaged a bi-national unitary state with early increased Jewish immigration. The proposals would not satisfy either side, he thought, but they represented "a fair and just approach." With the first phase of the conference over, the Cabinet now had to agree on final proposals for presentation to the two contesting parties.[24]

The government's prolonged delay in announcing a long-term policy had drawn heavy criticism in the Parliamentary debate on January 31. Four days after the London *Times* came out for partition in light of the continuing danger faced by British troops and police, Crossman charged that if by procrastination "we let Palestine go down in ruins it is a poor sort of humanity and democracy that we are practicing." From the other side of the aisle, Manningham-Buller agreed that the Mandate was no longer tenable. Having "broken our pledges to the Jews," Churchill, echoing Stanley, again urged the MPs to give definite notice that if the United States refused to take a half share of "the bloodshed, odium, trouble, expense and worry," HMG should lay the Mandate at the feet of the UN within six months.[25]

That afternoon, Palestine radio announced the evacuation which Cunningham had requested of Creech Jones four days earlier, "so that the Government and armed forces will not be hampered in their task of maintaining order." Evacuees joked that this Operation Polly really was an acronym for "Panic Over Lots of Lousy Yids," but Robert W. Hamilton, the mandatory's director of antiquities, privately excoriated the policy of "scuttle," which could only bring HMG and the British people "into contempt" and convince the Arabs to protect themselves, as before, by armed rebellion. *Al-Difa'a* termed it "a great defeat" for the local administration. Concurrently, launching Operation Cantonment, troops set up barbed wire fences enclosing extensive residential areas in Jerusalem. "It is our business to see that the King's writ runs in this country," Cunningham declared to Chief Ashkenazi Rabbi Isaac Herzog. A sense once more of alarmed uncertainty pervaded the *yishuv*.[26]

In a press statement on February 2, Myerson worried that the Jewish community found itself threatened with possible martial law, but they could not "all become informers" at the government's request to cooperate against terrorism. The Chief Rabbinate appealed to the dissidents to halt the spilling of innocent blood and placing the *yishuv* "in danger of ruin and destruction." Gurney's communication the next day with the High Commissioner's approval, asking the Agency and the Va'ad HaLeumi to "state categorically" whether they were prepared "within seven days" to publicly call on the Jewish community to aid in "locating and bringing to justice" the members of the terrorist groups, understandably sounded like an ultimatum. Alerted to the Agency's fear that both operations were preparatory moves to an action against the *yishuv* which would commence upon the failure of the London talks, Silver sought Marshall's help on the 4th to "restrain the British." The new Secretary of State confidentially told him of Acheson's reply on January 21 to Inverchapel, but gave no further indication of what was in his mind except to say that "too much had appeared in the press already."[27]

Myerson wired Lourie on the 6th that an immediate intensive propaganda drive in America was essential, emphasizing that the evacuation of civilians was a "smoke-screen" to destroy the Agency and crush the *yishuv*, perhaps with a view to establishing military bases in Palestine. In fact, Marshall was glad to hear from Gallman one day earlier that the Colonial Office thought Cunningham would only place certain areas under military administration if "disturbances" took place, and he advised that HMG issue a statement to calm the waters. Creech Jones indeed told Parliament the next day that the letter from Gurney was doubtless Cunningham's last effort to prevent the situation from getting out of control while the London talks were going on. This eased the tension suddenly.[28]

On February 7, the same day that Hagana members created three more settlements in the Negev, the Cabinet endorsed the joint memorandum of a day earlier by Bevin and Creech Jones for a five-year trusteeship leading to a unitary state, with a 4,000-monthly immigration for two years and then approval by the High Commissioner and a local Advisory Council. (The latter, Bevin explained to Marshall, would end the Jewish Agency's status of representing Jews worldwide.) Any dispute could be settled by a UN-appointed arbitrator. Persuaded by Bevin that "no hope" existed for an agreed settlement between Arabs and Jews, the members concluded that HMG's strategic needs would have to be secured by a military alliance with the new state of Palestine, as had been obtained with Iraq and Jordan. If there was no measure of acquiescence in the proposals when put forward to the contending sides, it appeared that reference to the UN would be necessary.[29]

Reluctantly, Creech Jones informed Cunningham, he had concluded that any scheme of partition satisfactory to the Jews would be "demonstrably unfair to the Arabs" owing to the present distribution of population. Moreover, even if HMG were prepared to face the "resolute hostility" of the Arab world by advocating partition, it was by no means certain that London could count on the support of the Jews. In addition, Britain would have little chance of securing the necessary two-thirds majority at the UN, and reliance on full U.S. support was "doubtful." This alternative plan, he concluded, would not meet Jewish claims for sovereignty, but made "reasonable provision" for immigration and development. It was consistent with the principles of the Mandate, but added the practical promise of evolving towards independence by building up "from the bottom" political institutions rooted in the lives of the people.[30]

Attempting not to be overwhelmed by "the grim conditions" in present-day Palestine, Cunningham strongly disagreed with the Cabinet's proposals from the angle of "practicality and constructiveness." The experience of twenty-two years had shown that every attempt at mixed councils and equivalents of all sorts had failed; the question of immigration would again become acute after two years; the scheme would require some form of military administration to stop terrorism and bring weapons on both sides under control," rigorously" if this could not be done by agreement. He believed more than ever that partition gave the only hope of averting violence, and doubted the strength of the implacability, determination, or means of the Arab states to help any section of Palestine Arabs "who would be foolish enough to rebel." Arab statements "can never be taken at their face value," added Britain's top official on the spot. If HMG intended, nevertheless, to impose the proposed plan, the UN should do so rather than the mandatory, which would sooner or later be condemned to a further period of vilification and danger such as had occurred recently in the country. As to granting independence in five years, Cunningham wished to remind the Colonial Secretary of the danger of making yet another promise which quite possibly HMG would not be able to carry out and then undoubtedly be blamed for non-fulfillment.[31]

The Agency rejected the plan when meeting with the two Secretaries on February 10, Ben-Gurion observing that it moved away from Morrison-Grady—which they had already rejected—in the direction of the White Paper. Palestine was the only place in the entire world where Jews could be free and independent. The Arabs in Palestine formed less than 2 per cent of the Arab nation and its territory 1 percent of Arab territories; if there were an "unavoidable" choice, it was only just not to submit the Jews to foreign rule. He could not read the creation of a Jewish state into the Mandate, Bevin responded. He had tried to find a way to independence, but was now filled with "absolute pessimism."

If they had to go to the UN, HMG would submit all the schemes put forward and hand back the Mandate without any recommendations at all. Ben-Gurion's comment that the Jews had presented a compromise in partition drew Bevin's rejoinder that the Agency had never produced a map. The British were prepared to put on the table a draft map of their scheme "without prejudice," he replied to Locker, on condition that the Jews present theirs at the same meeting. The Jews had no plan to which the Arabs would consent, Ben-Gurion asserted, since they did not even agree to the existence of the Jews. The delegation would present its proposals after having seen the British map. The two-and-a-half hour meeting was "relatively friendly," Beeley reported to Gallman, and while there was no prospect of the Agency representatives agreeing to the British proposals, he thought "no door is yet closed."[32]

That meeting took place the following evening, Creech Jones reported to Cunningham, "with most disappointing results." When Beeley, Brook, and Harris showed the Morrison-Grady map for the Jewish province as the type of area similar to that of Jewish local administration under the new scheme, Ben-Gurion, Shertok, and Horowitz rejected it as "a mockery" of their claims. Instead of their own map, they traced the area that they were prepared to accept as a viable Jewish state. Beyond the area shown in the map, it had to include Galilee, the Gaza sub-district, the Beersheba sub-district, and the eastern portions of the Hebron and Jerusalem sub-districts up to and including the Jerusalem-Jericho road. That state, covering all of Palestine but the Judean hills, would include 600,000 to 800,000 Arabs. The Agency's response confirmed our view, the Colonial Secretary noted to Cunningham, that apart from all other difficulties, any partition scheme that HMG could defend in the UN as not being "demonstrably unfair" to the Arabs would be unacceptable to the Zionists. The same day, the government announced that many industries in Britain would be closed down and electricity cut off for five hours each day in all but essential services because of the critically short coal supplies and the whole country virtually snowbound.[33]

Realizing that Bevin was handling the Palestine question in the government, Ben-Gurion successfully secured a meeting alone with the Foreign Secretary on the morning of the 12th to see if common ground could be found for a mutually satisfactory solution. Pressed to tell what were HMG's needs and fears in Palestine, Bevin (with Beeley at his side) admitted that the British had an interest in the Negev because it had oil.

Yet every time they started to drill, "you stick in your nose and establish settlements in that area." Jewish sovereignty, Ben-Gurion replied, could best be the guardian of such imperial interests in a direct arrangement with Great Britain. Truman, who "practically stands no chance of re-election," and the Republican Party both demanded immigration into Palestine and had genuine sympathy for the Jewish case. Public opinion in Britain and the world, the Agency Executive chairman added, would not agree to the progressive *yishuv*'s being subordinated to Arab rule. Bevin disagreed with Ben-Gurion's claim that the Arabs would not rebel against a Jewish state. He resolutely stuck to the position that it was not right to place 600,000 Arabs in a Jewish state that the Mandate did not call for. It was "humiliating" for HMG to maintain 100,000 troops, "keep our people in fortresses," and send illegal immigrants away: "We cannot go on." "I cannot say that he accepted my views—he does not quickly change his opinion," Ben-Gurion wrote to his wife Paula after the seventy-minute interview, but he thought that Bevin listened with "an open mind." If HMG was not ready to adopt a decision now about the ultimate status of Palestine, the Agency's memorandum of that day urged that it continue the mandatory regime "in letter and spirit."[34]

From there, the Foreign Secretary went straight away to meet with the Arab delegation, which already on the 10th had submitted its rejection of the British proposals and again demanded a Palestine state and a complete halt to Jewish immigration. Having seen that the Arab and Jewish representatives would not agree, he declared that it might be best for HMG to stand aside and let them work out their own solution. If not, the matter must go to the UN, where HMG could not mediate as it was doing now. In Bevin's view, the Arab states that were UN members could not disclaim all responsibility for the Mandate given by the League of Nations, which some of them had joined and which now had handed over the Mandate to the UN. Husseini warned that the Arab governments could not restrain their populations much longer, while Lebanese delegate Nadim Dimechkie defended the Arab case. There could be no compromise between right and wrong, Iraq's Jamali averred when recommending that the British withdraw, convinced that the Palestine Arabs could handle the situation against the Jews and gain Arab League support if necessary. Bevin spoke strongly about the White Paper and particularly with regard to its land restrictions, which he said would have to be removed and constituted a blot on British honor and conscience. The English press gave considerable publicity to Bevin's statement.[35]

The Jewish Agency made last efforts on the 13th to block Bevin's plan. Having formally rejected it in a lengthy memorandum that day, Ben-Gurion got support in the morning from Stanley for partition and then went with his colleagues that afternoon to meet the two Secretaries. Creech Jones opened by saying that, with both sides uncompromising, they might have to recommend to the Cabinet that the matter must be brought to the notice of the UN. Ben-Gurion offered, in order of preference, that western Palestine should be turned into a Jewish state at once (*à la* the Biltmore Resolutions); the Mandate continue until a Jewish majority could then consider an independent Palestine; or, as a last resort, a viable state created with boundaries such as the Jews had indicated during the meeting two days earlier—each possibility without disturbing the position of the Arabs. Rejecting all, a frustrated Bevin concluded that Britain should give up the Mandate to the UN with no recommendations, confessing to the international organization that HMG had not succeeded. It was "a great pity" that all their efforts at the London talks had led nowhere, Creech Jones declared, and the delegation would be told the Cabinet's decision in due course. Ben-Gurion's additional suggestion to Lord Chancellor Jowitt that evening for a return to the pre-White Paper period for at least five years, during which the High Commissioner would judge immigration based on economic absorptive capacity once the 100,000 arrived within the first two, met with a rebuff: the British would leave; the Jews might defeat the Arabs, "but our hands will be clean." "If you want to leave," the Agency Executive leader responded, "we shall not stop you."[36]

Bernstein equally met with a refusal when arriving at Bevin's office that afternoon, armed with McNarney's consent, in order to seek emergency immigration into Palestine for at least the orphaned Jewish children in DP camps. The chain-smoking secretary, "a heavy set, bullish sort of man" increasingly suffering from heart trouble, shot back in that large, cold room: "Tell President Truman to take them. Your country is rich, and can use more labor…. I'll take some in England. If the U.S. will give the lead, the South American nations will follow." Plain spoken as usual, he criticized Silver and the American Zionists for running the Jewish Agency, which wanted a Jewish majority to "dominate" the Arabs and was attempting to try his hand by violence. Short of a solution such as his plan, he would permit no new immigration. His offer of 96,000 immigrants in two years, plus the 21,000 who had already slipped in, would have been enough "to keep them busy for five years. Then the tension would be relieved, and I could work things out." To Bernstein's fruitless protests, he indicated that he was going across the street to recommend to the Cabinet that HMG refer the problem to the UN. The matter could not wait any longer: "We can't afford the manpower. Too many British soldiers there. Too many of them getting shot. Anti-semitism is growing here." The Foreign Secretary stood up, a young man hurried in to help him into an overcoat, and he headed for 10 Downing Street.[37]

On the morning of the 14th, the same day that Ben-Gurion wrote Bevin to support a Jewish state and an Arab one (or the Arab area joined to Jordan), the Cabinet took up the Bevin-Creech Jones report on the London talks and their joint advice to submit the Palestine question to the UN without a specific recommendation. He had entertained hopes when the negotiations began over the last eighteen months, Bevin commenced, but American Jewry now exercised great influence in the counsels of the Jewish Agency; Arabs and Jews had hardened their positions; the U.S. Government's "interventions had only increased our difficulties." He saw Ben-Gurion's talk with Jowitt as just another effort to obtain a Jewish majority in Palestine, which was bound to excite the "active hostility" of the Arabs there. Strachey and Dalton continued to favor the Jewish claims as more reliable in securing British strategic interests. Their colleagues demurred in view of Jewish terrorism, however, with Tedder alone objecting that leaving the decision to the UN would "undermine" the foundations of Commonwealth defense. For Attlee, the status quo should be maintained, including the 1,500-monthly immigration quota, until a UN decision. Ultimately, the Cabinet agreed to submit the issue to the UN, announce their reasons in Parliament early the following week, and have Bevin consider (in order to avoid further procrastination) whether preparatory measures could be initiated by the UN so that the General Assembly could proceed to a definite discussion of the problem when it next met in September.[38]

The two Secretaries relayed this decision in a brief meeting with the Arab delegation that same day, Bevin expressing his "profound regret" that HMG had to admit failure, for the first time in British history, to solve a problem of this kind. Requested to "apply their minds" to see if the question could be solved before the GA session, all the representatives present made "solemn affirmations" that they could not be a party to a plan in which the idea of partition was given effect in any form. They objected to continuing the 1,500 immigration quota per month, to which Bevin remarked that the entry would not "upset" the situation in Palestine very much until the UN reached a decision. This would be a very difficult period, Creech Jones stated, because of the divergence of interest between the two communities, who both felt they had right and justice on their side. Britain had always sought to retain the goodwill of both parties, he declared, and only wished to secure the happiness and prosperity of Palestine, but cooperation had in practice proved very difficult to obtain. On that note, the conference ended with mutual expressions of appreciation for the cordial and friendly spirit in which the negotiations had been conducted.[39]

On the 18th, Bevin shared with the Cabinet Marshall's request that delay be shortened by submitting the Palestine issue to the Trusteeship Council rather than the GA, and that the monthly quota be increased to 3,000. (Acheson, one day after meeting with Silver, had made a first suggestion along these lines to Henderson, adding that if the additional entry produced Arab violence, the United States could ask the Security Council to rule on that as a threat to the peace within its jurisdiction.) Advised that the Council would not be competent to discuss the matter since Palestine was not the subject of a trustee agreement, Bevin decided, in view of the U.S. Secretary of State's representations, to announce merely that the question would be submitted to the UN. Bevan stood out in favoring an increase in the quota during the interim period, noting that many DPs wished to get to Palestine and that terrorism or illegal immigration would not be halted. Creech Jones responded that since the Cabinet would have to consider various problems regarding the interim period, the parliamentary debate should be held first. Bevin then informed the House of Commons in a brief statement of the Cabinet's decision of the 14th, arrived at as "the only course now open to us." The UN, he explained, upon receiving the various proposals that were put forward at the conference talks for dealing with Palestine, would be asked for its recommendation as regards a settlement. "After two thousand years of conflict another twelve months will not be considered a long delay," he declared, a statement Truman later considered reflecting "callousness" and "a disregard for human misery."[40]

Foreign and Colonial Office advisers thought that reference to the Trusteeship Council might prejudice the future UN decision, Beeley informed Gellman the next day, as the GA might decide on an independent Palestine state or two states at once. Cadogan would be asked regarding certain procedural suggestions designed to get the UN started on the problem in advance before September. As for the Jews in the DP camps, while the Cabinet "sympathized deeply" with their plight, Bevin's prime adviser on Palestine thought that any increase in the 1,500 monthly would "tip the scales" in favor of the Jews between now and the UN decision. Not surprisingly, Bernstein failed in his request of Creech Jones to enable a substantial number of 25,000 Jewish child survivors and the rest of the 185,000 Jewish DPs in the U.S. zones of Germany and Austria, most of whom "intensely desired" to migrate to Palestine, to enter in the "very near future" before they suffered "another major catastrophe" in this grim winter. The British would also turn down Clay's endorsement of a Bernstein request that 3,400 certificates outside the fixed quota be issued for orphaned child survivors, stating that they would take no action while the UN was considering the Palestine question.[41]

Bevin's statement in Commons drew the expected responses. Churchill wondered how the Rt. Hon. Gentleman could justify keeping 100,000 soldiers in Palestine who were needed in Great Britain, and spending £30–£40 million from the country's diminishing resources upon "this vast apparatus of protraction and delay," and now announce that mandatory rule would continue until the UN would solve the problem to which the Foreign Secretary admitted he could not offer any answer after a year-and-a-half. A brief Jewish Agency statement explained that the government's conference proposal contained the principles of the 1939 White Paper, which explained why the Agency had proposed that if the government were unwilling or unable to frame a specific, permanent Palestine policy, it should for the time being observe the Mandate as it had done before 1937. Syrian diplomat Mardam Bey declared that Britain's submission to the UN "shall not influence in any way" the Arab League Council's decision at Bludan in June 1946 to submit the question to the Security Council or the UN should the negotiations in London fail. In fact, Creech Jones confided in Shertok on the 20th, as he had hinted one day earlier in a meeting with Ben-Gurion and colleagues, that he and Bevin thought a reference to the UN would pose a great risk to the Jews, as the Arab appeal for freedom would appeal especially to the younger nations. Bevin himself considered that body a forum where questions were not judged on their merits "but fall into the pool of intrigue." Shertok acknowledged the risks, but countered that the Jews had chances even on sentimental grounds, though they would not go out of their way to incur risks if these could be avoided.[42]

The UN, Weizmann put it well in a letter to Epstein on February 21, offered a great but last chance for the Zionists' appearance, as "there is no appeal from this tribunal." He realistically assessed that the financially strapped Labour Government would pull out of Palestine if Arab-Jewish relations became more acute, just as Attlee had announced on the previous day the Cabinet's decision for withdrawing by June 1948 from the burden of mediating India's Hindu-Muslim divide, but thought that the Zionists would find little support among the great powers in the UN if terrorism continued. According to Eytan's detailed analysis for the Agency Executive on February 25, in addition to the five Arab states, the USSR, Byelorussia, and the Ukraine could be discounted. There might be some chance of "catching" Czechoslovakia, Poland, and Yugoslavia, with South Africa and New Zealand the most hopeful among the Dominions. The five Asiatic countries—Afghanistan, China, India, Iran, and Turkey—were likely to be biased against the Zionists. Greece would probably not vote against Great Britain, but the Scandinavian countries and the three West Europeans in the Benelux Customs Union offered good prospects. The twenty Latin American republics were the most important bloc, the majority expected to follow the "American line," as probably would Liberia and the Philippines. Italy and Ethiopia were potential friends. The head of the Political Department, Eytan urged, had to issue orders for a program of work to be carried out as soon as possible.[43]

The United States could render effective assistance, but Weizmann correctly observed that "so far nothing has come from America's side which would justify greater hopes in the future." Although expressing to Neumann his very high opinion of Marshall as a man of great probity and integrity, Frankfurter had no knowledge of the new Secretary's attitude on the Zionist question, and felt that they were in the worst position they had ever been in. Indeed, Henderson had advised Acheson on the 17th to "move slowly" with a commitment, noting that Washington might not be able to persuade the GA to endorse any partition plan for a "really workable Jewish State" not recommended by London, and that any such attempt might weaken U.S. prestige and influence in the UN and react unfavorably in the end against the Jews. Arguing that the Agency's diplomatic representatives had to affirm that they desired no transition stage to independence (just as had occurred for Transjordan), Gelber stressed to the members of the American Agency Executive that short of being totally abandoned by HMG, the Zionists could not make progress in the UN without Great Britain or without the United States as a sort of sponsor, champion, or advocate. Since small, Jewish Palestine might become "a helpless pawn in a bigger game," he concluded by quoting his earlier memorandum of November 1946, the UN should not be conceived as a nostrum which would cure all diseases of the Jewish body politic merely by invoking its magic name: "There could be no greater illusion."[44]

The forty-two-year-old director of the Nation Associates went further, Lillie Shultz advising *Nation* publisher Freda Kirchwey at this time that their left-wing magazine should champion the Zionist cause as it had that of the Spanish Republicans against Franco. All progressive forces in the United States should divide America from Great Britain, argued the former chief administrator of the American Jewish Congress in a long, "strictly confidential" memorandum, thereby "batter" at London's intransigence and open the possibility of winning either Soviet support or neutrality. As a matter of international concern, the current Democratic Administration should bring the matter to the UN, its stance favoring partition, the 100,000, and other demands which the Zionists had already submitted to the mandatory government. China, Brazil, and possibly France would back the United States in the Security Council; the United States, if it wished to, could win to its side in the General Assembly the largest section of the Latin American bloc. Truman could gain back the liberals in the 1948 elections, as well as the Jewish vote without seeming to seek it, at no risk of Republican opposition on the issue. The British plan made this kind of action imperative, Shultz wrote one week later, and she already had positive feedback from the treasurer of the Democratic State Committee of New York, the wife of Poland's delegate to the UN, Epstein and Lipsky, and Mendel Fisher of the Jewish National Fund.[45]

Opening a full-dress debate in the Commons on February 25, Bevin accused Truman's October 1946 declaration of being intended to precede a "competitive statement" by Dewey of jeopardizing the negotiations, blamed the American Zionists and the Jewish Agency for obstructionist stands, declared that two viable states could not be created in Palestine, and asserted that the Mandate contained dual aims which could not be accomplished within a conflict. The Jews were a religious body and not a nation. He would prefer even now to deal with the problem on a humanitarian basis, the world to deal with the Jewish refugee problem, rather than go to the UN. Eschewing polemic, Creech Jones declared, as he recently had to the Anglo-Jewish Association and to the Board of Deputies of British Jews, that "we are not going to the United Nations to surrender the Mandate" but "asking their advice as to how the Mandate can be administered" and, "if it cannot be administered in its present form we are asking how it can be amended." Stanley responded by asking for a specific plan, warned of further delay, wondered about enforcement of a majority UN decision, and suggested that the Arabs be asked to accept increased immigration of Jewish women and children. Barbara Ayrton-Gould (Labour) recommended that the Hagana be legalized to combat terrorism and that 4,000 Jews be admitted monthly. An "alien government" could not continue ruling Jews and Arabs, Crossman charged; the two sides should fight it out. Instead of keeping Palestine under an arrangement with America "under another phony constitution," he declared, HMG should tell the UN that the Mandate was unworkable, and that it would withdraw its troops and administration at a certain date.[46]

Although outraged at what he would later call "a very undiplomatic—almost hostile—statement" by Bevin about the President of the United States, Truman had his press secretary issue a moderately toned release the next day noting that the White House had asked for the 100,000 ever since his letter to Attlee in August 1945, and that America's "deep and abiding" interest in Palestine was "shared by our people without regard to their political affiliation." Charles A. Eaton (R, NJ), chairman of the House Foreign Affairs Committee, found Bevin's attack against Truman "so fraught with passion and fear" as to make the finding of a solution a difficult matter. Senators Brewster, Taft, Hawks, Barkley, Magnuson, and Pepper on both sides of the aisle also sharply criticized the Foreign Secretary's remarks. Facing this barrage of criticism, Beeley told Gallman that Bevin had for the most part spoken extemporaneously, the remarks focused on rejecting the Zionist demand for a Jewish state. The Foreign Secretary deeply wished to liquidate the DP problem on humanitarian grounds, and would "undoubtedly" do his best to get the 100,000 into Palestine at the earliest possible date provided this could be done as part of a political settlement inside or outside the UN, or as part of an international settlement of the refugee problem as a whole. Bevin looked forward, Beeley added, to an early opportunity to discuss Palestine with Marshall at the impending fourth session of the Council of Foreign Ministers in Moscow.[47]

Far more critical to Truman at this point was his meeting at 10:00 a.m. on February 27 with a few Congressional leaders to get their approval for massive aid to Greece, where since 1945 HMG had helped maintain a royalist government in a civil war with Communist guerillas, as well as to Turkey. Inverchapel had handed a blunt *aide-mémoire* six days earlier to Acheson, conveying that the British, having already strained their resources to the utmost, wished to inform State that its assistance to those two countries would end on March 31. HMG hoped that the United States would assume both burdens, then totaling more than a staggering $400 million. British diplomats had sent informal warnings in the last months of 1946, and a September report by White House Counsel Clifford and his assistant George Elsey had concluded that Moscow's long-range aim was "the economic, military and political domination of the entire Middle East." Marshall and a forceful Acheson outlined the pressing need to the four Senators and three House members present that morning. Vandenberg (who had recently told Silver that he still preferred an "immediate" determination of Palestine on the basis of a "viable partition") responded sonorously that he and a majority on Capitol Hill would lend their support, but only if the President himself made the case and linked it explicitly to the survival of the Western democracies against the Soviet Union. When the crucial meeting ended a half-hour later, Truman informed Clifford that he was willing to "lay it on the line," and merely wished to see a speech draft before making a final decision.[48]

At Creech Jones's initiative, Bevin agreed that same day to sit down one last time with the Agency representatives. With Ben-Gurion now back in Palestine and Shertok in the United States, Goldmann advised that if the British wished to avoid the UN, they should accept an interim policy of admitting the 100,000 within a year and repealing the present discriminatory land laws, and "leave what would happen after that." If there were disagreement, then the way to the UN would always be open. When Bevin insisted that the Arabs should have a say over immigration beyond the 100,000, he replied that this undermined the idea of the Jewish National Home. There was no further basis for discussion, Locker remarked, if the Arabs had a veto over Jewish entry. Bevin stood firm: In two years' time, after the Jews got the 100,000, "the whole thing would start again," and the Jews would have an additional 100,000 in Palestine. He wished the burden of immigration lifted off British shoulders, and could not have the "pistol of illegal immigration held over his head." On that note Bevin left, heading for the long train ride (instead of an airplane flight) to Moscow at doctor's orders because of his heart condition. The conversation, Goldmann reported to Gallman, "had no positive results."[49]

Shertok lay his case before Marshall on the 27th, beginning with the assertion that sovereignty in Palestine could cure the world of "the Jewish malaise," provide a secure framework for the rescue of persecuted Jews, and create a constructive outlet for the energies of the Jewish people. They could not endure much longer any outside domination: "We must be masters of our own destiny." The Zionists' "work of nation-building" from the very foundations required the attributes of statehood, which could make a substantial social and economic contribution to the entire region. The over 200,000 survivors in DP camps, who wished to be transferred to Palestine, represented the most urgent problem. The Arabs never consented to additional Jewish immigration, but the "armies or hordes" of Iraq and Saudi Arabia would not march across deserts to Palestine, there to fight the British Empire. The Zionists sought a new understanding with London, which could only be achieved with the help of America, the greatest progressive world power. He hoped that the United States would press HMG now to abrogate the restrictive land laws and bring over the 100,000; taking the initiative of proposing a solution when the GA met in September should to be left for further discussion. Silent throughout, Marshall then assured his visitor of the "deep interest" of the U.S. government and himself in this matter. If the problem of Palestine should arise during the course of his conversations in Moscow with Bevin, he was sure that the statements which Shertok had just made would be helpful.[50]

Concurrent events bore out Ben-Gurion's warning, given in a final letter to Creech Jones before returning home, that "things cannot remain as they are in Palestine." On February 9, the wooden brigantine *LaNegev*

(To the Negev, with 647 passengers) was captured with the use of tear gas by a boarding party from the HMS *Chieftain* after a battle which left the German-born, twenty-five-year old British HaBonim member Herbert Lazar Laser dead. This ship's arrival and the three new Negev settlements, the Hagana announced, were "our reply to the threat of martial law." Three days after these passengers' transfer to Cyprus, the Hagana damaged a military landing craft used to transport refugees. The day that Barker relinquished his command (February 12), he confirmed the death sentence on Yehiel Drezner (also known as Dov Rosenbaum—twenty-four), Eliezer Kashani (twenty-three), and Mordekhai Alkoshi (also known as Alkahi—twenty-one) for bearing arms on the night of December 29, an apprehensive *yishuv* being led to understand that there would be a stay of execution pending the result of Gruner's appeal to the Privy Council. (The announcement was made two days later, after Barker had safely departed.) The Hagana and Irgun proceeded to engage in harsh kidnappings and counter-kidnappings.

On the 17th, the steamer *HaMapil HaAlmoni* (The Anonymous Illegal, with 807 passengers) was intercepted by two British warships and captured after a violent struggle. The next day, dissident land mines injured five soldiers; that night and the next, the Irgun attacked an RAF airfield and damaged in two places the pipeline of the Iraq Petroleum Company near Afula. On the 27th, the *Haim Arlosoroff* (carrying 1,378 survivors, including 664 from Sweden and 50 orphaned children, and named after the Agency's political director who was murdered in 1933) was intercepted by British warships; thirty Jews and eleven British seamen were injured in the wild battle. As the passengers were being transferred to a craft for deportation, a LEHI bomb exploded in the British Port Authority headquarters in Haifa, killing two and wounding four.[51]

The Arab Higher Committee, expanded in January by Haj Amin from the now defunct Arab Higher Executive to include more of his close associates and supporters, continued to stand by its unyielding call for immediate independence and recognition as Palestinian citizens only those Jews who were in the country prior to the Balfour Declaration, together with their descendants. In the last months, Danin informed Kollek, a "sizeable number of those who worked with us were killed. Jamal al-Husseini waves his sword." Most notable had been the murder the previous November of Fawzi Darwish al-Husseini, whose small Falastin al-Jadide group championed the League for Jewish-Arab Rapprochement and Cooperation's bi-nationalist state program spearheaded by Haim Margalith Kalvaryski, Ernst Simon, and others. Warned by Husseini of the danger of his activities, Fawzi had replied: "The day of politics by assassination among us is past." Following his murder, Jamal announced "My cousin stumbled and received his proper punishment." Others included Mufti opponents Mustafa Dajani, Sheikh Ali Shahin, and Muhammad Zeinati, as well as two connected with land sales to Jews, assassinations all directed, charged the Hagana weekly newspaper *Eshnav*, from Haj Amin's headquarters in Alexandria. Asked by the Syrian newspaper *Al-Ayam* about British reports of Arab terrorist organizations, Husseini replied that it was the duty of the Arabs to assume their own defense since they could not count on the British, the more so as the latter were not able to defend themselves in Palestine. Arab Revolt military leader and pro-Nazi collaborator Fawzi al-Kaukji, Public Information Officer Richard Stubbs publicly admitted on February 24, had "escaped the vigilance" of the British frontier control, and was now recruiting fighters in the country's Arab centers. The Hebrew press openly hinted that the mandatory authorities had acted as an accomplice.[52]

On March 2, "statutory martial law" was put into force by means of Operation Elephant over Tel Aviv, Petah Tikva, Ramat Gan, Bnei Brak, and a large sector of Jerusalem following a slew of Irgun attacks the previous day in which eighteen people were killed and twenty-five others wounded. Most of these—thirteen killed and twelve wounded—resulted from the bombing of the British army officer's club, known as Goldschmidt House, on King George V Avenue opposite the landmark Yeshurun Synagogue in central Jerusalem. The mandatory's official communiqué charged that the admittedly "severe measures," affecting some 300,000 people, resulted from the "the lack of cooperation" shown by the Jewish Agency and the Va'ad HaLeumi when asked to help bring to justice members of the terrorist groups. All commerce, deliveries, transportation, telephones, postal, bank and court services stopped; people were permitted to leave their homes for only three hours a day, when grocery stores and some pharmacies were allowed to be open.

Major General Richard Gale, responsible in Tel Aviv, denied any punitive motive to harm collective economic life, but government communications attest that this was the case. Locals readily pointed to Barker's non-fraternization order after the King David Hotel bombing. Weizmann did not doubt the sincerity of official statements that martial law had been imposed for purposes of security, he wrote Cunningham on the 4th, but he had equally no doubt that it was in fact leading to the "economic strangulation" of the country. Two days later, Churchill wondered in the House of Commons how any "coherent brain" could approve having at present three or four times as many British troops in "little petty" Palestine as in "mighty" India, or what "element of obstinacy" had forced this sustained effort "in the midst of general surrender and scuttle of British will power in Palestine."[53]

Expressing the *yishuv*'s "numbing shock" at the Goldschmidt House attack, a joint statement by the Agency and the Va'ad HaLeumi pointed out that they had made consistent efforts to combat terrorism, but the mandatory's immigration restrictions had not helped to relieve the tension in the country. The mounting strain, Myerson warned her Executive colleagues on the 14th, could well lead individuals to collaborate with the British. Declaring at the meeting that Bevin was "the most popular man" in Great Britain, Ben-Gurion also worried that reference to the UN was, like the Anglo-American Committee of Inquiry, just another delaying tactic. The next day, he drafted a telegram to Attlee stating "martial law absolutely futile and senseless unless really meant to punish whole community, ruin its economy and destroy the foundations of the Jewish National Home." It increased the resentment of the hard-hit population and created "fertile soil" for terrorist propaganda. To enforce the White Paper and maintain the racial land law, all the while keeping thousands in Cyprus camps and condemning thousands of Displaced Persons to degradation in Europe, Ben-Gurion charged, martial law "is latest turn of the screw" in Palestine's having been "turned into a Police State." In the name of "justice and sanity," he earnestly appealed to the Prime Minister to remove the root cause of unrest by abrogating the land law, facilitate substantial Jewish immigration, and thus re-establish the indispensable conditions for "orderly and decent Government."[54]

In fact, one day before Ben-Gurion's telegram reached Whitehall on the 18th, Cunningham and the army had decided to halt Operation Elephant, claiming that, in Creech Jones's words to the Cabinet, it had "reached the limit of its usefulness." The Palestinian Arab press viewed martial law's ending as a further British defeat. The local administration announced that 78 arrests had been made, including fifteen LEHI and twelve Irgun members; nine would be released within the month, but the two groups declared that no important members had been caught. Within a week of martial law's declaration, the Irgun and LEHI had carried out fifteen more attacks, resulting in the death of one soldier and the wounding of almost forty (including civilians). Fourteen more incidents were reported the next week, resulting in one soldier's death and fifteen others wounded. These included another Irgun attack on the Schneller Barracks in Jerusalem and a LEHI assault two nights later on a freight train, wrecking nineteen oil tank cars, and leaving one Arab worker dead and another wounded.[55]

"Govern or Get Out" had read the *Sunday Express's* front page headline on March 3. Churchill lashed out in the Commons to ask how long this "senseless squalid war" would go on against the Jews in Palestine, in which Attlee's government had squandered some £80 million to give the country to the Arabs "or God knows to whom," before some decision was reached. Gurney might respond to a worried Ben-Zvi that every British soldier murdered deferred the solution to the immigration question, while the Goldschmidt House attack pushed it off for a long time. His superior felt compelled to tell Creech Jones on the 16th that the Army, not wanting to impose martial law throughout the country and lacking enough troops to carry it out efficiently, apparently could not even protect themselves. The next morning, a few hours before martial law was lifted, the Jerusalem Military Court sentenced twenty-one-year-old Moshe Barazani of LEHI, caught with a hand grenade near the Jerusalem security perimeter on the 9th, to "be hanged by the neck till he was dead."[56]

The Mandate government's defense on March 3 of its stringent immigration policy notwithstanding, as well as renewed requests made of all the European governments concerned to prevent the departure of illegal immigrant vessels from their ports, three more such transports arrived that month. On the 9th, the *Ben Hecht* (597 passengers), the only ship sponsored by the Irgun and paid for with the proceeds of "A Flag is Born," was captured by three British warships without incident. Three days later, the *Shabtai Luzinsky* (with 823 passengers and named for a major *aliya bet* operative in Italy who recently had been killed in a road accident there) beached itself north of Gaza. Hundreds of local residents came down to the beach to mingle with passengers, who thus avoided arrest. Many residents were mistaken for refugees and sent to Cyprus, with some 460 locals returning home the next week. Having advised London on the 9th about secret information indicating that 25,000 Jews were ready to leave Europe for Palestine at short notice, Cunningham warned Creech Jones four days later that unless the quota were increased to meet this "real human issue," there is no way of stopping terrorism other than by "outright war with the Jews." On the 30th, the *Moledet* (Homeland, with 1,588 passengers) became disabled some 50 miles outside Palestinian waters and issued an SOS. Royal Navy units responded and took the ship under tow, soon bringing all to Cyprus.[57]

The same month, a secret memorandum reached the Canadian government about the *President Warfield*, a packet steamer that had carried travelers on the Chesapeake Bay between Norfolk and Baltimore from 1928 onward and then transported troops for the U.S. and Royal Navies during World War II. Former Lt. Commander of the U.S. Coast Guard and now Chief Engineer John D. Crabson, heading a crew of forty with twenty-four-year-old Isaac "Ike" Aronovitz (later Aranne) of Palestine as Chief Mate (and Hagana member), was told to leave the vessel after it reached Marseille. One more significant fact had been uncovered: the boat, bearing a Honduras flag (actually arranged by United Fruit Company president Sam Zemurray, who had been approached by Weisgal and Shind) was fitted with 1,000 Kapok life preservers put aboard in Baltimore before departing for the Mediterranean on February 27. The report did not disclose that Zemurray had also declared this United Fruit vessel, about to be decommissioned, as junk in order to place the purchase price within the range of the Brockton textile businessman Dewey Stone and his "Weston Trading Company," of which Stone was the sole stockholder, for the Hagana.[58]

Cabinet meetings in the last week of March reflected a growing loss of British control. Creech Jones announced on the 20th that only twenty-four suspected terrorists had been arrested, and that the *yishuv* continued its stance against cooperation with the authorities. "Terrorism is even worse now," Attlee pointed out. Tax and other revenue had been lost; four more escort vessels had to be brought to the Mediterranean to augment preventive measures against illegal immigration. In a remarkable admission, the Cabinet "considered that a more definite plan should have been made" to maintain order in the country until the UN session in September. The Chiefs of Staff, instructed now to do so, reported six days later that civil government should be continued for the present along with "intensified" military pressure against terrorists throughout

Palestine, martial law to be "selectively" re-imposed for a limited period where and when needed. The "insoluble" morale problem facing soldiers there added to the difficulty, one brigadier reflecting the view of several senior officers when recently asking, after Eban's address to the Imperial Defence College: "What vision could be set before them as a worthy object of their sacrifice and hardship?"[59]

Cunningham and G.O.C. Gordon MacMillan, recalled to London, told a concurring Cabinet on the 27th that no improvement in the situation could occur until a political settlement was reached. The 1,500 monthly immigration quota would remain in place, but martial law not be enforced over the entire country. Aside from a prolonged economic and social dislocation that would result, the latter would swing moderate opinion even further against HMG, as the Chiefs had concluded, and obtain more recruits for the Irgun and LEHI ranks. Confronted by the Stern Group's bombing of the Shell oil refinery in Haifa on March 31, which caused £400 million in damages and the loss of 16,000 tons of oil, Cunningham could do little more than announce on his own that the Palestine taxpayer would have to bear the costs. With security expenditures now nearly double the 1945 figure of £4.5 million, for a projected deficit in the mandatory's budget of some half a million pounds sterling that fiscal year, hopes to ease the administration's financial straits appeared dimmer than ever.[60]

A *New York Herald Tribune's* feature story on April 1 from its Frankfurt correspondent, forecasting a mass march by DPs on Palestine beginning with Easter week on the style of the biblical exodus from Egypt, was viewed with "considerable alarm" in Hilldring's office. Wahl had to "supply cold compresses to fevered brows" in the State and War Departments, whose officials expected to see a "bloody" movement immediately out of the camps. Bernstein quickly issued a statement, approved by the top military authorities, stating that no responsible Jewish leader or organization advocated such a "mass crusade," expressing his personal opinion that the U.S. Army would continue to show "humaneness" in receiving the inevitable flight into the U.S. zone by Jews fleeing persecution in eastern Europe, and calling for a substantial interim immigration into Palestine for DPs who "are determined to find a permanent home in their own land." The story as seen from Washington, which actually originated in a plan first raised by Eri Jabotinsky to his associates in the Bergson group's Hebrew Committee of National Liberation, further indicated that the DP situation was deteriorating rapidly. An imminent directive from Clay would require all DP camps to be stabilized immediately as to population, Fierst informed Wahl, but the border would remain open. The Army would continue to assist emigration movements (organized by *Aliya Bet*) on a small scale, but large train-loads of people would most likely not be expedited without difficulty.[61]

The day after this news exclusive appeared, Cadogan submitted a formal British request to place the Palestine question on the General Assembly's agenda at its next regular session six months hence. The official move followed an earlier suggestion by Trygve Lie, the former foreign minister in Norway's government-in-exile in London during World War II and currently the UN Secretary-General. Since "an early settlement" of the issue was desirable, some "preliminary study" should be conducted by the UN. This could be done, HMG proposed, by convening a special session of the GA as soon as possible. The session should confine itself to appointing a special committee, its task to investigate the Palestine problem and, under Article 10 of the Charter, make recommendations to the GA's regular session for its solution. The same day, Victor Chi-Tsai Hoo of China, Assistant Secretary-General, sent telegrams to all UN members except the United Kingdom, inquiring whether they agreed to the summoning of the special session for this purpose. The next day, Shultz sent a memorandum to Kirchwey outlining the practical steps to have the UN authorize "the establishment of a Jewish state with unlimited immigration in a viable part of Palestine." Acheson informed the United States' fifty-two diplomatic missions on the 4th that State was replying in the affirmative, emphasizing its hope that the agenda be confined to this question, thereby establishing a precedent that in general such sessions be confined to "speedy consideration" of urgent problems. Whitehall informed the U.S. Embassy in London three days later that restriction of the agenda to a single item was entirely in conformity with its wishes.[62]

Lie's original idea to set up a preliminary committee immediately, consisting of the five permanent Security Council members (the United States, the USSR, the United Kingdom, France and China) along with Czechoslovakia, Brazil and Sweden, and save the heavy financial output of a special session had met with a sharp rebuff from Washington.

Shertok liked the committee's proposed composition, as it would circumvent the arithmetical majority of the presumably anti-Zionist Arab or Muslim, Asian, Communist, and Catholic states. (New York City's Cardinal Spellman had privately told the sympathetic Wadsworth that while the Catholic Church strongly opposed partition primarily because "the whole of the land is sacred to Christ," a "regime of guarantees and safeguards" had to be given for the Holy Places and the Christian minorities if it were imposed.) Yet Acheson thought the absence of a special session of doubtful legal validity, and hesitated in light of HMG's refusal to offer specific proposals towards a solution. Lie also wished to give the Jewish Agency and the Arabs an equal voice before the committee, drawing Bevin's objection that the inclusion of a Jewish representative would set "a dangerous precedent" for the participation of non-governmental organizations in UN committees. He did agree with Lie about the committee's composition and that if the Jews did not participate, the Arab states should not either at this stage. British Embassy officials refused State's request for a concrete formulation of HMG's plans for Palestine, having reiterated simply on March 21 that "the Mandate is unworkable," and the United Kingdom would turn the matter over to the Assembly for a recommended solution whether in the form of a trusteeship, a unitary state, or partition.[63]

At this stage, some in the State Department propounded the idea of having Arab states included in the preliminary committee. Robert McClintock, Special Assistant to Dean Rusk, Director of the Office of Special Political Affairs, had first broached this in a memorandum to Henderson, with a copy to Acheson, on March 4. Hearing of Lie's original proposal from former Republican Senator from Vermont Warren Austin, now head of the U.S. delegation to the UN, he suggested that it be composed of the states elected to the Security Council, the Trusteeship Council, and the Economic and Social Council (the Big Five represented in all three). This special *ad hoc* group of twenty-nine would include three Arab states, and reflect the fact that the Palestine problem affected trusteeship, economic and social affairs, and security. Such a committee, McClintock advised, should not be expected to visit Palestine. Reading a *New York Herald Tribune* report of the same date about this possibility, Shertok had protested to a sympathetic Lie that the Arabs could not be a party to a case and sit, at the same time, in judgment on it. Epstein made the same point to Merriam. Yet Henderson actually "took for granted," Neumann and Executive colleague Hayim Greenberg concluded from an interview with him, that Arab states would be included. Shertok hinted to Henderson on April 3 that this might question the Agency's own appearance, leading to the response that no decision had yet been arrived at and that his objection would be borne in mind. Henderson also relayed State's assumption that Moscow would insist upon including the Arab states, although this might be "cover for their manoeuvre to out pro-Arab Britain."[64]

Andrei Gromyko, the thirty-eight-year-old Soviet Permanent Representative to the UN, had received cabled instructions on March 6 from Foreign Minister Vyacheslav Molotov to accept Lie's original proposal to set up a special committee. As formulated in a report eleven days later by Near Eastern specialists to Deputy Minister of Foreign Affairs Andrey Vyshinskii, Moscow's position called for annulling the Mandate for Palestine, the withdrawal of British troops in order to create "a normal situation," and the UN to work out a constitution for "a single independent democratic Palestine, which ensures that the peoples living there will enjoy equal national and democratic rights."[65]

Truman's forceful remarks before a joint session of Congress on March 12 that the United States should grant immediate economic and financial aid to Greece and Turkey, declaring that "it must be the policy of the United States to support free peoples who are resisting attempted subjugation by armed minorities or by outside pressures," convinced the director of the USSR Foreign Ministry's Near East Department that the United States "continues to interfere actively and openly in almost everything that goes on in the Middle East." The assessment three months ago of his mission chief in Syria and Lebanon, Daniil S. Solod, that Truman's efforts to carry out his own policy in the Eastern Mediterranean have "proved to be timid, ill-timed and unsuccessful," actions reflecting "the habits of a minor civil servant," was "plainly at variance with the facts." Nor could I. V. Samylovskii agree with Solod that Truman had given up direct handling of matters concerned with the Palestine question, or that the President's letter to Ibn Saud on October 25 could be considered his last intervention in Palestine affairs. Finally, he found it hard to accept Solod's conclusion, regarding the 100,000 figure which Truman had long proposed, that Palestine was unable to absorb "a meaningful number" of immigrants. He did agree that Great Britain had "no intention of letting Palestine go," but looked only for a solution which would allow HMG to "keep its own domination there for a longer period."[66]

The Arab states had already expressed their strong reservations about appointing a UN committee to study the Palestine case prior to its consideration by the GA in September. Iraqi Foreign Minister Jamali cabled Lie on March 11 that the Palestine question needed no further study, the Arabs accepted the 1939 White Paper's main principles, and neutral observers might consider a new committee as favoring the Zionists and shaking international confidence in the impartiality and justice of the UN. On the 24th, the Arab League Council had held the American and British governments responsible for the "present critical situation" in Palestine, "and for the grave dangers that threaten security and peace in this part of the world as a result of such a situation." The members pledged themselves to defend Palestine's independence, authorized the establishment of a committee for this purpose, and demanded a complete and immediate stoppage to Jewish immigration. The Iraqi delegation's call to break off diplomatic relations with Washington and London, together with criticism of Truman, was dropped from the final resolution.[67]

On April 6, Jamali handed U.S. Ambassador Wadsworth a message that he had telegraphed to the other Arab states, proposing a uniform communication to Lie expressing opposition to a special session focused on Palestine. If the session were summoned to declare that country's immediate sovereignty, Jamali added, Baghdad would welcome the session. When Wadsworth suggested that the GA did not possess the authority to declare Palestine's independence, and that the word "immediately" was ill-chosen in view of the British official request, Jamali modified the language to read that his government would endorse a session to the end that Palestine's independence be declared forthwith. Two weeks later, the diplomatic representatives to the United States of the five Arab states sent Lie their request for the inclusion of an additional item in the agenda, calling for an end to the Palestine Mandate and the declaration of the country's independence.[68]

Faced with the probability of a nineteenth commission to investigate Palestine, Shertok, like other Zionist leaders, found his own opinions in "a confused state." The British lion, he declared to Hadassah's National Board, "is dying very hard and he is still strong enough to deal with 600,000 Jews" in Palestine. The recent publication of memoirs by

Crum and Crossman about the Anglo-American Committee of Inquiry, particularly these two participants' unflattering portrayal of British actions, offered no comfort. Further, HMG was "entirely non-committal" when referring the problem to the UN. Not surprisingly, the Agency Executive had announced on March 24 that it would submit the 1946 World Zionist Congress' political plan to that international body, the Agency to insist on the full implementation of the Mandate, "but its representatives will also be empowered to discuss other possible solutions." (Ben-Gurion spent little time on deliberations about the UN, devoting himself from that month onward in a "seminar" about strengthening the yishuv's military capabilities against an inevitable Arab attack.) Others worried about a special session of the GA, which would enable the Arab states to take part in the proceedings from the very beginning.

Still smarting from what he privately termed "my political assassination" at the Congress in Basle, Weizmann wrote to Creech Jones that "UNO means almost endless procrastination," warned Kaplan that America would not act against England, and thought that a report in the press about HMG not going to be bound by a UN decision evidence that "Mr. Bevin has over-reached himself at this time." "However," he added to Wise on April 8, "there may be no limit to which this gentleman may go with impunity." Buxton had no confidence in Bevin's integrity, and warned the AZEC's Ben-Horin that Beeley's selection as one of the British operatives at the GA was equivalent to giving the Arabs a spokesman.[69]

Would their cause fare better in the General Assembly or in the Security Council? "Little probability" existed at present, Epstein told Welles, of obtaining the required two-thirds majority in the GA, as opposed to getting seven out of the eleven needed votes in the Council. The so-called "non-white" bloc in the Assembly was growing stronger and more cohesive every day; on March 26, speaking as the host before twenty-five Asiatic nations in New Delhi at the first Asian Relations Conference, Indian National Congress leader Jawaharlal Nehru proclaimed his future country's support of an Arab state in Palestine. In addition, the GA could do no more than recommend, whereas the Council could make binding decisions. An ultimate majority in the Assembly favorable to Zionist prospects was only possible if the United States took the lead and acted firmly against all Arab and British proposals, Menahem Kahany observed to the Executive. "The key is in the hands of the USA Government," he concluded, but judging by this first move, "the help we can expect from them is very problematic."

At the same time, an expert in international relations advised Gelber, the GA was much more flexible, the crucial Latin American delegates would take a strong line, and even the smaller European powers were more likely to do so. The Security Council, by contrast, was hamstrung by any member's veto and by great power rivalries, while it had to be proven that the Palestine situation posed a threat to international peace and security. Moreover, few of the problems placed before the Council, such as Iran, British troops in Greece, Spain, and the admission of new member states, had been properly solved by it. Whatever the answer to the fundamental question, the Agency had no choice but to wait until the member states replied to Lie's invitation.[70]

The American government's intervention in Greece and Turkey appeared to open an avenue to more active participation by the United States in the settlement of the Palestine problem. If the British felt the burden of keeping 10,000 troops in Greece, Epstein pointed out to Henderson, they certainly felt the weight that much more in keeping ten times the number in Palestine. It followed that if London brought the issue to the UN, he argued, Washington would then be in a stronger position to demand a pro-Zionist interim policy as regards immigration, colonization, and land purchase. Sack and Silver made the same point to receptive Senators, suggesting that State be asked to press Whitehall for a quid pro quo, which was "a natural and normal procedure in international relations."[71]

Soon after Dalton informed Commons that Great Britain had spent £46 million in two years for the maintenance of British troops in Greece and £52 million for military and police purposes in Palestine, Henderson thought that purely on financial grounds the British would not stay in Palestine. Yet critics of what would soon be called the Truman Doctrine, aimed to contain Communist threats to Greece, Turkey, and beyond during the "Cold War," as far apart ideologically as Laski and Baruch both concluded that the keeping of so many troops in Palestine while quitting Greece had nothing to do with dollars but with oil. Laski was especially caustic in his criticism, suggesting in the *Nation* an alternative to Bevin's Middle Eastern policy, which had made the Foreign Secretary the ally of both American Standard Oil and the Grand Mufti: "If he mingles imagination and resolution with the sturdy common sense he shows in a trade-union negotiation, he can throw away his fears, settle down to a sensible negotiation with Stalin and his colleagues, save Great Britain much obloquy, and dissolve a good deal of fantastic mythology which reads more like a legacy from Mr. Kipling than a sober estimate of contemporary realities."[72]

Henderson had acknowledged to Epstein that the possible new policy of the United States in Greece was "undoubtedly" connected with the American government's general policy in the Middle East. Marshall would discuss the general problem with Bevin in Moscow, he added. The global implications actually went much further, Acheson having told his Cabinet colleagues on March 7 that Greece was the key to "encirclement movements" in France, Italy, Hungary, and Turkey. The individual most responsible for its gestation and then securing approval from Congress, he presented the crisis in clear, dramatic terms that Friday morning: "If we go in we cannot be certain of success in the Middle East and [the] Mediterranean. If we do not go in there will [be] collapse in these areas. There is [the] possibility of military risk, but it is doubtful if this will occur." Truman immediately followed: "It means [the] U.S. going into European politics. It means the greatest selling job ever facing a President." Once his address on Capitol Hill ended five days later, the *New York Times* properly called the President's speech a "radical change [in American foreign policy] in the space of twenty-one minutes." Marshall did not, in fact, discuss Palestine with Bevin at the latest meeting of the Council of Foreign Ministers. Yet to prominent *New York Herald Tribune* columnist Stewart Alsop, America could no more limit its intervention in Middle Eastern recent affairs than the hopeful lady in the joke could remain just a little pregnant, and having begun the job in Greece and Turkey must go on to first stabilize the Middle East with the partition of Palestine.[73] The question remained: would the Truman Doctrine impact on that highly contentious, long-standing quandary as well?

The Zionist leadership refused to commit itself irrevocably in advance to adhere to the GA's ultimate recommendation. Addressing a plenary session of the Va'ad HaLeumi on April 1, Ben-Gurion declared that if a "more or less satisfactory settlement" were not reached, two primary forces would alone decide Jewry's fate in Palestine when the time of final decision were reached: "the strength of the *yishuv* and the drive of the so-called illegal immigration." The UN, he declared, did not have the authority, the tradition, the capacity, the force, or the experience to make decisions on complicated questions which were bones of contention between the different Powers, but immigration would continue and the Jewish state would arise: "No one can rob us of our right to independence in our homeland." Five days later, Shertok sounded the same note in New York when telling the National Committee for Labor Palestine that "we shall be masters of our destiny in the measure that we shall will so to be—and act accordingly without waiting." Rather than wait for the approval of an international authority before becoming a nation, he pointed out, all members of the UN "worked out their salvation by methods which have been found legitimate and appropriate." Voicing opposition to partition, Sneh advised the General Zionist labor organization that it was illusory to expect rapid and effective action from the UN, the British wished to keep the Mandate, and the Zionist movement should gear itself to continue immigration until a numerical majority of 1,000,000 was reached within the next five years.[74]

A similar militant tone came from the Arab camp. In Cairo, after a meeting of the Council of the Arab League, Husseini announced that if the UN decision were unfavorable to their cause, the Arab states would nevertheless continue the struggle for an Arab Palestine. The AHC decided to form local National Committees on the pattern of those set up during the 1936–1939 Arab Revolt in Palestine. On April 17–19, the political committee of the Arab League, meeting in Damascus, resolved to place on the GA's agenda for a special committee the abolishing of the Mandate and the Balfour Declaration, Palestine's independence, and an immediate stop to Jewish immigration. The Arab press reported that the attendees secretly endorsed the decisions of the Inchas and Bludan Conferences, as well as a plan to declare Palestine's sovereignty without considering the UN and to create a government-in-exile led by Haj Amin. Oriental Minister Walter Smart informed Whitehall that Azzam was very pessimistic as to any favorable results for the Arabs emerging from the proceedings, and Emir Feisal warned that any UN decision to "impose" more Jewish immigration and to promote the eventual establishment of a Jewish state in Palestine would not be accepted by the Arabs and "inevitably lead to armed hostilities." The results of an upheaval in the Middle East, he added, would be disastrous for both the Arabs and the British, who would "have to face the music" while the Americans remained outside the turmoil. Urged by Smart to impress moderation upon Arab colleagues, Feisal expressed his dearest wish that Arabs and British should cooperate at the General

Assembly meeting, but they could not go with HMG to the length of "committing suicide."[75]

The British wished to distinguish between accepting GA recommendations as to Palestine's future status and any which would involve action by His Majesty's Government. As regards the latter, Permanent Under-Secretary of State for Foreign Affairs Orme Sargent cabled to Bevin in Moscow on April 3: "We must reserve our freedom to accept or refuse." This might include, for example, a recommendation for a trusteeship by the Big Five, for which the Chiefs of Staff would have to be consulted first before the Cabinet could be asked to take this course. Sargent therefore proposed that, with Bevin's agreement, the Cabinet endorse a statement about HMG's freedom to "refuse the task of themselves administering any policy of which they do not approve." Beeley hinted to this approach in an interview with Goldmann, and the *New York Times* deduced from "an authoritative quarter" in London that "the British seem determined to reserve their position all along the line." Brigadier Clayton repeated to Eban the identical remark which he had made about the Anglo-American Committee before its report: there was no harm in referring the matter to the UN provided that HMG made it clear that they would not take the UN's advice if they did not like it.

Bevin, however, replied on the 11th that Cadogan hold back making such a declaration until "a suitable moment," which might not occur until discussion at the GA had actually begun. The Chiefs weighed in: "We should retain our essential strategic requirements in Palestine." Cadogan protested on the 24th to this stance: if he only gave "wait and see" as an answer when asked about British intentions, "no one [would] be satisfied," and he thought that the phrase about reserving HMG's position on enforcement seemed "otiose." Nonetheless, McNeil received the Cabinet's sanction to instruct its UN representative not to make a statement when the special session opened that committed the government regarding acceptance of the GA's final recommendations if carried by a two-thirds majority vote.[76]

Informed by Lie on April 13 that a majority of the GA members had concurred in the summoning of a special session, to be opened on April 28, the State Department considered that the committee selected to report back to the Assembly by September should be a small one of "comparatively disinterested states." Excluding the Big Five and the Arab states, the ten country representatives which it had in mind could offer "a fresh approach" and a consideration "not unduly influenced" by positions already taken by the more interested governments. A second choice, read the memorandum which Rusk drafted for Marshall to send Truman four days later, would be the Big Five and six of the smaller powers, again excluding the Arab states. Truman liked the first suggestion best, and agreed with the opposition of Acheson and associates in the Near Eastern Division to a committee consisting of governments on the Security Council, the Economic and Social Council, and the Trusteeship Council (which would include three Arab states) as "very little better" than a full meeting of the GA.[77]

A small committee of neutrals, Acheson remarked to a Canadian Embassy officer, offered the only possible hope of providing "a sane examination" of the Palestine question. To the Arabs' claim that they should have at least one representative, he said that "everyone" had a very special interest in the Palestine problem. Acheson felt "passionately" about this, thinking that the handling of the Palestine problem might be one of the main tests of the UN, and that it would be tragic if the special Assembly were to fail to lay down a hopeful course of procedure. A full-dress debate on the problem itself and a large committee would be the "two shoals" which could wreck the outcome. The approach to the Assembly, in his view, should be to "scare the bejesus out of them" that this was no longer a question of U.S. policy or British imperialism, but it was a serious question which "imperils the peace of the world."[78]

In discussing the importance of a successful resolution of this issue, Acheson mentioned to the Canadian diplomat that it would also do much to allay the criticism that the UN was by-passed in the Greek matter. The UN could not "under any conceivable stretch of the imagination" have coped with the Greek problem, he quickly added. Some on the Senate Foreign Relations Committee hearings about U.S. help to Greece and Turkey, contacted by Silver in the hope of achieving a quid pro quo in favor of Zionist interests, had already raised the Palestine issue at that time. In response, the State Department declared that it would be "unfortunate" to link the extension of aid to Greece with the Palestine problem. "Many months" would pass before the UN would be able to find a solution to the Palestine problem, its spokesman claimed, while the question of aid to Greece, as pointed out by the President, "is extremely urgent."[79]

The Jewish Agency opposed the appointment of a neutral committee, Shertok told Acheson on April 23, feeling that the Palestine question was primarily a "great power" question, while the small states would be too timid to make the bold decisions which the situation demanded. (In similar vein, the Dutch delegation's head told his own associates that a committee without the Security Council members would produce "an academic report whose importance would be marginal.") He also suggested that the United States present a resolution to the Special Assembly calling upon Britain to administer the Mandate faithfully, including the lifting of restrictions on immigration and land purchase; rebut the Arab proposal that a Palestine state be established forthwith; and support the Agency's request to appear on the Assembly floor in order to present the Jewish case. Unmoved, Acheson stood by State's preference for a small committee of neutral states, and, thinking that the special session should be limited to matters of a procedural character, would not be inclined to present or support any resolution relating to the "substance" of the case such as immigration. Agency participation would lead to "fruitless discussions obscuring issue" while Arab attempts to force discussions "would only result in their discredit." The Agency, he added, should be given every chance to present its views on substance to the committee that will emerge.[80]

The "vicious circle" of British repression breeding Jewish terrorism and terror leading to new repression, which Acheson acknowledged that day, validated Shertok's concern that the situation in Palestine might well become so desperate that consideration of the problem by the UN would become "a mere academic process." On April 3, death sentences were passed on Meir Feinstein (twenty) and Daniel Azulai (eighteen) for having taken part in the Irgun attack on the Jerusalem Railway Station the previous October. The four other Irgun fighters awaiting execution (Gruner, Drezner, Kashani, and Alkoshi) had remained in Jerusalem's central prison at the Russian Compound, all wearing crimson-gallows dress, awaiting what was hoped would be the Judicial Committee of the Privy Council's precedent-setting commutation of Gruner's sentence. MacMillan had announced that the execution of the three would not be carried out until Gruner's case before the Council was completed, and Political Officer Vivian Fox-Strangways told lawyer Max Seligman that he "did not believe that anyone wanted to see that poor chap die." Before the four were secretly transferred to Acre Prison on the 14th, Gruner told thirty-eight-year-old Irgun commander Begin in a smuggled letter that as "a faithful soldier" he accepted his fate "for the world knows that a land is redeemed by blood."

With Gruner's appeal still pending, and the four deprived of the traditional rite of a last meal and a rabbi's final visit, he was without warning brought to the gallows on the early morning of April 16 while singing the *HaTikva*. Drezner, Kashani, and Alkoshi followed at twenty- to thirty-minute intervals, each singing the Zionist anthem as well. Prior notice of the final sentence had not been given to them, their friends, or their lawyers. Their request to be buried in Rosh Pina's cemetery near Shlomo Ben-Yosef, the first Jew hanged by the British nine years earlier, was denied. The four bodies were delivered to the Jewish Community Council of Safed (Tsfat). A shocked *yishuv* heard the news over government radio at 7 a.m. Protest was muted because curfews had been placed over major Jewish cities. The Jewish Agency expressed its "profound shock and pain" and several Hebrew newspapers published the four names framed by black borders. At the same time, units of the Hagana, which had recently prevented extortion efforts by dissidents against shops and banks, stood in readiness to prevent any attempt "to impose on the public demonstrations of mourning." In Munich, an orderly demonstration of 500 Jewish DPs marched to the British Consulate carrying the Zionist flag and several banners, the largest of which read "Gruner's death will be avenged."[81]

On April 17, the *Official Gazette* published amendments to the Defence Regulations, signed two days earlier, stating that henceforth judgments and sentences passed by the Military Courts in Palestine or by the GOC would not be subject to appeal and may not be challenged before any Court. In addition, certain prison rules should not apply in the case of death sentences passed by Military Courts; both amendments were retroactive. "Yesterday my four Jews were hung," Barker wrote to Katie Antonius: "I hope the Arabs will no longer think we are afraid to hang Jews and to fight." In Alexandria, Haj Amin expressed the view that at last Britain was being firm with the Jews, and this act of the mandatory showed "courage." Major George Charlton, the Acre Prison warden, thought otherwise. Appalled by the shameful treatment accorded Gruner during his final hours, he refused to carry out the executions. P. J. Hackett, Commissioner of Prisons, and Andrew Clow, superintendent of the Nablus prison, took over in his stead. Irgun headquarters immediately issued orders to kidnap British soldiers in retaliation, its radio transmitter announcing that any "enemy subject" taken prisoner, army or civilian, would be tried by "a war court of the Jewish underground movement and, if condemned, "hanged or shot."[82]

Also on the 17th, MacMillan confirmed the death sentences on Feinstein and Barazani, and commuted the sentence on Azulai to life imprisonment. At 11:40 p.m. on April 21, prior to their scheduled execution the following morning, these religiously devout young men, Feinstein, a native-born *sabra* of Polish parents, and Barazani, an Iraqi immigrant, committed suicide in Jerusalem's Central Prison by detonating a hand grenade placed between their chests. They had requested the Irgun to smuggle in grenades in order to kill both themselves and their executioners on the way to the gallows and so avenge their four comrades in Acre Prison, but chose their ultimate fate in order not to risk the life of a rabbi who had insisted on accompanying them at dawn. In a last message, they called on their Irgun and LEHI fighters-in-arms to "carry the banner of revolt with honor and carry on until we redeem and are redeemed. We march to death proudly." Earlier last-minute appeals by Weizmann and Chief Rabbi Herzog to Cunningham were of no avail, Gurney officially conveying regret after the two deaths (as in Gruner's case) that the High Commissioner was "unable to intervene" in the matter. "That's two more less," wrote Barker to Antonius: "I'm all for them doing that—it saves a lot of bother."[83]

A new wave of shootings, bomb-throwing, and mine-laying by the Irgun and LEHI followed the hangings and the Feinstein-Barazani deaths. One British soldier was killed in an attack on a camp in Netanya on the 18th. Eight soldiers and civilians were killed and twenty-seven wounded when the Cairo-Haifa train was blown up near Rehovot on the 22nd. Two days later, four soldiers were injured by a land mine three miles south of Jaffa. Cunningham demanded that the *yishuv* cooperate with the authorities in preventing these acts or he would reimpose martial law; Ben-Gurion refused, and defended Agency criticism abroad against the mandatory as legitimate protests. A police inspector and three constables were killed and six wounded in a mine explosion at a police station in Sarona, near Tel Aviv on the 26th, the same day that Haifa police chief A. E. Conquest, long a LEHI enemy, was shot dead in Haifa. Only the jammed hands of a pocket watch's timing mechanism prevented a powerful LEHI bomb from exploding in the Colonial Office on the 16th; M. M. Collins, a Jewish businessman from England then visiting Tel Aviv, saved himself at the last minute on the 24th from an Irgun hanging in an orange grove by reciting Hebrew prayers. Any lull in our operations against "the British occupier of our country" would result from tactical considerations, Begin told Homer Bigart of the *New York Herald Tribune*, and no truce was possible until a free and independent Jewish state east and west of the Jordan was achieved. The UN discussions, in his opinion, would lead mainly to delay, much desired by the British, and if after eighteen months or more "some paper 'solution' were reached" but not to London's liking, "everything will be just where it is now."[84]

Shertok had advised Acheson on April 23 that a lifting of restrictions on Jewish immigration to Palestine might tend to break the "vicious circle" of repression and terrorism there, but British officialdom would not be moved on that issue. A very concerned McNeil had informed a meeting of the Dominion representatives at the beginning of the month that the threat of illegal immigration was increasing, as the organization in charge became more and more efficient. The ships being used were newer and much faster than the earlier ones, the passengers held papers that were apparently completely in order, and the British were extremely nervous to intercept the vessels as they zigzagged toward the coast lest the Royal Navy destroyers run aground. He spoke very bitterly about the failure of the French and the Americans to take adequate steps against the traffic in spite of "persistent" British representations, and hoped that the establishment by treaty of a twelve-mile limit for immigration patrols might be of "considerable advantage" in intercepting and diverting these vessels to Cyprus. Three weeks later, Lord Altrincham, formerly Minister Resident Middle East at the end of World War II as Sir Edward Grigg, declared to his colleagues that the responsibility for the situation in the Holy Land which led to referring it to the UN "is really due to the crimes of Europe and to sabotage by other civilized powers of our government in Palestine," who sabotaged it "by the encouragement of illegal immigration" and by "ignorant support of Jewish extremists."[85]

A similar suggestion to Shertok's, made by Weizmann to Crossman on March 12, had been passed by the Labour MP to Attlee. After a long delay, the Prime Minister sent a private response against making concessions on immigration:[86]

> It is not just a question of the terrorists. So far the Jewish Agency
> has shown no inclination whatever to stand up to the terrorists, but
> on every occasion reiterates a demand for an increase in immigration

or an alteration of the land regulations. They have also turned down every suggestion made. It is about time something came from them.

In relaying this to Weizmann on the 28th, four days after the Central Committee of Liberated Jews in the U.S. zone in Germany asked the UN via Lie to open the gates of Palestine—"the land of our forefathers and our hope," the extremely depressed Crossman wrote that he had every fear that Marshall would be inclined to back any active policy in Palestine which Bevin proposed. This would leave Britain with a new trusteeship agreement framed more to the Foreign Secretary's taste. The Americans, he went on, would now show consideration for Arab susceptibilities as much as Britain, but would be shrewd enough to avoid putting the United States in the position where Washington would have to undertake a policy "either harmful to domestic interest or objectionable to Standard Oil." Legalized partition or partition by force seemed to Crossman the only practical way out of the present difficulties, but he saw no prospect of HMG pressing for the former, while the Americans would be content to support it verbally and then to accept defeat "if this can be arranged."[87]

Aliya Bet would not be halted. On April 13, the Theodor Herzl (2,641 passengers, including 40 babies and 50 children under 10 years old) was intercepted by three destroyers eight miles off Tel Aviv. With streamers reading "Did you join the Navy to chase orphans?" and "The Germans destroyed our families and homes; don't you destroy our hopes," the old cable-laying steamship refused to halt. In the course of a three-hour battle, tear-gas bombs and gunfire from boarding marines killed Aryeh Dyerman (twenty-four) and Istvan Weiss (twenty-two) and wounded twenty-seven; Menahem Samet (twenty-eight) died in the hospital with his wife at the bedside. Two days later, the yishuv mourned the victims with a large procession to the cemetery that carried one banner only: "No power can stop immigration." On the 18th, one refugee was shot dead and six wounded in a demonstration on Cyprus in protest against the reduction of the monthly quota for Palestine from 730 to 350; a one-day hunger strike followed. Five days later, the 300-ton coastal steamer Sh'ar Yashuv (The Remnant Will Return, crammed with 768 passengers) was stopped by the British, who used tear-gas, batons, and knives but no fire-arms. Seven injured were taken off, one with a concussion. The rest were transferred to Cyprus, marking the thirty-first recorded Aliya Bet vessel since the Berl Katznelson's voyage in November 1945.[88]

By this time, the stance of the USSR regarding discussion at the UN had crystallized further, adding one more element to the March 17 report that had reached Vyshkinskii. The "Jewish question" in Western Europe could not be solved only by immigration to Palestine, proposed Deputy Director of the Middle East Department M. A. Maksimov on April 12 to his superiors, since "nothing short of the complete destruction of all the roots of fascism and the democratization of the countries of Western Europe will give the Jewish masses normal conditions of life." A collective protectorate under UN auspices, he advised, would be a "more fruitful" solution, although it must be remembered that the Arab and Jewish populations of Palestine were mature enough to be given full independence, that both opposed a protectorate in principle, and that each called for full independence and the creation of, respectively, a Jewish or an Arab state.[89]

Three days later, the Middle East Department of the USSR Ministry of Foreign Affairs endorsed Maksimov's points and the March 17 recommendations while analyzing the U.S. UK, Arab, and Zionist positions on Palestine. In its view, the United States sought air and naval bases in the Near East, as well as oil, in order to establish "American domination of the world." Truman's favoring a Zionist state depended partly on the two million Jewish voters in the United States and on American Zionist "capabilities." The British referred the question to the UN "in an attempt to gain time" while reserving its position with regard to the peoples of Palestine. With the Arabs and Jews at opposite sides, this memorandum concluded, the USSR had to support the demands of "progressive social groups" for the creation of an independent and democratic Palestinian state, the UN to lay the foundations "within a fixed time" towards this end.[90]

Truman chose to maintain a low profile in the matter. A request on April 14 to "His Excellency" from Bergson on behalf of the Hebrew Committee of National Liberation, seeking financial support for that group's transfer to Palestine and the initial cost of rehabilitation and resettlement there of the 200,000 "Hebrew displaced persons" now in the American zones of occupation in Germany and Austria, was referred to the State Department the next day. There is no indication that the President saw this letter, which was forwarded by his secretary to the Near Eastern Affairs department on the 22nd and filed on May 2. Truman rejected a recommendation from Gael Sullivan, Acting Chairman of the Democratic National Committee, that he discuss the forthcoming UN hearings on Palestine with Silver and a few representatives of principal Jewish organizations. As Sullivan reported to Sack on the 26th, the Chief Executive feared that he would be put in the position of trying to influence the United Nations delegates. In addition, if the Jews were received he would also have to see speakers for others (meaning the Arabs), and this in turn would "muddy the waters." Truman would also have to make a statement after seeing the Jewish delegation, but all he could say would be to reaffirm the stance which he had already taken, and he thought that unnecessary: Austin "knows his position," Truman added, and the State Department "is giving Austin a briefing." (Sullivan had no information as to the nature of the briefing.) The President would watch for pro-Russian support, Sullivan observed next, and that in turn "will make our position clearer." If Moscow, for example, took a pro-Arab attitude at the UN, the United States in turn would take an anti-Arab attitude. However, Sack informed Silver, Sullivan did not seem to have "a clear picture" on the Russian subject.[91]

When newly elected GA President Oswaldo Aranha, heading the Brazilian delegation, opened the special session on April 28, many continued to wonder if Britain would live up to the UN's recommendations should these ran counter to HMG's wishes. Henderson had privately thought that London "would not dare defy" the UN decision, as it could not afford to defy public opinion; it would be obliged either to agree or to surrender the Mandate. The next day, at the outset of discussion in the General (Steering) Committee, Asaf Ali (India), supported by Mahmoud Hassan Pasha (Egypt) and Gromyko, pressed for a positive declaration on the part of the British representative in light of a statement six days earlier in the House of Lords by Viscount Hall that he "could not imagine" the government carrying out a policy "of which it does not approve." Cadogan replied: "If it were a decision which we could not reconcile with our conscience, should we single-handed be expected to expend our blood and treasure in carrying it out? I am only going to make a reservation on that particular point, and I shall make it in proper terms in the Assembly." Not entirely convinced, Neftali Ponce (Ecuador) remarked later in the meeting that item one of the agenda "required a satisfactory explanation from the United Kingdom about the efficacy of the participation of the United Nations in the solution of the Palestine problem." When Ali asked if the British government would prepare a memorandum to the GA, Cadogan, against Aranha's desire not to go beyond the point of the agenda, promised to do so when making a statement of the case in general.[92]

Cadogan's side-stepping the basic question reflected the British Cabinet's uncertainty and its wish not to have a full-dress debate at this stage. "Why should we *alone* promise to carry out [a] decision?" Attlee queried on April 29 in agreeing with Bevin. Secretary of War Alexander did not want HMG to commit at all from the "defence angle," but Bevan thought that the Cabinet must accept the authority of the court. Attlee jumped in: "But this isn't a court." As members of the UN, Bevan riposted, we should share in enforcing the decision. The issue remained unresolved. Cadogan's associates agreed the same day with Whitehall against Cunningham's suggestion that the GA be asked to make some declaration deprecating acts of terrorism, since they wanted to avoid a discussion "of all the merits of the case." Introducing a special resolution, they noted, would turn the GA deliberations towards "the contemplation of past history and of the present unhappy state of affairs," rather than consideration of plans for the future, "and would thus needlessly complicate the proceedings." On the other hand, any GA resolution that secured passage could urge, pending a final settlement of the problem, that all parties, in the spirit of Article 2 of the UN Charter, rely on peaceful means for the attainment of their objectives and should discountenance terroristic acts. They hoped that it might also, at the same time, be possible and desirable to get the Assembly to pass a resolution supporting recent British representations to Lie that he request the member states to discourage illegal immigration. Time would tell.[93]

The speeches of four delegates that day in an auditorium at Flushing Meadows in Queens, refurbished site of the New York City Pavilion built for the 1939–1940 World's Fair, gave a foretaste of what might follow. Characterizing the Palestine Mandate a mistake and political Zionism "imperialism at its worst" that endangered peace everywhere, Jamali defended the 1939 White Paper, asked if "the rightful inhabitants of Palestine" should be subjected to a domination by "aliens, imposed by force, invasion and aggression," and called (as submitted by the Egyptian delegate and the other four Arab states on April 25) for the declaration of Palestine's independence. Herschel V. Johnson (United States) insisted that only the item originally proposed by Britain on April 2 should be considered at this session, the last chance for the solving of the Palestine problem in "a peaceful and fair manner." "Calm study" in an atmosphere free from pressure on the part of the great powers and from intrigues behind the scenes was essential, Austin's deputy argued, with the Arab states "and any other interested people" free to express their full views regarding a solution "at the proper time" in the regular session.

Charles Malik (Lebanon) reiterated the Arab request for a full examination of the subject in order to enlighten the committee selected before it set out to work; both the Arabs and the Jews agreed on the independence of Palestine, which the League of Nations Mandate had ultimately championed twenty-five years earlier. The Soviet Union, Gromyko declared, favored a consideration of the substance of this question at the present session, but not in the sense that a decision should be taken in accordance with the proposal championed by the delegation of Egypt with the support of the other Arab states. Aranha, Lie, Cadogan, Gromyko, and Johnson worked out a compromise plan whereby the Arab proposal would be withdrawn, with the substitution of a resolution that the terms of reference "will not exclude the possibility of this or any other solution which may be found appropriate," but the Arab delegates turned it down. After the proposal submitted by the Arab states was defeated late at night by a vote of eight to one (Egypt, the one Arab state represented on the committee) with five abstentions, the General Committee recommended that the British item be placed on the agenda of the Assembly for a vote on May 1, and that of the Arab states not be included.[94]

This first meeting of the General Committee boded ill for the Zionists. They had no official standing to refute the Arab presentation. The Jewish Agency's earlier request, made by Silver to Lie on the 23rd, to be recognized as a non-voting representative and appeal for a Jewish state was opposed by the American Council for Judaism. The Agency had succeeded in persuading the major U.S. Jewish organizations to let it be the sole advocate in this regard for the Jewish people before the UN, although the Hebrew Committee of National Liberation and the ultra-Orthodox Agudas Israel also requested to be heard, and a memorandum to the GA from HaShomer HaTsa'ir favored a bi-nationalist Palestine. Acheson had turned down Shertok's request that the United States take the lead in the special committee and issue an interim proposal advocating the immediate opening of Palestine to Jewish immigration. Russia, Shertok informed the Agency Executive's American section on the 14th, was "a dark horse and complete negative; she is out-side our reach." An indication of Moscow's attitude appeared ten days later in an editorial of the *Daily Worker*, official organ of the American Communist Party, which urged the GA to "assist in the formation of a joint Jewish-Arab state based on equal democratic rights."[95]

The Arab states, by contrast, presented a united front in following al-Khoury's stance to press for a full-dress discussion in the Assembly. If they could not prevent the formation of a special committee, they intended to seek representation on it. Their first objective would then be to influence the other committee members. Their second, a confidential Agency intelligence report disclosed on the 29th, was to watch the trend of the discussion so they could find out if and when it turned against them: "In that event they will be able to provoke an Arab revolt in Palestine before September." This time, Azzam and Arab Higher Committee secretary Emil Ghouri had declared, the revolt would be organized without giving any prior warning. Further, an Arab League bulletin quoted the text of a letter from Mahatma Gandhi declaring that if the Arabs, "a great nation known throughout history for hospitality and generosity," gave the Jews, "an intelligent, learned and active people," protection and hospitality "without the need of mediation, then you have fulfilled the traditions for which you are famous."[96]

While the composition of the special committee and its terms of reference remained to be decided upon, the "vicious circle" of repression and terrorism continued throughout Palestine. Haj Amin advised the Arab League to press at the UN for the country's independence, while the problem of Jewish refugees to be considered a world problem, for Palestine was unable to absorb "all those Jews" presently living there—"let alone another 15 million (*sic*) Jews." One of these *yishuv* residents, nineteen-year-old Asher Itzkovitz, a *ma'apil* from the Carpathian Mountains who had arrived aboard the *Yagur* in August 1946 as one of two Holocaust survivors out of his entire family, was killed on April 9 by an Arab mob as he made his way during Passover to the Western Wall in Jerusalem's Old City; an Arab constable saved Itzkovitz's companion. McDonald wrote to Hutcheson of the "police state" that he regularly witnessed during his visit there. In his opinion, a column in the *Palestine Post* on the 18th aptly captured the on-going domestic tension, along with this *cri de coeur*: "It is a pitiful reflection on the political and moral resources of the Labour Government that it should answer the challenge of the lawbreakers with a withdrawal of the law's protection from innocent and guilty alike." McDonald, like the U.S. official who sent a copy to State, thought the conclusion therein particularly strong: "The British people are a great and good people with the pride of a civic freedom perhaps unparalleled anywhere else in the world. Their government is not equal to them in virtue or in courage." Its author's overriding question had yet to be answered: "To what end?"[97]

Endnotes

1   Meeting, January 1, 1947, WO 32/10260; Meeting, January 2, 1947, FO 371/61762; both in PRO; Conference, January 3, 1947, 5/4, Cunningham MSS; *Memoirs of Field-Marshal Montgomery*, 421.

2   Memos, December 9, 1946, CAB 129/15; Bevin statement, January 2, 1947, CAB 195/5; Bevin-Shinwell memo, January 7, 1947, CAB 129/16; all in PRO; Cohen, *Palestine and the Great Powers*, 210–211.

3   L. K. (Kohn) note, January 1, 1947, S25/10551, CZA; Creech Jones memo, January 16, 1947, Annex 1, CAB 129/46, PRO; Conference, January 3, 1947, 5/4, Cunningham MSS.

4   Conference, January 3, 1947, 5/4, Cunningham MSS; Ben-Gurion interview at the Colonial Office, January 2, 1947, FO 371/61762, PRO.

5   Meeting, January 4, 1947, FO 371/61762, PRO.

6   Trevor, *Under the White Paper*, 297–298; Ben-Zvi memo, January 3, 1947, J1/33211, CZA; Myerson-Remez-Gurney meeting, January 7, 1947, BGA.

7   Menachem Begin, *The Revolt* (Los Angeles, CA, 1972 ed.), 254–255.

8   Attlee to Bevin, December 1, 1946, FO 800/475; Attlee "Near Eastern Policy" memo to Bevin, January 5, 1947, FO 800/476; both in PRO.

9   Bevin to Attlee, January 9, 1947, FO 800/476, PRO. On September 30, 1938, Hitler, Italian Prime Minister Benito Mussolini, French Premier Edouard Daladier, and British Prime Minister Neville Chamberlain signed the Munich Pact, which sealed the fate of Czechoslovakia, virtually handing it over to Germany in the name of peace. Upon returning to Britain, Chamberlain would declare that the meeting had achieved "peace in our time." Convinced that Hitler's territorial demands were not unreasonable and that Hitler was a "gentleman," he had persuaded the French to join him in pressuring Czechoslovakia to submit to the German *Führer*'s demands.

10   Dixon minute, January 10, 1947, FO 800/476; January 13, 1947 meeting, CAB 127/281; both in PRO.

11   Trevor, *Under the White Paper*, 298–300; Inverchapel to Bevin, January 7, 1947, FO 371/61762, PRO; *Palestine Press Review*, January 9, 1947; Ben-Gurion speech, January 11, 1947, J112/1203; JAEJ, January 12, 1947; both in CZA; *Palestine Post*, January 13, 1947.

12   Bevin memo, January 14, 1947, CAB 129/16; Cabinet meeting, January 15, 1947, CAB 128/9 and 11, and CAB 195/5; Epstein memo, c. January 21, 1947, A263/18, CZA; Creech Jones memo, January 16, 1947, CAB 129/16; all in PRO.

13   Bevin memo, January 13, 1947, CAB 129/16; Cabinet meeting, January 15, 1947, CAB 195/5; Beeley memo, January 16, 1947, FO 371/61858; all in PRO.

14   *FRUS, 1947* (Washington, D.C., 1971), vol. 5, 1000–1001, 1006; Inverchapel to Bevin, January 9, 1947, FO 371/61762, PRO; Epstien memo, January 12, 1947, S25/6618; Silver to Epstein, January 13, 1947, S25/6621; both in CZA; Acheson-Shertok interview, Jan. 15, 1947, 501/BB Palestine/1-1547, SD; Jewish Agency Executive, American Section, January 20, 1947, Z5/49, CZA; AZEC Executive, January 29, 1947, ZA.

15   *FRUS, 1947*, vol. 5, 1007–1008.

16   Frankfurter to Buxton, January 23, 1947, Box 40, Frankfurter MSS; Bevin to Inverchapel, January 17, 1947, FO 371/61763; Inverchapel to Bevin, January 21, 1947, FO 371/61764; both in PRO; *FRUS, 1947*, vol. 5, 1008–1011.

17   Cabinet meeting, January 22, 1947, CAB 195/5 and CAB 128/11; both in PRO.

18   *FRUS, 1946*, vol. 7, 717–720; *FRUS, 1947*, vol. 5, 1011–1014.

19   Va'ad HaLeumi meeting, January 20, 1947, J1/8028, CZA; Trevor, *Under the White Paper*, 300–304; Cunningham-Myerson et al. interview, January 27, 1947, 5/1, Cunningham MSS; JAEJ, January 28, 1947, CZA; *Palestine Post*, January 31, 1947; Ralph Windham, "Kidnapped Off the Bench," RG 72.16, 1784/4, ISA; Hoffman, *Anonymous Soldiers*, 374–376.

20   *FRUS, 1947*, vol. 5, 1015–1017; Meeting, January 27, 1947, FO 371/61747, PRO; Al-Khoury's address, A537/6/16/2, Anglo-Jewish Association Archives, London; Sasson memo, January 28, 1947, S25/7030, CZA.

21   *FRUS, 1947*, vol. 5, 1017–1021; Meeting, January 29, 1947, Z4/303/32, CZA; Abba Eban, *An Autobiography* (New York, 1977), 70.

22   *FRUS, 1947*, vol. 5, 1021–1023; Meeting, January 30, 1947, FO 371/61747, PRO.

23   *FRUS, 1947*, vol. 5, 1024–1028; Meeting, February 3, 1947, A289/84, CZA

24   *FRUS, 1947*, vol. 5, 1028–1030; Creech Jones to Cunningham, February 5, 1947, FO 371/61747, PRO; Jones to State, March 14, 1947, 867N.01/3-1347, SD.

25 London *Times*, January 27, 1947; *Parliamentary Debates, Commons*, 432, cols. 1306, 1326–1329, 1345–1352.

26 Hoffman, *Anonymous Soldiers*, 378–380; R. W. Hamilton, *Letters from the Middle East by an Occasional Archeologist* (Edinburgh, 1992), 1; *Al-Difa'a*, February 2, 1947, 47/784, HA; Herzog-Cunningham talk, Feb. 1, 1947, S25/5601, CZA. Operation Polly, transferring some 1,700 British civilians to Egypt, concluded successfully one week later.

27 Trevor, *Under the White Paper*, 306–308; Chief Rabbinate manifesto, February 5, 1947, Isaac Herzog MSS, Heikhal Shlomo, Jerusalem; Gurney to Myerson, February 3, 1947, S25/5647, CZA; Lourie to Agency Executive, February 4, 1947, 93.03/2270/5, ISA.

28 Myerson to Lourie, February 6, 1947, 93.03/2267/19, ISA; Gallman to Marshal, February 5, 1947, 867N.01/2-547, SD; *FRUS, 1947*, vol. 5, 1030.

29 Bevin and Creech Jones memo, February 6, 1947; Meeting, February 7, 1947; both in CAB 129/16; *FRUS, 1947*, vol. 5, 1035–1037.

30 Creech Jones to Cunningham, February 7, 1947, FO 371/61667, PRO.

31 Cunningham to Creech Jones, February 9, 1947, FO 371/61767, PRO.

32 Meeting, February 10 (February 12 memo), 1947, Z4/15214, CZA; FO 371/61873, PRO; *FRUS, 1947*, vol. 5, 1040–1042.

33 Creech Jones to Cunningham, February 13, 1947, CO 537/2333, PRO; *FRUS, 1947*, vol. 5, 1044; *Foreign Policy Bulletin*, 26:12 (February 21, 1947): 1.

34 Ben-Gurion interview with Bevin, February 12, 1947, 7/1, Silver MSS; David Ben-Gurion, "Cards On the Table Before Bevin," *JOMER*, December 25, 1964, 15–16; CO 537/2333, PRO; Ben-Gurion to Paula, February 12, 1947, BGA; Agency memo, February 12, 1947, Box 31/3, Arthur Creech Jones MSS, Rhodes House, University of Oxford, Oxford, England.

35 Arab statement, February 10, 1947, in Jones to State, March 13, 1947, 867N.01/3-1347. SD, Creech Jones to Cunningham, February 13, 1947, FO 371/61748, PRO; *FRUS, 1947*, vol. 5, 1043, 1046; M. S. (Shertok) conversation, February 13, 1947, A245N/207, CZA.

36 Jewish Agency statement, February 13, 1947, A263/18, CZA; Ben-Gurion, *JOMER*, January 22, 1965, 11–13; Meeting, February 13, 1947, Z4/302/32, CZA; *FRUS, 1947*, vol. 5, 1046–1047.

37 Philip Bernstein, "Bevin Says No," Bernstein MSS.

38 Ben-Gurion to Bevin, February 14, 1947, BGA; Bevin-Creech Jones memo, February 13, 1947, CAB 129/17; Cabinet meeting, February 14, 1947, CAB 128/9; both in PRO.

39 Creech Jones to Cunningham, February 15, 1947, FO 371/61749, PRO; *FRUS, 1947*, vol. 5, 1047–1048.

40 Cabinet minutes, February 18, 1947, CAB 128/9 and 195/5; both in PRO; *FRUS, 1947*, vol. 5, 1048–1049; Acheson-Silver meeting, February 14, 1947, 93.03/2268/25, ISA; *Parliamentary Debates, Commons*, 433, col. 985; Truman, *Years of Trial and Hope*, 183.

41 *FRUS, 1947*, vol. 5, 1053–1054; Bernstein memo, February 17, 1947, 800.4016DP/2-2047, SD; Abraham S. Hyman, *The Undefeated* (Jerusalem, 1993), 317.

42 *Parliamentary Debates, Commons*, 433, col. 989; Ben-Gurion, *JOMER*, February 5, 1965, 17; *FRUS, 1947*, vol. 5, 1055; Meeting, February 19, 1947, Z4/10381; Shertok-Creech Jones interview, February 20, 1947, S25/7568; both in CZA.

43 Weizmann to Epstein, February 21, 1945, WA; Eytan memo, February 25, 1947, S25/5343, CZA.

44 Weizmann to Epstein, February 21, 1945, WA; Neumann memo, February 18, 1947, Crum files, Neumann MSS; *FRUS, 1947*, vol. 5, 1051; Gelber memo, February 14, 1947, A263/18, CZA.

45 Lillie Shultz, "Memo on Palestine," February 4, 1947, MC280/238; Shultz to Kirchwey, February 11, 1947, MC280/287; both in Freda Kirchwey MSS, Schlesinger Library, Radcliffe College, Cambridge, MA.

46 *Palestine Post*, March 7 and 14, 1947; Creech Jones-Stein-Laski interview, February 14, 1947, Creech Jones-Board of Deputies meeting, February 17, 1947; both in C14/31, Board of Deputies of British Jews Archives, London;

47 Truman, *Memoirs, Years of Trial and Hope*, 2, 181–182; *FRUS, 1947*, vol. 5, 1057–1058; *JTA*, February 26–27, 1947.

48 *FRUS, 1947*, vol. 5, 32–39, 60–64; Clifford, *Counsel to the President*, 131–132; Vandenberg to Silver, February 17, 1947, Z6/93, CZA; McCullough, *Truman*, 539–542. Forrestal and Patterson agreed with Marshall that "immediate aid" should be given. The collapse of Greece in particular, Marshall believed, would create a situation "threatening to the security of the U.S." Marshall memo to Truman, February 27, 1947, PSF General, Box 129, HSTL.

49 Meeting, February 27, 1947, A263/18, CZA; *FRUS, 1947*, vol. 5, notes to 1058.

50 Shertok-Marshall conversation, February 27, 1947, 867N.01/2-2747, SD; *FRUS, 1947*, vol. 5, 1059. In press interviews, Shertok observed that, Bevin's statement in Commons on February 25 notwithstanding, Truman could not have upset the negotiations the previous October because there was no prospect of an agreed solution at the time, and the Foreign Secretary's

considering the Jews only a religious body indicated his lack of information on the Zionist problem and his incompetence to judge the issues and bring about a settlement. "The Jews," Shertok asserted, "had never empowered Mr. Bevin to decide what they are." *Palestine Post*, February 27 and 28, 1947.

51 Ben-Gurion to Creech Jones, February 26, 1947, Z4/15214, CZA; Trevor, *Under the White Paper*, 310–314, 316–318; *Palestine Post*, February 10 and 18, 1947; Calendar memo, February 14 and 16, 1947, 6/19-4kaf, Jabotinsky Archives; *Haganah, Jewish Resistance* 1 (March 15, 1947); JTA, March 2, 1947; Slutzky, *Sefer Toldot HaHagana*, 916–917, 1142–1146; Z. Gilad, *Sefer HaPalmah*, 742–743, 802–812; Arie L. Eliav, *The Voyage of the Ulua*, I. L. Taslitt, trans. (New York, 1969). For Arlosoroff's murder and its later political impact on the *yishuv*, see Penkower, *Twentieth Century Jews*, chap. 8.

52 Khalaf, *Politics in Palestine*, 129–132; Danin to Kollek, January 7, 1947, Z4/30972, CZA; Aharon Cohen, "Why Was Fauzi Husseini Killed?," *Mishmar*, January 3, 1947; Cohen to Elath, February 18, 1947, L35/133; Susan Lee Hattis, *The Bi-National Idea in Palestine during Mandatory Times* (Jerusalem, 1970), 305; Protocol, November 11, 1946, Box 45, Jerome Frank MSS, Sterling Library, Yale University, New Haven, CT; *Haganah, Jewish Resistance*, 1, March 15, 1947; *Al Misri*, February 18, 1947, S25/9033, CZA; *Palestine Affairs*, March 1947, 33; *Haganah, Jewish Resistance* 2, April 15, 1947.

53 Trevor, *Under the White Paper*, 318–322; Hoffman, *Anonymous Soldiers*, 387–390; *Palestine Post*, March 2, 1947; *HaBoker*, March 10, 1947; Weizmann to Cunningham, March 4, 1947, WA; *Parliamentary Debates, Commons*, vol. 434, col. 65. Told about the impending attack on Goldschmidt House, Ben-Gurion immediately ordered that the British be informed. The messenger arrived too late with this information. Aryeh Eshel, *Shvirat HaGardomim* (Tel Aviv, 1990), 42–43. For other actions against the *porshim* (dissidents) at this time, see report up to March 15, 1947, J18/82, CZA.

54 *Palestine Post*, March 3, 1947; JAEJ, March 14, 1947, CZA; Ben-Gurion to Attlee, March 18, 1947, FO 371/61894, PRO. Not finding a trace in the British archives of this cable, Michael Cohen speculated that "perhaps Ben-Gurion thought again about the political effect of admitting how vulnerable the Yishuv was to British sanctions." Michael Cohen, *Palestine and the Great Powers*, 239.

55 Creech Jones report, March 19, 1947, CAB 129/17, PRO; *Palestine Post*, March 17, 1947; Trevor, *Under the White Paper*, 322–323; Hoffman, *Anonymous Soldiers*, 391–393.

56 *HaAretz*, March 18, 1947; Ben-Zvi report, March 4, 1947, S25/28, CZA; Cunningham to Creech Jones, March 16, 1947, FO 371/61770, PRO.

57 PIO statement, March 3, 1947, S25/10488, CZA; McNeil memo, March 12, 1947, FO 800/487; Memo, March 25, 1947, FO 371/61768; both in PRO; Eri Jabotinsky report, March 10, 1947, Reuven Hecht MSS. (courtesy of R. Hecht); Slutzky, *Sefer Toldot HaHagana*, 1146–1147, 1107–1108; Z. Gilad, *Sefer HaPalmah*, 695–703; Nicholas Bethell, *The Palestine Triangle: The Struggle for the Holy Land, 1935–1948* (New York, 1979), 314–315; Trevor, *Under the White Paper*, 328–331; *Palestine Post*, Mar. 31, 1947; *Hagana Jewish Resistance*, April 15, 1947.

58 March 11, 1947 report, 84–85/19, Box 255, RG 25, PAC, Ottawa; Meyer Weisgal, *So Far, An Autobiography* (New York, 1971), 235–236; Stone interview, Box 2, Dewey Stone MSS, AJHS.

59 Meeting, March 19, 1947, CAB 129/17 and CAB 128/9; Meeting, March 20, 1947, and Chiefs of Staff report, March 26, 1947; both in CAB 129/18; all in PRO; Eban to Agency Executive, March 10, 1947, 93.03/2266/38, ISA.

60 Meeting, March 27, 1947, CAB 128/9, PRO; Hoffman, *Anonymous Soldiers*, 397–398.

61 New York to *Palcor*, April 1, 1947, S25/5232; Wahl to Kenen, April 1, 1947; Wahl to Klausner, April 14, 1947; both in A431/14; Bernstein to Kenen, April 9, 1947, A370/1043; all in CZA; Jabotinsky memo, April 1947, Box 6, Eri Jabotinsky MSS, Jabotinsky Archives; Wahl memo, April, 15, 1947, A431/14, CZA.

62 *FRUS, 1947*, vol. 5, 1067–1069; Shultz memo, April 3, 1947, MC 280/238, Kirchwey MSS.

63 *FRUS, 1947*, vol. 5, 1060–1064, 1066–1067; Shertok-Lie meeting, March 5, 1947, S25/5178, CZA; Wadsworth memo, January 13, 1947, 867N.01/1-3047, SD; Bevin to Cadogan, March 3, 1947, FO371/61769; Inverchapel to Bevin, March 21, 1947, FO 371/61770; both in PRO; Memo, March 21, 1947, Robert McClintock MSS, SD.

64 McClintock to Henderson, March 4, 1947, 867N.01/3-347, SD; Shertok-Lie meeting, March 4, 1947, S25/5178; Epstein-Merriam meeting, March 5, 1947, S25/6623; Shertok to Myerson, April 2, 1947, S25/3968; Shertok to Myerson, April 4, 1947, S25/3965; all in CZA.

65 *Documents on Israeli Soviet Relations*, 166–172.

66 Ibid., 158–164, 173. For the steps leading to Truman's address since he accepted the appeal of Marshall and Acheson on February 27, see *FRUS, 1947*, vol. 5, 63–110; Clifford, *Counsel to the President*, 133–137.

67 Jamali to Lie, March 11, 1947, FO371/61874. PRO; *FRUS, 1947*, vol. 5, 1064–1065, 1132; Arab League Council protocol, March 23, 1947, 2569/14, RG 130/15, ISA; Tuck to State, March 28, 1947, 867N.01/3-2847, SD.

68 *FRUS, 1947*, vol. 5, notes to 1068.

69 National Board, March 5, 1947, Hadassah Archives; Crum, *Behind the Silken Curtain*; Crossman, *Palestine Mission*; Agency Executive declaration, March 24, 1947, S25/10029, CZA; Ben-Gurion Diaries, March–November 1947, passim, BGA; Weizmann to Creech Jones, March 27, 1947; Weizmann to Kaplan, March 27, 1947; Weizmann to Wise, April 8, 1947; all in WA; Buxton to Ben-Horin, April 22, 1947, A300/16, CZA. For Ben-Gurion's "seminar," see David Ben-Gurion, *Pa'amei Medina*, M. Avizohar, ed. (Tel Aviv, 1993), chap. 2.

70 Epstein to Welles, March 14, 1947, S25/6618; Robinson at JAEJ, March 17, 1947, S25/5355; both in CZA; Adelson memo, March 28, 1947, 93/18/6; Kahany to Agency Executive, March 29, 1947, 93.03/2267/15; both in ISA; Adelson to Silver, March 18, 1947, 7/1, Silver MSS; Gelber memo, March 28, 1947, CF-political file, ZA. The presence of a delegation from the Hebrew University and the Va'ad HaLeumi established Jewish Palestine as part of the Asian Continent and as "a member of the family of nations of Asia." Bonné report to Myerson, April 30, 1947, S25/7485, CZA.

71 Epstein-Henderson talk, March 4, 1947, S25/6623, CZA; Silver to Myers, March 7, 1947, 4/3, Silver MSS; Memo, March 13, 1947, Robert Wagner MSS, Georgetown University, Washington, D.C.

72 Sack-Henderson talk, March 8, 1947, 4/3, Silver MSS; Sack to Shapiro, March 17, 1947, Box 3, Schulson MSS, NYPL; Baruch-Krock telephone conversation, March 25, 1947, Box 17, Arthur Krock MSS, Dept. of Rare Books and Special Collections, Princeton University Library, Princeton; Harold J. Laski, "Britain Without Empire," *Nation*, March 29, 1947, 353–356.

73 Epstein-Henderson talk, March 4, 1947, S25/6623, CZA; Cabinet meeting, March 7, 1947, Matthew J. Connelly files, HSTL; Clifford, *Counsel to the President*, 138–140; *New York Herald Tribune*, April 4 and 7, 1947.

74 Va'ad HaLeumi meeting, April 1, 1947, J1/7989, CZA; Sidney Hertzberg, "The Month in History," *Commentary* 3 (May 1947): 469; *JTA*, April 8, 1947.

75 Hertzberg, "The Month in History," *Commentary* 3 (May 1947): 369; Parshan report, April 19, 1947, S25/9033; "In the Arab Camp" report, April 23, 1947, S44/484; both in CZA; Campbell to Bevin, April 26, 1947, FO371/61875, PRO.

76 Sargent to Bevin, April 3, 1947, FO 371/61771; JAE American Section, April 3, 1947, CF-Washington Office, ZA; *New York Times*, April 3, 1947; Eban to JAE, April 17, 1947, 7/1, Silver MSS; Sargent to Bevin, April 23, 1947; Cadogan to FO, April 24, 1947; McNeil memo, April 28, 1947; all in CAB 129/18, PRO.

77 *FRUS, 1947*, vol. 5, 1072–1073.

78 Minute sheet, April 22, 1947, RG 25, series B3, vol. 2152 (pt. 3), PAC. State's first choice included a member each from Canada, New Zealand, Sweden, Belgium, Czechoslovakia, Brazil, Mexico, Colombia, Norway, and Siam.

79 Minute sheet, April 22, 1947, RG 25, series B3, vol. 2151 (pt. 3), PAC; *JTA*, April 4, 1947.

80 *FRUS, 1947*, vol. 5, 1073–1077; Elad Ben-Dror, "UNSCOP: Reishit Hitarvuto Shel HaUm B'Sikhsukh HaYisraeili-Aravi," PhD thesis, Bar-Ilan University, 2003, 30; Shertok to Myerson, April 24–25, 1947, S25/5353, CZA.

81 *FRUS, 1947*, vol. 5 1076; Begin, *The Revolt*, 261–272; Seligman letter to the editor, *New Statesman*, August 4, 1972, 160–161; Hoffman, *Anonymous Soldiers*, 400–402; Slutzky, *Sefer Toldot HaHagana*, 954–955; Wilkinson to State, April 22, 1947, 867N.01/4–2247, SD. For Shlomo Ben-Yosef, see Monty Noam Penkower, *Twentieth Century Jews*, chap. 9.

82 Trevor, *Under the White Paper*, 336; Barker to Antonius, April 17, 1947, P867/9, ISA; Parshan report, April 19, 1947, S25/9033, CZA; Hoffman, *Anonymous Soldiers*, 402; Bell, *Terror Out of Zion*, 199.

83 Begin, *The Revolt*, 273–274; Hoffman, *Anonymous Soldiers*, 403–404; Trevor, *Under the White Paper*, 337; Barker to Antonius, April 22, 1947, P867/9, ISA.

84 Slutzky, *Sefer HaHagana*, 918; J. Bower Bell, *Terror Out of Zion* (New York, 1977), 200–202; Cunningham–Ben-Gurion talk, April 23, 1947, BGA; *FRUS, 1947*, vol. 5, 1077; Yaakov Eliav, *Mevukash* (Jerusalem, 1983), 315–317; *New York Herald Tribune*, April 20, 1947. In a memorandum to all UN members but Britain "and her satellites," the Irgun called for the creation of a Hebrew Provisional Government. Memorandum, April 1947, Box 12/45, Palestine Statehood Committee MSS, Sterling Library, Yale University, New Haven.

85 *FRUS, 1947*, vol. 5, 1074; Robertson to Pearson, April 2, 1947, RG 25, series A12, vol. 2013 (pt. 2), PAC; *Parliamentary Debates, Lords*, vol. 147, col. 65.

86 Weizmann to Crossman, March 12, 1947; Crossman to Weizmann, April 28, 1947; both in WA.

87 Gringaus memo to Lie, April 24, 1947, 86 7N.01/6-1047, SD; Crossman to Weizmann, April 28, 1947, WA.

88 *Palestine Post*, April 14 and 24, 1947; Trevor, *Under the White Paper*, 338–340; Slutzky, *Sefer HaHagana*, 1147–1148; Z. Gilad, *Sefer HaPalmah*, 703–705.

89 *Documents on Israeli-Soviet Relations*, 174–175.

90 Ibid., 176–180.

91 Bergson to Truman, April 14, 1947, 867N.01/4-1447, SD; Sack to Silver, April 26, 1947, Box 3, Schulson MSS.

92 Sack to Silver, April 10, 1947, CF-State Department, ZA; Slawsom memo, April 26, 1947, AJC Archives; Cadogan to FO, April 29, 1947, FO 371/61775, PRO; Jacob Robinson, *Palestine and the United Nations* (Washington, D.C., 1947), 57–59.

93 Cabinet minutes, April 29, 1947, CAB 195/5; UK delegation to the UN to Butler, April 29, 1947, FO 371/61776; both in PRO.

94 *New York Times*, April 30 and May 1, 1947; *FRUS, 1947*, vol. 5, 1078. The five abstaining were the Soviet Union, Brazil, Czechoslovakia, India, and Poland. Polish delegate Josef Winiewicz said that he abstained because he was not prepared to vote on the motion before the Jewish people were permitted to participate in this Assembly. To this point, Aranha remarked, "I think they have the right to be heard by one of the organs of our organization."

95 *JTA*, April 16, 23, 24, 30, 1947; JAE American Section, April 14 and 21, 1947, Z5/47; Shertok to Myerson, April 17, 1947, S25.5356; both in CZA; Schenkolewski report, April 23–May 19, 1947, M. Schenkolewski files, October 46–April 47, Jacob Rosenheim MSS, Agudas Israel of America Archives, New York City.

96 Report, April 29, 1947, S25/5355; *Weekly Digest*, April 30, 1947, S25/9033; both in CZA.

97 Haj Amin to the Arab League, April 29, 1947, L35/23, CZA; Yisrael Meidad, "Pesah Damim," *Makor Rishon*, Musaf Shabbat, April 4, 2014, 17; McDonald to Hutcheson, April 20, 1947, L35/79; CZA; *Palestine Post*, April 18, 1947; 501. BB Palestine, SD.

7. UNSCOP, Two Sergeants, and the *Exodus 1947*

On May 1, 1947, UN headquarters, temporarily located in the Sperry Gyroscope plant at Lake Success, witnessed two significant votes in the first public taking of sides across the international arena regarding the Palestine question. In this northwest Long Island suburb twenty miles east of New York City, a location used by the General Assembly and the Security Council while architects prepared blueprints for a permanent UN skyscraper in Manhattan's Turtle Bay neighborhood overlooking the East River, the GA agreed that the British item regarding a Special Committee on "the future government of Palestine" be placed on its agenda and be referred to the First (Political and Security) Committee for consideration. During the afternoon of the same day, following an extended debate, the Assembly defeated inclusion of the Arab states' proposal that the Special Committee deal with "the termination of the Mandate over Palestine and the declaration of its independence" by a roll-call vote of 24 to 15, with 10 abstentions. Those in favor included the five Arab states, the Soviet Union, Byelorussia, Ukraine, Yugoslavia, Afghanistan, Argentina, Cuba, India, Iran, and Turkey.

The Polish and Czech representatives supported the Agency's request to participate in the meetings of the special session, but U.S. representative Austin reiterated Washington's position that the session should confine its activities to the "procedural task" of appointing a committee and instructing it to draw up recommendations for the next Assembly regular session in September. In his opinion, only a UN member state should be permitted to present its position before the GA plenary meetings; it would be "useful" for the Agency, which he felt should not be regarded as speaking for all the Jews of the world or even of Palestine, to present its views before the First Committee given its special status under the Mandate and the fact that the Arab states had presented their views. Lester Pearson (Canada) agreed with Austin's emphasis on procedure, and objected to Gromyko and the rest of the Soviet bloc advocating a full hearing in the GA for the Agency as the only Jewish organization to be granted this privilege. The attitude of that bloc, he informed Foreign Minister Louis S. St. Laurent, was consistent with its previous support of the Arab states' call for a discussion on the substance of the Palestine question, and was undoubtedly also influenced by the desire to establish a precedent for the participation of such non-governmental organizations as the Soviet-sponsored World Federation of Trade Unions. As amended by Cadogan, the U.S. resolution ultimately called for the General Committee to recommend to the Assembly that it ask the First Committee to decide on all the communications received. This proposal was adopted the same day by ten votes, with three abstentions (USSR, Poland, and Czechoslovakia).[1]

"Greatly pained" by Austin's stance, Shertok cabled Marshall on the 3rd that it opened the way for the Jewish Agency being "debarred from access" even to the Political Committee. The Arab attacks throughout the session on Zionist rights and interests without a single word spoken in the Agency's defense, together with the impending discussion of the terms of reference for the Special Committee, whose findings would "most vitally" affect the future of the Jewish people, entitled the Agency to participate in a consultative capacity at least in meetings of that Committee. As the one officially recognized public body authorized to represent Jewry vis-à-vis Palestine and having done so for the past twenty-five years, the Agency could not possibly agree to being relegated to a position of equality with "self-appointed," unrepresentative committees which had no standing whatsoever in Jewish life generally, or in Palestine in particular. In the interest of fairness and having confidence in UN deliberations, Shertok closed by appealing to the U.S. Government to support the Agency's claim and instruct its UN delegation accordingly.[2]

Austin had actually received his instructions earlier from Marshall, who had gotten approval from Truman for State's suggestion that a sub-committee might be designated to hear the views of non-governmental organizations of Palestine such as the Jewish Agency and the Arab Higher Committee "if it becomes necessary." That possibility, conveyed by a "very friendly but very frank" Henderson to Shertok at Flushing

Meadows, Shertok deemed "ridiculous." The Agency, he pointed out against Henderson's claim that the Arab Higher Committee would have to be heard on the same level as the Agency if the latter were granted the right to participate, had received internationally recognized status from the League of Nations. An *ad hoc* committee would be "an outrage," Silver told the Agency's American Section Executive, the State Department determined "to reduce us to the status of nobodys [*sic*] in the sessions." Henderson was worried by the terrific pressure placed upon him via AZEC-generated telegrams that were flooding Washington in favor of the Agency's speaking before the GA. We will have to "hammer away" with these people, Silver believed, to educate them "that ours is not the problem that will have to take care of 175,000 Jews [in the DP camps]. They are trying to push our case, to reduce it..." Shertok interjected at this point, "to a question of philanthropy." The Arab Higher Committee had made no application to be heard by the GA, and it had "been dragged in by the tail," Silver observed. The Arab states had made their case five times already, and we should not appear if the AHC is invited as a parallel to the Agency, he insisted.[3]

The GA considered the General Committee's report on May 3 and 5. The Latin American and Slav countries led the revolt against the attempt of the United States and Great Britain to leave the entire question up to the First Committee. The members first refused, by a vote of 39 to 8, with 7 abstentions, to accept a Polish-Czechoslovak resolution to give the Jewish Agency a hearing in the Assembly itself. Sava Kosanovic (Yugoslavia) supported this step as a symbol "that we, the free, peace-loving peoples of the world, after the victory over Nazi ideologies, would identify ourselves in understanding, in support, and in appreciation of those who were the first victims of the brutal Nazi-Fascist ideology of race supremacy and discrimination, the first victims of gas chambers and concentration camps." Enrique Rodrigues Fabregat (Uruguay), arguing, as Gromyko had on May 2, that the UN Charter did not bar the Agency from being heard in the full Assembly, introduced a compromise resolution that it be granted "a hearing" in the First Committee. At noon on the 5th, the U.S. delegation let it be known that, contrary to Austin's resolution of the previous week, it would support Fabregat's proposal. A joint resolution to that effect, along with sending to that Committee for its decision other communications received "of a similar character from the Palestinian population," was adopted by a vote of 44 to 7 (the Arab states, Afghanistan, and Turkey), with 3 abstentions (India, Iran, and Siam) and 1 absence (Costa Rica).[4]

Arab delegates were extremely angry with the joint resolution adopted at Flushing Meadows. Al-Khoury remarked that he did not know whether the UN was the proper agency to solve the Palestine problem. Speaking menacingly of the possibility that the 70 million Arabs surrounding Palestine would take matters into their own hands despite the efforts of the Arab governments to restrain them, the Syrian representative also severely criticized Aranha for requiring the GA to take a vote after the panel of speakers listed on Saturday had been exhausted. Other delegates, however, praised Aranha for being mainly responsible for cutting off procedural debate, and making it possible for the First Committee to take over. (In fact, Aranha had wanted the Agency to address the First Committee, and Lie told Shertok that it would be admitted there.) Since the First Committee, like the Assembly, was composed of one representative from each of the fifty-five member states, noted Herman Santa Cruz (Chile), the only real difference was that Pearson would preside as chairman, and the meetings would take place in a Lake Success room that was equipped for simultaneous translation.[5]

The joint resolution's use of the noun "hearing" was sure to provoke debate. Having sought in vain to amend it so that the Arab Higher Committee would be treated on the identical basis as the Jewish Agency, the five Arab states persuaded the AHC to request a hearing before the First Committee on the same grounds as the Agency. Consequently, the AHC asked to be permitted to attend the deliberations "and be heard on this problem." David Wdowinski, a leader of the Revisionist-Zionist Betar youth resistance movement in the 1943 Warsaw Ghetto Uprising and now responding on behalf of the Hebrew Committee for National Liberation (one of those seeking to be heard at the UN and claiming to be recognized by the Irgun leadership as its spokesman outside of Palestine), immediately declared that to invite the AHC to the United Nations would be "an invitation to avowed Fascists and known Nazi collaborators." Pointing to the ex-Mufti of Jerusalem as a war criminal listed at the Nuremberg Trials by some member states of the UN, he asserted that the international body's prestige would be "tragically reduced" in the eyes of the world "if these loathsome Nazis are admitted to its proceedings."

The U.S. and British delegations construed "hearing" to mean an appearance by non-governmental organizations in order to present their viewpoint, answer questions, and leave when done. State's Rusk said as much to Agency consultant Oscar Gass, comparing this to an appearance before a committee of Congress. The Arab states could be expected to support this view, but Agency representatives were divided on the matter, all visualizing the sitting in on the full Committee deliberations with the right to reply to statements that they considered wrong or contentious. Clarification of what constituted a hearing, Pearson told reporters, would constitute the "first major hurdle" of his Committee's work.[6]

On May 7, the First Committee resolved to grant a hearing to the Jewish Agency, the Arab Higher Committee, and to any other organization "representative of a considerable element of the population of Palestine." (At an emergency session, the GA approved this recognition of the AHC in order to counter the threat of a boycott by the Arab states of its proceedings, what a page one *New York Times* headline called "an appeasing move.") The vote on the much-battered Austin-José Arce (Argentina) resolution, which Pearson termed a "Manhattan cocktail," was 44 to 0. The abstention of the five Arab states, along with Turkey and France, however, led to speculation that either the Arab countries or the AHC, or both, might boycott the Committee sessions. Latin American countries joined with the Soviet Union and other Slav states in defeating the U.S. proposal to bar both the Agency and the AHC from discussing the substance of the Palestine question or the composition of the inquiry committee, and another to have Great Britain alone certify which of the rival organizations had the right to speak on behalf of "a considerable element" of Palestine's population. (Cadogan stated that he had "consented" to Austin's second proposal to grant the Agency a hearing, but that he had not requested it.) Alexandre Parodi (France) pointed out that a discussion of substance might well prolong the special session for weeks. His compromise resolution, reflecting the Quai d'Orsay's assumption that the Zionist case would be defeated "all along the line" and therefore instructed him to take a neutral stand, failed, however, by a vote of 23 to 19.[7]

The First Committee spent the week from May 7 onward at successive meetings about constituting and instructing the Special Committee, both issues producing considerable dissent. Austin advocated a small committee of seven nations, excluding the Big Five and the Arab states, while Gromyko proposed the permanent Security Council members and raised no objection to an Arab state. "If the United Nations can find a just solution which will be accepted by both parties," Cadogan stated two days later, "it would hardly be expected that we should not welcome such a solution," but HMG should not have the sole responsibility "for enforcing a solution which is not accepted by both parties and which we cannot reconcile with our conscience." On the 13th, a broadened committee of eleven assumed "neutral" states was finally agreed upon, consisting, in alphabetical order, of Australia, Canada, Czechoslovakia, Guatemala, India, Iran, Netherlands, Peru, Sweden, Uruguay, and Yugoslavia. The United Nations Special Committee on Palestine (UNSCOP) thus came into being.

Herschel Johnson (Austin's deputy) challenged Gromyko's proposal on the 10th that the Special Committee submit proposals "on the question of establishing without delay an independent State of Palestine," stating that this would prejudge the issue and that the Committee, without specific instruction, could make such a recommendation if it saw fit. The Soviet proposal failed on the 13th by a vote of 26 to 15, with two abstentions and two absences. On motion made by Parodi, the whole draft paragraph regarding the independence of "peoples of Palestine" as suggested by the American representative, instead of "population of Palestine" favored by the Arabs, Britain, and Russia, in an attempt to make the clause "as innocuous as possible" with the crucial "s" in "peoples" much to the Agency's liking, was deleted. Instead, the First Committee recommended that same day to the GA, the vote 46 to 7 (the five Arab states, Afghanistan, and Turkey), one abstention (Siam), and one absent (Haiti), that UNSCOP investigate all questions and issues relevant to the Palestine problem, conducting this in Palestine "and wherever it may deem useful." The latter phrase linking Palestine with the DP problem, championed by Poland, the Latin American states, the United States, and the Soviet Union, carried against the Arab objective (expressed by Beeley) to limit the inquiry to Palestine itself. UNSCOP was also charged to give most careful consideration to the religious interests in Palestine of Islam, Judaism, and Christianity, and to report with such proposals "as it may consider appropriate for the solution of the problem of Palestine" to the Secretary-General no later than September 1, 1947, so that the UN members could consider this by the second regular session of the General Assembly.[8]

The Agency's official appearance for the first time on behalf of the Jewish people before the organized community of nations began with

Silver's address on May 9 (in the absence of Ben-Gurion, then en route to New York) at the big horseshoe table of the First Committee. Beginning with the Mandate's commitment, backed by leading world statesmen, to give the Jewish people the opportunity "to reconstitute their national home in Palestine," the chairman of the Agency's American Section decried HMG's policy in recent years for having "grievously interfered" with and circumscribed the continuous growth of the Jewish National Home. Real feeling and emotion could be detected on many faces, hitherto an audience sitting in respectful silence, when he called for the immediate relaxation of the mandatory's restrictive immigration measures against the "war-ravaged" survivors "languishing in their misery" in DP camps while still waiting for salvation. The moderate tone of Silver's speech, which ended with the hope that representatives of the Jewish people would soon be a part of this "noble fellowship" of the UN, drew much praise.[9]

Shertok's appearance, when answering questions three days later, also garnered sympathetic coverage. His own statement that treating the Palestine and immigration issues in isolation from one another "would make as much sense as the study of hearts beating in disregard of blood circulation" echoed distinctly in newspaper coverage, which stressed his clear definition that the Jewish National Home's establishment constituted the process, with the Jewish state "its consummation." Small nations were especially pleased with Shertok's statement that Jewish Palestine was not an outpost of any foreign domination, and that the ambition of the World Zionist Organization was to integrate itself "into the modern structure of reviving Asia."[10]

The Arab Higher Committee's speakers received a different reception. On May 10 Henry Kattan spoke ably of Arab claims to Palestine as "their natural and inalienable right," and reviewed their "substantial contribution" to the Allied victory in the First World War (but remained silent about the Second). Claiming, contrary to the views expressed by many UN delegates, that the powers of a mandatory "cannot legally outlive the existence of the body [the League of Nations] delegating such powers," he also declared that the problem of the Jewish refugees was a humanitarian concern which had to be treated as such by the civilized world, divorced from the Palestine problem, and deemed it "absolutely essential" that HMG immediately stop all Jewish immigration to Palestine as inherently illegal. This Christian Arab closed with a

New Testament quotation from "the greatest of Masters" who rose "from that holy but today tortured land": "Do unto others as you would have them do unto you" (*Luke* 6:31).

In vivid contrast, Ghouri made a long and apologetic defense of the exiled Haj Amin's wartime collaboration with the Third Reich, and compared the former Mufti to liberators George Washington and South Africa's Jan Smuts. The AHC's secretary, also a Christian Arab, rounded off his appearance with a query: Did the Jews' questioning of the record of "an Arab spiritual leader" properly come "from the mouth of a people who have crucified the founder of Christianity?" These and related declarations drew Pearson's interruptions five times, along with his warning against making "controversial statements which provoke even more controversial replies." (Haj Amin's memoirs would applaud Ghouri's defense of his honor as a "big achievement" for the AHC at a forum in which "the whole word heard us.") A few minutes later, Jamali announced that the Arabs would physically fight against any UN adjudication not completely favorable to them. After all this, Eban reported to his superiors, few people in the hall were prepared to say that Jewish objection to being handed over to Arab domination was extremist or unreasonable. In the view of eminent American journalist Elmer Davis, the Arabs of Palestine had not vindicated their maturity for independence if these spokesmen reflected their views and inclinations.[11]

Gromyko's pronouncement on May 14, based on new instructions which he had received from Moscow only on the 4th and delivered the day before the special session ended, proved to be the major surprise of these Assembly deliberations. Listening to it in Jerusalem, Horowitz compared it to "a thunderbolt out of a clear blue sky." While continuing to maintain the Soviet line that a bi-national state was the best solution, he declared that if this were not realizable because of "the deterioration of relations" between Jews and Arabs, then UNSCOP would have to consider an alternative solution which, like the first, had its advocates in Palestine: the "partition" of that country into "two independent autonomous States—one Jewish and one Arab." The speech's most remarkable features included the omission of the standard Communist attack on Zionism; the admission that the Jewish people's desire for a state was "natural and justified" in light of their "indescribable" and "exceptional sorrow and suffering" during the last war in which they had been subjected to "almost complete physical annihilation," followed thereafter by their wandering about in search of means of existence and of shelter; and the omission of any suggestion for Jewish assimilation and reconstruction in Europe.[12]

Whitehall and State were taken aback by this startling turn of events. Certain until this juncture, together with his Whitehall colleagues, that Moscow would back the Arabs against partition, a suspicious Beeley assumed that the Soviets were preparing the way for some form of trusteeship in which they would be associated. The Russians had outsmarted the Americans and this would strengthen the *yishuv*'s extremists, thought a very surprised Gurney; Stalin was celebrating one of his "shining victories," remarked Gurney's deputy, V. Fox-Strangways. Rusk advised Acheson that Gromyko's speech, like the various Soviet statements throughout the two-week session, seemed "designed to straddle the fundamental issue." For an anxious Rusk, the Soviets succeeded in "playing both ends against the middle" in such a way as to gain credit both with the Jews and aspirations than that delegation's with the Arabs, leaving the USSR in an "excellent tactical position for the future." In his judgment, Stalin's regime would ultimately come out "forthrightly" on the side of the Arabs at a moment when it could "reap the greatest benefits" in the Muslim world.[13]

Having lost their earlier attempt to have the Assembly discuss Palestine's independence, the Arabs reacted strongly. Hearing Gromyko earlier defend the Agency's right to be heard before the GA, Azzam had remarked to a State Department official that the Soviets were trying "to back two horses." Confronted now by this radical switch, some Arab states stressed Gromyko's attack on the British and the Mandate, and construed the demand for a bi-national state as support for their insistence on a democratic Palestinian state (containing, in fact, a numerically frozen Jewish minority). The speech also increased the Arab effort to strengthen relations with Turkey, India, and Iran, with the aim of establishing a pan-Asian bloc against the great powers. In shock, the Arab press demanded a boycott of UNSCOP, with Iraqi newspapers united in calling Gromyko's latest remarks an "astounding blow to the Arab world." Jamali, who insisted on an interpretation of "one state and one people," announced that any UN decision about Palestine's future except independence would be "resisted" by the Arab states.[14]

The Jewish Agency hailed Gromyko's May 14 address as "an event of extraordinary importance" for accepting a number of basic principles guiding Zionists in their analysis. In his poem "A Telegram to Gromyko" two days later, Alterman spoke for a dazed *yishuv*, characterizing its reaction to the speech thus: "Sometimes it is a robust emotion, warm and good / of a swimmer who is fighting with the endless waves, / and suddenly he is tossed a lifesaver from the shore...." *Davar* and *HaAretz* both noted that it undermined the Foreign Office's appeasement of the Arabs in order to prevent their joining Russia against the West. HaShomer HaTsa'ir's *Al HaMishmar* indirectly argued against his second alternative by attacking the Agency Executive's championing of a Jewish commonwealth, while the Jewish Communists' *Kol Ha'Am* cabled Gromyko its pleasure over his proposal favoring the creation of an independent Arab-Jewish Palestine state. Wahl confided to Silver that his own talks with Gromyko before the speech already had shown "much more compatibility" between the Soviet delegation and Agency aspirations than Moscow's with the Arabs, which was in keeping with the "generous" Soviet attitude in repatriating many thousands of Polish Jews that made it possible to build up the Jewish DP population in Germany from 70,000 at the war's end.[15]

At the same time, adopting an objective analysis, Robinson cautioned his Agency Executive colleagues in New York not to rush to euphoria. There was nothing new in Gromyko's condemnation of the Mandate as an instrument of British imperialism, the American Section's international law expert began. Gromyko also "leaves us in the dark" concerning the rights of the Jewish people to Palestine, and he did not make clear that the Jewish DPs wished to emigrate there. Moreover, the Soviet representative omitted consideration of the key issue of future Jewish immigration. Finally, his statement that Arabs and Jews both had "historic roots in Palestine" was certainly a long way from accepting the unique historical connection of the Jewish people with that country. Still, the Agency had grounds for preparing a memorandum to sway Washington that Gromyko's speech demonstrated that the fear of "driving the Arabs into the arms of Russia" was not an intelligent motive for an anti-Zionist policy, while the *yishuv* and world Jewry would never be diverted from the consciousness that their destiny was "inseparably linked with the victory of democratic ideals and with resistance to all forms of totalitarianism."[16]

The very uncertainty of Moscow's real intentions led Ben-Gurion, then on a brief visit to New York in order to inform the GA that "a distinct Jewish nation" had arisen in Palestine having no conflict with the Arab people, to meet privately with Gromyko before returning home. The day before Gromyko's speech, he had proposed to the Agency Executive members in the United States that they should demand of UNSCOP a Jewish state where Zionist settlement predominated, with the rest of Palestine placed under a trusteeship "continuing the pro-Zionist clauses of the Mandate" until that part was ripe for independence as a Jewish state. Goldmann, who would accompany Ben-Gurion to see the Soviet representative, argued (with Shertok's backing) that no country would take on a trusteeship, and they should press UNSCOP for a good partition. Four days later, the Agency Executive chairman explained to Gromyko that an Arab majority in a single state would forbid Jewish immigration and stifle the *yishuv*'s development. He suggested that the two American engineers' plan to enable 1,2500,000 Jews to settle the country soon would benefit the entire population, to which Gromyko replied that it would undoubtedly be better for Palestine if the Jews ruled the whole country, but there would not be a two-thirds majority in the General Assembly for such a proposal. He thought Ben-Gurion's request for permission to send a Zionist delegation to Moscow unnecessary, since he was in New York. Greenberg had to report by cable to Locker that "Benartzi" (Gromyko) did not "add anything of importance to contents his address."[17]

Returning home, Ben-Gurion told the Agency Executive that Gromyko's speech left Russia free to support either Arabs or Jews at the General Assembly in September. Its overarching purpose was to gaining her main object—ousting of British influence from the Middle East. Cunningham heard of this meeting from a "highly reliable source." Reporting the contents to Creech Jones, he added that Ben-Gurion's conclusion "would seem to hit the mark and is more realistic than the views normally expressed by this generally most unrealistic politician."[18]

The deliberations leading to UNSCOP's creation did not ease the mandatory's worries in Palestine, as the Irgun's audacious attack on the afternoon of May 4 against the maximum security prison in Acre (Akko) made clear. In a joint operation with LEHI and coordinated with its men imprisoned inside, it blasted through the thick fortress walls that Napoleon's month-long siege in 1799 had failed to breach. Three members of the assault team, including leader Dov Cohen ("Shimshon") who had been commended for World War II service with British commando units in North Africa, were killed along with six prisoners who died in a gun battle with Sixth Airborne troops; two escapees were recaptured. Twenty-three prisoners out of forty-one dissidents selected for escape made it to freedom, but so did more than two hundred Arab prisoners, including nine who had taken part in the Arab Revolt a decade earlier. Another "suicidal" operation showing the "irresponsible character" of the terrorists, declared a Jewish Agency spokesman in Jerusalem; "an operation for liberation," retorted the Irgun's clandestine radio station. The greatly flawed operation, which was featured in the Anglo-American press, dramatically underscored Great Britain's growing inability to maintain law and order. "The law-abiding members of the community for political reasons have combined in deciding not to distinguish themselves from the members of the attacking forces," Cunningham resignedly wrote to his superior in an 8,000-word dispatch that the Colonial Secretary would read to the House one month later, "who thus emerge from within a civilian population at any moment with full initiative and every operational advantage."[19]

The dramatic raid also boosted the Irgun's image in the United States, a Ben Hecht appeal for funds to the Bergson group's American League for a Free Palestine especially roiling the diplomatic waters between London and Washington. In a full-page advertisement provocatively entitled "Letter to the Terrorists of Palestine," the famous Hollywood screen writer crowed that HMG had "pulled the UN trick" because they were frightened of the Irgun, and he went so far as to deliver this cry: "Every time you blow up a British arsenal, or wreck a British jail, or send a British railroad train sky high, or rob a British bank or let go with your guns and bombs at the British betrayers and invaders of your homeland, the Jews of America make a little holiday in their hearts." To a reporter from the London *Evening Standard*, Hecht went further: "Because you hanged Dov Gruner the British are going to get the pants kicked off them, the same as they got in Ireland. British hooligans can never run a country. They only hold the whip for a while." A furious Whitehall pressed its American counterpart to prevent such advertisements and fund-raising campaigns for "armed resistance," which also financed the illegal immigration to Palestine. In response, State declared that it could do nothing to halt these efforts, nor deprive the organizations involved of their tax-exempt status. Scant consolation came from a remark by Marshall, who on the 7th had declared that Truman's stand on Palestine remained U.S. Government policy, that such donations were clearly not charitable.[20]

The "Farran Case" reflected, as MacMillan later highlighted in his overview of this critical period, the further poisoning of relations between the mandatory and the *yishuv*. As a leader of the new Special Squads created from the police ranks to counter terrorism, wartime hero Major Roy Farran and three members of his squad abducted sixteen-year-old Alexander Rubowitz while he was engaged in pasting LEHI posters across Jerusalem walls on the evening of May 6. Their car sped away, but a gray felt trilby hat whose sweatband bore the embossed initials "Far-An" or "Farkan" was picked up at the scene. The *Palestine Post* published an account on the 22nd that clearly implicated the police, and Myerson would be able to assert correctly in a note to Cunningham one month later that the youngster had been kidnapped by Farran and some accomplices, taken down the deserted Jericho Road, "grilled" and tortured for about an hour, then murdered. (Soon thereafter, U.S. consul general in Jerusalem Robert Macatee transmitted to State a copy of Myerson's note.) A local British investigation revealed that Farran had confessed his role as the killer to his superior; Gurney and the acting attorney general agreed that he should be placed under arrest and charged with murder. Farran fled to Damascus, but eventually was persuaded to return to Jerusalem, where a military court would bar incriminating evidence on legal grounds and announce an acquittal verdict on October 2. He was whisked out of the country, received the Distinguished Service Order from King George V the following year, and subsequently, ever unrepentant, held the post of solicitor general of Canada's Alberta province. Rubowitz's body was never found.[21]

While the Special Squads were quickly disbanded in light of the international clamor that led to queries in Commons and drew Attlee's displeasure, *aliya bet* continued to be a great source of frustration for HMG. On May 17, the *HaTikva*, with 1,414 passengers, was intercepted and captured after a battle. Six days later, the *Mordei HaGetaot* (Ghetto Rebels), carrying 1,457 Jews, was stopped and boarded by the British off southern Palestine. All of its passengers were arrested. The *Yehuda HaLevi*, named after the legendary Jewish physician-philosopher of Medieval Spain whose poems yearned for Zion, arrived in Palestine with 399 survivors on the last day of the month after being intercepted by the Royal Navy. The immigrants were immediately transferred to Cyprus, whose expanded camps now held more than 14,800 refugees. An estimated 2,400 Jews had found their way into Northern Italy en route to Palestine in the last two months, reported the U.S. consul general in Genoa to Washington. The *President Warfield* was currently in

Genoa, capable of carrying 5,000 inhabitants, and known to be embarking illegal immigrants for Palestine, Attlee informed his Cabinet at the beginning of May, leading Creech Jones to declare that "every possible step" should be taken to prevent the arrival of such a ship in Palestine's waters. How to do so remained a matter for the Admiralty.[22]

The GA's special session adjourned on May 15 after adopting the First Committee's report by a vote of 45 to 7 (the Arab states, Afghanistan, and Turkey). After the Americans "took fright" at the British suggestion that they introduce a resolution for a truce in Palestine by all governments and parties concerned, Norway called for refraining from any threat or use of force that might "create an atmosphere prejudicial to an early settlement of the question of Palestine" pending action by the Assembly on UNSCOP's report. This was passed unanimously, with the Arab states abstaining.[23]

While the Irgun announced cessation of terrorist activities in favor of "political work" until the country's future status had been clarified, the Stern Group blasted three railroad bridges and two trains, and planted mines in various sections of the rail system. The Jewish Agency Executive in Jerusalem appealed to the *yishuv* to maintain peace, and declared that it would cooperate with the UNSCOP inquiry; Shertok pointedly referred to Gromyko's speech as "the most outstanding of a number of pleasant surprises" for the Agency at this session. The Palmah retaliated on the 20th against two villages harboring Arab bands engaged in robberies and killings of Jews, during which three Arabs were killed and several wounded, but the general reaction was that the incident had no political significance. Azzam Pasha, pleased that "our views are now better understood throughout the world," declared that the Arab states would take part in the Special Committee's investigations. Emile Touma of the Palestine Arab Communist party stated that it wanted a single, independent Palestine freed of British troops. Henry Kattan sounded the one discordant note from the Arab quarter, insisting that the instructions handed to UNSCOP had shifted the emphasis from a search for a solution to the situation in Palestine to one encompassing a solution for the problem of the displaced Jews of Europe.[24]

Encouraged by the special session, Austin recommended to Marshall on the 22nd that while the United States would not bring pressure "of any kind" on UNSCOP, he suggested that the government's objective should be "an independent Palestinian state" as a UN member, with guarantees for the civil and religious rights of all minority groups. Immigration might be as high as two-and-a-half percent of the country's present population for the first two years, and one percent per annum thereafter. Provision should be made for a period of perhaps five to ten years of preparation for independence, during which time Palestine should be placed under a UN trusteeship. Gromyko's sensational speech gave some indication that the Soviets would go along, at least in principle, with a solution of this kind, Austin concluded, as would the Arab states and "the more reasonable and better-balanced elements" of American Jewry and Jews in other countries. Acheson noted that the department's views had been discussed with Austin and were reflected in this document. Marshall, whom Ben-Gurion characterized to his Executive associates in Jerusalem the same day as a "sphinx" with regard to Zionist aspirations, initialed Austin's memorandum.[25]

Not surprisingly, Henderson got Acheson's consent on the 28th not to conduct "confidential exploratory conversations" with the Agency about Kaplan's request for $75–$100 million as a first stage to help in the absorption of 100,000 into Palestine and in the *yishuv*'s "businesslike development." When Shertok and Epstein met with Acheson and Henderson the next day to ask for a U.S. statement clarifying its present policy with regard to Palestine, and to have Washington suggest to UNSCOP that it recommend that the GA take steps for the "immediate inauguration" of large-scale immigration from Europe to Palestine before the ultimate solution of the problem had been decided upon, Acheson's reply was clear: the United States did not wish to be seen as pressuring a Committee which had been established on the theory that it could approach the subject "in a spirit of complete neutrality." Their suggestions, he added, would be carefully considered before a reply could be made to them.[26]

Truman continued to keep his own counsel. He had refused to see Silver and associates prior to the GA special session. State's views at this point were not conveyed to the President, who had received Marshall's summary on May 16 of the Assembly session, together with the Secretary's conviction that the results were "very satisfactory" to the United States and afforded "some ground for hope" that a "practicable solution" might be presented by UNSCOP to the Assembly in September. Four days earlier, Niles had made sure that Truman realized the significance of a Nation Associates' report from Kirchwey, sent to all Assembly members and the White House, with damaging evidence that some AHC and Arab representatives now at the UN were Hitler's allies, and that Haj Amin had taken an active role in Germany's mass murder of European Jewry. Thanking "Dave," he wrote directly on the memorandum "I knew all about the purported facts you mentioned and, *of course*, I don't like it." Recalling his frustration over the Anglo-American Committee and the Morrison-Grady reports, he went on: "We could have settled this Palestine thing if U.S. politics had been kept out of it." "Terror and Silver are the contributing causes of *some* not all of our troubles." The document itself "could have been used by us for the welfare of the world had not our own political situation come into the picture." Truman closed on this note: "I surely wish God Almight[y] would give the Children of Israel an Isaah [*sic*], the Christians a St. Paul and the Sons of Ishmeal [*sic*] a peep at the Golden Rule. Maybe He will decide to do that."[27]

As May came to a close, Bevin had the last word. Addressing the Annual Meeting of the Labour Party at Margate on the 29th, the Foreign Secretary revealed that HMG had not yet decided its Palestine policy, but he personally wanted to know whether all the other nations would also accept the UN's solution. He described the basic problem in Palestine as a reflection of "a Jewish-Gentile war," ranking these remarks, perhaps unconsciously, with his offensive November 1945 remark about Jews wanting "to get too much at the head of the queue." (Laski had hoped that Creech Jones would take any discussion on Palestine at the meeting, given Bevin's past "really quite indefensible utterances" and considering, so he wrote to Frankfurter, that "EB has got to a stage of anti-Semitism that is fantastic.") As to Britain's future attitude, the government was mainly responsible for the creation of the sovereign Arab countries, and they were reaching "real independence." He was trying to encourage considerable social and industrial developments in that part of the world so that the people living there would have great opportunity and the area carry larger populations than were the case at present. "We therefore cannot afford to lose our position in the Middle East," Bevin concluded. "Our Navy, our shipping, a great deal of our motive power for our industry in the shape of oil, are there...." Equally important, a leading Palestinian Arab noted, the Foreign Secretary repeated that nothing in the Balfour Declaration or in the Mandate permitted HMG to deprive Arabs of their rights, and that the answer to the persecution and plight of Jews, a product of Europe, should be solved by and in Europe. At the same time, editorialized the *Palestine Post*, whether Bevin's implied notice that nothing was to be allowed in Palestine except what Whitehall considered suitable, UN or no UN, would really produce "satisfactory results," even for Britain herself, was another matter.[28]

Yet even putting aside the increasing descent into chaos across Palestine, Bevin could not be oblivious to the onerous financial reality, as portrayed in Creech Jones' latest report on the subject to Cabinet colleagues, that the direct costs to public funds there of terrorist activities over the last two years had reached well over £5 million. The cost of security measures, including Operation Polly and the loss resulting from the reduced effectiveness of departmental services, was probably even higher. The annual expenditure of the Palestine government on security measures came now to more than £8 million in a budget totaling £25 million. This did not include the cost of maintaining the Cyprus camps, gratuities to dependents of officials killed in terrorist attacks, and security measures such as the requisitioning of private property. The Colonial Secretary estimated a deficit of £1 million in Palestine's budget for 1947–1948, quite apart from the considerable cost of measures directed against illegal immigration, government losses from territory action, and other security commitments. Some increases in general taxation must be made, he opined, but no conclusions were reached that day as to how to proceed.[29]

On May 29 the British succeeded in having Lie circulate Cadogan's note of the 23rd to the member nations of the UN requesting their active support in discouraging unauthorized Jewish immigration to Palestine. This move followed the advice of the State Department, which had earlier dissuaded London from doing so during the GA session, in arguing that UNSCOP should not be distracted from its work by this illegal traffic. Ben-Gurion would cable Silver to protest to Lie, who by his action "helps hostile act British government against principal sufferers Nazi persecution." Silver immediately did so, observing that the note was purposely submitted after the special session had ended, and that Cadogan's move was out of order while the matter of Palestine was *sub judice* and the Mandate still required HMG to facilitate Jewish immigration.[30]

UNSCOP had just begun its assigned task, as six of its eleven members met on the 28th behind closed doors to commence making recommendations on twenty-five questions which Lie had placed before them. Three hefty "working papers," prepared by the UN Secretariat, offered them documents, maps, and a background survey for examination. Dr. Jŏze Brilej, director of Yugoslavia's foreign ministry political department, already declared that he would insist that the group visit the Jewish DP camps, which had to be examined along with Palestine as one problem. His other colleagues, in alphabetical order by country, included John Hood, counselor in Australia's Department of External Affairs; Justice Ivan Rand of Canada's Supreme Court; Karel Lisicky, Czech Minister Plenipotentiary; Dr. Jorge García-Granados, Guatemala's Ambassador to the United States; Sir Abdur Rahman, Justice of India's Lahore High Court; Nasrollah Entezam, Iran's permanent delegate to the UN; Dr. Nicholas S. Blom, special advisor to the Netherlands foreign ministry; Alberto Ulloa, chairman of the Peruvian Senate's Foreign Relations Committee; Chief Justice Emil Sandström of Sweden; and Prof. Enrique Rodriguez Fabregat, Uruguay's permanent delegate to the UN. Lie appointed Victor Hoo, the Assistant Secretary-General, as his representative. Realizing that there would be a lot of drafting to be done for its reports, Hoo in turn selected Dr. Ralph Bunche, head of the Department of Trusteeship who had been instrumental in the UN's creation at San Francisco, as his "special assistant."

In closing the special session, Aranha had pledged the fifty-five General Assembly members to the finding of a "just solution" for the Palestine dilemma. HMG had failed to restrict the discussion to purely procedural matters and the Arabs' tactics were "exceedingly inept," Beeley concluded, but he thought that the substantive deliberations had a positive side as well: now both the UN and the American public could see for themselves that the central issue involved was not a struggle between a dependent population or Zionists against an imperial administration, but "a bitter contest" between Arab and Jew for control of Palestine. All told, the Assembly delegations at the special session had been pleased with the outcome, Sir Carl A. Berendsen of New Zealand reflecting their view: "This is only an approach, but it's a good approach."[31] Would the eleven neutrals chosen, not one possessing expertise about the Middle East and the Palestine question, live up to these hopes and expectations?

On the eve of UNSCOP's arrival in Palestine, Macatee cautioned Marshall and American missions throughout the Middle East that the mandatory, "living in pathetic seclusion in 'security zones,'" was "a hunted organization with little hope of ever being able to cope with conditions in this country as they exist today." It was extremely difficult to know where civilian government control began and that of the Army ended. The Jewish Agency, "the most extraordinarily complex non-governmental organization in the world," would presumably testify in its "usual comprehensive fashion." Efforts for illegal immigration, widely believed to be organized by the Agency, would continue, as would certain activities by the terrorist groups without endangering UNSCOP members themselves. Talk of boycotting UNSCOP by members of the Arab Higher Committee, which was "rather ineptly" leading the disorganized Arabs, had to be taken seriously. Without Arab testimony, any solution ultimately put before the UN by the fact-finders might well prove "abortive." Unless the members were "endowed with the wisdom of Solomon," these factors would try their "patience and mental faculties to the utmost." "They should not think this an ordinary dispute," the U.S. consul general concluded from his perch in Jerusalem.[32]

While the Arabs spoke of not testifying once they heard the lineup of the eleven-nation Committee, reported Homer Bigart for the *New York Herald Tribune*, Jewish hopes "soared." The Arab states thought only India and Iran "safe" for their cause, with Yugoslavia and Peru, each having a strong Muslim minority, "hopeful" allies. Nonetheless, the outgoing director of the Arab Office in Washington, Cecil Hourani, told Epstein that until the Arabs "physically crushed" the Jewish state on the first occasion of an international crisis, they would do everything to make its economic position "untenable." Two days later, Azzam Pasha told him that a Jewish commonwealth established in accordance with UN recommendations would fare no better than did the Crusaders and could not last any length of time, being of an "artificial nature"—surrounded by hostile Arabs and dependent upon the goodwill of foreign powers. The Agency actually felt confident of five states (Australia, Czechoslovakia, Netherlands, Sweden, and Uruguay) and hopeful of Canada and Guatemala. Judged purely on its academic and political merits, Eytan wrote to Horowitz, the Arab case was a "great deal more convincing," if only because "it is so much simpler than ours." The "two main points in our favor," he thought, were the Committee's going to view the *yishuv*'s positive achievements in Palestine, especially the *kibbutzim*, and "the sight of human misery" in the DP camps in Europe.[33]

As for other GA members, Eban found encouragement from his tour of France, Belgium, Holland, and Luxembourg, as did Comay after his "not unfavorable" meetings with New Zealand Prime Minister Peter Fraser and Australia Minister for External Affairs Herbert V. Evatt, whose views "more or less" coincided with those of the very pro-Zionist South African Premier Jan Smuts. On the other hand, chairman Sandström, seen by a member of the Swedish Zionist Association after he was chosen at Lie's initiative to chair the UNSCOP team, represented "a still unwritten page" with little knowledge about the Jewish question and the Palestine issue. The Dutch Zionist organization wrote that Blom and alternate A.I. Spits appeared sympathetic, although they spoke about Surinam's absorbing Jewish refugees, and expressed concern about Russia's attitude towards Zionism and the Jews in general. Adelson thought Granados a "first-class man" who could be counted on "to understand our point of view," but she did not know quite what to expect from Ulloa's alternate in Palestine, Arturo Garcia Salazar, in view of his position as Peru's Ambassador to the Vatican.[34]

Truman issued a statement regarding Palestine on June 5, the same day that the Secretary of State announced at Harvard University's commencement exercises what soon became known as the "Marshall Plan" for the economic rehabilitation of a war-torn Europe. A White House release called on every U.S. citizen and resident, "in the interests of world peace, and of humanity, meticulously to refrain" while the UN considered the Palestine problem "from engaging in, or facilitating any activities which tend further to inflame the passions of the inhabitants of Palestine, to undermine law and order in Palestine, or to promote violence in that country." The President, Niles confidentially told Epstein, "did not fall into the trap" when the British asked him to publish a statement which also included some reference to illegal immigration. Viewed as a response to two protests from HMG against newspaper advertisements by American Jewish organizations to raise money for terrorists in Palestine, Truman's statement received a favorable reaction from the Jewish Agency and by left and liberal sections of the *yishuv* press. The Irgun, however, hinted in a reproachful response that Washington was more interested in oil than in Jewish freedom, and vowed never again to be "the passive victims of international intrigue." At the same time, the Agency declared that those survivors who tried to come to their Promised Land did so with full legality under Article 6 of the Mandate, and that refugee ships would continue to arrive during the UNSCOP inquiry.[35]

The "crucial question at present," Comay wrote to a friend in Sydney on June 12, "is what Washington may do." Its representatives certainly "hedged" throughout the GA special session, and having for a decade or so "played a very double game—pro-Zionist in New York and pro-Arab in the Middle East," the State Department was "very unhappy" about having to take some positive line of action. In fact, a preliminary draft by Henderson on Palestine's future government, which McClintock had acknowledged to Rusk was "obviously designed to favor the Arab side of the case and will be distinctly unpalatable to the Jews," had been shared with Austin one week earlier. It closely resembled the latter's memorandum to the Secretary of State on May 22 except for a lower rate of immigration (one-half of one percent) of the estimated population as of January 1, 1947, after the first two years until the termination of the trusteeship. Having reviewed that memorandum on the "vexatious" Palestine issue, Marshall informed Austin on June 13 that once the First Committee decided not to hold hearings in the United States, State thought it preferable not to make any public statement "unless unexpected developments should take place." Since an agreed settlement "no longer appears possible" and "at least a certain degree of force" might be required to implement any solution, the department thought it would be wise to review the whole matter in order to make certain that any kind of a solution would be based "upon principles which can be defended before the world both now and in the future." "It is important," the Secretary ended, that we decide at the earliest possible moment what our basic attitude should be in regard to this serious problem."[36]

The American Zionist leadership tried, without success, to pierce State's wall of silence. The department informed Senators James E. Murray (D, MT) and Wagner, in response to their cabled request to the White House that Austin give full support to the Congress's repeated pro-Zionist resolutions, that "it would be premature" for the government to develop its policy in such a way as to "limit the full utilization" of UNSCOP's recommendations and its report. Senator Henry Cabot Lodge Jr. (R, MA) conveyed to the AZEC's Schulson that Senate Minority Leader Alben Barkley (D, KY) agreed with Truman that speeches in Congress on behalf of Zionism might appear as if the United States was "trying to influence the jury." Welles's radio address, drawing strongly on information from Epstein in calling for the United States to join the Soviet Union, particularly after Gromyko's latest GA speech, to work together for a Palestine settlement "in a spirit of cooperation," received no backing from State. Truman's declaration of last October 4 expressed "a hope," Henderson informed Sack on June 12, and since HMG "did not see fit" to accept the President's suggestion, it was "no longer effective," and the department "is now awaiting the developments." The next day, Marshall cabled twenty of State's diplomatic posts to emphasize that the government was not, at this stage, "supporting any solution in preference to another."[37]

On June 14, Congressman John F. Kennedy (D, MA), speaking in Boston before the New England Zionist Region's twenty-seventh convention, championed "the establishment of a free and democratic Jewish Commonwealth in Palestine, the opening of the doors of Palestine to Jewish immigration, and the removal of land restrictions, so that those members of the people of Israel who desire to do so may work out their destiny under their chosen leaders in the Land of Israel." This clarion call went far further than a private letter mailed from Palestine in 1939 to his father, then U.S. Ambassador to Great Britain, a strong supporter of Prime Minister Neville Chamberlain's policy of appeasement toward Hitler and an anti-Zionist, in which the Harvard College junior had opined that the White Paper "just *won't* work." In its stead, he had then advocated the country's partition into two autonomous districts, giving them self-government (Jerusalem to be an independent unit) while safeguarding British interests. Now the thirty-year-old Representative from the state's 11th Congressional district, making his first public address on the contentious issue, went on to add the following: "If the U.S. is to be true to its own democratic traditions, it will actively and dynamically support this policy."[38] Washington remained silent.

Four days later, Marshall informed Silver (in Henderson's presence) that the department could say nothing further at this time than that it was "anxious that a fair and equitable solution" could be found for the "extremely complicated" Palestine problem. In addition to the difficult international issues connected with it, he added, factors of "internal politics" came into play. To Wagner's request that the Nation Associates' documents pertaining to Haj Amin's collaboration with Germany in the killing of European Jewry be urgently published, Marshall replied that the U.S., British, and French governments had agreed to publish numerous material on Nazi and Fascist activities, some of which related to the former Mufti, just as soon as the "necessarily slow and arduous" work of analysis, translation, and classification had advanced to a stage where "an accurate and complete picture of events" would be given. Maintaining State's determination to avoid enunciating its policy during UNSCOP's investigation, Henderson told Silver separately that he was quite aware of the "deep interest" of many American citizens in the Palestine problem, and realized that "these emotions at times prompted them" to be extremely critical when the American government did not assume an attitude towards that problem which was "to their liking."[39]

Unknown both to State and to the Zionists, Eddie Jacobson again entered the picture at this time, following a telephone call to B'nai Brith Kansas City official A. J. Granoff from that fraternal organization's executive vice-President, Maurice Bisgyer and President Frank Goldman. They asked Granoff, Jacobson's lawyer and dear friend, if he knew anyone named Jacobs or Jacoby, who was supposed to be a very close friend of President Truman. "Yes, you mean a man named Eddie Jacobson," he replied. They wished to discuss with him the matter of 100,000 Holocaust survivors entering Palestine, for whom the Jewish Agency had asked their help, to persuade Britain to "lift up the bars and let these poor refugees in." "I don't know what in the hell I can do," said Jacobson when Granoff called him, but he readily agreed to a meeting. The two men flew from Washington, sat with Jacobson for several hours as Bisgyer explained the State Department's apparent agreement with Foreign Office policy, and he agreed to see the President soon thereafter. Going at his own expense after Granoff oriented him regarding the issue on humanitarian grounds, Jacobson met with Truman for the first of many unofficial meetings, all centered then on getting help for the remnants of Jewry still in the DP camps two years after V-E Day.[40]

In Palestine, the British administration had its hands full in trying to keep order and calm. Cunningham's expressed hope, when acknowledging Weizmann's good wishes on his sixtieth birthday, that they would work together in "bringing better times to this country" appeared an idle fancy. He failed in trying to persuade Husseini that the AHC's boycott of UNSCOP would only be taken by the world in general as flouting the UN, clearly place the Arabs at an initial disadvantage at the GA's full meetings in September, and give the impression that the AHC had no confidence in its ability to present its case. Hearing his "personal anxiety" that the Arabs should take every opportunity of countering Jewish pressure and influence, Husseini retorted that the facts were well known, there was no need for a committee, and that its members would be even more biased that its predecessors owing to the countries chosen to be represented on it. (One day earlier, Agency intelligence reported that the AHC had informed some members of the Palestinian Arab opposition parties that if they testified, their lives would be endangered.) If the UN decision went against the Arabs, he protested vehemently, the Arabs of Palestine would fight, and all his Arabs were prepared to die in this cause. Cunningham warned Husseini to be careful, as he was determined and ready to take strong action against him and anyone else who broke the peace or tried to arouse the Arabs.[41]

On June 13, Husseini officially informed Lie of its boycott owing to the fact that the GA special session had not called for the Mandate's termination and Palestine's independence, as well as its failure to separate the world Jewish refugee problem from that of Palestine. Azzam and the Arab states failed to persuade Haj Amin to recant; the AHC would stage a fifteen-hour strike in Jerusalem as the inquiry began its work. "I am afraid," Barker wrote to Katie Antonius, "your people do not appreciate their problems with a Western mind. Such a pity." Haj Amin was "a menace to the general Arab interests," Azzam told Epstein, with Cecil Hourani, director of the Arab League's Washington office, finding fault that his intransigency strengthened the claim "that Jews and Arabs cannot live within the same State." Brilej's surprise motion on the 17th to censure the AHC for its attitude was defeated by a 9 to 1 vote, with Granados abstaining, the members considering Sandström's radio appeal for cooperation and his assurance that UNSCOP came "with an open mind" sufficient.[42]

For its part, the Jewish Agency declared that HMG's stringent immigration rules fostered terrorism, and the Executive protested Gurney's obstruction since February in its laying of water pipelines to *yishuv* settlements in the Negev. Under new National Command head Yisrael Galili, the Hagana began independently of the British a "little *saison*" against the Irgun (the Palmah, then focusing on *aliya bet*, refused to participate), beating up suspected members, which in turn led the Irgun to react in kind. The Hagana foiled several Irgun operations against the British, including a planned attack on the military headquarters at

Citrus House in Tel Aviv on June 18, during which Hagana officer Ze'ev Verber was killed by a warning charge while probing a tunnel half-way to that headquarters, and a LEHI attempt on MacMillan's life. Twenty thousand, including many British, attended Verber's funeral in Tel Aviv. Told that the British would have to give special escort protection to the UNSCOP members, one police officer refused: "They are here to find out facts, let them go off with a mine, and then they'll have the real facts." To the press's surprise and annoyance, the mandatory insisted that its testimony at the Committee's opening session be held *in camera* for security reasons, even as both dissident groups declined to observe an interim truce in light of the "occupying authorities'" continued check on immigration and the death sentence passed by military courts against their fighters.[43]

UNSCOP's initial run-in with the mandatory came on June 16, when the military court in Jerusalem passed the death sentence by hanging on Irgunists' Avshalom Habib, Mayer Nakar, and Yaakov Weiss for taking part in the attack on the Acre Prison. Coinciding with the members' first official meeting at the YMCA, Granados, Fabregat, and Brilej wished to protest the sentence as an act that would "entail serious difficulties" for the Committee. The regular presence of armored cars, huge coils of barbed wire thrown about entire blocks of buildings, and Emergency Regulations allowing for arrest and imprisonment without trial had already given the UN team the clear impression of a police state that, Gurney testified, was spending almost $30 million a year (exclusive of army expenses) to maintain order. MacMillan privately noted to Granados that commuting the death sentences, as had been requested to the Committee in letters from family members of the condemned young men, would be interpreted by the terrorists as a sign of weakness; moreover; as a soldier, he dutifully had to obey the law; and a pardon was Cunningham's exclusive prerogative. Hood, Rahman, Sandström, and Rand thought UNSCOP had no right to intervene.

After five secret meetings, a compromise resolution, sent to Lie to forward to the mandatory government, observed that a majority of the Committee expressed concern that execution of the sentences might have "possible unfavorable repercussions" on the fulfillment of its task. In a cold, rebuking letter, Gurney wrote to the group on the 23rd that MacMillan had not yet confirmed the sentences, so that the Committee should have avoided "public comment." (This "sharp, almost brutal, retort" was what one might have expected from as "tough and formal-minded a person" as Gurney, McDonald wrote to Hutcheson.) One week later, Cadogan responded to Lie that it was the "invariable practice" of HMG not to interfere with the High Commissioner's discretion whether or not to exercise the Royal Prerogative of Pardon.[44]

Shertok's 75-minute factual presentation on the afternoon of the 17th, in the first public hearing on the stage of the YMCA auditorium, fluently made the Agency's argument that the "cornerstone of cooperation" between the *yishuv* and the British administration had been knocked out by the latter's restrictive policy toward Zionism contrary to the Mandate. Palestine, "the birthplace of the Jewish people," had seen "almost interrupted" effort by Jews to return to their original homeland. As a result of British restrictions, particularly from the 1939 White Paper onwards, the attempt of Jews to escape the Holocaust in Europe had been "one continuous tragedy." "Immigration absorbed itself"; "not one single Arab village had disappeared from the map of Palestine." Yet only 5 percent of the land was open to purchase by Jews, who paid two-thirds of the country's taxes, created their own economy, and owned 80 percent of Palestinian industry. The 640,000 Jews here had fifty-two countries of origin, but nearly half of the present population was either born in Palestine or brought up here; 18,000 children had settled in the country. Rahman pressed him on immigration and land transaction, but, Macatee reported home, Shertok answered "with his customary agility." Faced with Entezam's question about Jewish-Arab cooperation, Shertok asserted that political cooperation between Jews and Arabs in an independent unitary state in Palestine would be impossible. If subjected to an Arab majority with hostile leaders, the Jews felt that they would be left in the lurch. Hoo later declared privately that Shertok was "strong and clever," with Gurney's statement taking the defensive and the Jewish speaker the offensive. "I don't exactly know," he confessed, "what the other wanted to say."[45]

While the Committee members began their tours of the country, the Agency Executive met the next day in Jerusalem to vote on its stand before UNSCOP. It had already rejected the requests of the opposition leftist HaShomer HaTsa'ir and Ahdut HaAvoda, as well as of the centrist Aliya Hadasha, to appear separately before the Committee. Sneh's motion favoring a provisional international regime for five years that would insure the immigration of 1,000,000 and large-scale settlement failed by a vote of 8–2, with Shertok abstaining. The motion which drew the greatest support, reiterating the claim for all of Palestine as a Jewish state while simultaneously initiating steps to arrive at a compromise solution, was adopted, with Sneh abstaining. Ben-Gurion, awaiting clarification of internal issues within the political coalition, did not vote but expressed support for this position. By a vote of 6 to 1, with the rest abstaining, it was agreed that Weizmann could appear before the Committee as representing the Va'ad HaLeumi. Ben-Gurion, Shertok informed Macatee on June 19, would put forward in his open testimony the Agency's claim to all of Palestine on an historic basis, but in a private hearing declare that it would accept partition and present an outline for the latter if requested to do so by UNSCOP. This, Kohn soon clarified to a member of the U.S. consulate, meant that the Agency would consider partition "as a final political settlement." The Western Galilee and Jewish Jerusalem would have to be included, he emphasized.[46]

Trips around this troubled land decisively influenced some of the Committee members, Agency liaison officers Eban and Horowitz taking full advantage of the AHC's blunder not to participate. With the support of British liaison officer Donald C. MacGillivray, a Scot who served in Gurney's office, and now as Bunche's diplomatic aide, Horowitz convinced the team that the Jewish predominance in Haifa's industrial plants made it illogical to insist on seeing an equal number of Jewish and Arab factories. The immediate rapport that existed between charismatic, Argentinian-born Moshe Toff (later Tov) and fellow Latin Americans Granados and Fabregat kept the Agency always informed about the Committee's deliberations. Blom, a former colonial officer in the Dutch East Indies, was critical of the Administration's "just muddling through" and impressed by a large reception with Dutch-born Jewish settlers. Rand, animated by a liberal humanitarianism, appreciated long talks with Horowitz as they drove to Haifa and later the Dead Sea potash plants. Lisicky, who had secretly told the British in New York that they could "count upon his good will" and that he thought Bunche "a vague idealist and rather an inept man," appeared moderate if punctilious. Yugoslavia Senate President Vladimir Simic, Brilej's superior, was quiet and somewhat of a doctrinaire.

Former Guatemalan revolutionary Granados, stormy in temperament, was deeply moved by Tel Aviv, the barren Negev's Revivim agricultural phenomenon, and the Kiryat Anavim kibbutz outside of

Jerusalem. The sufferings of Jewish children in Europe especially moved the far more reserved Fabregat, who, like his colleagues, was stirred by the exploitation of child labor in an Arab factory in Haifa and the forced exclusion there of Jewish visitors in the group. Significant doubt arose about the chances for a mutual Jewish-Arab future in light of the strong "racial animosity" (Hood's phrase) exhibited by Arab authorities, while the impression received of the Arab sector's achievement was negative and disappointing. By contrast, the Bet HaArava settlement on what used to be pure salt land near the Dead Sea, where settlers conversed in different languages with their visitors, made a deep impact on all. So did the clean, dynamic Jewish settlements, as opposed to the dirt and backwardness of the Arab villages and towns. Sandström, Salazar, and Entezam remained impenetrable at this point, unlike the fiery Rahman, unabashed spokesman for the Arab cause despite Nehru's instructions that he maintain "complete impartiality." Most of the UNSCOP Secretariat joined in a lively hora dance with settlers in Ein Gev on the Kineret Sea. Still, until the resumption of public hearings in July, wrote Agency press officer I. L. Kenen in his diary, most were "properly" very careful not to commit themselves or to prejudge the situation.[47]

A meeting of UNSCOP members with Weizmann in his stylish Rehovot home on June 23 created the greatest impression, Bunche calling him "the conscience of the Zionist movement." The aged leader referred to his youth, his laying of the Hebrew University cornerstone in 1918 as "an act of faith," and to his successful meeting with Feisal in 1918, as well as one with Churchill and Attlee in 1937. He was a Zionist because only in Palestine could Jews be pioneers, rather than what antisemites in other countries dubbed "parasites," coming in "on the ground floor" to develop a hitherto desolate country and a modern language. Communist Russia, he replied to one of only a few questions from the captivated visitors, had a policy of "de-Judaizing the Jews," outlawing Hebrew and pressing for their assimilation. Gromyko's last speech at the GA was the best statement for the Zionist cause made by a non-Jew since the Balfour Declaration. The British presence in Palestine did not really increase Jewish security at all. Learning from the Jewish example how to farm, produce and market goods, the Arab population had steadily increased as a result of *yishuv* settlement—one of the main reasons for partition. Only the Jews could take care of terrorists within their camp, while a Jewish army of 50,000 with modern arms could be quickly raised and more than hold its own against 300,000 Arabs in a Jewish state. The addition of 50 to 70 thousand Jews per year would make the Jewish position secure for at least the next five or ten years. The Jews "could take care of themselves," Weizman emphasized, and "they were here to stay." Greatly moved, Bunche "referred to his feelings as a Negro and the emotional identity that Dr. Weizmann's description of Jewish destiny aroused in him." As Sandström and Rand drove back with Horowitz to Jerusalem, they sat silent and only murmured "Well, that's really a great man."[48]

Three days later, Sandström, accompanied by Hoo and Bunche, held a secret interview with Begin, who expressed his conviction that the Irgun would continue its legal revolt against the wish of the "British Occupation regime" to keep Palestine as a military base for itself. Its aims, which could only be achieved by force, included Eretz Israel as the homeland of the Jewish people on both sides the Jordan; the immediate repatriation of all Jews who wished to come to Palestine, with no need to transfer any Arabs from the country; and the creation of a Hebrew republic under a democratic government. A provisional Hebrew government, to be set up immediately, would focus on this repatriation, after which free elections would follow with full Jewish and Arab representation. In the Irgun commander's view, Arab opposition was instigated by the British themselves; he did not think the Arabs would actually go to war against the Jews. "We have lost six million people and every Jewish life is the more precious to us, but we fight for a purpose, to avoid subjugation and utter destruction." If the British executed Irgun men by hanging, his organization would do the same, also "fighting for the right of free men." He hoped that UNSCOP might hear some of the Irgunists imprisoned at Acre (Sandström replied frankly there was very little possibility), but added that he was not sure the Committee's intervention would produce any results. "Au revoir in an independent Palestine," Hoo remarked as the group took its leave. Shaking Begin's hand, Bunche exclaimed "I can understand you. I am also a member of a persecuted minority."[49]

The "persistent and successful" attempts of Jewish organizations at illegal immigration continued to worry Bevin. Creech Jones, agreeing with Cunningham, tried to press Whitehall with the need that UNSCOP report in time for the GA's regular session in September, and so bring to an end with the least possible delay the "present almost intolerable situation" in Palestine. Charting his own course, the Foreign Secretary sought Marshall's intervention on June 27, following Truman's "greatly valued" statement of the 5th, to have Washington tell U.S. officials in Europe to "discourage" this unauthorized movement. He and colleagues felt very strongly that the organizers of the traffic were not only endangering the peace and security of the Middle East, but now "flouting" the authority of the United Nations. The Secretary did not rush to reply, but Henderson had just informed Epstein of the department's conclusion that it would be "unwise" to engage in conversations along the lines proposed by Agency officials in the meeting on May 28 while UNSCOP was endeavoring to make "constructive suggestions" with regard to a solution for the Palestine question. The official response did not surprise Epstein, who knew of Henderson's growing influence on Marshall in light of Acheson's departure from the department, and particularly of his recently articulated anti-Zionist pronouncements "in no ambiguous terms" before two groups associated with the U.S. delegation to the UN. He had also told a member of the French Embassy that rumors of Azzam Pasha, whom he considered "a very reasonable and moderate man," spreading anti-French propaganda on the North African situation were probably due to the Zionists' "strong influence" over the press.[50]

Henderson and the U.S. military presented a serious challenge, Epstein warned Shertok. Should State adopt a partition plan (especially if this would be the plan adopted by the majority of UNSCOP), Henderson, in collaboration with the American military experts, would probably be the man to "bridge" the gap between Morrison-Grady and the Jewish Agency proposal ("Goldmann's Plan") of last year. Rifkind, sent by the Zionists to sound out Eisenhower on the issue, heard in an interview on June 24 that the U.S. Army Chief of Staff appreciated what the *yishuv* had done in Palestine and he favored a Jewish homeland, but thought that there was much to be said for Cyrenaica as the place for the Jews. He referred to the idea of an Arab *jihad*, as well as the question of Arab sabotage of U.S. oil pipe lines and communications. After presenting the Zionists' arguments, Rifkind gave Eisenhower an Agency memorandum (prepared by Eban and Shertok) arguing that a democratic Jewish state in Palestine would be in the strategic interests of the United States "against the contingency of war." It could mobilize three or four fighting divisions; provide heavy technical equipment through industrial and scientific capacities; and offer the only deep-water port in the Mediterranean at Haifa and a series of air bases in the Negev.

The five-star general passed this on to Lauris Norstad, director of the War Department's Plans and Operations division, who replied that Rifkind's views were not convincing. The belief of the former advisor on Jewish DPs that Arab reaction would be limited and temporary was "highly questionable," in Norstad's assessment, and he reiterated the Army's concern about "the adverse strategic impact on the security interests of the U.S." if Rifkind's conclusion turned out to be incorrect. This would be "most serious." Further, it was "questionable" that the Jews would be more inclined to develop a democratic state than the Arabs. Since Rifkind's arguments "do not hold up under serious analysis," Norstad advised that the memorandum should be merely noted and not submitted to Marshall.[51]

The weekend "orgy" of murder in Palestine, Macatee reported to State on June 30, while by no means unusual there, gave the UNSCOP group "some food for thought." Three soldiers were wounded on the 29th as LEHI, responsible earlier in the month for eleven "letter bombs" that had been dispatched from Italy to Cabinet members, Barker, Spears, and former High Commissioner Harold MacMichael, struck for the second successive day at the British forces. Twelve of its force surprised three soldiers and two officers sun-bathing on the beach at Herzlia. Before escaping under cover of a smoke bomb, they emptied their revolvers at the soldiers, while the officers were beaten. The attack came while Tel Aviv was still tense from LEHI's killing of three soldiers and the wounding of one the previous night in a daring attack in the center of the city. One soldier was killed and one wounded in Haifa at the same time, when Sternists fired into a bar frequented by British officers. The assaults were believed to be in retaliation for Rubowitz's murder.[52]

The "despicable" killings "darkened" all the Jewish achievements that the Committee had seen in Palestine, Bunche remarked to a Hagana informant, most recently its visit to the Hebrew University and the Hadassah Hospital. A shaken team, also contending with Arab press accusations that it was appeasing the Jewish terrorists by intervening on behalf of convicted men, stated in a communiqué that it had decided by nine votes (Australia and India abstaining) that such acts of violence constituted "a flagrant disregard" of the GA appeal on May 15. In addition, it unanimously expressed sympathy to Alan Major, assistant to the mandatory's liaison officer, for the battering he endured during an unsuccessful LEHI kidnapping attempt. The Irgun, according to a memoir by its own Shmuel Katz, persuaded its right-wing rival to post-pone such efforts for now, in order not to harm its chances of capturing British officers in the hope of halting the march to the gallows of Habib, Nakar, and Weiss.[53]

At the end of its second week, Macatee observed, UNSCOP had gotten acquainted with the Palestinian reality, but there also came "a certain quality of bewilderment at the maelstrom into which they had been thrust." Rampant Jewish terrorism continued; so did the firm Arab boycott. Feeling "decidedly slighted" by Haj Amin's dogmatic insistence on non-cooperation, the Committee announced on June 27 that "hence-forth they would not visit any more Arab places, for reasons beyond their own control." As for a visit to the DP camps, five strongly favored going (Guatemala, Uruguay, Holland, Yugoslavia, and Czechoslovakia) against three (Canada, Australia, and India). The Slav bloc also wished to visit the camps in Cyprus, whose internees had petitioned UNSCOP that they had "no other place in the world than Palestine." Hearing complaints from Palestine's Arab Communists about Gromyko's May 14 speech, Brilej replied to them that Moscow was forced to neglect the Middle East "for the time being" because it had to solve its prob-lems in Europe. At the GA in September, he added, it would demand a dual state with equal rights but not the bi-nationalism of HaShomer HaTsa'ir. Moreover, Brilej told one Arab journalist in a report that was then spread throughout Arab circles, Yugoslavia was one of the few countries which decided not to consider the ex-Mufti a war criminal. On another occasion, he privately expressed the fear that a Jewish state would become an outpost for American imperialism.[54]

Choosing to avoid joining in what turned out to be a boisterously welcoming reception for the Committee by Tel Aviv's residents, Rahman paid a private visit to Abdullah, who had informed Wadsworth that he favored a partition that would give him the Arab part of Palestine. While the Indian delegate was personally "well disposed" to the Arabs, he told HMG's representative in Amman, the Arabs' refusal to cooperate was having "a disastrous effect" on his colleagues, and he had failed to find anyone who could inform him of the Arab point of view. His Iranian asso-ciate advised the Arab consular representatives in Jerusalem to appear before UNSCOP, offering the inducement that if many Arab states were to be visited there would then be no time left for a tour of "concentra-tion camps" in Europe, and indicated that the Jordan government would receive the Committee. Rahman informed his colleagues of Abdullah's interest and his opposition to the AHC boycott.[55]

UNSCOP's third week in Palestine began with public testimony on July 4 from Ben-Gurion, followed by Weizmann's four days later. Confronted by undisguised hostility in questioning from Rahman, who had already conveyed to Sandström his opinion that Palestine and the Jewish DP problem were not directly connected and that democracy would not permit "foreigners" to settle in a country against the majority's will, the Agency Executive chairman emphasized the Zionists' desire to bring in 1,000,000 Jews immediately and undertake large-scale economic development that would also benefit the Arab parts of the country. They demanded the right to sovereignty in all of Western Palestine, with temporary UN supervision and enforcement during two or three years, but were ready to consider immediate partition that guaranteed a viable Jewish state. He noted the Mandate's acknowledgment of the enduring link of world Jewry to Eretz Israel during two millennia of unimaginable persecution, the collective memory that bound the Jewish nation and returned it to the Promised Land, observing that Englishmen did not know the facts about the *Mayflower*'s historic sailing to the New World but every Jewish child could retell the narrative of the Exodus from Egypt and the Passover holiday's concluding fervent wish "New Year in Jerusalem!." The Jews would attempt to work out a modus vivendi with the Arabs, he asserted, but "we will take care of ourselves" if threatened by force.

Weizmann, appearing in his private capacity yet certain that he spoke for "the overwhelming majority of the Jewish people everywhere," advocated partition as the only available solution combining the three qualities of "finality, equality, and justice." This solution, endorsed in a letter that he read from Smuts, should include the Peel Commission's proposal of the Galilee and the coastal plain plus the Negev and Jewish Jerusalem. (A subsequent letter to Sandström explained his opposition to the Morrison-Grady and Bevin plans.) Decrying both the White Paper and terrorism, he pleaded that UNSCOP not prolong the agony that had lasted a long time, hoping that once more "a message of peace will come out of this country, which is so sorely in need of peace." His "dignified" and good-humored presentation, as opposed to the aggressive stance taken by Ben-Gurion, charmed the delegates. As the nearly blind herald finished, the audience, the largest since the hearings began, broke out into applause which Sandström made no attempt to halt.[56]

At that moment, the mandatory announced that MacMillan had just confirmed the death sentences on Habib, Nakar, and Weiss. The entire Hebrew press declared the GOC's decision a "brazen challenge" to UNSCOP that would probably "drag the country into a whirlpool of blood." Weizmann drafted an appeal to Cunningham, although loathe to do so after his personal communication on April 20 for Barazani and Feinstein had met with no response. Now that the case was no longer *sub judice*, however, he saw no other way of preventing what he believed would be "a very grave error," since execution of death sentences had not stopped terrorism and, "particularly at this moment," would make things much worse than they were. The letter was not sent; Weizmann met Cunningham that afternoon in the hope that the High Commissioner would exercise the prerogative of mercy. The mission was to no avail. Nor would the High Commissioner talk to Myerson or to Herzog. Sandström refused to comment, stating that the fate of the three lay still in Cunningham's hands. The Irgun urged UNSCOP to prevent the murder of "Hebrew prisoners" which, if carried out, "will bring in its train the most serious acts of retaliation" even during the Committee's deliberations.[57]

Irgun operations head Amihai Paglin ("Gidi"), realizing that the condemned men might be hanged at any moment, immediately intensified its hunt for potential captives in a hostage-taking operation. At 12:30 a.m. on July 12, five masked men succeeded in abducting Sergeants Clifford Martin (nineteen) and Mervyn Paice (twenty) of 252 Field Security Section, affiliated with the Army Intelligence Corps, as they left the Gan Vered café in Netanya with Hagana officer Aharon Weinberg. They dropped the bound Weinberg in an orange grove, and brought the two officers to an underground bunker beneath a disused diamond factory near the city limits. The kidnapped men found themselves in an airless three-meter cube separated from the factory floor by three feet of sand, equipped with two oxygen cylinders so they could breathe, a mattress, some food, and one canvas bucket for use as a toilet. They were told of the consequences if the three Irgunists would be hanged, and advised that the entrance to the bunker was mined to discourage any thoughts of escape.[58]

As 5,000 First Infantry Division troops, with a considerable number of the Hagana, began just before dawn the next day Operation Tiger's intensive search of Netanya and some twenty different settlements and communities nearby, UNSCOP continued its hearings through the third and fourth week. Fishman, Herzog, and Agudas Israel presented Jewry's religious attachment to the country. Kaplan, Horowitz, and Agency head of the Trade and Industry Department Fritz (Peretz) Bernstein detailed the benefits that Palestine's Arabs had attained as a result of the *yishuv*'s development despite the mandatory's obstructionist measures, and declared that increased immigration would increase the country's economic absorptive capacity. The Anglican Bishop of Jerusalem, the Moderator for the Church of Scotland in Jerusalem, and the Jewish Women's Organizations all had their turn as well.

In private sessions, the Committee decided by a vote of 6 to 3 with two abstentions not to visit the Cyprus camps, and by a vote of 5 to 4 with two abstentions not to invite representatives of the deportees on that island, even as it agreed to make another approach to the AHC to give testimony and to send invitations to the Arab states to appear. Sandström, Hoo, and Bunche met secretly with the Hagana high command on the 13th, one day before it became known that the Committee would visit Beirut to hear from the Arab states. (Entezam pressed for this locale in order not to encounter the problem of possibly meeting Haj Amin in Cairo.) Magnes, Elie Eliachar of the Sephardic community, and the Communist Party of Palestine followed in the next two days. On the 16th, Sandström and Hoo heard Husayn al-Khalidi, a former mayor of Jerusalem and now secretary of the AHC, privately assert that the Jews had no historic rights to Palestine, which should become a democratic state with an Arab majority. The next day, Zalman Rubashov (later Shazar) spoke for the Histadrut, while Shertok sharply criticized the Administration's immigration and land purchase regulations. On the morning of the 18th, he summed up the Agency's case, pointed out the impracticality of bi-nationalism and of a Morrison-Grady settlement, requested the immediate elimination of the White Paper and a visit to the DP camps, and called for "the establishment of Palestine as a Jewish State." The two fundamental events in modern Jewish history—the destruction of European Jewry and the *yishuv*'s renaissance in Palestine—were "two poles which, between them, galvanized the Jewish national will into action." Permanent stability in Palestine could only come, he emphasized, by "satisfying the craving of the Jewish people" for sovereignty in their historic homeland.[59]

Thus the public hearings in Jerusalem came to a close. The UNSCOP delegates had gained little from Cunningham's informal address the previous day at Government House, when he remarked that the core behind "the fury and fire" of the Palestine controversy rested in a "bitter conflict" between Arab and Jew for independent domination, aided by the outside pressure from Arab states and diaspora Jewry, particularly in the United States. In the past two and-a-half years, he counted 291 incidents resulting in 316 deaths and 960 wounded, with no diminution to be expected in the escalation of violence. He fully agreed with Weizmann of the need for finality, the only answer an early political solution because "the sands are running out."[60]

The Agency Executive had offered the Committee a far more specific plan on the evening of the 14th when, during a meeting at Shertok's home, Ben-Gurion spelled out the need for the entire Negev, the Dead Sea area, Jewish Jerusalem, and the mountainous part of Galilee—all joined to the places where Jews were currently settled as the nucleus of any projected Jewish commonwealth. When a colleague, surprised at the map which Ben-Gurion drew on the spot, whispered "Biltmore," the Executive chairman snapped "Biltmore-Shmiltmore—we need a Jewish state." He foresaw a population of 600,000 Jews and 500,000–520,000 Arabs (excluding Gaza, Jaffa, and Nazareth) in this state. These boundaries, Shertok added, constituted the *minimum* Jewish claim. Now departing the YMCA auditorium on the 18th and with UNSCOP heading soon for Beirut, Sandström told reporters that he was glad the hearings in Palestine were over and done with, "but the next stage will be harder." Following the Cabinet's decision last winter not to give effect to a partition scheme, the British turned down his request for information about possible forms of partition.[61] Little did Sandström or others realize just how a drama then unfolding on the Mediterranean Sea would affect their difficult task, and especially HMG's prestige, in the days and weeks to come.

That same day, Shertok sent Sandström the gist of a radio broadcast from the ship *Exodus 1947*, the name (*Yetsi'at Eiropa*) which Sneh gave to the *President Warfield* as it was transporting well over 4,000 Jewish refugees to Palestine, urging that some UNSCOP members proceed to Haifa to witness the boat's arrival, ascertain the exact conditions on board, and hear a first-hand account of "the tragic occurrence." *Kol Yisrael* had picked up the vessel's transmission that, in the early hours of the morning, six British destroyers attacked the ship *outside* the territorial waters of Palestine. The ship was boarded and the refugees attacked with rifle fire and gas bombs. The Jewish casualties were one killed, five critically wounded, and about one hundred slightly wounded, mainly by gunfire. *Exodus 1947*, badly damaged and shipping water, was making its way to Haifa, and the refugees aboard appealed to UNSCOP "for intervention and assistance."[62]

The full broadcast at 7:30 a.m. from the Hagana's Captain "Ike" Aronovitz, who had departed one week earlier with 4,550 survivors (actually 4,554 with Colombia visas, including 655 children, on a ship meant for 600) from Sète in southern France, described how, seventeen miles from the shores of Palestine, six destroyers and one cruiser (the *Ajax*) suddenly opened fire at 2 a.m. on *Exodus 1947*, threw tear gas bombs, and rammed the ship from three directions. British naval forces finally succeeding in seizing the bridge, but a reserve steering wheel in the bottom of the ship enabled his vessel to be piloted in the desired direction of Palestine. On the deck, he declared, lay 1 dead, together with 5 dying, 20 seriously wounded and 200 less seriously. The hull was broken, the deck smashed; the pumps were working at full speed to dispose of the water inside. Resistance continued for more than three hours but, after sending an SOS to UNSCOP to witness at Haifa "the shocking crime against humanity and international law," Aronovitz relayed that he could not undertake the responsibility to continue to sail towards Haifa in light of severe leaking that put the "fugitives from death, survivors from the death furnaces" in danger of drowning.[63]

Attlee's Cabinet was determined to take "every possible step," as Creech Jones had put it on May 1, to halt such a vessel from reaching Palestine's waters successfully. Already on February 14, the oddly named Operation Embarrass had been launched by the British secret intelligence service (MI6) to plant explosives on five *aliya bet* boats beginning that summer. In the government's request in late 1946 of MI6 chief Sir Stewart Menzies, who suggested that these could be blamed on an invented Arab terrorist group called the Defenders of Arab Palestine, it was noted that "intimidation is only likely to be effective if some members of the group of people to be intimidated actually suffer unpleasant consequences." In all, one ship would be destroyed, two damaged, and the explosives discovered on the other vessels before they were detonated.

Whitehall actually thwarted an MI6 plan to place a limpet mine on the *Exodus 1947* with a three- to four-day delay in the hopes of disabling it. Yet the Royal Navy's determined assault with truncheons and light fire arms against a hail of food cans, potatoes, bottles, wooden boards, and metal bars ultimately led Yossi Hamberger (later Harel), the Hagana commander on board and Mosad representative, to order that the vessel be surrendered (against Aronovitz's wishes) lest it sink with the loss of so many on board.

Two Holocaust orphans, shot to death, lay on deck, fifteen-year-old Zvi Hersh Jakubowitz and twenty-three-year-old Mordekhai Baumstein. Second Mate, twenty-four-year-old William (Bill) Bernstein of San Francisco, in a coma from the bludgeoning which he had received at the wheelhouse when trying to halt Royal Marine boarders with a fire extinguisher, would die hours later on a Haifa hospital operating table. In a last letter to his brother on July 9, he wrote that "the chances are slim as far as getting through. We will do our best, but the important thing is that these people are out of Europe and will end up with their own people sooner or later." Bos'n Bill Millman, shot at close range, had his jaw shattered. As later recorded by First Mate Bernard Marks, club and gunshot wounds had left 146 refugees with injuries, 27 requiring hospitalization. In the late afternoon, the exhausted passengers reached Haifa under British escort with Marks at the steering wheel on the bridge, the Zionist blue and white flag flying fore and aft. Soon thereafter, Sixth Airborne Division troops transferred most of them to the *Ocean Vigour*, the *Runnymede Park*, and the *Empire Rival*. Converted into caged prison ships, the first crammed freighter left port that night and the other two early the next morning. The passengers assumed they that were headed for Cyprus, which the British, wishing to forestall resistance in transferring them from the *Exodus 1947*, had promised as the final destination.[64]

Sandström and Simic watched the *Exodus 1947*, gashed open at both sides, come quayside. Earlier that morning, guided by Hadassah Hospital director Dr. Chaim Yassky, they had visited the Agency's immigration hostel at Neveh Hayim near Hadera and then the internees in Atlit. The two men were deeply moved by stories from survivors who showed signs of nervous strain, especially from a young woman in that detention camp who asked, after declaring that she wished to live and give something to the country and her people: "By what right do you keep me behind barbed wire? I want a home." Hearing from Hoo of Shertok's request that some UNSCOP delegates be on hand for the *Exodus*'s arrival, they drove to the Haifa port. For two hours, they witnessed the "whole gloomy picture" of the stretchers coming down with the two dead bodies and then the many wounded, followed by the slow stream of men, women, and children passing through a disinfecting station before boarding the three freighters.

On the way back to Jerusalem, Simic was absorbed in his thoughts and did not say a word during the entire drive. Sandström turned to Yassky and remarked that without this trip an "important link" in the whole visit to Palestine would have been missing. When Yassky expressed a doubt if any force could stop the *yishuv* from bringing Jews to Palestine and added that he might yet see immigrants dropped by parachute, the chairman replied that perhaps soon there would be no need for such a step. (By then, as Sandström would soon tell Cunningham, he now favored partition.) As the Swedish judge entered UNSCOP's lodgings at Kadimah House, he concurred that the Arab states would not move their armies, but he did not think that the mandatory would arouse the Palestinian Arab population. The British, he believed, wanted to depart the country and were only looking for "an honourable way out."[65]

"Expected in Cyprus this morning," read the *Palestine Post* headline on July 20 about the three freighters' sailing, but none knew of Bevin's decision eight days earlier "to make an example" of the *Exodus 1947* and send it back to its initial departure point in France. (While the Central Committee of Liberated Jews in the U.S. zone in Germany announced that "no force will prevent us from striving to the only coast of hope," an official protest from the AHC Executive called for force to return the passengers to their "countries of origin.") Bevin had failed to persuade counterpart Georges Bidault to refuse all supplies and harbor facilities to the *President Warfield* and five other named ships, and when he heard that it had slipped out of Sète he presented the French foreign minister with a stiff letter demanding that the Quai d'Orsay give orders to receive the passengers, who he claimed had been encouraged by controllers seeking profit of "this infamous traffic," and disembark them. Neither knew that Abbé Alexandre Glasberg, a Jewish-born Catholic priest who had saved hundreds of Jews as a member of the French resistance during the war, used his contacts in the Interior Ministry to issue forged transit documents that enabled all to cross borders and enter the jammed vessel, or that within fifty-four hours the Colombian consul had signed on his own the entry visas to his country for each passenger. After Bidault agreed to receive the refugee passengers in France, Bevin called on Prime Minister Paul Ramadier to caution that French indulgence in the matter regarding Jewish "unauthorized persons and troublemakers" might well alarm and dismay the Arabs of French Africa, and he asked for support against the illegal immigration, which was "in any case largely a financial racket controlled from New York."

Ambassador Duff Cooper in Paris warned the Foreign Secretary on the 18th that forcible removal at a French port would likely provide "lurid anti-British propaganda," to which French public opinion would be susceptible in view of memories of German persecution of Jews under the WW II occupation. The man in the street, he added, ignorant of Palestine problems, "sees only in these illicit immigrants survivors of a persecuted race seeking refuge in their national home." Unmoved, Bevin shot back tersely the next day: "Guards have been instructed to use whatever force may be required in order to deliver immigrants into French hands."[66]

As soon as Martin informed Brodetsky on the 21st of this decision and an official announcement was made that afternoon about the action "taken in accordance with normal international procedure and the agreement of the French government," a steady cry of protest arose. Not bringing them to Cyprus would send the *Exodus 1947* refugees "back to complete despair" and strengthen the opposition in the *yishuv*, Brodetsky responded, eliciting Martin's response that the traffic, not bringing in large numbers, "was merely constant irritation," and "it would be convenient if the whole business could be forgotten." A Jewish Agency statement deplored the "needless and wanton act" against the *Exodus*'s "cargo of human misery," wondered how liberty-loving Frenchmen could accede to "so heartless an enterprise," and asserted that no amount of repression could stifle the urge of Jews for freedom in their own country. A three-hour general strike took place in every *yishuv* town, city, and kibbutz, with banners at a rally attended by 20,000 in Tel Aviv reading "piratical actions" would not halt Jewish immigration. Irgun broadcasts lashed out at "Nazo-British pirates" and "Adolf Bevin." Silver protested to Lie against the "shameful and inhuman action," and at a rally in Madison Square Garden, which drew 10,000, praised the Hagana and asked "is there no Truman policy for our people?" "The word is murder," wrote

I.F. Stone in *P.M.*; the British decision "is a heart-breaking one—as senseless as it is cruel," editorialized the *Washington Post*. Gurney, on the other hand, issued an official endorsement of the Royal Navy for carrying out "its lawful duty," a point which he repeated to Shultz, then visiting Palestine in order to gather additional material from Horowitz and others for Nation Associates memoranda.[67]

The American Zionist leadership kept trying to pin down Washington's stance on Palestine, without success. A Democratic delegation organized by the Nation Associates of six Senators and Congressman Celler had failed to draw any statement from Marshall other than that there had been no change in, or departure from, traditional American policy on Palestine, along with a restatement of his view that the United States should refrain from any declaration until after the report by UNSCOP. (For the same reason, he turned down Silver's request for issuing a statement on Palestine for the ZOA's fiftieth anniversary convention.) Informed of this meeting by Marshall, Henderson presented him with a memorandum advocating a Palestine state with an Arab majority, claiming that that plan "is based on principles of the character upon which the Charter of the United Nations is based." Epstein gave Rifkind a memorandum for Eisenhower explaining that the Arab states, with their ill-trained, poorly organized and equipped armies, would not be capable of joining in any united military action unaided against the *yishuv*. Americans for Haganah, set up with industrialist Abraham Feinberg as President and David Wahl its executive director, began a public relations campaign to support Jewish immigration to Palestine. Thirty Republican Congressmen, spearheaded by New York City's Jacob Javits, wrote a letter to Marshall and Austin which drew the Secretary's official response two weeks later: the government's views would be put forward when the General Assembly considered the Palestine problem.[68]

With an introduction to Clifford from Democratic National Committee executive director Gael Sullivan, who had failed to get Truman to send a message to the ZOA convention, Shultz informed the President's Special Counsel about Marshall's note of June 13 to twenty U.S. diplomatic missions abroad that the government did not have a Palestine policy. Clifford could not believe that it had been sent, both because it was inaccurate and because it should have been cleared by the White House first. She countered that a previous indication of this position had emerged from a visit with Robert A. Lovett, the highly regarded former War Department Assistant Secretary of State for Air and now Acheson's replacement, who remarked that Truman's statements were just "broad generalities for political purposes." "Bob Lovett is an honest man and he would be saying a lie if he said that," countered Clifford, who insisted that the President's declarations were not meant for political purposes, but because "we believe in the things he said on the subject." He concluded that he would find out the facts on the situation to satisfy himself, giving Shultz the impression from their first meeting that Clifford believed it very important to "keep the lines of authority straight," and that he would check upon the situation.[69]

Nor did "a terribly worried" Morgenthau, tapped by Montor to be the United Jewish Appeal's National Chairman, get satisfaction from a ten-minute telephone conversation with Truman on July 21 about the *Exodus 1947* refugees. His idea two months earlier for getting 100,000 Jews a year into Palestine by pledging to HMG $250 million a year for five years, proposed to Kaplan and Weizmann followers Simon Marks and Israel Sieff, had come to naught. Asking the President now to intercede at least long enough to resolve the issue on humanitarian grounds, followed by his talk to Marshall the next day, the former Treasury Secretary was discouraged at receiving no answer from either. Truman was "very sympathetic" and said that he would talk to Marshall, wrote Morgenthau in his diary. Ten days later, the State Department replied to Epstein's request to intervene by declaring that since HMG, as the Mandate holder, carried "full responsibility" for maintaining peace and order in Palestine, the U.S. Government count not "interfere" with the action of the British administration.[70]

In fact, Truman's own diary noted his feeling that "Henry had no business whatsoever" to call: "The Jews have no sense of proportion nor do they have any judgment on world affairs." He thought them "very selfish," caring not how many Estonians, Latvians, Finns, Poles, Yugoslavs or Greeks "get murdered or mistreated as DP as long as the Jews get special treatment." Truman's rant then picked up: "Yet when they have power, physical, financial or political, neither Hitler nor Stalin has anything on them for cruelty or mistreatment to the underdog [sic!]. Put an underdog on top and it makes no difference whether his name is Russian, Jewish, Negro, Management, Labor, Mormon, Baptist, he goes haywire. I've found very, very few who remember their past condition when prosperity comes. Look at the Congress attitude on DP—and they all come from DP." This private venting of spleen, written in an entry to be discovered in his Presidential library more than fifty years later, reflected personal irritation regarding Morgenthau (whom he did not like), the complex Palestine issue, and the intense pressure which he faced at the moment over Europe and the Soviet Union. A fundamental question remained: would the President's pubic actions speak louder that his private words?[71]

A hopeful answer for the Zionists came one week later. By coincidence, knowing that Hilldring was scheduled to retire from State on September 1, Fierst suggested to Niles that he advise Truman to name Hilldring as the President's representative on the U.S. delegation at the UN. A frustrated Sullivan, having "practically wrung his hands" over his inability to get anywhere with Truman in recent months on the Palestine question, was at the same moment open to Wahl's idea to have the President appoint someone whom he could trust to that position. This could counter Henderson's strong influence on Marshall, in whom Truman placed his personal trust. Crum was Sullivan's ideal choice, but he knew Truman considered that man's "outspokenness," although he was "doing a hell of a job," unsuitable for such a role. Wahl then spoke of Hilldring, who had been mentioned "very confidentially" to Niles.

On July 29 Niles, who told a worried Epstein that the Zionists had "no reason" to doubt Truman's "good intentions," sent a memorandum to his boss suggesting Hilldring "to carry out your policy on Palestine" at the UN and so counter the expected appointments of key delegation advisers Henderson and Wadsworth. Such a step could avoid further criticism about the U.S. delegation's Palestine stand "in those areas that gave us trouble last November." (One month earlier, Jewish Agency intelligence had found out that Wadsworth presented to Abdullah the Arab rebuttal against partition, a plan which the Jordan ruler favored.) Given the "unsympathetic" attitude of the two men regarding "the Jewish viewpoint," the announcement of their roles would engender "much resentment" and, on the basis of their "past behavior and attitudes," Niles frankly doubted that they would "vigorously carry out your policy." "Our temperamental friends, headed up by such people as Bart Crum and Silver," he ended, continued to spread the stories that Henderson misinterprets the President's policy, but Henderson had not, in Niles's judgment, satisfactorily answered Crum's charges. Thinking this had "some merit," Truman discussed it with Marshall and confidentially gave Lovett excerpts from Niles's memorandum; Hilldring was appointed as an alternate representative to the U.S. delegation soon after he retired from the State Department.[72]

The Arab states remained steadfast, as the UNSCOP members discovered when they met a delegation in Beirut on July 22. (Egyptian Prime Minister Nokrashi Pasha rejected Husseini's urging that the Arab League boycott the Committee, regarding this demand as presumptuous and foolish.) Speaking at the public hearing on behalf of all but Jordan, Lebanese Minister of Foreign Affairs Hamid Franjieh warned the Committee that any settlement that did not take into consideration Arab rights and feelings would be "doomed to failure and result in the most serious consequences." The Zionist program, intending to dominate Palestine and certain other areas in the region, constituted "a threat to peace." Past terrorist activities were evidence of the spirit which animated Jewish youth to conquer the country by force of arms, "which could lead the Jews and other innocent people to destruction." This, in turn, would undoubtedly provoke similar organizations to "repel Zionist aggression," and might well jeopardize the position of the Jews "hitherto living in peace throughout the Arab world."

They were united behind the demands of the Palestine Arabs for independence, Franjieh insisted. Against Haj Amin's memorandum to the Arab states that any Jew who entered after the Balfour Declaration would be considered an illegal immigrant, he limited this designation to those who entered Palestine against British law. Should a Zionist state arise, he added, the Arabs would "take effective measures to return the country to its lawful owners." Two memoranda, one replying to the Committee's questions and another submitted later via Camille Chamoun to UNSCOP, sounded the same theme. (The opposition National Bloc under Emile Eddé informed the group separately, as did Maronite Patriarch Antoine Aridah, of its support for a Christian Lebanese state alongside a Jewish state in Palestine, leading Haj Amin's Al-Wahda to describe Eddé as "a pawn of imperialism" and "a man open to betrayal.") "We want solutions that are just. Just solutions are not always based on compromise," insisted Iraq's Muhammad Fadhel al-Jamali, who compared the Zionists to the Nazis. Privately, Nuri al-Said proposed to Wadsworth a one-year UN trusteeship following the general principles of the 1939 White Paper.[73]

Abdullah took a line of "extreme discretion" when meeting an UNSCOP delegation two days later. Confronted by the strong opposition of Saudi Arabia and Egypt to his plan of a Greater Syria including Syria and the Arab areas of Palestine joined to Jordan in a federation with Iraq, he gave the disappointed group no lead as to his real views, although saying that "there were enough Jews in Palestine." (Hearing later of this interview, the Zionists were deeply disappointed that he did not even mention his "divide and annex" plan to endorse partition and absorb the Arab-settled areas in the country.) Asked if he would accept any Jews in Jordan, the king laughed and said, "That would be asking me to cut my own throat." There were many possible solutions to the Palestine question, he declared. "What was necessary was to adopt one solution and firmly enforce it," but in any solution "the incontestable Arab rights must be protected." Prime Minister Samir Pasha satisfied the visitors more with his suggestion that a constitution could be framed and guaranteed by the UN that gave the Jews all the necessary safeguards as a minority in the Palestinian state; he was noncommittal on the subject of possible Arab violence if faced by a decision unfavorable to their interests. Yet in a message to the Foreign Office, Abdullah soon confided that he hoped partition would be adopted, he being "perfectly willing" to take over all the Arab areas of Palestine or as much of them as were offered to him, and to withstand "any abuse and criticism" to which this action might expose him from the other Arab states. Samir Pasha agreed with this view, adding that the "considerable opposition" which might be expected from Haj Amin's supporters "would somehow be overcome at the time."[74]

Meanwhile, increased turbulence filled the Palestine air. A dusk-to-dawn curfew was imposed on the Jewish quarters of Jerusalem on the 22nd following a series of attacks on police stations and armored cars in the city, during which at least ten soldiers and policemen were wounded. A Palmah attack sabotaged the radar station on Haifa's Mt. Carmel which had tracked illegal immigration. An oil pipeline was damaged by the Irgun between Haifa and Afula, and a land mine seriously injured two British soldiers riding in a jeep nearby. On the 23rd, not long after an explosive set by the Palyam's Betsalel Drori put the Cyprus-bound deportation ship *Empire Life Guard* out of commission (a step approved by "Committee X" by a vote of 3–2), the government held a memorial ceremony in honor of the people killed in the King

David Hotel bombing, called by Information Officer Richard Stubbs "the most dastardly of outrages perpetrated by Jewish terrorists in Palestine." Operation Tiger throughout Netanya and environs, which Cunningham, following a Cabinet decision, dubbed "a controlled area" (rather than use the term "statutory martial law"), continued to affect 15,000 people who could not enter or depart an area of thirteen square miles.

Over a space of twelve days, nearly seventy separate incidents by the Irgun and LEHI claimed the lives of eight soldiers and police and injured eighty others. The country had not been subjected to such a "sustained onslaught" since the Arab Revolt. The fruitless search for the two kidnapped sergeants was called off on July 27; in a secret meeting with Netanya Mayor Oved Ben-Ami, Gurney had refused any guarantees regarding the condemned Irgunists, and Begin called off any future negotiations. After hearing vivid testimony the next morning from Rev. John Stanley Grauel, a thirty-year-old Methodist minister sent by the Hagana on the *Exodus 1947* in order to give the world a non-Jew's eye-witness account of that voyage, UNSCOP left for the Palais des Nations in Geneva, former headquarters of the League of Nations.[75]

On July 29, the three British freighters reached Port-de-Bouc, six days after War Veterans Minister François Mitterand announced that those who disembarked willingly would eventually be allowed to live in France or go elsewhere, but no one would be forced to land. The British had wished the landing to take place in isolated Villefranche, where it would be easier to disembark the passengers by force, but the Cabinet's Socialist majority ruled against Bidault, and Ramadier decided on Port-de-Bouc. Despite the temptation to escape their hot, cramped quarters, the refugees began a hunger strike and, encouraged by the charismatic HaShomer HaTsa'ir survivor and *briha* leader Mordekhai Rozman and a few Hagana men on board the boats, resolved to stay put. Journalist Ruth Gruber's reports to the *New York Herald Tribune* and her photographs used by the Associated Press and *Life* magazine of those in Cyprus and in the foul hold of the *Runnymede Park*, seized the public's attention. A sympathetic world press spread the word further, echoing former Prime Minister Léon Blum's strong attacks against HMG and the *New York Post* editorial's cry that "we must demand the death of British tyranny." A bed sheet on the *Empire Rival*, where many

Hungarians silently bore their Auschwitz-Birkenau branded numbers, read "We will go ashore in Europe only as dead men." Signs on the *Ocean Vigour* in English and French read "Open the doors of Palestine our only hope"; fifteen-year-old Yitshak Kraus climbed aboard its ten-meter-high mast and unfurled a Gordonia-Macabi Zionist-looking flag that he had secretly carried from Budapest aboard the *Exodus 1947*. "Unbelievably firm," Mosad director Meirov reported of the refugees' stand.

Despite the French press's harsh condemnations and Duff Cooper's begging Bevin to withdraw the boats from Port-de-Bouc, HMG's Foreign Secretary refused to relent. At the month's end, he told Cabinet colleagues that Palestine and Cyprus were out of the question. Creech Jones was seeking a suitable British colonial territory, while he was examining whether any of the refugees might be sent to the British zone of Germany. "No harm" would come if the British freighters stayed there for a few days, he added, and the possibility existed that their passengers "might decide eventually to go ashore peaceably."[76]

Habib, Nakar, and Weiss were hanged in Acre Prison in the early morning hours of that same July 29. "Do not grieve too much, What we have done we did out of conviction," they told their families through Haifa Chief Rabbi Nissim Ohana, who had heard each man's confession (*vidui*) a while before each went separately to the gallows singing the *HaTikva*. An inscription had been left on their cell wall: "They will not frighten the Hebrew youth in the Homeland with hangings. A. H. Thousands will follow in our footsteps." Next to it appeared the Irgun insignia of a hand gripping a rifle and the words "*Rak Kakh*" (Only Thus) against the background of a map showing the original territory of the Palestine Mandate, together with the three names in the order they were executed. Charlton, the warden who had served the government for twenty-five years, refused to carry out the executions and was immediately relieved of his post. Andrew Clow, acting superintendent, took over in his stead, with P. J. Hackett attending.

A *Palestine Post* editorial, echoed in the Hebrew press, denounced this act of "crass recklessness" which, together with the recent deportations, showed the determination of the British government to give the Jewish people "no quarter and to show them no understanding of their needs." Even as the bodies were buried in the Safed cemetery, the same location chosen for the four Irgunists in April, a Va'ad HaLeumi statement declared that an act of reprisal taken against the two innocent

British sergeants would be seen by Palestinian Jewry as a "bloodthirsty deed contrary to all human standards and as an unforgiveable sin against the Yishuv and the Jewish people." The Chief Rabbinate issued a more restrained statement, although in like vein. The commander of the Irgun thought otherwise.

Rejecting an appeal for mercy from Paice's father, Begin agreed with his military court's decision to hang the two intelligence officers without delay as members of the "British army of occupation, which was responsible for torture, murder, espionage and illegal entry into the Jewish homeland." Paglin and some comrades took the pair out of the bunker, hanged them, and then suspended the bodies in a eucalyptus grove at Tel Tsur with a mine placed underneath that spot. When the day passed and an intensive search by British and Jewish forces did not find the bodies, the Irgun disclosed the location to the Netanya Municipality and warned about the mine. The fall of Martin's body, cut down by Captain D. H. Galeti of the Royal Engineers on the morning of July 31, set off the mine, and the body was obliterated. Paice's body was hurled some distance away, while Galeti suffered serious wounds to his face and arms. Paice and Martin were buried the following day in the Ramleh Commonwealth War Graves Commission Cemetery.[77]

Swift reactions followed, beginning with Creech Jones's telling the Commons that in the long history of violence in Palestine "there has scarcely been a more dastardly act than the cold-blooded and calculated murder of these innocent young men." "The bestialities practiced by the Nazis themselves could go no further," announced the London *Times*. All sections of British Jewry condemned what the Anglo-Jewish Association called "a barbarous act." The Jewish Agency and the Va'ad HaLeumi railed against the "unprincipled men" who carried out "the foul murder," similar to what Myerson told Cunningham, although he was frustrated that her promise of a "strong and definite campaign" against the terrorists would (again) be undertaken independently of the mandatory's efforts. Responding to a British newspaperman's suggestion, Khalidi released a statement condemning "the most bastardly, cowardly, and fiendish act that has ever been perpetrated in this part of the world."

On the heels of the graphic front-page photograph in the *Daily Express* of the two sergeants hanging in the eucalyptus grove, antisemitic riots broke out in Liverpool, Manchester, Birmingham, Hull, Brighton,

Plymouth, Glasgow, and London. In Palestine, five Jews were killed and twenty-four others wounded as furious policemen and soldiers sought revenge in Tel Aviv and Jerusalem, and extensive damage was caused to many Jewish-owned shops before a tense calm was restored. Such conduct cannot be excused, Cunningham wrote to Creech Jones, but most of the British perpetrators were young, without the benefits of military service. Moreover, they had to work "in an atmosphere of constant danger and increasing tension, fraught with insult, vilification and treachery." It was therefore understandable that the murder of the two young sergeants "excited them to a pitch of fury which momentarily blinded them to the dictates of discipline, reason and humanity alike."[78]

Beyond the wave of revulsion that swept through England, the two hangings created a growing public consensus to quit Palestine as soon as possible. In the Commons debate on August 12, Labour's Michael Foot called for a troop withdrawal within three to six months; Stanley declared that the only alternative to partition, now advocated by the British press, was evacuation. "No British interest is involved in our retention of the Palestine Mandate," asserted Churchill one week earlier to an audience of 60,000 Tory sympathizers at Blenheim Palace. Dalton pressed Attlee to support bringing the troops out of the "wasp's nest" that was Palestine, the country a burden in terms of manpower and money, of no real strategic value, exposing young soldiers "for no good purpose to most abominable experiences," and "breeding anti-Semites at a most shocking speed." The Colonial Office's Assistant Secretary Trafford Smith, then visiting Palestine in order to smooth the waters between mandatory officials and UNSCOP, warned a colleague that there would be "a serious break" in the morale of the expatriate service if present conditions lasted beyond September. Both Martin and MacGillivray were convinced that partition offered the best solution, but freely confessed to Isaiah Berlin that Colonial Office opinion "counts for little these days." At the same time, Creech Jones felt compelled to advise the delegation soon to leave for the GA session that the "strong feeling now apparent in the country" and in the House for British withdrawal had to be taken into account.[79]

What to do in the interim remained unclear. Cunningham and MacMillan, backed by General John Crocker, Dempsey's successor, objected to imposing martial law throughout the country. At the most, thirty-five suspected Irgun sympathizers, including three mayors, were arrested on August 5 at the High Commissioner's suggestion. Beeley asserted to Eban that the government would be morally bound to accept a two-thirds majority decision of the General Assembly, but it could legitimately decline to accept the sole responsibility for enforcing the solution. In an interview with Crossman on August 4, Bevin expressed the feeling that the Jews had organized world public opinion against HMG and himself, and the whole Jewish pressure was "a gigantic racket" run from America. In a reference presumably to the hanging of the sergeants, the Foreign Secretary said that he would not be surprised if the Germans had "learned their worst atrocities" from Jews (*sic!*), and indicated his belief that the Negev was of strategic importance to Great Britain. Crossman's conclusion that Bevin's outlook, corresponding roughly with the *Protocols of the Elders of Zion*, showed him to be "insane" on this specific issue paralleled that of *News Chronicle* editor Gerald Barry, who told Eban that Bevin was so "rabid" in this matter that he would sooner bring British troops out of Germany than out of Palestine. The essence of Bevin's enraged remarks to Crossman was related to Eban, who passed them on to Niles for Truman's information and guidance.[80]

Bevin's extraordinary commitment, despite the increasing wish of British public opinion to relinquish Palestine, became even clearer with his decision, made in tandem with Attlee, to send the *Exodus 1947* passengers to Germany. These Holocaust survivors had remained in the three ships' holds for twenty-four days during an intense heat wave, refusing to disembark despite the shortage of food, the crowding, and the abominable sanitary conditions. On August 18, all on the boats except the young children staged a hunger strike despite the Hagana's urging not to do this in their greatly weakened state. Eventually, Bevin persuaded the Cabinet to return the would-be immigrants to the very soil where Hitler had first begun his war against the Jews. An announced ultimatum on the 21st that the passengers would be taken to a British-controlled port in Germany if they refused to debark in France, creating a "storm of protest" in the United States, led Lovett, appointed by Marshall to deal with Palestine, to informally request of Whitehall that the decision be altered. The British refused, as did the passengers; Bidault, charging that the 1939 White Paper breached the Balfour Declaration's pledge, refused to issue a second warning.

The next evening, as the ships left for Hamburg via Gibraltar, the Hagana sent word that the voyagers would be given priority for *aliya*. Those aboard the *Runnymede Park* hoisted a sheet bearing a Nazi swastika drawn on the Union Jack. As the last of the three vessels moved out of the harbor and the survivors sang the *HaTikva*, one Hagana young woman, standing near Gruber on the stone quay, said softly: "Now you will see the birth of a Jewish State." Protests from across the Jewish political spectrum and worldwide outrage ensued, *L'Humanité* speaking for many when labeling the entire scene an "Auschwitz on the seas." A newborn aboard the *Ocean Vigour* who died a few hours after birth received a burial at sea, with the three ships halting, their flags lowered to half mast, and the crews standing at attention. Once in Hamburg, Rozman and others would be forcibly removed from the *Runnymede Park*, as would the youngsters on the *Empire Rival*. Even on the *Ocean Vigour*, which contained most of the elderly, the weak, and the children, clubbing and the use of powerful water hoses were needed to drag refugees off that ship. All were then transported in Operation Oasis to two internment camps near Lübeck, and given the lower calorie rations of the Germans as further punishment.[81]

Goldmann drew UNSCOP's attention on behalf of the Jewish Agency to the "extreme gravity" of this situation, produced by the "inhuman action" of the Labour government, but Sandström and company were focused on discussions of Palestine's future. One of their sub-committees chaired by Hood had returned from a week's visit to Jewish DP camps in Germany and Austria, deeply moved both by the refugees' plight (10,000 alone facing "squalor and misery" in Vienna) and their determination, as seen in the testimony of more than seventy randomly chosen interviewees, to reach Palestine. The group quickly ruled out an Arab or a Jewish state in all of Palestine. Rand's firm opposition to hearing British representatives, his conviction that the Mandate's days were numbered, and his insistence on "a clear-cut solution" all carried great weight. His memorandum favoring partition and an economic union, the latter point swaying Blom, Lisicky, and Salazar, came to constitute the basis of the majority's recommendations, although Bunche's argument (advanced by Fabregat, as well as by Horowitz) that the Canadian's additional proposal for a central authority in Palestine to oversee basic concerns took away independence was more persuasive. Entezam,

Rahman, and Brilej—all voting with Salazar against a visit to the DP camps—found themselves in agreement on a federal, unitary state.

The partitionists, however, were divided over borders, with Salazar preferring complete independence for a tiny Jewish state, and Fabregat, with Rand's support, arguing for a sizeable territory. These two, joined by Granados, wanted the entire Galilee and the Negev in the Jewish state. Sandström and Blom agreed to the Galilee; Salazar favored part of the Negev. The main problem for this group, Gideon Ruffer (later Rafael) reported to an Agency colleague, was their felt need to decrease the Jewish area in order to lower the number of Arabs under Jewish control.[82]

The further deteriorating Palestinian reality of executions and terrorist retaliation greatly affected the UNSCOP delegates. For the moderate, circumspect Sandström, it underlined the need for a permanent solution. Bunche and Lisicky warned Horowitz that the hanging of the two sergeants had "entirely obscured" the powerful impression created by the *Exodus 1947*. Yet the first Arab attack against Jews on August 10, killing five and wounding seven in Tel Aviv, followed by another four days later which killed three Jews and wounded twenty-four in the Tel Aviv and Jaffa area, Lisicky acknowledged, in turn obscured that feeling. The early meetings of the members were therefore concerned with politics as "the art of the possible," Eban summarized, seeking to develop a solution far more in detail than the Peel Commission or the recent Anglo-American Committee, which one member dismissed as being "not so much a report as a Prayer to God by Magnes." Uncertain as to HMG's intentions or desires, they had to acknowledge the conclusion of the fledgling International Refugee Organization that options for Jewish refugee settlement abroad were almost nil, while General Clay and others indicated a rise in German and Rumanian antisemitism and a worsening of the DP inmates' condition and morale. Testifying before the Committee, Crossman pressed for partition including the Western Galilee to the Jews and an international force of contingents from different countries to implement UNSCOP's recommendations. Bunche, however, worried that this would take much time to organize, was more concerned with the viability of the Arab state; the reality of economic union which Rand pressed for; the number of Arabs in the Jewish state; and the very question of getting a two-thirds majority in the Assembly for any solution.[83]

Jerusalem posed a separate problem. Salazar, an ardent Catholic and Peruvian Ambassador to the Vatican, supported the idea of its becoming a third state. The possibility that it would be left out of the Jewish commonwealth led Kohn, Eban, and Horowitz to stress to Leon Mayrand, Rand's alternate, that "Zionism without Zion" would be "a body without a soul," depriving the Jewish state of its "historic aura," and it would be impossible to obtain Jewish support for any partition scheme which would not include the Jewish part of Jerusalem outside of the Old City walls; the same was said to Bunche and Richard Pech, Lisicky's alternate. Brilej was convinced by Horowitz's opposite argument that Jerusalem should not become a clerical reactionary enclave. Some other alternate members and Latin American pro-partitionists agreed. The compromise formula would finally be adopted favoring the internationalization under UN authority in a most restricted area of this special city holy to three major faiths. Yet, as the advocates for partition still had not resolved their differences regarding borders with only days left before the September 1 deadline, it appeared at this point that only a federal plan would reach the finish line. Hearing from Bunche that the Committee was "stuck," MacGillivray reported home that only Sandström thought the report would be ready in time.[84]

In Washington, both the Administration and State continued to maintain their outward silence. Marshall informed Bevin on August 7 that he had requested the Treasury and Justice Departments to study halting the solicitation for funds or outfitting of vessels for transporting illegal immigrants, and had reminded U.S. representatives in Europe to abide by the President's statement of June 5 in this connection. After he opined at a Cabinet meeting the next day that a British withdrawal from Palestine would be followed by a bloody struggle between Arabs and Jews, Lovett responded that the Jews would be successful in the first instance owing to their superior weapons, but the Arabs would reply with a protracted and bloody guerilla war, Truman interjected: he would make no statement on Palestine until UNSCOP reported. He had, so recorded Forrestal (now the first U.S. Secretary of Defense), "stuck his neck out on this delicate question" with his request for the 100,000 in the fall of 1945, and did not propose to do so again.

Two days after the President surprised Niles with the Medal of Merit, he endorsed State's informal intercession with London against sending the Exodus 1947 refugees back to Germany. At the same time, in reply to

Eleanor Roosevelt's private appeal that they be transported to Cyprus, Truman repeated what his diary had recorded after Morgenthau's telephone call a month earlier. (She rejoined, based upon an eyewitness report about Jewish orphans in the Cyprus internment camps, that cruelty seemed to be on the British, not Jewish, side.) On the 29th, Lovett warned the Cabinet that the GA's taking decisions by majority vote could constitute a danger to the United States, where the Asiatic countries could obtain the balance of power by joining the Muslim nations "and the black and white races," with Palestine an issue they found on which they could get together. He saw no prospect of any agreement between "the interested parties" in that country. While much emphasis had been placed upon the distress among the Jewish survivors, he added, an equal danger arose of solidifying sentiment among all of the "Arabian and Mohammedan" peoples against this country.[85]

The Zionists had good cause for anxiety, Epstein reported to his superiors. In a private conversation with Baruch, Marshall referred in "most unfavorable" terms to them over the hanging of the two sergeants, and declined to assist the *Exodus 1947*. Epstein heard directly from Turkey's chief UN delegate that Herschel Johnson privately conveyed State's probable intention at the GA to support cantonization along the Swiss model, thinking the Arab League a powerful factor in the Middle East and worried that every "uncautious (*sic*)" American step would push the Arabs toward Russia. The department turned down as "improper and unadvisable" Ambassador Lewis Douglas's suggestion (advanced by Goldmann) that the United States mediate between Britain and the Jews. Additional reliable sources led Epstein to conclude that if partition became UNSCOP's majority recommendation, State might apply Truman's October 1946 formula to "bridge the gap" between the proposals of HMG and the Agency while satisfying British sovereignty and the Arabs regarding their independent area. The department absolutely objected to sending U.S. troops to Palestine, and favored that British responsibility under UN control remain during the transitional period.[86]

Lovett's personal views further worried Epstein. In an hour-long interview on the 29th, the Under Secretary told the Agency's D.C. representative that the murders, robberies, and kidnappings in Palestine had become for him what Chicago had been for millions of people, concluding that "Palestine was a bad place where bad people were tolerated."

Whatever the reasons behind terrorism, that did not change the feeling of "democratic and peace-loving Americans." Lovett also referred to the danger of an Arab "holy war" in the event of a pro-Jewish resolution of the Palestine problem, and wondered if, instead of a "drastic" solution, a "gradual" bringing the Jews and Arabs to understand the need for cooperation although the political controversy remained unsolved would better lead to a rapprochement. Epstein emphatically insisted that only a clear decision supported by the UN's authority and backed by the American government could bring about a lasting solution for Palestine even though Jewish-Arab relations might become worse for some time before they could improve, and that there was no compromise between two alternatives facing Palestine's Jews: Haj Amin or independence. Lovett expressed his satisfaction over the government's wisdom in withholding any statement of policy until the UNSCOP recommendations were known, and praised Henderson for having been "most helpful" to him since he joined the State Department, and for maintaining the "proper perspective" on Palestine and other issues for the benefit of all parties concerned.[87]

By then, UNSCOP's delegates had come close to final voting on their report. Bunche worked around the clock drafting papers on the federal plan, partition, and holy places, and, totally disgusted with the shifting positions of the different advocates, told Hoo that he was leaving on the 26th. He had enough of being, according to one of his private notes, "a ghostwriting harlot!" Realizing that this departure would dash any hope of a report, Hoo protested strongly, and it was agreed that Bunche would depart three days later. This may well have swung the Committee to finally vote on the morning of the 27th, but with unexpected results. Salazar claimed that he would switch to support federation because the drawing of borders remained unsolved. Sandström, Rand, Granados, and Fabregat continued to back partition, but differed amongst themselves on boundaries and other issues. Hood (following instructions from Evatt, who, aspiring to a key position in the GA session, wished to adopt an image of objectivity on the Palestine conundrum) suddenly suggested that UNSCOP present the Assembly with most of the proposals without any recommendation. The ever-cautious Blom and indecisive Lisicky quickly supported this, drawing an objection from Sandström, the key supporter of partition, that each member should present his own report and its conclusions if no solution could be agreed upon.[88]

At this crucial point, the supporters of the federal plan, wishing their scheme to be part of the Committee's formal recommendations and thereby to be discussed in the GA, pressed for another vote that afternoon. With Entezam and Granados leading the way, the hesitant members reached a decision. Blom and Lisicky, joining the partitionists, made certain that both recommendations would be included in the report, thus enabling them to avoid making a clear-cut decision. Salazar reversed himself again to support partition in exchange for agreement to his priority—the internationalization of Jerusalem as a separate enclave. Seven delegates now backed partition but with precise boundaries yet to be decided upon, and the federal plan drew the same three advocates. Hood, who personally favored a trusteeship that would lead to a unitary state, again abstained. Bunche jotted down this note for himself: "Their artificial union—partition—won't have a shoo-in in the General Assembly. Federation won't either." None of the partitionists was elated, an "aghast" Granados realizing that a majority report without specific borders would be doomed to failure and the members themselves "appear ridiculous."[89]

While Bunche sat down and, without a break from 6:00 p.m. to 6:00 a.m., wrote all the three main chapters, Granados drew up a new plan on the 28th. Salazar consented to his agreement to endorse a free city of Jerusalem in exchange for extending the Jewish state's coastal strip to the Lebanese border and then have it run parallel to that border until it joined the Eastern Galilee. Granados also devised two narrow international corridors at points where the two states intersected, giving the Arabs Acre and the rest of the Western Galilee, with the Jews obtaining a connection between the coastal plain and Eastern Galilee and the southern corridor providing communication between the Negev and the Gaza area. The hardest task then fell to Paul Mohn, the Swedish deputy member and expert on territorial issues, who had to draw upon twenty-five Palestine maps strewn throughout his room and draft the borders of partition.

Mohn's diary relates that this withdrawn and taciturn figure, working on his own until very late at night, "tried to reconcile ideas that are irreconcilable: Hope for Jewish-Arab cooperation and fear of Jewish-Arab animosity." A Protestant minister father, profoundly shocked by the "Dreyfus Affair," had instilled in his son an awareness "of the tragic history of the Jewish people." Mohn's own diplomatic service in the

Middle East during World War II did not leave him particularly sympathetic towards the Arabs' national aspirations, while he was deeply affected by meeting Holocaust survivors in the DP camps who waited in suspense for the decision to establish the Jewish state, as well as by the "extraordinary success" of the Jewish settlement in the Negev. He suggested two seminal proposals for partition: assign Western Galilee to the Arabs and most of the Negev to the Jews, and have Granados's corridors become "points of intersection" ("kissing points" that MacGillivray had suggested to Mohn earlier). Jerusalem and Bethlehem would come under international control. In addition, he assigned Jaffa, despite its large Arab majority, to the Jewish state, because he did not believe in various forms of enclaves and corridors.

Rand's pledge to Horowitz before the final vote that he would not allow the Jews to be placed in a "territorial ghetto" helped secure all the partitionists' backing for Mohn's suggestion regarding the Negev. Mohn's final draft gave the future Jewish state 62 percent of the Palestinian territory. In his view, the six triangle-shaped areas (three each for the Jewish and the Arab states) in his "map of patches," joined at the intersection points in order to preserve the territorial integrity of the two states, would permit the two sides to live in peace or to "separate and turn their backs on each other." Bunche, with the help of John Reedman, the Secretariat's expert economist who championed an economic union in order to strengthen an Arab state, also prepared a note on the viability of the two states in Palestine. Exhausted and unhappy with his labors, personally preferring the minority plan and disappointed with the quality of the Committee members, he finally flew home on the 30th to his wife and two daughters.[90]

On August 31, UNSCOP sat down in the evening for its fifty-second meeting to formally adopt the report. The first part contained eleven unanimous recommendations, most importantly that the Mandate must be replaced as soon as possible by independence, and a clear majority for paragraph twelve: Granados and Fabregat refused to accept the "incontrovertible" postulate detaching Palestine from the Jewish problem in general by suggesting the settlement of Holocaust survivors elsewhere. Seven delegates (Canada, Czechoslovakia, Guatemala, Netherlands, Peru, Sweden, and Uruguay) backed an Arab and a Jewish state with economic union after a two-year transitional period with British administration under UN auspices, and a *corpus separatum* of Jerusalem-Bethlehem under international control. During that time, Britain had to admit 150,000 Jews. Three (India, Iran, and Yugoslavia) voted for an independent federal state under Arab domination with Jewish and Arab provinces and a common capital in Jerusalem, following a transitional period not to exceed three years and entrusted during that time to an authority designed by the Assembly. Hood abstained from supporting either the majority or the minority plans, explaining that, without having achieved unanimity, the Committee should send both recommendations to the General Assembly. Simic, the last to sign in alphabetic order, affixed his name at 11:55 p.m. As the clock struck midnight, the members filed out of the conference room on the fourth floor of the Palais des Nations. Fabregat embraced an anxious Horowitz waiting in the hall and, with tears in his eyes, said "It's the greatest moment in my life."[91] The curtain had fallen on the UNSCOP act of the Palestine drama, and all eyes now turned to Lake Success.

Endnotes

1 Pearson to St. Laurent, May 3, 1947, MG 26, J1, vol. 428, PAC; *FRUS, 1947*, vol. 5, 1078–1079.

2 Shertok to Marshall, May 3, 1947, 93.03/ 2268/25, ISA.

3 Marshall to New York, May 6, 1947, 501.BB/5-647, SD; *FRUS, 1947*, vol. 5, 1080–1081; JAE American Section, May 1, 1947, Z5/357; JAE American Section, May 2, 1947, Z5/2362; both in CZA.

4 *New York Times*, May 6, 1947; *FRUS, 1947*, vol. 5, 1079.

5 *New York Times*, May 6, 1947; JAE American Section, May 1, 1947, Z5/2362, CZA.

6 *New York Times*, May 6, 1947; Gass-Rusk meeting, May 6, 1947, 93.03/2268/25, ISA. While he personally favored the Jewish Agency's participation as any member except for not voting, Pearson told Shertok on May 4, he would insist on "complete clarity of definition in advance." JAE American Section, May 5, 1947, Z5/2359, CZA. Also see David Wdowinski, *And We Were Not Saved* (New York, 1963).

7 *New York Times*, May 7 and 8, 1947; Robison report, May 8, 1947, Robison MSS; Epstein to Jarblum, June 12, 1947, L35/126, CZA.

8   First Committee meetings, May 9 and 10, 1947, DAG-1/3.1.1-13, UN Archives, New York City; *FRUS, 1947*, vol. 5, 1080, 1083. Robinson, *Palestine and the United Nations*, 59–60 and Chap. 11; Pearson to Laurent, May 9, 1947, MG26, J1, vol. 428, PAC; Eban report, May 14, 1947, S25/5353, CZA

9   Robison report, May 9, 1947, Robison MSS.

10 Moshe Sharett, *B'Sha'ar HaUmot* (Tel Aviv, 1964), 63–72; Levenberg cable, May 13, 1947, Z4/30917, CZA.

11 Robison report, May 10, 1947, Robison MSS; Robinson, *Palestine and the United Nations*, 136–137; Ben-Dror, "UNSCOP," 27; Eban report, May 14, 1947, S25/5353, CZA.

12 *FRUS, 1947*, vol. 5, 1084–1085; Epstein to Shertok, June 20, 1947, S25/1694, CZA; Horowitz, *State in the Making*, 157.

13 Garran note, May 23, 1947, FO371/61777, PRO; Intelligence report, May 16, 1947, 115/58, HA; *FRUS, 1947*, vol. 5, 1088–1089. On the other hand, Henderson later told the AZEC's Leo Sack that the day after Gromyko's speech he had told the Russian "If you mean what you say, I feel that we can do business." Sack to Silver, June 12, 1947, Box 3, Schulson MSS.

14 *FRUS, 1947*, 3 (Washington, D.C., 1971), 577–578; Mapai circular, May 29, 1947, S53/12C; May 16, 1947 report, S25/5355; both in CZA; *HaBoker*, May 19, 1947; *JTA*, May 23, 1947; Iraqi newspapers, FO 371/61875, PRO; Agency report, May 23, 1947, S25/5355, CZA; 47/802, HA.

15 *New York Herald Tribune*, May 15, 1947; Natan Alterman, "A Telegram to Gromyko," *HaTur HaSh'vi'i, 1945–1948* 2 (Tel Aviv, 2010), 231–232; CID report, May 16, 1947, 115/58, HA; *JTA*, May 16, 1947; Wahl to Silver, May 15, 1947, A431/31, CZA.

16 Robinson memo, May 15, 1947; Memorandum, May 29, 1947; both in 93.03/2268/16, ISA.

17 JAE American Section, May 13, 1947, Z5/2362; JAEJ, May 22, 1947; Greenberg to Locker, May 20, 1947, Z4/10388/II; all in CZA.

18 Cunningham to Creech Jones, June 2, 1947, FO 371/61894, PRO.

19 Evron, *Gidi*, chap. 4; Bevin, *The Revolt*, chap. 21; *JTA*, May 5 and 7, 1947; *Palestine Post*, May 6, 1947; Irgun radio broadcast, May 7, 1947, IR-060, Begin Archives; Cunningham to Creech Jones, May 4, 1947, S25/10488, CZA.

20 *New York Herald Tribune*, May 15, 1947; Jones to State, June 4, 1947, 867N.01/6-447, SD; Epstein-Porter talk, May 8, 1947, Z5/2403, CZA; *New York Times*, May 20, 1947.

21 David Cesarani, *Major Farran's Hat, The Untold Story of the Struggle to Establish the Jewish State* (Cambridge, MA, 2009), Hoffman, *Anonymous Soldiers*, 416–

440; Giora Goodman, "Aharei 57 Shanim: Giluyim B'Farashat HaRetsah," *HaAretz*, April 6, 2008; Macatee to State, June 26, 1947, 867N.01/6-2647, SD. Seeking revenge, LEHI sent a parcel bomb addressed to R. Farran in Great Britain. His younger brother, Rex, who opened it on May 3, 1948, was killed by the explosion.

22 Slutzky, *Sefer Toldot HaHagana*, 1100; *Hagana Reports*, June 15, 1947, S25/5603, CZA; Heacock to State, May 19, 1947, 800/4016 DP/5-1947, SD; May 1, 1947, CAB 128/9, PRO.

23 *New York Times*, May 16, 1947; Beeley report, FO371/61780, PRO.

24 Slutzky, *Sefer Toldot HaHagana*, 1333; Arab Office Jerusalem memo, n.d., S25/7719, CZA; *JTA*, May 23, 1947.

25 *FRUS, 1947*, vol. 5, 1086–1088; JAEJ, May 22, 1947.

26 *FRUS, 1947,* vol. 5, 1090–1096.

27 Sack to Silver, Aug. 1, 1947, Manson files; Niles to Truman, May 12, 1947, and Truman's response, Palestine 1946–1947, Box 160, HSTL.

28 Robinson, *Palestine and the United Nations*, 60–61; *JTA*, June 6, 1947; Bevin to Creech Jones, May 9, 1947, Box 32/3, Arthur Creech Jones MSS, Rhodes House, Oxford University, Oxford; Laski to Frankfurter, May 2, 1947, Box 75, Frankfurter MSS; CID report, May 30, 1947, 47/639, HA; *Palestine Post*, May 30, 1947.

29 Meeting May 18, 1947, CAB 129/19, PRO.

30 Embassy to Whitehall, April 21, 1947, FO371/61805, PRO; Ben-Gurion to Silver, June 8, 1947, BGA; Silver to Lie, June 9, 1947, 93.03/2269/5, ISA.

31 *JTA*, May 28, 1947; Beeley report, FO 371/61780, PRO; *New York Times*, May 16, 1947. For an analysis of the delegates, see Ben-Dror, "UNSCOP," 43–54.

32 Macatee to Marshall, May 22, 1947, 501.BB Palestine/5-2247, SD.

33 *New York Herald Tribune*, May 15, 1947; Epstein to Executive, June 20, 1947, S25/4153, CZA; Epstein to Executive, June 20, 1947, 93.03/2270/5; Eytan to Horowitz, May 12, 1947, P-6916; both in ISA.

34 JAE London, May 5, 1947, Z6/84, CZA; Fraser to Comay, May 15, 1947, 93.03/2267/37, ISA; Comay to Kirschner, May 16, 1947, S25/22813, CZA; Katz to Neuman-Silver, May 29, 1947, 7/1, Silver MSS; von Amerongen and Davids to Friends, June 2, 1947, S25/5354, CZA; Cadogan to FO, May 16, 1947, CO 537/2336, PRO; Adelson to Yarden, May 29, 1947, A423/14, CZA.

35 *New York Herald Tribune*, June 6 and 9, 1947; Irgun statement, June 6, 1947, IR-082, Begin Archives; Epstein to Wise, June 12, 1947, Box 101, Wise MSS.

36 Comay to Schenck, June 12, 1947, 93.03/2266/15, ISA; McClintock to Rusk, May 21, 1947, 501/BB Palestine/5-2147, SD; *FRUS, 1947*, vol. 5, 1103–1105.

37 Marcy to Murray, June 4, 1947, Box 1, Schulson MSS; Welles address, June 8, 1947, S25/6621, CZA; Sack to Silver, June 12 and 17, 1947, Box 3, Schulson MSS; *FRUS, 1947*, vol. 5, 1103.

38 Kennedy speech, June 14, 1947, Box 28, David F. Powers Personal Papers; Kennedy to Joseph P. Kennedy, 1939, Presidential Papers, Office Files, Special Events Through the Years; both in John F. Kennedy Presidential Library, Boston. For Joseph P. Kennedy's anti-Zionism and some antisemitic remarks, see Penkower, *Palestine in Turmoil*, 2, 595–596, 613n99.

39 *FRUS, 1947*, vol. 5, 1105–1107; Marshall to Wagner, June 18, 1947, S25/6618, CZA; Henderson-Silver talk, June 19, 1947, 867N.01/6-1947, SD.

40 A. J. Granoff oral history, Aug. 9, 1969, HSTL; *Kansas City Times*, May 13, 1965; Granoff remarks, May 22, 1965, at Jacobson Memorial dedication, Tel Aviv (courtesy of A. J. Granoff).

41 Cunningham to Weizmann, May 5, 1945, WA; Cunningham to Creech Jones, June 7, 1947, FO371/61875, PRO; Cable, June 6, 1947, S25/5434, CZA.

42 Lie to Sandström, June 14, 1947, DAG.133/3.0.0. Box 6. UN Archives; Barker to Antonius, June 21, 1947, P867/9, ISA; Efraim Karsh, *Palestine Betrayed* (New Haven, CT, 2010), 81; *FRUS, 1947*, vol. 5, 1102, 1108.

43 Silver to Lie, June 9, 1947, 93.03/2269/6, ISA; *New York Herald Tribune*, June 2, 1947; Slutzky, *Sefer Toldot HaHagana*, 953–956; Z. Gilad, *Sefer HaPalmah*, 638–641; Philip Brutton, *A Captain's Mandate, Palestine: 1946–1948* (London, 1996), 99; Intelligence report, June 10, 1947, 115/58, HA; Kenen diary, June 13, 1947, 2267-16 Het Tsadi, ISA; Macatee to State, June 23, 1947, 867N.01/6-2347, SD; *New York Times*, June 18, 1947. The big *saison*, or hunting season, occurred against the Irgun after HMG's Middle East Resident Lord Moyne was assassinated by two Stern members on November 6, 1944. *Yishuv* support for it wound down by May 1945, given the continuing White Paper and Begin's principled refusal to become embroiled in a potentially dangerous civil war. See Penkower, *Decision on Palestine Deferred*, 306, 311, 320, 348.

44 June 18 and 22, 1947 meetings, UNSCOP files, UN Archives; Jorge García-Granados, *The Birth of Israel, The Drama as I Saw It* (New York, 1948), chap. 6; Robinson, *Palestine and the United Nations*, 261; McDonald to Hutcheson, June 26, 1947, McDonald MSS.

45 Sharett, *B'Sha'ar HaUmot*, 74–91; *New York Times*, June 18, 1947; *FRUS, 1947*, vol. 5, 1109–1100; June 19, 1947 report, 115/58, HA.

46 JAEJ, June 18 and 19, 1947, CZA; *FRUS, 1947*, vol. 5, 1111; Kohn-Porter talk, June 20, 1947, S25/5968, CZA.

47   Horowitz, *State in the Making*, Chaps. 25–26; McNeil to Sargent, May 28, 1947, FO 371/61779, PRO; Eytan cable, June 24, 1947, S25/5374, CZA; Granados, *The Birth of Israel*, Chaps. 7–11; Ben-Dror, "The Arab Struggle against Partition: The International Arena of Summer 1947," *Middle Eastern Studies* 43:2 (March 2007): 270; Toff to Lourie, June 24,1947, 4/3, Silver MSS; Eytan memo, June 27, 1947, S25/5374; Tchernowitz to Eytan, June 27, 1947, S25/5375; Epstein to Shertok, June 18, 1947, S25/5374; all in CZA; Kenen diary, June 18, 20, 22, 27, 1947; July 3, 1947; all in 2267-16 Het-Tsadi, ISA.

48   Hagana report, June 27, 1947, 115/58, HA; Bunche notes, June 23, 1947, Box 12, UNSCOP MSS, UN Archives; Horowitz, *State in the Making*, 177.

49   Begin-Sandström meeting, June 26, 1947, C14/20-2, Board of Deputies of British Jews Archives, London; Begin, *The Revolt*, 301. For Begin's later meeting with Granados and Fabregat, see Granados, *The Birth of Israel*, 155–160.

50   Mathieson to Baxter, June 19, 1947, FO 371/61939, PRO; *FRUS, 1947*, vol. 5, 1112–1113; Henderson to Epstein, June 25, 1947, 93.03/2268/25; Epstein to Shertok, June 24, 1947, 93.03/92/35; both in ISA; Epstein memo, July 2, 1947, S25/6595, CZA.

51   Epstein to Shertok, June 24, 1947, 93.03/92/35, ISA; Rifkind-Eisenhower talk, June 24, 1947, S25/6621, CZA; A.S.E. (Eban) and M.S. (Shertok) memo, May 29, 1947, 7/1, Silver MSS; D.E. memo, June 24, 1947, Rick-Riz (misc.) file, Box 88, Eisenhower Presidential Library, Abilene, KS; Norstad to Eisenhower, July 1, 1947, RG319, Box 93, P and O, 091 Palestine, Section I, Cases 1, National Archives, Suitland, Md.

52   *FRUS, 1947*, vol. 5, 1116; *HaAretz*, June 6, 1947; *JTA*, June 30, 1947.

53   Hagana report, June 29, 1947, 115/58, HA; Yassky to Shertok, June 30, 1947, S25/5374, CZA; Hoffman, *Anonymous Soldiers*, 453.

54   *FRUS, 1947*, vol. 5, 1116; Palestine report, June 29, 1947, Correspondents 1947 file, AJC Archives; Schieber-Schuller to UNSCOP, June 16, 1947, DAG-13/3.0.1, Box 13, UN Archives; Hagana report, June 29, 1947, 115/58; July 3, 1947 report, 47/655; both in HA; Shertok to Linton, July 11, 1947, S25/1695, CZA; Myerson to Shertok, July 31, 1947, 93.03/2270/3, ISA.

55   Hagana report, June 30, 1947, 115/58, HA; Epstein to Sasson, June 23, 1947, S25/1694, CZA; Pirie-Gordon to Whitehall, June 30, 1947, FO371/61875, PRO.

56   *JTA*, July 4, 8–9, 1947; Rahman to Sandström, July 1, 1947, Box 7, UNSCOP MSS; *FRUS, 1947*, vol. 5, 1117–1118, 1124–1126; Weizmann to Sandström, July 14, 1947, WA; Kenen to Lourie, July 12, 1947, Z5/475, CZA. Eytan thought, however, that Weizmann's mainly subjective approach, based on personal experience and knowledge, lacked the objective grounds for partition,

"which are really the essential ones." Perhaps, he advised Shertok, Howoritz, and Eban, this was a task on which the Agency would have to concentrate for Geneva. Eytan memo, July 9, 1947, S25/5380, CZA.

57 *JTA*, July 9, 1947; *FRUS, 1947*, vol. 5, 1126; Weizmann draft to Cunnningham, July 8, 1947, WA; Kenen to Lourie, Aug. 4, 1947, Z5/1337, CZA; Irgun to UNSCOP, July 8, 1947, Box 6, DAG.13/3.0.0, UN Archives.

58 Hoffman, *Anonymous Soldiers*, 453.

59 *FRUS, 1947*, vol. 5, 1126–1129; Fishman address, July 4, 1947, file 1, Y.L. Maimon MSS, Mosad HaRav Kook, Jerusalem; Hagana-UNSCOP meeting, A197, Box 1, Hoo MSS, UN Archives; Eliachar address, A430/229A, CZA; Slutzky, *Sefer Toldot HaHagana*, 983–984; Hagana memo to UNSCOP, July 11, 1947, Box 7; Meeting, July 13, 1947, A/AC/13/SR.23; both in UNSCOP MSS; Khalidi conversation, July 16, 1947, A/197, Box 1, Victor Hoo MSS, UN Archives; Intelligence report, July 20 1947, 115/58, HA.

60 Cunningham address, July 13, 1947, S44/564, CZA.

61 Meeting, July 14, 1947, A/197, Box 1, Hoo MSS; Ben-Dror, "UNSCOP," 146; *FRUS, 1947*, vol. 5, 1130; Beeley to Martin, July 19, 1946, FO371/61858, PRO.

62 Shertok to Sandström, July 18, 1947, with gist of the broadcast, S25/5380, CZA.

63 Radio message, July 18, 1947, S25/5380, CZA.

64 Keith Jeffery, *MI6, The History of the Secret Intelligence Service, 1909–1949* (London, 2010), 693–694; Bethell, *The Palestine Triangle*, Chap. 10; Bernard Marks memoir, June 29, 1993, SC-2837, American Jewish Archives; Morris Bernstein talk, n.d., F41/119, CZA; Meir Schwartz, *MiPort de Bouc Ad Hamburg: 50 Shana Le'Yetisyat Eiropa 1947—"Exodus"* (1997), courtesy of Prof. Meir Schwartz. The recent British television series "Foyle's War" featured the Defenders of Arab Palestine in the second episode of season nine, entitled "Trespass." The episode's telling of a bomb placed in the hall of the London Conference in September 1946 was based, in fact, on a LEHI planting of a time-bomb in the Colonial Office's Dover House on April 6, 1947. This was followed by twenty-one letter bombs to Attlee, Bevin, and other major officials two months later. See Yaakov (Yashka) Eliav, *Mevukash* (Jerusalem, 1983), 316–319; Christopher M. Andrew, *In Defence of the Realm: The Authorized History of MI5* (London, 2009), 357.

65 Yassky memo, July 18 (written 13 in error), 1947, A427/6, CZA; Cunningham to Creech Jones, July 20, 1947, FO371/61875, PRO.

66 *Palestine Post*, July 20, 1947; Yahil to Shertok (cable to Sandstrom), July 20, 1947, S25/5378, CZA; Bethell, *The Palestine Triangle*, 319–320, 334; Lucien

Lazare, *The Mission of Abbe Glasberg*, trans. L.M. Abrami (2016); Venya (Hadari), "MeiAhorei HaKela'im Shel Parasha Ahat...," *MiBifnim* 12:2 (August 1948): 290; CID report, July 19, 1947, 47/635, HA.

67 Martin-Brodetsky meeting, July 21, 1947, S25/2630, CZA; Fischer memo, July 23, 1947, 93.2/184/10, ISA; *Palestine Post*, July 22, 1947; Irgun broadcasts, July 23 and 27, 1947, C14/20-2, Board of Deputies of British Jews Archives, London; *JTA*, July 21 and 22, 1947; Silver to Lie, July 24, 1947, 7/1, Silver MSS; *JTA*, July 25, 1947; I.F. Stone, "The Word is Murder," *P.M.*, July 21, 1947; *Washington Post*, July 23, 1947; Gurney-Shultz interview, July 24, 1947, Freda Kirchwey MSS, MC 280/237, Special Collections, Radcliffe College, Cambridge, MA; Shultz to Horowitz, July 30, 1947, 691/6-P, ISA.

68 Meeting with Marshall, July 1,1947, S25/6621; Henderson to Silver, July 2, 1947, S25/6623; both in CZA; *FRUS, 1947*, vol. 5, 1120–1123; Epstein draft, July 3, 1947, 93/35, Het Tsadi, ISA; Shapiro memo, July 9, 1947, Box 3, Schulson MSS; American Jewish Agency Executive, July 21, 1947, Z5/53, CZA. Marshall to Javits, July 30, 1947, Box 2, Schulson MSS. Informing Shertok that Henderson told Celler that he personally supported partition plus the Negev, Epstein cabled that he regarded it "as Loy desire future alibi only." Epstein to Shertok, July 2, 1947, S25/1695, CZA.

69 Shultz memo, S25/6621, CZA.

70 Memo, May 20, 1947, Morgenthau Presidential Diaries, vol. 8, FDRL; Morgenthau remarks, July 24, 1947, UJA Executive Committee, MRD-1, 432. United Jewish Appeal Archives, New York City; July 22, 1947, vol. 8, Morgenthau Presidential Diaries, FDRL; Epstein to Myerson, July 31, 1947, S25/1695, CZA.

71 Monty Noam Penkower, "The Venting of Presidential Spleen: Harry S Truman's Jewish Problem," *Jewish Quarterly Review* 94:4 (Fall 2004): 615–617. Curiously, Truman's entry also stated that Morgenthau had brought a thousand Jews to New York "on a supposedly temporary basis and they stayed," when it was *Truman* who granted permanent entry for the 918 Jewish refugees interred in Fort Oswego, New York, since mid-1944, rather than return them to Europe as Roosevelt had intended. See Sharon R. Loewenstein, *Token Refuge: The Story of the Jewish Refugee Shelter at Oswego, 1944–1946* (Bloomington, 1986).

72 Sachar, *The Redemption of the Unwanted*, 217, 320–322; Wahl to Grossman, July 28, 1947, A431/6; Wahl to Crum, July 28, 1947, A431/18; both in CZA; Wadsworth-Abdullah talk, June 23, 1947, S25/9037, CZA, and 501. BBPal/6-2347, SD; Epstein memo, Aug.1, 1947, S25/6621, CZA; Truman to Lovett, August 6, 1947, PSF 184, HSTL.

73 Sandström meeting with Eban and Horowitz, August 1, 1947, 93.03/2270/1, ISA; *Palestine Post*, July 25, 1947; Granados, *The Birth of Israel*, 200–208; Ben-Dror, "UNSCOP," 197–199; Lotski report, July 29, 1947, Z5/5434, CZA; *Palcor*, July 28, 1947; Beirut to Whitehall, July 24, 1947; Memo, July 30, 1947; both in FO371/61876, PRO; Chamoun memo, n.d., Box 6, UNSCOP MSS; Memo, July 1947, S25/6621, CZA.

74 Bunche notes, July 24, 1947, A/197, Box 1, Hoo MSS; "In the Arab Camp," Aug. 3, 1947, S44/564, CZA; Piri-Gordon to Whitehall, July 28 1947; Pirie-Gordon to Whitehall, July 30, 1947; both in FO 371/61876, PRO. For Abdullah's Greater Syria plan, see "The Greater Syria Movement," January 10, 1948, RG 25-G2, vol. 84–85/19, PAC.

75 *JTA*, July 22–27, 1947; Z. Gilad, *Sefer HaPalmah*, 759–772; Slutzky, *Sefer Toldot HaHagana*, 975, 977; Hoffman, *Anonymous Soldiers*, 455; Berl Repetur, *LeLo Heref* (Israel, 1973), 344–345; Creech Jones memo, July 19, 1947, CAB 129/20, PRO; Hagana intelligence report, February 4, 1948, IR-062, Begin Archives; Grauel interview, July 28, 1947, DAG-13/3/01-2, UN Archives; *Grauel, An Autobiography as told to Eleanor Elfenbein* (Freehold, NJ, 1982). Also see Grauel to Villard, August 13, 1947, 92/36-Het Tsadi, ISA.

76 Bethell, *The Palestine Triangle*, 335–336; Venya, "MeiAhorei HaKla'im," 293–294; Ruth Gruber, *Destination Palestine* (New York, 1948), 74–101; Shertok to Myerson, July 31, 1947, 93.03/2270/3, ISA; July 31, 1947, CAB 128/10, PRO; *New York Post*, Aug. 7, 1947; Eitan Haber, "HaYeled ShehHeinif Et HaDegel Al Toren Oniyat-HaGeirush," 1964, 3050/6-G, ISA.

77 *Palestine Post*, July 30, 1947; *JTA*, July 31, 1947; Begin, *The Revolt*, 289–290; Irgun statement, July 1947, IR-062, Begin Archives; *HaMashkif*, July 31, 1947; Eshel, *Shvirat HaGardomim*, 170–190; Hoffman, *Anonymous Soldiers*, 455–457; Evron, *Gidi*, 271–282.

78 July 1, 1947, FO371/61782, PRO; *Palestine Post*, July 31, 1947; CID report, July 31, 1947, 47/756, HA; *FRUS, 1947*, vol. 5, 1134–1135; Myerson-Cunningham talk, July 31, 1947, S25/5601, CZA; Statement, July 30, 1947, 37/6/1B/5, Anglo-Jewish Association Archives, London; C14/32-1, Board of Deputies of British Jews Archives, London; Bethell, *The Palestine Triangle*, 338–340; Eshel, *Shvirat HaGardomim*, 192–198; Slutzky, *Sefer Toldot HaHagana*, 928–929.

79 Cohen, *Palestine and the Great Powers*, 245–246; Dalton to Attlee, August 11, 1947, PREM 8/623, PRO; Eban report, August 5, 1947, S25/464, CZA; Smith to Sabben-Clare, August 1, 1947, Trafford Smith MSS. (courtesy of Trafford Smith).

80 Cohen, *Palestine and the World Powers*, 247–248; Eban report, August 5, 1947, S25/464; Sachar, *Redemption of the Unwanted*, 215. The *Protocols of the Elders of Zion*, an antisemitic forgery purporting to describe a Jewish plan for global domination, was first published in Russia in 1903, translated into multiple languages, and disseminated internationally in the early part of the 20th century. The *Protocols* were claimed to consist of the minutes of a late nineteenth-century meeting where Jewish leaders discussed their goal of global hegemony by subverting the morals of non-Jews, and by controlling the press and the world's economies.

81 Bevin to Washington, August 16, 1947, CO 537/2313, PRO; Aviva Halmish, *Exodus, HaSippur HaAmiti* (Tel Aviv, 1990), chaps. 14–16; *Palcor*, August 22, 1947; *FRUS, 1947*, vol. 5, 1138–1142; Locker to Smith, August 21, 1947, S25/2638, CZA; *HaAretz*, August 10, 1947; *Kol HaAm*, August 13, 1947; Léon Blum, *Populaire*, August 1947, S25/2630; C2/562; Va'ad HaLeumi meeting, August 22, 1947, J1/7267; all in CZA; *Palestine Post*, August 24, 1947; Gruber, *Destination Palestine*, 108–126; Schwartz, *MiPort de Bouc Ad Hamburg*.

82 Goldmann to Sandström, August 21, 1947, 93.03/2270/12, ISA; Granados, *Birth of Israel*, chap. 21; Box 3, UNSCOP MSS; Meeting, August 5, 1947, S25/3890, CZA; Meetings, August 6–8, 13, and 15, 1947, DAG-13/3.0.1-2, UN Archives; Horowitz-Eban and Lisicky, August 22, 1947, 93.03/2269/21, ISA; Horowitz-Toff and Granados, August 19, 1947, 93.03/2270/1, ISA; Ruffer to Sharef, August 11, 1947, S25/500, CZA; Bunche to Hoo, August 15, 1947, A/197, Box 1, Hoo MSS.

83 Eban-Horowitz and Sanström talk, August 1, 1947, 93.03/2270/1, ISA; Horowitz-Lisicky, August 2, 1947, S25/5991; Eban and Horowitz and Bunche talk, August 3, 1947, S25/5970; Eban report, August 4, 1947, A427/9; all in CZA; Horowitz-Rand talk, August 6, 1947, 93.03/2266/24, ISA; Rufer to Sharef, August 11, 1947, S25/500, CZA; Sommerfelt memo, July 29, 1947, A197, Box 1, Victor Hoo MSS, UN Archives; Clay meeting, August 14, 1947, DAG 13/3.0.0., Box 3, UN Archives; Memo, Aug. 7, 1947, Box 3, UNSCOP files; Crossman talk, August 13, 1947, DAG-13/3.0.1, Box 2, UN Archives; Horowitz-Eban and Crossman-Bunche talk, August 13, 1947, S25/5970, CZA; Horowitz-Mohn talk, August 14, 1947; Shertok-Goldmann and Bunche talk, August 15, 1947; both in 93.03/2270/1, ISA; Horowitz, *State in the Making*, chap. 32.

84 Horowitz note, August 19, 1947, 93.03/2270/1, ISA; Horowitz, *State in the Making*, 212–213; Granados, *Birth of Israel*, 243, 245; Jewish Agency memo,

August 1947, S25/3965; First report, n.d., S25/5991; both in CZA; Ben-Dror, "UNSCOP," 267.

85 *FRUS, 1947*, vol. 5, 1136–1137, 1139; Cabinet meeting, August 29, 1947, Matthew J. Connelly files, HSTL; W. Millis, ed., *The Forrestal Diaries*, 303–304, 306; Roosevelt to Truman, n.d., and Truman reply, August 23, 1947, 4560; Roosevelt to Truman, August 30, 1947, 3773; both in Eleanor Roosevelt MSS, FDRL.

86 Shertok to Myerson, August 4, 1947, 93.03/2270/3, ISA; Epstein to Myerson, August 28, 1947 (two cables); Epstein to Myerson, August 29, 1947; all in S25/1697, CZA.

87 Epstein-Lovett interview, August 29, 1947, A427/6, CZA.

88 Brian Urquhart, *Ralph Bunche: An America Life* (New York, 1993), 148; Elad Ben-Dror, "The Arab Struggle against Partition," 284, 293n138.

89 Ben-Dror, "The Arab Struggle against Partition," 285–286; Ben-Dror, "UNSCOP," 332; Urquhart, *Ralph Bunche*, 149; Granados, *Birth of Israel*, 244

90 Urquhart, *Ralph Bunche*, 149; Granados, *The Birth of Israel*, 244–246; Horowitz, *State in the Making*, 218–219; Ben-Dror, "UNSCOP," 287–289, 302; Ofer Aderet, "Why the Mysterious Swede Who Drew Up Israel's Map Favored the Jews," *Ha'Aretz*, November 25, 2017; Reedman-Horowitz, August 20, 1947, 93.03/2269/21, ISA; Bunche-Green interview, Sept. 24, 1947, US/A/AC.14/6, UN Archives. MacGillivray had given Mohn a memorandum by Douglas Harris on partition, in which the British assigned the most limited boundaries to a Jewish state. MacGillivray to Martin, July 7, 1947, FO 371/61782, PRO; Ben-Dror, "UNSCOP," 255–257.

91 Meeting, August 31, 1947, DAG-13/3.0.0, Box 2, UN Archives; *Official Records of the Second Session of the General Assembly, Supplement no. 11, UNSCOP, Report to the General Assembly*, vol. 1 (New York, 1947); Horowitz, *State in the Making*, 223.

8. Partition

Even as the three ships transporting the caged *Exodus 1947* refugees steamed their way to Hamburg, *Aliya Bet* chief Meirov and Jewish Agency director in Germany Haim Hoffman (later Yahil) sought Ben-Gurion's permission to mount an extremist response when they reached port. Then attending the Zionist General Council's meeting in Geneva, Ben-Gurion rejected any such activity, including arson and mass resistance by DPs from the American and British zones, saying that these Holocaust survivors had done enough, and should not be involved in any operation that would likely end in more bloodshed than they had endured up to this point. Both Inverchapel and Cunningham had urged against a return to German soil, to no avail. Attlee defended HMG's decision and the condition of the "reception camps," responding in a letter to Sidney Silverman MP, who had warned the Cabinet that the "wholly indefensible" policy was making Whitehall the "object of ridicule throughout the world," adding that only in the British zone could accommodation be found "at short notice" for these illegal immigrants.

The forced disembarkations on September 7 by more than 1,000 helmeted British soldiers armed with machine guns, tear-gas pistols, high-pressure hosepipes, and steel-tipped truncheons drew an unprecedented wave of denunciation in the American press, which overwhelmingly voiced demands for a quick decision based on the UNSCOP majority recommendations in order to preclude similar tragedies in the future. Even anti-Zionist Near Eastern Affairs Division director Merriam, writing in response to Epstein's protest, expressed the department's hope that UN consideration soon of the Special Committee's report would result in a solution for the Palestine problem "which will prevent the recurrence of incidents such as those of the *Exodus 1947*."[1]

Jewish Agency officials quickly expressed their support for the majority report upon its release on September 1. The Zionist General

Council's resolution described the UNSCOP inquiry as "a serious attempt to arrive at a workable solution of the Palestine problem," and particularly applauded its recommendation for the creation of a Jewish commonwealth. Hearing that a proposed Jewish state would include the Negev, an ecstatic Ben-Gurion chided critics who thought the map a nightmare: "I only hope this nightmare comes true!" Even the dissenting HaShomer HaTsa'ir, Ahdut HaAvoda, and the Revisionists declared that it at least formed a basis for negotiation, although Magnes wept, telling a close friend that it would mean war and the end of everything for which he and followers stood against "dismembering" the country. Talking with a U.S. consulate official in Jerusalem, Myerson praised the "corridors" proposal as ingenious, although asserting to a press conference that including Western Galilee (and dropping Jaffa) would be a "better division" of the country for a Jewish state. Shertok had further reservations about the exclusion of Jewish Jerusalem, the long transition period, and probable Arab refusal to cooperate with an economic union holding up Jewish statehood, but believed that all efforts should be made towards its realization, with Jewry "facing great historic chance."[2]

A similar response, with the exception of the American Council for Judaism, came from across the Atlantic. The American Jewish Committee and the American Jewish Conference stressed the majority report's offering "the best practical hope" for the large-scale immigration of Holocaust survivors as the crucial reason to have the recommendations promptly adopted by the General Assembly. Silver cabled Swope that these were "quite satisfactory," and that "energetic support" from Washington was "indispensable" for success. With Morgenthau's intervention, Nathan made the case to a "strongly sympathetic" Eleanor Roosevelt at her home in Hyde Park. A New York Times editorial, whose Jewish publisher Arthur Hays Sulzberger had long doubted creating "a political state as a basis of religious faith," now declared itself ready to work and hope "most earnestly" for the success of the proposed new states by the UN, whose prestige was of "primary importance at this stage of the world's history."[3]

The Arabs sharply dissented. Musa Alami, while involved as head of the Arab Offices abroad in a bitter feud with Haj Amin over representing Palestine's Arabs, officially dismissed the Zionist case as "worthless"; declared that UNSCOP's terms of reference were prejudicial against the Arabs; rejected both reports; and warned that a Jewish state imposed by violence "would be opposed by violence," plunging the Middle East into a state of war that might precipitate "an international conflict of incalculable dimensions." Advised privately by Beeley that the Arabs should not again isolate themselves at the Assembly by taking up a "totally intransigent position," Alami responded through representative Edward Atiyah that amendments to the minority report—with Palestine remaining an Arab country—could secure Arab cooperation towards a GA endorsement, provided that a previous understanding with HMG were arrived at. The AHC, joined by the Palestinian Arab press, called on its "Arab sisters" to join in preventing the "destruction" which Zionist and imperialist ambitions would bring upon the "holy Arab nation." Jamali cautioned U.S. Ambassador Douglas that if the Assembly took a "wrong course," it would "mean the end of [the] UN for all Arab states"; if the GA accepted anything like the UNSCOP majority recommendation, a "bloody Arab uprising" would erupt against the Jews as "invaders" and against British troops should they interfere. Haj Amin went further, denouncing even the minority report as legitimizing the Zionist presence in Palestine and a "partition in disguise."[4]

Behind the façade of Arab unity, however, strife seethed. Abdullah confidentially informed Jewish Agency Arabists that he would be prepared to accept the majority report if he received the Arab "triangle" of Palestine. They also heard that Haj Amin wished to expand the borders of an expected revolt to encompass Jordan and thereby topple the Hashemite ruler. Nazareth's well-to-do Christian Arabs, fearing for their property and lives in the face of "the Husseini terror," sought to flee to Lebanon and the U.S. Sami Taha, the most prominent Palestinian Arab trade union leader, was fatally shot by an unknown assailant on the evening of September 12 in Haifa because, according to many in the local Arab community, he was targeted by the Husseini faction for his open support of Musa Alami. HaShomer HaTsa'ir's Arab department divulged that Taha had objected to Haj Amin's call for extended militant protests during the UNSCOP visit, worried about their deleterious impact on Palestinian Arab workers; he also called for an elected Arab Higher Committee. R. M. Graves, Jerusalem District Commissioner, recorded in his diary that Taha had recently called for collaboration with the *yishuv*, an "ample excuse for the average Oriental patriot for killing the traitor, who dares to utter such statesmanlike words." Taha's murder, reported British police headquarters there, made certain individuals "assassin conscious" that secret organizations under the dictates of the Husseinis had commenced to execute their program of "persons to be eliminated."

Rumors also circulated that the Iraqi gift of £100,000 to Alami in support of his Arab Construction Scheme, rather than the usual donation per year to the AHC for the purpose of buying Arab lands, derived from Baghdad's enmity towards Haj Amin for associating himself with the pro-German revolt of Rashid Ali in 1941 against the regime. Egypt and Saudi Arabia pressed London not to favor Abdullah's Greater Syria plan, while the pro-British Prime Minister Nuri al-Said favored the Hashemite dynasty's ambitions.[5]

Bevin at this juncture considered it impossible to foresee what solution could be found, so Henderson heard on September 9 when visiting the Foreign Office. Having earlier communicated to Ibn Saud that the Greater Syria scheme was a question for the Arabs to discuss among themselves, the Foreign Secretary expressed surprise that Washington had made things "so difficult" for HMG, seeing that the Near East was obviously of strategic importance. In his view, the United States bore a share of responsibility for the considerable bloodshed and loss of property in Palestine, as well as British prestige there. Again and again, public statements regarding the necessity of the 100,000 immigrants and other aspects had thrown London "off balance" when he had been endeavoring to make progress in resolving the "delicate" Palestine problem. The bulk of funds for terrorist activity and illegal immigration had come from America, discouraging the mandatory's attempts to maintain law and order in the Holy Land. For two years, he had tried "in a friendly way," but without success, to have the U.S. government halt the exemption from income tax donations to organizations so engaged. With Great Britain already facing many "grave" internal and international problems, Bevin thought that the chance of prevailing on his colleagues to implement the majority recommendations appeared highly doubtful. London would wait, he informed Henderson, until the Assembly's pronounced decision, and if the GA asked Britain to implement the majority report, the Cabinet would then answer to that request.[6]

Unprepared to commit HMG to Alami's proposal, Beeley was shocked at a "top secret and personal" cable received from Gurney to Creech Jones on September 8. The Chief Secretary's views about reducing the number of Arabs in the Jewish state to 400,000; favoring the economic union; shortening the transition period to a mere six months; holding down by force the Arab population of the Jewish state during that time; the "appalling events at Hamburg"; believing that there was "really no practicable alternative plan" to partition which would provide for an increased immigration rate of 6,5000 monthly from September 1 onwards; and approving Jerusalem under UN control—all made up an "extraordinary telegram." Writing to his Whitehall associates three days later, Beeley opined that the lengthy communication suggested the top officials of the Palestine Administration "are already packing their bags." The Cabinet had not yet carefully considered the full UNSCOP report, he informed Agudas Israel Executive Harry Goodman, and while he thought that Moscow would support the Yugoslav stand at the General Assembly for a unitary state, the Czech delegation appeared to have a free hand, and the American countries might favor the majority report that had been signed by all the Latin American delegates.

The entire British press, save for the *Economist*'s declaration that partition was "unworkable" and therefore HMG should have nothing to do with its enforcement, approved the majority plan explicitly or implicitly. The London *Times* went so far as to state that the majority report is "the more logical and on the whole the simpler," and was calculated to appeal to "the conscience of international opinion gathered in the General Assembly as an honest attempt to adjudicate between the two claimants to Palestine." Beeley remained skeptical.[7]

Azzam Pasha had no doubts that GA adoption of either plan would result in an Arab-Jewish war, and that only a joint U.S.-UK line of action could help the Arabs, "helpless" themselves against the Jewish hold on American public opinion, and avoid the "invidious" position of arranging a later retreat from an unrealistic UN decision. To Beeley, he advised that the British and another UN authority build up over a ten-year period the institutions of an independent Palestine state. Azzam rejected the arguments, put privately to him at the Savoy Hotel by Eban and Horowitz on September 15, that the majority recommendations would provide "finality and equality" and benefit regional development. The Arab peoples, he asserted to the pair, viewed Palestine Jewry, "an alien organism," as a temporary phenomenon that would eventually be ejected by the Arabs in the same manner as the European Crusaders after two hundred years of living uninvited in their midst. Realistically, he stressed, the question came down to whether the Jews could bring more force for the creation of a Jewish state than the Arabs could muster to prevent it. All were governed and directed by "historic forces," which would impel the Arabs to fight the Jewish foothold whether the fight redounded to their interest or not. He discounted Horowitz's appeal that choice allowed people to operate along the line of their greatest interests, and concluded that Arab agreement could only come by the Jews creating autonomous units within the framework of Arab society. If they refused to abandon Zionist aspirations, their only hope lay in the enlistment of predominant political power to suppress Arab resistance. Azzam's "forcefulness and fanaticism" stirred his visitors, but left them depressed, realizing that with this encounter "vanished the last effort to bridge the gulf." They saw looming ahead, Horowitz later recalled, forces pushing them toward "the brink of a sanguinary war, the outcome of which no one could prophecy."[8]

That same day, Marshall explained to the U.S. delegation at the General Assembly the quandary of either alienating the Arabs or being severely attacked for "pussyfooting" when adopting a public stand on Palestine. Against Eleanor Roosevelt's doubts over USSR support for the Arabs, he, Hilldring, and Henderson (present at Lovett's request) believed that the Russians would espouse a unitary state for the sake of expediency. Marshall agreed with the statement that Lovett and Henderson had drafted for his delivery to the GA, avoiding a definite position in favor of the majority report but praising the eleven unanimous UNSCOP resolutions and hoping for general agreement during the GA session. Hilldring wished the United States to go further in favor of that report while remaining prepared to amend it as the result of debate; Roosevelt thought it at least as important to think of the value of such support in promoting the success of the UN.

Implementation by U.S. troops had to be considered, Marshall pointed out, eliciting Henderson's agreement along with his charge that the UNSCOP report was "not based on any principle but was full of sophistry." Austin did not see how it was possible to carve out of an area already too small for a state a still smaller state, which would have to defend itself forever with bayonets against the Arabs "until extinguished in blood." Assuming that the delegation would support the majority report, he felt that it would be necessary to take the urgent next step and to support it with all the required help, including troops. Marshall's statement should be as clear as possible, Austin concluded, creating a "determined effort" early so that the Arabs would not get the idea that they would yet convince the delegation.[9]

On September 17, Marshall announced to the General Assembly that the United States intended to do everything within its power at this session to assist in solving the difficult Palestine problem, which required of all courage, resolution, and restraint. Commending highly the Special Committee on Palestine for its contribution, he saw its agreement on eleven recommendations, even if it did not reach unanimity on a number of issues including partition, as representing "definite progress." Any solution recommended by the GA could not be ideally satisfactory to the two peoples primarily concerned. While the final decision must properly await the detailed consideration of the UNSCOP report, Marshall added, the United States gave "great weight" not only to the recommendations that had met with the unanimous approval of that committee, but also to those which were approved by the majority of its members. The same day, after al-Khoury opposed setting up an *ad hoc* political committee on which every Assembly member would have the right to be represented in order to discuss the agenda concerning Palestine (Lie's suggestion of five days earlier to the General Committee), and after the British and American delegates favored its creation, the General Committee gave its approval.[10]

All the Arab delegations interpreted the Secretary of State's words as an "all-out" declaration of American support for the majority plan, Wadsworth reported to Johnson on the 18th. (A copy of that memorandum reached Truman as well.) He had urged the Arabs to understand that Marshall's "great weight" phrase did not imply a definitive commitment, and expressed the hope that their final word would be based on continuing recognition of "a broad mutuality" of Arab and U.S. interests in the Near East, but they were hardly mollified. Until then, argued the Syrian and Lebanese representatives, the U.S. Government—with the exception of the White House—had been neutral, but from this moment Marshall could not go back later on his remarks. No useful purpose would be served in discussing the terms of procedure in the UN with Wadsworth, Emir Feisal remarked, and no aspect existed on which further Arab-American cooperation was possible. To us, Lebanese Minister Charles Malik observed, "Palestine is *the* issue." Jamali warned that the Arabs would find means to oppose Jewish aggression, "even by force of arms," and he blamed the United States for giving in to Zionist pressure and thus being primarily responsible for present and future developments in Palestine. An adviser to the U.S. delegation, talking to a British counterpart the same evening, gained the additional impression that that delegation was not "entirely pleased" with Marshall's statement on Palestine.[11]

The Jewish Agency representatives to the UN had cause for anxiety as well. Shertok found encouraging Lie's private confidence that the majority recommendations would be approved as "there is no other solution," but Crum informed them that Hannegan could not deliver the Administration's backing for the report because Kenneth C. Royall, the first individual to be appointed Secretary of the Army, was afraid the United States would lose the oil in the Middle East. Roosevelt was "a tower of strength" within the American delegation, but John Foster Dulles—who actually thought that putting the Palestine issue before the GA offered "little hope of a constructive solution"—was being "cagey." Even given Hilldring's appointment (his pro-Zionist views were similar to Buxton's, Niles reported in confidence), the "evil spirit," in Shertok's opinion, of Wadsworth's presence was worrisome. Further, Shertok agreed with a newspaper headline that Marshall's statement suggested "qualified acceptance." At a subsequent delegation press conference following the Secretary's speech, Charles Bohlen, Alternate Representative for the delegation who was more prepared to give the Soviets a sphere of influence in Eastern Europe than accept Kennan's stronger "containment" policy, remarked that the United States might be inclined to consider the best points of the minority report.

Nor could Truman's support be taken for granted, nor was it known whether he would receive a joint Jewish delegation. The main question was now, Silver told a meeting of Jewish organizations on September 18, how to influence the President, a man who "is used to make a friendly gesture and then drops the matter. If this will be the case now, it means defeat." In addition, Robinson observed, securing an international police force for implementation in the interim period would not be easy, and in the meantime the British would remain.[12]

On September 20, 1947, the Labour Cabinet "approved generally" Bevin's view that he had been "reluctantly driven" to the conclusion that HMG would announce its intention to surrender the Mandate and, failing a satisfactory settlement, to plan for an early withdrawal of the British forces and administration from Palestine. There were "grave" disadvantages in carrying out either of the two UNSCOP reports or any alternative plan of partition, and he was not willing that Great Britain enforce a settlement which was unacceptable to either the Arabs or the Jews. Creech Jones, Dalton, Bevan, Noel-Baker, and President of the Board of Trade Stafford Cripps agreed against Shinwell's favoring the majority plan, while Alexander, whose Chiefs of Staff had emphasized the "overriding importance" of retaining the goodwill of the Arab states and of the Muslim world as a whole, noted that to maintain law and order until a specific date for withdrawal would require additional military re-enforcements. Hearing that the Air Staff wanted to remain in Palestine, Bevin said "Tell [them] that, if they want to stay, they'll 'ave to stay up in 'elicopters."

Three days earlier, Attlee had informed Bevin of his wish that an announcement should include a definite date for withdrawal, which should not be longer than six months. Now, seeing a close parallel between the present position in Palestine and the situation in India, whose Hindu majority was engaged in violent clashes with Muslim-dominated Pakistan over the Punjab after both countries had been declared independent on August 15, Attlee did not think it "reasonable" to ask the British administration to continue in Palestine. He agreed with Cripps that the official statement should not offer HMG's willingness to remain unconditionally until an authority selected by the GA declared itself ready to assume full responsibility. Creech Jones and Bevin set out to redraft the statement which the Colonial Secretary would deliver before the Assembly in six days' time.[13]

One week earlier, the International Subcommittee of the Labour Party Executive had unanimously resolved, following a motion by Bevan which Shinwell strongly supported, to have the party urge the acceptance of the general lines of the majority report. Chairman Laski had sent the resolution with a covering note to Attlee, saying that this was an honorable way out of "an intolerable impasse," and urging that Cabinet acceptance would relieve a "grave discomfort" in the party. Showing up at Transport House headquarters on the 24th, Attlee declared to its members that the majority report was "fantastic" because it gave the Jews more than any other committee had ever suggested; acceptance would repudiate Bevin; and there was no suggestion in the subcommittee's proposal that HMG should be aided in imposing the majority plan. To Laski's shock, Noel-Baker then accused the Jews of bringing all this on themselves by terrorism, and advised that they should "clear out" of Palestine, realizing that Zionism was "doomed," if they could not find terms of agreement with the Arabs. Attlee then disclosed the Cabinet's decision, sparking Laski's denunciation that it was nothing but a Foreign Office maneuver on behalf of the Arabs; he considered Bevin their "passionate advocate" since there was nothing left of his reputation, which the Foreign Secretary had staked on his Palestine policy, and he was revenging himself on the Jews in consequence.

Writing to Frankfurter, Laski was completely convinced that HMG proposed to "sell the Jews down the river," with Whitehall "hermetically" persuading the State Department to stand with it on the ground that, otherwise, the Russians would fill the vacuum and get the region's oil. Laski remained certain that the decision was a trick, based on the three assumptions that there would be no agreement on any plan at Lake Success, the United States would take no special responsibilities of any kind, and HMG would then be asked to stay on the understanding that history had "wiped out" both the Balfour Declaration and the Mandate.[14]

Henderson lost little time in advising Marshall that, while giving "serious weight" to the majority proposals, the government should make it clear that "our minds are by no means closed," and due importance would also be given to the view of other nations and particularly of the "interested parties." His long TOP SECRET memorandum of September 22, seeking to counter what he years later called the "very-pro Israel" stand on the 15th of most of the U.S. delegation, cautioned that advocacy of any partition plan would be certain to undermine Washington's relations with the Arab, and to a lesser extent with the Muslim world just when oil and communications facilities in the area were vital to U.S. and world interests; would necessitate major contributions in force, materials, and money to its implementation if adopted; and would be unworkable in the face of "fierce" Arab opposition. In addition, it would not dispose of the problem because disagreement over an economic union and other matters would send the "disagreeable matter" back to the General Assembly. Finally, it would ignore the principles of self-determination and majority rule advocated in the UN Charter and American concepts of government, and would recognize the principle of a Jewish "theocratic racial state" (the phrase raised one week earlier in a memorandum, stamped "Secret," by the anti-Zionist William Eddy, former U.S. Minister to Saudi Arabia and now a

Special Assistant to State), thus questioning Jewish identity outside of Palestine. Henderson added the assurance that his staff would loyally carry out Marshall's statement of September 15, continuing to endeavor to execute that decision in a manner that would minimize as far as possible "the damage to our relations and interests" in the region.

The very next day, the Secretary, backed by Johnson and Hilldring, declared to the principal Arab representatives that the U.S. delegation could not "throw the UNSCOP report out of the window." Marshall added, at the same time, that contrary to Chamoun's address to the GA on the 20th, he had made no commitment to favor partition. Rather, Washington would keep an open mind and hear all points of view before reaching any conclusions. Al-Khoury, who predicted at the meeting a similar "disastrous" fate for Zionist efforts to the one that had befallen the Crusaders, felt somewhat assured. Emir Feisal, however, told Johnson and State Adviser Paul Alling in strict confidence that he wished Marshall to know that "NO Arab Government" in the Near East would be able to "restrain the outraged feelings of its people" if a Jewish state were established in Palestine.[15]

Following a discussion of the U.S. delegation in Marshall's office on the morning of the 24th, attended by Roosevelt, Rusk, Bohlen, Hilldring, and department Legal Advisor Charles Fahy, the Secretary decided that the U.S. representative on the *Ad Hoc* Committee on Palestine would make no statement in the early phrases of the general discussion, and present the U.S. views for the first time only at the completion of the sessions on Palestine. The draft of this position should begin at once, embracing support of the majority plan with such amendments as were now believed by the U.S. Government to be "wise and essential to a workable plan." The plan should retain the provisions for partition and large-scale Jewish immigration. If the U.S. proposal did not receive a two-thirds vote of support in the GA, or if it were ascertained beforehand that this would be the case, then the government would consider two lines of action for what Hilldring's record of the meeting termed "the switch position": force a vote in the *Ad Hoc* Committee to demonstrate the absence of support for the majority report, or propose an alternate solution which would elicit the support of two-thirds of the members of the UN. (The possibility of placing Palestine under a UN trusteeship or some other form of supervision, McClintock had advised Rusk, would afford "a convenient opportunity" to get rid of the quasi-official position enjoyed by the Jewish Agency.) A tentative draft for an alternate plan should also be prepared. It was the "firm conviction" of those present that all this must be maintained in the "utmost secrecy."[16]

One day before articulating the British statement before the *Ad Hoc* Committee, Creech Jones, accompanied by Inverchapel and Hector McNeil, informed Marshall during an early lunch of its contents and the decision for an early withdrawal. The GA had voted on the 23rd by a show of hands (29 to 11, with 6 abstentions) in favor of creating that committee, the only speakers to take part, Jamali and Malik, opposed. HMG thought that no conflict existed between the UNSCOP conclusions and the broad objectives of British policy, Creech Jones began. His government was prepared to assume responsibility for carrying out any plan securing Arab and Jewish agreement. If the GA recommended a plan not acceptable to both contenders, London would not feel able to give effect to it. In that case, the UN would have to provide an alternative implementing authority. McNeil hoped that the United States would not react as it did in the case of Greece, thinking that the British were "walking out" on Washington. From his brief understanding of the imminent statement, Marshall responded that he thought that would not be the case. He personally was very sympathetic to the British dilemma and, without discussing the wisdom of the course which they had followed in "particular incidents," he felt that they had been the victims of "an impossible situation and considerable unjust criticism." The U.S. Government would deal with the matter at the "highest level," meaning by implication (which the Secretary did not explain further) that it would be treated as an international affair, and not permit "local political pressures" to determine the government's actions.[17]

Reaction to Creech Jones's declaration before the GA on September 26 came swiftly. Johnson acknowledged, so the Colonial Secretary reported to Attlee and Bevin, its "clarity, courage and helpfulness." The Syrian and Saudi Arabia delegates reacted "more than favorably," although they regretted that HMG was leaving the Arabs "a mess of our making." Jerusalem's *Al-Wahda*, seeing it as another example of British cleverness at not showing their true intentions, declared that the Arabs had decided to march, and nothing could stop them. First Jewish responses suspected a British design to perpetuate the mandatory's hold on Palestine, giving HMG in effect a veto. (Shultz's analysis on this key point, with which Hilldring privately agreed even as he told her to trust Marshall, led to Victor Bernstein's critical dispatch in *PM*.) "Evacuation is not an alternative to a solution," editorialized the *Palestine Post*, which castigated Britain's determination to "wash her hands" of the problem just when UNSCOP's partition solution was in sight. Still, echoing most U.S. newspapers, the *New York Herald Tribune* editorialized that the British decision was "as wise as it is honorable."

Churchill favored a quick withdrawal, charging the government with having wasted between £100–£150 million and the services of 100,000 troops in Palestine, gaining nothing but ill will there and in "every quarter of the world." Only the *Manchester Guardian* among the British press criticized Creech Jones's announcement, declaring it a "sorry" scuttle that left Jews and Arabs to fight it out between themselves. Gurney assumed that the statement was intended to force both Jews and Arabs to the realization that they must now reach agreement; failing that, he thought it feasible to abandon most of Palestine to "chaos and disorder" but that Christianity would surely expect HMG to see that Jerusalem and its Holy Places were not handed over to be fought for between Muslims and Jews. Leaving was not a bluff, Lord Chancellor Jowitt informed the Council of Foreign Relations in New York; political pressure at home made it impossible to stay, and he was "deeply apprehensive" over the future.[18]

The two contesting sides in Palestine girded for battle. Haj Amin threatened war, predicted victory "in the end," and strongly condemned both UNSCOP reports (he dubbed the minority report part of "the Zionist Imperialist plan"). The Arabs would never allow a Jewish state to be established in one inch of Palestine and "not a single Jew" would be allowed to migrate there, declared the AHC's UN delegation. Moderate reactions from al-Khoury and Chamoun in favor of some Jewish immigration were swept aside as the Arab League political council, meeting in Sofar near Beirut on September 16–19, warned that any attempt to create a Jewish state in Palestine would lead to bloodshed in the Middle East, and its members resolved to mobilize a pan-Arab army under the control of the League—not Haj Amin—in order to save Palestine and to donate £1 million to that cause. Still, the Egyptians balked at participating in any military action, while the Saudis refused to join an oil embargo.

Inspector General of the Palestine police Nicholas Gray bluntly warned Zaslani and the Hagana's Eliyahu Saharov of serious Arab trouble when implementation of the UNSCOP report began, and he declared that British forces would help the Jews only if the Agency provided full cooperation in "eliminating" the terrorist problem, especially as the Irgun had recently announced its intention to continue operations. The Agency would handle both matters on its own, the pair responded. "We Jews are perfectly capable of taking care of ourselves" against any "troubles" with the Arabs, Ben-Gurion declared publicly. When a member of the AHC Executive informed the press on September 27 that "the time had come when the Arabs should resort to force to defend their cause," the Agency countered that this first occasion since the UN's creation of member states threatening force against a prospective GA recommendation would be met by the *yishuv*'s "fierce, sustained, and justified resistance." Two days later, responding to Creech Jones's statement and the British killing of one man and wounding at least ten when halting the 446 refugees aboard the *Af Al Pi Khen* (In Spite of It All) and sending them to Cyprus, Ben-Gurion asserted that the Jewish people would consider no UN solution which did not provide for the "immediate establishment of a sovereign Jewish State."[19]

By the month's end, Jewish Agency officials privately sounded the alarm about Washington's uncertain stand. "President's attitude unknown severe struggle over essential majority scheme foreseen," Shertok cabled Myerson on the 21st; Epstein reported to Kaplan the following week that Henderson's department was exerting heavy pressure on Marshall to refrain from alienating the Arab world. They had no awareness that Forrestal, recently appointed the first U.S. Secretary of Defense, had objected in Cabinet to Hannegan's pitch for Truman to speak out in favor of 150,000 Jews to enter Palestine, and had asked the President (as he had after the last November elections) whether it would not be possible to lift the "Jewish-Palestine question" out of politics. It was worth trying, Truman replied, although "obviously" (so Forrestal recorded in his diary) the President was skeptical. An "unsatisfactory," "fairly disquieting" meeting with a taciturn Marshall on the 26th at Shertok and Silver's request yielded nothing further from the Secretary, who, reacting sharply to Silver's direct question as to the government's definite attitude in view of "disquieting" reports in the press, declared that the United States had bigger problems and the future of the UN was at stake. Four days later, State's "top secret" memorandum to Marshall discussed allotting Jaffa, Safed, and the southern portion of the Negev to the Arab state; suggested combining the best of the

majority and minority reports if neither secured a two-thirds majority vote in the Assembly; viewed the maintenance of goodwill within
the Muslim world as "one of the primary goals" of American foreign
policy; and emphasized the urgency of a definitive solution by the UN
"which the interested parties cannot expect by agitation and violence
to alter."[20]

The same memorandum to Marshall noted that while the Soviet Union
had thus far avoided taking a position, the U.S. Embassy in Moscow and
other observers were convinced that, "in the final showdown," Moscow
would support the Arab states, much as Gromyko had favored a unitary
state in his historic GA address of May 14. According to Lie's report to
Shertok two weeks earlier, Gromyko had privately told him that Russia
was not behind Yugoslavia's UNSCOP stand, but he refused to commit
himself on the majority report. Sneh learned from Czech Vice-Minister
for Foreign Affairs Vladimir Clementis that Prague had not yet given its
GA delegation final instructions, although he was more inclined to the
minority report's federal scheme. Semen Tsarapkin, Russia's delegate on
the *Ad Hoc* Committee, adopted in general a non-committal attitude when
queried by Epstein on September 19. Three days later, Shertok learned
from a reliable source that the Yugoslav delegate on that committee was
instructed to "keep silent," while his Russian, Pole, and Czech counterparts would vote for the majority recommendations

None knew that Molotov had sent a Top Priority cable (with a copy to
Stalin) on the 30th to Andrey Vyshinskii, head of the Soviet delegation to
the GA's Second Session, not to oppose the majority opinion. For "tactical
reasons," the Russian Foreign Minister explained further, "we did not want
to take the initiative" the previous May "in the creation of a Jewish State."
(The original text, crossed out by Molotov, read: "It was inexpedient for us
to take the initiative...") Consequently, Gromyko had received a directive
five months earlier to favor partition as a second option. Completely in
the dark about this crucial directive, the State Department's latest memorandum to Marshall concluded that "concerted opposition" of the Soviet
bloc and the Arab League states and their Muslim supporters could defeat
any proposal which did not command almost unanimous support of the
other members of the UN.[21]

The AHC and Agency representatives, invited by newly elected chairman Evatt to appear before the *Ad Hoc* Committee, immediately showed
their contrasting colors. Speaking on September 29, Jamal Husseini

called for the establishment of an Arab state comprising all of Palestine, with protection for each minority and a guarantee of worship at all Holy Places, the country's Arabs "solidly determined" to oppose "with all means at their disposal" the "dissection, segregation or partition of their tiny country." Three days later, Silver indicated acceptance of the majority report, despite the limited area given the Jewish common-wealth and Jerusalem's exclusion from that state, the Agency prepared to "assume this burden as one of the sacrifices intended to find a way out of the present intolerable impasse." The preliminary debate that followed found Uruguay and Panama favoring partition, Lebanon and Iraq opposed. Czech pro-British representative Lisicky prophetically warned that unless an independent force was instituted responsible directly to the UN, some other great power or powers must be persuaded to take the responsibility for enforcement.

Concluding that only partition "gave any promise whatever" of providing a settlement, the Canadian delegation sought a discussion on methods of implementation and enforcement. Its American counterpart, however, preferring to proceed on the assumption that all members were bound to cooperate in this regard, and that HMG would be responsible for suppressing any disturbances which might arise, vigorously objected in private to this suggestion. The delegation, advised by Lt. Genl. Mathew Ridgway that any recommendation on sending armed forces to Palestine had "very far reaching military implications to the U.S.," gave no public indication of where the U.S. Government stood.[22]

Behind this veil of silence and protracted delay, the State Department appeared in fact to shift towards the Arab position. On October 3, Jamali and Feisal conveyed to Wadsworth that the Soviet delegation, as well as a Polish representative, had approached the Arab states with an "explicit offer" to support the Arabs on Palestine if they would support Ukraine for the Security Council. If the United States could not now "guarantee the Arab position," they would feel compelled to respond positively to Moscow on this, as well as on other matters. Although Alling informed Malik that these intentions were "no less than a form of blackmail," Henderson reminded Lovett that the Arabs considered Palestine "the most important question in their international life," and they felt it their duty to use "all means available" in order to block the setting up of a Jewish state. At a meeting of the U.S. delegation on October 3, one day after Ben-Gurion called on the *yishuv* to mobilize for national security and the UN to render an immediate decision on a Jewish state, it was generally agreed that the majority plan would not obtain a two-thirds vote at present, in which case some form of UN trusteeship for Palestine might be desirable; the United States was committed to the encouragement of Jewish immigration to Palestine but not to support the creation of a Jewish state; and the delegation should not attempt to persuade GA members to vote for the majority plan. (Conveying his thoughts to the receptive Canadian Middle East specialist Elizabeth MacCallum, Wadsworth foresaw the GA appointing a governor for Palestine, the UN Trusteeship Council administering the territory "for a year or two.") At the end of the meeting in his office, Marshall indicated that he was thinking of issuing a press statement requesting the Congress to pass legislation for increasing immigration of DPs to the United States.[23]

State had also gained the Defense Department's support just then for shipping 335,000 tons of steel during the next two years for the construction by the Arabian American Oil Company (ARAMCO) of a 30-inch oil pipeline from Saudi Arabia to a terminus in Lebanon. Although the Commerce and Agriculture Departments argued that domestic needs had to be met first, State, with the Navy's support, argued that Middle East oil was vital for the country's own requirements and for the Marshall Plan's economic reconstruction of Europe, as well as for hampering Communist influence and intrigue throughout the Arab states. Lovett's memorandum to Marshall added that it would also raise the general economy of the Near and Middle East areas, making them "less vulnerable to outside pressures." Appearing on October 9 before the Senate Committee on Small Business, which questioned the Administration's favorable decision in the matter, Forrestal pointed to the rapid depletion of American oil reserves and an equally rising curve of domestic consumption. From 1939 to 1946, world oil reserves had gone up about 60 per cent while American discoveries added only about 6 per cent to that of the United States. Until new fields of substantial magnitude in the Western Hemisphere were discovered, he concluded, steel pipe for this venture should have preference.[24]

Shertok and Silver's unsatisfactory meeting on September 26 with Marshall, coupled with rumors of State's pro-Arab shift, generated Zionist pressure to secure Truman's endorsement of the UNSCOP majority report. Rosenman, alerted by Epstein, spoke with the heads of the Democratic Party in New York. Bronx party boss Ed Flynn, with the backing of state party chairman Paul F. Fitzpartrick, party treasurer Carl Sherman, and New York City Mayor William O'Dwyer, then telephoned Truman to discuss the need to regain Jewish support in next year's elections; he received "a favorable impression." Sullivan assured Kirchwey that he would continue to "battle all the way" on the Palestine issue to assure that "America's decision is on the side of justice."

Niles, updated by Epstein, and Clifford mobilized Cabinet members Hannegan, Attorney General Tom Clark, and Federal Security Agency Administrator Oscar Ewing to impress upon the President the importance of American support for the UN's international standing. Jacobson's private appeal for "my people" that "Harry" support at the General Assembly the need of 500,000 Jews in Europe to reach Palestine—"the only place where they can go"—vied with Truman's expressed thought at a Cabinet lunch on the 6th that "if they would keep quiet" then "everything would be all right." Confronted with Hannegan's political emphasis against Forrestal's pro-Arab argument, as well as scores of AZEC-organized telegrams and bi-partisan Congressional letters advocating for the Zionist cause, an angry Truman declared that hasty decisions would likely cause greater harm than benefit to the parties directly concerned. Nathan met with Hilldring and Bohlen and, in a confidential memorandum submitted on October 8 to Mrs. Roosevelt and Hilldring for the U.S. delegation, urged a "firm and forthright" statement favoring partition. She asked Niles to tell Truman of her fears that lack of support would harm the United States' good name in the UN, and question the President's credibility if his backing of partition would not guide the delegation's stand.[25]

Finally, meeting with Lovett, Niles, and Clifford in the White House on the 8th, Truman approved a statement that he had discussed with Marshall three days earlier in which the delegation would declare the government's support for a Jewish state. The same day, Truman replied to Jacobson that he did not think it proper to directly intervene "at this stage," particularly as a two-thirds vote was needed "to accomplish the matter sought." Marshall, he added, was handling "the whole thing, I think, as it should be and I hope it will work out all right." The Arab League Council's decision to send troops to Palestine's borders and resist Jewish statehood, reported in the *New York Times* on October 9, Truman later characterized as "belligerent and defiant." A draft by Rusk, sent the next day to the delegation, conveyed the President's emphasis to Lovett that Washington's financial and economic aid to Palestine would not be a direct U.S. contribution but only come under UN auspices, and that the United States would not "pick up" the United Kingdom's responsibility for maintaining law and order there. Any American participation regarding the latter would again be as a part of a UN "police force or constabulary." Lovett continued to share the State Department's misgivings about the latter phrase, agreeing with McClintock's view that this reference might be taken by the "more wild-eyed elements" on both Jewish and Arab sides as an invitation to man and finance small armies under the guise of police forces in the two new states.

Truman's military advisors, Niles soon informed Epstein, were advising him that the *yishuv* could not withstand an Arab invasion or even those states' support of the Palestinian Arabs, while the President worried that a large American force close to the Soviet borders might spur Stalin to send in troops, possibly leading to a full-scale conflict. Indeed, the U.S. Joint Chiefs of Staff recommended to Forrestal on October 10 a unilateral trusteeship as the "most desirable" means of checking Soviet designs and retaining the "good will" of the Arab and Muslim states.[26]

On October 11, the same day that Buxton, Crum, and McDonald released a statement together with some writers on Middle Eastern affairs that Arab warlike threats had "no substance," Johnson announced at the *Ad Hoc* Committee that his government supported the basic principles of the unanimous UNSCOP recommendations and the majority proposal. Using the opening phrases in Truman's letter to Ibn Saud on October 25, 1946, a regarding U.S. involvement and therefore responsibility in developing the Jewish National Home since World War I, an American representative for the first time before an international body made clear U.S. support for partition if adopted by the General Assembly. Maintaining law and order might require a "special constabulary or police force" recruited on a volunteer basis by the UN. At the same time, U.S. participation in implementation would only be as a part of a broad UN endeavor directed to this end, and—a reflection of State's reservations—that "certain geographical modifications" had to be made, such as Jaffa being part of the Arab state, in the majority plan.

Johnson's British counterparts quickly responded in private that the statement "was far from being fully satisfactory." They were "not enthusiastic" about partition, and thought that the United States should have indicated how such a plan, which would not have the support of both sides, was to be implemented. In a secret cable to Creech Jones, Bevin characterized the allusion to a constabulary as "ill-considered and ill-thought out." The Arab press went further, denouncing Truman for bowing to the Jewish vote and inheriting Britain's imperialist legacy, while asserting that millions of Arabs and Muslims would never submit to foreign conquest.[27]

Johnson's unequivocal statement came just at the right time for the worried Zionists. Sneh reported that his meeting on October 3 with Vatican Secretary of State Domenico Tardini, arranged via Abbé Glasberg with Monsignor Roncalli (later Pope John XXIII), had obtained the Holy See's willingness to be neutral and not to object to the voting preferences of the Latin American countries. Yet the concerns of Bidault that French support would endanger the country's hold on the 16 million Muslims under its colonial rule in North Africa made that deeply divided Cabinet's stand uncertain. Its continued abstention, influencing West European neighbors, and that of others would undoubtedly jeopardize a two-thirds majority vote. Tipped off on the previous day that the Chinese were going to make a statement opposing partition, Shultz got Fanny Holtzman, lawyer to that government, to persuade Ambassador Wellington Koo that this would lose them American public support and "incur the needless animosity of important persons here"; an outright opposition to the majority report was deleted from the delegation's statement the next day, although the equivocal tone left that country's vote still in doubt. (Holtzman had first presented the Zionist case to Koo in March.) In addition, Vijaya Lakshmi Pandit, Nehru's sister, had just spoken at the *Ad Hoc* Committee about India favoring Palestine as an independent state, the problem of the "displaced" Jews in Europe to be dealt with as a UN responsibility separated from the Palestine question.[28]

Although Johnson declared his assumption that all members would observe their obligation under the UN Charter to refrain "from the threat or use of force," Syrian army units moved slowly on October 11 to the Palestine frontier, with the Damascus press predicting an early formation of an Arab government under Haj Amin. The Syrian and Iraqi armies would occupy the Arab parts of Palestine simultaneously with British withdrawal, boasted the Syrian defense minister, who called the Hagana "the biggest bluff in history." (His prime minister, Salih Jabr, candidly told a British diplomat that he envisioned Abdullah taking over the whole of Palestine, giving the Jews "the necessary safeguards.") Reporting also that day about the Arab League summit in Aley,

Lebanon, which endorsed the Sofar resolutions, *Akhbar Al-Yom* editor Mustafa Amin quoted Azzam Pasha: "I personally wish that the Jews do not drive us to this war, as this will be a war of extermination and momentous massacre which will be spoken of like the Tartar [Mongol] massacres or the Crusader wars." Aside from Azzam's genocidal threat, the Aley conferees agreed upon a united Arab military command which marginalized the AHC, also vaguely promising weapons, money, and volunteers for Palestinian Arab independence, but turning down Haj Amin's call for a Palestinian Arab government-in-exile.[29]

On another worrisome note, Eytan cabled Sharef in Jerusalem about an Arab-British plan, Beeley its moving spirit, to force the UN into establishing an Arab state by leaving the territory and weapons to the Arabs and, through filibustering, preventing a two-thirds majority for partition at the *Ad Hoc* Committee. Jewish Agency intelligence also heard that Gurney told a secret meeting of the principal government departments that the mandatory administration was under no obligation to the population before evacuating Palestine. Consequently, the Postmaster General was to "simply burn the stock of stamps and let things be"; when the time came the gates of the prisons should be opened and its inmates "allowed to depart"; and such currency stock held by the government should be burned. The consequences of withdrawal without settlement, thus "leaving a vacuum," Cunningham advised his superior, would be "a disaster and a tragedy for the people of Palestine."[30]

The Soviets, deftly waiting first for the American response, formally declared Moscow's support for partition on October 13. Echoing Gromyko's May 14 statement to the GA, Tsarapkin spoke at the *Ad Hoc* Committee about the Nazi persecution of the Jews during World War II, and emphasized the right of the Jewish people, like the Arabs, to a state of their own in Palestine. Relations between those two contesting peoples had reached "such a state of tension" that it had become impossible to reconcile their points of view, which the "impracticable" minority plan had proposed. The questions of a frontier, government during the transition period, and the status of Jerusalem remained to be resolved, he noted, but if the GA decided on partition, "great progress" would have been made to a solution of the Palestine question as a whole. The statement, Vyshinski reported to Molotov with copies to Stalin and associates, was "well received" by the Jews, while the Arabs were "disappointed." Johnson publicly expressed "gratification" that this was similar to the American position, although the latter's proposal to create volunteer police units to maintain order during the transition period particularly drew the Arabs' fire. The Americans, Myerson was informed by her colleagues in New York, suspected that the Soviets wished to gain a foothold in the region, and were determined to oppose it. Unless the Russian intentions were satisfactorily clarified soon, this coded telegram added, Marshall intended to defer his final decision about attending the Foreign Ministers Conference in London the next month to discuss the future of Germany.[31]

The same day, Jamali told Advisor to the U.S. Delegation Samuel Kopper that since the United States was apparently no longer an ally of the Arab states and Russia did not seem to wish to be so, the six states would no long abstain, but vote on each matter in accordance with their own interests. Immediately following Johnson's statement, the U.S. draft resolution to have a GA sub-committee draw up a detailed plan for Palestine's future government in accord with the unanimous recommendations and the majority proposal heartened the Jews; the bombing of the U.S. consulate in Jerusalem drew no condemnation in the Arab press. Inverchapel conveyed to Lovett HMG's concern that a volunteer constabulary would hardly suffice to handle any major Arab disturbances, and, when asked if Britain would support the majority plan, evasively replied that he did not know if a country directly involved in the Palestine question would be expected to vote or not. Great Britain, Creech Jones made it clear when addressing the *Ad Hoc* Committee on the 16th, would continue to administer Palestine only if both sides agreed, and only for a limited transitional period in order to help them put the agreement in effect. Should the GA fail to arrive at a settlement agreeable to Arabs and Jews, HMG would proceed to plan the withdrawal of the British administration and its military forces. Any GA vote on the nature of a settlement, the Colonial Secretary stressed, should thus not be done independently of measures to implement it.[32]

Doubts about the sincerity of the American position on Palestine soon arose. The impression continued to be spread in Lake Success, observed I. F. Stone in *PM*, that the United States was not lobbying for the majority plan with countries that were dependent on its economic aid, such as China and Cuba, nor with the Latin American countries. (At this point, only Uruguay, Paraguay, and Bolivia had been instructed by their governments to support partition; Garcia-Granados adopted a strong pro-Zionist stand on his own initiative.) A "weak and equivocal" position behind the scenes, Stone added, would enable the Arabs and their definite supporters (Afghanistan, India, Iran, Pakistan, and Turkey) to block approval of the requisite two-thirds. Hearing two weeks earlier of Lovett's comment both to Proskauer and to Nathan that the United States must be ready with proposals for the interim period in the event of no two-thirds,

Shertok had already thought it an "open question" whether Washington was interested in obtaining the needed majority. State's Gordon Knox, advising the American delegation, candidly told Johnson on the 18th that the delegation was not receiving the department's "detailed views"; he suspected that his superiors did not wish the United States to adopt "clear cut attitudes" regarding boundary and future government issues because doing so "might lead to responsibility for implementation." McClintock proposed in a memorandum to Lovett two days later that, while firmly backing partition, some "sops" could be given to the Arabs, including "territorial adjustments"; a Greater Syria republic with its capital in Damascus; no Jewish immigration into Palestine during the interim period; and preventing American Jews from sending additional "supplies of war" to the new Jewish state.[33]

A lengthy article a few days later which also questioned America's commitment, appearing in the same prestigious New York Times that had applauded the highly rare American-Soviet agreement at this point, helped spark Marshall's authorization on October 22 to have the delegation "line up the vote" to support the American proposals. The State Department's Fraser Wilkins, Adviser to the delegation, did not interpret this, however, as "indicating that we should 'browbeat' the representatives of other countries at the UN into our point of view." This was in keeping with Henderson's telling Shertok on the 22nd that the U.S. delegation would not engage in "arm twisting" tactics to "corral" votes, as well as his response to Lovett the same day about the memorandum by McClintock, relaying that his department was unwilling to "carry the banner" for partition.

The suggestions therein would not have "the least effect" on the Arab attitude, Henderson asserted, while the United States would "inescapably" be "saddled" with the major if not sole responsibility for administration and enforcement, which he assumed neither Congress nor the American public were willing to undertake. The Near Eastern Division and, it was believed, other important government departments were unprepared to accept the "losses" to the U.S. position in the Middle East which would be bound to follow an "aggressive" partition policy. An unenforced partition, moreover, would lead to intervention from the Arab states, the Soviet Union, and, eventually, the United States "in one form or another." A complete stoppage of Jewish immigration would be impossible. Finally, assuming that the government's present policy of not "waving the flag" would continue, the two-thirds vote would probably fail. In that case, Henderson concluded, the United States or any other supporter of partition could seek some compromise plan. In the worst scenario, it would be in order to propose "a temporary trusteeship," along with "fairly substantial" immigration, "ending in a plebiscite" in Palestine.[34]

By then, the first phase of the general debate had ended, with Evatt's proposal for three sub-committees, adopted by the *Ad Hoc* Committee on October 21, reflecting his desire for a partition plan to be prepared unobstructed by the Arab states and their supporters. Number 1 was to draw up a detailed plan based on the U.S.-Swedish draft resolution favoring the UNSCOP majority recommendation, along with a Canadian amendment by Lester Pearson to consider implementation; Number 2 (against Fabregat's objection) to offer a plan for a unitary Palestinian state as proposed by Saudi Arabia and Iraq; and Number 3 on conciliation as proposed by El Salvador, to find ground between Jew and Arab on Palestine's future. On the 18th, after Shertok had risen one day earlier to counter the uncompromising speech of Pakistan's Mohamed Zafrullah Khan, Weizmann (aided by Eban's draft) had delivered a dramatic, personal plea for a sovereign, progressive Jewish collective in Palestine, thereby also relieving the survivors of "the darkest human tragedy of our time" who yet "linger amidst the memories of the past and the graveyards of the present." He made light of Jamal Husseini's assertion that the Jews were descended not from the Hebrew Kingdoms but from the Khazars of Southern Russia; sarcastically opined that he could not rival the contacts of the representatives of Iraq and Syria, who had equated the Zionist enterprise with Nazi doctrine, in that particular field; hoped for a real Arab-Jewish partnership and for resuming the traditional Anglo-Jewish friendship; and ended with Isaiah's prophecy about the return of one people to Zion in fulfillment of the Divine promise to "hold up a signal to the nations and assemble the banished of Israel, and gather the dispersed of Judah from the four corners of the earth."

At a recent Latin American caucus, Aranha had urged the delegates to remember that "somewhere the United Nations must break through the iron curtain of futility and paralysis." Yet the two rival sides were no closer together after three weeks of speeches, convincing a Jerusalem correspondent to report home in effect that "it is as if an irresistible force is about to collide with an immovable object." The time had now come for each of the GA's fifty-seven nations to take a stand.[35]

Sub-Committee Number 1 consisted of the United States, the USSR, and seven other nations, all of whom had expressed support for the UNSCOP majority recommendations, with Number 2 composed of the six Arab countries joined with anti-partitionists Afghanistan, Colombia, and Turkey. The American delegation had first persuaded the Jewish Agency to agree that wavering France and silent Belgium be part of the former, this to prevent the Arab argument that the committee was completely biased. Representatives Pedro Zuloaga (Venezuela) and Ksawery Pruszynski (Poland), prodded by Shultz, ably thwarted this move, however. Once the Russians' resolution to include Security Council members (that would have included Great Britain, Syria, and Colombia) was defeated, they followed suit.

Pruszynski, author of a laudatory book about the yishuv after his first visit to Palestine in 1931, had vigorously opposed his delegation's initial support for bi-nationalism, and now he worked as chairman to keep a homogeneous committee. Kirchwey and Nation writer Madeline Karr succeeded when warning Evatt that columnist Drew Pearson would report "a double cross" if he did not support this effort. Pruszynski quickly insisted on closed meetings that would be limited to its members, and that (at Shultz's suggestion) William Epstein, the sympathetic Middle East Section chief in the UN's Department of Political and Security Council Affairs, serve as his assistant. Since the U.S. delegation continued to delay its statement on implementation, working committees began tackling the issues of boundaries, economic union, and the city of Jerusalem. A caucus of Czechoslovakia, Guatemala, Poland, Uruguay, and Venezuela, later joined by the Russians, met separately to decide on procedures and on what they would like to have as the outcome of the Sub-Committee's deliberations.[36]

The American delegation had decided on October 22 to discuss with the British a shortening of the two-year transition period proposed by UNSCOP to July 1, 1948, the inclusion of Safed within the Arab state, and the southern Negev placed there as well. A memorandum to this effect, drafted two days later, added the proposed appointment of a commission to act as the UN's agent for the purpose of "facilitating the transition to independence." Constituent Assemblies were to be elected (women also to vote) by the populations of the two states in order to set up provisional governments. Lovett ordered Ambassador Douglas on the 25th to discuss this immediately with Bevin, while Johnson and Hilldring observed in a separate memorandum the next day that instead of possibly instituting a policy of "scuttle and run," HMG, which had voluntarily exercised the responsibility of the Mandate for so many years, could "hardly object" to a UN request to continue in control in that area for a few months longer. (When Brodetsky and Linton complained to Trafford Smith at this time about the presence in Palestine of the Arab Legion and the Jordan Frontier Force, the Colonial Office Assistant Secretary replied that the British wished to withdraw "decently and with fairness.")

Yet State's Division of Near Eastern Affairs considered the U.S. delegation's decisions to be based on the "highly questionable" assumptions that the British, together with the Arabs and the Jews, would cooperate in implementing the partition plan, fulfilling the UNSCOP unanimous recommendations by July 1948 and agreeing to the economic union. "Confusion will be worse confounded," Merriam observed to Fraser on the 30th, given the additional proposal for a GA Commission headed by a High Commissioner while the mandatory power still administered the country. If policy discussion of which Near Eastern Affairs was unaware had led to the delegation's decisions, Merriam added, it would like to know their substance.[37]

The individual who had the last word on that policy continued to maintain a wary silence. Aside from pro-partition advocacy from twenty-three governors and leading Republican Senators Vandenberg and Taft, a flood of telegrams, postcards, and telegrams reached the White House in this period. (The U.S. delegation itself received some 27,500 communications in like vein during the first week of October, including one from New York State Liberal Party chairman Adolf A. Berle Jr., a former Assistant Secretary of State and U.S. Ambassador to Brazil.) Reluctant to submit to such pressure, Truman wrote confidentially to Senator Pepper on October 20: "I received about thirty-five thousand pieces of mail and propaganda from the Jews in this country.... I put it all in a pile and struck a match to it—I never looked at a single one of the letters because I felt the United Nations Committee was acting in a judicial capacity and should not be interfered with."

On the opposite side, an unsigned message from Ibn Saud to Truman, received by State ten days later, declared that Johnson's October 11 declaration was "an unfriendly act directed against the Arabs" and "inconsistent" with President Roosevelt's assurances in 1945 to the desert monarch. Without doubt, he asserted, this would lead to "a death blow" to American interests in the Arab countries and cause "much bloodshed" between Arab and Jew, at the end of which a small Jewish state would "perish in a short time...die by famine," the result the same as that of those "crusader states which were forced to relinquish coveted objects in Palestine." Relying on Marshall, the individual he most respected, to handle this complex matter, Truman chose to hold off an official reply. He did send a message to the Union of American Hebrew Congregations noting that the world of religion owed "an incalculable debt" to Judaism, for the faith of "Israel" through the centuries in "one ever living and true God" had "quickened man's struggle toward spiritual heights."[38]

Bevin did not cast doubt on the British Cabinet's decision to withdraw, which he thought "still seems to be the only possible one," but he felt compelled to set out for Attlee on October 22 the problems to be considered before a definite date and procedure could be announced. When addressing Commons one day earlier, the Prime Minister had hinted at March 1949 at the latest, but Bevin's lengthy memorandum raised major questions relating to maintaining law and order; halting unauthorized immigration; Jerusalem; Cyprus detainees; threats by Arab governments to enter with armed forces; the Arab Legion; and to whom Palestine should be handed over.

The Ministry of Defence and the Colonial Office had not yet weighed in on these crucial issues when Bevin informed Douglas on the 28th that HMG would support "within reason" any proposal or recommendation concurred in by the Arabs and the Jews, but would not commit to assist in any implementation recommended by the GA until it had an opportunity to examine it carefully. State's suggestions three days earlier via Lovett, however, implied that if the British lent assistance in carrying out a program for Palestine, in the Foreign Secretary's judgment, it would lead to "disturbances, if not in fact, to violence and blood-shed." London did not at present contemplate announcing a withdrawal date for its forces and the termination of the mandate. Finally, Bevin expressed deep concern about two former United Fruit Company refrig-erator ships, the *Pan York* and the *Pan Crescent*, in or near Constanza, Rumania, for the alleged purpose of bringing some "18,000" illegal Jewish immigrants to Palestine. He did not disclose that British MI6 operatives had the previous month successfully detonated mines on the hull of the *Pan Crescent* when at berth in Venice, and only the alert crew's manning the pumps had saved it from sinking.[39]

While publicly insisting on the Aley Conference resolutions, a few Arab leaders sought what Nuri Pasha termed a "cantonal settlement" arrived at secretly with the Americans. Requested by Evatt to explore the possibility of conciliation by means of the third Sub-Committee, Nuri, attempting to eliminate Haj Amin's influence, got word from Feisal that Ibn Saud would be prepared to pursue the thought if the other Arab states concurred. Receiving this approval, Nuri broached the idea to Beeley, who transmitted it to the receptive Wadsworth on October 21. (Abdullah, with encouragement from British Minister Alec Kirkbride and Glubb, continued to favor his own annexing the Arab "triangle" area of Palestine and possibly the Negev once the British withdrew.) Beeley explained to Eastern Department acting head I.F. Garran that if the GA did not arrive at any recommendation or made an "ineffectual" one, the Americans would be driven to negotiate directly with the Arabs once the British withdrew—"a contact which would suit us well enough."

As for threats of direct action by Arab states, Bevin told his Middle East ambassadors that there "seemed to be in all their talk a good deal of whistling to keep their courage up." (Speaking with Johnson, Creech Jones thought them "largely bluff.") They should be told that any direct intervention in Palestine while the mandatory continued to be responsi-ble for administration there would be considered directed against HMG. If thought desirable, Bevin added, British representatives should also deny rumors that London had secret arrangements with any Arab gov-ernment about action by Arab forces in Palestine after the withdrawal.[40]

The two *Pans* appeared more worrisome to the British and their American counterparts at this moment in time. Already on October 11, in response to Cunningham's urging that future policy regarding ille-gal immigration be reconsidered at an early date, Creech Jones had pointed out that little hope existed for any cooperation from Bulgaria and Rumania, while the Turks, unwilling to do anything to embarrass themselves in their relations with Russia or to "leave them with large numbers of Jews on their hands," claimed that they could not halt passage through the Straits. (The British Ambassador's continued protests to Sofia against the likely embarkation of the *Pans* had no effect.) With Whitehall fearing little chance of UN help in this regard, the Colonial Office could only suggest mortgaging the legal immigration quotas of several months in advance, although realizing that "this would be tantamount to admitting defeat." British delegation advisor John Martin suggested to the Colonial Office's Trafford Smith that a staged military withdrawal might allow Jewish entry once abandoning the coastal area from Caesarea to Tel Aviv, but the immediate concern of both the Eastern Department and Cunningham was that the arrivals of the *Pan Crescent* and the *Pan York* in Palestine before withdrawal would undoubtedly "stretch" existing accommodation for illegal arrivals to the limit.

This anxiety increased greatly with a report, sent to the UK delegation, which then shared it with Chamoun, that the Soviets intended to send large numbers of highly trained operatives "owing no other allegiance than to the Kremlin" into an independent Jewish state. Receiving related information from the US Mission in Bucharest that Communist agents were among the 15,000 Jews aboard the *Pans*, and hearing of Bevin's reply to Douglas, McClintock, with Rusk's approval, recommended to Lovett on October 31 that the Jewish Agency be urged in "the strongest terms" to take immediate and effective measures to cease unsanctioned immigration into Palestine, and particularly immigration emanating from areas under Soviet influence.[41]

That very concern led to a consensus of opinion the same month when the British Joint Staff Mission met in the Pentagon with the U.S. Chiefs of Staff. General William "Monkey" Morgan happily reported to Montgomery that Washington, torn between keeping the Jewish vote in New York State and the oil interests, would give HMG "more sympathy and, therefore, help" regarding Palestine. (Indeed, a State Department memorandum for these talks asserted that it was essential to keep Ibn Saud's good will and that of other important Saudi Arabs so that the development of the "enormous national resource" of that desert kingdom's oil would be allowed to continue.) Both teams agreed on October 22 that since "a hostile power" should not be allowed to secure control of the western entrance of the Mediterranean, "a firm hold" had to be retained on the Middle East through "an agreed policy designed to strengthen and improve our mutual position." Accordingly, no GA recommendation would be acceptable that allowed Soviet influence "of any kind" in Palestine, and the only solution acceptable to both from a military point of view "is one which does not alienate Arab goodwill to the United States and Great Britain."

Assuming that HMG could "no longer hope to obtain its long-range strategic requirements in Palestine," the CIGS forwarded to Bevin two days later Montgomery's paper to the British military chiefs positing that orderly redeployment to safeguard the empire's vital strategic requirements in the Middle East required a longer stay in Egypt beyond the treaty figure of September 1949 until proper arrangements had been finalized in Libya, Cyprus, and the Sudan for the peace time deployment of one division and one brigade. Troops moved from Palestine might have to be temporarily accommodated, he added, in Germany, the United Kingdom, and possibly Greece.[42]

By October 26, the Soviet leadership had actually decided upon its proposals to Sub-Committee number 1. That day, Molotov forwarded to Stalin Vyshinski's suggestions for the transition period, along with his own advice to concur. These included that the Palestine Mandate be abolished as of January 1, 1948, British troops to be withdrawn within three to four months thereafter. During the transition period of one year, a Special Commission, drawn from the Security Council membership and operating in Palestine, would draw frontiers based upon the GA resolution for partition, and choose a Provisional Council for each state in consultation with the parties and organizations of the two sovereign entities. Elections would then take place within six months for a constituent assembly based on democratic principles, aiming to draw up a constitution and elect a government. The government councils would set up administrative bodies and an armed police force. Vyshinski had indicated that these proposals were basically in agreement with the opinion of representatives of the Jewish Agency. A handwritten notation by Alexander Poskrebyshev, Chief of the Special Section of the Central Committee of the Communist Party, appeared on the top of the first page of this document: "Comrade Stalin agrees."[43]

Shertok and his associates faced formidable challenges. They obtained an understanding from the Soviets except over a volunteer armed force and the Russians' preference for a Security Council Special Commission. They even heard from Tsarapkin that the Russians had privately criticized Simic for neglecting the Holocaust when proposing binationalism, and received the Soviet delegate's personal toast, raising bottles of vodka, "let's drink to the Jewish State." However, the Agency had failed to sway the French or the Belgians, with eleven more countries wavering in their support. A plea with the U.S. delegation to have the Jewish part of Jerusalem and the Western Galilee in the Jewish state did not succeed either. While telling Proskauer that the delegation was doing everything to ensure a final acceptance of partition, Marshall "waxed indignantly" about the preparation of the *Pans* and other ships in America. If this would not stop at the present delicate stage, the Secretary of State declared, he would "come out with a counter-blast" which would seriously imperil the entire position. Memoranda from the Nation Associates (provided by the Agency) about the wartime collaboration with the Third Reich of Haj Amin and several current Arab spokesmen, together with newspaper reports by I.F. Stone and others that the Arab nations would not jeopardize their oil sales to the West or unite in a strong attack against the *yishuv*, did little to alter the U.S. State and Defense Departments' shared perspective, the War Department's anti-Zionist Military Intelligence Division particularly suspicious of Soviet designs.

In Palestine, which witnessed a first armed confrontation between the Hagana and the Irgun, Ben-Gurion and Galili warned the Agency's Security Committee that £3 million had to be raised quickly in order to purchase weapons abroad and the *yishuv*'s military forces reorganized into battalions and brigades to meet a possible Arab invasion in "a war for life and death." The Palmah striking force headed by twenty-nine-year-old Yigal Alon, 3,000 at maximum strength, had at this point one rifle for three men and five grenades per fighter.[44]

Johnson's public statement on October 31 reiterated the U.S. delegation's decisions of one week earlier, assuming, Eban cabled journalist Jon Kimche, that Britain would cooperate with the smooth transfer of functions to the Jewish and Arab areas if the GA recommended partition. (Johnson had also assumed that both sides would maintain security in their respective areas, which McNeil doubted.) Yet, Eban soon wondered, "is this not to underestimate Bevin's resourcefulness and tenacity?" London had not given any such assurance, while Inverchapel, at Bevin's instruction, had raised with Marshall and Lovett the same day the question of illegal immigration. Rusk immediately informed Gelber, a past Oxford University contemporary, that if an *Exodus* incident ensued from the *Pans'* arrival in Palestine, State would speak out "sharply" against the Jewish Agency for not cooperating at this stage "in keeping matters quiet."

On November 2, Gelber conveyed the Agency's report (originating with the Mosad L' Aliya) that no departures from the Atlantic or Black Sea ports were expected during the coming five or six weeks, but he also stressed that the Agency did not have full control over "the Underground." Although pleased, Rusk warned that the Agency should do "its utmost" to restrain the Underground and avoid any appearance of "a tie-up" with Russia, whose chief aim was to undermine the Marshall Plan for Europe's reconstruction. If the two-thirds support were not gotten, he added, the Agency should now be giving serious thought to that eventuality. Such an outcome would be a "setback" to the United States itself, Gelber retorted, and the UN would become a "farce" if it failed to carry through a project which was so near a settlement. The Agency, he declared, had not considered the possibility of failure, and if the great powers permitted a vacuum to develop in Palestine, the Jews themselves would be compelled to fill it "and take over."[45]

Tsarapkin offered the Soviet plan on November 3, calling for termination of the Palestine Mandate on January 1, 1948, the British to leave no later than May 1, and the two new states to be established by January 1, 1949. The Security Council, he proposed, would appoint a special commission to oversee implementation with the assistance of local militias. (The U.S. delegation feared, *per contra*, that direct resort to the Council would enable Russia to sow confusion through use of its veto power, while Ambassador Bedell Smith in Moscow warned that it would enable them to "soften up" the area for "eventual straight Communist cultivation.") When Granados proposed a third plan calling for a transitional period under a General Assembly commission, bolstered by security forces from five small states, that would end not later than September 1, 1949, Shultz (with Shertok's approval) had the delegates of Poland, Guatemala, and Venezuela press for a compromise: a GA-named commission of small, pro-partition states responsible to the Security Council, along with an international police force. The Mandate would end by May 1, by which time the British armed forces would be withdrawn, with two independent states to be created no later than July 1, 1948.

With Pearson backing this concept, Sub-Committee 1 appointed a special working group consisting of the United States, USSR, Guatemala, and Canada to arrive at a compromise. Getting from Cadogan no promise of British help in implementation, a furious Johnson wondered at one meeting how the mandatory power could abandon its responsibilities. Pearson responded: "How can we prevent a nation from assigning bankruptcy?" Realizing that the British could not be forced to do something which they could not do, the Canadian succeeded in getting an agreement for which Shultz's earlier memorandum to Zuloaga served as the basis. Most regarded the compromise on November 10 as a major victory ("A miracle!," wrote *Yediot Aharonot* editor-in-chief Azriel Carlebach) at a time when Washington and Moscow were at loggerheads in all other UN committees, and it appeared that a major hurdle had been cleared.[46]

Three days later, however, Cadogan told Sub-Committee 1 that while the mandatory would continue to maintain law and order wherever its troops remained, its military forces, to be evacuated by August 1, 1948, would not be available as "the instrument for the enforcement of settlement in Palestine against Arabs or Jews." This "rather stubborn and uncooperative attitude" not to even assist in the "orderly transfer of functions" to the succeeding authorities, U.S. delegation advisor J. F. Green reported to Rusk and McClintock, would be "a complicating matter" whatever the GA outcome. In fact, Bevin had already wired Marshall that London would not stand for "playing the Russian game" to try to embroil British troops in repressive action there, and the Cabinet had approved the Chiefs of Staff's estimate that withdrawal would be affected by August 1.

Although the Agency sought the Mandate's end on February 1, the Sub-Committee accepted the date of August 1 and the establishment of two states by October 1. It would also agree unanimously on a UN Commission of five states (Guatemala, Iceland, Norway, Poland, and Uruguay) for implementing partition. Concurrently, the *New York Times* and other American newspapers reported a rumor (categorically denied by Whitehall) that London was planning to sequester £12.5 million of the mandatory government's financial balance upon the Mandate's termination, leading Weizmann to write to Smuts that this "high-handed procedure" was reflective of the "serious damage to British prestige" caused over Palestine, "a "test case" for the United Nations and a chance for HMG to "finish the Palestine story in honor and dignity." If an international police force were not forthcoming during the transitional period, Shertok announced, the Jews were ready to assume full responsibility for maintaining order, with aid required by the *yishuv* to secure weapons and vehicles.[47]

The British were set on withdrawal, but filled with uncertainty as to the outcome for Palestine. Having no doubts that the two-thirds majority would not be reached and that bloodshed would come in any event, Beeley thought that the only basis for a solution was a unitary state with autonomous Arab and Jewish cantons. If the United States were really concerned about keeping the Security Council out of the Palestine question, Bevin wondered, why did not Washington abandon its support of partition? Thinking that "to walk out leaving chaos must be surely a last resort," Cunningham advised that as the situation clarified, the mandatory would assist the UN Commission with administration and police until the latter was in a position to form its own government and police from such sources as the GA approved. Until the withdrawal, however, he posited that the Commission should be confined to planning for the transfer of power and the formation of a security force.

Since Bevin agreed with his and the UK delegation's assumption that the transferring of services to any provisional government or council, as Granados contemplated, would be "tantamount" to implementing partition, the Foreign Secretary urged Cadogan to delay "by all possible means" the dispatch of the Commission to Palestine until HMG was ready to hand over the Mandate. Realizing that it might be necessary to give a fixed date for the termination and always having harbored the view that this should coincide with the end of the civil government in Palestine, late in the evening of November 19 the High Commissioner ultimately offered that date to Creech Jones in a "top secret and personal" cable marked "most immediate"—May 15, 1948.[48]

Reports of Arab activity remained open to speculation. Arab correspondents claimed that their camp had obtained sufficient votes at this juncture to prevent partition (sixteen against and ten abstaining), but Azzam brought Feisal's cable from Lake Success to the attention of the U.S. *chargé* in Iraq that three South America states had deserted the Arabs under U.S. pressure. (Hearing this together with reports from Damascus and Baghdad that China and Cuba had done likewise, Johnson officially denied exerting any pressure, adding that Latin American states were subject to "considerable persuasion" by the "highly organized and well financed" Jewish Agency.) Azzam warned the U.S. Embassy in Baghdad that the Jews would face an "impossible war" against the Arab states, who would "come back eternally" to fight them "with characteristic Arab fury." Celebrated military analyst George Fielding Eliot warned in the *New York Herald Tribune* and other newspapers that 800,000 Jews in Muslim lands were in grave peril if fighting over Palestine between Jews and Arabs began. Sasson conveyed to Shertok from a reliable source that Egypt had decided to detain all Zionists in "concentration camps," with other Arab countries probably to follow, in the event of Jewish-Arab armed conflict in the Promised Land.

The British, Zaslani informed Myerson, appeared to favor work-ing with Musa Alami to implement the Morrison-Grady plan that Nuri al-Said supported, keeping Abdullah in the dark. For his part, the Jordan ruler met secretly with Myerson on November 17 at Naharayim, again proposed his "divine and annex" plan, asserted his hatred of Haj Amin and that he would prevent the passage of Arab troops through the king-dom, and explicitly declared his readiness to sign a written agreement with the Jewish Agency. Agency intelligence reported, however, that Azzam, wishing to dissuade Abdullah from his Greater Syria scheme, accepted the king's demand to restrain Haj Amin and hold a referendum on Palestine's future after the country's conquest, under Jordan's aus-pices and control.[49]

Eban's confidence that reaching decisions of economic union and boundaries would "not be difficult," expressed to *New Judea* editor Jacob Hodess in London on November 4, seemed premature. While the Agency succeeded after a long struggle in having Sub-Committee 1 agree unanimously to each state having its own personal bank, credit policy, import licenses, control of foreign exchange receipts and expen-ditures, and conduct international financial operations on its own faith and credit, the issue of boundaries proved far more difficult to resolve. Soviet insistence got the Lydda airport placed in the proposed Jewish state, but the Americans were emphatic that Western Galilee, the only place which the Arabs had for future economic development of any sig-nificance, had to remain Arab, as should Jaffa.

Johnson told a meeting of voluntary organizations that the bulk of the Negev should also go to the Arabs, as it was a mostly occupied Bedouin and desolate area that entailed "no sacrifice of material importance to the Jews." (A detailed Colonial Office memorandum in April for UNSCOP on partition had made the same claim about the "uncultivable" Negev.)

Direct appeals to Johnson, Lovett, and Henderson from Proskauer, who had publicly agreed with Johnson's statement that the U.S. delegation would not "twist anybody's arm" to vote for partition, that it would be "a tragic error" to deny the Agency's request for the southern Negev and Aqaba fell on deaf ears. Johnson and Rusk, operating on Marshall's instructions to Austin on the 12th about the Negev, tried privately to gain Shertok's approval on the assurance that only thus could the two-thirds majority be obtained. Following his rejection, the Zionist UN delegation decided at an urgent meeting in Weizmann's suite at the Waldorf Astoria Hotel to have him intervene personally with Truman, who alone had the power reverse the stance taken by the delegation under State's instruction. Epstein called Niles, and within less than an hour the nearly blind herald was informed that the President would be pleased to see him in an unpublicized meeting at noon on November 19.[50]

Unrelenting pressure from the British against Jewish illegal immigration played an important part in the deliberations of Sub-Committee 1. Replying at length to Bevin's memorandum of October 30 concerning 17,000 Jews about to sail aboard the two *Pans* and the possibility that the *Colonial Frederick C. Johnson* might leave from Norfolk, Virginia, for the same purpose, Marshall revealed one week later that State had urged the Agency to restrain "the Underground" as to the *Pans*, while definite steps had been taken to prevent the *Johnson's* departure. Faced with persistent newspaper reports that the *Pans* were soon to leave from Rumania, Shertok cabled the Agency's Maurice Fisher in Paris on the 14th to contact Meirov and secure his assurance that the two vessels would not depart in the coming four weeks. Transports continued from other quarters, with the *Aliya's* 182 young passengers successfully reaching Netanya undetected the next day, and the 794 immigrants aboard the *Kadima* (Forward) seized by the Royal Navy on the 16th, brought to Haifa, and then deported aboard the HMS *Runnymede Park* to Cyprus. Kopper's approaching Gelber (again at Rusk's order) about this traffic elicited the response that the Agency would do its utmost regarding the *Pans* to "let sleeping dogs lie" until the UN adopted a settlement scheme.[51]

A threatened denunciation by Marshall of the Agency's stance on these unsanctioned voyages, Shultz learned later, also led an anxious Shertok to retreat from his earlier request to have Jerusalem divided into three independent boroughs—a Jewish Jerusalem, an Arab Jerusalem, and the Old City, with free access, settlement, and worship, and the choice by Jerusalem's residents of citizenship in one of the two states. The U.S. delegation, as well as the Russians, had endorsed this earlier request, with Prusyznski proposing an international enclave for the Old City and Bethlehem analogous to Vatican City. Henderson, however, cabled Hilldring that the department considered such a tripartite division "impractical and undesirable." Aside from Christian opposition and the difficulty of dividing its population, he argued, administrative and municipal services, almost the whole modern commercial area, and important government buildings would go to the Jewish state, forcing the Arabs to build up an entirely new city in an area "mostly unsuitable for such construction." Palestinian Chief Rabbis Herzog and Ben-Zion Uziel cabled Smuts, Marshall, and Czech President Edvard Beneš that to separate Jewish Jerusalem from the Jewish state would deprive the latter of its spiritual center and historic roots. Yet Shertok, worried about Marshall's possible public reprimand and told by U.S. officials that it would be very difficult to obtain a two-thirds majority vote without the concession on Jerusalem, acceded to the Americans' insistence that the entire city and environs (as in the UNSCOP report) become an international *corpus separatum* regime under the Trusteeship Council.[52]

On the 19th, an ailing but optimistic Weizmann headed for his meeting at the White House, having told Epstein that Truman, whose dispatch of Earl Harrison to the Jewish DP camps was instrumental in leading to the UNSCOP majority report, would prove a "powerful champion" of the Jewish people at this hour of "crucial urgency." He had come to Washington with a long list of points for discussion, including Pearson's own request that the President issue a statement confirming the United States would play "its full part" as a Security Council member to take action in case of lawlessness in Palestine during the transition period. Instead, he followed Epstein's advice to take up only the matter of the Negev's southern port area of Elath (Eilat), figuring that the President could focus on this key issue and would not wish his guest to leave the Oval Office empty-handed.

While Epstein stayed outside with Clifford and Niles, Weizmann briefly thanked Truman for his past support and described the serious situation at the UN which could only be rectified if the United States stood by the government's declared policy. Hearing the Chief Executive reply that "we have to prove beyond all doubt that we are firm in our views and intentions," Weizmann then centered on Epstein's memorandum, a map of the Negev, and Walter Lowdermilk's plan for its advancement in order to show the desert area's importance for large-scale development and especially that Elath, historically linked in Jewry's history from the days of the Jewish Kingdom to the UNSCOP majority report, was indispensable for the Jewish state's gateway via the Red Sea to Asia and Africa. Truman's knowledge of the world and of Palestine in particular impressed Weizmann, who was delighted to hear his host declare that he would give clear instructions to the U.S. delegation about the Negev and Elath in accordance with the views that the Zionist movement's avatar had presented.[53]

Just before the 3 p.m. meeting of Sub-Committee 1 that afternoon, Johnson and Hilldring sat down with Shertok to inform him of Lovett's reaffirmed instructions that morning to advocate the transfer of the entire southern Negev to the Arab state. Johnson had actually suggested to the Committee one week earlier that Aqaba near Elath go to the Jews, which led Bevin to immediately wire Inverchapel to urge Lovett or Henderson to take effective action against this "rash" statement; "astonished" that Johnson had made such an "unrealistic" suggestion, Henderson undertook to insure that it was "quashed." At this point, Truman telephoned Hilldring to ask how things were going. Told that Hilldring and Johnson were not pleased with State's instructions, the President said that nothing should be done to "upset the applecart." (Hilldring added in an urgent call to Bohlen one hour later that Truman expressed agreement with Weizmann's views, and appeared to make it plain that he wished the delegation to go along with the UNSCOP majority report on the Negev.) A half hour later, Shertok was greatly relieved to hear from Johnson that no change was in the offing, while Weizmann subsequently wrote that "obviously the President had been as good as his word." When Lovett telephoned Truman that evening, Truman said that he had not at all intended to change State's instructions, but had merely been concerned that the United States should not "stand out as a useless minority" on this important issue. Writing the same day to the pro-Zionist Senator Elbert Thomas (D, UT), the President concluded thus: "I have about come to the conclusion that the Palestine program is insoluble but I suppose we will have to keep working with it."[54]

The next few days were marked by alternating new hopes and new discouragements for advocates of partition. On the 19th McNeil suggested to Bevin that if the two-thirds majority were not in sight by the end of the GA session, HMG should press Aranha and the *Ad Hoc* Committee to remain at work and consider some other plan. Calls for Jewish immigration elsewhere than Palestine continued despite the fact that only nineteen of the fifty-seven UN members had thus far joined the International Refugee Organization in charge of this issue, and not a single Arab state had done so. The Russians, Kirchwey warned Shertok, had come to feel that the Jewish Agency had conceded too easily to the Americans, with the U.S. Chiefs of Staff, the State Department, and the delegation's Dulles, who thought the UN had no legal right in this question, firmly opposed to Zionist objectives. While Johnson on the 22nd made his first formal speech in the *Ad Hoc* Committee in favor of partition, one month since the subcommittee on implementation had begun its work, New Zealand's Carl A. Berendsen declared that he was instructed to support that recommendation only on condition that the UN also assume responsibility for implementation. The delegates of El Salvador and Denmark (hitherto pro-partition) joined in support, leading the Dominican Republic's Henriques Urena to respond that abstention votes would mean the creation of a military administrative and economic vacuum. In sharp contrast to his usual calm, Johnson retorted strongly that the UN should "grasp the mettle" and go ahead. A frustrated Evatt adjourned the general debate that evening, stating that he hoped to reach a vote by the next night.[55]

On the 24th, Tsarapkin lashed into Britain's on-going reservations, saying they were "harmful, dangerous, and might involve great difficulties." State itself, Evatt told the Nation Associates' Madeline Karr, had replied to an inquiry from the Siamese delegation that it did not care how Siam voted, the same day that Shultz heard about Haiti and Liberia being instructed to vote "no." On the 25th, the Arab plan for a unitary state obtained 12 votes, with 29 against and 14 abstentions, although the Arab proposal that the question of legality be submitted to the International Court of Justice was defeated by a razor-thin vote of 21 to 20, with 13 abstentions and 3 absentees. An amended version of the UNSCOP majority plan with economic union, including Elath in the Jewish state and Beersheba (Be'er Sheva) and Jaffa in the Arab, was adopted the following day by 25 to 13 (the Arab states, Afghanistan, Cuba, India, Pakistan, Siam, and Turkey), with 17 abstentions, and 2 absent (Paraguay and Phillipines). This was still one vote short of the two-thirds majority required in the GA plenary.[56]

It was generally believed that some of the seventeen abstainers would back partition when the Assembly debate opened on November 26, although Feisal confided in Beeley that the Philippines, Liberia, and Greek delegates, who deliberately were "lying low" at this stage to avoid pressure, had promised their votes in the plenary to the Arabs. Gromyko defended partition as becoming of "profound historical significance" in meeting the "legitimate demands of the Jewish people," citing their close link to Palestine for "a considerable period in history," and their current position as a result of the recent world war, with hundreds of thousands still without a country. Yet, following a pro-partition speech from Sweden's Gunnar Hagglof, a first shock came when Carlos Romulo declared that the Philippine government could not support any proposal for "the political disunion and the territorial dismemberment" of Palestine. As onlookers debated whether this portended abstention or a negative vote, Vassili Dendramis of Greece announced that his government, noting the Arab opposition and the mandatory's attitude, would switch from abstention to vote "no." Haiti's Antonio Vieux, who a few months ago at the GA Special Session had given one of the most humanitarian speeches on Palestine, then delivered a third blow to the partitionists by moving from the abstention group to the opposition.

The Arabs crowed, Horowitz recalled, while Beeley was "radiant with joy." Fabregat, who spoke once again of the Holocaust survivors, especially children, who needed Palestine, failed to sway José Arce of Argentina to drop his abstention and join most of the other Latin America countries in favor. The Agency, needing at least five additional votes for partition, set out to work with the help of Lie and Aranha for a fillibuster by inscribing many new names on the speakers list. At 6 p.m., Aranha asked for a show of hands on whether or not a night meeting should be held. The Arabs and their supporters wanted it; the United States, USSR, Canada, Guatemala, and twenty more voted against. In light of the 24 to 20 result, the GA president ordered a postponement during the Thanksgiving Day holiday (the idea broached by Neumann to Hilldring during the lunch recess). Each side now had thirty-six additional hours to attain victory in the crucial vote.[57]

During this debate, Chamoun had condemned American influence in the Assembly as a "dark and obscure tyranny," but until then the United States had not taken decisive steps to influence other states to endorse its stand favoring partition. On the 24th, Lovett had called the White House with information from the U.S. delegation that its case was being "seriously impeded" by the high pressure exerted by Jewish agencies, including the use of bribes, and that, among others, Liberia (which had abstained) and Nicaragua (which had voted for) were being threatened with American economic sanctions. Truman immediately responded that he did not want threats or "improper pressure of any kind" to be used to coerce other delegations to follow Washington's lead. The Under Secretary of State telephoned Johnson and Hilldring that same afternoon to relay Truman's wishes, together with the President's reiterated insistence that American troops only be used as part of an overall UN force. Despite a report from Oscar Cox, who had talked to Lovett, that State's Norman Armour would "corral" votes for partition, Shultz heard from friendly Latin American delegates the same morning that no such attempt had been made.[58]

Given Aranha's precious, if limited, gift of time, the Zionist forces sought every possible avenue to marshal the required two-thirds majority. During the Thanksgiving holiday, President Manuel Roxas of the Philippines was contacted by his personal friend Julius Edelstein, a cable from Wagner and twenty-five other senators, another from Frankfurter and fellow Supreme Court Justice Frank Murphy, one from Weizmann, and a U.S. Congressman who cautioned that a "no" vote would cost the country American economic support. Harvey S. Firestone, Jr., pressed separately by Holtzman and Edward Stettinius, called Liberian President William Tubman to warn that he would not proceed to expand his rubber plantations, vital for that country's export trade, unless a "yes" vote were delivered. Shertok reminded the Ethiopian delegation that the *yishuv*'s newspapers had refused an Italian consul's request to halt criticism of Mussolini during the Italo-Ethiopian war of 1935–1936, which ended in that country's subjection to Fascist rule and Emperor Haile Selassie's passing through Jerusalem on his way to exile in England. (Under Egyptian threats regarding its Coptic Christian community, the pro-partition Selassie chose to abstain.)

After Nathan's intervention failed, Goldmann and Shultz, working separately, recruited Adolf A. Berle, Jr., counsel to the Haitian government, and Raymond Alexander, that country's Honorary Consul, to try to obtain a "yes" from Port-au-Prince. To insure that Ecuador would not switch its "yes" vote, Benno Weiser (later Varon), operating under Toff's direction, arranged for a flood of cables from Zionist committees of the whole South American subcontinent to reach the President and foreign minister in Quito. A last-minute effort by the acting head of that country's UN delegation for permission to vote against partition met with failure. Nicaragua dictator Anastasio Somoza Debayle, having been treated by a leading Boston surgeon at the intervention by the Stone brothers of Boston, influenced his and other Latin American countries to adopt the affirmative line.[59]

Not all efforts by the partitionists bore fruit. Appeals to Cuban President Ramón Grau San Martin from Morgenthau and Lehman, along with an intense campaign by the country's Hebrew Palestine Committee, failed to move the independently minded and pro-Arab UN delegate Guillermo Belt. (The latter reported in anger to State that one Latin American delegate had changed his vote to support partition in return for $75,000 in cash, and that another anti-Zionist delegate, perhaps the Costa Rican, had refused a $40,000 bribe but subsequently was ordered by his government to vote for partition.) Colombia delegate Alfonso López, despite the intervention with that country's President by the pro-Zionist minister of education, pressed repeatedly for a "no" and received Bogotá's permission to abstain. Baruch got former U.S. Ambassador William Bullitt to warn Ambassador Wellington Koo that voting "no" would cut off American aid to China. Taft's speech, made at Silver's request, to support a $60 million loan to China brought Koo to publicly back partition in the GA, but after the Arabs arranged a staged revolt of fairly large proportions on the Turkestan border, the government's minister of war (a Muslim) warned that this would jeopardize the country's borders with Muslim neighbors. Ultimately, his country would abstain, Koo told Bullitt, because of the large Muslim element among the Chinese.

Sufficient pressure on three political parties from Arab groups residing in Chile led to that country's switch from voting "yes" to a vote to abstain. Weizmann's cables to various Greek officials and intercessions by the Liberal Party's Dean Alfange, also chairman of the American Christian Palestine Committee, with that country's leaders did not succeed against a secret deal whereby a "no" vote brought the Arab pledge to support Greece on all future matters of interest to Athens. State had assured Greek delegates before they cast a negative vote that their country was free to vote "as she saw fit," and Athens also had to consider Pakistan's membership in the UN Special Committee on the Balkans and the "precarious position" of Greeks in Egypt. Nehru, with 30 million Muslims left in his new state, and seeing "no effective solution for the present" in Palestine, as he put it in replying to Einstein' appeal "to end the pariah status of Jews among peoples," turned down Weizmann's personal plea and instructed India to vote "no." K. N. Panikkar's repeated efforts to persuade his delegation and Nehru to at least abstain failed. Honduras and El Salvador did not live up to their promise to "banana king" Zemurray to support partition, and chose to abstain.[60]

The morning session on November 28 witnessed a shift in Arab tactics that appealed to a number of delegates, including those who had already declared in favor of partition. Beeley's advice the previous day to the Arabs that only their adoption of a softer line of compromise, which HMG would support, could stop a two-thirds vote for partition only impressed Jamali and Chamoun. Zafrullah Khan's own recommendation that they propose a unitary federal state with cantons drew more support except for Husseini, Feisal, and Yemen's El-Islam Abdullah, leading him to offer this proposal at the session. He focused on the need for conciliation, pointedly praising Magnes's "noble and wise" steps in this respect. Granados rebutted with an attack on the mandatory's failure toward that objective; charged that the AHC under the zealot Haj Amin would never agree to concessions; declared that the world had an obligation after the Holocaust to the Jewish people; and lauded the Zionist enterprise for already having laid the foundations for the spiritual, social, and political independence of a Jewish commonwealth in Eretz Israel. After Aranha halted thunderous applause from the galleries, largely filled by Jews, Jamali began with once again warning of the bloodshed to follow from a united Arab and Muslim world against a Jewish state. From then on, however, the Iraqi delegate changed to a moderate tone and called for the UN to make a greater effort at achieving an Arab-Jewish agreement based on justice and mutual understanding.[61]

A sudden, more serious development that afternoon raised the tension when France's Alexandre Parodi, having arrived at an understanding with the Arabs the night before, proposed on his own a 24-hour adjournment in the expressed hope of securing some conciliation between the warring parties. Epstein, who failed to persuade him not to make the speech, learned later that Jean Chauvel of the anti-Zionist Afrique-Levant Department and Claude de Boisanger of the Quai d'Orsay's conservative circle at the UN had convinced Parodi to thereby assuage the Arabs, and when later voting for partition have an "alibi." (Parodi later told French Zionists that he opposed partition because, thinking the proposed frontiers "undefensible," he worried about the fate of their grandchildren.) The same morning, the Zionist team had reckoned that it had the necessary partition votes regardless of how Greece and the Philippines would decide, yet the Nation Associates' Karr overheard Parodi say to the representative of France Press that he might abstain if his vote was not needed if Haiti voted "yes." Not able to take any chances, the Agency got the sympathetic Ambassador Henri Bonnet to try to put through a number of telephone calls to Parodi, without success. Bonnet accepted Kirchwey's argument that the adjournment was nothing more than "a stalling device" to give the Arabs time to try to rally more opposition, since one could not perform in twenty-four hours what had not been obtained in the past thirty years. Lovett told Epstein that he would take care of the matter, but nothing happened. Parodi's resolution carried by 25 to 15.

Poland's Oscar Lange immediately spoke out against, while López, contacted by the British and some Arab leaders, proposed postponing a final decision for a couple of months. The Americans not only failed to speak, Johnson had to nudge Austin to vote "no." That evening, Comay suggested to Shultz that Evatt be asked to return and refute Parodi's charge about the lack of effort to conciliate the two contesting parties, but the Australian by then was on a flight home. A procedural defeat was in the offing, since those who voted for adjournment might join with the thirteen who had backed the Arab plan on the 25th and call for postponement as the first item of business when the plenary session resumed the next day.[62]

Here, again, the involvement of Truman proved critical. The United States had to "crack the whip" as it usually did when vitally interested in GA proposals, a discouraged Alfange wrote to Silver on the 28th about State's not taking a leadership role for partition. Yet Truman's directive to Lovett on the 24th notwithstanding, the thirty-third President of the United States went into action privately. Some of Jacobson's diary entries hint at this development: "Received call from White House— everything OK" (November 26) and "Received call from his secretary not to worry" (November 28). Unsigned notes in the Truman files, attached to a memorandum dated November 20, read thus:

Palestine votes look a little better.
1. We have been in touch with *Liberian* minister to try to get the Government's instructions changed to support us.

2. I think we have *Haiti*.
3. We may get Philippines out of *No* into abstention or, with luck, yes.
4. *Cuba* still won't play.
5. *Greece* is uncertain but has the excuse of the Balkan Commission vote trade with Muslims.

Truman, also pressed by the Democratic National Committee's top leadership and in receipt of two recent letters from Weizmann to carry through partition as "a triumph of American statesmanship under your direction and initiative," would soon tell Jacobson and Granoff on one of their private visits to the Oval Office that he had been responsible for swinging the votes of several delegates. Hilldring confirmed this later to Epstein. Comay, too, would acknowledge shortly thereafter to a colleague that the President "became very upset and threw his personal weight behind the effort to get a decision.... It was only in the last 48 hours on Friday and Saturday that we got the full backing of the United States."[63]

Truman's closest aides, probably at times without his direct knowledge, intervened aggressively in these pivotal days. Clifford conferred with Philippines Ambassador J.M. Elizalde and other delegations, later declaring in interviews "it was because the White House was for it that it went through. I kept the ramrod up the State Department's butt." Henderson subsequently recalled Johnson's telling him of Niles's telephone call that Truman wanted the delegation to get all the votes possible, "that there would be hell if the voting went the wrong way." According to British delegation advisor with the Latin American countries H. R. "Shadow" (given his eye patch) Hadow, Austin called Elizalde saying that U.S. prestige was involved. Thirty years later, long-time Chicago Democratic boss Jacob Arvey confided that, hearing Mrs. Roosevelt's report to Rabbi Solomon Goldman that State Department officials were informing delegations that there would be "no resentment" if they did not vote for partition, he passed on this news to fellow-Jew Niles. Niles, in turn, informed Truman, who telephoned her at Hyde Park and received confirmation of the story. Word was then sent from the White House to certain delegates that the President's position was "positive and firm, and could not be diluted in any shape manner or form." Niles also tried through Greek-born businessmen Thomas A. Pappas, who in turn got 20th Century Fox President Spyros Skouras and others to join, to cable Athens to change that country's stand.

He also mobilized Baruch as well to threaten Parodi that a "no" vote would cause U.S. aid to be cut. More significantly, Blum's intercession (and that of Minister René Mayer) with the new Prime Minister Robert Schuman, after a trans-Atlantic message from Weizmann via Marc Jarblum, tipped the scales, as the French delegation received orders two hours before the crucial vote to back partition.[64]

Bevin, hearing from Cadogan on the 24th that the U.S. delegation was now pressuring other delegations and trying to "rush matters to a final vote with as little discussion as possible," vented his frustrations that evening during a dinner with Marshall and Douglas. After taking exception to Johnson's criticism of HMG and stating that a unanimous anti-British feeling against the Jewish influence in Palestine was due to the execution of the two British sergeants, "which would never be forgotten," he again charged that American Jewish intervention had made impossible his efforts to successfully solve the Palestine difficulty prior to its reference to the UN; remarked that the Balfour Declaration did not commit Britain to develop a Jewish state; and asserted that "many indoctrinated" Communists aboard the illegal Jewish vessels were seriously threatening Middle East stability. On the 28th, Bevin handed over to Marshall the British four-stage military withdrawal plan, with the civil administration to be maintained over the whole of Palestine until May 15, 1948. If the GA voted partition, he added, London did not want the UN Commission, "bound to have a disturbing effect on the Arab population," to arrive before May 1 because it would not suit these plans. Lovett authorized Johnson the next day to inform Cadogan that State agreed with this proposal, thus limiting the transition period to only two weeks.[65]

The GA session on November 29 at Flushing Meadows, with Aranha, Lie, and Under Secretary Andrew Cordier at the rostrum, began that Saturday afternoon with an address by Chamoun. Since a meeting of the Arab delegations that same morning, under the influence of the AHC's Husseini (he pointedly chose not to attend), had turned down his proposal that the GA vote to revive the principles of the UNSCOP minority plan, the Lebanese delegate now raised this on his own. Iceland's Thor Thors then rose to report on Sub-Committee 3's efforts at conciliation. In the same way that he had accepted the argument made by Eban in a visit to his hotel that morning, Thors stated that once the UN took a firm decision and the parties were faced with that fact, conciliation might come about. López had first tried to advance the Arab agenda with the support of the Chilean delegate, but the latter changed his mind and refrained from doing so. Al-Khoury, quoting Feisal's readiness to meet with Marshall to seek a possible conciliation, a step which Evatt had suggested at the beginning of that month to the Saudi prince, also urged such exploration. His charge of Jewish influence in the UN brought Aranha's gavel down, calling him to order, while alternate sections of the public galleries hissed and applauded.

Jamali called for an adjournment, with the *Ad Hoc* Committee reporting by January 31, 1948. Johnson and Gromyko firmly opposed these last-minute efforts. Aranha ultimately ruled that Chamoun's motion was a substantive matter which had to be voted on after the partition plan, and which would also need a two-thirds majority. On similar grounds, he pushed aside an adjournment motion with extraneous provisions by Iran's Mustafa Adl aiming to refer the matter back to the *Ad Hoc* Committee, which should report to the Assembly in "several weeks."[66]

At 5:35 p.m., Aranha called for a vote to partition Palestine into a Jewish and an Arab state that would become fully independent by October 1. The Jewish state of 5,500 square miles would currently be inhabited by 514,000 Jews and 352,000 Arabs, the Arab to cover 4,500 square miles that contained 804,000 Arabs and 10,000 Jews. (The 289 square mile enclave of Jerusalem (including the outlying villages Ein Karim and Abu Dis)—Bethlehem would have 105,000 Arabs and 100,000 Jews governed by the Trusteeship Council.) A five-man commission under Security Council guidance would "take over and administer" the areas evacuated by the mandatory authorities and finalize the borders, the British enjoined not to "prevent, obstruct or delay" its work.

A solemn hush descended on the hall as Cordier, in a clear, flat voice, began the roll call. "Afghanistan?" "No." "Argentina?" "Abstain." "Australia?" "Yes." "Belgium?" "Yes." "Bolivia?" "Yes." "Belorussia?" "Yes." And so it went on. France's loud *"Oui"* sparked an outbreak of applause in the hall, which Aranha sternly suppressed. Halfway through the alphabet "we knew that we were safely home," Eban later reminisced. The six Arab states, Muslim countries Afghanistan, Iran, Pakistan, and Turkey, along with Cuba, Greece, and India, opposed partition. Yugoslavia's "Abstain," the last vote, was followed by Cordier's announcement: "Thirty-three in favor, thirteen against, ten abstentions, one absent. The resolution is adopted." (By that morning, Siam's

Prince Subha Svasti had left for Bangkok, ostensibly on the grounds that a revolutionary coup had occurred in his country, but actually, according to Eban's later recollection, to avoid voting "no.") A seemingly unending roar of applause arose immediately after the passage of those brief six minutes showing a comfortable margin of five votes in favor, drowning out Aranha's gavel. Cadogan then expressed the hope that the UN Commission would communicate with his government so that arrangements could be made for its arrival and for the coordination of British plans for withdrawal.[67]

The Arabs quickly attacked the result, Feisal setting the tone by declaring that Resolution 181 (II), which included the opening of a port and hinterland not later than February 1, 1948, for "substantial" Jewish immigration, "destroyed the Charter." Saudi Arabia, he went on, considered herself not bound by the resolution, and reserved the right "to act freely in whatever way she deems fit." Jamali, followed by the delegates of Yemen and Syria, spoke in like vein. Egypt and Lebanon, although silent, joined them in leaving the hall, Azzam Pasha shouting at the door: "Any line of partition drawn in Palestine will be a line of fire and blood." Amidst continuous cheers, the GA then unanimously accepted Aranha's nominations for the Commission's membership: Bolivia, Czechoslovakia, Denmark, Panama, and the Philippines, and voted $2 million for its work. (The final selection was pushed through by the State Department, which refused to consider either Granados or Fabregat, and put forth the Philippines on the argument that at least one member should be able to develop some contacts on the Arab side.) Lange, Austin, and Arce praised Aranha's efforts, with Lie expressing confidence that out of all this work the UN would achieve real progress towards "a more securely peaceful world" in the ten months before the delegates met again for the GA's third session in Europe. At 6:57 p.m. it was all over.

Aranha returned to his suite at the Waldorf Astoria, where several Arab princes in the elevator were fuming with rage, hands gripping their daggers. Turning to his son-in-law, the Brazilian commented that such Arabs were unaware of the long-term consequences of the partition vote, a "turning point" in Arab history. "Nothing would operate the miracle of awakening the Arab world from their secular lethargy," he declared, "except that Israeli thorn embedded in its side."[68]

Pandemonium swept the Jewish world, which had been reciting *Psalms* during the Sabbath or sitting transfixed during the vote, glued to their radios as the "nerve-wracking" minutes went on. In the GA lobby, an admiring crowd gathered around the sobbing Silver, whose high-pressure AZEC campaign had witnessed triumph. "Mission accomplished," Jacobson tersely wrote in his diary that evening. Abraham Feinberg, rushing over from a *bar-mitsva* celebration to be with Weizmann at the Savoy-Plaza hotel, found him alone in his shirtsleeves. They embraced and, in tears, the aged Zionist chieftain said only "At last." Eban, his wife Suzy, Toff, and Shertok rode back in a car to Weizmann's rooms, all the way in silence because the moment was "overpowering," and persuaded him to attend a Labor Zionist rally, where thousands accorded him a rapturous homage. In Palestine, the first Jewish city began to celebrate with irrepressible joy for hours, quite a number of ecstatic celebrants getting rides on British military vehicles, with the poet Avraham Shlonsky exclaiming to colleagues seated at Tel Aviv's bohemian Café Casit on Rehov Dizengoff "Yehuda HaLevi did not merit this and I did!" Addressing a mass of people dancing the *hora* in front of Jewish Agency headquarters in Jerusalem's Rehavia quarter, Myerson observed the following day that the deliverance for which Jews longed for the past two millennia had arrived, "so great and wondrous that it surpasses human expression," and that the *yishuv* extended its hand in peace to Arab neighbors. The *HaTikva* burst forth, its words "to be a free people in our own land" suddenly acquiring a new meaning.

Exultation permeated the spontaneous, all-night celebrations in the DP camps in Germany, one reporter observing that "all the year's despair and hopelessness seemed to have been wiped out of the hearts of the Jewish remnant." In Rome, many demonstrators met at the Arch of Titus, victory symbol of the Roman destruction of Jerusalem in 70 CE, to pray and to announce that no longer were the Jews without a home. Budapest's Jews, like their co-religionists everywhere, wished each other *mazal tov* and raised the Zionist banner.[69]

Concluding with the Hebrew words *"Tehi HaMedina HaIvrit!"* (Long live the Hebrew state!) in his brief remarks at the Agency celebration on the morning of November 30, Ben-Gurion tenderly touched the Zionist blue-and-white flag, and shouted defiantly: *"Anahnu am hofshi!"* (We are a free people!). He issued a statement declaring that the General Assembly vote giving his people a sovereign commonwealth in part of its ancient homeland was "an act of historic justice, compensating at least partly for the unparalleled wrong to which the Jewish people were subjected for

1,800 years." It represented a "great moral victory" for the very conception of the UN, he thought, the international body standing for cooperation in the cause of peace, justice, and equality all over the world. He thanked the efforts of the two great powers, as well as the endeavors of many other nations who had brought about the decision. Thus was acknowledged the extraordinary agreement in the Cold War between Washington and Moscow, without which the denouement of November 29, 1947, would not have occurred, although he made no reference to the pivotal thirteen votes cast in favor by the Latin American countries.

Yet the Agency Executive chairman had not left his room at the Kalia Hotel in the northern Dead Sea area to celebrate after Resolution 181 (II) had passed, telling daughter Renana his fears of an encroaching war which would claim lives, perhaps from among the youngsters then dancing in the streets below. Would the Jews, he worried when speaking to Mapai's Executive Committee, even be capable of self-government or become embroiled in internal squabbles and strife?[70] The consequences of the historic partition vote, this supreme pragmatist keenly understood, could not be foretold.

The next day, the Arabs launched a civil war. A bomb thrown in Tel Aviv's central bus station killed five Jews and Arab gunmen ambushed two Jewish buses traveling from Tel Aviv to Jerusalem, killing seven. Two days later, an Arab mob looted and burned Jewish shops in Jerusalem's commercial center while the British police stood by ("mysteriously" even allowing "young lads" to pick up "their own stones for a second throw!," recorded Director of Antiquities R. W. Hamilton)—but disarmed Hagana members coming to the rescue and arrested sixteen of them for illegal possession of weapons. On the 8th, Hagana units stemmed a first orderly assault against Tel Aviv's Hatikva quarter, planned by Arab Revolt militia commander Hasssan Salameh who had followed Haj Amin to Nazi Germany in World War II, leaving 45–50 attackers dead. An AHC manifesto to Palestinian Arabs declared that "kingdoms are established over dead bodies and skulls," while Azzam Pasha announced that the Arabs would resist the UN decision by force, their armies preparing for victory and intending to invade Palestine after the British departure.

On the 9th, six Jews were killed near Gevulot in the Negev, the vast, sparsely populated area which comprised 80 percent of the Jewish partitioned state and which Ben-Gurion insisted had to held against all adversity. Ten died in an ambush against a Kfar Etzion convoy on the Jerusalem-Hevron road two days later, fourteen in a convoy to the besieged Ben Shemen village two days after that by Arab Legion soldiers. The acquisition of weapons was "now matter of life death," Ben-Gurion cabled Kaplan in urging £300,000 without delay. Isolated *yishuv* settlements in the Negev were particularly vulnerable, six Jews killed in the Beersheba area alone on December 15. Four days later, the final words to the waiting Jewish nation from the silent young girl and boy in Alterman's poem "Magash HaKesef," who fell in battle against their implacable enemy, captured the grim reality: "We are the silver platter upon which the Jewish State was served to you."

Beyond Palestine, Muslim Brotherhood leaders, repeating the call from the *ulema* religious faculty of Cairo's Al-Azhar University for a world-wide *jihad* (holy war) against Jews, spearheaded huge demonstrations in Cairo, Damascus, and Baghdad. Rioters in Aleppo killed 75 Jews and wounded several hundred while setting fire to synagogues and houses. A pogrom against Aden's Jewish community left 76 dead, 78 wounded, and scores missing, the local British-trained Aden Protectorate Levies, meant to protect the colony, actually responsible for many of the Jewish deaths. Rioting in Bahrein left one woman killed and sixty-seven Jews injured, with girls raped and dozens of houses and many synagogues and schools being torched. We will not stop the battle, Azzam told a large gathering in Cairo, "until victory has been achieved and our enemy has been thrown into the sea." This violent, widespread response went far beyond Aranha's reaction to the initial assaults: "when you perform an operation, a little blood must flow."[71]

Retaliatory actions by the Irgun quickly followed, the Hagana maintaining its focus on defense and *aliya bet*. Taking up Begin's published order to attack the murderers' bases, his followers launched the first counter-attacks: thirteen Arabs were killed at Tireh, near Haifa, on December 11; twenty were killed and five wounded by a "barrel bomb" at Jerusalem's Damascus Gate the next day. On December 13, six Arabs were killed and twenty-five wounded by bombs placed at the Alhambra Cinema in Jaffa; five were killed and forty-seven wounded by two bombs at the Damascus Gate; seven were killed (including two women and two young children) and seven seriously wounded in an attack on Yehudiya. A few days later, ten Arabs were killed by a bomb at Jaffa's Noga Cinema. Opposed to these tactics, a Hagana manifesto called for peace, similar to Sasson's appeal to Azzam Pasha on December 5, to no avail. The Hagana high command occasionally veered from its policy of restraint (*havlaga*) in order to have Palmah units destroy centers of guerilla activity. Its "illegal" immigration efforts continued all the while, the *HaPortzim* (They who breach) evading the Royal Navy blockade and landing its 167 passengers on December 4 at the mouth of the Yarkon River. On the 22nd, the *Lo Yafhidunu* (They will not frighten us), with 884 passengers, was intercepted. Six days later, the *Kaf Tet B'November* (680 passengers) met the same fate.[72]

For Bevin, as he put it to Iraqi Senate President Nuri Pasha on December 11, HMG's hands were tied "by embarrassing commitments" so long as it held the Palestine Mandate. The British administration, he asserted, would be withdrawn "at the earliest feasible moment" in order that London could "disentangle" itself from these, and freely pursue a consistent policy towards the Middle East as a whole. To do so, the Cabinet had agreed one week earlier that the UN Commission should not arrive before May 1, 1948: an earlier sharing of authority would be "intolerable" and that body's arrival would probably provoke Arab disturbances and consequently upset the Chiefs of Staff four-stage withdrawal plan. (Lie thought that the Commission would be ready to depart about the end of January, Goldmann informed Inverchapel.)

Furthermore, as Bevin made clear to the House of Commons on the 12th, he could not open a port, as proposed for February 1, 1948, in the GA's partition Resolution 181(II), to receive Jewish immigration before HMG lay down the Mandate. A halt to Jewish immigration until the Commission's arrival in May, Bevin told Marshall, would enable the British to proceed in "an orderly way," also perhaps making it possible for the mandatory to provide a port on the Palestine coast for legal immigrants after the UN group's take-over of the country. When Marshall expressed his belief that the Jews would no longer proceed with illegal immigration, since "it must be a dead loss to them and would be of no pressure value," Bevin questioned this, and urged that the U.S. Government restrain the Jewish Agency and publicly condemn the unsanctioned traffic while urging the Jews to "remain patient." Such a step, he added, would incidentally "steady" the Arabs.[73]

The Arab states were quickly informed in confidence and with "great frankness" of the withdrawal outline in the hope that they would do nothing to interfere with an orderly British exit or to force the mandatory to take measures to "suppress disturbances" in Palestine. The appeals of *yishuv* leaders, on the other hand, for weapons and armored cars to protect their convoys and settlements, as well as to remove the Arab Legion from Palestine and halt arrests of Hagana defenders, were regularly denied at a time when Agency intelligence reports revealed that the Arab League political committee's recent gathering in Cairo had secretly assigned quotas per state for funds and weapons, decided to create training camps and arsenals in Syria, and appointed Iraqi General Ismail Safwat to head the Arab Liberation Army (ALA)—his first announced goal to "destroy the Jews of Palestine and purify this nation of them completely." Haj Amin, left out of the meeting, remained deeply suspicious that Safwat's proposal would lead to land grabs in Palestine by Jordan, Egypt, and Syria. Indeed, Azzam acceded to the king's demand to restrain Haj Amin and hold a referendum on Palestine's future under Amman's control.

The Arab states, in condemning the partition resolution, declared openly their firm resolve "to enter the battle which has been imposed upon them, and, God willing, to proceed with it to its successful end." At the same time, Abdullah warned Iraq's Regent Abd al-Ilah that if he permitted Iraqi forces to enter Jordan's territory, his arch enemy Ibn Saud and possibly Syria would demand this as well, and then the Iraqi kingdom would be occupied "before Palestine had been conquered." The killings continued in the Holy Land, with ninety-three Arabs, eighty-four Jews, and seven members of the British security forces dead in the first two weeks after the partition vote. Arab guerillas from Lebanon, Syria, and Jordan began to drift across the borders into Palestine. Still, Creech Jones thought it proper to maintain a balance by telling the Commons that "serious disturbances" in that country were due mainly to Arab "resentment," leading to "serious loss of life," but that Jewish reaction to these attacks "has further inflamed the situation."[74]

Truman tried to steer clear of the quickly deteriorating situation in the Holy Land. Drafting a reply to Weizmann's personal assertion before the GA vote that the Zionists had not gone beyond the limits of "legitimate and moderate persuasion" and did not intend to be used as a channel for the infiltration of Communist ideas in the Middle East, he expressed regret at the unprecedented "pressure and propaganda" that he had faced, which "did not please me a great deal." It showed, he went on, that "the people for whom we had done the most" had no confidence in the integrity of the White House. Then, as on other occasions having gotten his frustrations out in initial correspondence, Truman chose not to send the response dated December 1. Instead, expressing his great appreciation for Weizmann's letter eight days later testifying to the Jewish world's "profound sense of gratitude to you and your Administration" for the initiative and leadership which led to the Assembly's historic decision, he added that it was "very essential" that restraint and tolerance be exercised from now on if a peaceful settlement in the Near East was to be obtained. To Morgenthau's telegram of thanks, Truman cautioned "Henry" that the Jews must now display "tolerance and consideration" for "the other people" in Palestine with whom they would "necessarily" have to be neighbors.

Hearing reports of pressure from U.S. officials on the Philippines and Haiti delegates to vote for partition, he asserted to Lovett that such groups would put the UN "out of business: if "this sort of thing" continued, and he was "very anxious that it be stopped." In like vein, Truman turned down the AZEC's request, sent via Senator Brien McMahon (D, CT), that he be the guest of honor at a Zionist victory gathering, having Connally advise the Congressman of his feeling that "the American Delegation did its duty. We went through. I feel that we should not celebrate."[75]

The victors harbored no such compunctions. In the course of a dinner arranged in Gromyko's honor by the American Committee of Jewish Writers, Artists and Scientists (a Soviet "front" organization), Neumann paid tribute to Gromyko's initiative in getting the Jewish Agency admitted to the GA sessions and to the key Soviet role in attaining Resolution 181 (II). Gromyko, in turn, reiterated to the nearly 1,000 guests that the Soviet attitude was dictated primarily by the unprecedented suffering of the Jews during the last world war, and their great need for a refuge and security after the global conflict. At the official Zionist celebration in New York's Manhattan Center on December 2, featuring the "Three Musketeers"—Fabregat, Granados, and Zoluaga, Neumann quoted a line from Italy's national anthem, written by Goffredo Mameli a century earlier and adopted by that country the previous year: "The graves open up and the dead arise!"[76]

The Jewish Agency Executive cabled Aranha its deeply felt gratitude for his "sagacious and energetic conduct to which constructive outcome present session is in large measure due," while thanking Evatt for his "wise and untiring guidance." Nathan lauded Shertok for his "most outstanding" performance, which made the positive decision possible; Frankfurter thought that Epstein, who had sent an album of Hagana songs in appreciation to several who contributed to the victory, merited "a very special share" of the glory. Senator Henry Cabot Lodge Jr. (R, MA) hailed Silver's "historic" achievement of "such enormous significance." Reginald Coupland, first to advance partition to colleagues on the Peel Commission in 1937, congratulated Weizmann for the attainment of his goal after so many "perverse delays," and hoped that he would impress the new commonwealth with the stamp of his statesmanship so that it could show the world "what the Jews can do when restored to their historic home."

Thanked by Shertok for his "outstanding share" and being "spontaneously active all the time" towards the triumph achieved, Sullivan replied to "Moshe" that it would be one of the "heartwarming satisfactions of our lives" to have played a part in "bringing about here on earth 'more stately mansions'" in Palestine. He also applauded Kirchwey for her "calmness, clear vision and clean fighting spirit," and despite the many "booby-traps ahead," he had no fear of the outcome. Bonnet wrote Frankfurter that he was glad the UN was able to take a courageous decision for a courageous people. "The dawn which had remained a drab gray has become a glorious crimson," Buxton told Ben-Horin: "God does seem to be in his heaven."[77]

Forrestal, however, convinced that domestic party rivalries had dictated the U.S. stance for partition, sought to take Palestine "out of politics." He tried in this regard to sway J. Howard McGrath, Senator (D, RI) and Democratic National Committee chairman, including with a confidential report by the Central Intelligence Agency (CIA), created by Truman in September to advise the National Security Council, which predicted an Arab victory within two years against a Jewish state. Having failed, he argued before Truman's Cabinet on December 1 that the Administrations' support of partition was "fraught with great danger" for the country's future security as the result of alienating the Arab and possibly Muslim worlds. The Chief Executive repeated his firm opinion that American armed forces not be used towards implementing the GA resolution, but Forrestal doubted how this could be avoided if the UN asked for U.S. participation. Hearing Byrnes confirm that Niles and Rosenman had influenced Truman to drop the Morrison-Grady report in light of Dewey's imminent pro-Zionist speech during the

Congressional elections, he found it "most disastrous and regrettable" that American foreign policy was determined by the contributions which "a particular bloc of special interests" might make to the Democratic Party funds. When Vandenberg and Dewey were not forthcoming either in his quest to obtain non-partisan action on the Palestine question, Forrestal decided to let the subject drop for the time being.[78]

The U.S. War Department's top officials did not, Secretary Royall already having prepared a few days before the historic vote a memorandum on the implications of the Palestine issue for the country's security interests. Noting that the Joint Chiefs had twice urged against jeopardizing U.S. influence in the strategic Near East region and against committing American troops to maintain law and order in Palestine, he suggested that an alternate solution be prepared in case the two-thirds majority vote would not be achieved. A possible UN trusteeship had to be considered along with all its ramifications, the National Security Council (NSC) to receive the recommendation of the State, Army, Navy, and Air Force Departments on this subject "as a matter of highest priority." On December 5, ARAMCO's Washington, D.C., representative informed the War Department that any provision of arms to the Jewish state would force an immediate withdrawal of his company and all other Americans in the area, and he handed a copy of Duce's telegram about the negative impact of the partition vote throughout the Arab world, which had also been brought to Truman's attention the previous evening. General Albert C. Wedemeyer, Army Chief of Plans and Operations (P and O) and the recipient of ARAMCO's information, who had one day earlier privately expressed concern about "the Jewish influence, not only in our country, but in all "money-making areas of the world," greatly feared that American military support, without which a Jewish state could not long survive, would alienate the Arabs and further the Soviet cause.[79]

On December 9–10, William Eddy found no dissent when, reporting to the Policy Planning Staff and to members of the Joint Strategic Survey Committee about his latest trip throughout the Middle East, he asserted that the Arabs would without any difficulty "throw the Jews out" by starving them once the British departed. The Jews in the other countries would be "in a bad way" whenever the war broke out, and the Arabs would prefer to have the USSR come in than have a Jewish state. American Jews and American money were "the firebrands," in his characterization. The former Marine Corps colonel and U.S. Minister to Saudi Arabia, now a consultant to ARAMCO, recommended that the government pursue a "strictly neutral" policy in the Arab-Jewish dispute. This, he thought, might within ten years regain the United States' favored position in the Arab world—"a position essential to its security."[80]

Duce's "top secret" memorandum to ARAMCO president William F. Moore on December 22, relating his welcome visits with major Arab leaders immediately after the GA partition vote, made the American oil companies' position eminently clear. To the head of Egypt's Misr Bank he confided that he had advised Washington of the dangers inherent in partition, the decision for which the U.S. President had not made with "a thorough understanding of the consequences," and he had wired ARAMCO that Washington had "set the woods on fire" with its endorsement. My conferees did not think that partition was a practical solution of the problem, he told Azzam Pasha, who in turn declared that the Arabs would "drive the Jews into the sea," even if it took them two hundred years. Duce promised to convey to the State Department the Arab League secretary-general's alternative compromise plan for a token "Vatican State" in Palestine to be given to the Jews. Duce reiterated to all his listeners that ARAMCO wished to continue developing their oil resources for mutual benefit.

If we could get "this Palestine matter" settled and the pipeline built, he assured Feisal, greatly increased quantities of oil beyond the current 300,000 barrels a day in Saudi wells could be moved. This would also result in the building of additional refining capacity in the north, much to the benefit of Syria and Lebanon. A "most affable" Feisal responded by saying that the Arabs were determined to "eliminate" the Jews from Palestine, and that "no stone would be left unturned" to force this to a conclusion. Nuri Pasha, like Azzam, noted the "difficulty" in Arab governments' preventing the massacre of Jewish populations within their boundaries. Individuals like myself and Middle East experts in the U.S. Government who knew the region best, Duce told King Farouk's Chef de Cabinet Ibrahim Abdel Hadi Pasha, were opposed to partition. He felt that it "would not work," that military operations in Palestine would ultimately result in tragic consequences for the Jews in many countries, and that it would lead to the rise of antisemitism in many countries of the world.[81]

The State Department's Middle East experts, anxious about the rising turmoil in Palestine and accepting on November 30 HMG's position that the UN Commission should not arrive before May 1, agreed fully with Duce's assessment. Already on November 10, Marshall had written "OK" on Henderson's confidential memorandum recommending the suspension of exports of arms and ammunition to Arab states and Palestine. Lovett, Armour, and Merriam, among others, had concurred earlier to this proposal "so long as the tension continues." If Arabs used weapons of U.S. origin against Jews or vice versa, Henderson argued then, "we would be subject to bitter recrimination." State issued an official statement to that effect on December 5 along the lines of Henderson's earlier recommendation that morning, and the following day Lovett cabled Marshall in London that the Jewish Agency would likely request Washington soon to permit the export to Palestine from the United States of military supplies in light of the "recent disorder" in Palestine and threats from Arab states. Marshall consented to State's suggestion that, in that case, the Agency should be advised to make such requests to the mandatory and thereafter to the UN Commission.

Hearing this, Michael Wright of the Foreign Office "warmly" welcomed the step, although on the 17th he gave Ambassador Douglas a top secret memorandum declaring that HMG would deliver war materials to Middle East states under prior treaty obligations. Any new orders from Palestine or Arab countries would be "scrutinized with great care," and if hostilities broke out in the region, the whole question would be reconsidered. The British forces intended to leave no war-related stores in the course of their evacuation, he added, opining privately that the basic problem was that both sides in Palestine, as proven by the recent "disorders," had hidden away too many weapons. Consequently, HMG did not favor more arms imports.[82]

Henderson therefore proved evasive on December 8 when Shertok, accompanied by Epstein, urged the need for the Jewish authorities to be prepared militarily to take over gradually from the British as the latter withdrew their armed forces. Resolution 181 (II), after all, had provided for the establishment of armed militia by the two provisional government councils in order to keep internal order, and that any threats to peace by the neighboring Arab states were to be referred to the Security Council. All types of small arms, planes, machine guns, mortars, anti-aircraft, and tanks were essential, he declared, together with military advisers. If the Jewish authorities could not obtain assurances of help from the United States, they would perforce be obliged to turn elsewhere. (Ben-Gurion had in fact dispatched Ueberall to Europe for this purpose just before the vote, and valuable understandings had been reached with some Prague sources when Paris possibilities did not materialize.) Marshall had established the ban on weapon exports already in November, Henderson responded, and, contrary to recent press reports, the U.S. Government had given only $8,000 in light arms for internal security and police forces to the Arab states since the end of World War II. Transmitting a record of this conversation to Lovett and Armour, Henderson advised that no recommendation be made pending further clarification of Mr. Shertok's "tentative views."[83]

The Hagana's request for arms swiftly followed. Forrestal received a "personal and confidential" appeal from Celler, who wrote to "Jim" that it would be "tragic" if U.S. inactivity in this regard led to the negation of the UN decision. Former director of the wartime Office of Strategic Services (precursor to the CIA) William "Wild Bill" Donovan informed the Secretary of Defense that a Hagana member had recently come to his law office asking for arms and munitions, without which Palestine's Jewish community would be "hard put" to resist Arab attack, but the Hagana did not wish to enter into any arrangement with the Russians. In a second conversation with Henderson, Shertok told the sympathetic Franklin D. Roosevelt, Jr., State's director of Near Eastern Affairs intimated that "considerable discussion" would have to determine if the required equipment should be given to the Jews directly, or perhaps the UN Commission would be the competent organ to deal with the matter.

Two of Forrestal's advisors had said in an exploratory talk with Zionist representatives that the issue would first have to be settled with the State Department, and that unless the question could be brought within the framework of U.S. obligations as a Security Council member, the matter would require Congressional authority. Shertok's reply that the Jews asked for help in implementing a UN decision and for protecting themselves against those who defy it appeared to satisfy Special Assistants Max Leva and John Ohly. It was one thing, Shertok ended, for the U.S. government to say that they were not prepared to send troops to Palestine. It was quite another for Washington to deny arms to the Jews when they were attacked and ready to defend themselves.[84]

State's Near East specialists, having crossed swords with the pro-partition group in the U.S. delegation at the GA, went further now to seek without delay a review of American policy on Palestine. Before the vote,

Merriam and associates had drafted, with McClintock's basic assent, what he termed "our switch trusteeship proposal" for a five-year period if the two-thirds majority did not materialize. The chief of the Near Eastern Division now proposed that Truman issue a statement in order to "restore the situation following the recent shambles in New York" and to "forestall disaster" to the UN and to U.S. interests. The President would completely disavow any "undue pressure" that was brought on countries to support partition, and any person or organization exerting "unauthorized" pressure hereafter would be prosecuted to the full extent of the law. Further, that the United States did not consider the UN to have the right to enforce a settlement of a political problem involving the "friendly peoples" of Palestine without the free consent of the majority of both of that country's communities. If their consent could not be obtained, the problem should be reviewed, the UN asking the British to "carry on" pending other arrangements, while Washington would not "be amenable to political blackmail, either international or domestic" in this matter.[85]

Not surprisingly, on December 17 State offered a draft, prepared at the NSC's request, which offered two alternative recommendations. In the first, the United States would urge that the Palestine problem be referred back to the GA because partition was impossible to implement, with a UN trusteeship to be proposed if Jew and Arab could not support a "middle-of-the-road" position. In the second, it would declare that in view of the "manifest impossibility" of implementing partition, no steps were to be taken to that end, American troops would not be sent for its enforcement, and the arms embargo should be maintained. Goldmann heard from the U.S. Embassy in London that Marshall told his staff he thought it may have been a mistake supporting partition.[86]

State also kept pressing the Zionist Executive, following Bevin's repeated requests, to halt illegal immigration at the present time and especially the sailing of the *Pans*. Shertok assured Henderson on December 8 that the Agency would "take all steps in its power" to prevent such movement, but that the provision of a seaport and an increase in the present rate of legal immigration were essential to accomplish this purpose. When a few days later Johnson (transmitting a message from Marshall), Armour, and Henderson individually expressed to Shertok the government's deep concern and "earnest desire" against the *Pans*' possible departure, he repeated that while it also opposed the two boats' exit, the Agency had no "absolute control" over the departure. He noted the crisis forcing Rumanian Jews, who had sold all their belongings, to flee into Bulgaria (thanks to ransom "exit permits" arranged by the Mosad's Shaike Dan with the Bucharest authorities), and dismissed British and U.S. War Department charges of Communist infiltration within those aboard as "a cruel joke." Ben-Gurion, Myerson, Moshe Shapira, and Isaac Gruenbaum of the Executive in Jerusalem agreed with Shertok to halt the two boats, Sneh and Eliyahu Dobkin dissenting. Meirov, accepting the unanimous view of his operatives on the ground, returned home in an effort to change Ben-Gurion's mind. The latter proposed that he fly to the United States to speak with Shertok, his brother-in-law, and the other Executive members. Yet a sudden morning call to Meirov from Venya Pomeraniec (later Ze'ev Hadari) in Paris, warning categorically that any further delay would cancel the entire mission, brought the Mosad chief's decisive order: the *Pans'* should leave Constanza for the port of Burgas, Bulgaria, immediately; the passengers would reach there by train. The dye was cast.

The two vessels, to be called *Atsma'ut* (Independence) and *Kibbutz Galuyot* (Ingathering of the Exiles) at Ben-Gurion's suggestion, sailed on the 26th from Burgas with 15,706 passengers, including 4,000 orphans. Four British destroyers and two cruisers intercepted them as soon as they exited the Dardanelles. Strained negotiations between the Agency in Jerusalem, the two Palyam captains, and the British followed while Zemurray's former banana boats flying the Panama flag continued eastward. On the 30th, McClintock drafted a suggested statement about the *Pans* for Lovett's use at his afternoon press conference declaring that the department "deprecates" clandestine immigration to Palestine, particularly as Resolution 181(II) provided for "substantial" Jewish immigration at an early date. The Acting Secretary of State chose not to use McClintock's paragraphs. The same day, an agreement was finally reached whereby the *Pans*, the Hagana still in charge of the *ma'apilim*, would steam with British sailors on the bridge direct to the Famagusta port in Cyprus.[87]

The year ended with yet another example of Palestine's rapid slide into daily violence and chaos. On the 30th, four days after an Arab ambush in Bab-el-Wad on a Jerusalem-bound convoy whose weapons had been confiscated earlier by the British killed seven, including Youth Aliya's acting director Hans Beyth, and injured nine, Irgunists threw two bombs at a crowd of Arab workers who were standing in front of the Haifa Oil Refinery, killing eleven and wounding dozens more. An angry crowd butchered thirty-nine of their Jewish co-workers in revenge, and wounded another fifty before British troops restored order. No arrests were made. In punitive reprisal, some Palmah soldiers and Hagana men from Haifa attacked the village of Balad ash Sheikh and its satellite village Hawassa, from which most of the killers had come. There were more than sixty dead, including women and children. When the newly formed left-wing Mapam party criticized the indiscriminate killing, Ben-Gurion responded thus: "We are at war.... There is an injustice in this, but otherwise we will not be able to hold out." Husseini's counter stance was clear, the AHC leader telling *Al-Wahda* on the 30th that once the last Palestinian Arab had been martyred, the Arab states would continue the struggle until victory. Cunningham thought the Arab League's plans a recipe for disaster, leading to "the destruction" of Palestine. The mandatory would not be able to enforce law and order as long as Jewish attacks on Arabs continued, Gurney told Myerson. "Terror is prevalent" and "normal life" for Palestine is disappearing, U.S. consul in Jerusalem Robert B. Macatee wired Marshall the next day, but compared with what may be expected in the future "it is a period of relative quiet." The UN Commission, he concluded, will be attempting a "well nigh impossible task." To any observer, the future was doubtless fraught with dangerous unpredictability.[88]

Endnotes

1   Yahil to Avigur, July 31, 1966, A382/10; Epstein memo, September 11, 1947, A427/6; both in CZA; Silverman to Attlee, September 3, 1947; Attlee to Silverman, September 6, 1947; both in C14/32-1, Board of Deputies of British Jews Archives; Silverman to Attlee, September 10, 1947, 71/24/1, MS239, Special Collections, Hartley Library, University of Southampton, England; *Palestine Post*, September 9, 1947; Hamlin memo, September 26, 1947; Merriam to Epstein, September 15, 1947, both in S25/2630, CZA.

2   Resolutions, September 3, 1947, S25/1807, CZA; *FRUS*, 1947, vol. 5, 1143–1144; Yigal Lossin, *Pillar of Fire: The Birth of Israel—A Visual History*, Z. Ofer, trans. (Jerusalem, 1983), 481; Magnes draft statement, n.d., 138, Judah

Magnes MSS, Central Archives of the History of the Jewish People, Jerusalem; Miller to Rosenwald, February 5, 1953, ACJ files, ZA; Shertok to Kirschner-Gerig, September 4, 1947, 93.03/2270/14, ISA.

3 Proskauer-Blaustein to Marshall, September 10, 1947, Box 8, Proskauer MSS; Palestine Sub-Committee, September 10, 1947, Paris-Palestine file, AJC; Conference statement, September 2, 1947, 867N.01/9-347, SD; Silver to Swope, September 1947, Manson files, AHS; Nathan memo, September 6, 1947, 93.03/2267/32, ISA; Nathan memo, September 5, 1947, Box 3765, E. Roosevelt MSS; *New York Times*, September 1, 1947.

4 Alami statement, August 30, 1947, FO371/61877; Beeley memo, September 5, 1947, FO 371/61952; both in PRO; *Davar*, September 3, 1947; *FRUS, 1947*, vol. 5, 1144; Beirut to Bevin, September 17, 1947, FO371/61529, PRO.

5 Maimon report, September 14, 1947, S25/9013; HaParshan report, September 10, 1947, S25/9034; Rosenberg to Myerson, November 5, 1947, S25/9215; all in CZA; *HaAretz*, September 14, 1947; September 16, 1947 report, S25/3300; Arazi to Fisher, November 7, 1947, S25/1699; both in CZA; Report, November 15, 1947, Mapai MSS, Beit Berl, Kfar Sabba, Israel; R. M. Graves, *Experiment in Anarchy* (London, 1949), 84; Fforde report, September 13, 1947; Mechan report, September 23, 1947; both in 47/667; Calder report, September 4, 1947, 47/665; all in HA.

6 Bevin-Henderson talk, September 9, 1947, FO 800/476, PRO; *FRUS, 1947*, vol. 5, 498–499; Bevin to Ibn Saud, June 5, 1947, RG 25, G2, 84–85/19, vol. 199, PAC.

7 Beeley memo, September 5, 1947, FO371/61952; Gurney to Creech Jones, September 8, 1947; Beeley notes, September 11, 1947; both in FO371/61878; all in PRO; Goodman note, September 9, 1947, AIWO London 1947, Jacob Rosenheim MSS, Agudas Israel of America Archives, New York City; *Palestine Post*, September 7, 1947; September 2–7, 1947 summary, P345/1442A, RG 65, ISA; London *Times*, September 2, 1947.

8 Douglas to Marshall, September 15, 1947, 501.BB Palestine/9-1547, SD; Beeley memo, September 13, 1947, FO 371/61879, PRO; Eban report, September 19, 1947, S25/2965, CZA; Horowitz, *State in the Making*, 234–235.

9 *FRUS, 1947*, vol. 5, 1147–1151. For the delegation's preliminary discussion of U.S forces regarding implementation of Article 43 of the UN Charter, see September 13, 1947 meeting, Palestine File-1, Robert M. McClintock MSS, SD.

10 *FRUS, 1947*, vol. 5, 1146, 1151. For a good summary of the general debate on Palestine during September 17–22, see Robinson memo, September 26, 1947, Z6/95, CZA.

11 *FRUS, 1947*, vol. 5, 1152–1153; Wadsworth to Johnson, September 18, 1947; Wadsworth to Henderson, September 18–20, 1947; both in 501.BB/9-1747. SD; Wadsworth memo, September 18, 1947, PSF 184, HSTL.

12 JAE US, September 17 and 18, 1947; both in Z5/59; JAE American section minutes, September 22, 1947, Z5/2365; all in CZA; Dulles draft, February 2, 1947, II-Correspondence UN file, John Foster Dulles MSS, Rare Books and Special Collections, Princeton University, Princeton, NJ; Buxton to Ben-Horin, September 20, 1947, A300/16, CZA; Meeting, September 18, 1947, World Agudas Israel Organization Archives, Jerusalem; John L. Harper, "Friends, Not Allies: George F. Kennan and Charles E. Bohlen," *World Policy Journal* 12:2 (1995): 77–88.

13 Attlee to Bevin, September 17, 1947, FO 371/61878; Bevin memo, September 18, 1947; Alexander memo, September 18, 1947; both in CAB 129/21; Cabinet minutes, September 20, 1947, CAB 128/10; all in PRO; B. Pimlott, *Political Diary of Hugh Dalton*, 414.

14 Letter to Shertok, September 17, 1947, Z6/85, CZA; Laski to Frankfurter, September 27, 197, Box 75, Frankfurter MSS.

15 *FRUS, 1947*, vol. 5, 1153–1162; Henderson to Armour, May 28, 1975, 1/55, Norman Armour MSS, Eddy memo, September 13, 1947, 6/2, William Eddy MSS; both in Dept. of Rare Books and Special Collections, Seeley G. Mudd Manuscript Library, Princeton University. That same year, Eddy joined the Arabian American Oil Company (ARAMCO) as a consultant.

16 *FRUS, 1947*, vol. 5, 1162–1163; McClintock to Rusk, September 22, 1`947, 501.BB Palestine/9-2247, SD.

17 *FRUS, 1947*, vol. 5, 1164; Robinson to JA Executive, September 30, 1947, S25/5470, CZA; Creech Jones statement, September 26, 1947, FO 371/61789, PRO.

18 Creech Jones to FO, September 27, 1947, FO 371/61790, PRO; *Palestine Post*, September 28, 1947; Wadsworth to Johnson, September 26, 1947, US/A/AC.14/4, UN Archives; Shultz Strictly Confidential memo, 28, 95–96, A427/8, CZA; *Palestine Post*, September 28 and October 8, 1947; FO to New York, Sept 25, 1947, FO 371/61878, PRO; Jowitt address, September 30, 1947, Records of Meetings, vol. 8, Council on Foreign Relations Archives, New York City.

19 Ben-Dror, "The Arab Struggle," 285; OAG to Creech Jones, September 22, 1947, FO371/61878, PRO; Report, September 3, 1947 S25/5601, CZA; Karsh, *Palestine Betrayed*, 86–87; Adelson memo, September 15, 1947, 93.03/2266/5, ISA; Report, September 26, 1947, S25/9020, CZA; Macatee to State, September

4, 1947, 501.BB-Palestine/9-447, SD; Irgun statement, September 19, 1947, 8 Klali/21, HA; *JTA*, September 23, 1947; *Palestine Post*, September 28 and 30, 1947; *Palcor*, September 28 and 29, 1947.

20 Shertok to Myerson, September 21, 1947, S25/1696; Epstein to Kaplan, September 29, 1947, S53/25; both in CZA; W. Millis, *Forrestal Diaries*, 309–310, 322; JAE US, September 26, 1947, Z5/ 59, CZA; Shertok to Myerson, September 30, 1947; Lourie to Linton, Oct. 2, 1947; both in 93.01/2180/5, ISA; *FRUS, 1947*, vol. 5, 1166–1170; Ben-Gurion-Shertok telephone call, September 30, 1947, S44/564, CZA.

21 *FRUS, 1947*, vol. 5, 1169–1170; Sneh to JA in Washington, September 29, 1947, S25/1698, CZA; Shertok to Myerson, September 18 and 22, 1947; both in 93/01/2180/5; Epstein memo, September 19, 1947, 93.03/92/35; all in ISA; *Documents on Israeli-Soviet Relations*, 226–227.

22 Meeting, September 29, 1947; October 2, 3, and 6, 1947; all in DAG-1/3.1.1-12, UN Archives; Report, October 2, 1947, Robison MSS; Ilsley statement, October 14, 1947, Z6/95, CZA; Memo, December 27, 1947, MG26, J4, vol. 310, PAC; Ridgway to US Army Chief of Staff, October 6, 1947, RG319, 091 Palestine, Box 93, NA.

23 *FRUS, 1947*, vol. 5, 1171–1176; *Palcor*, October 2, 1947; MacCallum memo, October 7, 1947, RG25-62, vol. 84–85/19, PAC. State's specialist on postwar planning, Harley Notter, went further, advising that the United States support a unitary, independent Palestine "with its present frontiers." Notter to Johnson, October 6, 1947, Box 1, Dean Rusk MSS, NA.

24 Mattison to Henderson, August 28, 1947; Hoffman to Loftus, September 3, 1947; Lovett to Marshall, September 8, 1947; Memo, September 22, 1947; all in Box 4, William L. Clayton MSS, HSTL; W. Millis, *Forrestal Diaries*, 323–324.

25 Eilat, *HaMa'avak Al HaMedina*, 2, 254–258; Sullivan to Kirchwey, October 6, 1947, A427/1, CZA; Jacobson to Truman, October 3, 1947, PSF, Box 184, HSTL; W. Millis, *Forrestal Diaries*, 323; Natan memo, October 6, 1947, 93.03/2267/32, ISA; Lourie to JAE US, Oct. 8, 1947, Z6/95, CZA.

26 Epstein, *HaMa'avak Al HaMedina*, 2, 256–257; Truman to Jacobson, PSF, Box 184, HSTL; Truman, *Years of Trial and Hope*, 183; *FRUS, 1947*, vol. 5, 1177–1179; JCS Memo, October 10, 1947, 092 Palestine, RG 218, NA.

27 Buxton et al., October 11, 1947 statement, A300/16; Johnson address, October 11, 1947, S25/5353; both in CZA; *FRUS, 1947*, vol. 5, 1180; Bevin to Creech Jones, October 14, 1947, FO371/61791, PRO; *HaAretz*, October 14, 1947.

28 Baruch Tenenbaum, "A Comforting Sense of Deja-Vu," *Jerusalem Post*, April 25, 2013; JAE US, October 1, 1947, Z5/2369, CZA; Shultz, "Confidential

Report," 25–26; Holtzman to Koo, March 12, 1947, Z6/93, CZA; Holtzman to Koo, October 11, 1947 (two letters), Fanny Holtzman MSS, 5/13, American Jewish Archives; Meeting, October 11, 1947, DAG-1/3.1.1-12, UN Archives.

29 *FRUS, 1947*, vol. 5, 1286, 1179; "Report from the UN," October 9, 1947, S25/5353, CZA; Beirut to Cairo, October 11, 1947, FO141/1233, PRO; David Barnett and Efraim Karsh, "Azzam's Genocidal Threat," *Middle East Quarterly*, 18:4 (Fall 2011), 85-88; Memo, October. 1947, S25/9020, CZA.

30 Eytan to Sharf, October 11, 1947, S25/1698, CZA; Memo, October 1947, 93.03/2267/41, ISA; Cunningham to Creech Jones, October 8, 1947, FO371/61960, PRO.

31 Meeting, October 13, 1947, S25/5460, CZA; *Documents on Israeli-Soviet Relations*, 227–228; Reuter, October 13, 1947, J112/1072, CZA; Jewish Agency N.Y. to Myerson, October 15, 1947, 93/01/2180/5, ISA.

32 *FRUS, 1947*, vol. 5, 1180–1184; *Palcor*, October 16, 1947.

33 I. F. Stone, "Warning Against A Sell-Out on Palestine," *PM*, October 19, 1947; Meeting, October 10, 1947, S25/5460, CZA; JAE US, Oct. 5, 1947, Z5/59, CZA; Shertok to Myerson, October 8, 1947, 93.01/2180/1, ISA; *FRUS, 1947*, vol. 5, 1186–1192.

34 *New York Times*, October 15 and 20, 1947; *FRUS, 1947*, vol. 5, 1195–1199.

35 Meeting, October 7 and 21 1947, DAG-1/3.1.1-12, UN Archives; October 18 and 22, 1947, both in S25/5460, CZA; *Isaiah* 11:12; Robison reports, October 18 and 21, 1947, Robison MSS. According to a *PM* report, Aranha also warned the Latin American delegates then that failure on their part to support the U.S.-USSR agreement on partition would be a further heavy blow to the weakened United Nations. *PM*, October 9, 1947.

36 Shultz, "Confidential Report," 22–24, 29, 33–40; Karr memo, October 24, 1947, A427/6, CZA; "Line-up on Palestine," The *Nation*, October 25, 1947.

37 *FRUS, 1947*, vol. 5, 1200–1215, 1217–1219; Interview, October 22, 1947, Z6/95, CZA.

38 Vandenberg to Taft, October 8, 1947, Robert A. Taft MSS, Library of Congress, Washington, D.C.; *New York Times*, October 7, 1947; Memo, October 6, 1947, US/A/AC.14/40, UN Archives; Truman to Pepper, October 20, 1947, CF, Box 59, HSTL; *FRUS, 1947*, vol. 5, 1212–1213; Truman to Aronson, October 27, 1947, Executive minutes, Union of American Hebrew Congregations Archives, New York City.

39 Bevin to Attlee, October 22, 1947, FO 800/487, PRO; *Palestine Post*, October 23, 1947; Foreign Office to DC, October 29, 1947, FO371/61793, PRO; *FRUS, 1947*, vol. 5, 1215–1216; Danny Goldman and Michael J. K. Walsh, "Stranded

in Bogas, Cyprus: The Affair of the Pans, January 1948," *Journal of Cyprus Studies* 15 (2009): 45–46.

40 Beeley to Burrows, October 22, 1947, FO37161792, PRO; *FRUS, 1947*, vol. 5, 1192–1194; Kirkbride to Bevin, October 11, 1947, FO371/61881, PRO; Memo, October 21, 1947, 93/163/4, ISA; Beeley to Garran, October 11, 1947, FO371/61948; Bevin to HMG Representatives, October 16, 1947, FO 371/61882; both in PRO. Memo, October 30, 1947, Box 1, Rusk MSS. Worried that chaos would ensure after the British withdrawal if no kind of administration were in place, Cecil Hourani proposed a bi-nationalist solution once the "extremist" Arab Higher Committee and Jewish Agency were "kept out of the way." The Eastern Department's Garran retorted that the British would not help in maintaining order, which also went against HMG's declared intention of withdrawing "lock, stock, and barrel" if there was no UN settlement. Garran memo, October 30, 1947, FO371/61952, PRO.

41 Creech Jones to Cunningham, October 11, 1947, Cunningham MSS; Sterndale-Bennett memo, January 31, 1948, FO371/68516; Eastern Dept. to Beeley, October 17, 1947; Martin to Trafford Smith, October 20, 1947; both in FO371/61894; Sinclair to Falla, October 22, 1947, FO 371/61793; all in PRO; Memo, October 22, 1947, McClintock MSS; Cunningham to Creech Jones, October 29, 1947, FO371/61894, PRO; McCintock to Lovett, October 31, 1947, Box 1, Rusk MSS.

42 Morgan to Montgomery, October 17, 1947; Memo, October 16, 1947; Montgomery to Bevin, October 24, 1947; all in FO800/476, PRO; *FRUS, 1947*, vol. 5, 553.

43 *Documents on Israeli-Soviet Relations*, 235–236.

44 JAE US Executive, October 26, 1947, 93/64/9, ISA; Yuval to Ben-Gurion, October 26, 1947, S25/5353; Eytan to Gelber, October 23, 1947, Z4/475; J. L. (Linton) memo, Brussels visit, S25/5353; all in CZA; *JTA*, November 2, 1947; *FRUS, 1947*, vol. 5, 1216–1217; Drew Pearson, "Mufti Plots Battle in U.N.," *New York Daily Mirror*, September 19, 1947; Lourie to Shultz, October 10, 1947, A427/5, CZA; I. F. Stone, "What Price Arab Oil?," *Nation*, October 4, 1947, 358–360; Epstein to Kollek, October 28, 1946, L35/97, CZA; Slutzky, *Sefer HaHagana*, 958, 1328–1329; Va'ad HaBitahon, October 28, 1947, S25/9347, CZA.

45 *FRUS, 1947*, vol. 5, 1219–1230; Creech Jones to Bevin, Oct. 30, 1947, FO371/61793, PRO; Memo, October 30, 1947, Box 1, Rusk MSS; Eban to Linton, November 3, 1947, 93.01/2180/5, ISA; Eban to Hodess, November 4, 1947; A194/13, CZA; Gelber to JAE US, November 5, 1947, 93.03/93/6, ISA.

46 *FRUS, 1947*, vol. 5, 1231–1238, 1241–1246, 1252–1253; Shultz, "Confidential Report," 47–55; Wilkins to Merriam, November 6, 1947, 501.BB Palestine,

SD; Krasno interview with Epstein, October 22, 1990, UN Archives; Pearson to St. Laurent, November 10, 1947, RG25, G2, vol. 84–85/19, PAC; Shultz to Zuloaga, October 28, 1947, L35/137, CZA: Azriel Carlebach, "HaKongress Roked," *Yediot Aharonot*, November 12, 1947.

47 *FRUS, 1947*, vol. 5, 1259–1261, 1263–1264; Green memo, November 15, 1947, Box 1, Rusk MSS; Bevin to Marshall, November 12, 1947, FO371/61794; Cabinet meeting, November 11, 1947, FO371/61794; both in PRO; *Palestine Post*, November 18, 1947; Weizmann to Smuts, November 15, 1947, WA; *Palestine Post*, November 17, 1947.

48 Beeley-Agudas Israel interview, November 6, 1947, Shenkolewski files, June 1947–March 1948, Rosenheim MSS, Agudas Israel of America Archives, New York City; *FRUS, 1947*, vol. 5, 1253–1254; Cunningham to Creech Jones, November 5, 1947, FO 371/61794; Cunningham to Creech Jones, November 12, 1947, FO371/61887; Cunningham to Creech Jones, November 15, 1947; Bevin to UK delegation, November 18, 1947; both in FO371/61888; Cunningham to Creech Jones, November 19, 1947, FO371/61889; all in PRO.

49 Sasson to Shertok, November 5, 1947, 93.01/2180/4, ISA; *FRUS, 1947*, vol. 5, 1240, 1248; Damascus to FO, November 14, 1947, FO371/61887, PRO; Sasson to Myerson, November 9, 1947, S25/4015, CZA; Dorsz to State, November 5, 1947, 867N.01/11-647, SD; *New York Herald Tribune*, November 21, 1947; Sasson to Shertok, November 5, 1947, 93.01/2180/4, ISA; Zaslani to Myerson, November 16, 1947, S25/5353; Abdullah-Myerson meeting, November 17, 1947, S25/4004; both in CZA; Efraim Karsh, *Palestine Betrayed* (New Haven, CT, 2010), 97.

50 Eban to Hodess, November 4, 1947, A192/13, CZA; November 3, 1947 meeting, DAG-1/3.1.1-13, UN Archives; Gass to Kaplan, November 4, 1947, 93.01/2206/9, ISA; Shultz, "Confidential Report," 59–60, Halperin to Lourie, November 4, 1947; Proskauer to Johnson, November 11, 1947; both in 93.03/2269/29, ISA; Colonial Office memo, April 1947, DAG-13/3.1.0:2, UN Archives; *FRUS, 1947*, vol. 5, 1251, 1255–1256, 1259, 1267–1270; Eliahu Elath, *Israel and Elath, The Political Struggle for the Inclusion of Elath in the Jewish State* (London, 1966), 17–18.

51 *FRUS, 1947*, vol. 5, 1247–1248; Shertok to Fisher, 93.01/2180/6; Gelber to JAE US, November 19, 1947, 93.03/93/6; both in ISA; *Palestine Post*, November 17, 1947.

52 Shultz, "Confidential Report," 56–59; Shertok to Lisicky, November 15, 1947, 93.03/2266/35, ISA; Herzog and Ben-Uziel cable, October 29, 1947, P580/48, Leo Kohn MSS, ISA; *FRUS, 1947*, vol. 5, 1250–1251.

53 Gelber to Weizmann, November 14, 1947, WA; Elath, *Israel and Elath*, 18–22. For Lowermilk's plan, see Walter Lowedermilk, *Palestine: Land of Promise* (New York, 1944).

54 *FRUS, 1947*, vol. 5, 1270–1292; Cadogan to Bevin, November 14, 1947; Bevin to Inverchapel, November 17, 1947; Inverchapel to Bevin, November 18, 1947; all in FO371/61888, PRO; Weizmann, *Trial and Error*, 458–459; Truman to Thomas, November 19, 1947, OF 204 Palestine, Box 913, HSTL.

55 McNeil to Bevin, November 19, 1947, FO 371/61889, PRO; Eytan to Sharef, November 6, 1947, S25/463, CZA; Kirchwey to Shertok, November 19, 1947, MC280/237, Kirchwey MSS; Report, November 22, 1947, Robison MSS; *Ad Hoc* Committee meeting, November 22, 1947, DAG-1/3.1.1-12, UN Archives.

56 *Ad Hoc* Committee meeting, November 24, 1947, DAG-1/3.1.1-12; meeting of November 25, 1947, DAG-13/3.1.0:2; both in UN Archives; Shultz, "Confidential Report," 76, 86; Cadogan to Bevin, November 25, 1947, FO 371/61890, PRO. The Netherlands' abstention was motivated principally by its concern for relations with the millions of Muslims in Indonesia, then part of its colonial empire in the Far East. For Belgium's "yes" vote, see Eilat, *HaMa'avak al HaMedina*, 434–435. Prime Minister Paul-Henri Spaak told the British shortly before the vote that while he feared that partition with U.S. military enforcement would lead to war, no alternative proposal had been offered. Rendel to Bevin, November 26, 1947, FO371/61795, PRO.

57 Cadogan to Bevin, November 25 and 27, 1947; both in FO371/61890, PRO; Horowitz, *State in the Making*, 299; Report, November 26, 1947, Robison MSS; Neumann, *In the Arena*, 251; Shultz, "Confidential Report," 95. Enrique Corominas, second-in-command on the Argentine delegation, objected to Arce's views. Adelson memo, August 4, 1947, UN 1946–1948, ZA.

58 Cadogan to Bevin, November 27, 1947, FO371/61890, PRO.; Memo, Connally to Truman, November 25, 1947, Box 184, PSF Palestine-Jewish Immigration, HSTL; *FRUS, 1947*, vol. 5, 1283–1284; Shultz, "Confidential Report," 99.

59 Carlos P. Romulo, *Forty Years, A Third World Soldier at the UN* (New York, 1986), 65–68; Neumann, *In the Arena*, 252; Davis memo, December 12, 1947, 501/BB Palestine/12-1247, SD; Weizmann to Roxas, November 27, 1947, WA; Larabee-Villard talk, November 26, 1947, 867N.01/11-2647, SD; Dennis-Kopper talk, November 25, 1947, Policy Planning Staff Studies, Box 1,Tab A, no. 19, SD; Shultz, "Confidential Report," 86–92; Adolf A. Berle, *Navigating the Rapids, 1918–1971*, B. B. Berle and T. B. Jacobs, eds. (New York, 1973), 579–580; Benno Weiser Varon, *Professions of a Lucky Jew* (New York, 1992),

147–163; Adelson memo, January 2, 1948, 126/160-Het Tsadi, ISA; Sachar, *The Redemption of the Unwanted*, 222.

60 Morgenthau to San Martin, November 29, 1947, 93.02/2267/30, ISA; Lehman to San Martin, November 28, 1947, Palestine folder 1946–47, Lehman MSS; Edy Kaufman, Yoram Shapira, and Joel Barromi, *Israel-Latin American Relations* (New Brunswick, NJ, 1979), 145; Thompson memo to Henderson, December 18, 1947; Kennan memo to Lovett, January 19, 1948; both in Policy Planning Staff Studies, Box 1, Tab A, no. 19, SD; Shultz, "Confidential Report," 27–28; Weizmann cables, November 27, 1947; Alfange to Green, November 26, 1947; both in 93/3-Het Tsadi, ISA; Santiago to State, December 2, 1947, 501.BB Palestine/12-247; Jernegan memo, December 3, 1947, 501/BB Palestine/12-347; Kelley to State, December 3, 1947, 867N.01/12-347; all in SD; Einstein to Nehru, June 13, 1947, and Nehru reply, July 11, 1947; both in 92/34-Het Tsadi, ISA; Weizmann to Nehru, November 27, 1947, WA; Epstein to Gourgey, January 19, 1948, Z6/60, CZA; Eilat, *HaMa'avak al HaMedina*, 433–434, 442.

61 Eilat, *HaMa'avak al HaMedina*, 449–452. Three years later, Haj Amin's representative in Haifa disclosed that the ex-Mufti had wished to contact the Agency via Mordekhai Eliash to suggest negotiations on a plan that did not include partition. The Agency replied that "it would not deal at all with this murderer." *HaAretz*, July 27, 1950.

62 Cadogan to Bevin, November 28, 1947, FO371/61890, PRO; Epstein to Klinow, December 11, 1947; L35/126; Epstein memo, January 14, 1948, S25/6595; both in CZA; Fisher to Shertok, January 20, 1948, 93.03/128/10, ISA; Shultz, "Confidential Report," 100–102; Epstein, *HaMa'avak Al HaMedina*, 454–456.

63 Alfange to Silver, November 28, 1947, 93/9, 3-Het, ISA; Jacobson diary, November 26 and 28, 1947, Jacobson MSS; Donovan, *Conflict and Crisis*, 329–330; Weizmann to Truman, November 25 and 28, 1947, WA; Jacobson diary, December 8, 1947, Jacobson MSS; Shultz, "Confidential Report," 108–112; Eilat, *HaMa'avak al HaMedina*, 439; Comay to Gering, December 3, 1947, 93.03/2266/15, ISA; Lillie Shultz, "The Palestine Fight—an Inside Story," *Nation*, December 20, 1947, 675–678.

64 Clifford interviews, August 27–28, 1949, and October 10, 1949, Josephus Daniels MSS; Eban S. Ayers diary, November 28, 1947; Henderson interview, June 14, 1973, Oral History Collection; all in HSTL; Hadow to Beeley, December 7, 1947, FO371/68528, PRO; Arvey to Penkower, May 26, 1977 (in the author's possession); David B. Sachar,"David Niles and American Policy," Harvard College senior honors thesis, 1959, 54, 73; Eilat, *HaMa'avak*

al HaMedina, 430–432; Marc Jarblum, "Ktsat Zikhronot," *HaPoel HaTsa'ir*, November 6, 1962, 4–5.

65 *FRUS, 1947*, vol. 5, 1287–1290; Bevin to Inverchapel, November 26, 1947, FO371/61795, PRO.

66 Epstein to JAE, November 29, 1947, S25/5353, CZA; Epstein, *HaMa'avak Al HaMedina*, 452–465; Abba Eban, *Abba Eban, An Autobiography* (New York, 1977), 97–98; Comay to Gering, December 3, 1947, 93.03/2266/15, ISA; *FRUS, 1947*, vol. 5, 1293–1294; Evatt to Marshall and to Feisal, both November 1, 1947, Evatt MSS, Flanders University, Adelaide, Australia; *Palestine Post*, November 30, 1947.

67 Cohen memo, May 20, 1948, (8)11.10.95, HaShomer HaTsa'ir Archives, Merhavia, Israel; Eban, *Abba Eban*, 97, 99; *Palestine Post*, November 30, 1947; Hutschnecker memo, May 8, 1973, K14a/92, CZA. Abstaining were: Argentina, Chile, China, Colombia, El Salvador, Ethiopia, Honduras, Mexico, the United Kingdom, and Yugoslavia. For the abstentions of Mexico and Yugoslavia, see Eilat, *HaMa'avak Al HaMedina*, 441–444. For that of Argentina, see Toff to Epstein, December 20, 1947, Z5/3465, CZA.

68 *Palestine Post*, November 30, 1947; *New York Times*, November 30, 1947; Ruth Gruber, *Witness* (New York, 2007), 158; Comay to Gering, December 3, 1947, 93.03/2266/15, ISA; De Costa to Hutschnecker, July 7, 1970, K14a/92, CZA.

69 November 29, 1947, Jacobson Diary; Feinberg-McKinzie interview, August 23, 1973, Oral History Collection, HSTL; Suzy Eban interview, "November 29, 1947: The Story of a Vote," Toldot Yisrael (Jerusalem, 2009); Eban, *Abba Eban*, 99; Hayim Hefer and Noga Terkel, *Shurot Shurot* (Bet HaPalmah, Tel Aviv, 2008), Lossin, *Pillar of Fire*, 491, 495; *JTA*, December 1, 1947; Secretary's report, December. 10, 1947, 93.2/184/9, ISA. The poet Yehuda HaLevi of Medieval Spain had written of his yearning for Eretz Israel.

70 Zipporah Porath, *Letters from Jerusalem 1947–1948* (Jerusalem, 1987); *JTA*, December 1, 1947; Ben-Gurion, *Pa'amei Medina*, 503; Ben-Gurion speech, December 3, 1947, BGA. Ben-Gurion used the phrase "Hebrew state" because the official name had not yet been decided upon by the *yishuv* leadership.

71 *HaAretz*, November 30, 2014; Schedule, December 1–15, 1947, S26/4148; Karsh, *Palestine Betrayed*, 101–102, 105; Hagana report, December 10, 1947, S25/9210, CZA; "The Arab World" and "Arab World Affairs," nos. 11 and 12, December 1947 reports, S25/9051, CZA; Robert Philpot, "As Jews Evacuated from Aden Bloodbath, A Daring Mission to Rescue a Torah Scroll," *The Times of Israel*, December 11, 2017; Hamilton, *Letters from the Near East*, 25; Va'ad HaBitahon, December 11, 1947, S25/9344,

CZA; *New York Herald Tribune*, November 30 and December 15, 1947; *HaAretz*, November 30, 1947; Zaslani to Myerson, December 15, 1947, 65/4-Het Tsadi, ISA; *Mishmar*, December 17, 1947; Ben-Gurion to Gurney, December 23, 1947, S15/48; Banin to WJC, December 14, 1947, C3/18/3; both in CZA; *New York Times*, December 6, 1947; Ben-Gurion to Kaplan, December 14, 1947, S25/1700, CZA; Natan Alterman, "Magash HaKesef," *Davar*, December 19, 1947; *Jihad* declaration, n.d., FO371/61580; Eliachar to Samuel, Jan. 31, 1948, FO 371/68366; both in PRO; Zulov to Jewish Agency secretary, Jan. 20, 1948, A116/861, CZA; Karsh, *Palestine Betrayed*, 105; Hutschnecker memo, May 8, 1973, K14a/92, CZA.

72 Begin, *The Revolt*, 337–338; Sasson to Azzam Pasha, December 5, 1947, P573/1, Leo Kohn MSS, ISA; Hagana order, December 3, 1947, S25/5603, CZA; Slutzky, *Sefer Toldot HaHagana*, 1376–1379, 1414–1415; *Jerusalem Post*, December 5 and 14, 1947.

73 Bevin-Nuri Pasha interview, December 11, 1947, FO371/61797, PRO; *House of Commons*, December 11–12, 1947, Vol. 445, cols. 1221 and 1406; Cunningham-Myerson interview, December 17, 1947, A289/125, CZA; Bevin-Creech Jones memo, CP (47) 320, December 3, 1947, CAB129/22; December 4, 1947, CAB 195/5; Inverchapel to FO, December 4, 1947, FO371/61790; Bevin-Marshall talk, December 4, 1947, FO800/487; all in PRO; *FRUS, 1947*, vol. 5, 1298–99, 1301–1302.

74 FO to representatives in Arab countries, December 4, 1947, FO371/61890, PRO; Zaslani to Shertok, December 4, 1947, S44/716, CZA; Slutzky, *Sefer Toldot HaHagana*, 1358; Ben-Gurion to Jewish Agency, December 27, 1947, S25/1700, CZA; Muhammad Khalil, *The Arab states and the Arab League* (Beirut, 1962), 550–551; Philip Matttar, *The Mufti of Jerusalem* (New York, 1988), 125–126; Karsh, *Palestine Betrayed*, 96–97, 105; cabled report, December 20, 1947, 93.03/2269/27, ISA; Bell, *Terror in Zion*, 255; *House of Commons*, December 11, 1947, vol. 445, col. 1222.

75 Weizmann to Truman, November 28, 1947, WA; Truman draft to Weizmann, December 1, 1947, HSTL; Williams to Penkower, January 27, 2014 (in the author's possession); Weizmann to Truman, December 9, 1947; Truman to Weizmann, December 12, 1947; both in WA; Truman to Morgenthau, December 2, 1947, 93.03/2267/30, ISA; *FRUS, 1947*, vol. 5, 1309; Sack to Silver, December 1, 1947, Box 3, Schulson MSS.

76 Neumann, *In the Arena*, 254; *American Hebrew*, January 9, 1948.

77 Neumann, *In the Arena*, 255; Executive to Aranha, December 1, 1947, S25/5353; Executive to Evatt, December 2, 1947, S25/9667; Nathan to Shertok, December

5, 1947, S25/1545, all in CZA; Frankfurter to Epstein, December 8, 1947, 92/35-Het Tsadi, ISA; Epstein note, January 21, 1948, L35/86, CZA; Lodge to Silver, December 2, 1947, Box 3, Schulson MSS; Coupland to Weizmann, December 3, 1947, WA; Shertok to Sullivan, December 3, 1947; Sullivan to Shertok, December 5, 1947; both in 93.03/2269/29, ISA; Sullivan to Kirchwey, December 5, 1947, A427/1, CZA; Bonnet to Frankfurter, December 1, 1947, WA; Buxton to Ben-Horin, December 2, 1947, A300/16, CZA.

78 W. Millis, *Forrestal Diaries*, 344–349; Thomas W. Lippman, "The View from 1947: The CIA and the Partition of Palestine," *Middle East Journal* 61:1 (Winter 2007): 17–28.

79 Royall memo, November 24, 1947, 091 Palestine, RG 319, Box 93; Arnold to Wedemeyer, December 5, 1947, P and O 004/sec. II, Cases 19, RG 319, Box 16; both in NA; Joseph W. Bendersky, *The "Jewish Threat", Anti-Semitic Politics of the U.S. Army* (N.Y., 2000), 379.

80 Meeting, December 9, 1947, Policy Planning Staff Studies, Box 32, RG 59, SD; Meeting, December 10, 1947, Palestine, RG 218, NA.

81 Duce to Moore, December 22, 1947, S25/448, CZA. Obtaining a copy of this letter, the Jewish Agency passed it on to Shultz, whose Nation Associates featured it in a June 1948 memorandum entitled *Oil and the State Department Policy on Palestine* (New York, 1948).

82 *FRUS, 1947*, vol. 5, 1249, 1290, 1297, 1300–1301, 1315; Henderson to Lovett-Armour, December 5, 1947, 867N.01/12-547, SD.

83 *FRUS, 1947*, vol. 5, 1303–1304, Avriel, *Open the Gates!*, Chap. 24. According to the AZEC's Akzin, however, the value of U.S. weapons to the Arab states amounted to $41 million. Akzin to Welles, 93.03/66/4. ISA.

84 Celler to Forrestal, December 10, 1947, Box 23, Celler MSS; Donovan to Forrestal, December 16, 1947, 091 Palestine, Box 93, RG 319, NA; Shertok to Roosevelt Jr., December 24, 1947, 93.03/2268/21-II, ISA.

85 McClintock memo, November 13, 1947, Box 1, Rusk MSS; Merriam to Henderson, November 14, 1947, 501.BB Palestine/11-1447; Merriam to Henderson, December 11, 1947, Box 1, Rusk MSS; all in SD.

86 *FRUS, 1947*, vol. 5, 1313–1314; Linton to Jewish Agency Jerusalem, December 22, 1947, S46/590, CZA.

87 *FRUS, 1947*, vol. 5, 1304, 1312; Meirov to Shertok, December 4, 1947, Avigur 16; Ben-Gurion diary, December 2–29, 1947, 80/183/6; both in HA; Yigal Avidan, "L'khol Ish Yesh Mekhir," *Makor Rishon*, September 27, 2014, 50; Shertok to Ben-Gurion, December 12, 1947; Ben-Gurion to Shertok,

and Shertok to Ben-Gurion, both December 1, 1947; Executive to Shertok, December 20, 1947; all in S25/1700, CZA; Shertok-Rusk talk, December 19, 1947, 867N.01/12-1947; Shertok to Armour, December 26, 1947, 867N.01/12-2647; both in SD; Klarman cable, December 27, 1947, 4/6/195-Peh, Jabotinsky Archives; FO371/61855. PRO; Abba Naor, "HaYonim El Arubotehem," *MiBifnim*, 13:3 (November 1948): 496–501; Zeev (Venya) Hadari and Zeev Tsahor, *Oniyot O Medina* (Tel Aviv, n.d.); Danny Goldman and Michael J.K. Walsh, "Stranded in Bogas, Cyprus, The Affais of the Pans, January 1948," *Journal of Cyprus Studies* 15 (2009): 41–64; Slutzky, *Sefer Toldot HaHagana*, 1184–1188.

88 *Hadassah Newsletter*, January 1948; *Palestine Post*, December 31, 1947; Report, December 30, 1947, S25/4037, CZA; Benny Morris, *1948, The First Arab-Israeli War* (New Haven, CT, 2008), 102–103; Slutzky, *Sefer Toldot HaHagana*, 1383, 1543; Karsh, *Palestine Betrayed*, 83, 106; Gurney-Myerson interview, December 29, 1947, S25/7725, CZA; *FRUS, 1947*, vol. 5, 1322–1328.

9. Civil War

As the year 1948 dawned on Palestine, tragedy roiled beneath the surface. The mandatory's casualty list for the past month of December had reported the killing of 204 Jews, 208 Arabs, 6 other civilians, 12 soldiers, 2 Jordan Frontier Force members, 1 Arab policeman, and 12 Jewish Supernumerary Policemen, with 407 persons seriously wounded and 593 slightly. Scant hope existed for a peaceful resolution in the land, so riven with conflict, as the Arab world immovably rejected the yishuv's appeal for compromise and its claim to national sovereignty. Hagana forces repulsed an Arab attack on Tel Aviv, inflicting severe casualties, and killed at least four Arabs (the police figure, although the Hagana claimed many more) in retaliation for the murder of forty-one Jews in Haifa a few days earlier. Four Jewish passengers were wounded when Arab snipers opened up on a bus traveling from Jerusalem's center to the Givat Shaul area; a Jewish bus was attacked in Haifa, while three Jews were wounded in that city when Arabs blasted a cold storage plant. Thirty-five Negev settlements, comprising over 6,000 Jews, were completely cut off and faced the possibility of "certain death." Excoriating the mandatory government for not distinguishing between attackers and those attacked, Ben-Gurion declared that the yishuv would defend itself and the frontiers of the Jewish state in this "savage war against our very existence."

A Stern Group bombing on the 4th of the Najada and Futuwwa guerilla center in Jaffa killed more than 70. Three days earlier, Fawzi al-Kaukji officially established the Arab Liberation Army (ALA) under the Arab League's aegis, calling from Syria for "jihad to help the persecuted Arabs of Palestine." "Only a change of policy" could stop violence, declared AHC secretary Emil Ghoury. He added in a frank interview with foreign correspondents that the nucleus of a militia of more than 24,000 for the "liberation" of Palestine had already been organized locally, to be joined by volunteers from other Arab countries for a war that would start "at the convenient opportunity."[1]

Jerusalem, "which has been, and must remain the heart of the Jewish people" in Ben-Gurion's recent phrase to the Histadrut Executive Committee, and under Arab siege since the UN partition vote, faced particular strife. Up to January 11, a total of 150 persons were officially reported to have been killed there, and at least 350 known to have sustained injuries. The central post office ceased operating because Jewish and Arab employees feared attacks from each other. Arab threats that Jews leave their homes on pain of death led to Lower Katamon being almost entirely evacuated. Jewish supply convoys under Arab attack failed to reach the metropolis for three successive days; constant shooting from Sheikh Jarrah against buses led to a considerable loss of Jewish lives in the vicinity of the Hadassah Hospital and the Hebrew University on Mt. Scopus. The mandatory authorities were finally persuaded to secure that road, enabling the burial at the Jewish cemetery on the Mount of Olives of fifty-three bodies accumulated over one week. Firing soon resumed, however, leading to eight more Jewish wounded and a nurse killed; a Magen David Adom ambulance carrying six of those wounded to Hadassah was shot at from a military transport containing soldiers of the Arab Legion.

Snipers regularly fired from the Haram esh-Sharif, other mosques, and churches on the 1,700 Jews living in the Old City. Arab barricades at Jaffa Gate prevented some 200 Jews from reaching their homes there. On the 3rd, a bomb enabled Arabs to enter the Warsaw Houses and, before being driven out by the Hagana, succeed in killing one Jew and wounding four. House-to-house army searches that followed led to the finding of a small quantity of arms and the arrest of fifteen in the Jewish Quarter. Four days later, a Jewish Agency liaison officer with the British army "strenuously" recommended to his superiors that at least the young children be evacuated, then raised the additional "presumptuous" thought that perhaps all the Jewish inhabitants, most demoralized, should leave.[2]

An Agency liaison representative in Jerusalem got the impression that the army wished to take great care not to offend the Arabs, rather than restore law and order. Indeed, Lt. Col. T. McLeod, commander of the Second Battalion of the Highland Light Infantry, suggested that the Hagana reduce its forces in the Old City, populated by 20,000 Arabs. The British officer in charge of Jewish Supernumerary Police in the Galilee turned down a request that armored cars be permitted for escort duties on the frequently attacked main northern road. He claimed that this would only annoy the Arabs, who had none; Arab snipers could not be stopped from shooting whenever they pleased; and Jewish bus service should stop, since too many people would be killed otherwise.[3]

Hearing Bevin privately declare that HMG was determined to withdraw from Palestine "so that Arabs and Jews should remain alone to face each other and the hard facts," Victor Khoury informed Lebanese foreign minister Riad Solh that official circles in London thought a solution of the question would be attained on the basis of a federal state. Nor was Beeley discouraged about the current situation, provided that the conflict could be kept within the land holy to the Jewish, Muslim, and Christian faiths. During conversations in London, he expressed the feeling that the number of local fighting men on both sides would be "relatively small," and that war would force the Jews to make concessions in the Galilee and the Negev. Attlee's government was anxious to begin talks with the UN bodies on Palestine, Bevin's primary advisor on Palestine added, and still hoped to end the Mandate at any early date, depending on the wishes of the five-man UN Commission.[4]

Bunche, serving now as Principal Secretary to the Commission, foresaw a number of considerable difficulties in trying to achieve its primary tasks. While the British were "clearly" not entitled to tell its members when they could arrive in Palestine, he asserted in a memorandum to Lie on January 5, the Commission might well be confronted with "a tendency toward indefiniteness" on London's part with regard to dates and specific commitments, and an attitude of "studied aloofness" with respect to implementing the details of GA Resolution 181 (II). Establishing liaison with Palestine's Arabs posed a "tough problem," including the question as to what security the Commission members might have to offer not only for themselves, but for those willing to deal with it if the personal risks were not "prohibitive," Perhaps the most challenging test would be the absence of an adequate armed escort force for the delimitation of boundaries, given the opposition of irate Arab villagers, while it would be "very unwise" to accept a probable Hagana offer to provide such a force. Arab non-cooperation would force the Commission to function, for the time being at least, as a virtual government, thus requiring a much larger Secretariat to assist that body. Soon after arriving in Palestine, Bunche ended, the Commission should make it clear to the peoples of Palestine and of the region generally that it intended to objectively fulfill in every respect the Mandate given it by the UN whatever support it received, confident of success in completing the tasks assigned to it within the time limits specified, and to the ultimate benefit of both Arabs and Jews.[5]

Lie strongly believed that the partition plan should be carried out, and thought that with the two chief antagonists of what observers termed the Cold War in Europe between Washington and Moscow at least on the same side in a major crisis, the UN would have a chance to act with full effect and authority. In this spirit, he stated to the UN Palestine Commission members at their first public meeting on January 9, at which Lisicky was chosen chairman, that they were entitled to assume that the Security Council would use "every necessary power" to back them up. The Assembly resolution, taking account of likely armed Arab resistance, had requested the Council to "determine as a threat to the peace, breach of the peace or act of aggression, in accordance with Article 39 of the Charter, any attempt to alter by force the settlement envisaged by this resolution." Privately, Lie initiated Secretariat studies on various possible ways in which an international force might be provided, sounding out smaller member nations about contributing contingents to a UN force and drafting a statement (which he never issued) for limited infantry units from each of the Council's Big Five powers. He also had legal advisers begin preparing a paper which argued that the Council had the power to undertake the responsibilities requested by Resolution 181 (II).

The Agency quickly appointed Shertok to provide any information that the Commission might require, as did London by designating Cadogan, but the Arab Higher Committee officially responded that the resolution, obtained under US pressure with various delegations, "is null and void," and that the UN had no jurisdiction to recommend partition. Considering the Balfour Declaration, the Mandate, or any imposition of "international alien immigrants" on their country to be "an act of aggression and invasion," it concluded that the Arabs of Palestine would never submit or yield to any power going to Palestine to enforce the resolution of November 29, 1947: "The only way to establish partition is first to wipe them out—man, woman and child."[6]

The State Department's serious doubts about partition surfaced in hints given a few days earlier when Eban and Epstein called on the

Division of Near Eastern Affairs to elicit further U.S. support towards its implementation. Very much concerned with the type of incidents now taking place in Palestine, such as the December attacks relating to the Consolidated Refinery in Haifa, Henderson warned that a continuation of terrorist activities which resulted in the killing of innocent people would have a "brutalizing" effect, and cause many to have serious doubts as to whether the Arabs or the Jews were "sufficiently mature" to govern themselves. Replying to Eban's requests regarding Jewish immigration and security prior to the departure of British forces, Rusk stressed that the establishment of a *modus vivendi* between the Jews and the Arabs was the most important issue for consideration at this time. He believed that his guests were well aware of the many legal difficulties attendant on further deliberation of the Palestine problem in the Security Council. Successful implementation of Resolution 181 (II) "hinged on" the working out of details with the Jews, the British authorities, and the Arabs. For this reason, urged the director of the Office of Special Political Affairs, both Jews and Arabs should attempt to settle the problems regarding Palestine as best they could by themselves, and should only fall back on UN action "as a last resort."[7]

The High Commissioner's major concern at that moment was the likely illicit import of arms and munitions by the two contending parties. On January 1, 406 of 537 passengers evaded arrest when the *HaUmot HaMeuhadot* (the United Nations) beached at Nahariya, but the two *Pans*' arrival in Cyprus the same day had definitively indicated the Royal Navy's failure to stem the unauthorized refugee transports. Now Cunningham sought from Creech Jones, with a copy of his telegram sent on January 2 to the embassy in Washington and all of HMG's postings in the Near Eastern capitals, information on arms shipments so that suspect vessels might be intercepted when entering Palestine's territorial waters and directed into Haifa for special examination. Intelligence sources showed that the Jews were trying to buy munitions in the United States, Poland, and Czechoslovakia. Their wealth, influence, and "the sympathy with which their cause is widely regarded," he noted, indicated that they would continue to export weapons from the United States surreptitiously despite the arms embargo, while countries in the Soviet zone would probably not be deterred from this trade. The Arab states, he added, were providing weapons and intended to smuggle more across the land frontiers to Palestine's Arabs. Reports, which might well be exaggerated, spoke of 10,000 rifles having already been sent to the Arabs in Palestine, with a greater number on the way. Hopefully, accurate intelligence would enable large consignments to be intercepted and seized from those engaged in the clandestine endeavor.[8]

The accidental dropping of one of twenty-six cases being loaded the next day as "used industrial machinery" aboard the *SS Executor* in Jersey City's Pier F, disclosing that the cases contained an estimated 65,000 lbs. of TNT and another fifty-one cases ready for shipment on the same ship to Jewish firms in Palestine, quickly corroborated Cunningham's fears. Traced to Philip Alper and a few others, U.S. authorities also seized fifty-nine tons of war surplus explosives from a firm in New Jersey and from trucks traveling in New York State. Press reports indicated that another seventy-three tons were said to be on the high seas. Two weeks earlier, a communication from Hagana head commander Galili to Eliyahu Saharov in Europe, with Ben-Gurion's approval, had succeeded in obtaining a shipment of desperately needed light weapons and bullets from Italy to the Tel Aviv port.

Realizing now that the U.S. disclosure threatened a much larger *rekhesh* (purchase) operation that Haim Slavin had masterminded, the Jewish Agency formally stated that all such transportation was done in full conformity with American law. Further, it was proud to give aid to the embattled Jews of Palestine threatened by the ex-Mufti, who had collaborated with Hitler in the destruction of 6,000,000 Jews in Europe, and who now called the Arab world to carry on his work of "massacre and extermination" in defiance of the UN partition vote. Intensive negotiations behind the scenes ultimately led to the arrest of Alper and five young men, who were put on probation for one year with the stipulation that they did not have to report to a probation officer but were not to violate any law during that period. The sympathetic judge ruled that they were trying "to provide means of defense to otherwise helpless people," but FBI surveillance put an end to these shipments.[9]

The *yishuv*, by now an organized, motivated, homogeneous, and semi-industrial emerging state, appeared ready for the first stages of war. With the aid of machine tools purchased in the United States. between 1944 and 1946, secret Hagana factories were producing two- and three-inch mortars, submachine guns, grenades, and bullets in large numbers. Its 35,000 members, including 2,100 Palmah soldiers (and 1,000 reservists), would be reorganized and expanded in these months to consist of twelve brigades. Most of the over 25,000 Palestinian Jews who had served in the British Army during World War II contributed vital experience to the Hagana. Further, in emergency the Irgun's 2,000–3,000 members and the Stern Group's 300–500 fighters might coordinate their operations with this formidable militia force.

Yet Ben-Gurion, most responsible for the Hagana's transformation after the war and keenly aware that the armies of the Arab states posed the threat of destruction to Palestinian Jewry, had to contend with an unavoidable reality: artillery, tanks, armored cars, and combat aircraft were all lacking. Ammunition for Hagana ranks was also in short supply, some fifty rounds per rifle and six to seven hundred rounds per machine gun. Not surprisingly, shortly before the key UN vote Galili declared to colleagues on the newly formed Defense Committee that the Hagana sought to maintain a purely defensive policy, retaliation preferably limited against Arab perpetrators, so that "the hostilities do not expand over time or over a wide area." Huge sums of cash had to be obtained quickly if Avriel, Saharov, Tuvya Arazi, and others engaged in *rekhesh* abroad were to succeed in the purchase of heavy weaponry to meet the decisive battles soon to be waged for statehood.[10]

The country's Arab community, overwhelmingly agricultural villagers loyal to family, clan, and occasionally region, could hardly compete with the *yishuv* in terms of a burgeoning modern infrastructure, national bodies, weapons, and trained military manpower. Montgomery had posited at the end of December that the Jews would "in the long run" be "thrown out of Palestine" unless they came to terms with the Arabs, but fissures along social, political, and religious lines left the country's 1.2–1.3 million Arabs without a unified command and control. Unable to overcome the trauma of the Arab Revolt (1936–1939), their cause had been further weakened by Haj Amin's flight from Palestine in October 1937, his support in April 1941 of the pro-Nazi revolt in Iraq, and his subsequent alliance with the Third Reich during World War II.

The former Mufti had good reason to be wary of the Arab League, which rejected the proposal for his leading a Palestinian government in exile and/or over the entire country, and insisted (as Eban informed Bunche) that all non-Palestinian commanders be responsible to Damascus except for the AHC's appointment of Abd al-Qadir al-Husseini to oversee the Jerusalem area. Dismissive of Kaukji as an old mercenary, he hoped for 10,000 Muslim Brotherhood volunteers, and relied in the meantime on lightly armed bands of 200–500 local fighters each, notably that of al-Qadir al-Husseini (Haj Amin's favorite nephew) in the Jerusalem hills, Hassan Salameh's in the villages around Lydda and the Judean foothills to the east, and Abu Ibrahim al-Saghir's in lower Galilee. These bands rarely cooperated with each other, however, and tended to alienate the peasant villagers with their heavy-handed, often brutal, behavior. In addition, Haj Amin's continued terrorism against adversaries, Husseini gunmen killing some prominent members of the political opposition, drove the Nashashibi faction and its pro-Abdullah allies out of political life. Under these joined circumstances, Palestine's Arabs entered the war bereft of an effective, national military organization.[11]

Nor had the Arab League leadership, for all its resolutions and public pronouncements, resolved internal divisions *vis-à-vis* Palestine. Baghdad supported Amman's designs; Cairo, Damascus, and Riyadh did not. The Arab states were unlikely to go the length of war, Middle East specialist Elizabeth Monroe reported for *The Scotsman* after a recent tour of the region. Home concerns came first, Ibn Saud disclosing that the pressure put upon him by the other Arab countries to oppose American oil interests on account of U.S. support for Zionism had been "heavy but unavailing." Egyptians engaged in diplomatic talks with London about the constitution of the Sudan were thinking in terms of their "minimum requirements" for resuming talks on a wider treaty. Abdullah's uncertainty when pressed by League representatives to support a joint invasion gave Sasson reason to write the Jordan monarch that his annexing the Palestine "triangle" could work in tandem with the Jewish Agency's partition endorsement. (Shertok privately approved the principle of continuing Jewish financial and diplomatic support for Abdullah—provided that the king could be trusted.)

The regular Arab armies, totaling about 100,000, were poorly trained and not unified as to weaponry or command. As for volunteers, Hagana intelligence reported that up to January 2 the total number joining the ALA in Damascus came to 15,733, but only a small number actually had received training; the balance were men whose enthusiasm "may not survive continued bickering and indecision of the leaders." Moreover, the League, with Solh backing Kaukji, objected to Haj Amin's wish to institute an Arab government in Palestine under his direction.[12]

HMG's policy at this juncture with regard to the GA recommendation on Palestine, characterized by opposition leader Oliver Stanley in private conversation as a "cacophony," remained difficult to ascertain and assess. Horowitz concluded from extensive personal talks that the Colonial Office, favoring partition, wished to end the Mandate "decently" in "dignity," and with as little friction as possible. Whitehall and the military echelons, on the other hand, were greatly anxious about its impact on oil, bases, and relations with the larger Arab world. Pressed by Ambassador Kirkbride to approve Abdullah's claims and his wish to intervene contrary to the Arab League's decisions, the Foreign Office implicitly agreed by replying on January 11 that the king should be given "vague generalizations" about supporting his desire to see "a stable and democratic settlement" in Palestine.

At the same time, Agency Arabist Ezra Danin reported to Sasson about a plan attributed to Brigadier I. N. Clayton, liaison with the Arab League at HMG's Embassy in Cairo, about the League covering the expenses of the Arab Legion, which it expected would occupy all of Palestine. The Jews would then be offered a settlement on the lines of the Morrison Plan, with the British holding on only to air bases in Jordan. Clayton and Beeley confided to U.S. Ambassador Jones their hope that the Security Council would do its utmost to prevent the spread of fighting in the Middle East, leaving the two Palestine parties to their own military resources while the Council in effect would "quarantine" Palestine and the UN Commission suspend its work until Arabs and Jews reached a sufficient measure of agreement. The Palestine Arabs and the Arab states could then be persuaded to recognize the area of the Jewish state, moderate Jews also accepting more "practical" boundaries. "It might take two years" for the contenders to "tire sooner or later of the conflict which they both seem to be courting so assiduously," Clayton said; Beeley was inclined to think that it might not be so long.[13]

In Palestine, despair began to take hold in the highest government circles. No government could always maintain law and order, Cunningham told Ben-Gurion, and he did not wish to harm Jews or Arabs. Yet the Hagana attack on the Hotel Semiramis in Katamon on January 5, intended against the Najada headquarters but mistakenly blowing up the wrong wing of the hotel and killing fourteen civilians, including Spanish vice consul Manuel Travesedo, led him to have the Public Information Office condemn the Hagana's taking credit for this "dastardly and wholesale murder of innocent people." He urged the Colonial Office to arrange the early appointment of a governor for

Jerusalem and for some international armed force, believing it unthinkable that the Holy City should just be left to become "a cockpit of internecine strife" and "lapse into a pitched battlefield." Writing to former High Commissioner Harold MacMichael, Palestine Chief Justice William Fitzgerald, fearing "an appalling conflagration," agreed with the Jewish Agency's claim that the sooner the UN Commission arrived to negotiate the British departure from power the better, greatly fearing that the situation would develop into a Spanish Civil War and declaring that HMG's "sacred trust in the Holy Land" should not end thus.

Gurney's advisor for security affairs felt compelled to advise the International Committee of the Red Cross that in view of the present "state of insecurity" in Palestine, its earlier approved visit to detention camps not take place, at least for the time being. Authoritative Whitehall sources reported on the 15th about the Palestine government's recommendation that Britain surrender the Mandate six weeks earlier than the planned date of May 15, worrying that the whole machine of civil administration might collapse before then because of continuing strife. Half of the mandatory's thirty-two departments had already been immobilized for weeks at a time owing to insecurity, and less than one month's supply remained of certain types of fuel oils essential for transport because of the closure of the Haifa refineries after the massacre of Jewish workers there.[14]

"The situation is deteriorating daily," wrote Captain Philip Brutton home on January 10, the vacuum created by a steady British withdrawal inevitably filled with blood. An Irgun bomb killed fourtenn Arabs and injured nineteen outside Jaffa's town hall on the 5th. Another two days later at Jerusalem's Jaffa Gate killed seventeen and wounded over fifty. More than two hundred ALA men crossed the Syrian border on the 9th and attacked Kfar Szold and Kibbutz Dan in the Upper Galilee; stout defense and a British troop of armored cars and the Irish Guards sent by MacMillan beat back this first attack on a *yishuv* settlement. The same day, eleven Hagana men were killed, one of them decapitated, in an ambush near Gan Yavneh.

On the 14th, a thousand Arabs under al-Qadir al-Husseini's command attacked Kfar Etzion, largest of the four *kibbutzim* in the bloc called Gush Etzion; 130 Arabs were killed but the settlement's ammunition and medical supplies were low. Hagana reinforcements left late the following night from Jerusalem, twenty-eight kilometers away. Refusing a few times to abort their mission, the presence of this Mountain Platoon was discovered near Surif on January 16, five kilometers from Gush Etzion. After a battle that lasted seven hours against hundreds of armed Arabs who descended from the surrounding hills, the entire relief force of thirty-five under the command of Danny Mass, having run out of bullets began throwing stones at their attackers, was massacred, their bodies brutally mutilated and stripped by the local villagers. One of the dead fighters was still clutching a stone in his hand. British forces, which had made no effort to stop the fighting, later transferred the dead for a communal burial in Kfar Etzion.[15]

Not prepared to go "like sheep to the slaughter" as Ben-Gurion put it to Cunningham, the *yishuv*'s leaders charged that the mandatory government's declared "neutrality" was actually designed to work in the Arabs' favor. The Hagana officer responsible for the Hotel Semiramis bombing had been removed, Ben-Gurion privately told the High Commissioner, and the Agency publicly regretted the loss of innocent lives, but the government had said or done nothing about the Arab Legionnaires who mowed down fourteen Jews at Beit Nabala on December 14, the massacre of the thirty-five sent to reinforce Kfar Etzion, or the killings of the eleven near Gan Yavneh.

Notwithstanding the presence of over 80,000 troops and secret British military intelligence reports (obtained by the Hagana) disclosing accurate knowledge of foreign invaders and their exact deployment, 10,000 Arabs, some under German officer command and including fascist Yugoslav Muslims, crossed into Palestine with little difficulty. Arms searches of Jews continued despite Gurney's promise to Myerson that they would be stopped, V. Fox-Strangways of the Chief Secretary's office declaring that approval had been given for *two* licensed weapons to be carried on every Jaffa-Tel Aviv highway Egged bus to Jerusalem on condition that no other arms were held on the vehicle, and that searches might be carried out at any time to insure that this condition was observed. Armored cars were refused, roads not protected, and Jewish weapons for self-defense confiscated. The Arab Legion remained in Palestine, also absorbing most of the 3,200 members of the disbanded Jordan Frontier Force, and the Jews in Jerusalem's Old City were still held hostage under Arab blockade.[16]

French intelligence sources informed the Jewish Agency on the 13th that Clayton had recently concluded arrangements with Solh stipulating that British forces would leave Jewish settlements in the Galilee, giving a free hand to Kaukji after concentrating its troops in Haifa. The following day, London announced that it would honor its treaty pledges of sending considerable armaments to Egypt, Iraq, and Jordan, leading a concerned Royall to advise Forrestal that such deliveries should be "actively" observed in light of the American arms embargo and U.S. interests in the area.

Cadogan informed the UN Commission that the functions and authority of Palestinian civil government had suffered a "very severe diminution," and "it would be optimistic" to hope for any improvement in view of recent developments. When ARAMCO could not fulfill its contract obligation to pay Ibn Saud a great amount of British gold sovereigns, he agreed to accept dollars at the rate of exchange of the "free market" in Jedda, 30 per cent above the official rate, HMG by this simple manipulation greatly increasing that monarch's income. Without offering indisputable evidence, British representatives repeated that "hundreds of militant Communists" were aboard the two *Pans*. Epstein countered by providing relevant facts to newspapermen, endorsing Shultz's suggestion to have the Nation Associates document a record of British actions, and informing Tsarapkin that the Jewish commonwealth would stay "strictly neutral" in the present "complex international circumstances."[17]

The U.S. State Department appreciated Great Britain's request, officially transmitted on January 5, to take all possible steps for the "common interest" of both countries to both "reassure the Arabs" and persuade the Jews, "even though it means the exercise by the latter of considerable restraint," to make good in deeds their words of friendship to the Arabs. Ever since the past May, the department had received the sobriquet "Foggy Bottom," not only for the low-lying neighborhood on the Potomac River to which State moved, but also for its use of a specialized lexicon which allowed diplomats to disagree while still maintaining the façade of courtesy and cordiality. On Palestine, however, its mandarins left little doubt that they were united against the partition vote and in search of an alternative.

Already on January 2, Henderson and Rusk had cleared a summary by two officers in the Near Eastern department recommending the rejection of any unilateral U.S. action towards implementing partition. They also proposed considering either a Security Council request of an advisory opinion from the International Court of Justice or the United States initiating a call in the Council of a Special Session to reconsider the question if it became apparent that enforcement of partition would be impossible without the use of outside force, and opposing any further Soviet expansion into Palestine. Given Arab anti-American sentiment arising from U.S. support at the GA of partition and its effect on oil supplies for Washington's European Recovery Program (also called the Marshall Plan) against Soviet expansion, the memorandum added that discussions should be initiated at a high level with ARAMCO officials over proposals that might be made to reincorporate in some country other than the United States, without any pressure put on the oil companies to take any action which they regard as "a poor risk" in view of the existing political situation in the Middle East. Time was pressing, for five days later Herschel Johnson had urged State to determine, in conjunction with the military branches, what action the United States should take to provide the Council with armed forces in implementation of Article 43 of the UN Charter.[18]

War Department intelligence chief Col. Robert McDowell expressed to Epstein and Eban his view that Palestine's Jews, whom he doubted could hold the Negev, were the attackers, but it was Forrestal who took the lead in Washington's anti-Zionist camp. On the 6th, the Secretary of Defense, hearing from the president of Socony Vacuum that his company and associate companies Texas, Standard of California and Standard of New Jersey would suspend work on the oil pipeline and collateral developments in Saudi Arabia because of the "disturbed condition" in Palestine and the indications of its continuance, expressed his deep concerns about access to Middle East oil for U.S. requirements in war and in peace. The same day, he sent Truman a memorandum about the vital strategic need for American air bases in the Mediterranean and its environs "against nation X."

Informed by Henderson of "the great pressure" that had been put on him and on Lovett to obtain votes for partition, confirmed by Kermit Roosevelt when asserting in the *Middle East Journal* that U.S. interests in the Middle East and those of political Zionism were in "conflict," Forrestal took the opportunity at a Cabinet meeting on January 16 to emphasize that the American public should be told about the "overriding importance" of access to Middle East oil reserves. Within a week, he drafted a paper for Lovett about the need for a bipartisan foreign policy, continuing the arms embargo, objecting to unilateral implementation of partition by the United States, and not allowing the situation either to do "permanent injury to our relations with the Moslem world" or to end in a "stumble into war."[19]

A luncheon which Forrestal gave for Brooke Claxton, Canada's Minister of Defense, at the Pentagon on the 14th, attended by Chief of the Army Eisenhower, Secretaries John L. Sullivan (Navy), W. Stewart Symington (Air), and Royall (Army), Admiral William D. Leahy and others on the Joint Chiefs of Staff, and Joint Staff director General Alfred Gruenther, reflected their shared grave concern over the outbreak of "serious" local hostilities in Palestine. Eisenhower estimated the probable need of four U.S. divisions to prevent the overrunning of the Jewish areas by the Arabs; otherwise, the UN would encounter so severe a defeat that "it could scarcely survive." Yet the oil supplies of the Arabian peninsula would be lost and the Arab League might also then gravitate into the Soviet orbit. If, on the other hand, the U.S. did not take action to support the Jews, the Russians might seize the opportunity to do so, allowing them to control not only the greatest oil reserves in the world, but the whole strategic situation from the Persian Gulf to the Central Mediterranean.

The best way, Eisenhower noted, would be for the United States to send about six divisions to the Middle East and keep them there permanently, but that was completely out of the question even if the army had the divisions to send, which it did not. Two or three divisions would still require partial mobilization to take place, causing a "tremendous hubbub," which would be very likely to develop into a strong antisemitic feeling in the country. None disagreed with Eisenhower's assessment or offered "a way out," but Claxton found the tone of the conversation, sympathetic towards British difficulties, "hostile to Jewish aspirations in Palestine and at times verged on being anti-Semitic in general." Zionist claims were summarily dismissed as propaganda, with the importance of Middle East oil, which Forrestal said constituted two-thirds of the world's known oil reserves, uppermost in their minds at most points in the conversation.[20]

Truman, who had given Forrestal permission to make an "informal attempt" to secure Republican agreement on the broad principle that the Palestine issue should be above America's domestic political considerations, faced two related questions on this topic at the White House news conference on January 15. In a brief reply, he thought that American troops would not be sent to Palestine, but an international police force created to serve with the United Nations plan, "to which all of us are working." He favored whatever was necessary for the UN to use and "enforce its mandates." The President, wrote reporter RTE to his editor, thus "reaffirmed" the official policy of the United States to support the partition decision, and Marshall had not publicly dissented from this view. Off-the-record, RTE went on, the Secretary of State did not respond to a letter which he had received from Wedemeyer against partition, and Hilldring still thought that the GA resolution was "the right and the only solution." The UN "ought to stick" to that decision, Hilldring told this reporter, for "if half a dozen nations can frustrate the decision of the United Nations then where is the United Nations?" Unless some bipartisan agreement arose on Palestine—"a remote possibility at best," it appeared to RTE that on the basis of Truman's statement the use of a UN force, rather than removal of the arms embargo, would seem to be the course.[21]

On January 20, Director of State's Policy Planning Staff George Kennan presented to Marshall and Lovett his colleagues' recommendation that the United States take no further initiative in carrying out or aiding partition. Memorandum PPS/19 opposed sending any forces for implementation; favored continuing the arms embargo; and advised that if the partition plan showed no prospect of success without the use of outside armed forces, the United States should propose that the matter go back to the General Assembly. Given the present "irreconcilable differences" between the two rival sides, also leading to widespread rioting in the Arab world and the loss of U.S. prestige in the region, it noted the danger of serious unrest and instability which Moscow would exploit there and throughout the troubled region unless a workable solution could be developed. Support of partition would jeopardize U.S. air base rights, oil so vital to the success of the Marshall Plan, and American educational institutions in the area. The Jewish state's ability to survive "for any considerable period of time" against the Arab states, the approximately 400,000 Arabs resident in the proposed new Jewish state, and in lesser measure from Muslim neighbors was "improbable."

Given these circumstances, the American UN delegation should cooperate in working out any possible settlement designed to encourage "pacific settlement" between Palestine's Arabs and Jews, or investigate the possibilities of other suggested solutions such as a federal state or trusteeship, which would "not require" outside armed force for implementation.

The entire issue, in the staff's opinion, was not a proper question to refer to the International Court. Henderson and Grady approved this change of policy, Kennan added, but Rusk had yet to see this final draft or commit himself to it.[22]

The next day, after agreeing "in general" with the conclusions set down by Forrestal in the memo on bipartisan foreign policy, Lovett showed him PPS/19. Lovett's supplementary comments gave Forrestal the impression that State was "seriously embarrassed and handicapped" by Niles's activities in going directly to the President on matters involving Palestine. Forrestal responded that Marshall had to take on the issue firmly, removing it from the realm of domestic politics. Lovett in turn disclosed that a telephone call to him from Niles, relaying New York lawyer Morris Ernst's hope that the arms embargo would be lifted, as well as a New York Congressman's inquiry about Truman's stand on the matter, led him to ask Connelly to give a message to the President requesting that he release no such statement without first advising the State Department.[23]

Rusk's response to PPS/19 emphasized that a major reversal of U.S. policy, requiring the approval of Truman and leading Congressmen, had to delineate a "new situation" that had arisen after November 29, 1947, which mandated reconsideration. That could arise, he suggested, if the two provisional governments were not constituted by April 1, 1948, as stipulated in Resolution 181 (II). Whether the Security Council was entitled to use armed force to carry out a GA *recommendation* (his emphasis) remained a serious question, and the United States should have "no hesitation" in criticizing the United Kingdom's "present irresponsible attitude" in not cooperating with the UN and rejecting in effect the Assembly resolution. Given that large-scale fighting in Palestine would ensue were no solution reached and the British withdrew, he suggested consideration of a UN trusteeship for the whole of Palestine, with the United States taking its fair share of the fiscal and security responsibility for the trust territory.

Kennan, in turn, took issue with Rusk's criticism of the British and his proposing talks with the United Kingdom, pro-partition nations, and more moderate Muslim governments in order to persuade the Arab states not to frustrate the GA resolution. He wished to extricate the United States from the "ugly realities" of the Palestine problem, the inevitable state of violence to come mainly due to "the Jewish leaders and organizations" who had pushed "so persistently" for their objectives. A trusteeship that Rusk had suggested might arise, Kennan concluded, but a "hands off" policy at present, which might indeed involve a loss of prestige both for the United States and the UN, would be worth it "if we can thereby regain the full independence and dignity of our position in this confused and tragic question."[24]

Rusk's sharp condemnation of Britain's stance at the UN found a ready echo in Bunche's comments at the Commission's meetings in the third week of January. He found Cadogan's statement that the group could arrive only two weeks before the mandatory's departure and not be permitted use of any British members of the Palestine Administrative Service an "indefensible" position. Asked how the UN body could recruit administrators in two weeks' time to take over when the mandatory administration left, Cadogan's reply that he did not know revealed, in Bunche's phrase, the Britisher's "sheepishness" at its greatest. Even the pro-British Lisicky told Cadogan privately that adhering to that time table was "beyond human possibility." The British also informed Bunche that they could not open up a port to unlimited Jewish immigration, as stipulated for February 1 in the partition resolution, because it was "impossible to lay down the Mandate piecemeal," and it would introduce the "most serious deterioration" in the security situation in Palestine and hamper both the maintenance of administration and the withdrawal process at large.

Bunche had every intention, Austin reported to Marshall, of urging the Commission to expose the British position through a first report to the Council at the month's end, and to demand that a "showdown" take place before the members left for London and Palestine. The Commission members decided to give Cadogan an opportunity to answer pointed questions before judgment were passed, but they did resolve that their report would point out the impossibility of meeting the April 1 deadline for the establishment of provisional governments because the United Kingdom would not permit the Commission to arrive until shortly before the British exited Palestine.[25]

The State Department's plans received public attention when James Reston, reporting on January 27 in the *New York Times*, revealed the concern of Defense and State that Truman's partition endorsement was "influenced by the political strength of pro-Zionist organizations in key political centers of this country." The title of his article,

"Bipartisan Policy on Holy Land Seen," echoed the thrust of Forrestal's continuing efforts to halt this influence. Worried that the same groups might convince the Administration to implement the November resolution by sending troops to Palestine, the newspaper's chief diplomatic Washington correspondent went on, the two departments insisted that U.S. strategic interests in the Middle East should not be jeopardized by current policy. The "hostile Moslem response" to partition threatened oil, which Forrestal had testified before the House Armed Services Committee's Special Subcommittee on Petroleum was in short supply, so vital to the European Recovery Program. The Administration was not backing away at present from partition, Reston noted, but both Defense and State were strongly opposed to any action that might antagonize the Arab world.[26]

Eleanor Roosevelt saw this approach as placing the UN's future position at stake. A recent two-part series in the *New York Post* had pointed to Henderson as the "man in the saddle: Arabian style" dictating an anti-Zionist policy, and another in the *New York Herald Tribune* reported State's instructing the American Consulate in Jerusalem to take up the passports of any American citizens found engaged in the fighting, but Reston had now linked State and Defense as firm opponents of the partition plan. The United States, which had "led" in the acceptance of the UN majority report, should support an international police force, Roosevelt wrote to Truman two days later, and provide "modern implements of war such as tanks, airplanes, etc." which were "essential to the control of Arabs." Britain sought only "to please the Arabs," in her opinion, and the UN had to be strengthened now as an instrument of peace. In like vein, Acting UN Secretary-General Byron Price had urged the U.S. delegation to back an international force to carry out partition, while Welles and American Association for the United Nations (AAUN) director Clark Eichelberger also championed dropping the American arms embargo, each separately viewing the issue as a crucial test for the success of the UN. Truman promptly replied to Roosevelt that he and Marshall were trying to work on an implementation plan, while agreeing that her words about the British "were correct as they can be. Britain's role in the Near East… has not changed in a hundred years."[27]

While State and Defense pressed their joint effort to undermine the U.S. commitment to partition, Myerson launched her own drive across the United States to obtain Palestinian Jewry's urgent need for $25–$30 million within two to three weeks for the purchase of weapons. Thanks to Montor, she first appeared on the evening of January 25, two days after her arrival from Jerusalem in the worst snow blizzard New York City had seen in years, before the General Assembly in Chicago of the Council of Jewish Federations and Welfare Funds. Her dramatic eye-witness description of the *yishuv*'s will to fight "until the very end," together with her charge that American Jews could decide if it or Haj Amin would emerge victorious—"don't be too late," electrified the audience. Hearing that they could help participate in the joy of laying "the cornerstone of the Jewish State," making their people's millennial dream a reality, they cheered, wept, and began to declare financial pledges. Community donations came in rapidly to United Jewish Appeal offices. Morgenthau's strong support, first with some recalcitrant JDC Executives and then in parlor meetings across the major cities, and Montor's dedicated tenacity would be pivotal in the weeks ahead. For Beeley, however, Myerson's press conference at Lake Success the following day, appealing in effect for U.S. military intervention in favor of the Jews and playing off America against Britain, could only cause satisfaction to one major power: Soviet Russia.[28]

For most of the harried Agency Executive members in New York, Weizmann's presence might alone bring about a change of mind in Washington. The pressures of the British, the Arab states, the oil lobby, and State-Defense officialdom, joined to an impotent UN Commission and particularly the fact that contacts with the White House had practically broken down—all spelled potential disaster for Zionist hopes. Seeing that, as he put it later, the Jews were going to be "urged back into the vacuum of tutelage" after having been placed on the threshold of statehood, Eban sent on his own initiative a cable on January 23 urging Weizmann to come to New York: "everything depending on outcome negotiations here." Joseph Ivor Linton, who had worked with Weizmann in London for years at 77 Great Russell Street, accompanied him to the White House in December 1945, and sat with him at the 1946 Basle Congress, called the Dorchester Hotel suite with the identical request at the urging of the Weizmann Institute's Josef Cohn.

Greatly annoyed and dreading New York's cold winter weather, Weizmann noted that he no longer held any official position in the Agency, and was about to return to Rehovot, where he hoped to spend the rest of his life at the Institute pursuing scientific work. So furious that he slammed down the receiver, Weizmann turned to his wife Vera and said, "We have just left New York, and the idiots now want us to go back." Finally, with her encouragement, he agreed to do so (at Weisgal's suggestion) if the appeal were to be repeated officially by the Executive in New York. Receiving Ben-Gurion's approval, Shertok had Eban extend the request, and Weizmann sailed on the 29th aboard the *RMS Queen Mary*.[29]

All the while, the prospects for Palestine's future grew dimmer. British detonations of some Hagana defensive positions in the Old City resulted in the murder by Arabs of two Jews; Arab snipers in Abu Kabir killed another two Jews in Tel Aviv on the 18th. On January 20, eight Jews were killed in Yehiam, seven Jewish Supernumerary Policemen who were not permitted to use armored cars out of their neighborhood near Yazur on the 22nd, and an additional ten Jews three days later. Yet Cadogan declared in a closed session of the UN Commission on the 21st that the violence in Palestine was due to the Jews, and that the AHC was cooperating with the Administration by reigning in Arab extremists. The Colonial Office's Palestine section head Trafford Smith frankly remarked to the Commission that "a revised plan of partition" was needed; mandatory Under-Secretary John Fletcher-Cooke added that the Jews would have to withdraw to the coastal plain from Tel Aviv to Haifa after the fighting, leading Bunche to point out that this was about the small area proposed in the second revision of the 1937 Peel Plan.

Five days later, Gurney informed Herzog that the authorities were prepared to protect the Jews in the Old City, provided that the Hagana and the "armed dissidents" left the area. After two thousand years of exile and the murder of 6,000,000 Jews in Europe under Hitler, Herzog replied, the Jews could not entrust their safety to others, and resolved to live with God's help. More sympathetic and candid than the Chief Secretary, Cunningham remarked to Silver that he was sorry his term of office was "ending on a note of failure." A few days later, the Arab League recommended that "the Arab nations occupy all Palestine with their regular armies when British troops leave Palestine."[30]

A Whitehall spokesman asserted that UN plans for Palestine did not contemplate the establishment of a Jewish militia, which Shertok had urged on the UN Commission, because 45 percent of the population in the projected Jewish state was to be Arab. (One week after Bevin reached an agreement with his Colonial and Defense counterparts on the 24th to keep to the Mandate termination date of May 15 and troop withdrawal by August 1, the Foreign Office told its UN delegation that sending an international force to Palestine would provoke the Arabs, and start a conflagration in the region "with incalculable consequences.") "Shallow sophistry," retorted the Agency Executive in Jerusalem on the 25th. The service of those Arabs who wished to enlist in that militia would be accepted, but their refusal to cooperate could not render the entire plan inoperative, and made effective Jewish defense even more urgent. The effect of this strategy, it went on, "is to render the Jews of Palestine defenseless" while HMG continued to supply arms to the Arab states and denied them to the Jews. The British were attempting to turn Palestine into "a death trap," the official reply concluded, in which the Jews would be forced to surrender to England's own Palestine scheme "or go down fighting for their very lives." "My government cannot allow" the formation of armed militias from the residents of each state or permit provisional governments to function prior to the termination of the Mandate, Cadogan stated categorically to the Commission on January 30, and "would not regard favorably" the Commission's arrival earlier than two weeks before then.

The final day of the month witnessed the interception of 279 Jewish refugees aboard the *Lamed Heh Giborei Kfar Etzion*, named in honor of the 35 Hagana fighters who had been killed in the Hevron hills on January 16. With the 1,500 entry quota per month remaining in force, they would be transferred to the detention camps in Cyprus on the same day that Resolution 181 (II) had called for an open port in Palestine to receive Jewish immigration.[31]

The UN Palestine Commission's first monthly report on February 2 indicted Great Britain in effect for circumventing the partition resolution, but was couched in weak terms and failed to make a single recommendation. It did not "find satisfactory" HMG's insistence that the group should only come two weeks before the Mandate's termination, thus not allowing it to work towards the creation of militias, the security of Jerusalem, two Provisional Councils of Government by April 1, and the Economic Union. The report did reveal Cadogan's secret testimony accusing the Jews of conspiring to "consolidate the advantages they gained in the General Assembly" by waging a terror campaign to intimidate the Arabs, but asserting that the Arabs would fight back and not "be tamed." Yet Per Federspiel (Denmark), who informed the Americans that he personally preferred a federal state, and Lisicky had with difficulty prevailed upon their colleagues not to accept Bunche's wish to castigate HMG for obstruction. Lisicky told Knox of the U.S. delegation that he was thinking of an arrangement, sponsored "discretely" by London and Washington, allowing Abdullah to send troops to maintain law and order in Palestine with the understanding that there might be a plebiscite in Palestine regarding its possible annexation to Jordan. In turn, Abdullah would "tolerate" the existence of a Jewish state smaller than the boundaries laid down in the GA recommendation. "This is pretty much OK," noted McClintock on the possibility just raised.[32]

The Commission's subsequent report on security, drawing upon information from Cunningham and the Jewish Agency about large Arab armed incursions into Palestine, as well as the Arab Higher Committee's statement on the 4th to Lie that Palestine's Arabs "will never submit or yield to any power going to Palestine to enforce partition," came to two conclusions. First, "powerful Arab interests" were deliberately attempting to "alter by force" the Assembly recommendation—"tantamount to waging war" against the UN, which had also asked the Security Council to determine any such effort "as a threat to the peace, breach of the peace or act of aggression" in accordance with Article 39 of the UN Charter. Second, an urgent need existed for the Council to provide an adequate, international armed force if the Commission were to be enabled to implement the resolution and maintain law and order in Palestine when authority was transferred to it. The Council had to act promptly in order to carry out the partition resolution and to avert "great bloodshed and human suffering" in Palestine. "A dangerous and tragic precedent" would be established, the second report concluded, if force, or the threat of the use of force, were to prove "an effective deterrent to the will of the United Nations." To Pearson, Lisicky described this report as a "declaration of impotence" which did nothing more than present the facts, and he expressed personal disappointment at the stand taken by the UK Government.[33]

State Department officials, moving rapidly away from Washington's official support of partition, took issue with that analysis. Knox stressed to Austin that the United States was in no way committed to use or contribute to the use of force to implement Resolution 181 (II). Rusk, now directing the Office of United Nations Affairs, recommended in a "top secret" memorandum on February 3 that the United States should support any measures "falling short of the use of armed force" by the Security Council to restrain external aggression against Palestine from the contiguous Arab states. If partition could not be implemented without force, the United States should then support calling a Special Session of the GA to reconsider the entire problem, with the probable outcome that a UN trusteeship for Palestine would be proposed and "terminable" when the Jewish and Arab communities of Palestine could agree on a *modus vivendi* either for a unitary federated state or for partition. The same day, he informed Austin that the Council should not consider a threat to peace, breach of peace, or act of aggression regarding Palestine until after its examination of the acts themselves and in light of "surrounding circumstances prevailing at the time."[34]

Following Henderson's call to him for a "reconsideration of the entire question," as put forward in Kennan's PPS/19 memorandum, on February 11 Rusk sent Lovett a memorandum drafted by McClintock and entitled "Shift to New Position on Palestine." It proposed that the U.S. or another delegation at the Council call for a special GA session, with the Americans prepared to support a trusteeship for Palestine, administered by the UN or the remaining three of the Allied and associated Powers of World War I (the United States, United Kingdom, and France), until such time as the Jews and Arabs could come to an agreement. The same day, Lovett received the Policy Planning Staff's paper "The Problem of Palestine," advocating that a special GA session consider a new solution in the form of an international trusteeship or a federal state, with provision for Jewish immigration in either case. State submitted that paper as a working document to the National Security Council, along with the understanding that it did not necessary represent the department's final views.[35]

Still, when pressed by Canadian Ambassador Humphrey H. Wrong on the 4th as to the U.S. delegation's stand when Palestine would come before the Security Council, Lovett had noted that the GA resolution was a recommendation, while Rusk added that the only way under the Charter in which the UN could become legally responsible for the enforcement of partition would be for the whole of Palestine to be placed under trusteeship and for "a fresh decision" to be taken to partition Palestine. The immediate objective, Lovett declared, should be to secure a "cooling-off" period until the whole situation could be reexamined, the British ideally to keep their forces in Palestine for a further period and the GA to "take another look" at the problem in the light of the failure of its first proposal. State could not propose this to the Commission because, as he put it, "there were Zionist spies everywhere."

When Wrong reminded his listeners of Johnson's pledge before the partition vote that the United States would fulfill its responsibilities as a member of the Council, Lovett replied that no American forces had been promised or implied, and he thought that the dispatch of even a small force as part of an international contingent would result in a wave of antisemitism in the country. Moreover, Russian military assistance could be invited "by one side or the other" if matters went on as they were. There was "enough truth" in the charges that the British were arming the Arab states, he stated, to make the U.S. position "most uncomfortable" in enforcing their embargo on weapons to the Jews. In an election year, the Ambassador later wrote to St. Laurent, the U.S. Administration was not likely to take a public initiative towards the adoption of another scheme that would certainly be represented by the Zionist leaders as a betrayal.[36]

Up to this point, Marshall had not made up his mind. At a press conference on the 11th, he declared that the U.S. Government stood by its earlier position on partition, and that no instructions had been or would be given to Austin to reiterate the American stance. To Epstein, this statement indicated that the American role would be that of "wait and see," allowing other Council members to press for "reconciliation." That Truman did not ask Ibn Saud and the Iraqi Premier to desist, as news commentator Drew Pearson said in a radio broadcast the previous evening, reflected the kind of appeasement policy reminiscent of the 1930s, which had led to "the most disastrous consequences." Every effort had to be made, he urged Shertok, to ascertain whether or not a directive had been issued to the US delegation and its nature.[37]

Speaking at the National Security Council meeting the next day, Marshall announced that State had just outlined for him three alternative courses as a guide to American policy: direct abandonment of U.S. support for partition; "vigorous support" for its forcible implementation by the Security Council, which would involve the use of "substantial" American forces—either unilaterally or jointly with Russia; or refer the question back to the Assembly and attempt to "reshape" the policy. The last did not mean surrendering the "principle" of partition, but adopting some "temporary expedient" such as trusteeship, or a joint Anglo-French-American mandate with a revision of the partition decision along the lines of the original British cantonal plan. These were simply the alternatives suggested, he noted, and none of them carried as yet his approval. Replying on the 12th to a letter from Congressman Jacob K. Javits (R, NY) and twenty-nine other members of the House of Representatives, Marshall asserted that the various Arab states had committed thus far "no overt acts" to endanger the maintenance of international peace and security in the terms of the UN Charter; the United States had to await the Council's decision regarding the Commission's report on security; and the President and he continued to regard the solution of this "immensely difficult problem" as a UN solution, to which end the United States would contribute as "a member and steadfast supporter" of that international organization.[38]

Nor had Truman taken an unequivocal stand since the partition vote. At a meeting on the 4th with U.S. Ambassador to Iraq Wadsworth, an inveterate anti-Zionist ever since serving in the latter half of the 1930s as the country's Consul-General in Jerusalem, he indicated that the Grady effort in the summer of 1946 to implement the unanimous Anglo-American Committee report had failed because of "British bullheadedness and the fanaticism of our New York Jews." Both parties had not changed. He could say that the United States would not send weapons to the Near East and would only act through the UN. With "a categorical ejaculation," so read Wadsworth's account to State, he confirmed the Ambassador's wish that after the National Security Council's consideration, the country's Near Eastern representatives could say that no American troops would be sent to Palestine to impose partition.

When Wadsworth sought approval for the assertion that the UN should reconsider partition, since the Jewish-Arab cooperation presumed by the GA was "nonexistent," he replied that was for the UN to decide in the light of experience. He appreciated Wadsworth's hopes for Iraq's development of the Tigris-Euphrates Valley, but added that there was nothing much constructive anyone could do if the Arab leaders started sending their armies into Palestine. Only a UN international police force should enter, if needed. The United States would not send troops unilaterally into Palestine, Truman declared, but the Arabs had to first assure him before getting "categoric [sic] promises" that they would not either. "Seeing the picture" as Lovett and Marshall did, Truman remarked, he felt that he could "go along" with what the State Department might recommend.[39]

Unaware of Truman's actual views but keenly worried about Zionist prospects, Jewish Agency Counsel David Ginsburg hosted a three-hour meeting on the evening of February 3 with associates to discuss future strategy. The group, consisting of Shertok, Gass, Cohen, Nathan, Gilbert, Epstein, the Agency's Moshe Yuval, and Ginsburg law partner Harold Leventhal, decided to join a "rational argument" for the U.S. Government to support partition with political pressure on both parties against accepting a new position on Palestine "less considerate of Jewish needs and desires." Marshall would be approached by Donovan, Hilldring, and Roosevelt, she also to indicate her views to Truman. A letter signed by prominent Americans to the President, emphasizing the immorality of abandoning partition and its deleterious impact on the UN's future prospects, together with Weizmann's seeing Truman and Marshall, were also advised. Dewey, Taft, Vandenberg, Barkley, Harriman, Dulles, McGrath, and Welles would be approached. (Dulles, as Dewey was informed, was in fact "distinctly out of sympathy with the Zionist point of view," saying that the partition resolution was "railroaded" through the UN by the U.S. delegation.) All instruments of the press and radio would be utilized, and the Washington group would meet further on a regular basis for clarifying its position and for collaborating to get the most effective presentation possible.[40]

"A big conspiracy is brewing in Washington" seeking to reverse the U.S. position on Palestine, Epstein wrote to Kirchwey three days later. Particularly active were Henderson's circle and some prominent Defense Department officials led by Forrestal, along with Wadsworth and Duce. Truman would not see Senator James E. Murray (D, MT), who had just blasted the government's arms embargo and the State Department's "mixture of unbecoming timidity toward the Arabs and thinly-disguised disapproval toward the Jews." Sullivan, sent by Kirchwey to talk to Truman, reported back that the President would say nothing more than that he was "working on a plan" to see partition achieved, while Forrestal believed Washington should "eat crow" on Resolution 181 (II) and that sending American troops would mean the "biggest wave" of antisemitism which the country had ever imagined. State and Defense did not care about the elections, Sullivan concluded, and everything came down to bases, oil, and the whole problem of building up America's position vis-à-vis Russia.

Proskauer's meetings with Truman and Lovettt, calling for a lifting of the embargo and obtaining British cooperation as envisaged in the November resolution, got nothing more definite than the President's saying that no change had occurred in U.S. policy, the government was studying the question of an international police force, and Washington desired to "reconcile" between "moderate Jews and moderate Arabs." When Proskauer asked if reconciliation meant the Jews' sacrifice of territory, Truman replied negatively, but gave no further indication of the content of their plan. Niles told Epstein that "Ishemet" (Truman in Hebrew code) was inclined to issue a statement to deny rumors about a change in policy, but "Mazkir" (Secretary Marshall in Hebrew code) objected as an unnecessary concession to public pressure and harmful to the Administration's prestige.[41]

The State and Defense departments' viewpoint gained traction. In a conversation with Baruch and Franklin D. Roosevelt, Jr., Forrestal expressed the War Department's opposition to a UN force for fear of Russian penetration into Palestine; hoped that some British troops would stay on after August 1 for internal security and against a possible Soviet plot; and declared that vital U.S. oil and strategic interests required peace with the Arabs. He indicated the possibility of Arab acquiescence if only the Tel Aviv area, to have an international status similar to Vatican City, remained Jewish. Washington officials and the *New York Times*'s Herbert L. Matthews accepted the British line that Moscow intended to send masses of Jews to Palestine to establish a Communist regime in the future Jewish state, beginning with the *Pans*, notwithstanding a public declaration by the British general commanding the Cyprus camps that not one Soviet spy was to be found among the more than 15,000 passengers on those two boats.

Lie, giving Shertok and Silver his opinion that the British were trying to sabotage the GA majority vote, supported an international force of Great Powers to implement partition, but Marshall and Lovett feared Communist infiltration even through units of Soviet satellite countries. After a talk with Eleanor Roosevelt, Hilldring turned down Morgenthau's request to intervene with the Near Eastern "boys," doubting the value of "feeding me into a meat grinder" that would produce no results and "leave me impotent for any future usefulness." Articles by

Reston, leading syndicated columnists Joseph and Stewart Alsop (*New York Herald Tribune*), and Caroll Binder (*Minneapolis Star Tribune*) trumpeted the State-Defense position. "It was perfectly clear," Epstein told Tsarapkin when informing him of Duce's activities, that if it were left in the hands of Forrestal and Lovett, then one might say "in advance" that when the question was discussed in the Security Council, the United States would adopt a position favorable to the Arabs.[42]

As their ultimate card, the Zionists and their supporters counted on Weizmann to turn the tide with Truman. At first, the aged leader arrived at New York City's Waldorf Astoria Hotel on February 4 in a belligerent mood. "Why did you drag me to this frozen waste when I might have been in Rehovot?" he shot at Eban that evening as a blizzard swirled outside on Park Avenue. The danger at Lake Success and the fact that not a single contact at the highest government levels had been possible since November were described in reply, Truman refusing to even receive a Zionist delegation in the White House. Weizmann decided to seek an interview, and released a statement to the press declaring he had no doubt that the UN, with the support of the U.S. Government and other governments concerned, would overcome the difficulties in Palestine which had been raised "through a violent attempt to overthrow a just and lawful international decision." When he fell ill the next day with a chest complaint and developed a high fever, his doctor advised that he remain in bed for some time, and Weisgal warned that the group was taking a serious risk because Weizmann had shown on a previous visit that his health was sensitive to that metropolis's winter climate.

Wishing to make his stay in America as brief as possible, Weizmann had Frankfurter and Ginsburg draft a letter to Truman for an appointment. Knowing that the President was about to leave for a trip to the Caribbean, and recalling Truman's "kindness and understanding" when they last met, he asked on the 10th for a few minutes' meeting in light of the fact that if the present trend of events were not halted, the Palestine crisis "might well end in catastrophe, not only for my people but for Palestine and indeed the United Nations."[43]

Two days later, Truman had Connelly reply that the President greatly regretted that he would be unable to do so before Weizmann returned to Palestine. Scheduled to depart Washington on the 20th for a few weeks' trip, his calendar between now and then was completely filled. A meeting at this time was out of the question, and the President sent "his very best wishes." "So disturbed" at the ever-mounting Zionist pressure, Truman later wrote, he gave instructions to his staff that he would not see Weizmann. The same day, queried at a press conference concerning partition, Truman replied that he had no comment. Asked whether there was any disposition to "soften" the plan, he responded that "The United States Government is supporting the United Nations. That is as far as I can go."[44]

In the meantime, violence in Palestine had unquestionably escalated, Consul General Robert B. Macatee informing State on the 9th that more than 1,000 persons were reported to have lost their lives and more than 2,000 wounded since the GA November 29 vote. The future looked bleak, with the mandatory government "admittedly in a state of disintegration"; the Jews, none of whose attacked settlement defenses had been pierced, determined to establish their state; and the Arabs, despite "a great deal" of internal dissension, encouraged by the steady arrival of armed bands into the country and the clamor in the Jewish press of U.S.-UK alleged "sabotage" of the UN decision. Local British officials, adamant in their refusal to help implement the partition resolution in any way, "cannot get out of Palestine too soon." The police had no sympathy for the Jews, while the army seemed generally occupied with minimizing any casualties that it might receive from the Arab-Jewish conflict, employing decisive force most often only when disturbance seemed likely to become widespread. As to the possibility of the Commission controlling matters, Macatee ended, one of the highest ranking officials summed up the local British attitude: when it arrived, Palestine "will go up in smoke."[45]

The recent bombing of the offices of the *Palestine Post*'s offices on Jerusalem's HaSolel (later HaHavatselet) Street off Zion Square, ordered by al-Qadir al-Husseini, reflected the steady decline into chaos. Fawzi el-Kutub, who had studied demolitions in Nazi Germany during the 1930's and became one of the key people in al-Husseini's headquarters in Bir Zayit twenty kilometers north of Jerusalem, had prepared the half-ton TNT explosive which two British army deserters loaded at Beit Hanina onto an army vehicle driven by Abu Khalil Janho on the night of February 1. Army deserters Corporal Peter Madison and Captain Eddie Brown, who later said that his brother was killed by the Irgun, followed the truck in a stolen CID car for their escape. The blast at 10:58 p.m.

destroyed the *Post* press and offices, also gutting two adjacent buildings. About forty people were injured; four died of their wounds. Acting
editor Ted Lurie and three staffers managed to get out the paper on the
Liphshitz printing press nearby with a special two-page edition the next
day, the furious front-page British-born columnist Roy Elston, a former
Colonel on Whitehall's staff in the Middle East now writing under the
pseudonym David Courtney, defiantly proclaiming that "truth is stronger than TNT and burns brighter than the flames of arson." A CID report,
historian Uri Milstein discovered years later, relayed that the Arabs saw
this attack as proof of their commando's efficiency. It encouraged them
to dare more, al-Husseini turning again to el-Kutub, with their next
target to be the congested thoroughfare of Ben-Yehuda Street.[46]

Tensions hardly abated over the next two weeks. The same *Palestine
Post* special edition reported on day-long explosions in Arab and Jewish
quarters, two robberies in Tel Aviv, the Hagana foiling an assault from
strong Arab formations concentrating in the village of Beit Safafa
against the Mekor Hayim suburb, and Hagana attacks against the Arab
villages of Kabri and Tarshiha, from which gangs had left to murder
nine men of the Yehiam settlement and killed a number of Jewish
Supernumerary Police. Jewish bus passengers died when shot at by an
Arab Legion camp near Haifa. Kohn's request to arm Jerusalem's Jewish
civil guards and permit them to search army and police vehicles was
refused (that guard's Yehuda Kashayoff was killed by a soldier near the
Jewish Agency headquarters on February 5), and officialdom denied a
British involvement in the *Post* bombing. After all people between the
ages of seventeen to twenty-five in the *yishuv* had been called up for full,
active service, usually in the Galilee or the Negev, men between those
of twenty-five to forty were now receiving the call. Jerusalem's main
water pumping station at Ras-el-Ain was virtually taken over by some
600 well armed Iraqis, leading Jerusalem District Commissioner R. M.
Graves to acknowledge before long that security forces "are not inclined
to drive them out by force."

On the 10th, a strong Arab attack on Yemin Moshe led to one British
officer killed and three wounded, six Arabs killed and sixteen wounded,
and one Jew killed and six wounded. Two days later, four Hagana men
were arrested then "released" unarmed near St. Stephens Gate, where
they were lynched by an Arab mob and their bodies mutilated. On the
14th, the Hagana raided the village of Sasa, deep in Arab-held territory

near Lebanon, destroying thirty-five houses and killing more than sixty. That and two additional raids on three bridges convinced an angry Cunningham that the Hagana had increased its reprisal operations, indifferent to civilian casualties.[47]

The mandatory's sense, as conveyed by Cadogan to the UN Commission on January 21, that to the Arabs in Palestine "the killing of Jews now transcends all other considerations" found corroboration in and beyond the country's borders. *Reynolds News* reported on the 8th Haj Amin telling Muslims that it was not enough to overcome the Jews of Palestine, but to "exterminate them because they constitute a menace to Arabs." Three days later, Husseini reiterated in Egypt's *Al Masri* his warning that special commando squads would attack the Commission's members upon their arrival; that the AHC rejected Chamoun's proposal for Palestine as a federal unitary state; and that Palestine's Arabs would only accept "the extermination of the Zionists and complete independence for the whole of Palestine."

The "complete intransigence of all the Arabs at present" and the "folly" of their rejecting any policy of negotiation or conference constituted Cunningham's warning to Abdullah, who, State was informed, permitted 700 armed Syrians to cross from Jordan to Palestine. The pro-Arab Minister to Saudi Arabia James R. Childs explained to Feisal that the United States supported partition because of past official support for Zionism; the majority UNSCOP report; public opinion strongly stirred by "the mistreatment of Jews in Europe and the intense desire of surviving Jews to go to Palestine"; and the impossibility of postponing the solution any longer in light of the current situation and the British decision to withdraw. Feisal responded in turn that the kingdom and other Arab states would refuse to accept a Jewish state under any considerations—with "continuous warfare" the result, compelling Childs to inform State that no assurances or arguments could be offered to alter Ibn Saud's "implacable hostility and opposition" to a partition of Palestine.[48]

The increasingly grave situation prompted Ben-Gurion to cable Shertok on the 12th that the entire initiative of the Arab forces of war against the *yishuv* had passed into the hands of the Arab states, which were continually sending numerous bands across the northern and eastern frontiers, including Jordan. Various sources and Hagana intelligence disclosed that these well-trained, well-equipped contingents were under the command of well-educated Arab officers assisted by Europeans, mainly German technicians. (Hundreds of volunteers under Kaukji's command had centered in Nablus and Tubas nearby at the end of January, preceded by two battalions of the ALA arriving in the North, all of these trained in Syria.) Although lacking definite information as to details, the *yishuv* expected "serious attacks." The Iraqi colonel sent by the ALA to command the Jaffa front in December had halted negotiations in that city towards peace with the Jews, dismissing the mayor's earnest warning that without agreement Jaffa would be destroyed by answering that he did not mind the city's destruction if the Arabs secured the destruction of Tel Aviv. The Arab attacks encouraged by British "sabotage" of the November UN resolution, declared an AZEC national conference of 800 Zionist leaders from thirty five states on the 16th, mandated that the government approve a Jewish militia and stop the arms embargo in order to "vindicate the integrity of American policy."

The next six weeks were "extremely critical if not fateful," Ben-Gurion warned Shertok, as "goods" from Ueberall and Arazi could only be expected at best after six to eight weeks: "Time fatal factor." He closed by urging the immediate arrival of an international force or at least the dispatch of equipment by the UN or by the United States. Eliminating the references to the Ueberall-Arazi efforts and to time being a fatal factor, Epstein sent a copy of the cable soon thereafter to Marshall, the Commission, and the members of the Security Council.[49]

State persisted in its retreat from partition, McClintock preparing a brief memorandum for its meeting with the National Security Council on the 13th which indicated that "a new situation" in Palestine would make an alternate plan to partition "imperative," That novel circumstance could include the refusal of the Palestinian Arab population, the Arab governments, or the United Kingdom to cooperate, or the failure of Security Council members to join in carrying out the November 29 resolution. Villard, now a State member on the Policy Planning Staff, was advised the next day to say that there would not be sufficient votes in the Security Council for implementation in the absence of pressure, and the government should not exert any such pressure.

On the 17th, State proposed in an NSC draft that the United States should continue to support partition short of the use of outside armed force, while the disagreeing military members called for another solution to the Palestine problem, with a special GA session convened to reconsider the situation. The draft then continued by proposing that in the event of the GA's reconsideration, the British should be urged to continue to exercise HMG's Mandate over Palestine and a trusteeship should be administered by the UN Trusteeship Council, with an international force to maintain internal order during a transitional period. Receiving this draft two days later, Lovett told the Policy Planning Staff to hold the paper for the present, and to his staff remarked that he "does not know what the Department's policy is."[50]

Marshall, less acquiescent than Truman in replying on the 16th to Eleanor Roosevelt's letter requesting that the embargo be lifted and the Jews and any UN police force be equipped with modern armaments as "the only thing which will hold the Arabs in check," declared that Jews and Arabs were committing acts of terror and violence. He went on: The political situation in this country "does not help matters"; American weapons to Palestine and neighboring states would led to the further shedding of blood; and we should approach the problem through the UN rather than unilaterally. Responding the same day, she agreed that the United States should do whatever the UN asks of us, but was "seriously worried" that Forrestal advises the President that even if the UN suggested a police force with equal quotas for all nations, the Defense Secretary would feel that should Russia enter he had to mobilize the United States "fifty per cent for war at once." She considered this "utter nonsense" and did not understand it very well. Marshall did not reply, but at a press conference on the 19th remarked that no change in policy had transpired with regard to the embargo on shipment of arms to Palestine. When asked if the United States would continue to support partition, he replied thus: "The whole Palestine matter "is under constant consideration."[51]

Although a friend of Marshall's told the Agency's Gideon Ruffer that the Secretary considered the *yishuv*'s military performance a cause for worry and disappointment, thinking that a first clear Hagana victory would deter the Arabs from further attacks, the Hagana's performance at Tirat Zvi in the Beit Sh'an Valley on February 16 should have made Marshall pause in judgment. Against the 600-man First Yarmuk Battalion commanded by the ALA's Captain Muhammad Safa, 115 defenders held off repeated charges, mortars, and machine guns for seven hours. They were aided by a pouring rain that turned into thick mud, a miracle in the eyes of the religious settlers. The Arabs retreated, a British armored column arrived, and Safa agreed to leave if the British first fired off mortars and machine guns so that he could later claim he departed under duress. Fifty-seven ALA dead and much weaponry were left behind, the Jews suffering one dead and one wounded. News of the defeat swiftly spread through Arab Palestine, leading to demoralization. And in the North Galilee, the Palmah ambush of an ALA bus from Lebanon killed sixteen, all victim to the rifle shots of nineteen-year-old demolitions expert Netiva Ben-Yehuda. The ALA's hope for easy victories had proven a chimera.[52]

Lisicky still hoped that the Security Council would support the Commission's request for an adequate international armed force to help implement the partition resolution. At a press conference on the 17th, when asked if the Commission would go to Palestine without an armed force, he avoided a direct reply but declared that his group "believes in its work," It was up to the Council to decide, in consultation with military experts, how such a force should be constituted. "It is possible that this is the last time you are meeting the 'five lonely pilgrims,'" he told the reporters, adding that he wished to emphasize the word "lonely." Rebuffing suggestions as to the difficulties and the shortness of time involved in setting up a police force, he said all that was involved was "the will" to do it. He recalled that at the close of the last press conference he had quoted the Latin words *"Dum spiro spero"* (While I breathe, I hope). The same day, the UK representative at the UN Economic and Social Council revealed a British proposal that the Council call on member states to notify the UN of steps they had taken to absorb their share of European refugees. He refused to comment on a question seeking to define the relationship between Britain's desire to clear the refugees out of Europe and her equally strong desire to keep them out of Palestine.[53]

Attlee's Cabinet stood its ground, accepting the advice of MacMillan and Cunningham that the Commission should arrive a fortnight before the mandatory's departure from Palestine but welcoming a small advance party. Bevin had his private secretary inform worried citizens that an earlier exit than May 15 had proven impossible without imperiling the success of the very complicated operation of withdrawal, but that everything possible was being done so as to incur no unnecessary risk to British lives. Creech Jones reiterated in the House of Lords that

British forces would not be used to impose any solution "which is not freely accepted by both parties in Palestine," and the Cabinet approved his going to defend HMG's position before the Security Council. Bevin did not express objection to Jordan Prime Minister Tawfik Pasha's private confidence on February 7 that the Arab Legion would enter Palestine's Arab areas after May 15 to "ensure stability". One week later, McNeil informed the World Jewish Congress's Alexander Easterman that "under no circumstances" would the British agree to any militia operating in any Palestine area under their control.

Talking on the 16th with former Palestine Attorney General Norman Bentwich, who hoped for Christian church leaders to intervene for the peace of Jerusalem, Bevin harked back to the Morrison proposals and the Federal Plan as still "the way out," and said that the British people would not stand for soldiers or police remaining in Palestine. Middle East experts planned to create facts in Palestine which would force the *yishuv* to accept any British or Anglo-American mediation towards the Morrison Plan or at least a smaller Jewish state, Zaslani cabled Sacharov, accomplished by allowing considerable Arab troop infiltration and eliminating both Haj Amin and Abdullah in favor of a settlement that would meet with the Arab League's approval.[54]

On the 19th, one day after Joint Chiefs director Gruenther reported to Truman and officials of State and Defense that the forcible application of partition would entail between 80,000–160,000 troops at a time when American military power was seriously limited, Truman heard from Marshall that a draft for Austin's forthcoming address to the Security Council would soon be ready for his review. Told that Lovett had taken "a careful approach" toward the reaching of a conclusion, Truman assured Marshall that whatever course State considered the right one, it could "disregard all political factors." Prepared by McClintock at Rusk's request and receiving the approval of Lovett, Austin, Rusk, Henderson, Legal Advisor Ernest A. Gross, and Policy Planning Staff Deputy Director George H. Butler, the penultimate draft, with Marshall's participation, noted that policy would conform to and be in support of UN action on Palestine. The Security Council's enforcement action, it emphasized, was authorized by the Charter "to keeping the peace and not to enforcing partition." In any event, it concluded, the Council should make every effort to obtain a result "which is acceptable to the Jews and Arabs of Palestine."[55]

Truman received the draft on the evening of the 21st aboard the Presidential yacht *Williamsburg* in Puerto Rico. One day earlier, Eleanor Roosevelt had written to him, sharply disagreeing with Forrestal's stance that any American volunteering in an international police force would lose his citizenship, particularly as those who had enlisted in the Canadian forces before World War II did not. (A few days later, she would agree to co-sponsor with Welles, Lehman, and Senator Elbert D. Thomas Eichelberger's AAUN petition calling on the UN to enforce the partition resolution.) Palestine's Chief Rabbis Herzog and Uziel had urged Truman to secure partition in order to discourage Arab aggression and "prevent the Holy Land from being turned into a shambles." He also had just received a telegram from Jacobson via Connelly, drafted with Granoff's help after B'nai Brith President Frank Goldman had called Jacobson to intervene as "the last hope," asking him to meet with the "very old and heartbroken" Weizmann, whom Truman had once told Jacobson was "the greatest statesman and finest leader that my people have."

This cable arrived right after a supporter of Wallace for the presidency in November trounced the Democratic candidate in a Bronx Congressional by-election, Reston and others agreeing that Jewish voters angry at Washington's Palestine policy and the embargo had accounted for the stunning upset. The President "talks Jewish and acts Arab," Wallace said publicly afterwards, and he told the House Foreign Affairs Committee that American money should be withheld from Great Britain until the latter stopped sending arms to the Arabs. Washington pundits predicted that Wallace would follow this up when campaigning in cities with sizeable Jewish populations, Republicans and Democrats alike now "sharply aware" that the Palestine question was one of the election issues of 1948.[56]

State's draft, aside from the text for Austin's speech, had also sought Truman's consideration and approval for "some form" of UN trusteeship if partition could not succeed without enforcement and the Palestine matter would go back to a special session of the General Assembly. That development, in State's opinion, would show that Palestine "is not yet ready for self-government," and perhaps the United Kingdom would have to be asked to retain the Mandate pending further UN action. Without commenting on this possibility, Truman cabled Marshall on the afternoon of the 22nd that he approved in principle the draft speech's "basic position." At the same time, he wished to make it clear that nothing should be presented to the Council which could be interpreted "as a recession on our part from the position we took in the General Assembly," and he called for seeing the final draft of Austin's remarks.[57]

Lovett gave Shertok on the 21st no inkling of State's shift, what McClintock handwritten notes for the NSC meeting a week earlier had termed a "drastic step." His guest delineated HMG's negative attitude at the Security Council toward implementing partition, and the mandatory's acquiescence in, if not encouragement of, Arab designs in Palestine. As one example, the Administration, although receiving a forty-eight-hour advance notice from the Agency that a band of 700 or 800 Arabs would leave Irbid in Jordan via one of two bridges over the Jordan River to attack the *yishuv*, left that bridge in the Arab Legion's control, and the assault against Tirat Zvi took place. London, Shertok observed, had not expected the recommendations of the Anglo-American Committee or of UNSCOP, and never realized that the Jews were determined to establish a state, the "best means" of maintaining peace in the region, and to defend themselves "to the last."

Pressed by Shertok, Lovett said that he could not answer at the present time whether the UN would provide weapons and an international armed force for implementing the GA recommendation, and declared that the United States, not prepared to take unilateral action, considered the Palestine problem one for the UN to handle. Epstein, also present, assumed that Lovett was thinking along the lines of "conciliation" because he had asked Shertok whether the Agency had talked to the British and to the Arabs, but the point remained uncertain. The next day, Shertok's letter explained to Lovett the "unbridgeable gulf" that existed between the warring parties, as evinced in Azzam Pasha's talk with Eban and Horowitz after publication of the UNSCOP report and the AHC's continued refusal to discuss partition; the Agency's viewing "with the greatest alarm" rumors about "freezing" the Palestine situation so that a new effort of conciliation might be undertaken; the *yishuv*'s strenuous objection to any prolongation of the Mandate; and the immediate need for preparing a Jewish armed militia and, if possible, an international force adequate in composition and size.[58]

"The new ghastly outrage" that had just occurred in Jerusalem, Shertok also observed to Lovett on the 22nd, rendered the position "unprecedentedly critical," and made clear that any deliberate attempt to give a further lease of life to British rule was "tantamount to courting disaster." At 6:30 that morning, three stolen British trucks and an armored police car, driven by four army deserters (two from the *Palestine Post* bombing) and two ex-policemen and carrying 3,500 pounds of el-Kutub's explosives, stopped on Ben Yehuda Street near two hotels that housed Palmah troopers. The trucks blew up, leveling four buildings and killing 58 people, almost all civilians, and seriously wounding 32 more. The attackers escaped in the armored car, but a manifesto soon circulated by the British League Palestine Branch made clear that its members had done so, having taken a sacred vow in the Church of the Holy Sepulchre, "where our Lord Christ was crucified by the impenitent ancestors of those very Jews who now aspire to mastery of this country," to "annihilate all Jews": "We will finish Hitler's job!" Calling on all nations to "arise and smite" the Jews, the Arabs to unite and liberate their country, Britons to drive out "the Jewish-dominated Labour government," and British soldiers and policemen to join the League, it ended with "Rule Britannia!"

Months later, one of the deserters revealed to a *Cincinnati Times-Star* reporter that al-Qadir al-Husseini had picked the spot as the densely populated center of the Jewish Quarter in the New City. The twenty-three-year-old "Tommy" claimed that the Britishers carried this out in revenge against the Irgun and Stern Group killings of their countrymen. "It was a bloody good show after all," he concluded when seeing newspaper photographs of the carnage. Irgun and Stern gunmen quickly took revenge, killing sixteen British troops and policemen.[59]

The same day as the Ben Yehuda Street bombing, HMG announced that it would block Palestine's sterling balances, amounting to about £100 million, thus removing that country from the sterling area. £7 million would be available for working balances and for current Palestinian needs until May 15, the disposition of sterling balances after that date to be the subject of consultation between Cadogan and the UN Commission, later with the Economic Board to be established. Should successor governments in Palestine desire it, the British would be prepared to discuss with them the question of readmission to the sterling area. The unilateral step, observed Anglo-Palestine Bank board chairman Sigmund (Eliezer) Hoofien-Horowitz, would curtail Jewish imports from sterling area countries and impair confidence in the banks and currency, causing avoidable credit stringency and consequently a probable rise in the cost of living. The director of State's Office of

Financial and Development Policy decided, however, not at present to "endorse or criticize" the £7 million figure, and that no reply should be made to the British at this time.

Concurrently, a State official on detail to the Mission at the UN informed Austin that the Arab states, feeling strongly that reconsideration of the Palestine question was necessary in order "to bear methods of conciliation," still believed that proposals such as Chamoun's of November 29 (which the AHC flatly rejected) did offer "real hope." While these delegates could not publicly espouse such a course, Samuel K. C. Kopper added, he thought that they would be willing to accept a trusteeship over all of Palestine and compromise on Jewish immigration "if it appeared that there was no possibility of the establishment of an independent Jewish State."[60]

With still no word from Truman, a recuperating Weizmann vented his spleen for more than ninety minutes on Creech Jones. Confined to the Waldorf Astoria hotel suite, he warned that the position being created in Palestine appeared to resemble that in the Spanish Civil War, with the Arabs and the ex-Mufti substituting for Hitler and Mussolini and the British for Franco. The Jews in the Negev, the Galilee, and Tirat Zvi, for example, would never agree to evacuate alive, and the Jews would find arms "by hook or crook": the one alternative to the Jewish state was "extermination." Bevin was "apparently suffering from a Hitler complex in his hatred of the Jews, and Weizmann would say if venturing a prophecy that the Foreign Secretary would suffer Hitler's end. If the *yishuv* had weapons they could hold their own. The Americans were taking the British line, yet if it came to a war, Great Britain, permitting Arabs to enter "in hordes" from the north and leaving Palestine in "organized chaos," would be isolated, and the Jewish people's animosity should not be underrated. As for oil, it could be produced by synthetic means; the oil companies working in Arab lands "had married themselves to a corpse and the corpse would eventually drag them down." He hoped to see Truman and Marshall, and would not mince matters with them either.

What the Jews had created in Palestine was very dear to him, Creech Jones responded, and he had insisted from the beginning that implementation machinery should accompany the partition recommendation. Still, addressing the Security Council six days later on the 24th, the Colonial Secretary repeated that prior to May 15 HMG could not open a port to Jewish immigration; transfer areas in stages to the Commission, which would only be allowed to arrive two weeks beforehand; or permit the formation of a militia under the control of a Provisional Government of the future Jewish state. He reiterated the British policy of not opposing the GA decision, but of not undertaking, alone or in association with others, to impose that decision by force.[61]

Austin's remarks at the Council earlier that day, following Truman's final approval to Marshall late on the night of the 23rd, emphasized that it was directed by the UN Charter to keep international peace and not to enforce a political settlement, in this case partition. The government, he added, reaffirming support for Resolution 181 (II), wished to have the Council's permanent five members (the United States, Soviet Union, United Kingdom, China, and France) look at once into the question of possible threats to international peace arising out of the Palestine question and to consult with the Commission, the mandatory power, and representatives of Palestine's Arab and Jewish communities as to implementing that resolution, as well as to call upon all governments and peoples, "particularly in and around Palestine," to take all possible action to prevent or reduce "the disorders" now occurring there.

The same day, a Policy Planning Staff paper for Marshall and Lovett cautioned that strategic interests required that no policy be championed which tended to "strain" British relations with the Arab world and "whittle down" the British position in the Arab countries. "A vigorous and collective national effort" could prevent the area from falling under Soviet influence, in Kennan's opinion, but "a fairly radical reversal" of the trend of our policy to date had to be effected if the United States was not likely to be held responsible for the protection of the Jewish population in Palestine against "the declared hostility of the Arab world," or to be confronted with sharing that responsibility with the Russians. In either case, he concluded, the "clarity and efficiency" of a sound national policy for that area would be "shattered."[62]

The night before, Truman had also shared with Marshall a statement which he intended to release publicly after Austin's speech.[63] That moment, coinciding with the violent Communist *coup d'etat* that abruptly seized power in Czechoslovakia and the reported death of its pro-Zionist foreign minister Jan Masaryk, had now arrived:

> The Palestine problem has been, and is the deep concern of this Government. It has been given the most careful consideration by me,

the Cabinet, and other responsible Government officials. The U.S. position has been developed through long and exhaustive study and many consultations.

This position has been accurately presented by Ambassador Austin in his speech before the Security Council of the United Nations today.

The following day, Austin introduced a draft resolution to the Security Council which mirrored exactly the position taken in his speech. He did this at the earliest possible moment because Colombia's Alfonso López had already on the 24th offered one for appointing a committee of two permanent and three non-permanent Council members to first ascertain if an agreement between the Jewish Agency and the AHC could be reached, which would enable the Commission to "discharge its functions and responsibilities in due course" without the use of force. López's resolution also sought to examine the advisability of the Council calling an extraordinary GA session for the purpose of "reconsidering" Resolution 181 (II) "as a whole or in part," and for the United Kingdom to postpone its termination of the Mandate to July 15, 1948, and, accordingly, its arrangements for the evacuation of its troops from Palestine. Not pleased with Austin's resolution, Chamoun expressed to Kopper his concern whether the Council would implement partition while seeking to maintain peace. Egypt's Mahmoud Bey Fawzi, like Syria's al-Khoury, claimed that the GA was not competent to act on the question of Palestine, and he even warned the Commission members that they would not be safe in Palestine, although "to the Arabs in Palestine the killing of Jews now transcends all other considerations."

Speaking to Rusk the next day, Parodi and Belgium's Joseph Nisot objected to the draft resolution on a different ground, stating that the Council could not accept the GA partition plan prior to the permanent members' investigation which Austin had advocated, or accept in advance the GA resolution's standard as to what constituted a threat to the peace. Amending Austin's resolution, Nisot would soon introduce another to that effect. It was clear from Nisot's earlier remarks, Rusk informed Lovett, that Belgium did not wish to approve partition again at this point in light of the altered conditions in Palestine which had arisen since November 29.[64]

Austin's speech and subsequent resolution hinted at State's move towards a retreat from partition. "Equivocal," "hedging," and taking a conciliation approach that "could well be upheld by everybody," remarked Rose Halprin to the Hadassah Executive board. "Double talk," Kirchwey communicated to Senator Charles E. Tobey (R, NH); her telegram urging Truman to put an end to this "double cross" was not relayed to the President. "Outrageously hypocritical" declared Celler, who asserted that no further committee studies were needed. "Inexplicable wobbling" of our State Department, wrote Proskauer to Robert Goldman, President of the Union of American Hebrew Congregations, who agreed that after the GA and the United States had spoken in November, the "very life" of the UN and the "good faith" of the United States were involved. This represented a victory for Ambassador Wadsworth, Sullivan told Shultz. Welles, concluding that the government now officially appeared to accept British objectives, was shocked.

Parodi, French Embassy First Secretary Jean-Pierre Benard informed Epstein, relayed to Paris his opinion that it signaled partition is "dead." He further suggested that a trusteeship regime would probably be set up in Palestine, at least temporarily, to prevent "complete chaos" after May 15, with the Americans favoring British troops staying on until a final settlement were reached. Amazed to hear Lovett stress to some Washington correspondents on the 24th that the United States was vitally interested in establishing peace in Palestine prior to and as a condition of successfully implementing partition, the pro-Zionist *Washington Post* editor Herbert Elliston concluded that the government had completely revised its position, leading him to feel that a UN trusteeship might be the solution to prevent the further deterioration of conditions in Palestine. Rusk had expressed the same thought to an off-the-record luncheon with a group of journalists at Lake Success.[65]

Refusing to answer detailed questions about Palestine at his press conference on the 26th, Marshall declared off-the-record that "in this highly emotional period of extreme bitterness and violent attacks" he intended to see that there would be "no bending" by his department, when guiding its UN delegation, "to any military threat or to any political threat so long as I am Secretary of State." The department, he concluded, intended to leave matters entirely to Austin so that there would be "no confusion in expressions and sentences used." One day later, Henderson told Epstein that efforts for peace were such a "sacred thing" that no attempt should be missed to renew them time and again. If only the British, Jews, and Arabs were to meet, he remarked significantly, it might bring something "new and satisfactory" to all parties concerned. Then, looking at Epstein, he corrected himself and said that he certainly did not mean to suggest that partition should not be the basis of discussion at such a meeting.

Yet speaking with one of Inverchapel's embassy staff, Henderson confided that State viewed Austin's proposal to establish a five-power Council committee as a means to establish that any attempt to implement partition by force was likely to result in a threat to international peace, thereby perhaps preparing the ground for "a new approach" to the whole Palestine problem. That approach towards "Peace in the Holy Land," a greatly relieved Phillips has just written to the sympathetic Henderson, could be a federated state with limited immigration, which in itself would assure the Arabs that they would not be dominated by the Jews. Before long, Marshall would show Phillips's letter to Truman.[66]

Lovett had "set Loy Henderson straight," so McClintock informed Rusk on the 27th, about the future alternatives which confronted the UN as to Palestine. If the Security Council could do nothing "constructive" about the Palestine problem, a special GA session might make a new recommendation along the lines of a possible trusteeship. The British might or might not be amenable to pressure asking that they stay on to maintain law and order for a while longer, but the United States could not formulate policy on the assumption that they would concur. As a second possibility, the Council would find (and there seemed to be "ample evidence" on hand already) that the situation in Palestine threatened international peace and security, leading to the UN's dispatch of forces there after May 15. If, on the other hand, nothing had occurred to change the partition recommendation, the Commission might go to Palestine under those terms and seek by negotiation to carry out partition with economic union. In that case, however, it should be made clear that the UN forces were there to maintain international peace and not to enforce partition.

Lovett, who seemed to clearly envisage the possibility that some UN international force would have to be made available in Palestine, also advised Henderson and McClintock the same day not to send a telegram which they proposed to the Arab capitals and to the American consulate in Jerusalem. Their original draft had asserted that policy, as indicated in Austin's speech, would be in support of UN decisions, and because the Government was "a sincere friend" to the Arab world and was equally determined to maintain international peace and security, it counseled those states not to persist in sending troops and weapons or in making warlike declarations that would require the Council to dispatch armed forces to Palestine in order to remove such threats. "This is a good time for everyone to sit tight," he decided.[67]

Truman, whose "agonized indecision" according to the Alsops was reflected in Austin's stand, had come to the same conclusion. In a letter to "dear Eddie" on the 27th from the Navy's Submarine Base in Key West, Florida, he wrote that while he was very sorry a greatly crowded schedule did not let him see Dr. Weizmann, there was nothing that the Zionist leader could say that Truman did not already know. He also had made it a policy not to talk with anyone regarding the Palestine situation until the Security Council had had a chance to act on the suggestion for a police force to enforce partition. For two and a half years, the President went on, that situation "has been a headache for me," The Jews were "so emotional" and the Arabs "so difficult to talk with" that it was "almost impossible to get anything done." The British, of course, had been "exceedingly noncooperative" in arriving at a conclusion, while the Zionists had of course expected "a big stick approach on our part," and naturally had been "disappointed when we can't do that." Truman then concluded: "I hope that it will work out all right, but I have about come to the conclusion that the situation is not solvable as presently set up; but I shall continue to try to get the solution outlined in the United Nations resolution." Knowing Truman as he did, Jacobson got the feeling that this long-time friend would not change his mind. He decided that the best thing to do was to wait until the President returned to the White House.[68]

This steady turn of events shook the pro-partition camp. Criticizing what he termed the "counselors of caution," Welles warned in the *New York Herald Tribune* that a refusal to enforce partition would bring war, Soviet troops into the region, and, in appeasing Arab violence, start the UN on the path of the League of Nations, which had caved in to Japan on China, to Italy on Ethiopia, and to Hitler on Austria and Czechoslovakia. Shultz urged that the Nation Associates prepare a factual presentation showing proof of British and American complicity, together with a program to break up the preponderance of anti-partition votes in the Security Council and to involve the American people to demand that Truman, "the one leverage which is left to us to prevent an American double-cross," perform on Resolution 181 (II).

The trouncing which the Wallace candidate had given the Democrats in the Bronx was worth as much as one armored division to the Hagana, Lowenthal wrote to Agronsky, but facing a growing movement for compromise called for "violent and aggressive action and demands now in the *yishuv*" so that world opinion could recognize that partition itself was on the Zionists' part a surrender and compromise. If worst comes to worst, he felt that it would be best "to be *forced* into becoming part of a unitary Arab state," and then bring in immigrants, arms, and means to seize the government just before or at the outbreak of the "forthcoming world war. We may just have time enough...."

"At a place strangely called Lake Success," Rifkind told the Federal Court Press Association, "neutral Neros are fiddling while Jerusalem burns." Deeply concerned over the "planned American double-cross on partition," Kirchwey cabled Silver and Shertok for reassurance that the Agency would not fall into State's trap leading to a compromise of the partition resolution. In reply, Shertok noted that he had said clearly before the Council on the 27th that no concession whatsoever would be forthcoming on the Agency's part, the partition resolution already a "most far-reaching compromise."[69]

The last week of the month augured no better in Palestine. The Administration quickly denied British involvement in the Ben Yehuda Street bombing, leading the *Palestine Post* to editorialize that the moral was clear: no confidence existed any longer in the mandatory government in its ability to maintain law and order, in its declarations, and in its control over its own forces. Authoritative Arab sources reported to the Agency that during the last four days some 700 additional volunteers had crossed into Palestine, headed by about 50 officers who had been granted six months' leave by their governments. General Taha al-Hashimi, just appointed to command the ALA recruits, was according to a British Intelligence report the individual who "undoubtedly did more than any other Iraq politician to further both the German and the ex-Mufti's plans in Iraq" regarding the pro-Nazi Rashid Ali revolt in 1941. Richard Koebner, chairing the Hebrew University's Modern History department, reflected in a public letter the *yishuv*'s urgent need for an international force to halt Jerusalem's impending "wholesale slaughter and destruction," warning that other than the city's Jews being massacred, Zionism will then be no longer; the victims would include the claim of the Arabs to be part of the civilized world and the belief in British competence everywhere; prove USA politics to have acted irresponsibly; and kill the UN. No action had been taken on Herzog's plea that Gurney arrange a truce for the Old City.[70]

The *yishuv* would emerge victorious against the Arab forces provided that weapons arrived before May 15, Ben-Gurion wired Shertok on the 27th. That remained uncertain, even as Hagana intelligence possessed proof that the British in Palestine were recruiting for the Arab Legion. The next day, 982 Holocaust survivors aboard the *Bonim V'Lohamim* (Builders and Fighters), like the 679 on the *Yerushalayim HaNetsura* (Jerusalem Besieged) on the 12th and the 696 aboard the *L'Komemiyut* (To Independence) on the 20th, were intercepted and transferred to Cyprus. On February 28, as well, twenty soldiers accompanied by a British constable and three Arabs in uniform entered the Hagana position at the HaYotzek factory opposite Holon, confiscated all weapons, and left. Arabs who had gathered outside immediately opened fire. Some Hagana men escaped, but eight were hit and "subsequently butchered." The following day, the LEHI's blowing up of a troop train near Rehovot killed twenty-eight British soldiers and wounded dozens more.[71]

Aware that the State-Defense stance focused on the danger of Communist infiltration into the Near East and the fear of jeopardizing U.S. oil needs by alienating the Arab governments, Zionist advocates circulated for Forrestal and other key Washington officials two memoranda on how partition would affect U.S. security and how its implementation should be effected under Washington's initiative and leadership. As to the first concern, they argued that Arab rulers would strenuously resist any increase of Soviet influence, knowing perfectly well that such increase would spell the doom of their present feudal regimes. Jews, many refugees from communism, were most unlikely to covet the status of a Soviet satellite; Jewish society in Palestine was wholly the product of free enterprise, while the system of collective farming and cooperative management of industry were the results of a voluntary choice of methods, not state compulsion found at the root of Soviet communism. The absence of an international force, moreover, would only increase the prospect of a Russian foothold.

Cancellation of the American oil concessions, the second anxiety, was out of the question for Ibn Saud, whose regime was almost entirely dependent on oil royalties and on American economic and political help. For all the Arab countries, "the cow is more anxious to be milked than anybody is to milk it"; Syria and Lebanon, both in dire financial straits, had scarcely any prospect for solvency except through the proceeds of pipeline concessions, and the same was true for Iraq and Kuwait. Independent American oil producers, moreover, had just pointed out that the domestic petroleum industry could maintain the increased demands and create satisfactory reserves if sufficient steel were supplied the industry and the price for crude oil remained fair. Recently, the president of Socony Vacuum Oil company, which had joined with Jersey Standard Oil, had written a letter to the *New York Times* pointing out that the Western Hemisphere had more oil than in the rest of the world, the Gulf States alone having reserves in excess of that of the whole Arabian peninsula, but the steel which these independent companies needed for development had been shipped to Saudi Arabia.

In fact, the *Oil and Gas Journal* observed that the country not only replenished the reserves which the United States had used in the year 1947, but definitely added approximately two billion barrels to the country's future reserves. Besides, in a war, the Russians were much closer to oil under the ground in Arabia than the Americans six thousand miles away. Further, a Special Committee to Investigate the National Defense Program had showed that ARAMCO, the strongest critic in the oil industry against partition, had overcharged the U.S. Navy for petroleum supplies to the tune of many millions of dollars, and a recent Senate committee disclosed that the company had deprived the U.S. Treasury of large sums of corporation taxes.[72]

The third argument to counter the State-Defense position, embraced by Roosevelt, Welles, Lehman, and others in support of the AAUN manifesto, asserted that a retreat from Resolution 181 (II) would undermine the prestige of the UN in general and of the United States, partition's recognized sponsor, in particular. Eichelberger, a member of the five-man committee which had prepared the first U.S. working draft for the UN Charter, took the lead, first writing to Rusk on the 19th that jettisoning that rare Soviet-U.S. agreement presented not only a threat to, but an actual breach of, international peace and security: how could any small state in the future believe that the UN would protect it? Destroying collective security under the UN would strike a greater blow to American security than by temporarily offending the Arab states. Repeating this in a telegram to Marshall three days later, he urged the Secretary to brush aside "all counsels of delay, timidity and legal hair splitting" and give "vigorous leadership" to the

Security Council in this crisis. Eichelberger disagreed with the stand of long-time AAUN supporter Morris Lazaron, a major voice for the anti-Zionist American Council for Judaism, and with Austin's statement of the 24th, which lacked moral fervor, said nothing calculated to give the slightest offense to Britain and the Arabs, and just repeated steps for conciliation that had been "futile" in the past. Two days later, he convened an emergency meeting at the Waldorf Astoria where a resolution unanimously adopted by sixty-two national groups, including the American Federation of Labor and the Congress of Industrial Organizations, called on the U.S. Government to sustain the GA resolution on Palestine. The present situation, it went on, constituted a threat to the peace of the world, which had to be prevented as provided for under Articles 39 and 42 of the UN Charter. The U.S. Government should support an international police force; permit the immediate purchase by the Jewish Agency of military equipment and its shipment to Palestine, to be used by a Jewish militia; and (a new idea) recognize the Provisional Government of the Jewish state as of April 1 in accordance with the GA resolution.[73]

The U.S. military sharply took issue with these views, Wedemeyer providing Royall at the beginning of the month an updated "Top Secret" report arguing that partition, "dangerously contrary" to basic American interests, should be replaced by trusteeship. Public opinion would change dramatically if the "ventriloquism and unethical pressures used [by Jews] in their earlier persuasion were authoritatively exposed." Without "strong and continuing external aid," it argued, the new Jewish state would collapse under an Arab onslaught, culminating in "the probable extermination of a vast number of human beings, among whom will be thousands of blindly-trusting Jewish colonists." The use of U.S. troops, guaranteeing that commonwealth's survival, would perhaps benefit "world Jewry," but the loss of American soldiers' lives would unleash an "almost certain surge of violent anti-Semitism in this country." G-2 Army Intelligence warned on the 26th that American Zionists had precipitated the crisis in Palestine; that Soviet penetration could be checked with the continued arms embargo; that Russian agents had infiltrated the Jewish refugees coming to Palestine; and that the Arab League states, their security interests coinciding with those of the United States and Britain, would remain "definitely oriented toward the Western Powers."

Two days later, a CIA report, after obtaining the approval of the Intelligence Agencies of the Departments of State, Army, Navy, and Air Force, concluded that partition could not be implemented, that the British had prevented full-scale security measures out of the desire not to antagonize the Arab states, and that only the Soviets would gain from sending international troops to Palestine. It concluded that if the Security Council failed to agree to any action whatsoever, the issue would probably return to the GA, where any new solution would have to be acceptable to the Arabs, who would probably be willing to make some concessions on the basis of the UNSOP Minority Report.[74]

Their British counterparts concurred with the overall military assessment. On the 26th, the Chiefs of Staff Committee decided that without peace, the current GA partition plan was "unworkable": the economies of both states would be ruined, the power and water supplies for large Jewish areas were in the Arab state, and rail communications could be halted. The proposed Jewish state, based on a coastal plain some twelve to fifteen miles in width and dependent upon sea communications terminating in the port of Haifa, would be in a naturally weak military position, while the Arab state, in the hill mass of central Palestine, would be relatively strong. A "less disastrous outcome" might result if the present UN plan were altered, only thus the Arabs "deflected from their present policy": the Southern and Eastern Arab states in Palestine to be incorporated with Jordan, the Northern Arab state with Syria/Lebanon; the partition plan boundaries amended to give "a reasonable corridor" to the port of Jaffa from the Southern state; Aqaba ceded back to Saudi Arabia in return for Jaffa and Saudi support; and possibly other "minor adjustments as necessary" made in the Jewish boundaries.

The next day, the Joint Intelligence Committee took account of the strength of all potential forces and the four-phrased evacuation program: the Gaza Civil District by February 29; Jerusalem, Lydda, and part of Samaria by May 21; the remainder of Samaria and Galilee by June 30; and the enclave around Haifa by July 31. It considered that in view of the unfavorable terrain, the lack of communications, and the "disjointed arrangement" of its territories, the proposed Jewish commonwealth "would be military unsound." Assuming the problem would be settled by force of arms between Arabs and Jews, neither side would be able, without considerable outside assistance, to achieve an early decisive victory. A Jewish state in Palestine could be established with the assistance of a UN force, the Committee concluded; the Jews would not be able to establish a Jewish state in Palestine solely by their own efforts.[75]

Cunningham did not entertain great hope. Writing to Martin of the Colonial Office on the 24th, he was rather inclined to think that matters in Palestine would crystallize somewhat on the lines of Eastern Galilee to Syria, Samaria and Hebron to Abdullah, and the south to Egypt, with the center remaining uncertain. He had previously told Bevin that the Arabs would win in the end, but since then he was much less certain, purely due to the "apparently military ineptitude" of the Arabs. Rather than being able to paralyze the Jews, who depended entirely on open communications, at the moment they could only think of "killing the Yehudis"; the Jews were winning at that game, as more Arabs were being killed than Jews. He thought that the Arabs should be able to make both the Huleh and the Negev "untenable," and the Jews able to hold the coastal plain, so it might well all end in a partition more on the lines of what the British would consider fair. As for "Poor Jerusalem!," the only alternative to keeping that city as much out of the conflict as possible was to have the UN Commission set up a Jerusalem state, but Haj Amin was said to believe in "creating chaos," and had been instrumental up to the moment in blocking the mandatory's efforts to have a truce in the Old City. It was a pity, he added, that the Arab states complied in letting him control this area.[76]

The Parliamentary Labour Party's Foreign Affairs Group had just passed resolutions urging Attlee's government to back the creation of an *ad hoc* force composed of units supplied by member-nations to enforce partition, seeing the issue as "a decisive test" for the whole future of the UN, but Bevin stood firm. Four days later, hearing Ambassador Douglas confide that the U.S. Government was trying to "extricate itself from the impossible position they had gotten into," the Foreign Secretary reiterated that the mandatory would not stay in Palestine after the already announced date. He would share with Marshall any personal ideas about how to help, but the Jews and the Arabs would have to give up "a good deal." Perhaps, however, everyone had been put in such a difficult position owing to U.S. policy, he remarked, that "they might all like to get out of it."[77]

Nor did the picture in the Security Council look at all promising come the end of February. "Exceedingly depressed" about UN developments and the forthcoming discussions on Palestine before the Council, Lie publicly warned on the 27th that failure to carry out partition would injure UN prestige and lead to a general loss of confidence in its ability to solve world problems. Egypt's Mahmoud Bey Fawzi cautioned, however, against an international force, stating that Palestine's Arabs were so trampled upon that the Arab states might just have to rush to their rescue. An "advance group" of the Commission, which had left for London on the 22nd, heard the same "gloomy and sinister note" in the Colonial and Foreign Offices as had been sounded by their colleagues in New York: the safety of the group led by Pablo de Azcárate y Flores, who stressed that he was working for partition "because I am a friend of the Arabs," demanded that they respect and observe in the "strictest and most scrupulous manner" what regulations the British authorities in Palestine thought fit to adopt as to their residence and, above all, their movements.[78]

Trafford Smith went further, writing to Under-Secretary of State for the Colonies Thomas Lloyd that the Jews' true hope of salvation lay in accepting for the present whatever compromise the Arabs were willing to concede. He suggested, for example, minority status with a certain amount of immigration in a unitary Arab state under UN safeguards. There was, however, little or no hope of the Jews taking "so sensible a course." If they did accept, the Zionist movement would "split from top to bottom," and the terrorists would "start blowing up" the individuals who advocated moderation. Unless the situation at Lake Success took a quite unexpected turn, Smith saw no real alternative to war in Palestine on a fairly large scale after May 15—the only good result being that both sides might be "more willing to see reason after a certain amount of blood-letting." Understandably, correspondent Anne Robison concluded thus after the first week of Council deliberations: "The atmosphere at the United Nations reflects the atmosphere in Palestine itself—everywhere there is apprehension and gloom."[79]

On March 1, the mandatory government issued a strongly worded communiqué, declaring that "the continuance of indiscriminate murder and condoned terrorism can lead to the forfeiture by the Jewish community of Palestine in the eyes of the world to be numbered among the civilized peoples." Coming on the heels of the LEHI murder of twenty-eight soldiers on a British troop train, it accused the Jewish Agency, "an international body," of breaking the laws of Palestine and those of other countries in which it has operated, and castigated the increase "in numbers and barbarity" by Jewish terrorist groups. The Jewish Agency riposted that numerous Arab attacks on Jews had never been officially condemned, and that the government had seen fit to deflect attention from its failure to maintain law and order, as well as its continuing the White Paper on limited immigration, by attacking and vilifying the Agency just when the *yishuv* was in "the throes of a life and death struggle against Arab aggression." Jerusalem area commander Brigadier C.P. Jones quickly issued a statement to the effect that he was going to shoot into any quarter from which shots were fired, and not examine who started the shooting.

Sensing that the chances of an Arab-Jewish truce were small, the Palestine correspondent for the American Jewish Committee concluded that "the lamps of civilized orderly government are one by one going out in this country, and are being replaced in each sector by the candles of autonomy, leaving many dark spots yet to be lighted." This month, Tel Aviv magistrate Helmut Lowenberg went on to observe, would show whether the UN and the Jews "have been sacrificed to the scare of the third war, or whether there is a vestige of reason and moral [sic] left in world politics."[80]

The UN Commission's advance party, arriving in Jerusalem two days later, received a rude, uncomfortable awakening. Azcárate, former Spanish Republic Ambassador to the Court of St. James, found their quarters near the YMCA filthy, severely limited in furnishing and cooking utensils, and, the members feeling "like animals in a zoo," effectively cut off from everyone and surrounded by yards and yards of barbed wire, along with floodlights and security police. In an informal statement soon thereafter at a press conference, which Arab leaders did not permit Arab journalists to attend, he stressed that their mission was "chiefly administrative and technical"—not political, to study and begin the preparations needed to transfer the present administration to the new regime at the end of the mandate. Unlike the luxury of the Kiryat Shmuel quarter's Kadimah House in which the UNSCOP team had lived, Eytan observed to Shertok, these six individuals were "being made to feel the Government's ire." Nonetheless, Azcárate already concluded by the 12th, and so informed Bunche, that the Arabs could not "destroy or get rid" of the present Jewish population of over 600,000, and most probably could not prevent it from increasing by immigration on a more or less large scale. An Arab state containing as a "minority" the current *yishuv* was "simply unworkable."

Partition, which he had favored ever since the Peel Commission offer of 1937, appeared "the most reasonable formula," the solution "for the time being" offering more chance of making possible "peaceful collaboration" between Arab and Jew. Indeed, the boundaries between the "real war zones" of the two warring communities showed that partition was being carried out in fact and "making progress every day." The Jews, in particular, were prepared to take over a great number of public services without any difficult whatsoever. Given this reality, Gurney privately suggested to Azcárate that the Commission drop the implementation of a formal plan for partition, focusing instead on administering Jerusalem and on the three essential services of post, customs, and civil aviation.[81]

As for the present military situation, Commission expert Col. Roscher Lund of Norway discounted the Arabs' ability to organize themselves in units and to possess technical skill in the handling of complicated machinery. None of the neighboring Arab countries would eventually be able to use their whole forces in Palestine, while the political feelings between those states "are not too amicable and they have, to a certain degree, to watch each other." Reporting further to Bunche, the former Chief of Norwegian Intelligence during World War II praised the Jews' morale and noted that they were "fighting with their backs to the wall," but he also advised Agency liaison officer Vivian (Chaim) Herzog of his worry about the strategic weakness of the *yishuv*'s position on the coastal plain, and thought it unsound to hold isolated Jewish settlements. Lund proposed that Shertok suggest to the Security Council that the Scandinavian force of 10,000 men at present in Germany under British command should be utilized for the task of policing Jerusalem. He also showed Herzog a letter from the Norwegian minister in Cairo saying that the Americans were backing a cantonization plan with the approval of Arab circles there.

If the expected war dragged out, Lund's first memorandum continued, the Jews would have the main advantage, receiving heavy weapons and reinforcements of manpower. No interference from outside forces in the first period would most probably end in a stalemate with heavy losses on both sides. If, however, he concluded, troops to any extent worth mentioning came from the Arab countries in the first stages of the fighting, the Jews "may be practically exterminated in Palestine as they have been in many areas of Europe in the last ten years."[82]

The Attlee Cabinet's decision, first communicated on February 7 that the UK delegation at the UN should express no opinion on any proposals made in the Security Council for an international force to impose partition and abstain from voting on this issue, remained in force. Cunningham's repeated request to Creech Jones that Palestine's frontiers could be closed against Arab infiltration by pressure at the highest political level fell on deaf ears, Whitehall insisting that the Arab League would reply that these bands were not under its control and would disobey an order to withdraw. Lisicky wished Gurney to state that if his private views were those of HMG, the Council should be officially so informed; no such declaration was forthcoming. Beeley and Clayton, Zaslani discovered in London, were actively championing the Morrison Plan with their Arab contacts. Inverchapel endorsed the appeal from Hadassah's Rose Halprin to have British forces protect the road leading to its hospital on Mt. Scopus, where twelve incidents of Arab shooting had already taken place between December 30 and February 26; Whitehall did not reply.[83]

Smuts cabled an urgent plea on the 8th for Attlee that HMG not sit back while the Palestine situation end in "a dreadful massacre" of Jews and Arabs, in which the Jews might at first prevail only to run finally the risk of "extermination" by the combined Arab forces. The Prime Minister answered ten days later that the two communities in Palestine had not cooperated "at all" with the Administration for the past few years "in spite of all our efforts to get them to do so." The government had done everything possible to help the United Nations in their work at every phase "short of implementation of the partition plan," but it was "not in our power" to prevent the consequences of the UN's approval of that plan. The Cabinet had decided with regret that it could not leave a military force in Jerusalem, but it was working for a truce to be observed there. Some of the functions exercised by the Central Government were being devolved to the local municipalities, where civil guard and police forces were being established. "I feel sure," Atlee ended, "that, in the light of what I have said, you at any rate will not regard our attitude as unhelpful."[84]

The *yishuv* certainly thought otherwise. Refused the use of reconnaissance planes to haul supplies to isolated Jewish sectors, one even shot at by the British to bring it down, Hagana intelligence also discovered that Gurney chose not to ask London to free funds for the import of necessary fuel and fuel products after the shutdown of the refineries. Hearing Fox-Strangways discount the Arab danger to the Jews in rather scathing terms in order to warn that the real threat lay inside their own ranks, Kohn replied that, engaged in "a life and death struggle" against Arab aggression, the *yishuv* could hardly be expected to start an internecine war among Jews. (At the same time, a grenade thrown by one Hagana member on the 4th at an Irgun meeting in Tel Aviv to collect funds injured about 200 persons. The zealous youth was court-martialed, but head commander Galili thought a union of forces with the dissidents impossible of achievement.) Sensing that the future of the Jewish state depended upon the Jews themselves, especially given Austin's recent declaration to the Security Council opposing an armed enforcement of partition, the leadership went ahead with intensive mobilizing of the twenty-two to twenty-five age group and formed a Provisional Government with a thirteen-member Cabinet.[85]

Notwithstanding the warnings of the Chief Secretariat's J.G.F. Sheringham to Herzog that only conceding to the ex-Mufti that all of Jerusalem be the capital of the Arab state would save the Jews from "annihilation," the Hagana drew up Plan Dalet (D) on March 10. This defensive plan aimed to relieve the city and, in the event of expected Arab attack, to gain control of the areas of the Jewish state assigned by the partition plan, and to "defend its borders and those blocs of Jewish settlement and such of the Jewish population as were outside the partition borders." As historian Yoav Gelber has pointed out against claims by later advocates of the Palestinian Arab "narrative" that the plan intended an "ethnic cleansing" and expulsion of all Arabs from the country, only Arab villagers who offered active resistance in these areas were to be expelled. Following statements by Creech Jones in Commons and Cadogan before the Council which he labeled "sabotage" of the partition decision, Ben-Gurion cabled Shertok on the 11th to stress to the Commission that the UN should authorize the immediate delivery of weapons to the *yishuv*; recognize its Provisional Government

Council; restrict British troops after May 15 to a defined area for their withdrawal; and take effective measures to prevent the further entry of Arab League armed forces into Palestine. Otherwise, the United States and all other UN members would share responsibility for "impending catastrophe." Following Chamoun's proposal to the Commission of a federal state, Shertok would do so six days later.[86]

The Arabs, firm as ever in their opposition, took heart from the recent Council deliberations and expressed confidence in the failure of partition. Entering Palestine on the 6th with a large, well-armed contingent and liaison officers headed by a former pro-Nazi collaborator in Syria, Kaukji soon told *Al-Ahram* that the ALA was fighting for "the annihilation of the Zionists," a phrase repeated by Haj Amin to Jaffa's *Al-Sarih* in declaring that the Arabs would continue fighting "until the Zionists were annihilated and the whole of Palestine became a purely Arab state." Their cause received a boost when eleven Christian groups in Palestine denounced the partition plan as a violation of the sacredness of the Holy Land and the natural rights of the Arabs, "the people of the country." Syrian Defense Minister Ahmad al-Sharabati informed U.S. Minister Robert Memminger that it would probably be unnecessary to defeat partition since the Jews now appreciated the strength of the Arabs, who could overrun all of Palestine within two weeks after the British left. "We are determined finally to get rid of the Jewish danger— no state, no political existence, no immigration and nothing whatsoever," trumpeted an *Al-Difa'a* editorial. In its reply to Lie's questions, the AHC "categorically" rejected any form of partition, insisting on one independent state for the whole of Palestine. The fighting did not let up, Hagana armored cars entering al-Faluja thirty kilometers northeast of Gaza City in an effort to halt attacks on convoys to the local *yishuv* settlements, killing thirty-seven villagers and wounding scores more at the cost of seven Jewish dead and four wounded.[87]

Two days after stating that the Arabs were determined "to get rid of the Jews once and for all," al-Qadir al-Husseini successfully carried out his boldest attack to date. An explosion on the 11th partially wrecked the Jewish Agency headquarters and killed ten persons, including Jewish National Fund director Leib Jaffe, and wounded ninety others. Armenian-American Anton Daoud Kamilyo (a Christian Arab also known as Abu Yusef), the U.S. consulate's regular Arab chauffeur, drove a green Ford flying the Stars and Stripes and carrying in the trunk another of el-Kutub's lethal bombs in two packages with grenades placed on top, parked the car at the main entrance, and made a quick exit by the back door. Receiving a considerable award from al-Husseini, including cash and tickets for his family and himself to Central America, he fled in a taxi a few minutes before the 200 lbs. of TNT went off, and reached the safety of Egypt.[88]

Convinced by now that the Security Council could not proceed with partition, and that its members' agreement to attempt conciliation "will prove fruitless," Marshall advised Truman on the 5th that the Council would most likely refer the Palestine problem to an immediate special session of the General Assembly for fresh consideration. He instructed Austin the same day to speak out strongly against the Belgian resolution (deleting Austin's first resolution about the Council's implementing partition), but abstain from voting in order to avoid any question of a veto. He also asked Austin to consider State's draft, which he should soon propose, that if a special GA session found conciliation unsuccessful, "until the people of Palestine are ready for self-government they should be placed under the trusteeship system of the United Nations." The first of Austin's resolutions of February 25, calling for the Council to accept the GA partition resolution as a basis for action, failed to achieve a majority of seven votes that afternoon. In effect, the members thus tacitly refused to accept the three requests made of the Council by the GA on November 29, the other two empowering the Commission to implement partition if the Council found the Palestine situation constituting a threat to international peace and security.[89]

At noon on March 8, the same day that Truman declared he would be a candidate for the Presidential election in November, Marshall told Austin that the President had approved the draft speech "for use if and when necessary." McClintock informed Lovett later that the offices of Henderson and Rusk had prepared detailed trusteeship agreements for either a direct UN trusteeship or a trusteeship of the three legatees of World War I (the United States, United Kingdom, and France). In addition, Marshall let Epstein know that his request to export light armor plate to Palestine for the *yishuv*'s need of protected vehicles against Arab attack would run counter to the embargo. Lie objected to the U.S. delegation's insistence that partition had to be implemented by peaceful means, telling Austin on the 13th that this was impossible, and if it were not enforced, "the UN would go downhill rapidly to nothing."

Nonetheless, given that the situation in Palestine "grew daily more fraught with danger to international peace," and fearing that Gromyko's proposal, having the Council deal with the question of security in Palestine before any review of the November resolution, would be linked to partition's implementation after May 15, Marshall sent Austin a TOP SECRET US URGENT telegram three days later: he should deliver the statement which Truman had approved so that the Council, divesting itself of responsibility for Palestine, could proceed to consider the security problem there divorced from the political issue of partition with economic union. He closed: "The time factor is imperative and Council must act without delay."

With Austin hesitant about overturning Truman's original support for partition, Rusk and Ross got him "back on track" on the 17th by agreeing to have him add in the statement that trusteeship "would be a temporary measure and without prejudice to whatever future settlement were arrived at by agreement between the peoples of Palestine." Austin then alerted Cadogan, Parodi, and China's Tingfu Tsiang—but not Gromyko, who thought that all attempts at conciliation by a special committee were valueless—to the impending reversal of US policy. All four delegations (Trafford Smith taking an active part as well) then took part in preparing the final draft of his speech.[90]

Hearing from various sources of State's objective, the pro-partitionists countered in various ways. Clifford, aided by suggestions from Lowenthal and Niles, drafted a lengthy memorandum to Truman on March 8 which advised that, uninfluenced by election considerations, endorsing the GA recommendation of November 29, 1947, was "in complete conformity with the settled policy of the United States" and "best for America." He argued that implementing partition—the Assembly resolution adopted largely at Truman's "insistence," backed by both political parties, offering the best hope of a permanent solution, and strengthening the U.S. position vis-à-vis Russia—was crucial to the UN's future and to the country's cementing alliances with South America and Western Europe. Benjamin V. Cohen, State's former Counselor, contributed two long articles to the *New York Herald Tribune* positing that the Security Council had the authority to carry out the Assembly's recommendation, and offering this admonition: "If the charter is to live, we must not exalt the letter which killeth and destroy the spirit which giveth life."

Eichelberger, whose AAUN reprinted these articles for wide circulation, warned Austin that British "sabotage" and American "timidity," even as the Arabs openly announced their intention of using force to prevent the carrying out of the Assembly resolution, had "dangerously weakened" the authority of the UN. Proskauer wrote to Lovett and to Austin endorsing the AAUN position. Frankfurter and Rosenman, Epstein cabled Ben-Gurion, had joined Cohen in using their personal contacts with the Administration in favor of the GA recommendation. The Jewish War Veterans of the United States, first to offer volunteers to implement partition and then forwarding compasses and binoculars for Hagana use, resolved to send a Friendship Train to the camps in Cyprus and to Palestine.[91]

Their varied efforts to sway Truman did not succeed. When Sullivan, pressed into action by the Nation Associates' Karr, tried to mention Forrestal's role in the forces against partition, the President "shut him up rapidly." Writing to Shultz, Karr observed that Truman had isolated himself from anyone but his "kitchen cabal," which included military aide and poker card partner General Harry Vaughan, a known antisemite, and the equally bigoted Snyder, so that his position on Palestine could not be good. *Collier's* Washington representative Bill Hillman informed Ruffer that during Truman's Caribbean trip, he had said to Hillman that he was the sponsor of partition and still believed that this was the solution, but did not know what should be done to implement it in the face of strong Arab resistance. He hoped that "something can be worked out" (one of Truman's favorite phrases), and had appealed to the Arab rulers to maintain peace—to no avail. The President told Senator Murray that he did not want to talk about the Palestine problem at this time, and would not want to see a group of pro-Zionist Senators. Replying to a personal letter from Senator Francis J. Myers (D, PA), who claimed that Austin's February 24 speech was replete with "vague generalities and legalistic double-talk which the public can't understand," Truman replied that he naturally was not happy over the implication "that I might be ducking any issues." "This is not my manner of meeting a situation," he emphasized, and he invited the Senator for a private talk in the future to clarify the matter.[92]

Truman's outburst at the start of his press conference on March 11 reflected the personal umbrage taken at the mounting pressure and what he would later describe as the "rather quarrelsome and emotional ways" in which he was asked by "the Jews" (immediately qualified in his memoir as "the extreme Zionists") and others to support partition. He began with a vigorous denial of what he termed a vicious statement by a columnist in a New York paper that the President had said the Jews of New York were disloyal to their country, and reiterated that it was "just a lie out of whole cloth." Listeners readily understood the reference to a column three days earlier by Drew Pearson, who had reported that a New York City publisher, whose wife was Jewish, asked Truman for further clarification. "When you speak of New York Jews," he interrupted, are you referring to such people as Bernard Baruch or my wife? Truman glared, according to Pearson's report, assured his visitor that he did not mean to include these two, and then "abruptly changed the subject."

Ted Thackrey, editor of the *New York Post* and husband of publisher Dorothy Schiff, had in fact been summoned to the White House to explain his newspaper's strong support for a Jewish state in Palestine. Since Thackrey knew Truman in Kansas and was not Jewish, the President, speaking freely, said that there was "no way to please" the "goddamned New York Jews." Subsequently, Thackrey declared that Pearson's reference to disloyalty was "inaccurate," but that the story in general was not made up out of whole cloth.[93]

On March 10, Lie told a press conference that decisive action to partition Palestine into Jewish and Arab states was still possible now. Two days later, as the UN Commission reported that Palestine would likely suffer "severely from administrative chaos and widespread strife and bloodshed" at the termination of the Mandate and the Trusteeship Council approved a draft Statute for the City of Jerusalem, Dewey Stone visited with Weizmann in New York City. The Zionist avatar was troubled by Truman's refusal to grant him a meeting. Stone returned to Boston to attend a Zeta Beta Tau fraternity dinner at the Parker House Hotel, where he and B'nai Brith President Goldman were being honored. Hearing a disconsolate Stone confiding Weizmann's distress about Truman's stand, Goldman replied that, by coincidence, he had just visited Kansas City, where he presented a B'nai B'rith award to Eddie Jacobson, who, he went on, was deeply interested in and concerned about Jews. Goldman offered to call Jacobson to urge him to intervene with Truman. Stone and Goldman borrowed a handful of quarters from others at the dinner, went to the hotel lobby's pay station telephone for privacy, and phoned Jacobson. Stone invited Jacobson to meet him at the Waldorf Astoria as soon as possible. The two men met for breakfast the next morning, where Stone briefed Jacobson on the issues involved.[94]

Jacobson took a train for Washington that same Saturday and, without an appointment, walked in on the President of the United States. Connelly had urged him not to discuss Palestine, but he quickly responded that he was determined to discuss this very subject with his old friend. After a few minutes of personal talk about their families and Jacobson's business, Jacobson brought up the Palestine issue. Immediately, he subsequently wrote, Truman became "tense in appearance, abrupt in speech, and very bitter in the words he was throwing my way." Hearing Truman say that he was satisfied to let the matter take its course through the UN, Jacobson tried to argue "from every possible angle," also reminding Truman that he had expressed reverence for Weizmann, now an "old and sick man" who had made his long journey to the United States expressly to see the President. Remaining "immovable," Truman replied how disrespectful and mean certain Jewish leaders had been to him, leading Jacobson to think that his dear friend was "as close to being an anti-Semite as a man could possibly be." Shocked that some Jewish leaders should be responsible for Truman's attitude, Jacobson was "completely crushed" at the firm, angry refusal to receive Weizmann.

Suddenly, Jacobson's eyes caught on a statue of Andrew Jackson resting on Truman's desk. "Harry, all your life you have had a hero," he began, and you are probably the best read man in America on the life of Andrew Jackson. "I too have a hero, a man I never met but who is, I think, the greatest Jew who ever lived." Having studied his past, "I agree with you that he is a gentleman and a great statesman as well. I am talking about Chaim Weizmann." A very sick man, "almost broken in health," he has traveled thousands of miles "just to see you and plead the cause of my People." You know, Jacobson continued, that he had absolutely nothing to do with the fact that some American Jewish leaders insulted you. "It doesn't sound like you, Harry, because I thought that you could take this stuff they have been handing out to you.... If you will see him you will properly and accurately be informed on the situation as it exists in Palestine, and yet you refuse to see him." Truman began drumming with his fingers on the Oval Office desk, then swiveled his chair and looked out the window at the Rose Garden. Jacobson knew the sign: Truman was changing his mind. All of a sudden, he swiveled himself around again, looked at Jacobson straight in the eyes, and said "You win, you baldheaded son of a bitch. I will see him. Tell Matt to arrange this meeting as soon as possible after I return from New York on March 17." He then pressed the button for Connelly to enter, and set up an off-the-record meeting so that the press and public would know absolutely nothing about it. Jacobson went straight to the Statler Hotel and, for the first time in his life, drank two double Bourbons alone before going to his room to tell Goldman and Bisgyer about the appointment for Weizmann.[95]

The next day, Jacobson, accompanied by Bisgyer, met Weizmann for the first time. Weizmann had already told Parodi, who favored a federal state and was anxious that the Jews would be "massacred" by the millions of Arab forces, that numbers were not decisive: "The trouble with the Egyptian army is that its soldiers are too lean and its officers too fat." He remained convinced that if the Jews stood firm they would win through, and so when told by Jacobson of the future meeting with Truman, he gave "the sweetest smile" Jacobson had ever seen. Informed that the interview was arranged so that it would not be too much of a strain on his health, Weizmann replied that he was ready to travel at any time. There was no hurry, the unassuming haberdashery store owner pointed out, because Weizmann could not go until the President returned to the White House after addressing a Saint Patrick's Day dinner at New York's Astor Hotel, so he would have a few days to recover his strength for the journey to Washington. The next day, Jacobson spent a half hour with Weizmann over a cup of tea, and fell immediately under the old man's spell. He left the apartment, Stone later recalled, completely prepared "intellectually and emotionally" to exercise further influence on Truman.[96]

On the 15th, Jacobson called Connelly from New York and finalized the meeting for March 18, Weizmann to enter through the East gate in order to avoid the press. Weizmann wished Jacobson to accompany him, but this idea was abandoned because (as Connelly pointed out) the press would readily identify Jacobson, and because he had to be "saved" to see Truman again in case the meeting with Weizmann did not go well. A "completely exhausted" Jacobson returned to Kansas City, where his brother had just been admitted to the local hospital, while Weizmann took counsel with Kirchwey and a few other close associates. Wishing him good luck one day before the crucial appointment, she pointed out that Truman's speech to Congress that afternoon restated the country's allegiance to the UN and to keeping the door open to the Soviet Union and to all countries genuinely cooperating in the maintenance of peace. It followed that the one area of fundamental agreement between Washington and Moscow, which lay with the GA resolution on the partitioning of Palestine, should be protected for its intrinsic importance and because it might conceivably lead to the enlargement of the areas of agreement.

Recalling the conversation that she and Shultz had with Weizmann on the 14th, "Freda" also stressed the value in underscoring that the *yishuv* would not fail to accept assistance, even if unsolicited, from "the countries of the East" if it were betrayed by the so-called democratic world. Finally, she advised, hearing from a usually reliable source that Truman considered the report of the Anglo-American Committee "his bible," a report that could create the perfect background for relegating the Palestine question to the Trusteeship Council, it might be worthwhile for Weizmann to explore this angle as well.[97]

Weizmann's interview that Thursday, for which he had asked twenty-five minutes and Truman graciously extended another twenty when this time proved to be insufficient, raised his spirits. As Weizmann soon told Shultz, he requested the lifting of the embargo, a directive to the U.S. delegation to ask for the immediate dispatch of the full UN Commission for Palestine in order to implement partition, and indications to the Arabs that Washington opposed their assaults upon the *yishuv*. His wife Vera added in a diary that he also asked for free immigration into Palestine. Truman responded that the lifting of the embargo was under discussion and he hoped to be able to tell him in a few days some good news, while he had already sent messages to the Arabs as Weizmann had suggested and the matter was being taken up with Ibn Saud. In general, he expressed agreement with Weizmann, and promised that he would do everything possible. Weizmann talked about the potentials of industrial development in Palestine and the need for land if the future Jewish immigrants were to be cared for, and impressed upon Truman the importance of the Negev to any future Jewish commonwealth.

Truman explained in plain language why he had at first put off seeing Weizmann, and that his primary concern was "to see justice done without bloodshed." When Weizmann left the Oval Office, Truman later wrote, "I felt that he had reached an understanding of my policy and that I knew what it was he wanted." In Eban's concise telling: "The President gave his visitor a specific commitment. He would work for the establishment of a Jewish State, of which the Negev would be part."[98]

Hearing in the course of this interview, as related in his autobiography, that "the President was sympathetic personally, and still indicated a firm resolve to press forward with partition," Weizmann left for New York "happy and gratified." Bisgyer related this some hours later to a greatly relieved Jacobson. The illness and "constant seesawing of events," which plagued Weizmann ever since he reached New York almost six weeks earlier, had produced in him what Vera termed "a black, even cosmic mood of despair."[99] Now, thanks to Jacobson, the doors to the White House had been opened. At another critical moment, Weizmann's personal appeal to the decisive American voice had again reached a receptive ear. The clouds had lifted—or so it appeared to the Zionist herald and his intimate circle on March 18, 1948.

Endnotes

1   *JTA*, January 2 and 5, 1948; Karsh, *Palestine Betrayed*, 161; *New York Times*, January 1, 1948; Myerson to Gurney, January 8, 1948, S25/4057, CZA; Morris, *1948*, 90; *New York Herald Tribune*, January 1, 1948; Slutzky, *Sefer Toldot HaHagana*, 1545.

2   Rosenberg to Myerson, January 4, 1948, 687/2-P, ISA; Herzog memo, January 6, 1948, Isaac HaLevi Herzog MSS, Heikhal Shlomo, Jerusalem; Warhaftig to Trusteeship Council, January 11, 1948, A297/35, CZA; Gluckmann report, January 4–7, 1948, 687/3-P, ISA.

3   McLeod interview, January 2, 1948, A297/35, CZA; Rosenberg to Myerson, January 4, 1948, 687/2-P; Khouri to Solh, Dec. 29, 1947, 65/8-Het Tsadi; both in ISA.

4   Horowitz report, Dec. 31, 1947, BGA; Report, January 12, 1948, S25/3569, CZA.

5   Bunche to Lie, January 5, 1948, DAG-13/3.1.0:2, UN Archives.

6   A.W. Cordier and W. Foote, eds., *Public Papers of the Secretaries-General of the United Nations, 1, Trygve Lie, 1946–1953* (New York, 1969), 105–106, 108–109; Nakhleh to Lie, January 19, 1948, S25/5176, CZA.

7   *Foreign Relations of the United States* (hereafter *FRUS*), `1948, vol. 5, part 2 (Washington, D.C., 1976), 537–539.

8 Cunningham to Creech Jones, January 2, 1948, FO371/68635, PRO.

9 Slutzky, *Sefer Toldot HaHagana*, 1518–1520; FO371/68635, PRO; *JTA*, January 12, 1948; Chancery to Eastern Department, February 18, 1948, FO371/68635, PRO. The story of *rekhesh* operations in the United States is dramatically told in Leonard Slater's *The Pledge* (New York, 1970). For other efforts, see Pinhas Vazeh, *HaMesima—Rekhesh* (Tel Aviv, 1966).

10 Morris, *1948*, 84, 86–88, 99–100. A Hagana-Irgun understanding was impossible at this time, given kidnappings of and violence against each other's members, and particularly when the Irgun charged that its rival had caused the death of the Irgunist Yedidya Segal, which the Hagana in turn called a "blood libel." *HaMashkif*, January 18, 1948; Irgun broadcast, January 18, 1948, A203/187, CZA; *HaBoker*, January 19, 1948; Galili remarks at Va'ad HaBitahon, January 18, 1948, S25/9345, CZA.

11 Morris, *1948*, 81–83, 89, 91; Memo, January 3, 1948, 93.170/8, ISA; Heydt to Shertok, S25/1701, CZA. For a Palestinian sheikh's negative opinion of Haj Amin, see Report, January 28, 1948, FO37168501, PRO. For the Arab Revolt, see Penkower, *Palestine in Turmoil*, 2, and for Haj Amin's wartime activities, see Penkower, *Decision on Palestine Deferred, passim*.

12 Elizabeth Monroe, "Arab states and the Strife in Palestine," *The Scotsman*, January 10, 1948; Eban to Bunche, March 16, 1948, 41.0, 45516/13, ISA; Report, January 17, 1948, S25/3569; Sasson to Abdullah, January 11, 1948, S25/9038; Danin to Sasson, January 4, 1948, S25/3569; all in CZA; Epstein memo, n.d., "Notes on the Military Strength of the Arab Countries," 21/35-Het Tsadi, ISA; HetReports, January 8 and 11, 1948, L35/19, CZA.

13 Jewish Agency London report, January 13, 1948, Z4/21282, CZA; Cohen, *Palestine and the Great Powers*, 326–330; Danin to Sasson, January 4, 1948, Z4/31282, CZA; Jones memo, January 2, 1948, 867N.01/1-648, SD.

14 JAEJ, January 6, 1948, CZA; Cohen, *Palestine and the Great Powers*, 309; press release, January 6, 1948, S25/4013, CZA; Cunningham to Lloyd, January 15, 1948, FO371/68531, PRO; Fitzgerald to MacMichael, March 2, 1948, MacMichael MSS; Grimwood to ICRC, January 4, 1948, G59/I/GC/16, International Committee of the Red Cross Archives (hereafter ICRC), Geneva; *Palestine Post*, January 16, 1948.

15 Philip Brutton, *A Captain's Mandate, Palestine: 1946–1948* (London, 1996), 116–117; *The Scotsman*, January 5, 1948; Bell, *Terror Out of Zion*, 267; Report, January 19, 1948, S25/4050, CZA; Slutzky, *Sefer Toldot HaHagana*, 1410–1411, 1431–1432; Gol Kalev, "Aborting Was Not an Option," *Jerusalem Post Magazine*, January 19, 2018, 12–15. The four *kibbutzim* of the Etzion bloc were

Kfar Etzion, Masu'ot Yitshak, Ein Tsurim, and Revadim. Among the thirty-five was Moshe Avigdor Perlstein, a former Bnai Akiva counselor and graduate of Yeshiva University. He was the first American killed in the Palestinian civil war. In August 1949, kibbutz Netiv HaLamed Heh (Path of the Thirty-five) was founded by former Palmah members at a key point along the route which the convoy had traversed that fateful night. That November, the decomposed bodies, twelve identified by Rav Aryeh Levin by means of a rarely performed biblical lottery attributed to the Vilna Gaon (*Goral HaGra*), were brought to the Mt. Herzl cemetery in Jerusalem and buried in a separate section.

16 JAEJ, January 6, 1948; Ben-Gurion to Cunningham, January 8, 1948; Jewish Agency statement, January 6, 1948; both in S25/4013; Teneh report, April 6, 1948, S25/9671; Report, February 27, 1948, S25/3991; Fox-Strangways to Myerson, January 16, 1948, S25/7725; all in CZA; Slutzky, *Sefer Toldot HaHagana*, 1345.

17 Fisher to JAEJ, January 13, 1948, S25/1701, CZA; Royall to Forrestal, January 15, 1948, Palestine 1948–1949, William Leahy MSS, RG218, NA; Cadogan statement, January 14, 1948, S25/10458, CZA; "Anglo-American Competition in the Middle East," June 21, 1948, 93/65/13, ISA; Shragai to Jewish Agency, February 21, 1948, S25/1702, CZA; *Documents on Israeli-Soviet Relations*, 259. For Shultz's plan of action, see her "Memorandum on Palestine," January 29, 1948, MC280/238, Kirchwey MSS. She also had Congressman John A. Blatnik of Minnesota insert into the *Congressional Record* her lengthy article which appeared that day in the *Nation* about the U.S.-UK "conspiracy" against Palestine. *Congressional Record*—Appendix, January 30, 1948, A647–649.

18 *FRUS, 1948*, vol. 5, part 2, 533–536; "Policy Problem Summary, Palestine," January 2, 1948, Box 1, Rusk MSS; Johnson Memo, January 7, 1948, Box 1, McClintock MSS; both in SD.

19 Epstein-Eban memo to the Executive, January 7, 1948, S25/5354, CZA; Forrestal memo, January 6, 1948, PSF156, HSTL; Millis, *The Forrestal Diaries*, 356–360; Kermit Roosevelt, "The Partition of Palestine, A Lesson in Pressure Politics," *Middle East Journal*, 2:1 (January 1948): 1–16; Cabinet meeting, January 16, 1948, HSTL.

20 Memorandum, January 14, 1948, MG 26, J4, vol. 310, PAC.

21 *FRUS, 1948*, vol. 5, part 2, 542; RTE to Bermingham, January 31, 1948, 65/13-Het Tsadi, ISA.

22 *FRUS, 1948*, vol. 5, part 2, 545–554.

23 Ibid., 360–361.

24 Ibid., 556–562, 573–581.

25 Austin to Marshall, January 17, 1948, Box 1, McClintock MSS; Ruffer to Sharef, January 19, 1948, S25/5354, CZA; Meeting, January 19, 1948, DAG.1/1.1.3, Box 1, UN Archives; Falla to Bunche, January 20, 1948; Meeting, January 21, 1948; both in DAG-13.3.1.0, Box 3, UN Archives; Smith to Martin, January 22, 1948, FO71/68530, PRO; *FRUS, 1948*, vol. 5, part 2, 554–555.

26 James Reston, "Bipartisan Policy on Holy Land Seen," *New York Times*, January 27, 1948; Forrestal testimony, January 19, 1948, *Investigation of the National Defense Program* (Wash., D.C., 1948), 25448–25450.

27 Charles Van Devander and James A. Wechsler, "Man in the Saddle; Arabian Style," *New York Post*, January 19 and 21, 1948; Shulson to Akzin, January 23, 1948, Confidential files-AZEC, ZA; Price-Ross conversation, January 27, 1948, Box 1, McClintock MSS; Welles to Akzin, January 26, 1948, Box 129, Sumner Welles MSS, FDRL; Eichelberger to Dulles *et al.*, January 28, 1948, Box 66, Clark Eichelberger MSS, Manuscripts and Archives Division, New York Public Library, New York City; AAUN memorandum, January 29, 1948, Z5/409/1, CZA; Roosevelt to Truman, January 29, 1948; Truman to Roosevelt, February 2, 1948; both in file 4560, Eleanor Roosevelt MSS, FDRL. Truman spoke in a similar vein at this time to Representative John Blatnik and to Senator Murray. Kerr to Shultz, February 2, 1948, A427/2, CZA.

28 *Living UJA History: Irving Bernstein* (Jerusalem, 1995), 5–13; Myerson, "A Report from Palestine," January 25, 1948, MRD-1, 37/2, UJA Archives, New York City; Montor interview with Monty Noam Penkower, June 8, 1977 (in the author's possession); Beeley note, January 27, 1948, FO371/68533, PRO.

29 Abba Eban, "Tragedy and Triumph," in M.W. Weisgal and J. Carmichael, eds., *Chaim Weizmann, A Biography by Several Hands* (London, 1962), 304; Joseph I. Linton, "Memories of 1948," n.d. (my thanks to Dr. Josef Cohn for a copy); Vera Weizmann, *The Impossible Takes Longer* (London, 1967), 221; Shertok to Ben-Gurion, January 26, 1948, S53/226, CZA; Meeting, January 30, 1948, DAG-13/3.1.0.1-5, UN Archives.

30 Slutzky, *Sefer Toldot HaHagana*, 1344, 1406, 1416; *Mishmar*, January 18, 1948; Austin to Marshall, January 27, 1948, Box 1, Rusk MSS; Gurney-Herzog interview, January 26, 1948, S25/28; Cunningham-Silver talk, January 27, 1948, A289/125; both in CZA; "Summary of Proposals," March 8, 1948, Box 13, Clark Clifford MSS, HSTL.

31 *JTA*, January 25, 1948; Bevin to Defence Minister, February 12, 1948, FO800/487; Beeley (?) to Falla, January 31, 1948, FO371/68531; both in PRO; Shertok at meeting, January 15, 1948, DAG-13/3.1.0.1-4; Meeting,

January 21, 1948, DAG-13/3.1.0.1; both in Box 3, UN Archives; *Palcor*, January 29, 1948; *HaMashkif*, February 2, 1948.

32 *Palcor*, February 2, 1948; Knox memo, February 3, 1948, Box 2, Rusk MSS; UK delegation memo, February 4, 1948, RG 25, G2, vol. 84–85/19, PAC; Eban-Horowitz to Bunche, February 1, 1948, Z5/409/1, CZA.

33 Memo, February 4, 1948, RG25, G2, vol. 84–85/19, PAC; Commission report, February 9, 1948, DAG-13/3.1.0:3, UN Archives; Pearson to St. Laurent, February 14, 1948, RG25, G2, vol. 84–85/19, PAC.

34 *FRUS, 1948*, vol. 5, part 2, 586–592.

35 Ibid., 600–603, 617–625.

36 Wrong to St. Laurent, February 4 and 5, 1948, RG 25, series A-12, vol. 2093, part VI, PAC.

37 *FRUS, 1948*, vol. 5, part 2, 625–626; Epstein to Shertok, February 16, 1948, L35/135, CZA.

38 Millis, *The Forrestal Diaries*, 371–372; Javits *et al.* to Marshall, February 10, 1948; Marshall to Javits, February 12, 1948; both in Box 2, Schulson MSS.

39 *FRUS, 1948*, vol. 5, part 2, 592–599. For Wadsworth, see Epstein to Roosevelt, February 5, 1948, L35/94, CZA, and Penkower, *Palestine in Turmoil* and Penkower, *Decision on Palestine Deferred*, passim.

40 Consultation memo, February 4, 1948, 93/127/1, ISA; Sherwin to Dewey, February 4, 1948, 5:271/27, Thomas Dewey MSS, University of Rochester Library, Rochester.

41 Epstein to Kirchwey, February 6, 1948, L35/129; Kerr to Shultz, February 3, 1948, A427/2; Murray statement, February 4, 1948, A427/10; all in CZA; AJC memo, February 5, 1948, Box 8, Proskauer MSS; Epstein to Ben-Gurion, February 10, 1948, L35/120; Epstein to Lourie, February 10, 1948, Z6/2250; both in CZA.

42 Epstein to Ben-Gurion, February 4, 1948, S25/1702; Lifshitz memo, c. February 15, 1948, A116/89; both in CZA; Lowenthal to Max, February 12, 1948, P-140, Box 7, Wise MSS, AJHS; Ruffer to Sharef, February 10, 1948, 93.03/64/18, ISA; Hilldring to Morgenthau, February 6, 1948, Z6/2250, CZA; *New York Times*, February 15, 1948; *New York Herald Tribune*, February 9 and 11, 1948; *Star-Journal and Tribune*, February 8, 1948; *Documents on Israeli-Soviet Relations*, 262.

43 Eban, *Chaim Weizmann*, 304–305; Press statement, February 4, 1948, WA; Linton, "Memories of 1948"; Weizmann to Truman, February 10, 1948; Vera Weizmann diary; both in WA. Newspaper men Herbert Bayard Swope and George Backer came two days earlier to polish the text, and Josef Cohn flew to Washington to deliver it personally to the White House.

44 Connelly to Weizmann, February 12, 1948, WA; Truman, *Memoirs*, vol. 2, 188; *FRUS, 1948*, vol. 5, part 2, 626.

45 *FRUS, 1948*, vol. 5, part 2, 605–612.

46 *Palestine Post*, February 2, 1948; A298/98, CZA; Gershon Agron, *Asir HaNe'emanut* (Tel Aviv, 1964), 160–168; Esther Hecht, "Media in a War Zone: Stronger Than TNT," *Jewish Herald*, April. 3, 1996.

47 *Palestine Post*, February 2, 1948; Council to Shertok, February 4, 1948, 127/2-Het Tsadi, ISA; Memo, February 2, 1948, P573/1, Kohn MSS; Kohn to Fox-Strangways, February 6, 1948, S25/4019, CZA; Report, February 1948, Palestine Correspondent report, AJC Archives; Condensed Survey, February–May 15, 1948, A289/125, CZA; British intelligence report, January 28–February 11, 1948, 65/8-Het Tsadi, ISA; Herzog memo, February 15, 1948, S25/4065; Kohn to Shertok, February 18, 1947, S25/1702; both in CZA; Brutton, *A Captain's Mandate*, 121; Report, February 14, 1948, CO537/3903, PRO.

48 Report, January 29, 1948, A/AC.21/7, UN Archives; Reynolds report, February 8, 1948, L35/65; Egyptian press, February 11, 1948, S25/5354; both in CZA; Cunningham report, February 22, 1948, Smith MSS (courtesy of Trafford Smith); Macatee to State, February 9, 1948, Box 2, Rusk MSS; Aidé-memoire, February 5, 1948; Childs to State, February 7 and 10, 1948; all in Box 1, McClintock MSS.

49 Ben-Gurion to Shertok, February 12, 1948, CZA; DAG-13/3.1.0:4, UN Archives; Press release, February 16, 1948, Z6/49; Epstein to Marshall, February. 14, 1948, L35/11; both in CZA.

50 *FRUS, 1948*, vol. 5, part 2, 627–629, 631–632.

51 Joseph P. Lash, *Eleanor: The Years Alone* (NY, 1972), 127–128.

52 Ruffer to Sharef, February 10, 1948, 93.03/64/18, ISA; Slutski, *Sefer Toldot HaHagana*, 1412–1414; Morris, *1948*, 106; Aryeh H. Bar Natan, "Av Ketana K'Khaf Ish," *Makor Rishon*, April 27, 2012; Brutton, *A Captain's Mandate*, 121–122.

53 Press conference, February 17, 1948, 7143/8-Het Tsadi, ISA; *JTA*, February 18, 1948.

54 Cunningham to Creech Jones, February 4, 1948; Beeley memo, February 6, 1948; both in FO371/68531; FO371/68501; Creech Jones memo, February 4, 1948, CAB 129/24; February 5, 1948, CAB 128/12; Bevin to Kirkbride, February 9, 1948, FO800/477; all in PRO; Easterman memo, February 14, 1948, Z6/2250, CZA; Bentwich to Taylor, February 10, 1948, Myron Taylor MSS, FDRL; Bentwich to Weizmann, February 17, 1948, 2/14, Robert Weltsch MSS, Leo Baeck Institute, Center for Jewish History, New York City; Zaslani to Sacharov, February 15, 1948, S25/20636, CZA.

55 *Forrestal Diaries*, 376; *FRUS, 1948*, vol. 5, part 2, 632–633, 637–639, notes to 648–649.

56 Lash, *Eleanor Alone*, 128; Herzog and Uziel to Truman, February 20, 1948, S25/5354, CZA; Jacobson to Cohn, April 1, 1952, WA; Granoff to Marcus, January 3, 1968, SC-6610, AJA; Jacobson to Truman, February 21, 1948, Jacobson MSS, HSTL; Reston, "Palestine Issue Put High in Bronx Wallace Victory," *New York Times*, February 19 and 20, 1948; *JTA*, February 25, 1948; Hadani memo, February 24, 1948, Paul O'Dwyer MSS, Special Collections, Jewish Theological Seminary Library, New York City. The AAUP manifesto of February 10, 1948, is in Box 66, Eichelberger MSS.

57 *FRUS, 1948*, vol. 5, part 2, notes to 637, 640, 645–648.

58 Ibid., 627, 640–643; Linton to Locker, February 22, 1948, WA. Lovett did share with Forrestal the gist of Austin's future speech. Diary, February 22, 1948, Forrestal MSS.

59 *FRUS, 1948*, vol. 5, part 2, 647; A116/89; S25/4151; both in CZA; Kohn to Shertok, February 24, 1948, 86/8; British League manifesto, February 1948, 573/1-P; both in Kohn MSS; D. Allen, *Cincinnati Times-Star*, October 18–19, 1948, ZA; Morris, *1948*, 108.

60 UK delegation statement, February 21, 1948, DAG.13/3.1.0.1, Box 1, UN Archives; Hoofien-Horowitz note, February 23, 1948, Z6/49, CZA; *FRUS, 1948*, vol. 5, part 2, 634–636, 643–645.

61 Memo of interview, February 18, 1948, WA; Creech Jones to FO, February 21, 1948, FO800/487, PRO; *FRUS, 1948*, vol. 5, part 2, 654.

62 *FRUS, 1948*, vol. 5, part 2, 651–657.

63 Ibid., 651.

64 Ibid., 654, 657–659, 661–664; UN Report, February 25, 1948, Robison MSS; Pearson to St. Laurent, February 27, 1948, MG26, 51, vol. 440, PAC.

65 Executive meeting, February 25, 1948, Hadassah Archives; Kirchwey to Tobey, February 27, 1948, A427/2; Kirchwey to Truman, February 25, 1948, L35/137; both in CZA; *JTA*, February 25, 1948; Goldman to Proskauer, February 25, 1948; Proskauer to Goldman, February 27, 1948; both in 1/3, Robert Goldman MSS, AHA; Shultz memo, February 25, 1948, A427/6, CZA; Welles to Akzin, February 25, 1948, Box 129, Welles MSS; Epstein memo, Mar. 1, 1948; Epstein-Elliston conversation, March 1, 1948; both in Z6/4/5; Kerr memo, February 25, 1948, A427/6; all in CZA.

66 *FRUS, 1948*, vol. 5, part 2, 665–666; Epstein-Henderson interview, February 27, 1948, Z6/4/5, CZA; Inverchapel to FO, February 25, 1948, FO371/68534, PRO; Phillips to Henderson, February 25, 1948, 55M-69(38)/18, Phillips MSS.

67 *FRUS, 1948*, vol. 5, part 2, 660–661, 664–665.

68 J. and S. Alsop, "The Wriggling President," *Washington Post*, February 27, 1948; Truman to Jacobson, February 27, 1948, Jacobson MSS; Jacobson to Cohn, April 1, 1952, WA.

69 *New York Herald Tribune*, February 17, 1948; Shultz memo and Shultz to Kirchwey, both February 18, 1948, MC280/238, Kirchwey MSS; Lowenthal to Agronsky, February 20, 1948, S44/565, CZA; Rifkind remarks, February 26, 1948, 24/10, Jacob Billikopf MSS, AJA; Kirchwey to Silver-Shertok, February 25, 1948; Shertok to Kirchwey, Mar. 1, 1948; both in 93/129/10, ISA; Moshe Sharett, *B'Sha'ar HaUmot, 1946–1949* (Tel Aviv, 1964), 157–171.

70 *Palestine Post*, February 23, 1948; Jewish Agency Arab Section report, Mar. 1, 1948, 93.03/179/18, ISA; Epstein to Editor, February 26, 1948, L35/87, CZA; Koebner to Friend, February 25, 1948, Box 5, Weltsch MSS; Herzog to Gurney, February 27, 1948, S53/2146, CZA.

71 Ben-Gurion to Shertok, February 27, 1946, 93.03/117/20, ISA; Confidential report, February 26, 1948, A289/125, CZA; Slutski, *Sefer Toldot HaHagana*, 1463–1464; Sacharov to Shertok, Mar. 1, 1948, S25/1703, CZA.

72 "Note on Palestine Policy," January 30, 1948, Confidential files-State Department, ZA; "Palestine Partition and United States Security," February 1948, Julius Klein-Palestine, Jewish War Veterans Archives, Wash., D.C. Taubman to Weisgal, February 7, 1948, Z6/49, CZA; Herold to Ben-Horin, February 12, 1948, PAC, McDonald MSS.

73 Eichelberger to Rusk, February 19, 1948; Eichelberger to Marshall, February 22, 1948; Eichelberger to Lazaron, February 24, 1948; Memo on American position, February 224, 1948; AAUP Resolution, February 26, 1948; all in Box 66; Eichelberger to Rusk, February 27, 1948, Box 67; all in Eichelberger MSS.

74 Bendersky, *The "Jewish Threat,"* 380, 382; *FRUS, 1948*, vol. 5, part 2, 666–675.

75 Chiefs of Staff Committee, February 26, 1948, FO800/487; JIC study with appendices, February 27, 1948, RG25, series A-12m, vol. 2093, part V, PAC.

76 Cunningham to Martin, February 24, 1948, FO371/68535, PRO.

77 Johnson to Bevin, February 24, 1948, FO371/68635; Top secret memo, March 1, 1948, FO371/64848; both in PRO.

78 McNaughton to St. Laurent, February 20, 1948, MG26, J1, vol. 440, PAC; *Palestine Post*, February 27, 1948; Pablo de Azcárate Y Florez, *Mission in Palestine, 1948–1952* (Washington, D.C., 1966), 6–7; Azcárate diary, February 26, 1948, DAG13/3.1.0.5, UN Archives.

79 Smith to Lloyd, February 26, 1948, FO371/68535, PRO; Robison Report, February 27, 1948, Robison MSS.

80 Official communiqué, March 1, 1948, S25/7725, CZA; Jewish Agency statement, March 2, 1948, 86/8, ISA; Kohn to ? (signature is not clear), March 3, 1948, S25/1584, CZA; Lowenberg, "Report from Palestine," March 1948, AJC Archives.

81 Azcárate diary, March 11, 1948, DAG-13/3.1.0:2, UN Archives; Eytan minute, March 5, 1948, 125/15-Het Tsadi, ISA; Azcárate press conference, March 9, 1948, S25/5354, CZA; Azcárate memo, March 12, 1948; Interview with Chief Secretary, March 13, 1948; both in DAG-13/3.1.0:5, Azcárate report to Bunche, March 15, 1948, DAG-13/3.1.0:3; all in UN Archives; Azcárate talk with Eytan and Kaplan, March 15, 1948, S25/5354, CZA. From "a very special source," the Agency received a copy of Azcárate's March 12th memo, 65/4-Het Tsadi, ISA.

82 Lund memo, March 15, 1948, DAG-13/3.1.0.1, Box 2, UN Archives; Herzog-Lund talk, March 10 and March 16, 1948; both in 41.0-116/24, ISA; Herzog to Shertok, March 17, 1948, S25/1558, CZA.

83 FO to UK delegation, March 2, 1948, FO371/68529, PRO; Herzog to Shertok, March 18, 1948, S25/1703, CZA; FO371/68366, PRO; Bunche to Azcárate, March 17, 1948, DAG-13/3.1.0, Box 5, UN Archives; Zaslani memo, March 7, 1948, S25/7706, CZA; Inverchapel to FO, March 4, 1948, FO371/68503, PRO.

84 Egeland to Noel-Baker, March 8, 1948; Pumphrey to Watson, March 18, 1948; both in Ref. A.S.16/1/1, PRO.

85 "Yeruham Report," February 1948–May 15, 1948, A289/125, CZA; Kohn memo, March 3, 1948, 86/8; British intelligence report, February 25–March 10, 1948, 65/7-Het Tsadi; both in ISA; *JTA*, March 3, 1948; Va'ad HaBitahon, March 2, 1948, S25/9347; Va'ad HaLeumi, March 1948, J1/7195; both in CZA.

86 Herzog-Sheringham interview, March 5, 1948, ISA; Netanel Lorch, *The Edge of the Sword: Israel's War of Independence, 1947–1949* (New York, 1961), 87–89; Yoav Gelber, *Komemiyut V'Nakba* (Ohr Yehuda, 2004), 152–153; Ben-Gurion to Shertok, March 10 (should be 11), 1948, S25/1703; Agency release, March 17, 1948, S25/5354; both in CZA; Shertok statement, March 17, 1948, DAG-13/3.1.0.1-3, UN Archives.

87 British intelligence report, February 25–March 10, 1948, 67/5-Het Tsadi, ISA; Robert Werdine, "The Truth About the Nakba," *Times of Israel*, May 17, 2012; *New York Post*, March 3, 1948; Memminger to Marshall, March 1, 1948, Box 2, Rusk MSS; Arab press excerpts, April 2, 1948, 7143/8-P, ISA; *Al-Sarih*, March 9, 1948, L35/65, CZA; AHC statement, March 10, 1948, DAG-13/3.1.0.1, Box 3, UN Archives; *New York Times*, March 15, 1948.

88 *JTA*, March 12, 1948; Kohn to Macatee, March 16, 1948, S25/4151; Ruffer to Elias, March 12, 1948; Egyptian newspaper interview, April 9, 1948; both

in S25/1584; all in CZA; Brutton, *A Captain's Mandate*, 127; Broadmead to Burrows, March 31, 1948, FO371/68630, PRO.

89 *FRUS, 1948*, vol. 5, part 2, 679–685; Pearson memo, March 6, 1948, MG26, 54, vol. 310, PAC; Memo, March 5, 1948, A427/9, CZA.

90 *FRUS, 1948*, vol. 5, part 2, 697–723, 725–737; Marshall to Epstein, March 8, 1948, Z6/49, CZA; *JTA*, March 12, 1948; McClintock memos, March 8 and 9, 1948, Box 2, Rusk MSS; Cadogan to FO, March 17, 1948, FO371/68538, PRO. Rusk had already on March 2 informed Cadogan of State's intentions. Cadogan to FO, March 3, 1948, FO371/68535, PRO.

91 *FRUS, 1948*, vol. 5, 687–696; Benjamin V. Cohen, "The United Nations and Palestine," *New York Herald Tribune*, March 16–17, 1948; Proskauer to Lovett, March 1 and 18, 1948; Proskauer to Austin, March 15, 1948; all in Box 8, Proskauer MSS; Eichelberger to Austin, March 3, 1948, Box 120, Eichelberger MSS; Epstein to Ben-Gurion, March 6, 1948, S25/1703, CZA; Press release, March 7, 1948, Julius Klein MSS, Jewish War Veterans Archives, Washington, D.C.

92 Karr to Shultz, March 9, 1948, A427/2, CZA; Ruffer to Shertok, March 11, 1948, 65/3-Het Tsadi, ISA; Sullivan-Shultz talk, March 15, 1948, MC280/238, Kirchwey MSS; Myers to Truman, March 4, 1948; Truman to Myers, n.d.; both in PSF, Box 160, HSTL.

93 Truman, *Years of Trial and Hope*, vol. 2, 188; *JTA*, March 12, 1948; Oliver Pilat, *Drew Pearson, An Unauthorized Biography* (New York, 1973), 183–184.

94 *JTA*, March 11, 1948; *FRUS, 1948*, vol. 5, part 2, 711; Stone to Bisgyer, August 3, 1970, Box 2, Dewey Stone MSS, AJHS.

95 Jacobson to Cohn, April 1, 1970, WA.

96 V. Weizmann, *The Impossible Takes Longer*, 227; Eban, *Chaim Weizmann*, 309; Jacobson to Cohn, April 1, 1970.

97 Jacobson to Cohn, Apr. 1, 1970; Kirchwey to Weizmann, March 17, 1948; both in WA.

98 Shultz memo, March 18, 1948, MC280/238, Kirchwey MSS; Truman, *Years of Trial and* Hope, 189–190; Eban, Chaim *Weizmann*, 306; V. Weizmann, *The Impossible Takes Longer*, 228.

99 Jacobson to Cohn, April 1, 1970; V. Weizmann, *The Impossible Takes Longer*, 227.

10. Statehood at Long Last

On the afternoon of March 19, 1948, Austin exploded the State Department's political bombshell in the Security Council. With partition no longer a viable option, he told the stunned spectators, a temporary trusteeship for Palestine should be established under the Trusteeship Council "to maintain the peace, and to afford the Jews and the Arabs of Palestine further opportunity to reach an agreement regarding the future government of that country." "On what basis can the United States expect reconciliation at this stage of the game when the fires of hate and nationalism have been fanned to a white heat?" whispered a New York journalist under his breath. While Jewish Agency colleagues around the conference table sat dazed, Silver expressed their sorrow that "a revision of an international judgment, maturely arrived at after prolonged and objective investigation and discussion, can be extorted by threats and armed defiance," and he declared that the Jewish people would move forward in the spirit of the General Assembly's November 29 resolution and "do everything dictated by considerations of national survival, as well as the considerations of justice and historic rights." The French and Chinese delegates gave general support to the U.S. reversal, but Gromyko stated that the Big Four had no right to modify the Assembly's partition recommendation, which should be fulfilled.[1]

Lie reminded the Council that UNSCOP had discussed the question of trusteeship for Palestine when raised by Australia's John Hood, but dropped the idea once concluding that both Arabs and Jews would oppose it, thus requiring larger UN forces to enforce a settlement. Were the Big Powers prepared to see to implementation? Austin's response that the Americans were "of course" ready to back up any UN decision drew laughter from the press gallery. By this time the Secretary-General was so disappointed in the turn of events, including Austin's proposal of a special GA session to consider the U.S. position pending new efforts to find an agreed solution and therefore to suspend the Commission's efforts to implement partition, he suggested to Austin that they both resign as a measure of protest. Austin responded that he would not do so, and advised Lie to follow the same course. Shortly afterwards, Gromyko expressed to Lie his hope and that of his government that this dramatic step would not be taken.[2]

Reflecting the American press in the main, including the non-Zionist *New York Times*'s sharp critique of the "inept" shift which caused American prestige to suffer a "severe blow," a *PM* editorial entitled "Betrayal" foresaw that as a result of this "Black Friday," the guns would be turned in Palestine upon the Jews, who had been supporting the UN. "As Truman's sorry effort to betray the UN into impotency continues," the newspaper went on, "its tragic but fumbling course becomes clear," and a full-dress Congressional investigation could not be much longer delayed. Coming out in favor of Associate Supreme court Justice William O. Douglas for the presidency, columnist Max Lerner blasted Truman as a man whose heart "bleeds in public" for the Jews of Europe and Palestine, yet who "lets over a million of them rot in Europe" and who abandoned several hundred thousand of them in Palestine to the mercies of "an Arab war of extermination." He and other liberals would not trust a man "who talks big about the UN and then cynically knocks the props from under it."[3]

The AZEC's Harry Shapiro immediately wired the ZOA to send the "largest possible" number of wires and letters immediately to Truman protesting this "shocking reversal" of Administration policy and "a blow at the heart" of the UN, and to wire or telephone Senators and Congressmen urging them to voice their protests publicly without delay. Jewish War Veterans' commander Brig. General Julius Klein, noting the support of the American Legion as well for partition, publicly warned that this example of the United States' "broken faith" and "ignoble surrender" played into the hands of Soviet Russia, reenacted the appeasement of Hiter at Munich in 1938, and rewarded the former Grand Mufti, the oil interests, and power politics. On behalf of the AAUN, Eichelberger charged that the UN Charter gave ample authority to the GA and the Council to maintain peace, and that the present Democratic Administration had not condemned the threats of aggression by the Arab states or supported the "moral and spiritual right" of the few remaining Jews of Europe after the Holocaust to have their homeland

and to have a voice in the UN. The American retreat now would appear, he ended, to be a retreat from the President's message two days earlier to Congress to support and strengthen that world body.[4]

A shocked Truman, his diary for March 19 records, believed that State had "pulled the rug from under me today." Having first heard of this reversal when reading the newspapers, he continued, "I am now in the position of a liar and a double-crosser. I've never felt so in my life." Acknowledging that he had approved Austin's speech while on vacation, he still believed that people "on the third and fourth levels" of the department "have always wanted to cut my throat. They've succeeded in doing it." He thanked Marshall for forwarding Phillips's letter to Henderson, which he read "with a lot of interest." Two days later, Truman wrote to his sister Mary Jane that, as had occurred with his militant speech before Congress regarding the Soviet Union, the "striped pants conspirators" in State had "completely balled up" the Palestine situation, but "it may work out anyway in spite of them." And this to his brother Vivian: "I think the proper thing to do, and the thing I have been doing, is to do what I think is right and let them all go to hell." To Crum, he wondered, referring to Weizmann, "what am I to say to that nice old man? You know I told him I would stand by a Jewish state. What must he think of me?" The following morning, Truman subsequently wrote in his memoirs, he sent Rosenman to see Weizmann and tell him that "there was not and would not be any change in the long policy he and I had talked about."[5]

His reference to "the long policy" suggests that Truman, also contending at the same time with the Soviet *coup d'etat* in Czechoslovakia, Moscow's aggressive designs in Germany and elsewhere, and his call to Congress for a U.S. Selective Service recruitment law, did not realize the full significance of the draft of Austin's statement when he had approved it on March 8. In addition, as emerged from a meeting which he convened the next day of Clifford and his aide Eben Ayers, Connelly, Bohlen, Rusk, and Charlie Ross, the President's childhood friend and press secretary, Truman had assumed that Austin, who told him that he had spoken on instructions from State, would announce the alternative plan after a Council vote had demonstrated "the impossibility" of putting over the partition plan. The public, therefore, had receiving no earlier "warning," and Truman was now placed in "the most embarrassing position" of his Presidential career. "They have made me out a liar and a double-crosser! We are sunk," he remarked. He doubted that Marshall knew of Austin's speech, so Ayers's diary recorded, "or would have done it without talking to him." "Telling the truth of the matter would make the President appear vacillating and/or ignorant of a most important matter," and would have to be accompanied, as a memorandum by Ross noted, with "a wholesale repudiation" of the State Department. The first impulse of the assembled was to call a cabinet meeting on the 21st in order to respond to this dilemma, but that would soon be abandoned because the press was likely to build it up as "a crisis meeting," only muddying the troubled waters further.[6]

A later, undocumented, popular account asserts that when Clifford informed Truman that Marshall and Lovett (both out of Washington at the time) had not told subordinates to inform the President when Austin's speech was to be delivered, Truman immediately called Marshall on the 20th. "With restrained anger," he asked the Secretary to issue a statement without delay that the trusteeship proposal was a temporary measure until partition could be carried out. At a press conference in Los Angeles the same day, Marshall did not go that far, declaring that he had received Truman's approval for trusteeship as "the wisest course to follow," and that (just as Austin's speech declared) it would be established "without prejudice" as to the eventual political statement which might be reached for Palestine. The next day, Truman wrote in his diary of the confusion caused by State's handling of the trusteeship issue: "I spent the day trying to right what has happened. No luck. Marshall makes a statement. Doesn't help a bit." On the 22nd, he told the Secretary that he was "so much exercised" in the Palestine matter for one reason: although he agreed earlier to Austin's statement, had he known when it was going to be made "he could have taken certain measures to have avoided the political blast of the press."

Officials in State, long-time opponents of partition, thought differently. Getting the green light from Marshall on the 16th for Austin to deliver the statement, seeing that already on February 25 a majority vote for partition had failed in the Council, hearing the UN Commission declare on March 18 that it had failed to obtain "any compromise" between Arabs and Jews and that the Council's Big Four favored suspending the partition plan, and not informed of Truman's meeting with Weizmann the same day, they felt no need to consult the White House further. Unlike Truman, Marshall and Lovett's subordinates did not take a domestic backlash into account.[7]

Misunderstanding and befuddlement did, in fact, spark a political backlash. New York State Democratic Chairman Fitzpatrick had sent Truman on the very day that the President returned from the Caribbean vacation a new platform for political action, including that he give full and active support to partition. Other party leaders had warned that the President could not carry New York and other key states in November unless he did so. Now Senator John J. Sparkman (D, AL), who had supported Truman despite his civil rights program, asked him to withdraw as a Presidential candidate. At the annual meeting of the Hebrew Sheltering and Immigrant Aid Society (HIAS), Truman's name was greeted soundly with boos, the 2,000 attendees going on to adopt a resolution that the trusteeship proposal "is tantamount to nullification" of the U.S. decision to back partition as settling the Palestine problem "in a way that would have been satisfactory and just."

Several New York delegates to the forthcoming Democratic Party's Presidential convention made their feelings known that, under present conditions, they should not be required to vote for Truman in July. Discussions with high party chieftains disclosed that they wished for "a northern revolt" of this kind in order to convince the President not to make the race but to persuade Eisenhower to run. Speaking as New York State chairman of the Liberal Party, Berle condemned Truman for the Administration's switch on the Palestine question. Senator Pepper urged his fellow Southern Democrats to take no action until the national convention, and then give their support to the party's nominee. The state ticket in Illinois would be sure to lose if Truman headed the ticket, aides to former boss Edward J. Kelley warned. A "revolt in California" was reported as well. Senator Edwin C. Johnson (D., Colo.) declared publicly that Truman's candidacy would handicap the party. Sullivan, telling Shultz that "Forrestal had won," confirmed to her that a revolution against Truman was "brewing" in Washington.[8]

State had actually tipped its hand over Palestine before Austin's speech, Rusk first remarking in an off-the-record conference ten days earlier that the United States, in accepting the partition plan, had "wittingly gambled" that there would be "no outside aggression nor extensive strife within Palestine," and had resolved that partition could not be enforced by the UN. He confidentially told Cadogan on the 17th that the United States thought trusteeship would last "for as short a period as possible." A meeting the next day of American Jewish Committee officials with Berle, former Librarian of Congress Archibald MacLeish, and *Life* managing editor Jack Jessup concluded that if "private" information concerning the U.S. position on Palestine confirmed that Washington could no longer support partition, it would be "imperative" for American Jews and American Jewish organizations to speak out "at once and unequivocally" in support of American policy. A half hour after the Big Powers had consulted over Palestine shortly before Austin's speech, Rusk insisted in a press conference that the GA recommendation was "an integral plan" that could not now be implemented by peaceful means. The continued war in Palestine, he replied to Shultz, had "changed the conditions" since Johnson's declaration before the Assembly vote that no reason existed why the Jewish state could not be established, and the Trusteeship Council would have to take measures to enforce its decisions if there were no peace after May 15. What was the difference between the United States declaring that a GA recommendation could not be carried out by force and its readiness to participate in imposing a Trusteeship Council decision, queried Tom Hamilton. Rusk's "mumbled" reply did not satisfy the *New York Times* reporter, and he and Shultz left the discussion.[9]

Jacobson, informed by Granoff on the afternoon of the 19th about the country's reversal of position at the UN, was speechless and in a state of disbelief. Numerous telephone calls to him that followed spoke of what "a terrible traitor" the President had been in betraying the Jewish people and in violating his promises. All blamed Truman for Austin's statement. He had "explicit faith" in his friend, Jacobson responded, and it would remain unshaken until Truman himself told him differently "with his own lips." Heartsick and worried, Jacobson stayed home in bed the next two days, returning to his store on Monday. There he received a telephone call from "the good Doctor." "Mr. Jacobson," Weizmann began, "don't be disappointed and do not feel badly." In his opinion, Truman had not known what was going to happen in the UN when he and Weizmann spoke the day before. Weizmann saw what had transpired as "just another letdown" in a long life that had experienced one disappointment after another, and he made this personal request: "Don't forget for a single moment that Harry S. Truman is the most powerful single man in the world. You have a job to do, so keep the White House doors open." Uplifted by this message, Jacobson felt renewed encouragement, as he later wrote, "to go on with the work which Fate put on my shoulders."[10]

Weizmann's statements to his closest acolytes suggested far less certainty regarding Truman. "Never before in my life have I been on such a fool's errand," Cohn later recalled Weizmann saying frequently during this stay in New York. His feeling of complete frustration came across vividly in his letter to Doris May, secretary of the Jewish Agency offices in London. Booking passage on the *Queen Mary* for April 7, he wrote to her on the 23rd that "the trip here was not very successful." The "unexpected and sudden let down" by the U.S. Government would have "tragic effects," he feared, "and the only thing which is left for us to do is to go on with our own work and await better times." Trusteeship, a "still-born project produced on the spur of the moment by some fertile mind in the American State Department," was "an insincere attempt to placate some part of Jewish public opinion, but I don't think anybody is being taken in by it." Two days later, acknowledging Halprin's gifts for Purim, he observed that, unfortunately, this year's festive Jewish holiday lacked a Mordekhai, but with *Pesah* (Passover) in a month's time, the real feast of liberation, he hoped that the next four weeks would bring some clarification in the confusion created by the British and American "statesmen." Truman, in Weizmann's view, was no Mordekhai.[11]

State's proposal for a UN trusteeship, Rusk told Jebb after Austin's speech, envisioned a "neutral" Governor selected by the Trusteeship Council and given wide powers, including his appointment of an administration and an advisory council on which presumably Arabs and Jews would be represented. The new administration would have, *inter alia*, power to collect taxes and maintain order, and the UN would supply the deficit if insufficient money were raised locally. The Governor would recruit a police force, which could be augmented by forces from the United States, the United Kingdom, and France (three permanent members of the Security Council), for these represented the allied and associated powers who had figured in the constitution of the Palestine Mandate. Rusk then made a strong appeal for British support for this plan, which would at least keep the Russians out of Palestine except to the extent that they would participate in the Palestine trust if they chose to join the Trusteeship Council. If HMG did back the proposed scheme, Rusk asked, would the British still maintain their proposed dates for evacuation? The ball had been returned once again to London's court.[12]

The U.S. Government's change in attitude towards Palestine, Henderson explained to the British Embassy's John Balfour the next morning, "had been perfectly logical." Assuming originally that partition could be implemented "without undue disturbance," State had come to realize that, with events having "entirely disproved" this hypothesis and partition by force unable to obtain the requisite Security Council votes, some other solution had to be sought. Since a temporary trusteeship offered the only practical means of "holding a solution" which threatened the peace and stability of the entire Middle East, Henderson entered "an earnest plea" that HMG might assist in its preparation or the possibility of taking some eventual share in its implementation. Otherwise, it might prove impossible to secure enough votes for the United States proposal, with subsequent "conditions of chaos" resulting in Palestine and elsewhere in the region. Balfour concluded that State preferred trusteeship by a small number of powers with the grant of virtually autonomous powers to the Governor, he to be installed by May 15, in order that internal order in Palestine should be effectively maintained.

Henderson was open to any alternative suggestions, the United States solely interested in starting "the ball rolling" towards a fresh approach to the problem. Personally, Henderson thought it necessary to "slow down the tempo" of the British withdrawal in order to enable the necessary arrangements for the successful installation of the Governor, keeping other powers aware of the need for the speediest possible action in such an event. He repeated the hope that Palestine could now be treated within the "wider framework" of securing British and American interests in the Middle East.[13]

In amplification of what Henderson told Balfour, Inverchapel conveyed to Bevin his view that Truman and Marshall had felt constrained to give "greater weight" to the views of Forrestal and the Chiefs of Staff in light of a rapidly deteriorating international situation. In addition, they had come to realize that the pro-Zionists could only be conciliated at the price of losing the support of an even greater number of voters who would certainly react "most vehemently" against any shedding of American blood in a Jewish cause. Third, given the fact that even many loyal Democrats now despaired of Truman's re-election, the President himself might well have lost patience with all domestic pressures and arguments which had militated against an assessment of the Palestine problem "on its own merits." The Ambassador did not think that, whatever may have been Washington's motives on earlier occasions, the Administration was now seeking to relieve its own embarrassments at HMG's expense. Henderson, he added, had told Balfour that the Administration would pursue its proposals whatever the Congressional and public clamor.[14]

The reversal of U.S. policy found a few adherents. The anti-Zionist American Council for Judaism kept in touch with Henderson, who urged its leaders to send a strong letter of support to Marshall. Lessing Rosenwald wrote to Austin; Lazaron spoke on radio across the country, and shared his views with the receptive Samuel McCrea Cavert, General Secretary of Federal Council of the Churches of Christ in America. The Committee for Justice and Peace in the Holy Land, founded in February by Kermit Roosevelt and former Barnard College dean Virginia Gildersleeve to lobby against partition in the belief that it went against America's national interests and common justice, advocated the resettlement of Holocaust survivors in the United States and elsewhere. Magnes, who wrote to the anti-Zionist historian of nationalism Hans Kohn that the United States was finally "on the right track," and his colleague Hebrew University professor Ernst Simon pressed for their Ihud Association's binationalist program. Jacob Rosenheim, president of the ultra-Orthodox Agudas Israel, urged his followers in Palestine not to participate in "an illegal Jewish government of an illegal state" opposed to religious tradition, and to favor trusteeship "without the frivolous game with statehood." Former *Jüdische Rundschau* editor and ex-Agency Executive member Robert Weltsch, as well as Yale University law professor Eugene Rostow, although not advocates of trusteeship, believed that the American switch necessitated the return of Weizmann and his associates' to the Zionist helm in place of Silver and Ben-Gurion. For Rostow, writing to Frankfurter, the latter had "overrated their own strength and underrated that of their enemies."[15]

Eleanor Roosevelt reacted to Austin's speech with a letter on the 22nd to Marshall, offering to resign her post on the UN Human Rights Commission because she felt compelled to air her thoughts in public. Aside from the United States' "moral obligation" to the Jews under the Balfour Declaration, her greatest concern was the damage done to the UN itself, which at the present time the United States had "more or less buried." She sent a copy to Truman the same day, decrying as well the American trend to prepare for "an ultimate war" against the Russians, with whom she thought some arrangements could be made by using U.S. economic power to obstruct their political advance. The Democratic

Party, Roosevelt added, was currently in a "very weak position," with the Southern revolt against Truman's recent call for civil rights for all American citizens, as well as the big cities and many liberals "appalled by our latest moves."[16]

Roosevelt's resignation would have been a calamity for the embattled Truman, who summoned the senior State Department officials for a "clarification" at the Cabinet room on March 24. The previous day, Ewing, whose group to re-elect Truman had heard Nathan warn of the reversal's negative effect on the President's chances, had received no response from Truman when conveying, as did McGrath, this domestic reality and the *yishuv*'s critical need to have the arms embargo lifted. Now, hearing Henderson argue that partition would jeopardize the country's interests across the Arab world, Truman cut in by commenting that the United States had not proposed partition and that he was not convinced by Henderson's argument. The atmosphere was charged, read Ross's notes on "Dark political days...," with the dislike between Henderson and Niles as they exchanged words. After Ewing posited that the reversal had impaired faith in the American government, especially among the small nations, Marshall said that State was working on obtaining a truce in Palestine, Rusk adding that it would have a definite answer by April 7.

The general understanding, according to Clifford's summary of the meeting, was that if State could not report success by that date, steps would be taken to rescind the embargo. Truman asked Clifford to prepare a statement for his press conference the next day. With State shunted aside from contributing to this task, Henderson authored a lengthy memorandum to Marshall explaining the department's embrace of trusteeship, together with its hope for British cooperation if Zionism and Palestine would not be made an issue in the coming Presidential campaign.[17]

Truman's statement on March 25, authored by Lowenthal and then reviewed by Clifford, Bohlen, Rusk, McGrath, Ewing, and Niles, repeated Austin's point that trusteeship had been put forward because partition could not be carried out by peaceful means at the present time. U.S. troops were not to be sent for its enforcement, both on UN Charter grounds and as a matter of national policy. Trusteeship was not proposed as a substitute for partition, but as an effort to fill the vacuum soon to be created by the mandate's termination on May 15.

Not prejudicing the final political statement, it would establish the conditions of order essential to a peaceful solution. An immediate truce had to be reached between Palestine's Arabs and Jews "if we are to avert tragedy," and the United States was prepared to take its share of responsibility if the UN agreed to its proposal. Open warfare was "just over the horizon" otherwise, the declaration ended, and the country's regard for the UN, for the peace of the world, "and for our own self-interest" did "not permit us to do less."

The same day, replying to Roosevelt, Truman made the same points of his statement in imploring her not to resign. The UN was humanity's best and perhaps only hope for peace, he added; it and the United States needed her. Truman's heartfelt letter moved Roosevelt deeply, and she resolved to remain at her post. She did criticize trusteeship in her column *My Day* while en route to London for the unveiling, in the presence of King George VI, Churchill, and Attlee, of a statue of FDR in Grosvenor Square. The American Council for Judaism secretary Elmer Berger, on the other hand, feared that "Mr. Truman kicked over the pail again" when he insisted that the U.S. Government had not abandoned partition. The statement, in his view, only served the "dangerous purpose" of playing with the "so-called" Jewish vote, and that any chance of the Arabs accepting a peaceful acceptance of partition was lost.[18]

"It should be clear that it is not only the resolution of the UN that is in jeopardy," Shertok warned the American section of the Jewish Agency Executive on March 20, "but the physical existence of the *yishuv*." Hearing Pearson confide that he thought Ottawa would accept the American proposal, which would "hold things in order" for two to three years, Eban, who authored a paper pointing out to the Council the problems of trusteeship in Palestine, asked the Canadian diplomat: "At the cost of how many killed?" Expressing "regret and astonishment" at the U.S. reversal, the Jewish Agency and Va'ad HaLeumi resolved in a joint statement three days later to oppose any scheme designed to prevent or postpone statehood. Chief Rabbi Herzog told the *New York Times*'s Dana Schmidt that despite the "deep shock" of the U.S. reversal, the Jewish people "will weather this storm as it has met so many calamities in its long history of martyrdom… assured beyond any shadow of doubt of its national destiny and trusting in Our Father in Heaven, who doth not sleep nor slumber."

At the same time, Ruffer's assumption that the Arabs now had "a green light" to proceed with aggression appeared borne out by the killing of another 81 Jews in the week ending March 21. Perhaps "the only way now to arrive at a final solution of the Palestine problem," a despairing Cunningham wrote to Creech Jones the next day, was for both sides to fight it out, "and if that is the case the proposals are only putting off the evil day. The position of the UNO will become the same as ours as Mandatory over the past 25 years. This would seem disastrous both for UNO and Palestine." Beeley, too, feared that trusteeship would see "an indefinite prologation of the condition of the latent war," which had now lasted for twelve years.[19]

On the 25th, Weizmann broke his two-months' silence since arriving in New York City by blaming the United States for increasing the confusion and bloodshed, and for inciting further Arab violence by submitting to the pressure of violence. Noting that Truman had assured him that the United States stood by partition, he announced that he would soon leave for Palestine, counting it "a privilege to be with my people in this hour of crisis." If left alone to face Arab aggression, he remarked, "we shall not shirk the struggle," for if the *yishuv* went down, "the ideals of international order would perish with us and force would prevail against justice as an arbiter of human destiny." The British had let foreign Arab forces cross into Palestine, where they continued to prepare "in leisure" to make war against the Jews and against the GA recommendation. In so doing, the mandatory government had acted against its own best traditions, "and left a tragic legacy to the country's future." The conditions which made the last months of the Mandate so tragic, Weizmann continued, were likely to apply to any new trusteeship. He had repeatedly attempted during the last quarter of a century to seek agreement over Palestine with the Arabs, but those leaders denied the Jews their fundamental right to freedom and development despite the "hallowed traditions and historic links" which bind the Jewish people to that country. Thanks to Niles, a copy of the letter reached Truman.[20]

Indeed, the Arab leadership remained adamant against any consideration of a Jewish state. Syrian President Shukri al-Quwatli was hopeful for a new basis of Arab-American cooperation, Wadsworth informed Marshall, for partition could never be accepted by the Arabs. Chamoun said the same to the Council after Austin's speech, declaring that the Arabs would insist on "total independence for Palestine undivided and democratic." Ibn Saud got word to Bevin, who passed it on to Marshall, that he was "so pleased" Austin's proposal showed that the U.S. Government did not support the partition plan. While Ben-Gurion and the Agency Executive were prepared to consider a truce, which the United States, the USSR, France and China urged on both contending parties, the Arab Higher Committee's New York representative, Isa Nakhleh, announced that it would only accept an alternative plan to establish a single independent state in Palestine. The AHC also insisted that a truce for Jerusalem, put forward by Graves at the end of February, required the exit of the Hagana from the Old City.

The Arab League's political committee concluded that the AHC should submit statements and information to the Security Council on the basis of the rejection of partition, Azzam Pasha announced, while the Arab state delegates could best collaborate with the Council by joint action for the prevention of illegal Jewish immigration. They were prepared to accept a compromise, he added to the British ministry in Beirut, "when and if [the] Zionist spirit had been well and thoroughly broken." Haj Amin made this crystal clear from his perspective by having Bevin receive "An Arab Charter for Palestine," which declared that that country's Arabs were determined to see that the Jewish "hordes" from foreign lands over the past twenty-five years, "instigated and directed by the international Zionist cabal," would never succeed in establishing their sovereignty "on one inch of Palestine soil."[21]

All was not well at this point, however, with the Arab world's stand on Palestine. While each state focused primarily on its own concerns, the Arab League schemed to bypass the ex-Mufti, Musa Alami favoring the Morrison-Grady plan and Clayton proposing that the League bequeath parts of Palestine to Egypt, Jordan, and Lebanon. Nakhleh, worried that the UN would never be able to reach "any intelligent or just solution" for Palestine, advised former AHC Executive member Izzat Darwaza, who had resigned in opposition to Haj Amin's methods, to press for the declaration of the independence of an Arab Palestine and strike at the root of Zionism" independently of the UN "as if it has never existed." Yet a somber report on the 23rd by Major General Ismail Safwat, commander of the Arab League Military Committee, informed Mardam, chairing the League's Palestine Committee, that its forces in Palestine, whether trained volunteers or armed Palestinian guerillas (meaning members of Abd al-Qadir al-Husseini's *Jihad al Muqaddas*) who operated independently of the ALA, could not achieve a "decisive" military victory against the well-armed and well-trained *yishuv*. All they could do was prolong the fighting for a certain period in accordance with the reinforcements they would receive and the weapons available to them.[22]

Azcárate thought that talk of trusteeship, just when the two contenders were already fighting and ready to engage in open war as soon as the Mandate ended, sounded "at least unreal." Writing a long, personal letter to Bunche, he asserted that partition was an on-going reality, the Arabs and the Jews controlling their own respective zones while "killing and destroying each other." The Jewish state was virtually in existence, and he did not think that even the Arabs themselves had any doubt about it. As opposed to a Jewish Central Administration capable, on the whole, of taking over control of most of the services, there was no such thing on the Arab side. Azcárate foresaw a sort of "war of secession," internationally legalized and which, therefore, should have been internationally supported; UN military support appeared out of the question.

The only practical possibility of avoiding this war, in Azcárate's opinion, would be for Washington and London to pressure the Arab states to accept partition and halt arms deliveries to their kin in Palestine, and to prevent all possible acts of aggression or provocation of the Jewish armed forces against the Arabs. Graves's truce effort for Jerusalem, which he thought the "cornerstone" of any realistic solution of the Palestinian problem, had to be tackled at the top political level. Personal experiences in the Spanish Civil War dominating his whole thinking, Azcárate told Eytan, he was "desperately eager" to save Palestine from the suffering which Spain had undergone a decade earlier. An international administrative nucleus in Jerusalem could be "a sort of common platform" for eventually covering parts, or even all, of the country, he thought, with Lund considering a force of 8,000 to10,000 men indispensable to carry out this task.[23]

The British Cabinet's official response on the 24th that it would continue to adhere to its neutral attitude greatly disappointed Marshall and his department. Beeley had already advised Creech Jones five days earlier that there was little if any hope as to a temporary trusteeship, and State's private request that HMG should help to provide the military backing for this proposal was "extremely dangerous." A truce and suspending the Commission's work were steps in the right direction, he added, leading to a special GA session. Bevin and colleagues, High Commissioner for Canada Norman Robertson reported to St. Laurent, were "really obsessed" with the special risks and responsibilities that concurrence in any new compromise scheme might thrust upon them beyond May 15. Indeed, Bevin implied this when addressing the Commons on the 23rd. "HMG's policy is now simply to get out of Palestine as quickly as possible without regard to the consequences in Palestine," Cunningham frankly put it to his superior two days later. Strong pro-partition statements by Welles and Evatt did not please either capital, particularly after the *New York Times* reported that Marshall had told a closed meeting of the Senate Foreign Relations Committee that the reversal was due to partition's requiring heavy military forces possibly for a long period, its implementation very probably making use of "large bodies" of Russian troops, which in turn would threaten Greece, Turkey, and the Arabian oil fields essential to the United States and to the entire European Recovery Program.[24]

Taking questions at a press conference on the 25th, Truman remarked that his position with regard to Jewish immigration into Palestine had not changed, but he believed that the first thing to do was to restore peace in the country and arrange a settlement that would halt the bloodshed. He also hoped that trusteeship would produce the kind of peaceful settlement that would result in there not being any need for the proclamation of "the Jewish Government." The United States policy, the President concluded, was to back up a UN trusteeship by all possible means, but that did not necessarily mean sending American troops to Palestine.

One hour later, Marshall publicly reiterated State's search for peace in Palestine through a trusteeship, but avoided discussion on the military force needed for its implementation. He tried the next day to persuade Shertok and Epstein of State's sincere designs, but they thought the truce would not solve "anything basic," and displayed considerable doubt that the trusteeship would help the situation. Responding to what he considered Gromyko's "irresponsible" charge at the Council on the 30th that Austin's statements were preparing the ground to "bury" the partition plan, Lovett felt it "most desirable" to get the maximum number of Council votes possible and obtain the United Kingdom's support for the U.S. proposal calling for a special GA session. Hutcheson's public endorsement of the trusteeship plan was certainly welcome at the White House and Foggy Bottom, although Bevin privately thought that Truman's March 25 statement had only convinced the Arabs that the President sought the immediate entry of the 100,000 and partition later on.[25]

In the meanwhile, the violence only intensified in Palestine. At least 23 Jews and 19 Arabs were killed on March 24 in fierce battles, the major one when a force of 800 Arabs attacked the Neveh Ya'akov settlement in the eastern part of Jerusalem. Another developed when several hundred Arabs isolated a twelve-vehicle Jewish convoy near the Bab-el-Wad (Sha'ar HaGai) valley on the road ascending from Tel Aviv to Jerusalem, killing at least twelve Jews and wounding thirty. Fourteen Arabs were killed and six wounded in two heavy engagements with Hagana units between Magdiel and Kfar Saba that same morning. Five Arabs were killed and two injured near Majdal, while nine other Arabs were seriously wounded in Jerusalem when a hand grenade exploded in the Old City. Seven Jews died during an attack on the Arab village of Mughar, near the Lydda airport, with a Jewish armored car blown up and all its occupants, including one woman, burned to death. Fourteen in a Hagana convoy to Atarot were killed on the 25th. Two days later, 46 Hagana men in a convoy on the road from Nahariya to Kibbutz Yehiam in the Galilee were killed; a 30-hour battle later that day near Neveh Daniel resulted in 15 Jews killed and 50 wounded, with 135 Arabs killed and scores wounded.

Some thirty Arabs were killed on the 28th during a Haganah raid on the Arab village of Sandala, near Jenin. The administration issued a warning that it would never again attempt to rescue Jews attacked by Arabs in a situation similar to that of the Jews trapped in the ambush near Neveh Daniel, set up by Abd al-Qadir al-Husseini, charging that Danny Mass and his men had left Jerusalem for Kfar Etzion without informing the mandatory authorities, and the Jews had disregarded warnings not to return along that route because the Arabs had erected barricades to halt them. The government's press release also revealed that 210 Jews were rescued, including 40 who were slightly wounded. Most of the Hagana's armored trucks, used to maintain the connection between Tel Aviv and Jerusalem, were lost in that attack, and the British subsequently handed over the convoy's weapons to the Arabs. "This was the most terrible day since the war began," Ben-Gurion wrote to Shertok on the 28th, before even aware of the Neveh Daniel tally of fifteen dead. Three days later, a convoy from Hulda to Jerusalem lost twenty-four Hagana fighters.[26]

On the last day of March, too, the transshipment and deportation to Cyprus of 737 visaless Jewish refugees, including 132 children, apprehended aboard the *Yehi Am* (The Nation Shall Live) two days earlier, was completed without incident. This offered no consolation for Weizmann, who wrote to Frankfurter of the venerable Rabbi Levi Yitshak of Berdichev calling the God of Israel to a *Din Torah* (rabbinic court) in order to give an account of why the Almighty persecuted the Jewish people so much. "I am sure the great rabbi felt considerable relief after having spoken thus," he went on, "and it is very unfortunate that even this sort of comfort is not given to us, and we have to carry the pain in us until the heart breaks and the moral force begins to ebb." The Jews had suffered more than 900 fatalities and 1,858 wounded up to this point, as compared with that Arabs' 967 and 1,911 respectively, losses proportionally twice as heavy as the latter in light of the *yishuv*'s population being roughly half of the Arab counterpart; its security position overall was extremely precarious. Weizmann closed on this despairing note: "Every day some new hope is being dangled before our eyes, and when the sun sets, it is nothing but a mirage. How long, oh God, how long?"[27]

On April 1, the Security Council, by a unanimous vote, adopted the US resolution calling upon the Arab and Jewish armed groups in Palestine to cease acts of violence immediately, and requesting the AHC and the Jewish Agency to make representatives available to the Security Council for the purpose of arranging a truce. The Council also adopted, by nine affirmative votes and two abstentions (the Soviet Union and the Ukraine), the American resolution requesting Lie to convoke a GA special session starting April 16 to consider further the question of Palestine's future government. Shertok's impassioned plea to the Council that it was not yet too late to implement the GA's partition recommendation, and that the U.S. truce proposal gave the false impression that both sides were at fault while 7,500 armed Arabs had invaded Palestine and Arab states were voting appropriations to supply arms and men for the Palestine conflict—"the current and salient feature of the country's disturbed condition," fell on deaf ears.

In reply, Egypt's Mahmoud Fawzi emphatically denied participation of the Arab states in the Palestine struggle, and declared that the Arabs would oppose any truce meant to keep the peace by armed force during the partition of the country. Gromyko alone declared that the Council was not empowered to order the Palestine Commission to suspend its activities in the interim, as only the GA could revoke these powers.[28]

Three days later, the Commission resolved to continue its work, aware of the possibility that the Special Session might produce no alternative plan for partition. That included the selection of a Provisional Council of Government, beginning with the observations of Panama member Eduardo Morgan that no difficulty existed regarding the creation of such a council in the Jewish state, and that the Security Council take action against "the aggressor" Arab groups resorting to force against the UN resolution. Only Denmark's Federspiel dissented, thinking that any formal resolution even hinting at political action might only serve to inflame passions in Palestine when truce efforts were in progress. For the immediate future, Azcárate recommended to Bunche that a truce, beginning with Jerusalem, be sought between the Agency and the Arab League, not the AHC; that the present administrative structure of Palestine in which *de facto* partition had been to a considerable extent carried out be respected and maintained; and that Jewish immigration be limited during the truce negotiations to the Jews interned in Cyprus. Privately, Lund warned Herzog that it would be "highly naïve" of the Jews to withdraw the Hagana from the Old City and leave the Jewish civilians to the mercy of the Arabs, despite all promises given by the British, and he expressed the feeling that the Jews "stood a chance" of setting up their state because he did not believe that anything very definite would emerge from Lake Success.[29]

On the 5th, one day after more than 50,000 American war veterans held a mass demonstration with 250,000 onlookers at Madison Square Park urging the UN to uphold partition, Austin invited the Council members (excepting the USSR and the Ukraine) to his office, where he presented the American plan for a temporary Palestine trusteeship. Calling for their responses, he announced that the fifteen General Principles did not commit the United States at this stage. Perhaps most tendentious were the points that the agreement would be of "indefinite" duration subject to "prompt termination" whenever the Arab and Jewish communities agreed upon the country's future government, and that the Governor-General would be given the authority to call upon states to assist when necessary towards the maintence of security in Palestine. ("We must not be drawn in at this stage on an American commitment," State informed its delegation in New York regarding the second issue.) We seek a truce, Rusk informed the UN Division of Public Liaison, because the Arabs were better armed, and the Jews would "undoubtedly be slaughtered" in the event of large-scale fighting. Most of the Council members present initially critized the plan's vagueness, while Pearson wrote home that a trusteeship agreement could not even be concluded without UK concurrence.[30]

While awaiting their official reactions, Henderson proposed four days later that "moderates and temperate" individuals like Magnes and Azzam Pasha be invited to the United States as soon as possible to possibly break "the present log jam" in the UN. The "extreme public positions" taken by the Jewish Agency and the Arab Higher Committee regarding sovereignty, he argued, made it increasingly difficult for them to modify their positions sufficiently for arranging a UN truce and interim governmental machinery after May 15. (Herzog heard from George Fielding Eliot that Marshall was loath to regard the American Zionist leaders as representatives of the *yishuv*, while Vandenberg told *Detroit Jewish News* publisher Philip Slomovitz in deepest confidence that the Secretary was prepared to resign because of their pressure unless Truman yielded to him.) Having requested Bevin and Bidault on the 9th to join in sponsoring the American proposal, Lovett approved Henderson's suggestion the next day, and telegrams to that effect were dispatched to Jerusalem and Cairo.[31]

Azcárate thought the Jewish Agency-Va'ad HaLeumi statement on March 23, opposing "any proposal to prevent or postpone the establishment of a Jewish State," injudicious. If the *yishuv* would lack the means of preventing the creation of a trusteeship in Palestine, Ben-Gurion's declaration of March 21 offered the Arabs the possibility of putting the UN on their side simply by accepting the trusteeship. Their joint claim that trusteeship would "necessarily" entail the "continuation of a foreign military regime in the country" was not true; the UN did not "unanimously" accept the end of the Mandate, which would terminate by a decision of the mandatory power; and a Provisional Jewish Government functioning in cooperation with UN representatives depended as well on UN intentions and decisions. Similarly, he found

Ben-Gurion's statement of March 21 that the Jewish state's establishment depended upon the *yishuv*'s ability to decide the issue "by force" in Palestine, not upon the GA decision of November 29, "most unlikely" to occur without any international support. So far, Azcárate noted, the Jews were not even able to secure a regular food supply to the 100,000 Jewish inhabitants of Jerusalem. Finally, the Agency Executive chairman's closing assertion that "we shall not agree to any trusteeship, whether temporary or permanent, even for the briefest period," he privately deemed a "most unwise and imprudent statement!!"[32]

Nor did the Arab attitude towards trusteeship offer much solace. In a talk with Azcárate, the Egyptian Consul favored a maximum period of 2–3 years, but with Cyprus's 30,000 imprisoned Jews to be absorbed within the Arab states. Husseini notified the Security Council on the 9th that the Arabs would not negotiate any truce with the Jewish Agency because the AHC did not consider the Agency as representing Palestine's Jews. Haj Amin violently rejected it outright, writing to the three Palestine Commission consuls that all of Palestine was a holy place to the Arabs, to be protected against the intruder. Prime Minister Mahmoud El Nokrashy Pasha advised U.S. Ambassador S. Pinkney Tuck in Cairo that the definite duration of the trusteeship had to be stipulated together with guarantees against an increase in Jewish armaments, numbers, and land purchase in Palestine, accompanied by an assurance that trusteeship would not jeopardize Arab "national aspirations" towards the final, complete independence of Palestine as a "united Arab nation."

The Arab League, Azzam Pasha declared to Tuck on April 18, did not support the American plan of temporary trusteeship, which it considered would serve only "to create a new regime and bring about another phase of trouble between Arabs and Jews." The League favored, as a practical matter, a continuance of the British Mandate, since HMG military forces aided by the UN's "moral and material backing" could lead to the final disarmament and creation of "a new Palestine state." Azzam added to Campbell that Jewish immigration had to cease in the meantime, and if civil war broke out the Arabs were confident of success, although it might take years, owing to their "inexhaustible" manpower reserves.[33]

Azcárate also had a few significant reservations about the American "fifteen points," which he transmitted to Bunche on April 7. Its call for a cabinet and democratically elected legislature sounded unreal, giving the "very wrong and dangerous" impression that elections could be held at once. Maintaining law and order in Palestine required something more substantial than "locally recruited police and volunteer forces," particularly because these would be insufficient from the first moment of the truce; an international police force of volunteers was "indispensable" at the very start. Immigration and land purchase should not be negotiated in consultation with Jewish and Arab communal representatives, but left in the Governor's hands. Arrangements had to be made at once to provide the trusteeship with a solid and stable financial basis. The trusteeship's "indefinite duration," a formula difficult to be accepted by Arabs and Jews, should be changed to one year, leaving it to the Trusteeship Council to decide about prolongation on the basis of a proposal submitted to it by the Governor. Termination of the trusteeship to occur when the two warring communities had agreed upon a plan of government suggested that there would in the future be one government and one country. The Jews might conclude that all possible partition was eliminated, while that suggestion contradicted point one's assertion that a temporary trusteeship would not prejudice the "rights, claims, or position of the parties concerned" or the character of the eventual political settlement.[34]

At this point, the Agency Executive in New York City entertained scant hope for the UN deliberations. Shertok thought the U.S. plan "rudimentary," had no definite provisions for enforcement, would perpetuate outside rule, and would only introduce "an element of confusion" in Palestine. In Eban's assessment, a mood of deep cynicism, disillusionment, and despair pervaded the GA, with the U.S. leadership discredited, the Arabs forced to welcome the trusteeship proposal as a move against partition but very wary of its implications, and the question of enforcement even more insoluble than under partition. Husseini had stated that his people would not agree to a cease-fire unless Hagana forces withdrew from Jerusalem and a truce was extended to all of Palestine. The American delegation was working very hard for the latter, insisting that there be no proclamation of Jewish statehood after May 15, and then permitting a limited Jewish immigration thereafter.

Eban thought the British position more realistic than that of the United States, with London reconciled to partition—but a smaller Jewish state, not helping the United States on trusteeship because HMG wished to keep it and the USSR out of Palestine, and wanting to give predominance to the Arab state by including in it the Galilee and the Negev. Unless the United States was prepared to enforce its plan, he concluded, it would not be able to muster the necessary two-thirds vote for passage. Yet, upon hearing Parodi's private dissatisfaction that the British attitude really rendered the whole UN discussion "futile," London instructed its delegation on the 7th to say that the United Kingdom would not veto an approved trusteeship agreement if secured by May 15, but would not commit "in any way" to take part administering or enforcing it or any other settlement. Cadogan announced this the same day at Austin's second informal meeting, which revealed that no delegation had done any work on a possible trusteeship.[35]

On April 10, the Palestine Commission reported to the GA that it could not fulfill its assignment because of "the armed hostility of both Palestinian and non-Palestinian Arab elements, the lack of cooperation from the mandatory power, the disintegrating security situation in Palestine," and the Security Council not furnishing it the necessary armed assistance. Azcárate and Lund would stay on for a while, but two other members of the advance party returned to New York. Council chairman López had recently reported to the members convening again at Austin's office that his talks in two meetings each with Husseini and Shertok separately regarding a truce had produced no common ground, "illegal" Jewish immigration the crux of the problem, with Husseini against any partition and opposing Jewish immigration during the truce and Shertok insisting on partition for the sake of the *yishuv*'s "self-preservation" when the British departed. He suggested that, under these circumstances, the Council should appeal for a truce and ask the United Kingdom to keep the Mandate for some time longer. Both sides, López thought, were "too worked up emotionally" to listen to reason, and he doubted that an Arab-Jewish agreement would be reached at the present time. The only specific suggestion made at the meeting was Austin's emphasizing that the truce should be on "a stand-still basis," including immigration, and that it should not be employed to impose any political statement, but only to institute peace and order, and to establish a temporary government in Palestine to take over from the mandatory.[36]

Gromyko was absent at the first two informal meetings in Austin's office, but on the 9th Molotov had sent Stalin for his approval, with copies to a few other prominent Politburo members, the impending instructions to their chief UN representative for the GA Special Session.

Gromyko was to defend the partition resolution, point out that the Security Council had not exhausted all the resources at its disposal to put this into practice, and charge HMG with hampering the Commission's work in Palestine. As for the U.S. trusteeship proposal, by repealing the November majority decision, it would aggravate the Jewish-Arab struggle in Palestine and "intensify unrest" in the region, compromise the GA's position, and leave the country in a "semi-colonial position." Finally, it contradicted the principle of autonomy, and was marked by distrust of the local population independently to organize Palestine's administration on a democratic basis.[37]

When Gromyko did attend the third private meeting at the U.S. delegation's headquarters on the 12th, at which the Commission's role was debated, he protested the discussion of a truce at such a venue, and wondered if this was done to have some delegations avoid embarrassment. López countered that he was fully within his rights to take advice from the other Council members in this manner. The same day, Evatt informed Austin of Australia's continued support for partition, that recommendation's lack of success due less to fighting in Palestine and more to the "vacillation" that had taken place in the attitude of some the powers most concerned and to the absence of "positive restraints" on the Arabs, which all UN members had the duty to exercise in carrying out the GA decision. Frazer sent similar instructions to his minister at Washington and the UN Department, hoping as well that the "great powers" would give partition their support.

The mandatory administration, Cadogan admitted at López's next meeting on April 13 (to which Gromyko was not invited), had "disintegrated" to the point where it was not possible for the British to delay further their departure. Pressing for a truce and an international trusteeship, Azcárate, continuing to favor partition as the formula which "reduces to a minimum" the friction between Arabs and Jews, sent a cable to Lie and Bunche the next day which ended: "Consider most unfair for Jews continue encouraging establishment state without providing appropriate international military assistance to defend it against Arab attack."[38]

While the Jewish Agency and the AZEC mounted an offensive against the trusteeship proposal, fully agreeing with Fabregat's private warning that any new victorious plan would ultimately mean that the *yishuv* would be "completely liquidated" and the Jews should therefore not yield "one inch" on partition's "irrevocability," Weizmann resolved to write to Truman in the hope of inducing the President to recognize the Jewish state whose establishment the U.S. Government was at that moment trying to prevent. The logic of partition and its "virtual... crystallizing" in Palestine, his letter began on April 9, compelled him to go on record against the idea of trusteeship, "a leap into the unknown." Hearing from Ginsburg that the State Department was thinking of asking the British to carry on, which he thought "the worst possibility of all," Weizmann decided to add a paragraph about his trembling to think of "the wave of violence and repression which would sweep Palestine" if rule continued under the British or indeed any foreign rule. Certain that Truman would not be a party to "the further disappointment of pathetic hopes" shared by the 100,000 Holocaust survivors still in the DP camps, he declared that the choice for the Jewish people was "between statehood and extermination." "History and providence have placed this issue in your hands," Weizmann concluded, "and I am confident that you will yet decide it in the spirit of the moral law."[39]

Truman chose not to answer the letter. (Lovett, sent a copy by Weizmann, would acknowledge it after two weeks with the expressed hope that the UN's action would lead to the "restoration of peaceful conditions" in Palestine and to agreement between Arabs and Jews resident there "on their future government.") The President and Marshall had recently received from Forrestal the estimate of the Joint Chiefs of Staff, who thought that a complete effective truce was impossible because of the "extremists" on both sides; that 100,000 troops, aside from destroyers and considerable air support, would be needed to impose and supervise trusteeship; and that even if the United States provided 46,800 of these soldiers, it would necessitate at least partial mobilization, overextend the army, require a supplementary budget, and could not be fully deployed prior to May 15. In addition, the Standard Oil company of New Jersey's board directors had just released a public statement (which McClintock placed in State's "Palestine File") about the vital necessity of Middle Eastern oil for Western Hemisphere oil supplies and the European Recovery Program.[40]

On the other hand, rising sharp criticism was heard from such as the independently-minded Senator Wayne Morse (R, OR), who warned that reversals by the United States and others would prevent the UN from surviving as an instrumentality for maintaining peace, a charge echoed in Congressman John F. Kennedy's public castigation of the trusteeship plan as "one of the most unfortunate reversals in American policy" and in his demand to lift the embargo so that the Jewish people in Palestine could "defend themselves and carve out their partition." Truman also had to contend with a movement within the Democratic Party, including Franklin D. Roosevelt, Jr. and Chicago party boss Jacob Arvey, to champion Eisenhower's candidacy for the presidential election come November. On the 9th, he declared at his weekly press conference that he had no comment to make about Palestine other than that it was pending before the UN, or whether the Administration was considering any modification of the arms embargo. Hearing that the lack of detail in the General Principles "considerably disturbed" Austin, McClintock informed him that Lovett had personally signed off on the truce proposal, and that it had been cleared by the White House.[41]

At the same time, when Jacobson visited him at the White House on the 12th, one day after the haberdashery store owner conferred with Weizmann, Truman reaffirmed strongly his earlier promises to the Zionist leader, and gave his former business partner permission to communicate this to Weizmann. He also had Ewing investigate the status of Palestine, the report concluding that the Arabs' claim that Palestine had been theirs for thousands of years was not true, and that in international law a conquerer could choose how to dispose of land obtained in war: the Allies had done so after World War I with Palestine, thus making the Jews' title to it "indisputable." Ewing's brain trust for Truman's reelection, at a meeting attended by Clifford, Niles, and Interior Under-Secretary Oscar Chapman, also advised Truman to appoint Hilldring to a senior post at the State Department and send Henderson to head an embassy abroad. Truman consented to the first suggestion, not to the second. After numberous telephone calls from Weizmann, one from Eleanor Roosevelt, and a cable from Morgenthau, the reluctant, sick Hilldring agreed to serve. Truman would announce at the month's end his new appointment as Assistant Secretary of State for Palestine reporting to Truman and Marshall directly, much to Forrestal's considerable worry and "the greatest astonishment" of all the Arab representatives.[42]

Weizmann was convinced that the Arabs could not carry out effectively and systematically any military campaign against the Hagana. He sent to quite a few people the current report by the *Economist*'s Intelligence Unit entitled "Middle East Morass," which highlighted the corruption prevalent within the Arab countries' ruling circles and their being consequently prone to Soviet infiltration. He was greatly strengthened after hearing from US Col. Mickey Marcus, who had just returned from secretly designing, at Ben-Gurion's request, a command and control structure for the Hagana and bolstering the *yishuv*'s weakest points in the Negev and the Jerusalem area, that as soon as the Hagana possessed some pieces of heavy artillery, the whole Arab "war of liberation" would collapse.

When Austin, Ross, and Philip Jessup of the US delegation visited Weizmann's sick-bed at the Waldorf Astoria to say how dangerous it would be for peace if the Jews of Palestine proclaimed a state on May 15, he replied that Palestine Jewry "would be off its head if it postponed statehood for anything as foolish as the American trusteeship proposal." Further, he considered the *yishuv*'s intention to proclaim statehood as soon as the Mandate ended "thoroughly justified and eminently realistic," a conviction which he repeated when Parodi conveyed to him the "veiled threat" that the United States would send cruisers to the Mediterranean in order to enforce the arms blockade. Quoting a remark of Baron Edward de Rothschild, he told Trafford Smith that "*Les Américains sont les gens qui vous lâchent,*" and expressed amazement that they had not produced a single great man since President Woodrow Wilson. When Rosenman, also a member of the small committee planning Truman's re-election campaign, approached him with an offer to help on condition of strict secrecy, Weizmann readily agreed. Various short memoranda, drafted by Linton and typed by Cohn in the hotel suite, were given Rosenman to brief this "newcomer" for action at the appropriate moment.[43]

An atmosphere of unreality appeared to engulf the latest UN developments when juxtaposed against the escalation of what Azcárate characterized to Bunche as the "minor war" between Arab and Jew in Palestine. On April 1, the first shipment of Czech weapons, arranged by Ueberall and hidden under a mountain of onions aboard the small vessel *Nora*, arrived just in time for Palmah soldiers heading for the decisive battle for the road to Jerusalem. Soon after these 10,000 rifles, 2,500,000 rounds of ammunition, and 500 machine guns reached the Tel Aviv port, paid for thanks to Myerson's highly successful campaign across the United States, the Hagana launched Operation Nahshon to clear the Tel Aviv-Jerusalem highway. (The first DC-4s intended for arms deliveries to Palestine, arranged by Kollek's team in New York, also arrived from Prague in Operation Balak with 200 Czech guns, 40 machine guns, and 150,000 bullets.) The Irgun obtained a substantial amount of weaponry when assaulting a British army base near Pardes Hanna on the 6th, also killing six soldiers including the commanding officer, a personal friend of the High Commissioner. The key al-Qastal village, dominating the western entrance to Jerusalem 10 kilometers away, ultimately fell on the 9th to the Palmah after the occupying, sizeable Arab forces spontaneously left for Jerusalem to join thousands at the funeral procession of Abd al-Qadir al-Husseini, who had been shot by a Palmah sentry when climbing up just before dawn to urge the forces of his right wing to advance. Large Jewish convoys, aided by Palmah units under Yitshak Rabin clearing Arab forces northeast of the Tel Aviv-Jerusalem road (Operation Harel), began reaching the long-besieged city.[44]

Jerusalem school teacher Bajhat Abu Gharbiyya, who had fought with Abd al-Qadir during the Arab Revolt and was part of his *Jihad al Muqaddas* fighters at al-Qastal, later wrote that the Palestinian Arabs' best commander had been in Damascus when the Hagana first captured the village on April 3. While sending the brief order to re-occupy the village because "Qastal is Jerusalem," Abd al-Qadir tried to persuade General Safwat, Riad al-Solh, Azzam Pasha, and Syrian defense minister Ahmad al-Sharabati to suppy his fighters with weapons. The Military Committee continued to claim, however, that it did not have them. When he asked for some of the artillery that had been supplied to Kaukji, he met with a persistent refusal, as he did when requesting that Kaukji artillery be ordered to come to Qastal's aid. On the evening of the 6th, with the two sides exchanging bitter recriminations, Abd al-Qadir shouted to the Committee members before returning to al-Qastal, "You're all traitors, and history will record that you lost Palestine."[45]

Bemoaning Abd al-Qadir's "irreparable loss," Abu Gharbiyya did not know that Kaukji had actually met on April 1 with the Hagana's Yehoshua Palmon at Nur-Shams, a former prison camp near Tulkarm. Although the ALA commander began by charging that the Zionists sought to dominate Palestine and all the other Arab countries, with Zionism a "bridgehead" for foreign intervention in the region, and Palmon countered by advocating the benefits of partition, their discussion clearly indicated that both opposed the ex-Mufti's designs for Palestine. Palmon would later recall saying at the time that the Hagana opposed Haj Amin and his commanders, including Abd al-Qadir, not the Arabs on principle, and that he received Kaukji's promise not to intervene to help Abd al-Qadir. Soon after their secret meeting, Palmon heard on Arab radio that Kaukji had kept his word by turning down Abd al-Qadir's request for heavy weapons. Kaukji also pledged to Palmon that he would only mount one attack to avenge his earlier loss at Tirat Zvi, thereby breaking his promise to Cunningham not to take further offensive action until May 15. Hearing this, the Hagana command thought that he would advance on the Beit Sh'an Valley, but Kaukji turned his forces to Kibbutz Mishmar HaEmek in northern Israel's Emek Yizrael instead.[46]

Founded in 1926 by HaShomer HaTsa'ir youth from Poland, Mishmar HaEmek was well prepared for a battle that began on April 4 and lasted eleven days. Intending to clear the way from Jenin towards the conquest of Haifa, Kaukji began with a barrage from seven artillery pieces (the first used in the war) supplied by the Syrian army. Two days later, most of the women, along with the wounded and children of the kibbutz, were evacuated with British aid to other *kibbutzim* nearby, and a mandatory-brokered ceasefire for twenty-four hours began. During that time, with the Hagana's 640 soldiers facing 2,500 attackers, the Jews fortified the badly damaged kibbutz and dug trenches around its perimeter. Kaukji reported on the 8th that Mishmar HaEmek had been captured; this "conquest" was celebrated in Arab newspapers, which also reported heavy casualties among the Jewish forces. The ALA, which actually had yet to enter the kibbutz, sent terms to the Hagana saying that they would raise the siege, regroup, and move toward Haifa, if in return the Jewish fighters would agree not to retaliate against the nearby Arab villages. The Jews declined the offer, and the Arab offensive resumed on the 8th.

That same night, the Hagana launched a counter-attack under the commend of YItshak Sadeh and captured al-Ghubayya al-Fawqa in a fierce battle. In the next days, soldiers of the Palmah and the Hagana's Alexandroni and Carmeli Brigades captured several other villages near Mishmar HaEmek and nearby Ein HaShofet; all of them were destroyed. Forced to retreat to Jenin, Kaukji later claimed falsely that Russian non-Jews had assisted the Hagana, aided by ten twin-engined bombers "of the American type." The ALA Druze Battalion's attack on Kibbutz Ramat Yohanan, undertaken at Kaukji's request to relieve the pressure on his own forces, also failed against the Carmeli Brigade. The Arab villages in that area were razed, and Palestine's Druze would throw in their lot with the emerging Jewish state.[47]

With a general collapse of Arab morale in Palestine extending to the ALA, Abdullah wired the Arab League Political Committee that he would undertake the rescue of Palestine with the Arab Legion. With the opposition of Mardam Bey and Haj Amin overcome by Azzam and Nokrashy Pasha, Safwat arrived in Amman with a letter from Azzam asking the king to coordinate details with the ALA commander, Azzam telling a London *Times* correspondent that he saw no alternative to the condition that Palestine must be taken over as a whole and remain an Arab state. Little emerged from the talk, however, and Safwat returned to Damascus. The next day, Abdullah told a press conference that he and the Arab Legion were prepared to fight "to the end" against the Jewish and Russian danger threatening Palestine, Jordan, and the entire world.[48]

An attack the same day in a joint Irgun-LEHI operation of about 120 men against the village of Deir Yassin, located between al-Qastal and Jerusalem and having checkered relations with its adjacent Jewish Givat Shaul neighbors, had more far reaching consequences. With marginal assistance from Hagana commander David Shaltiel in Jerusalem, the poorly trained fighters responded to fierce resistance in house-to-house fighting from the inhabitants, including women, by blowing up buildings and storming them. A truck with loudspeaker, meant to advise the villagers to flee south to Ein Karem, sank in a ditch; the warning in Arabic may not have been heard. ALA members who resided nearby did not at any point come to the aid of their brothers. The digging of graves for the local victims proving difficult due to the rocky ground, some bodies were burned in an effort that was not particularly successful. Much property was then looted to aid Jews who were in dire straits due to the war.

The Jewish Agency denounced the attack in a letter to Abdullah as an unforgiveable atrocity, with the Hagana, the Chief Rabbinate, and the *yishuv* press taking a similar stance well before subsequent international propaganda against alleged Jewish wartime immorality. The attackers suffered four dead and several dozen wounded. The Arab dead in battle numbered close to 110. No deliberate massacre or rapes had taken place, but subsequent Irgun statements more than doubled that number to inflate the "victory," as did the British for their own ends, while Arab horror stories in news agencies did so in order to encourage fighting spirit and rally the Arab world's support against the *yishuv*. As Eliezer Tauber has shown, the complete opposite occurred. Deir Yassin, like the loss at Mishmar HaEmek and the death of Abd al-Qadir al-Husseini, would mark the beginning of the complete collapse and defeat of Palestinian Arab society.[49]

Deir Yassin had other critical effects, beginning with further panic flight from Palestine's towns and villages. Ben-Gurion himself noted that it had propelled flight from Haifa when the *yishuv*'s battle for that strategic stronghold would begin not long thereafter, while the Hagana, in summarizing the Arab flight in the next two months, pointed to Deir Yassin as a "decisive accelerating factor." British intelligence came to a similar conclusion. More immediately, hundreds of Arab militiamen from Jerusalem and environs alongside Iraqi soldiers, taking revenge for Abd al-Qadir's death and Deir Yassin (Arab shouts of "*Minshan Deir Yassin*" [For Deir Yassin] could he heard), attacked seventy-eight doctors, nurses, academics, and Hagana men in a ten-truck convoy on April 13 passing the neighborhood of Sheikh Jarrah on its way to the Hadassah Hospital. Although warned regularly beforehand by Hadassah and Agency officials of this possibility, and calling that entire day for help from a mandatory garrison two hundred yards away, no British help arrived until after five hours. Only thirty-one bodies were recovered and buried; the rest "had turned to ashes."[50]

As for the Palestine administration's claim of neutrality, the French consul informed Azcárate that every evening a British tank parked at its door showed no "signs of life" when Arabs in the Old City moved against the Jewish neighborhood of Yemin Moshe, but shot at the Jews whenever they started to retaliate. Lourie conveyed to Bunche on the 14th that the British, in the process of evacuation, had recently begun turning over to the Arab Legion large quantities of armored cars, mortar bombs, ammunition, and petrol. The British imposed oil sanctions on the *yishuv* while providing oil to the Arab states. Refusing an appeal by the Board of Deputies of British Jews to immediately recognize the Hagana and allow a Jewish military under UN authority to acquire arms, Atlee delared on the 18th that HMG "had no reason to suppose" that a small and infrequent supply of weapons to the regular forces of the Arab states "have been or are unlikely to be put to an improper use in Palestine." The mandatory government soon announced that British troops would be withdrawn on May 1 from the Palestine-Egyptian frontier, worrying the Hagana that Egyptian "volunteers" would as a result cross into Palestine to fight with the Arabs. Despite Bunche's protest, it also impounded the Palestine Currency Board's funds of approximately £50 million to help cover such costs as the maintenance of the Cyprus refugee camps and the severance pay of the British civil staff.[51]

The Hagana's radical turn turn to offensive operations, called for by thirty-one- year-old Chief of Operations Yigal Sukenik (later Yadin) on April 1 to implement Plan Dalet and marking the second stage of the civil war in Palestine, witnessed a major *yishuv* victory in Tiberias. Between April 8 and 9, sporadic shooting broke out between the Jewish and Arab neighborhoods in that city. On the 10th, the Haganah launched a mortar barrage, killing some Arab residents. The local National Committee refused the offer of the ALA to take over defense of the city, but a small contingent of outside Arab irregulars moved in. During the next week, units of the Golani Brigade and the Palmah's Third Battalion attacked with dynamite and mortars, and refused to negotiate a truce, while the British chose not to intervene. Newly arrived Arab refugees fleeing from Khirbet Nasir ad-Din told of atrocities and twenty-two civilians being killed there, news which brought panic to the residents of the city. Ignoring pleas by the local Jewish leadership to stay, the entire Arab population of Tiberias (6,000 residents, or almost half of the population), acting on orders of the Nazareth National Committee, was evacuated under British military protection on the 18th, some going to ALA-held Nazareth and others to Jordan; the abandoned Arab homes were looted. This denouement triggered in turn the complete evacuation of a number of Arab villages nearby, among them al-'Ubeidiya, Majdal, and Ghuweir Abu Shusha.[52]

Across the Atlantic 6,000 miles away, Truman continued to feel very strongly that he would try "to do something" about Palestine before the GA session ended. Two top leaders of the Democratic Party heard him confide on the 14th about a change in personnel, which Shultz guessed might involve Henderson and the appointment of a special representative to handle the Palestine question (clearly a reference to Hilldring). Yet he also thought that carrying out the partition resolution would not garner sufficient votes in the Security Council, a remark which she understood was based on "a very thorough briefing on the part of our opponents." A copy of "Middle East Morass," perhaps sent via Weizmann, was deposited in Truman's Confidential File within the White House Central Files. A telegram from Kirchwey told him that the U.S. truce proposal "dishonored" his pledged word that the Administration was still committed to partition.

Weizmann's effort to secure an interview with Niles's intercession did not succeed, but Rosenman had far better fortune. He had spoken to and received a letter on the 19th from the Zionist avatar for Truman's consideration about Palestine's Jews "being in a better position to look after ourselves in the territory of the Jewish State" if there were a UN truce for Jerusalem. Rosenman also received a memorandum via Cohn which called for warning the Arab states not to commit aggression; the Commission to proceed posthaste to Palestine; and the granting of facilities to the Hagana, which should be recognized as the Jewish milita, to obtain adequate weaponry. The next day, Rosenman had a long discussion with Truman, and reported two days later to Weizmann via telephone that the President would intervene regarding Jerusalem.[53]

Rosenman also passed on the information that Truman, who had received Louis Dublin of the Hadassah Physicians Committee on the 21st, had never heard about the murder of the doctors a week earlier, "railed" against the British, and was "horrified" at the Arab atrocity, asking "What does it gain them to do that sort of thing?" The President had also expressed indignation at the "ineptitude" of the Zionists regarding the negotiations for a cessation of the hostilities. The American public, Truman remarked, was getting the impression that they did not wish to sit down and talk. He could not understand their "inflexibility," and felt that it would be to their great advantage to have a "peaceful atmosphere" established in which matters could be further discussed. Truman's main concern, Dublin recorded, was what would happen after May 15 in that war-torn country.[54]

Confronted by the forward UN movement towards a truce and trusteeship, Crum, with feedback from Epstein and Lourie, sent Clifford a note (written from Hagana headquarters in "Kibbutz 14" a few floors above New York City's Copacabana nightclub at 14 East 60th St.), followed by a memorandum on the 22nd of points to improve the two proposals. Aside from Truman's sponsoring an immediate truce and trusteeship statute for the City of Jerusalem and the Vatican's being notified of these secret attempts, it posited that the Jewish state had become a reality. Under these circumstances, an international trustee-ship at this stage was "impracticable" and impossible of implementation except with the help of large forces, leading to the conclusion that a free vote in the UN would reaffirm the partition plan. Truman could then properly say that the basic U.S. policy was to support the UN decision, thereby recapturing much of the public goodwill lost by the "seeming reversal" of America's stance on Palestine. Hilldring should be given full power by the President to secure this objective, and the Arab states cautioned that United States' economic sanctions would be leveled against them in the event of any acts of aggression. The UN should immediately establish a border watch or commission to insure against such forces invading Palestine, no Russians or Russian substitute needed on this commission. Crum also sent Weizmann a copy and one to Rosenman for presentation to the President.[55]

The next day, defending Austin's announcement to the UN about supplying U.S. troops for a Palestine police force, Truman declared for the first time at a news conference that, as Commander-in-Chief of the country's armed forces, he had the authority to do so without prior Congressional approval. Vandenberg, chairing the Senate Foreign Relations Committee, replied to colleague Brewster that he had not been consulted before Austin's declaration, but that the President had sent U.S. troops abroad in over 100 cases during the last 150 years, and that the limit of presidential authority in this field had never been clearly defined. Brewster and Pepper criticized the Administration for reversing its Palestine policy, Brewster assailing the continuing arms embargo and observing that "several thousand" young men had volunteered to participate as part of a special UN police force, but that Truman had never seen fit to take up this offer; Pepper called on the government to recognize the Jewish Provisional Government.

Responding to a petition from about 5,000 members of the bar protesting the U.S. reversal of support for partition, Austin replied that the United States, which had worked "faithfully and constantly" for partition, saw that it could not be implemented "by pacific means" and that the UN had no armed forces to do the job. Asserting that nobody would abandon the people of Palestine to "nothing but anarchy when the mandatory power moves out," Austin declared that "all of us should get together to patch up this government and administer it until some arrangement can be made."[56]

What also occurred on that April 23, Eban revealed fourteen years later, "contained a massive refutation of all the 'hard-headed' theories which deny the personal and human factor in international relations." In the late afternoon of the first Passover Seder night, Weizmann received a telephone call from Rosenman, who had just returned to the Essex House from Washington. Indicating that a leg injury prevented him from coming to the Waldorf Astoria, he urged that Weizmann come to see him at once. While Cohn waited just outside the bedroom, Rosenman related that Truman had called him into the Oval Office and began by saying quite simply, "I have Dr. Weizmann on my conscience." The President then went on to aver that he had not realized on March 18 when speaking to the Zionist leader that the State Department had gone so far in abandoning the partition plan. He wished to "find his way back" to the GA resolution of November 29, and if the Special Session could be "surmounted" without reversing partition and if a Jewish state were declared, he would recognize it immediately. Truman stipulated one absolute condition: he would deal only with Weizmann. For that reason, Weizmann had to postpone his departure for about three to four weeks so that Truman could receive him as soon as he was ready for an official announcement. Proceeding directly with his wife and Cohn to the Seder at the home of Lola and Siegfried Kramarsky, Weizmann maintained his silence about this remarkable revelation until, excusing himself right after dinner, he shared it "in absolute secrecy" with his closest associates upon returning to his hotel suite that same evening.[57]

Two days later, Weizmann sent Rosenman a secret memorandum asserting that the President's intentions might be thwarted by the "rapid development" of events transpiring at Lake Success, the adoption of a UN trusteeship agreement making it more difficult for Truman to recognize the Jewish state after May 15. Jessup had recently pressed the GA's Committee Number One to permit night sessions so as to speed up discussions. (His effort to immediately refer the U.S. plan to the Trusteeeship Committee failed, opposed on the 21st by Australia, the Soviet Union, the Ukraine, Byelorussia, Poland, and Yugoslavia.) Truman's stated willingness two days earlier to send U.S. troops had not helped the situation, because it meant that the Administration was now prepared to enforce trusteeship against the Jews. Furthermore, the killing of one G.I., even advertently, in action against Palestinian Jews would have disastrous effects. Given that an invasion of the Arab Legion might tragically aggravate the position, the United States could intercede with London regarding this British-officered, financed, and equipped force, and do much to prevent Abdullah's threat in this respect by warning him that it would withdraw support for his membership application to the UN and refuse the king any future financial assistance. Finally, the government could point out to Iraq that while it might consider aid to relieve great distress and hunger there, it would not support that country's aggression and "military adventure" in Palestine.[58]

As Weizmann had observed, the pertinent UN bodies pressed forward on a truce and on trusteeship. Speaking before an off-the-record conference of non-government organizations on the 16th, Sayre, American president of the Trusteeship Council, defended State's new position as not a switch but "the facing of realities in an honest way," and he declared that the ultimate solution might be partition—which the United States had not "as yet" dropped, a federal state, or perhaps an ultimate trusteeship. The next day, the Security Council adopted a resolution calling for a truce in Palestine while reminding HMG of its responsibility to maintain peace and order, with Parodi confiding in Austin his fear that no final GA solution would have the United States and United Kingdom blockading Palestine's coast, leaving the Jews to be massacred by the Arabs. The Trusteeship Council adopted a Draft Statute for the City of Jerusalem as a *corpus separatum* four days later.

On the 20th, Carl Berendsen (New Zealand), Gunnar Hagglof (Sweden), John Hood (Australia), and Gromyko (Stalin having approved Gromyko's memorandum of the 9th) proposed a reversion to partition. However, the Council passed a U.S. resolution (which Truman had approved earlier that day) on the 23rd establishing a Truce Commission made up of Belgium, France, and the U.S., all operating consular officers in Jerusalem, to supervise the carrying out of the truce and to report back to the Council by the 27th. Russia, the Ukraine, and Colombia abstained in the vote. On the 28th, the GA Political Committee agreed by a vote of 38 to 7 that the U.S. working paper of a draft trusteeship agreement for Palestine would be referred to the Fourth (Trusteeship) Committee for detailed discussion. The latter advocated the rapid establishment of a temporary trusteeship in Palestine, to be administered by the Trusteeship Council through a strong Governor-General, this to be without prejudice to the eventual political settlement there.[59]

Bevin, Ambassador Douglas reported to Lovett, was "deeply concerned" by the "dangerous possibilities" in the Palestine situation. The Foreign Secretary had gathered from a talk the previous week with Goldmann that "he and his group" were trying to push for a settlement along the lines of the Morrison cantonal plan, but, while particularly anxious that the United Kingdom's position be not interpreted as non-cooperative, Bevin was "at his wit's end to know what to do." The Conservative Party, as Churchill had already told Douglas, would vigorously oppose any suggestion that British troops be retained in Palestine, and most of the Labour MPs would be equally opposed. Bevin believed with Creech Jones that there was virtually "no prospect" of an effective truce, while the Colonial Secretary reported from New York his opinion that trusteeship (as the Agency had observed) required as many troops, or more, than partition. Creech Jones also thought that the proclamation of a Jewish state on May 16 was a factor that had to be taken into account, a view which Beeley believed was "quite right" based on Epstein's telling him that the Zionist leaders would be compelled by their followers to do so even if the UN did decree some alternative solution to partition.

Lovett was encouraged by a *New York Times* story on the 21st about British willingness to consider using its forces beyond May 15 to execute a Security Council political and military truce, but Whitehall, believing that an agreed truce was "most unlikely," indicated two days later that while not prepared to enforce a truce, it might consider a supervisory role until August 1 if both sides were to accept one. (Bevin warned Creech Jones that the news story may have originated with Goldmann, and the UN delegation should be especially careful in their dealings with him, whom the Foreign Secretary had known for a long time and considered that "he is not reliable.") The UN discussions, Gurney penned in his diary, seemed to be "more and more futile and unreal." For the duration of the Mandate, in any event, exactly as Cadogan had told an informal Council meeting on April 14, the legal Palestine immigration quota of 1,500 per month would be continued. Thus, the 798 passengers stopped aboard the *Tirat Zvi* on the 12th, the 782 captured on the 24th off Haifa on the *Mishmar HaEmek*, and the 550 taken from the *Nahshon* two days later near Haifa after fierce resistance, which left a number of people injured, were all transferred to Cyprus.[60]

Completely in the dark about Truman's innermost thoughts, Henderson pressed Lovett to champion a temporary trusteeship for all of Palestine, while Rusk informed Fawzi Bey of the department's having given considerable thought to Egypt's becoming part of the possible UN police force. Henderson sought a policy of persuading moderate American Jews to break the hold of "a minority of extreme Zionist leaders," who he felt continued to push Palestine Jews into "an extremely nationalist position"; encouraging the Arab League and Arab countries to adopt a "conciliatory and reasonable attitude" of cooperation with the Jews; impressing upon Britain and other democratic countries the need to back the U.S. position, that Presidential candidates and Congress remove Palestine from domestic politics and give that issue its rightful place as "a dangerous and difficult international problem." In McClintock's own view, the establishment of a "hard core" of security from Jerusalem to the Mediterranean, maintained by UN forces, would bring about a *de facto* partition of Palestine, with the Jewish state centered on Tel Aviv and extending north along the coast to almost, if not including, Haifa. "I should not care," he ended this memorandum to Lovett on the 22nd, "if Jordan, Lebanon, Syria, and Egypt took over the rest of the country."[61]

The capture of Haifa by Jewish forces that same day validated Lovett's notation "I think you are wrong" regarding McClintock's preliminary proposal for the borders of the Jewish state. Speaking with Canada's UN delegation, Weizmann pointed to the Hagana's triumph in Operation Bi'ur Hametz (the burning of leavened bread prior to Passover) as illustrating the weakness of the Arab forces. Already demoralized by the Hagana's killing of Mohammad ibn Hammad Al Huneiti, commander of Haifa's Arab militia, when ambushing a convoy to the city on March 17 with fifteen tons of weapons and explosives, the local Arabs found little reason to place stock in the ALA forces for largely deserting before the decisive battle. On the 18th, commanding officer Major-Gen. Hugh Stockwell informed Agency liason officer Harry Beilin that he would begin evacuating the British forces, quickly leading the Hagana to prepare for a three-pronged attack on the Arab neighborhoods. On the night of April 20, he officially announced to Beilin and ALA commander Amin Izz al-Din Nabahani that all forces would withdraw to the airport, port, and main areas of the city, and that they would not interfere in clashes between Jews and Arabs. Al-Din Nabahani promptly left for Damascus to report to ALA headquarters, leading to further Arab demoralization, especially when two prominent members of the Haifa Arabs' National Committee also departed.

Hagana propaganda broadcasts and swift shell bombardment proved decisive, with the British later praising the "smoothness" of the Hagana operation and its ability to achive victory with a relatively small number of Arab casualties, 50–100 killed in two days rather than 5,000. Local Haj Amin-dominated Arab leaders urged all Arabs to leave the city (Jewish mayor Shabtai Levy pleaded that they stay), and large numbers did so in panic, the British providing transport to Lebanon and Acre. 15,000 civilians were evacuated during April 21–22; by mid-May only 4,000 of the pre-conflict 70,000 Arabs would remain.

The Arab states protested vigorously to Whitehall that the British withdrawal ran counter to their understanding by which they had agreed to refrain from intervening in Palestine before May 15, and accused Stockwell of giving the Jews a considerable advantage for which the Arabs were not prepared. Azzam informed Campbell that if the "massacres" continued and the British forces could not give protection, the Arab states would be forced by their public to intervene militarily and could hardly be accused of an act of aggression. To Fares al-Khoury's accusations in Committee One about a massacre in Haifa, Shertok relied on Sasson's information to counter that Arab commanders had initiated the mass flight, and that the Jews wished Arabs to live in full security in the Jewish state.

HMG Consul General Cyril Marriot defended Stockwell's position, saying that the British forces were "so run down" that they could not maintain law and order in addition to ensuring a safe evacuation. The Arabs had brought on the situation in Haifa, Cadogan told the Council on the 23rd, because large numbers of ALA men had filtered into the city. The local Arabs were not fully behind the fighting effort, reported U.S. Consul Aubrey E. Lippincott to State, and a large number of the country's Arabs were "entirely depending" on outside forces to settle this dispute. The Arab forces were "quite amateur," lacked essential discipline, and their sense of organizational supply and tactics was "almost nil." For the time being, he concluded, the Jews would probably achieve successes in the field, but the whole matter "is a different story" if outside armies invaded. Here again, however, signs of disorganization were evident, with "as yet no signs of discipline and training comparable to that of the Jews." Cunningham reported explicitly for the first time a "collapse of Arab morale" in Palestine, the British Embassy informed Canadian Ambassador H. H. Wrong. At the same time, the

High Commissioner's personal assessment had concluded that Zionism "has exhausted its usefulness to Great Britain and has become more of a liability than an asset."[62]

Faced with the major defeats at Mishmar HaEmek, Tiberias, and Haifa, the AHC and all the states of the Arab League resolved on April 23 at a meeting in Serka, Jordan, to accept a trusteeship along the Morrison lines and have Haj Amin recognized as the representative of the Palestinian Arabs. If not, they would issue a joint Declaration of Palestine Independence the same time that the Jewish Agency issued its declaration of "a Hebrew Republic"; thereby "war will be legalized by war of one government against another." The Arab states would each send 2,000–3,500 soldiers from their regular armies under Abdullah's command, Iraq and Egypt giving the largest financial contributions, also sending a small part of their air force. The AHC alone would choose the occupation army to remain in Palestine temporarily. The Arab Legion might occupy before May 15 only those areas in Palestine that today were regarded as strictly Arab territory. Jewish minorities in Arab states would not be attacked nor their property confiscated. The ex-Mufti's role was clear, Zaslani noted: he had been chosen by Egypt's King Farouk and Ibn Saud as a "watchdog" over Abdullah. The resolutions concerning Palestine were given to Cunningham three days later.[63]

That same morning, the Defense Department's Ad Hoc Palestine Committee relayed to Leahy the result of its discussion with McClintock, Henderson, and some of their associates as to armed force requirements in order to secure Jerusalem, an evaluation which Rusk had requested, as well as to secure the Tel Aviv-Jaffa-Jerusalem area against illegal activities (short of all-out civil war) by "dissident elements" among the Jews and Arabs. The first called for 32,644 Army soldiers, the second 38,622, along with a total air force commitment of 1,000 men for each. The Committee having ruled out a partial occupation of Palestine as militarily unsound, the one significant comment made was that no additional advantage was apparent in adding the Tel Aviv-Jaffa area (the CIA's plan) to the Jerusalem one. Henderson firmly opined that the time was propitious to initiate talks in Washington on the Combined Chiefs of Staff working level in securing the Jerusalem area. Brig. General M.H. Silverthorn insisted that Haifa be used as the main port of supply for any contingent based in Jerusalem, with the latter's water supply protected by a company of troops and the force, divided between the

United States, United Kingdom, and France, also patrolling the Haifa-Jerusalem highway. The Trusteeship Council, McClintock immediately advised Rusk, would be well advised to recommend that the temporary trusteeship be promptly established for the entire country.[64]

The State Department ramped up its efforts, "plugging away hard" in a skeptical Creech Jones's characterization, to obtain a truce and an interim trusteeship. Following talks with Proskauer, who found an understanding spirit in Lovett, and Fawzi Bey, Austin drew up draft articles for their review. State backed a call for a Jerusalem truce along with an international 1,000 volunteer police there, advanced by Parodi on the argument that it would be a scandal of the twentieth century if 2,000 years of civilization were destroyed. On the 26th, the GA approved a resolution that the Trusteeship Council study "suitable measures" to protect the city and its inhabitants, and submit wihin the shortest time proposals to that effect. An Australian amendment to refer action on Jerusalem to a GA Sub-Committee rather than the Trusteeship Council was defeated (26 against, 20 in favor, and 7 abstaining), taken as an indication that the United States might find it impossible to reverse partition and have trusteeship adopted by the required two-thirds majority. At the same time, Rusk had to admit on the 26th to organizations accredited to the UN that the United States had found "no takers" to cooperate in the sending of troops. Proskauer, also impressed by a letter to the *New York Times* by Einstein and former Chief Rabbi of Berlin and Theresienstadt Ghetto survivor Leo Baeck endorsing Magnes's truce call so that, in their words, Palestine's Jews not "permit themselves to be driven into a mood of despair and false heroism which eventually results in suicidal measure," pressed Shertok and Ben-Gurion to support the overall truce effort.[65]

Lovett went much further in a frank, off-the-record talk on the 28th with Goldmann, in whom, he began, "the State Department has great confidence." Thinking that the Palestine situation might easily lead to "a general conflagration" with terrible repercussions on the world scene, he warned that if the Zionists prevented a truce, the United States would block any help being given to them, and publish a White Paper incriminating them (along with the British and the Arabs), which would do "great harm" to America's Jews and increase antisemitism in the country. While the Arabs could not annihilate the Jews, he conceded, the *yishuv* would be the losers in a long dragged-out war.

Lovett then made a thinly veiled threat. If the Zionists did not accept the truce, the U.S. Government would do "everything" to prevent any facilities being given to the fighting parties through American money or other forms of American help: "We will not allow the Arabs or the Jews to go on fighting with the help of American dollars." The truce led to partition *de facto*, and a little later *de jure*, he declared, and if the Jews turned to the Soviets, which he characterized as committing suicide, the United States could take certain measures to check the Russians from coming into Palestine. As Goldmann took leave after an hour had passed, Lovett repeated his warning about the government preventing any help being given to any one of the parties if no truce emerged, also explaining its position publicly and indicating "the follies" of all the parties involved. (Shertok soon cabled Ben-Gurion about the White Paper, "with grave effects for us," and the intimated "financial reprisals.") Lovett repeated to Inverchapel the possibility of a U.S. "financial embargo," even while noting that the Jews appeared to have gone further in agreeing to a truce for Jerusalem than had the Arabs. Cunningham made the same last point to his superior, observing that while the Agency Executive had agreed on the 9th to a cease-fire for Palestine as soon as the Arabs would do so, for they had started attacking the Jews, a reply from the AHC to his urgent request had still not been received.[66]

After a long talk with Goldmann the next day, Rusk relayed to Lovett that his visitor apparently supported a truce along the U.S. lines and was most anxious for some special arrangement for Jerusalem. That Zionist spokesman was opposed to trusteeship, Rusk observed, and believed that truce and trusteeship should be dealt with separately. On his own intiative, Goldmann stated to Rusk that he planned to urge Proskauer to bring in other American leaders such as Lehman to "moderate" the situation. From things he said and corroborated by other sources, Rusk went on, it was clear that Silver led the "intransigent" school, and was primarily responsible for State's difficulties on a truce. At the right moment, Goldmann had added, the United States should "crack the whip" and insist on a "reasonable" truce. He and I agreed, Rusk ended, that State should develop the area of agreement somewhat further before using "drastic action."[67]

The British government stuck resolutely to its timetable. It urged the Arab capitals not to undertake any aggressive acts, to be told in turn that the Jews were "on the offensive everywhere," attacks which, if continued, would make it difficult for the Arab forces to refrain from retaliatory action. Bevin, with Attlee present and in agreement that "all this aggression came from the Jews" and "after all Palestine was an Arab country," told Douglas on the 28th that London would use all influence possible to deter Abdullah, whose annual subsidy from HMG totalled $8 million, from moving Jordanian armed forces across the Palestine frontier.

Yet Arab Legion units had already attacked Neveh Ya'akov on the 18th, fired on Jerusalem's Talpiyot and Mekor Hayim neighborhoods ten days later, and exchanged artillery shelling for three days against the Hagana's taking control of the Gesher police station in the Beit Sh'an Valley until ordered to return to their barracks. (Clayton viewed the Legion's march into Palestine as the best guarantee for security following the British evacuation, Tuck informed Marshall, and he suggested amalgamating Jordan and Palestine as an excellent solution to the Palestine problem.) Bevin's remarks to the Commons on the 28th that Britain intended to withdraw the Arab Legion from Palestine before May 15 but that he refused to interfere with the delivery of arms and munitions to Arab states until the UN decision was received, adding "the Jews have the best arms," drew a comment by Maurice Edelman M.P. that "murder will be committed before you do anything." The Foreign Secretary immediately rejoined to cheers that "the British sergeants were not hanged by Arabs," then urged the Jews and the Arabs that the best way for both to settle this was to stop fighting.

Feeling "let down by the Army" in Haifa, a furious Bevin on his own had Montgomery order MacMillan to retake Jaffa against a successful Irgun assault and return it to the Arabs before May 15. (On second thought, he wired Creech-Jones that Stockwell's decision not to intervene more actively was "probably inevitable in the circumstances," but it naturally "makes things most difficult for us with the Arabs" when asking them not to intercede while the mandatory was responsible for law and order.) Beginning on the 29th, Major G. J. Hamilton directed the shelling of the Irgun headquarters in Tel Aviv with artillery, Cromwell tanks bearing 75-mm guns, and Spitfires also machine gunning the Irgun units in Jaffa's Manshiyya quarter for two days. This led to the killing of 70–80 Irgunists and an Irgun retreat, while forcing the Haganah to permit an escape route on the main Jaffa-Jerusalem road for the Arab civilian population. The latter had already been demoralized by the

Hagana's capture in Operation Hametz of the Arab villages surrounding Jaffa, as well as by the continuing mortar bombardment of Palestine's largest Arab city by a joined Hagana-Irgun effort (the Va'ad HaPoel HaTsiyoni had on the 12th approved an operative agreement between the two forces by a vote of 39 to 32) soon thereafter. The British also forcibly dislodged the Hagana from Jerusalem's Sheikh Jarrah, through which Arab bands had been "pouring into Jerusalem without check," on the pretext that it was vital for the army's projected evacuation route.[68]

Only the United States could bring effective persuasion to bear upon the Jews for a truce, Bevin told Douglas. He thought it "not proper" that the Americans pressed HMG to "get reason" with the Arabs, who were being "provoked," but did nothing with regard to the Jews, whose present action was the "direct outcome" of U.S. policy. The British were prepared to reconsider "their entire position" about helping the Jews and Arabs in an effort to settle their differences if a truce could be arranged, Bevin added, "on the understanding that they are not left in a solitary position of responsibility." Attlee went further, comparing the Jews with Hitler's method of putting people in Germany as tourists, then the *yishuv* giving them training to become soldiers.[69]

Both belligerent camps stood firm. Challenging China's Tsiang, key backer of the U.S. plan who placed on the same level the Arab armed incursions and Jewish illegal immigration, Silver had informed the Political and Security Committee on April 22 that the *yishuv* would establish the Jewish state officially on May 16 right after the end of the Mandate. In response, Malik asserted that the Arabs would oppose anything except a unitary Arab state, and Abdullah publicly urged all Arab nations to "join my army in a movement to Palestine to retain the Arab character of that country." On the 26th, replying to Fabregat's defending the November 29 partition vote for having acknowledged the birth of a Jewish nation—"How could they stop a river from flowing, a child from growing?," Husseini declared that the country's Arabs would proclaim the whole of Palestine an independent state on May 16 unless in the meantime the GA created a temporary trusteeship that would lead to a sovereign unitary state. Shertok countered the next day, asking the UN to prevent an invasion of Palestine by Jordan at the Mandate's end, and rejecting the American trusteeship proposal.

On the 28th, Prince Feisal spoke on behalf all the Arab delegates meeting in his apartment when telling Rusk and Jessup that Jewish immigration could at most continue at 1,500 per month, but it had to "cease altogether" after the truce. Azzam said the same to the British in Cairo. The following day, Shertok wrote to Marshall that the Jews would not defer statehood or agree to a truce that allowed the British to remain in Palestine and the Arabs—but not the Jews—to continue obtaining weapons for eventual use against the Jews.[70]

On the last day of the month, Truman told Rusk that, as he wished to get the Palestine matter "settled" rather than approach it from the point of view of personal political considerations, he agreed with State that an immediate truce there seemed to be the government's fundamental objective. In addition, it was "fundamental" that the truce should not be used as "a cloak" for a change in the military position of either warring side. After Rusk pointed to "extremists" like Silver, who unlike Goldmann, Shertok, and Jewish leaders in Palestine, made a "formidable war party" which "complicated" the department's task considerably, the President said that he wished Marshall to know he was ready to take whatever steps the Secretary thought would hasten the completion of a truce, prepared to "go the limit" in helping the UN bring this about. "If the Jews refuse to accept a truce on reasonable grounds they need not expect anything else from us" he replied to Rusk's statement that the Arabs might accept the truce and the Jews would not, which might then create "difficult problems" for him. The Arabs should be told that our policy was firm, Truman concluded, and be reminded that "we have a difficult political situation within this country." Expressly stating his concern over the Russian aspect of the situation, he ended by saying "go and get a truce"—there was no other answer to this situation.[71]

The same day, Austin sent Marshall a copy of the latest telegram to the Security Council from the chairman of the Palestine Truce Commission, Belgian Consul Jean Nieuwenhuys, beginning with "general situation Palestine deteriorating rapidly." Government departments were closing daily and normal activities coming to "a standstill." While the Jewish Agency was acting as a central authority for the *yishuv*, the Arab areas depended on the municipal authorities within the townships and villages. The intensity of fighting was increasing steadily; camps and areas vacated by the British were immediately becoming battlegrounds. Hagana operations on a larger and more important scale than Haifa were expected shortly, with rumors tending to increase the "nervous tension" in the country.[72]

This assessment appeared to corroborate Cunningham's latest "appreciation" of the situation to Creech Jones that the Agency, finally deciding to establish a Jewish state out of fear of a U.S.-imposed trusteeship, would launch an all-out offensive against the Arabs "to demonstrate Jewish military strength." For their part, the Arab states secretly resolved on the 30th to make five army divisions and six bomber planes available for their forthcoming invasion, with the Arab League allocating £1.5 million to finance the "opening stages" of the operation. Asked by Nieuwenhuys to desist from any military decisions or acts, Abdullah charged that current Jewish aggression and the presence of thousands of Palestinian Arab refugees who had "flooded" his and other Arab kingdoms called for the Truce Commission's compelling the Jews to halt every aggression and abandon the idea of establishing the Jewish state, thus making possible "a peace in the Holy Land." In the meantime, Lourie wrote Eytan, the discussions continuing in the GA Political Committee were "almost incredible in their apparent futility," with an atmosphere of "cynicism and gloom" hanging over the whole meeting.[73] Now, with the clock ticking relentlessly, only a fortnight remained until the Palestine Mandate would come to a close.

On the morning of May 1, given a massive push by Shertok to move from the obscurity of back-room draftsmanship to explain directly before the GA's Committee One why the defeat of the U.S. trusteeship proposal was important and urgent, the thirty-three-year old Eban asserted that Jewish sovereignty was already a reality in everything but name. Over the years, the world Zionist movement had created solid, coherent institutions in Palestine now poised at the threshold of sovereignty, and it also possessed a certificate of national legitimacy from the very international organization that was now debating the wisdom of its recent partition vote. His peroration affirmed that to prevent Jewish statehood would be a grotesque exercise for a UN pledged in the Charter's Article 76 to the advancement of dependent territories towards self-government; need more military force to prevent Jewish statehood than to let it take its course; and leave the future government in Palestine "still suspended in the old fog of uncertainty, with no vision of finality ahead."

The Americans' "violent reversal" of policy also ran counter to mankind's conscience haunted by the spectacle of Jewish survivors still languishing behind barbed wire, who desired to be citizens of a Jewish society in which their capacities and ideals "will be fully at home," and above all be a blatant acceptance of illicit force as the arbiter of international policy, thereby covering the UN in universal derision. The time had come, he asserted, for the emancipation of "two historic peoples from a long period of tutelage," freed from "a straitjacket of imposed unity" to a position of independence between both parties that would allow for a vision of mutual cooperation. "Congratulations," Gromyko soon told Eban in his booming bass voice during a luncheon in Lie's Forest Hills home, "you have killed American trusteeship."[74]

The U.S. trusteeship proposal fared little better in other quarters. Husseini and Iraq's Khalidy objected to the US trusteeship proposal as an attempt to impose partition indirectly, their opposition leading Belgium's Pierre Rykmans to be "not disposed" to accept it; France's Roger Garreau was "lukewarm" and wanted some other "special international regime." Fawzi Bey told Rusk that the Arab states might have to enter Palestine to "establish law and order" after May 15, Feisal adding in another interview that they "could not ever" accept a Jewish state, which would be "an abcess to the political body of the Arabs." A scheme to have Jerusalem placed under the International Red Cross's flag and a truce arranged for the entire country, recorded by Azcárate, drew Husseini's quick response: "No Partition!!"

Creech Jones conceded to Ross, Austin, and Parodi on May 2 that discussion of the matter had not convinced many governments that trusteeship was feasible in the absence of available forces to implement it and of a Jewish-Arab agreement. He personally thought that a good solution would have Abdullah's forces partitioning the country along a line running across to and including Jaffa (leaving the Jews a coastal state running from Tel Aviv to Haifa), placating Ibn Saud by giving him Aqaba, ceding to Syria the northeastern corner of Palestine, and "liquidating" Haj Amin. The Colonial Secretary quickly went on to say, at the same time, that this would be "power politics," and "we could not 'intrigue' in such a matter," although he thought that the Jews would agree to Jewish sovereignty over the restricted area which would result. Brazil's Eduardo Anze Matienzo suggested to the Americans that the UN order that matters be held in status quo until the next regular GA meeting, and that the United States, United Kingdom, and France be asked to assume joint control until that time. The pro-Arab Arce proposed that a sub-committee create a provisional UN regime after May 15, pressing for an Arab-Jewish agreement based "upon a free, independent state in Palestine."[75]

On May 6, a GA vote of 35 to 0 (with 17 abstentions) approved the Trusteeship Council resolution, passed one day earlier by a vote of 9 to 2, to have the mandatory appoint a neutral Special Municipal Commissioner to take over the entire Jerusalem administration ten days hence. Berendsen saw no sense in having a new official take over necessary but "minor tasks," "a man of straw, whose feet rest, not on any solid ground but upon the brittle ice of continued Arab and Jewish agreement." Julius Katz-Suchy, Poland's delegate and a Jew, continued to maintain that the partition recommendation was still on the books as the GA decision, and he questioned from where this man's legal authority would come. A sub-committee of Committee One began discussing the creation of a provisional government, Parodi proposing that it last only a few months, Tsiang deeming trusteeship "reactionary" and in general unpopular, and Tsarapkin thinking that even bare consideration of the French proposal in effect ignored the November 29 recommendation.

"It must now be reported," Ross relayed to State about a meeting on the afternoon of the 6th with Parodi, Creech Jones, and Nisot, that "a basis for agreement on truce terms has not been found." Hearing Creech Jones declare that recent military successes had made the Jews determined "not to budge" from statehood and unlimited immigration, while "inflamed public opinion" would sweep aside any Arab government in compliance with UN decrees, Parodi thought the situation "hopeless." His government would never permit French boats to do what British boats "have done to the Jews," he confided to Austin. The Colonial Secretary offered nothing further to a closed meeting of the subcommittee the next day other than "at this late hour, what is not possible by consent is not possible at all."[76]

Rusk had tried another tack. On the morning of May 3, he proposed to Lovett that an immediate cease-fire begin in Palestine on the 5th, with the Mandate extended for ten days, and an airplane furnished by the President fly to the Middle East with representatives of the AHC, the Arab states, and the Jewish Agency joining members of the Truce Commission to conclude a truce during that time. Truman agreed to make available his plane "Sacred Cow," a receptive Shertok was informed, and U.S. Consul Thomas Wasson in Jerusalem transmitted the message to the Jewish Agency. Upon consulting his colleagues, Shertok wrote to Rusk the next day that they did not consider warranted "the somewhat spectacular proceeding now suggested." They had already indicated their readiness for an immediate cease-fire if the Arabs would do likewise, while this proposal apparently ignored the Security Council's Truce Commission and would prolong the Mandate, which the Agency "could not possibly accept" even (as Ben-Gurion put it) for ten days.

Shertok's reply persuaded Rusk to inform Lovett that the Agency, in light of the Jews' present military superiority in Palestine, would prefer to "round out" its commonwealth after May 15, becoming "the actual aggressors" against the Arabs in Palestine. He thought Creech Jones's proposed solution to Parodi on May 2 of a *de facto* partition "the wisest course of action," seeking a *modus vivendi* between Abdullah and the Agency. Asked about press reports that his effort to settle the Palestine issue had failed within the last twenty-four hours, Truman replied on the 6th that he did not think so, and that the United States was doing "everything it can" to get that problem settled peacefully. Asked if he was still trying to persuade the British to remain in Palestine after May 15, the President answered that he had been in no communication with the British except through the UN, and that he did not know what the UN had asked the British to do.[77]

London turned down Rusk's sudden idea flat. Bevin declared in Commons on the 4th that HMG would not depart from its position to retain the Mandate until May 15, despite Marshall's expression to Inverchapel of "very strong hope" that HMG would agree to the Mandate's extension "in the general interests of peace." Until that date, he emphasized, the Palestine authorities would not tolerate aggression, as witness their halting Jewish attacks in Jaffa and preventing the country's invasion by Arab countries. The Jews have become "very truculent," Bevin wired Creech Jones, even as he urged UK Ambassadors to press that Cunningham's efforts for a truce over all of Jerusalem be accepted by the Arab governments, who "should not rely on us to save them from the results of their own intransigence."

Douglas's conviction that Britain would not be placed in a position of "a solitary acceptance of responsibility" found support in Beeley's speaking to the American delegation about the "great legal and time-consuming difficulty" of amending the Mandate deadline. Any extension would "harden" the respective positions of the warring parties, in Beeley's opinion, and greatly impair the chances of a truce. Fearful that the unlikely prospects for a truce or trusteeship would make Palestine "for many years to come" a "breeding ground for international bad feelings," he added that HMG's reinforcement in the last few days of troops to aid the imminent withdrawal would be misinterpreted were the Mandate to be extended. Whitehall's Michael Wright explained to Douglas that HMG had decided on the new units and authorized the military to take a "tougher line" because it did not wish the Mandate to end "in turmoil." If the Jews advanced in Katamon "one inch, we will crush them," Gurney confidentially declared. On the 5th, Beeley confirmed to Ross that the withdrawal deadline was midnight May 14, which the British had tried to keep top secret for military reasons.[78]

State found encouragement in Marshall's private talk with Magnes and Rusk's with Goldmann, who separately had each urged the United States to press for a truce and a trusteeship. Thinking the Hebrew University president's appeal on the 4th for trusteeship, a UN representative for Jerusalem, and a Governor General for all of the country "the first account of the Palestine situation in which he could believe," the Secretary arranged for his off-the-record meeting with the President the next morning. Rusk appreciated Goldmann's private advice two days later that Marshall intervene at once, and speak "bluntly" to Shertok and possibly Silver of the department's determination to pursue a truce policy in Palestine, although Truman might be moved by "internal political considerations" to add promises or qualifications which Goldmann thought "might not help in this situation." Ross had, indeed, heard Silver and Shertok insist on a guarantee that the Jews could establish their state at the end of the truce period, and that if the Arabs proclaimed a state for all of Palestine on May 15, the Jews would then feel free to revert to their original position and proclaim likewise for a Jewish commonwealth.

McClintock and Leonard Meeker of State's Office of the Legal Adviser even prepared a UN resolution threatening economic sanctions, recalling Lovett's threat to Goldmann, against violators of the truce in Palestine. State's Policy Planning Staff, consistently opposing partition, agreed that in view of the probable failure to reach a solution by May 15, a "serious explosion" would occur immediately after the Mandate ended. On the 6th, Truman approved State's draft of proposed articles for a three-month truce under the Commission's authority, during which time no steps were to be taken by Arab or Jewish authorities "to proclaim a sovereign state in a part of all of Palestine or to seek international recognition therefor," which was handed the following day to the Agency and AHC representatives in New York.[79]

Yet reports still circulated in the State Department and the White House to the effect that Shertok had agreed to conditions for a military truce and "political standstill" in Palestine, forcing him to write to Marshall on the 7th in an effort to clear up this "persistent misunderstanding." Reminding the Secretary that his letter of April 29 had made it clear that the proposed truce deferred Jewish statehood and threatened to prolong British rule in Palestine, he noted that private individuals (a hint to Proskauer, Magnes, and Goldmann) had differed with the Agency's line, but they did not represent the Jewish people of Palestine, bore no constitutional responsibility for its future, and were not in a position to give effect to the policy which they advocated. In response to an urgent call from the Agency Executive in Palestine, he was about to fly there for consultation with colleagues, who alone would have to decide on the truce proposal as a whole. The Agency was still prepared to accept a cease-fire throughout Palestine, he concluded, provided the Arabs did as well. Rusk quickly observed to Marshall that Shertok's wish for an interview before his departure was of "considerable significance." The bitter debates between moderates within the Agency favoring a truce, such as Goldmann, Epstein, and possibly Shertok himself, and "more extreme elements" such as Silver and Ben-Gurion pressing for the immediate establishment of the Jewish state "by force if necessary" made such a meeting important before the basic decision would be made upon Shertok's arrival in Palestine.[80]

Clifford, who received from Rosenman one day later a copy of Shertok's letter to Marshall, had already on the 4th prepared some penciled notes about the question of American recognition of the anticipated Jewish state. These posited that it was consistent with U.S. policy from the beginning; a separate Jewish sovereign entity, to be set up shortly, was "inevitable"; "We must recognize inevitably. Why not now?"; and State's trusteeship resolution did not stop partition. Truman, receiving from Clifford on the 7th a draft public statement for the next Presidential press conference on May 13 to announce his intention to recognize the Jewish commonwealth, telephoned Marshall for his views. The man he called "the greatest living American" objected strongly, however, leading Truman to say that he wished to have a meeting the next week on the subject. Turning to Clifford, Truman remarked that after the Secretary would most likely take a very strong position at the meeting, he wished Clifford to make the case for recognition. "You know how I feel," he said. Present it as though you were making an argument before the Supreme Court, Truman added: "I want you to be as persuasive as you can possibly be."[81]

In a conversation with Rusk the next day, Clifford urged that the United States take no position until the 15th which would "tie the hands" of the government after then, argued that there was strong indication in Palestine of actual partition now, and observed that there was just as much danger of continued conflict under a trusteeship substitute as under the existing November 29 resolution. If the United States were seeking an armed truce without a political truce there would be no difficulty. Rusk disagreed, pointing out that the Jews currently held about only one-third of their projected commonwealth as described in that resolution (the Negev was not under their control), and he indicated that the problem would be simpler if last November the delineation of the Jewish state had been different. The government's principal effort was directed towards a truce, he stressed, armed and also political in the sense of excluding the proclamation of two independent states. Unconvinced, Clifford moved forward to prepare a statement for the inevitable confrontation with State six days later, Truman as heretofore to decide the outcome.[82]

On the 8th, the same day that Rusk told Lowenthal "partition is a dead duck" as far as State was concerned, Shertok, accompanied by Epstein, made his final case to Marshall. Noting that Creech Jones had just given him the impression that Abdullah's Arab Legion would only occupy the Arab section marked out in the November resolution, predicted that the Jews would have their state on May 15, and believed that Abdullah would not commit aggression against the Jews, Shertok added that Glubb assistant Col. Desmond Goldie had met with the Hagana's Shlomo Shamir and Nahum Spiegel (later Golan) in order to convey Abdullah's wish to "avoid clashes without appearing to betray the Arab cause." Concluding that as a result of the Shertok-Creech Jones talk there was "a very limited possibility" of the Agency's accepting a truce, Marshall realized that the Agency was prepared to gamble on a "now or never" basis to declare a Jewish commonwealth on May 15 and on the possibility of an arrangement for partitioning Palestine with Abdullah.

After Lovett set forth State's position at length, Marshall warned, as a military man, that it was very dangerous to base long-range policy on temporary successes in the field of battle. No assurance existed whatever, as he had discovered subsequent to his failed talks throughout 1946 with Communist leader Mao Zedong and Nationalist head Chiang Kai-shek to seek unification for China, that the tide would not turn against them in the long run. Should that occur, they had no warrant to expect help from the United States. Thanking the Secretary for "his sincerity and his wisdom," Shertok promised to convey this admonition to his associates in Jerusalem.[83]

Bevin, in response to Marshall's queries after the Shertok interview, asserted on the 10th to Douglas that he did endorse a truce effort, thought the U.S. proposals sound, and had advised the Arabs to accept them. (Poland and Guatemala served notice the same day, however, that they would feel free after May 15 to recognize the Jewish state if it were proclaimed.) If Abdullah's troops moved into Palestine at all, the Foreign Secretary thought that they would confine their movement only to "the legitimate and clearly recognized Arab portions." He would continue to hold Abdullah back, had instituted "vigorous steps" to end the Jewish attack on Jaffa and to keep the Jews out of the Arab quarters in Jerusalem, and would like to keep the Jews away from the Arab areas.

There would develop, Bevin believed, a natural "sorting out of Palestine" which would set the conditions under which a truce, established under a UN resolution, could be made effective. If this ensued, he was contemplating an immigration of 4,000 Jews a month from Cyprus. If a truce held, Abdullah's soldiers in the Arab areas and the Hagana forces might provide the militia to preserve order and administer the affairs of Palestine. If the proposed truce for Jerusalem were obtained, Bevin thought that it would facilitate an extension to all of Palestine. Finally, he believed that Jaffa and Haifa should be open cities, with Gaza reserved for the Arabs. The same day, Whitehall instructed its UN delegation to work with the Americans to remove the legal basis for the proclamation of a Jewish state while allowing for a naval blockade of the Palestine coast.[84]

Shertok dashed off for his waiting plane to Palestine in order to be present at the critical meeting of the *Minhelet Ha'Am* (People's Administrative Council), which would soon decide as the Provisional Government Cabinet on whether or not to declare statehood as soon as the Mandate expired. At a meeting of the Agency Executive's American section on the night of the 3rd, Silver, Neumann, Halprin, and Mizrachi's Wolf Gold had opposed his and Goldmann's favoring a discussion of the U.S. truce proposal and using the "Sacred Cow," although all voted against trusteeship and extending the Mandate. The *yishuv*'s recent military successes in securing Safed and Jerusalem's Katamon area (Hagana Operations Yiftah and Yevusi), along with a telegram from Lourie indicating that Crum's visit with Truman on the 10th had been promising and that Clifford advised "we go firmly forward," had altered Shertok's anxious mood to one of optimism.

Ben-Gurion, set on the proclamation and fortified by private cables from Crum and a majority of the American Agency Executive to push for statehood and another from Epstein conveying Welles's agreement, had asked Weisgal, about to return to New York after a brief visit in Palestine, to find out "at once" what Weizmann thought about declaring independence. Weisgal placed the call during the ramshackle Dakota's brief stopover at Nice, and received this reply in a clear and short Yiddish from the man he always called "the Chief": "*Vos warten zey, die idioten?*" (What are they waiting for, the idiots?). Weisgal immediately sent back a one-word cable to Zaslani: "Yes."[85]

When the *Minhelet Ha'Am* opened its crucial deliberations on the morning of May 12, Shertok began by summarizing his conversation with Marshall. The Secretary had pointed out the military risks involved in declaring statehood, but no "virtual ultimatum" had been made threatening sanctions, as erroneously reported by Jon Kimche from Tel Aviv and which Epstein strongly denied. Further in Shertok's judgment, "nothing prejudicial to fund-raising" by the Democratic Party "would be allowed in an election year." Ben-Gurion argued that acceptance of the Americans' demand for a cease-fire would not check the Arab states' invasion, the Arab Legion already moving towards Jerusalem. Myerson reported on her secret visit to Amman two days earlier with Danin, during which she sharply rejected a worried Abdullah's private appeal that the Jews delay their independence for one year, after which the country would be united with Jordan in a "Judeo-Arab" kingdom where Jewish memebership in the Parliament and Cabinet could reach fifty percent. Sukenik candidly informed his listeners that at least one-third of the mobilized *yishuv* combatants lacked weapons, there was very little long-range armament, and only a few locally-made three-inch mortars and anti-tank weapons augmented by a small number of 20-mm guns were at Palestine Jewry's disposal. Galili, on the other hand, declared that the *yishuv*'s military situation would likely improve in seven to ten days.

By a close vote of six to four, recorded by Cabinet secretary Sharef as the night session ended, the American truce proposals were rejected—implying that a proclamation of sovereignty would follow in two days, and the name "Israel" chosen for the new state. The six included Mapai's Ben-Gurion and Shertok, Mapam's Mordekhai Ben-Tov and Aharon Zisling, Mizrachi's Moshe Shapira, and the General Zionists' Peretz Bernstein. The four included Mapai's Kaplan and David Remez, the Progressives' Felix Rosenbleuth (later Pinhas Rosen), and the Sephardim's Bekhor Shitrit. The group also agreed with Ben-Gurion that its declaration of independence would not specify any borders of the new sovereign entity.[86]

By this time, with State's latest initiatives not gaining traction, the voices for recognition reaching the White House had gained significant momentum. Dean Alfange's confidential letter on the 5th to Truman's military aide and long-time friend Maj. Genl. Harry Vaughan asserted that only this step, gaining the Jewish vote, would swing the New York State to the President, while the *yishuv*'s military victories had "knocked the props" from under the trusteeship proposal, allowing Truman to say that events in Palestine had reversed the trusteeship plan. (A copy reached Lowenthal, whose memoranda at the same time for Clifford raised many of these arguments.) Rabbi Samuel Thurman of St. Louis, after discussing Palestine with Truman on the 7th, told reporters that he was "very much encouraged" by the talk, and said that he did not think the President had really departed from partition as the ultimate solution for the Palestine problem. While expressing bitterness the next day to Sulzberger about the the New York Zionists, whom he regulary confused with New York Jews, Truman, like Lovett, appeared to blame Bevin for "an arbitrary and stubborn position."

On the 11th, Niles showed Truman a public opinion poll indicating that 80 percent of the press favored immediate recognition, as did a majority of both parties in Congress and of state governors. The same day, Mrs. Roosevelt, prompted by the Zionists that the Soviets would recognize the new state as soon as it was declared, wrote Truman that "it would be a mistake to lag behind Russia," and then she added in a handwritten postscript: "I personally believe in the Jewish State." Prominent Jewish figures, including Lehman (who had consulted with Silver), Baruch, and Proskauer, also deluged Truman with appeals for recognition. Rusk even telephoned Jessup to say that with Palestine's existing Jewish community "running its own affairs," apparently "going to get an open shot at establishing itself," he did not think that "the boss" (Truman) would ever put himself in a position of opposing that effort when U.S. opposition might be the only thing "that would prevent it from succeeding."[87]

The showdown in the Oval Office on May 12 commenced at 4 p.m. on a cloudless, sweltering day. Earlier, the UN plan for an interim regime for Palestine died after both the Agency and AHC rejected it, Jaffa was placed under Tel Aviv's municipal authority, and the British officially announced that the Mandate would terminate on May 15 at 12:01 a.m. Lovett and especially Marshall started with a criticism of the Jewish Agency's hardening attitude, and argued that the United States should continue supporting the UN trusteeship resolutions and defer any decision on recognition. Armed with numerous memoranda by Lowenthal and advice from Niles (who was also present together with a sympathetic Connelly), Clifford responded by first saying that a truce would probably not occur, while "the actual partition of Palestine had taken place without the use of outside force." The press statement that he proposed Truman make the next day, which should be delivered before the Soviets recognized the Jewish state, would restore the President's earlier stance for support of partition.

Lovett immediately countered: The Security Council was still discussing a truce; premature recognition would be "highly injurious" to the UN and, as a "very transparent" attempt to win the Jewish vote, also to the President; and the United States would be "buying a pig in a poke," not knowing what kind of a state would be set up. Reiterating some of these points, Marshall interjected that Clifford's counsel was based on domestic political considerations, while the Palestine problem was international, and should the President follow this advice, he would vote against the President if he cast a vote in the coming elections. An ensuing silence fell on the room, the Secretary's last statement coming very close to an explicit threat to resign.

Knowing that he had to stop the meeting, Truman declared that he would deal with both sides of the problem himself, then said to a very agitated Marshall "I understand your position General, and I'm inclined to side with you in this matter." He then initialed State's resolution, mainly drafted by Rusk and Jessup, for a truce and a UN Commissioner for Palestine. Once Marshall left the room, Truman turned to Clifford, and said, using one of his favorite Missouri farm phrases, "Well that was rough as a cob. That was about as tough as it gets. But you did your best." When the young counsel asked for his approval to test the waters one more time, Truman suggested "we let the dust settle a little—then you can get it again and see if we can get this thing turned around. I still want to do it. But be careful. I can't afford to lose General Marshall." To Niles, who said he was sorry that Lovett and Marshall had claimed that the Jewish state would be Communist, Truman replied that he should not pay any attention to that charge, "they are always making it… those two men mean well but they follow their subordinates." He agreed with Niles that Western recognition should precede that of the Soviet bloc "to give it the right slant from the beginning." At the same time, he wrote thus to former Senator Joseph F. Guffey (D., Pa.) after receiving a Jewish Philadelphia businessman's urging that Truman recognize the Jewish commonwealth immediately upon its creation: "You'd be surprised how many letters of this sort I get and how easy it is for people on the outside to settle this almost insoluble question."

To Clifford's surprise, Lovett called him shortly after the tense conference had ended, saying that it would be a great tragedy if Truman and Marshall were "to break over this issue" just in these most difficult months of the Cold War. He invited Clifford for a drink at his home that evening, as he wished to talk to him more about the issue. Knowing Lovett to be a sensible and thoughtful man, a delighted Clifford sensed that he was willing to try to find a solution to "this dreadful turn of affairs." The Under Secretary sought some compromise over the next two days if State and Truman could modify their positions, but Clifford insisted while nursing his bourbon and branch water that the President, whose views he had accurately presented, was not going "to give an inch." "Well then," Lovett responded, "let's see what can be done at State." On that slightly encouraging note," Clifford left for home. Marshall in the meantime had sent a "US URGENT" telegram to the U.S. Embassy in Stockholm asking if the Swedish government would object to the appointment of Count Folke Bernadotte as a UN Commissioner for Palestine. The same day, Shertok wired Silver of the date and venue for proclaiming the new state of "Israel," the 14th at 4 p.m. in Tel Aviv, with thirteen on the Provisional Government's Cabinet and thirty-seven to be the Provisional Council.[88]

Hearing from Clifford the next morning about that evening talk, a pleased Truman advised that he keep encouraging Lovett "to work on the General." In the middle of the day, Lovett called with a new suggestion: recognize the new state but delay announcing or implementing it for an unspecific period. "That's a nothing approach, Bob," Clifford shot back without even consulting Truman, as the President was "rock solid" about not going to "budge an inch" in his basic view. Lovett next proposed a *de facto*, rather than full *de jure*, recognition. Again without consulting Truman, Clifford said that this was an issue on which he felt his group could yield to State. The rest of the day ended without a resolution to the crisis, Marshall telling reporters, as State's Wilkins had advised him, we have to wait to see who does what when the Mandate ends. Queried a day later at his press conference about what he would do when the Jewish state would be proclaimed on the 14th, Truman replied curtly, "I will cross that bridge when I get to it." As he listened to the President's reply, Clifford thought, "We reach that bridge tomorrow."[89]

The pressure for recognition did not let up on the 13th, even when Jessup's proposal for a UN mediator (first approved with the British and Canadian delegations after the United States dropped its trusteeship proposal) was forwarded, despite Soviet objection and the Agency's rejection, to Committee One for voting the next day. The biggest massacre of Jews in the Palestine armed conflict had just occurred after two Arab Legion companies and hundreds of Arabs from nearby villages had killed 24 Kfar Etzion badly outgunned defenders on the 12th, murdering the next day 106 men and 27 women, including some after they had surrendered. (Only four survived the assault, three saved by Legion officers, and a fourth escaped to Kibbutz Masu'ot Yitshak.) This did not deter Lehman from pressing Truman for recognition "as promptly as possible" and Niles from reporting to Truman that a presidential grant of recognition before Arvey's scheduled mass meetings to celebrate the Jewish state's creation would be "a great opportunity for acclaim for the President." Arvey also wrote to Truman in this vein. Truman received a telephone call from Flynn to the same effect regarding three hundred such meetings across the country. When Niles told Truman that he and Lowenthal were trying to forestall any negative references to the

President at those meetings, Truman replied that he would show the two of them his appreciation for all their efforts.[90]

Clifford contacted Lovett on his own initiative that day, Lowenthal's diary later recorded, noting that while State had won the decision at the May 12th Oval Office conference not to announce recognition before an official request from the Zionists had been submitted, the question remained "whether and when we should recognize after application is made." The State Department was considering this question, Lovett replied. The same afternoon, Weizmann wrote a personal letter to Truman, which reached him thanks to Niles, asking for prompt recognition from the American government, whose leadership taken "under your inspiration made possible the establishment of a Jewish State," and thinking that the world would regard it "as especially appropriate that the greatest living democracy should be the first to welcome the newest into the family of nations." As for the Palestine police stores worth over £1 million, Gurney, whom Lund blamed for all the British "intrigues," threatened to leave the keys at the doorstep of Azcárate's headquarters when the UN officials refused to receive them at first but then relented. (Azcárate currently thought that the Jews should create effective Jewish independence now, and issue a proclamation of statehood six months later so as not to greatly harm the possibility of "normal neighborly relations" with the Arabs later on.) In the name of the Agency Executive, Dobkin extended to Cunningham "a heart-felt God-speed" on his imminent departure from Jerusalem and from Palestine.[91]

Arab military prospects as the Mandate's end drew near did not appear promising. Reporting from Cairo, Ambassador Tuck concluded that Arab morale had "almost totally collapsed" in Palestine; depression and frustration were "rampant" in most surrounding Muslim countries as the result of Jewish successes everywhere, the "ineptness" of Arab military leaders, the failure of the Arab League to agree on a concerted program and unified command, and the failure to acquire arms abroad. It was also feared that the Arab armies would be "soundly defeated" by the Jews, further sparking the fall of some governments as a result of "rising passions" among the Arab populations. Even so, the "moderate" Azzam and others continued to insist on a maximum of 1,500 Jews monthly during the period of a general truce, and refused Cunningham's request to open the Tel Aviv Jerusalem road. The young Palestinian

Arab Captain Michel Issa, head of the Ajnadin Battalion, had to order a retreat of his troops from Jaffa because ALA commander Major Adil Najmuddin left secretly by sea with all his Iraqi and Bosnian Muslim soldiers from Yugoslavia after they had looted several shops there.

Following Kaukji's loss at Mishmar HaEmek, the disbandment of the ALA, and Safwat's resignation, the Arab League agreed to have Abdullah, who dismissed the Arab Higher Committee, lead the invasion, as the king put it, in order to "enforce peace against the Zionist terror bands." A very reluctant Nokrashy, pressed by the Muslim Brotherhood-directed mass demonstrations and by Farouk's wish to restore Arab pride and his country's predominance, ultimately on May 8 joined the cry for battle. British intelligence, Wasson relayed to State, expressed "considerable doubt" that Arab armies other than the Arab Legion would do more than cross Palestine's frontiers and "await developments."[92]

While Ben-Gurion was making final preparations for declaring the new Jewish state, reborn after two millennia, in Dizengoff House on 16 Rothschild Boulevard, then home to the Tel Aviv Museum of Art, on May 14 at 4 p.m. so as not to violate the start of the Sabbath in Palestine two hours later, Clifford pressed on to secure Truman's recognition. Telling Lovett in the morning that the President would be satisfied if Marshall agreed not to oppose this step, he asked Epstein on his own to write a letter by noon to Truman on Jewish Agency stationery, with a copy to Marshall, requesting that the United States recognize the new state but claiming nothing beyond the borders outlined in the November 29 resolution. Clifford suggested that Epstein consult lawyers David Ginsburg and Benjamin Cohen for the draft, he and Epstein adding a rhetorical flourish about "the deep bond of sympathy" which had existed and become strengthened over the past thirty years between the U.S. Government and the Jewish people of Palestine.

Having the "Jewish state" typed in the letter because he did not yet know the name of the sovereign commonwealth, Epstein sent office worker Peggy Lieberson, who had just heard on the short-wave radio Ben-Gurion proclaiming the new entity to be called "the State of Israel," to intercept aide Harry (Zvi) Zinder at the White House gates. The pair returned immediately to Epstein's office, where, to save time, he crossed out those two words, penned "State of Israel" in their stead, and sent Zinder off to Clifford's office with the revised document and a copy to Marshall. Aided by Niles, a tense Clifford next drafted both a reply to Epstein's request and a Presidential statement, then called Lovett for a meeting between the two of them to resolve the matter. Lovett suggested the small F Street Club, to which he belonged, for their luncheon venue.[93]

The seventh and last High commissioner had left Government House in Jerusalem precisely at 8 a.m. Palestine time. Cunningham reviewed a guard of honor, drove to Kalandia landing field in an armed column with Spitfires circling overhead, and flew to Haifa, where he would board the HMS *Euryalus* at midnight bound for Malta. His farewell radio broadcast the night before had expressed his "great sadness" that an Arab-Jewish peace had not been secured under the Mandate, alongside the constant desire that "cooperation, good-will and amity" might be established between HMG and Palestine's inhabitants "to our mutual benefit in the future." The Union Jack had already been hauled down from the top of the King David Hotel, one wing of which had housed the Secretariat and British Army Force Headquarters; Hagana units, informed early that morning by town commander Brigadier Charles Jones that no troops would be left in the city by 4 p.m., quickly took control of the city center.[94]

In Tel Aviv, the Declaration of Independence, read on the Hebrew date of 5 Iyar 5708 by Ben-Gurion in his high-pitched voice while two large Zionist flags on either side of Herzl's portrait loomed behind him, emphasized that Eretz Israel was "the birthplace of the Jewish people" who had returned to their ancestral soil, and who had gained international recognition for their right to a "national revival in their own country" like all other nations. "*Medinat Yisrael*," the name chosen by the *Minhelet Ha'Am* to begin functioning on May 15 at 12:00 midnight Palestine time, would stand for "the principles of liberty, justice and peace as conceived by the Prophets of Israel."

The exile of 1,888 years came to an end with Ben-Gurion first to sign the typed document (later copied onto parchment) and Shertok the last of another thirty-six to sign according to the Hebrew alphabet, Fishman emotionally proclaiming the traditional blessing to the Almighty "who has kept and sustained and brought us unto this time." The *HaTikva*, sung spontaneously at the start of the ceremony, resounded again at its close after thirty-two minutes thanks to the Palestine Philharmonic Orchestra crammed in the balcony. News arrived that the surviving males of the Etzion bloc were all headed for captivity in Jordan, but also that Jaffa and the entire Western Galilee had been captured; the Hagana called for vigilance with "no panic, no complacency" as "the enemy threatens invasion." "I feel no gaiety in me," Ben-Gurion uttered to Cabinet secretary Sharef, "only deep anxiety as on the 29th of November, when I was like a mourner at the feast."[95]

Back in Washington's F Street Club dining room, Clifford, shown by Lovett Foggy Bottom's proposed statement that the President was considering the subject of recognition, responded that this would not do. While Marshall and you were away, he said plainly, the department had placed the President in a "very unfair," "unnecessary" position with Austin's announcement of March 19. "Speed is essential to preempt the Russians," he added. Ultimately, the two men worked on a draft for a *de facto* recognition, Lovett then reviewing it with Bohlen, Kennan, Rusk, and some others. Having obtained Marshall's agreement not to oppose recognition, much to Truman's satisfaction, he called Clifford a while later to add in the draft the word "provisional" in describing the new government of Israel.

Lovett still sought delay of a day or two, claiming that "indecent haste" would especially have a detrimental effect on the Arab world, and the U.S. delegation at the UN and some helpful governments had to be informed beforehand. Staunchly against postponement and worried about possible leaks to the public, Clifford called back to say that Truman wished to "take action on recognition" after a number of people had advised him not to permit the situation where "no internationally recognized government or authority in Palestine" would exist after 6 p.m. Eastern Standard Time, and "title would be lying about for anybody to seize." The President, he relayed a little while later, was under "unbearable pressure" to recognize the Jewish state promptly. Lovett, to whom Marshall had deputed the entire issue, and his associates arrived at the language of a White House press release around 5:30 p.m., a half hour before the Mandate would come to an end.[96]

Lovett then called Clifford, asking that the announcement be delayed until Austin got advance word of it and the GA session would end about 10 p.m. Ten minutes later, Clifford, who was with Truman at the time, relayed to State that the President would issue the statement shortly after 6 p.m. An astounded Rusk pointed out that this would "cut right across a standstill," for which the delegation at the UN had been working for weeks, and for which State already had forty votes. Nevertheless, Clifford replied, these were Truman's instructions, leading Rusk to call Austin. "To hell with it," responded the disgusted chief of the U.S. delegation, and he simply went home without telling his associates. At 6 p.m. Marshall informed Bevin and other capitals of the impending move, and he quoted Truman's statement in replying to Epstein's official letter soon thereafter. Truman's *de facto* recognition, penned by Clifford and Charlie Ross even before Epstein's letter arrived, came at 6:11 p.m—only eleven minutes after the Mandate had expired. Pale, worried-looking, and gaunt for the last two days, Epstein at last relaxed and gave a first sign of tears of joy.

That same moment, a delegate raced into the GA hall waving an Associated Press ticker- tape release giving Truman's statement. Jessup sent Betty Gough of his staff to find that ticker tape in Lie's empty office, while the embarrassed Sayre was caught speechless. Gough quickly retrieved the crumpled piece of yellow ticker tape from the wastebasket, and Jessup, smoothing the page out as best he could, read it from the podium. Granados, acting on his own, quickly declared that his government would grant full *de jure* recognition to Israel. Shortly afterwards, Lovett wrote the following: his own protests against this "precipitate action" and its consequent deleterious relations with the Arab world appeared to have been "outweighed by considerations unknown to me, but I can only conclude that the President's presidential advisers, having failed last Wednesday evening to make the President a father of the new state, have determined at least to make him the midwife."[97]

While Truman, thinking of his April pledge to Weizmann, said to an aide: "The old Doctor will believe me now," and then placed a first telephone call about his decision to Niles "because I knew how much this would mean to you," "pandemonium" (Rusk's description) struck the GA hall. Silver had silenced his audience briefly when announcing the creation of the Jewish state, yet debate had been continuing on the resolution posed by Jessup for a mediator's appointment. Now Porter McKeever of the U.S. delegation literally sat on Belt's lap to keep him from going to the podium to withdraw Cuba from the UN. Four minutes later, Marshall ordered Rusk to fly to New York and "prevent the U.S. delegation from resigning *en masse*." Some of Marshall's friends advised him to step down from his office, but the Secretary replied that "you do not accept a post of this sort and then resign when the man who has the Constitutional authority to make a decision makes one. You may resign at any time for any other reason but not that one."

Arab delegates Fawzi, al-Khoury, and Malik spoke harshly against Truman's action, while those of Canada, China, and a number of the Latin American states felt, as Austin reported to Marshall, that they had been "double-crossed." Eleanor Roosevelt would write to the Secretary that Truman's speedy recognition had created "complete consternation" in the UN, and she would not have wanted it done without the prior knowledge of her delegation associates and without "a very clear understanding beforehand with such nations as we expected would follow our lead." Marshall replied that "we were aware here of the unfortunate effect on our situation with the United Nations, which is much to be regretted. More than this, I am not free to say."

After the U.S. resolution for a mediator was adopted at 8:30 that evening by a vote of 31 votes to 7 (the Arab and Muslim nations) with 16 abstentions (the Soviet bloc), Jessup hurried back to Manhattan in his car, feeling that "the record of the United States was sullied." "Diplomacy by surprise is a dangerous practice," he wrote subsequently. In Whitehall's view, so Beeley reported to Austin, it was "not correct to consider" that the November 29 resolution established a legal basis for the creation of a Jewish commonwealth. Marshall later told Truman that State felt the United States "had hit its all-time low before the UN," while Roosevelt wrote him that seldom had she seen "a more bitter, puzzled, discouraged group of people" than the U.S. delegation, "just nonplussed by the way in which we do things." "There was not much else to be done," the President replied, given "the vacuum in Palestine" and the Russians "anxious to be the first to do the recognizing." In his memoirs, Truman added that some of that department's career men should not have been surprised at his decision if they had "faithfully supported my policy." "They almost put it over on you," Lovett said to him after Truman's announcement of recognition.[98]

At 6:01 p.m., the Zionist blue and white flag had been hoisted over the Jewish Agency headquarters in Washington, with a similar ceremony held the same time at the Agency's headquarters in New York City. Epstein told the first gathering that "it is the purpose of the State of Israel to become a democratic, peace loving and law abiding member of the family of nations. We will make our contributions to the welfare, prosperity and progress of the world and especially of the Middle East." An exhausted, triumphant Weizmann sent a message from his hotel room expressing "love and admiration to all sections of the *yishuv*," charging that "it will be our destiny to create the institutions and values of a free community in the spirit of our great traditions which have contributed so much to the thought and spirit of mankind." A telegram arriving the next day from Ben-Gurion, Myerson, Kaplan, and Remez acknowledged that he had "done more than any other living man" towards the Jewish state's creation, and they looked forward to his becoming its first President. As chairman of the Agency's American section, Silver declared that "the Jewish State must translate Jewish precept into action. The prophetic teachings must come alive in a progressive democracy whose example will shine throughout the world."[99]

In Palestine, the Hagana's SHAI intelligence service warned of an impending air-raid on Tel Aviv by Iraqi aircraft stationed in Jordan. Its report added that 6,000 Iraqis and Arab Legionnaires "will invade country tonight... they will come by the new road Jericho-Ramallah." "Generally reliable" French intelligence in Beirut had informed Kohn and associate Hayim Berman that the Arab states would invade simultaneously on May 15 with these forces: Egypt (8,000–10,000), Iraq (6,000–8,000), Jordan (5,000 of the Arab Legion), Syria (3,000), and Lebanon (2,000). Iraqi General Nur al-Din Mahmud, appointed by the Arab League's Political Department at its meeting in Damascus between May 11–14, would lead the combined Arab assault the next day. By midnight, Naharayim on the Jordan-Palestine border announced that the Legion had occupied its hydroelectric power plant, and threatened to shell the adjacent kibbutz, Gesher. Egypt's decision to join in the invasion, reported Kirkbride to Bevin two days earlier, had "dispelled" Abdullah's moderation. A few hours later, he reported from Amman that "the Arabs here are now full of optimism and in no mood to listen to any advice." Haj Amin's spokesman, Ahmed Shukairy, announced the Arabs' goal as "the elimination of the Jewish State." "This will be a war of extermination and momentous massacre which will be spoken of like the Mongolian massacre and the Crusades," predicted Azzam at a Cairo press conference as the Arab invasion began.[100]

Ever the realist, Ben-Gurion's last entry in his diary on May 14, 1948, noted that the fate of the new state "lies in the hands of the security forces." At 5:00 the next morning, having been awakened a few hours earlier to hear of Truman's recognition, he woke again to broadcast from a Hagana transmitter while the bombing by Egyptian Spitfires over Tel Aviv, killing one and injuring five, echoed into his microphone.

He immediately left to inspect the damage. Seeing on his countrymen's faces concern but no tears or panic, Ben-Gurion returned to the Red House on the city shoreline and compressed his feelings into a terse phrase: *"Eileh Ya'amdu"* (These shall stand). The inevitable, first Arab-Israeli War had begun.[101]

Endnotes

1   Report, March 19, 1948, Robison MSS; *Palestine Post*, March 21, 1948.

2   *Palestine Post*, March 21, 1948; Lie, *In the Cause of Peace*, 170–171.

3   *PM*, March 20 and 24, 1948; *New York Times*, March 22, 1948.

4   Shapiro to ZOA, March 20, 1948, UN Reconsiderations files, ZA; Klein statement, March 21, 1948, Jewish War Veterans MSS; AAUN statement, March 21, 1948, Box 120, Eichelberger MSS.

5   Harry S. Truman Post-Presidential Papers, Memoirs File, Diaries, Box 643; Truman to Marshall, March 19, 1948, PSF 184; Truman to sister, March 21, 1948, Truman Papers Pertaining to Family, Business, and Personal Affairs, Family Correspondence file, Box 20; Truman to Vivian, March 22, 1948, Family Correeespondence File, Truman J. Vivian, Box 282; all in HSTL; Frank interview with Crum, July 14, 1949, Gerold Frank MSS, NYPL; Truman, *Years of Trial and Hope*, 190; Eilat, *HaMa'avak Al HaMedina* 3 (Tel Aviv, 1982), 625–626.

6   Millis, *The Forrestal Diaries*, 387–398; Memo, March 29, 1948, Charles Ross, MSS; Eben Ayers diary, March 20, 1948; both in HSTL.

7   Dan Kurzman, *Genesis 1948, The First Arab-Israeli War* (New York, 1970 ed.), 126; *FRUS, 1948*, vol. 5, part 2, 739–740, 748–749; Diary, March 21, 1948, HSTL; Marshall to Bohlen, March 22, 1948, 501.BB Palestine/3-2248, SD.

8   *New York Herald Tribune*, March 21 and 22, 1948; *New York Times*, March 23 and 25, 1948; Sullivan-Shultz conversations, March 22 and 24, 1948; both in MC280/238, Kirchwey MSS.

9   FJP (Pratt) to McDonald, March.10, 1948, McDonald MSS; Trotter memo, March 10, 1948, RG18, 38/8, Presbyterian Historical Association, Philadelphia; Cadogan to FO, March 17, 1948, FO371/68538, PRO; Bennett to Slawson, March 18, 1948, Palestine files, AJC Archives.; Rusk briefing, March 19, 1948, MC280/238, Kirchwey MSS.

10   Jacobson to Cohn, April 1, 1952, WA.

11   Josef Cohn, "Report on Dr. Weizmann's Visit to the USA"; Weizmann to May, March 23, 1948; Weizmann to Halprin, March. 25, 1948; all in WA.

Mordekhai and Esther were the Jewish heroes who saved their people from vizier Haman's decree to murder all the Jews in King Ahashveirosh's Persian empire.

12 UK delegation to FO, March 19, 1948, FO371/68539, PRO.

13 Inverchapel to FO, March 20, 1948, FO371/64848, PRO.

14 Ibid.

15 Thomas A. Kolsky, *Jews Against Zionism* (Philadelphia, PA, 1990), 184; Rosenwald to Austin, March 23, 1948, file 124, American Council for Judaism (hereafter ACJ) MSS, University of Wisconsin Library, Madison; Lazaron address, March 31, 1948, RG18, 16/13, Presbyterian Historical Association; file 6044, Morris Lazaron MSS, AJA; Virginia Gildersleeve, *Many a Good Crusade* (New York, 1959), 409, 186; Gildersleeve to Taft, March 30, 1948, Virginia Gildersleeve MSS, Special Collections, Columbia University, New York City; Magnes to Kohn, March 31, 1948, Box 38; Magnes to Austin, March 25, 1948, file 2/11; both in Robert Weltsch MSS, Leo Baeck Institute, Center for Jewish History, New York City; Ihud statement, March 28, 1948, 999/28/20, ISA; Magnes to Gildersleeve, March 8, 1948; Simon draft, 1948?; both in Ernst Simon MSS, 4/1751, National Library of Israel, Jerusalem; Rosenheim to Va'ad HaPoel, March 22, 1948, Eretz Israel III, Jacob Rosenheim MSS, Agudath Israel of America Archives, New York City; Weltsch to Hexter, March 20, 1948, 4/1751/K5, Simon MSS; Rostow to Frankfurter, March 22, 1948, Box 99, Frankfurter MSS.

16 Lash, *Eleanor*, 129–130,

17 Eilat, *HaMa'avak*, 3, 632–634; *FRUS, 1948*, vol. 5, part 2, 755–757; Ross memo, March 29, 1948, HSTL.

18 *FRUS, 1948*, vol. 5 part 2, 759–760; Berger to Binder, Box 30, ACJ Archives; Eilat, *HaMa'avak*, 634; Roosevelt to Marshall, March 22, 1948, Box 4560, Eleanor Roosevelt MSS, FDRL; Lash *Eleanor*, 130–131. Marshall's reply, repeating the gist of Austin's statement, added that he would have Rusk explain further to her what had dictated State's action. Marshall to Roosevelt, March 24, 1948, Box 4560, E. Roosevelt MSS.

19 JAE American Section, March 20, 1948, Z5/2384, CZA; A.S.E. (Eban) memo, March 25, 1948, DAG-13/3.1.0.1, Box 3, UN Archives; Herzog statement, March 24, 1948, P573/1, Kohn MSS, ISA; *Jewish Agency Digest*, March 28, 1948, ZA; Cunningham to Creech Jones, March 22, 1948, FO371/68539, PRO; Jones to Lovett, Rusk, and Henderson, April 1, 1948, McClintock-1, McClintock MSS. Head of the Eastern Department, B.A.B. Burrows, thought it "absurd" to think

that trusteeship would work, considering that "tempers have become so hot" on both sides. Burrows' minute, April 2, 1948, FO371/68540, PRO.

20 *Palestine Post*, March 26, 1948; Linton, "Memories of 1948." I am grateful to Josef Cohn for giving me a copy of this valuable memoir.

21 *Palestine Post*, March 16, 1948; Graves to Gurney, March 9, 1948, DAG-13/3.1.0.1, Box 2, UN Archives; Robert M. Graves, *Experiment in Anarchy* (London, 1949) 213; Wadsworth to Marshall, March 18, 1948; Childs to Marshall, March 22, 1948, both in Box 1, McClintock MSS; Report, March 24, 1948, Robison MSS; Shertok to Lie, March 16, 1948; AHC statement, March 25, 1948; both in S25/5354, CZA; Boswall to Bevin, March 19, 1948, FO371/68539; UK delegation to FO, March 30, 1948, FO371/68541; both in PRO.

22 A.K. (Aharon Cohen) report, March 30, 1948, (2) 11.10.95, HaShomer HaTsa'ir Archives, Givat Haviva, Israel; Lutski to Epstein, March 24, 1948, S25/7733, CZA; Nakhleh to Izzat, March 25, 1948, 361/4-P, ISA; Hollingworth interview with Azzam Pasha, March 28, 1948, S25/9020, CZA; Walid Khalidi, "Selected Documents on the 1948 Palestine War," *Journal of Palestine Studies*, 27:3 (Spring 1998): 62–72.

23 Azcárate to Bunche, March 19, 1948, DAG 13/3.1.0.1, Box 1, UN Archives; Herzog to Shertok, March 23, 1948, S25/1703, CZA; Eytan-Azcárate talk, March 24, 1948, 93.03/125/16; Azcárate to Commission, March 25, 1948, 8/95/14-Het Tsadi; both in ISA. For Lund's views, see Herzog–Lund talk, March 31, 1948, S25/5634, CZA, and Lund memo, March 31, 1948, DAG-13/3.1.0.3, UN Archives.

24 Marshall to Douglas, March 26, 1948, FO371/68540, PRO; *FRUS, 1948*, vol. 5, part 2, 765–767; Robertson to St. Laurent, March 24, 1948, MG26, J1, vol. 441, PAC; FO to Washington, March 23, 1948, FO800/487; Beeley to Bevin, March 21, 1948, FO371/68540; Bevin to UK delegation, March 24, 1948, FO371/64848; all in PRO; Cunningham to Creech Jones, March 25, 1948, III/2, Cunningham MSS; Sumner Welles, "Elements of Security," *Washington Post*, March 30, 1948; Evatt statement, March 22, 1948, Z6/49, CZA; Washington to FO, March 25, 1948, FO371/64848, PRO.

25 *JTA*, March 26, 1948; *FRUS, 1948*, vol. 5, part 2, 761–763, 775–776; Eilat, *HaMa'avak*, 647–648; *Houston Chronicle*, March 26, 1948; London to Marshall, March 27, 1948, 501.BB Palestine/3-2748, SD.

26 *JTA*, March 25, 29–31, 1948; Harry Levin, *Jerusalem Embattled* (London, 1997 ed.), 15–35; Brutton, *A Captain's Mandate*, 129; Hagana report, March 30, 1948, S25/8918, CZA; Ben-Gurion to Shertok, 93.03/117/20, ISA; Slutzky, *Sefer Toldot HaHagana*, 1145–1146.

27   Weizmann to Frankfurter, March 31, 1948, WA; Karsh, *Palestine Betrayed*, 118.

28   M. Medzini, ed. *Israel's Foreign Relations, Selected Documents 1947–1974* (Jerusalem, 1976), 129; *JTA*. April 2, 1948; Sharett, *B'Sha'ar HaUmot*, 173–191.

29   *JTA*, April 4, 1948; Morgan statement, April 1, 1948, DAG-13, 3.1.0.1, Box 5; Azácarte to Bunche, April 1, 1948, DAG-13/3.1.0.1, Box 1; both in UN Archives; Lund-Herzog conversation, April 2, 1948, 41.0/116/24, ISA.

30   Press release, April 1948, Jewish War Veterans MSS; *FRUS, 1948*, vol. 5, part 2, 800–804, 811–812. For the initial responses during that meeting, see Kopper to Henderson and Rusk, April 5, 1948, Rusk-2, NA; Rusk meeting, April 4, 1948, Palestine-US, AJC Archives; Karr to Lillie (Shultz), April 6, 1948, A427/2, CZA; Pearson to Ottawa, April 5, 1948; Pearson to Wrong, April 6, 1948; both in RG 25, series A-12, vol. 2093, part V, PAC. Also Bunche's pencilled notes, DAG-13/3.1.0.1, Box 5, UN Archives.

31   *FRUS, 1948*, vol. 5, part 2, 804–807; Herzog memo, April 1, 1948, 41.0/116/24, ISA; Sack to Silver, April 8, 1948, Box 3, Hyman A. Schulson MSS.

32   Azcárate memoranda, March 21 and 23, 1948, DAG-13/3.1.0:5, UN Archives.

33   Conversation, April 6, 1948, DAG-13/3.1.0:5, UN Archives; *JTA*, April 9, 1948; Gelber to JAE, April 8, 1948, Z5/430, CZA; *FRUS, 1948*, vol. 5, part 2, 804n; Campbell to FO, April 17, 1948, FO371/68543, PRO.

34   Azcárate memo, attached to Azcarate to Bunche, April 7, 1948, DAG-13/3.1.0.1, UN Archives.

35   McNaughton to St. Laurent, April 7, 1948, MG26, J1, vol. 440, PAC; National Board meetings (April 4 and 5, 1948), April 28, 1948, Hadassah Archives.; Lawford to FO, April 5, 1948; FO to New York, April 7, 1948; both in FO371/68541, PRO; Austin to Henderson and Rusk, April 7, 1948, Rusk-2, SD.

36   *FRUS, 1948*, vol. 5, part 2, 809–811, 825; McNaughton to St. Laurent, April 10, 1948, MG26, J1, vol. 440, PAC. For the two meetings with Husseini and Shertok, see April 7 and 8, 1948, 93/1-Het Tsadi, ISA.

37   *Documents on Israeli-Soviet Relations*, 269–270.

38   McNaughton to St. Laurent, April 13, 1948, MG26, J1, vol. 44, PAC; Evatt to Austin, April 12, 1948, H.V. Evatt MSS, Flanders University, Adelaide, Australia; UK High Commissioner in New Zealand to FA and UN Department, April 13,1948, FO371/68543, PRO; Azcárate to Cunningham, April 21, 1948, DAG-13/3.1.0, Box 5A; Azcárate to Lie-Bunche, April 14, 1948, DAG-13/3.1.0.1; both in UN Archives. I thank Flanders University for making a copy of Evatt's telegram available to me.

39   Fabregat-Gruenberg interview, April 14, 1948, 93.03/129/4, ISA; *FRUS, 1948*, vol. 5, part 2, 807–809; Eban, *Chaim Weizmann*, 307. For the Jewish Agency's detailed critique of the US temporary trusteeship plan, see Eban to Ross, April 12, 1948, 93.03/95/14, ISA.

40   Lovett to Weizmann, April 24, 1948, WA; Diary, April 4, 1948, Forrestal MSS, Princeton University Library; Forrestal to Truman, April 4, 1948, PSF 184, HSTL; Memo for Chief of Staff, April 23, 1948, RG 319, Box 93, 091 Palestine, NA; *FRUS, 1948*, vol. 5, part 2, 813n, 832–833; Press release, April 20, 1948, McClintock-2, McClintock MSS.

41   *JTA*, April 4, 1948; Condemnation of US Policy Regarding Palestine by Young J.F. Kennedy, autograph manuscript, http://www.shapell.org/manuscript/jfk-partition-plan-1948-truman; Forrestal memo for Truman, March 26, 1948, PSF Daily Sheets 88, HSTL; Arvey to the author, May 26, 1977; *JTA*, April 9, 1948.

42   *Washington Post*, May 6, 1973; Ewing oral history with J. R. Fuchs, May 2, 1969, HSTL; Eilat, *HaMa'avak*, 682; Weizmann, *The Impossible Takes Longer*, 230; Inverchapel to FO, FO371/64849, PRO; Conversation with Nakhleh and Belt, April 29, 1948, Box 20, Frank Corrigan MSS, FDRL.

43   Cohn report, Feb.–May 1948, WA; *Economist* Intelligent Unit, "Middle East Morass," April 8, 1948; Eban, *Chaim Weizmann*, 309; Smith to Martin, April 12, 1948, Smith MSS; Weizmann, *The Impossible Takes Longer*, 230.

44   Azcárate to Bunche, April 1, 1948, DAG-13/3.1.0.1, Box 1, UN Archives; Avriel, *Open the Gates!*, 345–352; Pinhas (Pinik) Vazeh, *HaMesima—Rekhesh* (Tel Aviv, 1966), 171–186; Ben-Gurion, *Yoman HaMilhama*, 1, G. Rivlin and E. Oren, eds. (Tel Aviv, 1982), 331, 349; Kohn to Shertok, April 9, 1948, S25/1704, CZA; Slutzki, *Sefer Toldot HaHagana*, 1526–1527, 1562–1563; *JTA*, April 21, 1948; Halil al-Sakakini, *"KaZeh Ani Rabotai!,"* Gideon Shilo, ed. (Jerusalem, 1990), 231.

45   Walid Khalidi, "Selected Documents on the 1948 Palestine War," *Journal of Palestine Studies* 27:3 (Spring 1998): 72–85; Karsh, *Palestine Betrayed*, 120–121.

46   Report, April 1, 1948, 65/4-Het Tsadi, ISA; Palmon interview for the Hagana Archives, November 10, 1953, P28/33, Central Archives for the History of the Jewish People, Jerusalem.

47   Uri Milstein, "Al Mishmar HaEmek," *Segula* 36 (May 2013): 20–29; Morris, *1948*, 133–138; Report, April 21, 1948, 105/31, HA; Ben-Gurion, *Yoman HaMilhama*, 356.

48   Kirkbride to FO, April 16, 17, and 19, 1948, FO371/64849, PRO; *HaYom*, April 18, 1948.

49   Eliezer Tauber, *Deir Yassin: Sof HaMitos* (Jerusalem, 2017); Morris, *1948*,
      126–127; Benny Morris, "The Historiography of Deir Yassain," *Journal of Israeli
      History* 24:1 (March 2005): 79–107; Statements, April 11 and 12, 1948, P573/1,
      Kohn MSS; Fletcher-Cooke to Bunche, April 20, 1948, DAG-13/3.1.0:4, UN
      Archives; McNaughton to St. Laurent, April 21, 1948, MG266, J1, vol. 440,
      PAC. HaShomer HaTsa'ir's Aharon Cohen wrote to AHC secretary Husayn al-
      Khalidi one week later in hopes of some understanding, but received no reply.
      Cohen to al-Khalidi, April 14, 1948, (8)11.10.95, HaShomer HaTsa'ir Archives.

50   Morris, *1948*, 127–129; Slutzky, *Sefer Toldot HaHagana*, 1397–1398;
      Salomon to Lisicky, April 15, 1948, DAG 13/3.1.0, Box 1, UN Archives.
      Magnes acknowledged to MacMillan that the arrival of Brigadier Jones
      saved 28 Jews, 20 of whom were injured. Magnes to MacMillan, April
      18, 1948, Box 73, Jerome Frank MSS, Sterling Memorial Library, Yale
      University, New Haven (CT). The thirty-one victims who could be identified
      were buried individually. The remaining forty-seven Jews were purportedly
      buried in a mass grave in Jerusalem's new Sanhedria Cemetery. However, in
      the mid-1970s, Yehoshua Levanon, the son of one of the victims, discovered
      that a commission of inquiry that had been convened at the time of the
      attack reported that only twenty-five were buried in the mass grave and
      twenty-two victims were missing. Going in search of the missing bodies,
      in 1993 he met an Arab who had participated in the ambush, who claimed
      that the attackers had buried stray body parts in a mass grave near the
      Lions' Gate. In 1996 Levinson petitioned the Israeli High Court to force the
      Defense Ministry to set up a genetic database to identify the twenty-five
      bodies buried in the Sanhedria cemetery. The mass grave was never opened.
      Jerusalem Post, October 28, 1996.

51   Azcárate note, April 10, 1948, DAG-13/3.1.0:5, UN Archives; Lourie to
      Bunche, April 14, 1948, S25/5176, CZA; *JTA*, April 21, 1948; Bunche to
      Fletcher-Cooke, April 13, 1948, DAG-13, 3.1.0, Box 2, UN Archives; "Oil
      Sanctions," June 16, 1948, 93/65/6, ISA; Lillie Shultz, "Britain's Stake in an
      Arab Victory," *Nation*, May 29, 1948, 595–598.

52   Slutzky, *Sefer Toldot HaHagana*, 1456, 1566–1569; Morris, *1948*, 138–139;
      Karsh, *Palestine Betrayed*, 123; Zaslani to Shertok, April 27, 1948, 93/128/4,
      ISA; Harry Levin, *Jerusalem Embattled* (London, 1997 ed.), 81–83.

53   Shultz to Kirchwey, April 15, 1948, MC280/237, Kirchwey MSS; "Middle
      East Morass," OF39, White House Central Files, HSTL; Kirchwey to Truman,
      April 14, 1948, 129/1093, ISA; Weizmann to Frankfurter, April 13, 1948;
      Weizmann to Rosenman, and memo, April 19, 1948; both in WA; Judge R.

report, April 22, 1948, Z6/2250, CZA.

54   Judge R. report, April 22, 1948, Z6/2250, CZA; Dublin report, April 22, 1948, Hadassah (I-578), RG 4, Box 21, AJHS.

55   Lourie to Crum, April 21, 1948; Crum to Clifford, April 21 and 22, 1948; Crum to Rosenman, April 22, 1948; all in 69/5-Het Tsadi, ISA.

56   *New York Times*, April 23, 1948; *JTA*, April 23, 1948; Lawyers' Petition, April 22, 1948, Box 1, Paul O'Dwyer MSS, Library Archives, Jewish Theological Seminary, New York City.

57   Cohn report, February.-May 1948, WA; Eban, *Chaim Weizmann*, 309–310.

58   Weizmann memo for Rosenman, April 25, 1948, WA.

59   Memo, April 16, 1948, CF Political Files, ZA; Discussion outline, April 16, 1948, Francis Sayre MSS, Box 13, Library of Congress, Wash., D.C.; Greenberg to Klein, April 21, 1948, Klein files-Palestine 1948, Jewish War Veterans MSS; *FRUS, 1948*, vol. 5, part 2, 827–828, 837, 852; Austin to Marchshall, April 17, 1948, Rusk-2, Rusk MSS; UK-UN to FO, April 20, 1948, FO371/68544, PRO; Shultz memos, April 22, 1948, MC280/238, Kirchwey MSS; New Zealand High Commissioner to Commonwealth Relations Office, April 21, 1948, FO371/64849, PRO; Medzini, *Israel's Foreign Relations*, 133–134.

60   *FRUS, 1948*, vol. 5, part 2, 822, 826, 837, 839, 847, 850–851, 855–857; Bevin-Douglas talk, April 21, 1948, FO800/487; Creech Jones to Bevin, April 20, 1948; New York to FO, April 22, 1948; both in FO371/68544; all in PRO; McNaughton to St. Laurent, April 21, 1948, MG266, J1, vol. 440, PAC; Beeley to Burrows, April 24, 1948, FO371/68546; Bevin to Creech Jones, April 23, 1948, FO371/64849; both in PRO; Diary, April 23, 1948, Gurney MSS, St. Anthony College, Oxford University, Oxford; The Palyam and Aliya Bet Website, www.palyam.org/English/Hahapala/List_of_ships/.

61   *FRUS, 1948*, vol. 5, part 2, 833–834, 836–837, 841–842, 845–846. The full record of the Rusk-Fawzi Bey talk indicates that, like Truman, Rusk also declared that the United States had not abandoned its support for partition. Considering it "a fair and equitable solution," he remarked, the United States would be free, as all governments, to express its views on the merits of the eventual political solution "at some later date." Rusk memo, April 20, 1948, Rusk-2, Rusk MSS.

62   *FRUS, 1948*, vol. 5, part 2, notes to 846; McNaughton to St. Laurent, April 27, 1948, MG26, J1, vol. 440, PAC; Slutzky, *Sefer Toldot HaHagana*, 1569–1573; Gelber, *Komemiyut V'Nakba*, 147, 164–167; Morris, *1948*, 138–147; Moti Golani, "Britanya V'Hakhra'at 'Milhemet HaEzrahim' B'Eretz Yisrael: 'Mifneh Haifa,' April 1948," *Tsiyon*, 1999, 455–494; Zaslani to Shertok, April

23, 1948, 93/127/2, ISA; Campbell to FO, April 22, 1948; Marriot to FO, April 23, 1948; both in FO371/68544; Marriot to FO, April 25 and 26, 1948, FO371/68545; all in PRO; Sasson to Shertok, April 23, 1948, S25/8182, CZA; *FRUS, 1948*, vol. 5, part 2, 838–839; Wrong to St. Laurent, April 24, 1948, MG26, J1, vol. 443, PAC; "An Analysis of the Palestine situation, April 1948," Cunningham MSS; Karsh, *Palestine Betrayed*, chap. 6.

63   Zaslani cable, May 1, 1948, 93/128/15, ISA; Landau memo to Weizmann, April 27, 1948, WA.

64   Silverthorn to Leahy, April 26, 1948, with Memo of April 24, 1948, CCS 092Palestine, RG218; McClintock to Lovett, April 26, 1948, Rusk-3, Rusk MSS; both in NA.

65   Creech Jones to Bevin, April 28, 1948, FO371/68546, PRO; *FRUS, 1948*, vol. 5, part 2, 858–859, 864–868, 871, Box 8, Proskauer MSS; Rusk to Lovett, April 24, 1948, Rusk-3, Rusk MSS; Austin to Marshall, April 27, 1948, McClintock-2, McClintock MSS; Garreau interview, April 26, 1948, Rusk-3, Rusk MSS; *JTA*, April 19 and 27, 1948; Rusk remarks, April 26, 1948, 7/1, Silver MSS; Shertok to Ben-Gurion, April 29, 1948, S25/1558, CZA.

66   Goldmann-Lovett conversation, April 28, 1948, Z6/2759, CZA; Shertok to Ben-Gurion, April 29, 1948, S25/1558, CZA; *FRUS, 1948*, vol. 5, part 2, 869; Chronological account, April 3–24, 1948, 93/125/15, ISA; Kohn to Fox-Strangways, April 9, 1948, S25/5176, CZA. Cunningham reported further that Jerusalem's Arabs were either under no control or were acting under the orders of a number of Iraqi and Syrian military leaders whose activities were "quite uncoordinated" by either the AHC or the local Arab National Committee, with Arab thieves looting government property and shooting British police to get weapons. Cunningham to UKDEL US, April 25, 1948, FO371/68545, PRO.

67   Rusk to Lovett, April 29, 1948, Rusk-3, Rusk MSS.

68   *FRUS, 1948*, vol. 5, part 2, 876–877; Memo of conversation, April 28, 1948, FO800/487, PRO; David Tal, *War in Palestine, 1948: Israeli and Arab Strategy and Diplomacy* (London, 2004), 202; Tuck to Marshall, April 25, 1948, Rusk-3, Rusk MSS; Bevin to Creech Jones, April 27, 1948, FO800/487, PRO; *JTA*, April 29, 1948; Cunningham to Creech Jones, April 29, 1948, FO371/68545, PRO; *The Memoirs of Field-Marshal Montgomery*, 424–425; Kenneth W. Bilby, *New Star in the Near East* (New York, 1951), 28–29; Evron, *Gidi*, 306–343; Khalidi, "Selected Documents," 100–101; Morris, 1948, 150–152; Karsh, *Palestine Betrayed*, chap 7 and 173.

69   Bevin to Washington, April 30, 1948, FO371/68546, PRO; Wasson to Marshall, May 5, 1948, Rusk-3, Rusk MSS.

70   Shertok-Rusk talk, April 9, 1948, 93.03/129/6, ISA; *Palcor*, April 22, 1948; Report, April 26 and 28, 1948, Robison MSS; *FRUS, 1948*, vol. 5, part 2, notes to 873, and 874–876; Cairo to FO, FO800/487, PRO. Rusk, in turn, proposed to Feisal a monthly Jewish immigration quota of 4,000 during the truce, "based on compassionate grounds." Rusk to Feisal al-Saud, April 29, 1948, Rusk-3, Rusk MSS.

71   *FRUS, 1948*, vol. 5, part 2, 877–879.

72   Ibid., 880, and notes to 876.

73   Douglas to Marshall, April 29, 1948, Rusk-3, Rusk MSS; Slutzky, *Sefer Toldot HaHagana*, 1370; Kirkbride to FO, April 29 and 30, 1946; both in FO371/68546, PRO; Nieuwenhuys to Abdullah, April 28, 1948, 125/15-Het Tsadi; Lourie to Walter, 93.03/126/9; both in ISA. Cunningham's latest report went further in comments that Bevin told Douglas were "extremely sinister" and should be taken into account when dealing with the Palestine problem. The High Commissioner charged that the internal machinery of the Jewish State included staff for press censorship and all equipment of "a totalitarian regime," and that persecution of Christian Jews and others who offend against national discipline had shown a marked increase, and in some cases had reached "mediaeval standards." Bevin-Douglas conversation, April 29, 1948, FO371/68546, PRO.

74   Eban address, May 1, 1948, Jewish Agency files, ZA; Eban, *Personal Witness*, 142–143. A member of another friendly nation said afterwards that "trusteeship was so dead that if it were dropped on the floor, it would not bounce." Linton to Brodetsky, May 2, 1948, Z4/20029B, CZA.

75   UK delegation to FO, FO371/68546, PRO; *FRUS, 1948*, vol. 5, part 2, 887–888; Azcárate notes, May 2, 1948, DAG-13/3e.1.0:5, UN Archives; Ross to Marshall, May 2, 1948, Rusk-3, Rusk MSS; Matienzo-Maleady talk, May 3, 1948, Box 20, Frank Corrigan MSS, FDRL; Nenim Nat 5m 1948m 999/31/16, ISA; *JTA*, May 6, 1948. Cunningham thought the Red Cross plan for a general truce in Jerusalem "impracticable." Myerson and Kaplan interview with Cunningham, May 6, 1948, S25/634, CZA.

76   *The Arab states and the Arab League*, 556; Report, May 6, 1948, Robison MSS; Austin to Marshall, May 6, 1948, Rusk-3, Rusk MSS; French paper, May 6, 1948, DAG-13/3.1.0.5, UN Archives; Ross to Marshall, May 6, 1948, 501.BB Palestine/5-648, SD; Douglas to Marshall, May 10, 1948, Rusk-3, Rusk MSS.

Cunningham supported the IRC proposal, but the Palestine Commission members did not. Memos of May 11, 1948, S25/5176, CZA.

77   *FRUS, 1948*, vol. 5, part 2, 891–895; Shertok to Ben-Gurion, May 3, 1948, A312/18; Ben-Gurion to Shertok, May 4, 1948, S25/1553; both in CZA; *JTA*, May 7, 1948. The draft of Truman's prospective announcement regarding Rusk's novel suggestion, sent by Lovett to Clifford, is in Box 13, Clifford MSS. Shertok and especially Goldmann favored the "Sacred Cow" and truce proposal; Neuman, Silver, and the Revisionists' Joseph Schechtman strongly opposed. The American Zionist leadership ultimately opposed. Klarman letters, May 5, 1948, Yosef Klarman MSS, Box 1, Jabotinsky Archives, Tel Aviv; Memo, May 6, 1948, Palestine and Zionism-2, Sulzberger MSS.

78   *FRUS, 1948*, vol. 5, part 2, 896–897, 906–907; Bevin to Creech Jones, May 1, 1948, FO800/487; Bevin to Cairo, May 1, 1948, FO371/68546; both in PRO; Memo of talk, May 2, 1948, 867N.01/5-248; Douglas to Marshall, May 3, 1948, McClintock-2; both in SD; Bevin-Douglas talk, May 4, 1948, FO800/487; Inverchapel to FO, May 4, 1948, FO371/68547; both in PRO; Kaplan to Shertok, May 5, 1948, S25/1559, CZA; Ross to Marshall, May 5, 1948, McClintock-2, McClintock MSS. In addition, Bevin noted, HMG would be accused by the "whole world" of "double dealing" if it agreed to extend the Mandate for ten days, and the "parties" involved would no doubt "spin out the talks for the extra period and so on." Bevin to UK delegation, May 4, 1948, FO371/68547, PRO.

79   *FRUS, 1948*, vol. 5, part 2, 901–904, 917–923, 929; Journal, May 5, 1948, A. A. Goren, ed., *Dissenter in Zion, From the Writings of Judah L. Magnes* (Cambridge, 1982), 488–497; Bancroft to Rusk, May 5, 1948, Rusk-3, Rusk MSS; Memo, May 6, 1948, Policy Planning Staff, Box 32, SD. The American UN delegation soon told the British that the United States was prepared if necessary to cut off supplies of dollars to the Jews in Palestine. UK delegation to FO, May 8, 1948, FO371/68549, SD.

80   *FRUS, 1948*, vol. 5, part 2, 929–935.

81   Ibid., notes to 929, and 906; Clifford, *Counsel to the President*, 5–6. Rabbi Samuel Thurman of St. Louis, after meeting with Truman on May 7, told reporters that he did not think the President had really departed from partition as the "ultimate solution" for the Palestine problem. *JTA*, May 9, 1948.

82   *FRUS, 1948*, vol. 5, part 2, notes to 929, and 906, 935–936; Clifford draft statement, May 9, 1948, Subject file, Clifford MSS.

83   Lowenthal diary, May 8, 1948, Abraham Feinberg MSS, 1885/4-P, ISA; *FRUS, 1948*, vol. 5, part 2, 940–941, 945, 973; Sharett, *B'Sha'ar HaUmot*, 226–229; Memo, A289/129, CZA.

84　*FRUS, 1948*, vol. 5, part 2, 941, 955–956; *JTA*, May 11, 1948; Bevin-Douglas talk, May 10, 1948, FO800/487; FO to UK delegation, May 10, 1948, FO371/68549; both in PRO. For Moshe Toff's activity at this very moment to secure Guatemala's recognition, see Memo, May 12, 1948, L35/81, CZA.

85　JAE US meeting, May 3, 1948, Z5/43, CZA; Crum to Ben-Gurion, May 5, 1948, 93.02/2180/15, ISA; JAE US to JA Palestine, May 7, 1948; Lourie to Ben-Gurion, May 10, 1948; both in 93.03/2180/15; Ginsburg to Silver, May 11, 1948, 93.03/69/5; all in ISA; Lourie to Shertok, May 11, 1948; Epstein to Ben-Gurion, May 11, 1948; both in S25/1553, CZA; Weisgal, ... *So Far*, 262–263; Silver et al. to Ben-Gurion, May 13, 1948, 2237/50, ISA. Reading the Nation Associates' report "The British Record on Partition," Welles concluded that the mandatory's stand represented British policy "at its most shortsighted and at its least intelligent." Welles to Kirchwey, May 1, 1948, 66/4-Het Tsadi, ISA.

86　Minhelet Ha'Am meeting, May 12, 1948; Epstein to Shertok, May 12, 1948, 130.9/2308/6; both in ISA; Ben-Gurion, Diary, May 11, 1948, BGA; Sharef, *Three Days*, 99–107, 121–123; Ben-Gurion, *Yoman HaMilhama*, notes to 412.

87　Michael J. Cohen, *Truman and Israel* (Berkeley, 1990), 208–211; Lehman memo, May 7, 1948, Lehman MSS; *JTA*, May 9, 1948; Sulzberger memo, May 8, 1948, Box 58, Arthur Krock MSS, Princeton University Library; Lehman to Truman, May 13, 1948; Lehman to Neumann, May 14, 1948; both in Genl. Corresp. 1948, Lehman MSS; Philip C. Jessup, *The Birth of Nations* (New York, 1974), p., 273.

88　Communiqué no. 156, May 12, 1948, 41.0/124/30, ISA; Clifford, *Counsel to the President*, 9–17; *JTA*, May 13, 1948; *FRUS, 1948*, vol. 5, part 2, 972–982, including Elsey note on Clifford statement, May 12, 1948; Clifford statement, George Elsey MSS, HSTL; Lowenthal Diary, May 12 and 13, 1948; Truman to Guffey, May 12, 1948, OF204 misc., HSTL; Shertok to Silver, May 13, 1948, 93.03/88/15, ISA.

89　Clifford, *Counsel to the President*, 18; Wilkins-Jessup interview, July 21, 1988, Library of Congress, D.C.; *JTA*, May 13, 1948.

90　New York to St. Laurent, May 12, 1948, MG, J4, vol. 397, PAC; Jessup statement, May 13, 1948, DAG-13/3.1.0.1, Box 5, SD; Trafford Smith, "Last Days of the Palestine Mandate at Lake Success," May 3 and 12, 1948, Trafford Smith MSS, St. Antony's College, Oxford; Jessup, *The Birth of Nations*, 275–276; Austin to Marshall, May 13, 1948, 502.BB Palestine/5-1348, SD; May 13, 1948 report, Robinson MSS; David Ohana, *The Origins of Israeli Mythology: Neither Canaanites Nor Crusaders* (Cambridge, 2012), 104;

Morris, *1948*, 169–171; Cohen, *Truman and Israel*, 215; Arvey to Truman, May 12, 1948, OF 204D-misc., Box 776, May 1948 file, HSTL. The bodies of the Kfar Etzion victims were left unburied until, one and a half years later, the Jordanian government allowed IDF Chief Rabbi Shlomo Goren to collect the remains, which were then interred in one communal plot at the Mount Herzl military cemetery in Jerusalem.

91   Cohen, *Truman and Israel*, 216; Weizmann to Truman, May 13, 1948, WA; Gurney, Diary, May 13, 1948, Gurney MSS; Eytan-Azcárate meeting, May 12, 1948, S25/5634; Dobkin to Cunningham, May 13, 1948, S25/9392; both in CZA. For Azcárate's views three months later, see his "Notes on the Palestinian Question," Cairo, August 1948, DAG-13/3.1.0:5, UN Archives.

92   Tuck to Marshall, May 13, 1948, McClintock-2, McClintock MSS; Khalidi, "Selected Documents," 99–105; "In the Arab Camp," May 3, 1948, S25/9046, CZA; Karsh, *Palestine Betrayed*, 174–175; *Palestine Post*, May 12, 1948; Wasson to Marshall, May 13, 1948, Rusk-3, Rusk MSS; Report from Henderson, May 5, 1948, FO371/68551, PRO; "Arab Information," May 11, 1948, S25/2968; Silver et al. to Ben-Gurion, May 13, 1948, 130.9/1127/50, ISA. At the same time, French intelligence reported that Syria, Lebanon, Saudi Arabia, and Egypt had decided to let Abdullah, assisted by Iraq, enter Palestine; assassinate Abdullah; and intervene with their armies and form a "Mufti Government." Fisher to Ben-Gurion, May 8, 1948, S25/1559, CZA. Nokrashy told Bernadotte at the end of the month that his government had reluctantly decided on war "when it became apparent that no settlement could be worked out." Folke Bernadotte, *To Jerusalem* (London, 1951), 24.

93   Clifford, *Counsel to the President*, 18–20; Ginsburg-Postal interview, October 20, 1967, Bertha Schoolman MSS, Hadassah Archives; Epstein to Shertok and Epstein to Lourie, both May 14, 1948, 93/126/7, ISA; Epstein to Truman, May 14, 1948, Confidential File, State Department file, Correspondence File Palestine, Box 37, HSTL; Elath, *HaMa'avak*, 772–774.

94   Zeev Sharef, *Three Days*, J. L. Meltzer, trans. (London, 1962), 256–260, Schnurman report, May 17, 1948, S25/10526, CZA.

95   Ibid., 281–289; Ahareleh Visberg, "Hayom BaYom HaZeh MaMash," *Yisrael HaYom*, April 15, 2013;

96   May 15, 1948, Lowenthal Diary; *FRUS, 1948*, vol. 5, part 2, 1005.

97   *FRUS, 1948*, vol. 5, part 2, 990–991, 1006–1007; Dean Rusk, *As I Saw It* (New York, 1990), 150–151; Jessup, *The Birth of Nations*, 280–281; David Ginsurg interview, Oct. 20, 1967, Schoolman MSS, Hadassah Archives;

Elath, *HaMa'avak*, 773, 779. The Guatemala government quickly sent a cable to the new State of Israel approving Granados's declaration. The document bearing Truman's signed approval at 6:11 p.m. for the statement on May 14 is in the Alphabetical Correspondence file, Charles Ross MSS, HSTL.

98   Eban, *Chaim Weizmann*, 312; David B. Sachar, "David K. Niles and United States Policy," Senior Honors Thesis, Harvard University, 1959, 1; Vera Weizmann, *The Impossible Takes Longer*, 234–235; *FRUS, 1948*, vol. 5, part 2, 993, 997, 1013–1015; Rusk, *As I Saw It*, 150–151; Jessup, *The Birth of Nations*, 277–291; *Official Records of the General Assembly, 1948*, II (New York, 1948), 27–47; Roosevelt to Marshall (copy to Truman), May 16, 1948, and Truman to Roosevelt, May 20, 1948; both in PSF Personal File, E. Roosevelt, Box 272, HSTL; Truman, *Years of Trial and Hope*, 193–194.

99   Eilat, *HaMa'avak*, 781–784; *JTA*, May 16, 1948; Eban, *Chaim Weizmann*, 312–313.

100   Yoav Gelber, *Jewish-Transjordanian Relations, 1921–1948* (London, 1997), 283; Arab Section meeting, May 13, 1948, S25/5634; Berman-Kohn to Zaslani, May 12, 1948, S25/9390; both in CZA; S. Segev ed., *MeiAharei HaPargod* (Tel Aviv, 1954), 62–63; Larry Collins and Dominique Lapierre, *O Jerusalem!* (New York, 1972), 408; Karsh, *Palestine Betrayed*, 209.

101   Ben-Gurion, *Yoman HaMilhama*, 427–428.

Conclusion

Two hours after Cunningham's bulletproof, armor-plated, black Daimler limousine and motorcade wove their way through Jerusalem's quiet streets to Kalandia airport and then a flight to Haifa port for the last time, the ancient Holy City area effectively to fall under Arab control once the General Assembly had turned down proposals to guarantee Jerusalem's internationalization, an amazed Eytan reported that the British "no longer exist even as a concept, and it requires an effort of the imagination to convince oneself that there was ever such a thing as a Mandatory Government." Only the Red Cross standard atop the King David Hotel and a sign on the YMCA perimeter showed that anyone was taking its place. Bullets flew across King George V Avenue, but this made less of an impression than the emptiness of the entire area. The Truce Commission, almost completely cut off from the world, had so far achieved nothing; member J. W. MacCabe experienced great difficulty even in getting national flags to be mounted for the separate countries involved in that body's effort. The UN Palestine Commission, after holding seventy-six meetings, would adjourn *sine die* three days later.

Acknowledging publicly the original recognition of the Jewish National Home by His Majesty's Government some thirty years ago, Ben-Gurion expressed his wish for the resumption of friendly relations with the British Commonwealth, recalling the important part played by the Dominions in the GA's historic decision recognizing Palestinian Jewry as a nation. Despite the attack of the Arab states, including the Arab Legion "for whom London could not entirely disclaim responsibility," he confidently believed that "the State of Israel will establish good neighborly relations with them and become a stabilizing and progressive factor in [the] Near East as well as [a] unifying link between East and West."[1]

The Arab world, however, continued to trumpet the clarion call of war. At the same time that the regular forces of five states mounted their invasion of the country, the Arab League governments officially declared that they found themselves "compelled to intervene in Palestine solely in order to help its inhabitants restore peace and security and the rule of justice and law to their country, and in order to prevent bloodshed." "The aggressive intentions and the imperialistic designs of the Zionists," their statement of May 15 added, resulted in atrocities and the exodus of "more than a quarter of a million" of Palestine's Arab inhabitants from their homes and in their taking refuge in the neighboring Arab countries. The only solution of the Palestine problem, echoing what these governments had declared before the 1947 London Conference and the UN, remained "a unitary Palestinian State, in accordance with democratic principles." On the 18th, an Egyptian air force attack on Tel Aviv killed 42 civilians and wounded 100 in the central bus station. "Zionist immigrants won't conquer this world," Azzam Pasha confidently asserted to the *New York Times* lead foreign correspondent C.L. Sulzberger shortly thereafter, the Arabs having driven back all of Palestine's conquerors in the past, much as he had told the *New York Herald Tribune*'s Kenneth Bilby in April, that the Hagana "eventually will be worn out and will dissolve like ice." Even Abdullah now pronounced that no ground existed for the claim to independence by "the Jewish affinity [*sic*] in Palestine."[2]

Trygve Lie thought otherwise, deeming the invasion by the Arab states "the first armed aggression which the world had seen since the end of the war." Convinced that the UN could not permit such action to succeed and at the same time "survive as an influential force for peaceful settlement, collective security and meaningful international law," the Secretary-General wrote to the Foreign Secretaries of the Big Powers on May 16, one day after Shertok applied to Lie for the State of Israel's admission to the membership in the "family of nations," to "take account of the extreme seriousness of the situation… and of the necessity for prompt action at this crucial moment" in keeping with the Charter's Article 24 conferring on the Security Council primary responsibilities for the maintenance of international peace and security "in order to ensure prompt and effective action by the United Nations." Yet U.S. and Soviet efforts to have the Arab states condemned by the Council secured only five votes; Great Britain opposed any international action to halt the fighting. A cease-fire resolution one week later, along with three other appeals, met with prompt Arab rejection.

By then, Uruguay, Guatemala, Nicaragua, Czechoslovakia, Poland, and Yugoslavia had also recognized the existence of the new Jewish state. In Russia's according full *de jure* recognition on May 18, the first government to do so, Molotov wrote to Shertok of Moscow's hope that "the creation by the Jewish people of its own sovereign state will serve the cause of the strengthening of peace and security in Palestine and the Middle East and expresses its confidence in the successful development of friendly relations between the Soviet Union and the State of Israel."[3]

Defending their mandatory record to the last, a joint statement from the Colonial and Foreign Offices, neither of which had thought partition would achieve a two-thirds majority in the UN, acknowledged that HMG's failure to reconcile Jews and Arabs and to prepare them for self-government had eventually witnessed a UN policy which aroused determined Arab resistance without the pro-partition governments prepared to enforce that General Assembly recommendation. Receiving no cooperation from the Jewish community, 84,000 British troops had proven insufficient to maintain law and order "in the face of a campaign of terrorism waged by highly organized Jewish forces equipped with all the weapons of the modern infantryman." Since V-E Day, 338 British subjects had been killed in Palestine, while the military forces there had cost the British taxpayer £100 million. The renewal of Arab violence following the announcement of November 29, 1947, and the "declared intentions of Jewish extremists" showed that the loss of further British lives was inescapable.

In light of HMG's decision not to enforce partition against the declared wishes of the majority of Palestine's inhabitants, the statement went on, London decided to relinquish the Mandate and prepare for the earliest possible withdrawal from that country of all British forces. Required at the same time to hold apart two peoples "bent on open war" and to guard the country's frontiers against the weapons and supporters which both Arabs and Jews attempted to introduce, as well as to negotiate with the UN the transfer of British authority and functions, it was inevitable that "not all of these tasks were fully accomplished." (Whitehall's erroneous assumption, similar to the State Department's position, that the Soviet bloc would support the Arabs, went unmentioned.)

The government of Palestine still made attempts at mediation and arranging a truce, particularly in Jerusalem, in which it achieved "some measure of success." Although British responsibility for Palestine had now ceased, HMG earnestly hoped that some compromise might yet be possible which would prevent the destruction of all that had been achieved over the years and which would enable the country's people to live at peace and to govern themselves. Toward this end, the Colonial and Foreign Offices concluded, the British government was "still prepared to give every assistance in their power, short of imposing by force a solution not acceptable to both peoples."[4]

Attlee's farewell message of gratitude to the Palestine administration at the termination of the Mandate, echoing his defense of government policy in a "strictly confidential" communication to Brodetsky as president of the Board of Deputies of British Jews in March 1948, sounded a similar note. Writing to Cunningham on May 11, the Prime Minister conceded that the "high hopes" with which HMG took up the Mandate "have not been fulfilled." He bade farewell to the peoples of Palestine under conditions "tragically different from those to which it has been our purpose to lead them." The conclusion read thus:

> But even in this time of our greatest disappointment, when so much of constructive work done over so many years for the benefit of all communities is threatened with destruction, the officers of the Palestine service do not have cause for any sense of personal failure. History will honor their achievements. Faced by the most intractable problem, rewarded by baseless calumnies, imputations of partiality and often personal danger, they have established traditional, legal public service which should be of lasting value to successive authorities.

An editorial in the *Palestine Post* rejoined that his statement reflected "the very self-righteousness which has caused Britain's departure to take place in an atmosphere of resentment and ill-will instead of the enthusiasm that greeted Britain's advent." [5]

Bent on a peaceful withdrawal, GOC MacMillan issued Proclamation No. 1 of 1948 on May 15 (actually printed on April 20), announcing that the "occupied area" would be under his military jurisdiction until August 1.

All persons in the said territory had to abstain from any actions of a nature "calculated to prejudice" the interests or safety of His Britannic Majesty's forces "or to disturb the public peace" necessary for the safety and exit of those forces. All requisitions of services or property which might be "necessitated by the military exigencies" would be the subject of full compensation. He had already told the Truce Commission that "the Arabs are in bad shape and need breathing space," and felt that Abdullah would be "jolly careful" not to risk his army in battle with Jews. Meeting with Mayor Levi and others in Haifa two days later, the Lieutenant-General presented liaison officers of his own staff so that the "normal life of an important town" could continue alongside the security of his troops and "their quick and orderly evacuation" from that enclave.

Matters would in fact move forward so smoothly that on June 30, a full month before the scheduled date, the Union Jack was lowered at 12:43 p.m. at the port offices in Haifa harbor as a Royal Marines bugler sounded the General Salute and the last British troops embarked. MacMillan and staff were present at the ceremony and left a few minutes later. Since December 1947, some 115,000 tons of military stores and equipment had been shipped from Haifa, with 137,000 tons sent overland, and now British authority in Palestine had ended. Members of the Hagana immediately occupied the port installations, one Jewish official noting that "the British went out of their way to hand over in good order." When the evacuation had been completed, Ben-Gurion formally hoisted the flag of the State of Israel aloft. [6]

Far removed from this battlefield, Jews the world over celebrated their people's sovereign rebirth. Thousands attended meetings in Britain, France, Germany, Austria, Italy, Poland, Rumania, Czechoslovakia, Hungary, South Africa, and Argentina. An AZEC mass gathering in New York City's Madison Square Garden received a message from the nearly blind Weizmann, just chosen President of the State of Israel, noting the closing of "a two thousand year chapter of injustice, homelessness, and frustration in our history," and remembering "the six million martyrs of the last and bitterest trial of our exile as we enter the new era in a spirit of rededication to the fundamental truths of our prophets and sages." The blue-and-white Zionist banner, fashioned from a frock belonging to the wife of 2nd Baron Melchett, Henry Mond, was displayed in Weizmann's honor outside of the Waldorf-Astoria Hotel for the first time. Neumann hailed Truman's immediate *de facto* recognition of the Provisional Government of Israel, which he said came as a reward for the courage and faith of the Jewish people, who dared to reclaim their national heritage in the face of Arab aggression from all sides, while Morgenthau declared that the new commonwealth gave all Jews, particularly those in desperate straits, a constructive program on the "road to self-sustenance and self-realization."

In Germany's DP camps, hysterical Holocaust survivors shouted "*Genug DPs shoin, tsait mir birger fun Yisroel!*" (Enough already DPs, time we are citizens of Israel!). On behalf of the 24,000 *ma'apilim* in Cyprus, JDC representative Morris Laub and Jewish Agency officials agreed after discussions with British officials that the twelve detention camps would be emptied by August 1, the *Pan* York and *Pan Crescent* to take them home to Israel. By June 1, however, none had left, the British refusing to let men of military age leave the island for Haifa port.[7]

Bevin's inner convictions at that moment surfaced in an interview with Sulzberger on May 24. He remained certain that the Palestine conundrum was "solvable": a loose central authority such as the one proposed in the Morrison-Grady plan of provisional autonomy, leading Jew and Arab to live together through economic necessity and development, would eventually bring all "into a harmonious whole." He had intended the scheme to be tried for five years, but Truman's sudden declaration on the eve of Yom Kippur 1946, intended to forestall Dewey's pro-Zionist statement and issued against Byrnes's advice, put an end to that promising prospect. The vote for partition, won by threats to China, for example, about losing a needed loan from Washington, was "thoroughly wrong"; the sudden U.S. switch to trusteeship in March 1948 had been done without consulting London. The Arabs had agreed to a truce, the Foreign Secretary went on to claim, and he had "cleared the way" for a settlement along partition lines by sending in combat troops to stop the Jews in Jaffa, drive them out of Acre, and restore order in Jerusalem. "The stage was all set" when Truman abruptly recognized the State of Israel, "and it was all off, the Arabs blew up."

Expecting the Arab states to occupy the Arab-partitioned part of Palestine, Bevin did not consider that they were invading foreign territory when their troops entered the country. These armies had to do so, or the Jews "would have killed Palestinian Arabs." The Arab Legion "did not fire a shot" until it got to Jerusalem, where the Jews had violated the truce. Israel, he insisted, "is not a state, not a 'third party', and has no legal existence." Moreover, the 70 million Moslems in Pakistan "must not be antagonized." He wanted a cease-fire now, after which Jews and Arabs would be "unscrambled," each going back into regions due to them under partition. The Zionists "want to rule and crush the Arabs," he believed, whereas Jews and Arabs "can live together." He saw the Zionists as Fascists or Communists, while the two peoples would be "like Czechoslovakia." Five divisions would be needed to impose partition on both sides, and if there were going to be a world war, it would be because of the White House, never because of the State Department. He had never spoken so openly about this to anyone, Bevin ended, but did so because he had been impressed by Sulzberger's "good faith and trusted him."[8]

Other prominent Britishers were less certain of the outcome. "The many frustrations one met in Palestine," Cunningham wrote not long thereafter of that "burden" to a despairing Creech Jones, were "much mitigated by the confidence you were to repose in our work, and that made possible the only claim I feel we can make that we maintained British prestige to the end." Yet Canada's Department of External Affairs, in reviewing the UK Fortnightly Summary on May 14, 1948, reported the general feeling that the Mandate "is ending on a note of exasperation, disappointment, and failure." Former diplomat and MP Harold Nicholson jotted this in his diary the day after May 14: "All the pleasure I might have felt at this realization of the hopes of Zionism is clouded by the fear of war and the humiliation we have suffered." Shocked at the mandatory's "scuttle," going "one better" than Louis XIV's "*après moi le deluge*" by "leaving a time bomb" upon its departure to "blow up the dam" that Britain built up, Jerusalem mayor R.M. Graves recorded in his diary "I can't comment without profanity."[9]

Outraged by the position in which HMG had found itself, with British officers directing the gunfire upon Jerusalem and British armies being used by the Arab Legion, Churchill also minced no words during a meeting with the *New York Times*'s Anne O'Hare McCormick in criticizing the actions of Jewish terrorists in Palestine and the manner in which they outraged British feeling, which had induced "almost a spirit of hatred." At the same time, he felt that Britain was in an "unwarranted and unneutral [*sic*] position," and he felt ashamed when recalling that HMG had invited the Jews to Palestine ever since the Balfour Declaration had been enunciated. What was happening now, he repeated over and over, was not the British people or the acts of bad men. The present government was "merely uninformed and not skillful." Duff Cooper, who had advised against Bevin's sending the *Exodus 1947* back to Germany in order "to teach the Jews a lesson," considered this "fearful muddle" one of "the worst chapters in British history." Had we come down firmly on the side of the Jews we could have made a national home for them. The Arabs would have accepted the situation, his diary for May 22 read, but the Foreign Office "is always frightened of the Arabs and our Middle East experts love them."[10]

At this juncture, Truman still considered the Anglo-American Committee of Inquiry report the "correct solution" to the problem, confessing this to Crum one day after Ben-Gurion announced Israel's independence, and thinking that "eventually we are going to get it worked out just that way." ("Texas Joe" Hutcheson, who thought Bevin acted "like a bull in a china shop" and wondered whether "England is going to hell in a handbag," also believed that that report was "both statesmanlike and just.") He knew the document almost by heart and had reviewed it from time to time, the President told Magnes, then pressing the American Jewish Committee to support the U.S. effort in creating a Temporary Central Administration in Palestine and an Economic Union including the Jewish Agency's Jordan Valley Authority proposal, on May 6: "It was a thousand pities that that report had not been carried out. We might have been spared much of this present misery."

Very bitter that the Jews had refused his offer that the rival leaders fly aboard the "Sacred Cow" to the much contested area so that the Jews and Arabs could continue their discussions of the Palestine dilemma, Truman revealed a personal dream that Jews, Moslems, and Christians, whose lives were based more or less upon the same moral code, might get to understand one another better. This, he added, might also help to "lift the world from the materialism which was holding the world down to the ground and might destroy it." Russia would then not have "a spiritual leg to stand on." Jews and Arabs were "spoiling things," however, not giving these three major religious communities a chance to have confidence in one another. "That is one of the reasons why I deplore so deeply this conflict in the Holy Land," he confided. Taking leave of the Hebrew University president, Truman said rather emphatically: "Dr. Magnes, we won't give up! We shall hang on to this until we find a way. That is our duty."[11]

Responding to Weizmann's letter of May 13 two days later, Truman sincerely hoped "that the Palestine situation will eventually work out on an equitable and peaceful basis." Yet to Rabbi Thurman of St. Louis he soon wrote that "it looks as if the Palestine (*sic!*) situation is very dark this morning, although we recognized the Jewish free state as soon as they organized a Government and asked us for recognition." At the same time, notwithstanding Ambassador Douglas's view from London that the sudden *de facto* recognition of the Jewish state without previously telling the Attlee government constituted the "worst shock so far to general Anglo-American concert of policy," Truman did not even react to this acute warning. In reply to Alfange on the 18th, he wrote that the Jews, in common with the Irish and the Latin Americans, were "very emotional," but the President of the U.S. had to be very careful not to be emotional or to forget that he is working for 145 million people primarily "and for peace in the world as his next objective."[12]

The Security Council would finally adopt a cease-fire resolution on May 29, to last four weeks, but the fighting raged on across Palestine. Welles publicly blasted the Administration for continuing to delay full *de jure* recognition of the new Jewish commonwealth, and for announcing McDonald in June as the country's first Mission Representative to Israel only after the Soviet Union had declared its own appointee, Pavel Yershov, as Minister to its Legation. The State Department had, in fact, proposed a pro-Arab nominee; Truman, pressed by Niles and with support from Hilldring and Clifford but without consulting a consequently resentful Marshall, preferred "his own man" in Tel Aviv.

The arms embargo, which hurt the *yishuv* militarily more than the Arabs, continued. Sharply taking issue with a Council resolution of July 15 to invoke Article 39 of the UN Charter against any military force breaking a cease-fire order, the U.S. Joint Chiefs of Staff objected (as they had ever since June 1946) to any Soviet or Soviet-satellite armed force entering Palestine or for U.S. forces to be committed there. State's Middle East specialists, while accepting Epstein as the Special Representative (soon Ambassador) in Washington of the Provisional Government of Israel, backed Bernadotte's final plan to have Israel ceding most of the Negev to Abdullah in exchange for obtaining a part or the whole of western Galilee. (The UN mediator, empowered to promote "a peaceful adjustment" of the situation, was killed by a team of the Stern Group on September 17, just after completing his report.)

This plan fully satisfied Bevin, who persisted in seeking an "entente cordiale" with Washington, a position which Douglas "slavishly" advocated to the receptive Marshall.[13]

Britain's stubborn refusal to recognize the State of Israel, even after the Chiefs of Staff had by the autumn of 1947 chosen Cyrenaica on Libya's eastern coast as their main base of Middle Eastern operations once the talks with Cairo over revision of the Anglo-Egyptian Treaty had broken down, infuriated some prominent voices on the Albion Isle. Crossman, reminding Attlee of his proposal in the winter of 1946 that the only solution for Palestine was a test of strength between Abdullah and the Jews (the Prime Minister had then dismissed this as "Machievellian"), observed in early September that the only two Middle East armies which had stood the test of war were the Jews and the Arab Legion. One by-product of non-recognition, he added, was to provide a "last ray of hope" to the extremists and weaken the hands of the realists. Writing to Frankfurter two months later, Laski felt a "mixture of anger and humiliation" at Bevin's policy, after whom Attlee was the worst and then Commonwealth Secretary Noel-Baker. The Foreign Secretary's "fantastic vanity," responsible for London's "unbreakable hostility," could be checked, he suggested, if Truman wrote privately to Attlee that this hampered good Anglo-American relations.

On December 10, Churchill lashed out in Commons against HMG's "surly boycott," especially given Israel's driving the Arabs out of a larger area than was contemplated in the partition scheme and nineteen countries having recognized either *de facto* or *de jure* the new, effective Jewish government. In addition, "a sorry reward for all our efforts" would ensue if HMG's stance, also requiring by treaty to support Jordan if that country were attacked, created a "deep divergence on a critical issue" between London and Washington. For every reason, it was in Britain's interest to be represented at Tel Aviv as it was at Amman. "It is lamentable," the leader of the parliamentary opposition concluded, that this should have been so long delayed."[14]

Intensive Zionist lobbying as the 1948 presidential election drew near engineered once again a reversal of Washington policy. Truman had given a general endorsement to Marshall's statement at the Paris meeting of the General Assembly on September 21 in favor of the Bernadotte plan. Democratic politicians and intervention by Epstein, Niles, Clifford, Klein, Blaustein, Jacobson, and Silver's AZEC unrelenting drive, joined to Dewey's open challenge that Truman had not kept faith with the Democratic platform favoring the partition boundaries and *de jure* recognition, eventually swung the tide. In his last speech of the campaign on October 28, with two paragraphs added by Stone and vetted by Rosenman, Truman reaffirmed in the critically important city of New York his support of the party platform, and lauded the people of Israel for creating out of a barren desert "a modern and efficient state with the highest standards of western civilization," thereby demonstrating that their state "deserves to take its place in the family of nations." Prodded by Governor Lehman and Mayor O'Dwyer, he instructed Clifford and Ewing to draft instructions to Marshall not to issue any statement supporting sanctions against Israel, much to Eleanor Roosevelt's approval, forcing the British and the Chinese to withdraw their backing as well. Truman's political upset, a triumph defying most pollsters and the *Chicago Daily Tribune*'s front-page headline in bold letters "Dewey Defeats Truman" on the morning of the early election results, owed much to Feinberg's financial contributions to the President's triumphant "whistle-stop tour." He actually lost New York—the first President since Woodrow Wilson in 1916 to be elected without taking the Empire State, but the Midwest and West bore him to victory.[15]

Israeli successes against the Arab states' invasion, ultimately securing about 6,500 square kilometers beyond the original partition borders and running counter to earlier dire predictions by Montgomery, the CIA, and other leading military and diplomatic experts in London and Washington, proved decisive in the coming months. Truman's warning on December 30 that his government might have to reconsider its sponsorship of Israel's application for admission to the UN if General Allon's forces did not withdraw from their crossing into Sinai, intended by the President to prevent a British military intervention against Israel, achieved the desired effect. On January 7, 1949, the Israelis, suspecting hostile intentions, shot down five British Spitfires, then engaged in reconnaissance flights over Egyptian territory while the Israeli forces were still in Rafa. Bevin, "mindful of American opposition and the reticence of British public opinion," chose not to endorse a military option, the possibility in any case rendered academic by an unconditional ceasefire that Bunche, appointed by Lie to succeed Bernadotte, brought about between Israel and Egypt on January 7.

"Still incapable of coming to terms overnight" with the new Jewish commonwealth, the British failed in a last-ditch effort to persuade Washington that the Negev should be under their control. As late as January 28, Bevin and Attlee defended their policy in a lengthy debate before the House of Commons. Following Israel's first elections for the Constituent Assembly (soon to be called the *Knesset*) on January 25, Truman acceded to Bevin's request that both governments recognize Israel and Jordan, extending *de jure* six days later with Jacobson, Goldman, and Bisgyer present at the ceremony. Confirmed at Truman's request by the Senate on March 18, McDonald was appointed Ambassador Extraordinary and Plenipotentiary, thereby becoming the first Ambassador accredited to the new state.[16]

The British refused to concede defeat. Well after refusing to open the Tel-Aviv port on February 1, 1948, for the open admission of survivors, to permit the early arrival of the UN Palestine Commission, to protect Jewish convoys for besieged Jerusalem, or to curb the incursion of Arab guerilla bands, their Consul in Haifa had persisted in addressing his communications for the Provisional Government of Israel to the "Jewish authorities in Tel Aviv"—to have them regularly returned unopened. The ever frigid Cadogan even took to addressing Israel's representatives at the UN as "the Jewish authorities in Palestine." When Eban saw him reading the Bible on a sea voyage, he commented thus to the UK delegate: "I presume you are reading about the God of Abraham, Isaac, and the Jewish authorities." He received an icy stare in return.[17]

One week before Cunningham's final departure, the BBC cabled its correspondent to send more dispatches about the collapse of government services, "as we want to impress on the British public the fact that complete disintegration is taking place in Palestine." The film of Ben-Gurion reading the Declaration of Independence, which Yigal Lossin found at Pathé News when preparing the "Pillar of Fire" 1981 series for Israeli television, was not deemed newsworthy enough to show the British cinema audiences of 1948. At his first meeting with Bevin, Ambassador McDonald found his host "quite unreconstructed." Banging his fist on a table, the Foreign Secretary unleashed a diatribe against the Jews being "ungrateful" for what HMG had done for them in Palestine, snapped at Truman's stance regarding the Anglo-American Committee report, and charged the Jews with alienating British opinion by their attitude toward Arab refugees. At the UN, Cadogan opposed or delayed ceasefire resolutions when the Arabs appeared to be winning in the early stages of the conflict, but later stood for firm action when the Jews assumed control.

London would hold back *de facto* recognition of Israel until May 13, 1949, four months after the last of the Cyprus detainees reached Israel, having abstained on March 4 when the Security Council voted 9 to 1 (Egypt) in favor of Israel's membership in the UN. By a vote of 37 to 12 on May 11, with the United Kingdom and 8 other nations abstaining, GA President Evatt, who had so skillfully seen to Subcommittee One's unanimous pro-partition report and to the critical vote taken within three days after it had been submitted, announced that the body had approved Resolution 273 on Israel's application for membership. Responded now Foreign Minister Moshe Sharett on behalf of the new commonwealth: "The responsibility entailed was awesome; the vision for the future was uplifting." The following day, the individual who had masterfully commanded the Zionist ranks at the UN and received Marshall's rare tribute raised the Israeli flag alongside those of fifty-eight other member nations outside the UN headquarters, Permanent Delegate Eban at his side. Finally, confronted with the reality of a vibrant State of Israel, His Majesty's Government granted it *de jure* recognition on April 28, 1950.[18]

How had all this come to pass? At the end of World War II, Eban later reminisced, the Jews of the world were "wallowing in the fearful anguish of the Holocaust," its visual effects having an effect that went far beyond the mere statistical enumeration of the victims. Their promised National Home, recognized in the Balfour Declaration and in the Palestine Mandate for its historic connection to the Jewish people, was being assailed by regional violence and by "international alienation." The three major victorious powers—the U.S., Britain, and the Soviet Union—showed no intention at first of recognizing the Palestinian *yishuv* as a political reality. Attlee, Bevin, Truman, Marshall, and many others of high rank viewed the Jewish people as only a religious entity, much as had Washington and London during the years of the *Shoa*. (Asserting that Bevin's stand in this regard flew in the face of all historical facts and "inspired prophetic utterances," Chief Rabbi Herzog cabled the London *Times* that "national freedom will lead to revival Jewish spirituality.") "There wasn't a single ray of light on the horizon," Eban went on to recall. The Jewish spokesmen at the UN Conference at San Francisco were humiliatingly seated in some distant balcony, looking down at the fifty member nations, none of which had made anything like the sacrifices demanded of this one people by its own annihilation across a European landscape of contiguous evil. Yet, looking ahead to three years later, the first Representative to the UN of the State of Israel could not point to "a transformation of fortune as abrupt and as speedy and as providential" in the history of any other nation.[19]

First and foremost, Palestine's 600,000 Jews played the vital role in this denouement. Viewing Zionism as the legitimate movement of national return by an indigenous people intimately connected to that land for over three millennia and revolting against the litany of victimization which had plagued Jewish history for centuries past, they had transformed the country from a primitive and corrupt Ottoman backwater into what they rightly called *HaMedina BaDerekh* (the state-in-the-making). Its firm infrastructure already established in the 1930's, the *yishuv* continued to flourish economically during World War II, with impetus particularly given to industrial progress. Its on-going achievement thereafter under the aegis of the Jewish Agency deeply impressed both the Anglo-American Committee of Inquiry on Palestine and the UNSCOP delegates, and ultimately the required majority which endorsed a Jewish commonwealth during the General Assembly of November 1947. Ben-Gurion, unwavering in his will to make the state a reality, carried the budding nation on the shoulders of his imagination and the wings of his vision.

At least as significant, a native-born generation of Palestinian Jews, Anita Shapira has shown, absorbed an "offensive ethos" which prepared this youth to use force for realizing the idea of sovereignty on the land of their ancestors. Alterman's *"Zemer HaPlugot"* (Song of the Squads), a poem written only three years after his *"Shir Boker"* (Morning Song) in 1934, reflected the sense that peace would be brought by the rifle, not by the blade of the plow. Haim Gouri, the dean of Palmah-era Hebrew verse and a friend of the ill-fated Danny Maas, epitomized their heavy, ultimate sacrifice in *"Hinei Mutalot Gufeinu"* (Here Lie Our Fallen), *"HaRe'ut"* (The Friendship), and *"Bab-el-Wad"* (the steep gorge in the valley, today's Sha'ar HaGai, where Arabs ambushed convoys bringing essential supplies to the besieged Jewish residents of Jerusalem). The feeling of *ein breira* (we have no alternative), epitomized as the ethos of Yitzhak Lamdan's 1927 poem *"Masada"* and Shertok's final words to the Mapai Central Committee on May 11, 1948, captured the hearts of this collective entity, its back to the wall in a war for national survival. Their shared sentiment also fueled the Ayalon Institute, a Hagana clandestine bullet factory on Kibbutzim Hill north of Rehovot, which from 1945–1948 produced over 2,500,000 bullets, and a scientific corps (HEMED) created by Ben-Gurion in early 1948 which produced explosives for mines and grenades, as well as anti-tank weapons, under the direction of Efraim Katchalsky (later Katzir), later fourth President of the State of Israel.[20]

Shertok, facing Marshall just before flying home for the crucial vote of the *Minhelet Ha'Am* on declaring independence, spoke for the belief of the *yishuv* and of the Jewish people in general that it was "either now or never," and that their determination to achieve statehood was "unshakeable." Converted by the Holocaust, world Jewry embraced the Zionist thesis that their anomalous position as a homeless people had made the Jews expendable in the years of the *Shoa*, and that they, like all other peoples, had the right to national self-determination. This sense galvanized the unprecedented march in July 1946 of 8,000 British Jews to Trafalgar Square in protest against their government's sanctioning the broad "Black Sabbath" operation.

Jews had a common purpose and a single hope, Eban with reason told Bunche during the UNSCOP visit to Palestine. The urge to bring remnants of the *Shoa* to reach Palestine linked the JDC and the American Jewish Committee's Proskauer, who saw no "political schizophrenia" in supporting a Jewish state, with the *briha* emissaries and young Palestinians of the Jewish Brigade whose trucks were camouflaged by Moving Orders boasting the name of RASC TTG Company as the issuing authority, outsiders having no idea that the latter three letters, ostensibly British, were a secret code for a wily Arabic-Yiddish hybrid, *Tilhas Tizi Gesheften*, which literally meant "kiss-my-ass business." In agreement were binationalist advocates like HaShomer HaTsa'ir ideologues and Magnes, who wrote to colleague Buber that the unbearable sufferings which the Jewish people have had to endure "have deprived us of the capacity to be patient" and made them fall "prey to the Fata Morgana of the state." Neither would compromise on unrestricted Jewish immigration.

Al Robison and colleagues of the Sonneborn Institute and Materials for Palestine, the latter incorporated by former OSS agent Nahum Bernstein under New York State regulations, contravened U.S. law in raising weapons for Palestine's Jews. Others worked ceaselessly like Joe Boxenbaum in making large boats available for *aliya bet* and Al Schwimmer in smuggling dozens of wartime surplus planes and recruiting their crews to reach the Hagana. Sam Zemurray used his United Fruit Company contacts to gain crucial Central American countries' support for the GA vote in November 1947. Judge Jerome Frank of the U.S. Court of Appeals for the Second Circuit, an advocate of U.S. isolationism until the Japanese surprise attack on Pearl Harbor and an early supporter of the American Council for Judaism, joined Rifkind, Murray Gurfein, and five other distinguished jurists prior to that vote in authoring *The Basic Equities of the Palestine Problem*'s effective defense of the Zionist interpretation of the Balfour Declaration. Myerson's mission in early 1948 to raise millions of dollars from America's Jews for the *yishuv*'s armed struggle, gaining vital help from Morgenthau and Montor, quickly achieved its unprecedented objective in their desire to become partners in a people's sovereign reawakening. So, too, the 4,922 women and men volunteers of *Mahal* from 59 countries, 123 of whom (among them 4 women and 4 non-Jewish fliers) would be killed in battle or missing-in-action and hundreds more wounded.[21]

A wave of support from non-Jews for realizing the Zionist dream mounted in these same years. Brando's taking part in "A Flag is Born" was one with Frank Sinatra's passing money on one occasion from Kollek, then under FBI surveillance, to an Irish sea captain setting sail with munitions for the embattled *yishuv*. Meyer Lansky, known as "the Mob's Accountant," got the approval of "Murder Inc." head Albert "The Mad Hatter" Anastasia to have Hagana weapon shipments leave the Mafia-controlled New York waterfront and to sabotage similar Arab transfers. More than 100 leading American Christians of all denominations sent "A Message to Israel" on May 27, 1948, declaring that "biblical prophecy has indeed been fulfilled in our time." Feeling privileged to watch the rebirth of a nation "which has been moribund for 2,000 years," Buxton thanked Byrnes thus for tapping him to take part in the Anglo-American Committee: here is "something portentous and exhilarating—'manifest destiny,' 'the inevitability of history,' a conflict between the traditional East and the progressive West, a token of the possibilities of the United Nations." In like vein, Eleanor Roosevelt wrote on the day that the Israeli flag was added to the other standards outside of the UN area at Lake Success that "there was a lump in almost everybody's throat, I think, at the thought of a new nation being born and one whose people had suffered greatly." Churchill captured the mood best, declaring thus to Creech Jones in the lengthy Commons debate on January 26, 1949:[22]

> Whether the right hon. Gentleman likes it or not, and whether we like it or not, the coming into being of a Jewish State in Palestine is an event in world history to be viewed in the perspective, not of a generation or a century, but in the perspective of a thousand, two thousand or even three thousand years. That is a standard of temporal values or time values which seems very much out of accord with the perpetual click-clack of our rapidly-changing moods and of the age in which we live. This is an event in world history.

The survivors of the Holocaust, their individual universes ripped asunder and their pasts forever obliterated, contributed in great measure to the unfolding drama. Having chosen to end the long night of Jewish exile, the clear majority of this remnant resolved to make for Eretz Israel. More than 70,000 crossed national borders to crowd into boats for that arduous, oftentimes perilous, journey against the mighty British Royal Navy, their officially masked identity as "Displaced Persons" revealed in a novel sense: human beings now "Destined for Palestine." Representatives of the Anglo-American Committee, UNSCOP, Intergovernmental Committee on Refugees, Red Cross, and UNRRA came to acknowledge both their unwavering resolve and gritty European realities, as did Harrison, Eisenhower, and some military commanders in the DP camps. Asked by the Anglo-American Committee team what would be their second choice after Palestine for future entry, more than half of the 10,000 yet housed in the former Bergen-Belsen camp wrote "Crematorium." Hilldring's deep interest in the survivors' welfare, enabling the persistent efforts of Fierst, Wahl, and a few others, proved instrumental in keeping critical U.S. zones open in Germany, Austria, and Italy, and in his subsequent activity at the United Nations.

Their pressing ordeal explains why the armed showdown between the *yishuv* and the mandatory authorities became inevitable from 1946 onwards. The Attlee cabinet's decision in the autumn of 1945 to restrict the survivors' entry into Palestine to a mere 1,500 per month—the Prime Minister would insist on maintaining this quota even after submitting the Palestine conundrum to the UN—galvanized the three *yishuv* undergrounds to unite for several months in *Tenuat HaMeri* against what was now viewed as the occupying power. This continuation of the White Paper, Shertok and colleagues regularly observed at the time, had made "futile" any attempts by the Jewish Agency to curb terrorism. The survivors' on-going grim plight, dramatized by the Kielce pogrom (sparking a spontaneous mass exodus to Western Europe which Attlee and Whitehall still thought was organized to encourage illegal immigration to Palestine), also helped persuade the beleaguered Jewish Agency executive in Paris that August to retreat significantly from the 1942 Biltmore Program and champion "a viable Jewish State in an adequate area of Palestine."

Convinced that British edict had prevented "tens of thousands" of Jews from escaping the Holocaust, the survivors' three central committees in the occupied zones of Germany urged UNSCOP in July 1947 that, for their and their children's safety and peace, the establishment of a Jewish state in Palestine "is an absolute necessity." The saga that same month of the *Exodus 1947*, whose protracted resistance by the passengers was greeted by the *yishuv* with "surprised admiration" and which convinced Ben-Gurion after Bevin's decision to forcibly send them back to Germany that "we could hope for nothing more" from HMG, became symbolic of British insensitivity and of the whole Jewish race in dispersion. It dramatically, quintessentially seized the eye and wrenched the mind to sway world opinion in favor of Jewish statehood.[23]

Speeches at the UN increasingly joined the pressing humanitarian need of the *Sh'eirit HaPleita* to the political aspect of "the Jewish problem," Whitehall and Foggy Bottom dissent, as well as Arab protest, to the contrary notwithstanding. Aside from Gromyko's remarkable May 14, 1947, address and his later again acknowledging on November 26 the Jews "deep historical ties" with Palestine, Union of South Africa Prime Minster Jan Smuts, who had played a vital backroom role in the drafting of the Balfour Declaration, made this very claim to his delegation one month earlier. Fabregat, who would at Eban's request launch the filibuster that gave the Jewish Agency three additional days to gain the votes for the requisite two-thirds majority at the General Assembly, pressed the *Ad Hoc* Committee on Palestine a half-year later for the immediate entry into Palestine of 30,000 Jewish children, including some 4,000 orphans, in light of the 1.5 million others who were murdered in Hitler's "Final Solution of the Jewish Question." Josef Winiewicz, noting the massacre of six million Jews—one-third of world Jewry at the time, declared the same day on behalf of his country that "from their fellowship of suffering was born a moral solidarity to which Poland will adhere." Lie later recalled his being deeply moved by the pogroms suffered by the Jews, the Dreyfus Affair, and the fact that every one of his Jewish friends had been killed in the gas chambers.[24]

The rare consensus between the United States and Soviet delegations at the UN during the Cold War on this linkage made the partition vote of November 1947 possible. Undoubtedly setting its sights on filling the Palestine vacuum upon HMG's departure as a means to reach the Mediterranean and the Persian Gulf, Moscow accelerated Jewish emigration from the satellite countries of Eastern Europe and channeled crucial weaponry to the *yishuv* via Czechoslovakia. The highly unlikely American-Russian accord received fundamental support from the fact that of the 33 countries who would vote in favor of creating a Jewish state, a full 13 were Latin American or Caribbean. With the exception of Cuba and Greece, all opponents were either Muslim or Asiatic countries.

In a larger sense, concluded the *New York Times*'s UN bureau chief Thomas Hamilton, the partition decision "may be ascribed to the general feeling at Lake Success that something had to be done for the oppressed Jews of Europe." Palestine seemed the only area in the world which could and would take any considerable number of Holocaust survivors. Years later, Sharett put it this way: "Morally, our claim to independence need by no means have been buttressed by the graves of the millions, yet factually the nexus between doom and deliverance was patent. Without the torment caused to the conscience of the world by the catastrophe, it is extremely doubtful whether the General Assembly of the UN would have passed its epoch-making Resolution."[25] In the end, two historic trends had converged to bring about the ultimate vote: achievement in Zion and the Holocaust in Europe. The Jews now had to seize the option offered, join as one in battle whose end could hardly be foreseen.

The outcome for Palestine's Arabs differed radically. Bereft of leadership and of unity, this community held onto loyalties which centered on local bonds and were hampered by factional feuds. Native guerilla groups rarely cooperated with one another, while their manner of method often alienated the peasantry. The Husseini clan saw to the killing of major opponents, just as Haj Amin had during the Arab Revolt that was an unmitigated defeat one decade earlier, while his alliance and that of other leaders in the Arab camp with Hitler during the Second World War delegitimized the former Mufti in the eyes of many governments during this vital period. The intransigence of the Arab Higher Committee (AHC) to boycott UNSCOP, thereby abdicating the field in Palestine to the Jews, constituted a major error. In addition, the Arabs' agricultural base could not compete with a semi-industrial *yishuv*; their local committees were no match for the Jewish Agency's varied institutions and its organizational ability to raise funds; and they lacked a centralized, sophisticated armed force such as the Hagana. The Palmah's striking success during the Night of the Bridges in June 1946 at crippling the country's connection to neighboring countries, to be succeeded by the *yishuv's* ability a few months later to set up eleven Negev settlements simultaneously overnight, the latter the brainchild of Hagana Finance Department head Levi Shkolnik (later Eshkol), had no possible parallel in this world.[26]

Many Arabs fled Palestine during the stage of civil war from November 29, 1947, to May 14, 1948, for various reasons. Theirs was not a premeditated and organized exodus. Those leaving included much of the middle and upper class families seeking a safe haven early on; *fellahin* fearing Jewish reprisals for Arab ambushes; city dwellers who were deserted on occasion by Arab Liberation Army commanders; panicked masses in Jaffa, Safed, and elsewhere, especially after the Deir Yassin carnage (whose atrociousness both Irgun and Arab broadcasts exaggerated) and the fall of Tiberias followed by that of Haifa and Jerusalem's Katamon area; and those told to do so on occasion by the Husseinis or the invading Arab forces with the promise that they would soon return. In more than one instance, invading Arab guerilla bands took weapons away from the local Arabs.

Palestinian doctor Ghada Karmi later observed that each locality and village had its own militia, ignored AHC orders, and behaved autonomously. The diary of Anwar Bey Nusseibeh, AHC secretary in charge of the Jerusalem area's defense, is replete with sharp criticism of the Arab Liberation Army leadership, and he concluded that "in my overweening conceit.... I underestimated the strength of my enemy and overestimated the strength of my own people." Most of the peasantry chose to stay out of the fighting, Efraim Karsh has shown; peace agreements with the Hagana became increasingly commonplace. ALA commander-in-chief Safwat noted with astonishment on March 23, 1948, that the Jews "have not attacked a single Arab village unless provoked by it." At various times before that summer, Ben-Gurion, Shertok, and the JNF's Yosef Weitz all expressed surprise or astonishment at the instantaneous, swift mass flight, especially from the main Arab centers of Haifa and Jaffa. Most of the Druze villages in the Galilee threw in their lot with the Jews. Some forced expulsions of Arabs would take place after May 14, notably in Lydda (now Lod) and Ramleh, but a general order to that effect was never issued by the Israeli cabinet or the army.[27]

Paradoxically, the Arab states further weakened the cause of Palestinian nationalism. Traditional rivalries forestalled unity, with Egypt and Saudi Arabia opposing Iraq and Jordan in mutual distrust, and each focusing on internal matters. Ibn Saud refused to halt oil supplies to the United States; Egypt focused on obtaining Sudan in negotiations with the British; Abdullah sought a Greater Syria which Glubb favored but Damascus sharply opposed. Moreover, the Arab League downplayed Haj Amin's standing, refusing his calls in October 1947 and February 1948 for a Palestinian government under his direction, and made the major decisions in Cairo (not Jerusalem) as to resisting the Zionist enemy. Thus the charge of Abd al-Qadir al-Husseini, shortly before returning from Damascus—without getting his requested artillery—to the al-Qastal battle and his death there in April 1948, that the leader of the League's military committee was a traitor who would be condemned by history; the bombastic and unsuccessful Kaukji, Kirkbride later declared, "did his side great harm."

The outright rejection by the AHC and the Arab states of both UNSCOP plans, concluded a classified State Department official's report for the National War College the following October, created "the worst possible psychological atmosphere" in the General Assembly. Only the call to Palestine's independence as one state controlled by its present majority brought all the Arab states together, pressured by their masses and the radical Islamist Muslim Brotherhood (*Ikhwan al-Muslimun*), in a murderous hatred of Jews. At the same time, concludes Walid Khalidi, their military intervention, but for which the whole of Palestine would have been conquered by the Zionists in 1948, had come "too little and too late."[28]

Their inflexibility proved regrettable even to Beeley and other pro-Arab advocates like McClintock, while Cunningham wondered to Creech Jones one month after the General Assembly vote if the League truly had the Palestinian Arabs' interests at heart. Advising the Arab capitals on May 6, 1948, to accept the U.S. proposal for a ten-day cease-fire, Bevin warned that if they continued "holding out for 100% of their demands while blaming us for everything that goes wrong, they will once again lose every advantage which they might gain by early and realistic decisions," just as they had in refusing his proposals at the London Conference and waiting too long before putting up their own compromise proposals at the GA November session. The sympathetic Rusk, asked by Truman and Marshall to seek a political and military truce by May 15, later reminisced that he had obtained a Zionist agreement to accept 2,500 immigrants a month, only to hear an outright refusal from Prince Feisal of Saudi Arabia on behalf of the Arab delegation: "If we agree to twenty-five hundred, the Jews will simply bring in twenty-five hundred pregnant women, and that will mean five thousand!"

A consistent refusal to accept any compromise, whether the Anglo-American report, the Morrison-Grady plan, or either of the UNSCOP recommendations, did not stand the Arab states in good stead within the international political arena. Genocidal threats against the Jews of Palestine from the truculent Jamal Husseini and supposed moderates like Azzam Pasha were fulminated while memory of the Holocaust was stark fresh, the U.S. Military Tribunal in Nuremberg just then concluding that approximately 2,400 SS *Einsatzgruppen* soldiers had murdered 2,000,000 human beings, mostly Jews: "A Jew was killed simply because he was a Jew." At the same time, savage assaults took place against Jews in a few Arab countries. This only harmed the Arab cause further.[29]

A confluence of factors brought about the British decision to refer the Palestine quagmire to the UN in February 1947, a decade after the Peel Commission had declared the Arab and Jewish claims irreconcilable, the Mandate unworkable, and partition the best solution, and finally to leave the country. In grave financial straits after World War II and greatly dependent on an American loan however onerous

the terms, HMG could no longer maintain an enormous military garrison facing a determined *yishuv*, the Hagana, the guerilla strikes of
the Irgun and LEHI insurgents which, in Buxton's phrase, "dramatized the situation," and growing widespread public sympathy for the
survivors and *aliya bet*. (Supporters of that "illegal traffic," Creech
Jones declared in the full House debate after the GA November vote,
did "infinite mischief, aroused fierce passions among the Arabs, and
made our task of administering the Mandate extremely difficult.") In
early 1947, Truman acceded to London's abrupt request to take over
its major role in the Greek civil war against pro-Communist forces;
HMG would approve independence to India that August, a key factor
in Attlee's views to his cabinet one month later that Palestine be
evacuated by a definite date and so possibly force Arabs and Jews to
resolve their differences as he believed had occurred between Muslims
and Hindus. [30] Independence for Burma (January 1948) and Ceylon
(February 1948) followed.

The egocentric, insensitive Bevin rashly thought that, just as he had
strongly controlled the trade unions earlier, he could stake his political
reputation on negotiating a Palestine solution. All the while he sought
to bend his mighty will to frustrate the Jews, who he believed, for all
their sufferings, should not "get too much at the head of the queue."
"The hell with the Jews," he told Philip Bernstein and aide Herbert
Friedman in February 1947, a tirade strewn with profanity and crude
antisemitic overtones. When Ben-Gurion that same month made an
appeal to the Hebrew prophetic ideals of justice, Bevin sneered, saying
that he did not need to be told about Hebrew profits. A serious heart condition, at times leaving this physically huge man completely exhausted,
helps explain his short temper and the violent outbursts of a leader who
could not bear to see his working-class "Tommies" being killed in Palestine.
Failure over the contentious issue embittered him greatly, recalled
Whitehall UN Advisor Gladwyn Jebb, and pique followed. Truman's
individuality in this aggravating matter, to which he simply attributed
Jewish political pressure, exasperated the impulsive Foreign Secretary.
In this connection, as Norman Rose observes, he also did not grasp that
Truman, a seasoned politician, was mindful of a key fact: lobbying and
ethnic politics "were legitimate and long-standing traditions in American
electioneering practice." Kirchwey, Shultz, and others capitalized on this
reality in steady contacts with the Democratic Party leadership.[31]

What of the Balfour Declaration, the Palestine Mandate pledges, and the Third Reich's destruction of European Jewry? The first Bevin dismissed as "really a Power Politics" declaration that did not take into account the Arabs and which he considered the greatest mistake in the Empire's imperial history. He and Whitehall colleagues adamantly believed, as did Attlee, that London's prior commitments to the Jews did not entail statehood and that the few survivors could and should assimilate, dispersed in a peaceful world. Speaking in the wartime cabinet about "non-repatriable refugees" as early as May 16, 1945, then Home Secretary Morrison advised to "send Jews elsewhere" to territories other than Palestine if available. McNeil took the same position at the UN Conference on Refugees in May 1946, adding that the Jews could contribute "a valuable and even vital element" to the "future civilization" of the countries of Central Europe and that no distinction should be made between the various minorities existing in any country. At most, suggested Brigadier I. N. Clayton of HMG's Cairo Embassy that February, Britain could diminish the pressure of world Jewry by creating in Palestine a Jewish token-state, "a Jewish Vatican." In addition, British officials increasingly equated Zionism with communism, which had significant impact on the U.S. State and Defense Departments as the Cold War escalated.[32]

Years later, Bevin's chief adviser on Palestine acknowledged that the Holocaust was a turning point in British policy, but for which "there would have been a different settlement." At the end of April 1948, Beeley had told Austin it was "inevitable" that the Jews would, after considerable fighting, be able to consolidate a state of restricted size running from Tel Aviv to Haifa and going inland fifteen or more miles. He subsequently concluded that "we did not comprehend the special situation of the years 1946–47 and the significance Zionism held for the displaced and the immigrants of that period." Weizmann went further, thinking that the change in feeling and sentiment in Great Britain in relation to Palestine from the days of Balfour, Lloyd George, Smuts, *et al.* was mostly the fault of Bevin, whom he considered "a powerful ignoramus."[33]

The UN partition resolution—which Bevin, still aiming for a binational state, did not forecast—also contributed decisively to the British exit from Palestine in a postwar world increasingly opposed to colonialism. Evatt reflected the view of many delegates when cabling the Australian delegation in April 1948 that "the major issue is standing of

United Nations and United Nations' decisions," and Berendsen pressed his colleagues to implement the partition recommendation lest their inconsistent lead result in "inevitable confusion and dismay." More caustically, Pearson wrote to the High Commissioner for Canada in London the same month that HMG's policy of "non-intervention" and "mind your own business" while placing the GA under the obligation of recommending a solution to the problem "seems to me a pretty cynical method of behavior."

"The only morally sound position for the Secretariat now to take was to support partition," Bunche told Lie and other colleagues on April 22, "since the partition process had already gone very far." Yet the very same day, Bevin advised New York lawyer Morris Ernst that partition "must be dropped to satisfy the Arabs"; a Palestinian state ultimately created; and about 100,000 survivors brought to Palestine over an 18-month period, another 100,000 to the US and so many to the UK, and the remainder from an original 250,000 to France and elsewhere. Shortly thereafter, he and Attlee told Douglas that "after all, Palestine was an Arab country." Reflecting the attitude of the French government, Parodi raised with Austin one day later the "very serious question" of British motives "in this whole affair," with particular reference to Abdullah and his activities.[34]

Some British soldiers killed Jewish civilians, disarmed four Hagana members and left them to be butchered by an Arab mob, and helped in the *Palestine Post* and Ben Yehuda Street bombings of February 1948. Deadly revenge was sought after the King David Hotel bombing and the hanging of two sergeants; vulgar antisemitic epithets became more common in the ranks. British artillery was missing for six hours on April 13 when Arabs, including Iraqi soldiers, massacred the Hadassah medical convoy on its way to Mt. Scopus, but was available to force the Irgun to retreat from Jaffa and the Hagana from its complete conquest of Jerusalem's Sheikh Jarrah area. The Arab Legion, still under MacMillan's direct command, attacked the Etzion bloc shortly before the Mandate's end. Three months after the bombing of the Jewish Agency headquarters that March, twenty-two-year-old Robert Kennedy, hailing the "undying spirit" and "unparalleled courage" of the Jews, reported for the *Boston Post* that a leading Arab League official told him of British officers quickly admitting through their guard post the Arab responsible after he freely told what he had done, along with their remark "nice going."

The overwhelming majority of British soldiers, however, exhibited remarkable restraint despite regular, often deadly, provocation. The likes of Barker, who thought that the Jews would eventually be "eradicated" by the Arabs, and of Farran, as well as MI6's campaign to throttle unsanctioned immigration by placing bombs on *aliya bet* vessels, proved to be exceptions to the rule. The armed forces, at their height of 100,000 one-tenth of the British Empire's entire army now occupying a territory the size of Wales, could have brought Jewish terrorism to a quick end if allowed to employ their full power. Yet, as J. C. Hurewitz aptly put it, "it was a police state with a conscience."[35]

Cunningham and his political superiors were not prepared to contemplate unleashing the military upon the *yishuv*, as Montgomery wished, and resorted ultimately to what the *yishuv* derisively called "Bevingrad" defensive fortifications. The fear of a massive strike by the British armed forces, which would have been nothing short of disastrous, had driven Weizmann to successfully demand Sneh's resignation from the Hagana high command, as well as to urge moderation upon an increasingly impatient *yishuv*. That would result in his losing the mantle of leadership to the more militant Ben-Gurion and Silver at the World Zionist Congress in December 1946. This rejection (to be followed by a vindictive Ben-Gurion not having him later sign Israel's Declaration of Independence) was a trauma, wrote friend George Weidenfeld, "which haunted him to his death." One month later, Ben-Gurion told *yishuv* emissaries that Britain's imperial policy would not change, and a Jewish state had to be established and built immediately.[36]

Testifying before the Anglo-American Committee, Chief Secretary Shaw frankly remarked that "it has never been clear where we are really heading." In like vein, when asked by Montgomery what was really wrong with Palestine, the imperturbable Gurney replied that, surrendering over the last thirty years to the pressure of American Jewry or Arab rebellion, it was "merely a lack of policy with which nobody agrees." (In the introduction to a private "Postscript," the mandatory's last Chief Secretary would also claim that "no evidence existed" to substantiate the statement that 6,000,000 Jews had been killed in Europe, and "whether or not this is true, it was open to Jews there to resume life in their own countries.") In the end, as Benny Morris has written, the Attlee cabinet concluded that it could not afford to alienate Washington

(Bevin's primary concern in the Cold War) over a highly emotional issue that "was not a vital interest."[37]

Truman far sooner than HMG grasped the Holocaust's impact, articulated with clarity in his letter of October 25, 1946, to Ibn Saud, and eventually understood its transformation of Zionism into a political movement ready to resist all opposed to the realization of Theodor Herzl's dream. Deeply stirred by the unparalleled, methodical annihilation of European Jewry by the Germans and collaborator nations during the recent global war, he pressed for the large admission of survivors to Palestine. Harrison's recommendation for the 100,000, coming after personal letters on the President's own initiative to Churchill and Attlee in this regard, only strengthened his inner conviction.

In the fall of 1945, he agreed to an Anglo-American investigation on the condition that Palestine serve as its central focus, and announced his approval of that report's unanimous proposal for immediate entry of that number without consulting London or referring to the vague recommendation of a unitary state. In September 1946, the same month that Truman wrote his wife Bess that "there is no solution for the Jewish problem," a personal report to the President about the Jewish refugees in Europe by Edwin Pauley took the 100,000 figure for granted. His public statement on the eve of Yom Kippur 1946, urging "substantial" Jewish immigration into Palestine (but not Jewish sovereignty there), reflected both his awareness of the importance which financially strapped Democratic Party leaders placed on the Jewish vote in the Congressional elections and of bi-partisan support, mirroring public appeal far beyond America's five million Jews, for the plight of the survivors. "My only interest," he wrote to Senator George shortly thereafter, "is to find some proper way to take care of these displaced persons."[38] While Attlee and Bevin saw this as a double-cross and seethed, the U.S. delegation at the UN would come to share Truman's view and his support for statehood.

Clifford's virtuoso performance, its apex arrived at with his successful pressing of Lovett, who had threatened the independently-minded Goldmann at the end of April 1948 with financial sanctions against the Zionist movement and publishing a dossier of its pressure tactics at the UN, played a decisive part in the outcome. "I just received a cable from Palestine," Niles told him on May 16, 1948, that they are going to change the name of their new state to "Cliffordville." This suave, softly-spoken man, who would become the most eminent Washington lawyer/politician of his generation, received valuable help from Niles, Lowenthal, Rosenman, Ewing, Crum (then national chairman of Americans for Haganah), and a few other aides in Truman's familiar entourage.

The forty-one-year-old Special Counsel to the White House convinced his boss that humanitarianism—the President's lodestar on this vexatious issue, political motivation, and the national interests of the U.S. did, indeed, coincide. Truman's pivotal role in frustrating State prior to the GA vote of November 1947 (he spoke "vigorously" to the U.S. delegation at Lake Success, Niles informed Buxton) and after the department's embrace of provisional trusteeship in March 1948, a diplomatic reversal which Thomas Mann considered "the most humiliating and revolting political event since the treachery perpetrated on Czechoslovakia in 1938," reflected this fundamental belief. The simple sincerity of Jacobson—aided by Granoff, his former business partner whose contribution Truman subsequently declared was "of decisive importance," and the tactful charisma of Weizmann ("one of the wisest people I think I've ever met," he later recalled) were instrumental in countering his great irritation with the aggressive pro-Zionist campaign spearheaded by Silver, an AZEC crusading effort which Welles strongly praised. The concurrent efforts by Truman and Niles, supported by State and the American Council for Judaism, to have Jewish refugees find shelter in the U.S. had not yet borne fruit.[39]

Given all this, combined with a desire to strengthen the fledgling UN and to forestall the Soviets in recognizing a new state that had already proven itself on the battlefield, Truman chose to disregard the misgivings of Marshall, the warnings of Forrestal, and the anxieties of the oil companies, and to move on his own. His "thunderbolt" recognition of the new Jewish commonwealth after State's trusteeship proposal had "died stillborn," coming one day following Weizmann's request for the same (the letter brought to Truman thanks to Niles), brought the initiative back to the White House. It received an enthusiastic American press and Congressional response. When honored at Kansas City's Hotel Muehlebach in December 1961 by local businessmen, Truman, who kept a quotation from Mark Twain on his desk—"Always do right. This will gratify some people and astonish the rest," thought that he did not deserve any special credit for this step. In his opinion, "the creation and recognition of the State of Israel was right."[40]

The individual personality of the then occupant of the White House must be taken into account. An unpopular Chief Executive, he had to contend with the initial popular image of an accidental, virtually unknown President, living in FDR's giant shadow and completely untried in foreign affairs, who had risen from the Pendergast political machine of Kansas City to the mightiest office in the land. The victorious Republicans in the 1946 Congressional elections continued to joke that "to err is Truman"; many Americans were not "wild about Harry." Truman's suspicion that the mandarins in government did not take him seriously, the self-revealing phrase "these people forget who is President of the United States" often on his lips, helps explains his resentment of those whom he contemptuously labeled "the striped-pants boys" of the State Department. Bevin's snide, impulsive remark about his domestic motives regarding Palestine's political future afforded another personal irritation, which he years later characterized as "a pretty raw, ignominious thing to say." Always carrying in his wallet the lines of Alfred Lord Tennyson's poetic dream for "the Parliament of man" (*Locksley Hall*), Truman ultimately stood by the GA recommendation, authorized by Article 14 of the UN Charter.

His concern, as he told Weizmann in March 1948, "to see justice done without bloodshed" explains his steady opposition to committing U.S. troops to Palestine and his approval of State's arms embargo on the Middle East. His cabinet tirade against Jews in July 1946 and in a diary entry at the height of the *Exodus 1947* drama, echoing personal letters about the business acumen of "Hebrews" and "kikes," owed much to his rise from a prejudice-ridden small town in the Midwest. At the same time, the month of his *de jure* recognition would also witness his supporting a loan from the Export-Import Bank to Israel of $100 million (later increased to $135 million) that he had promised Weizmann during their meeting on May 25, 1948. Two years later, he would sign a bill under which Israel was to receive almost $65 million, of which $50 million was earmarked for the relief and resettlement of Jewish refugees. In July 1952, shortly before leaving office, he signed an appropriation bill whereby Israel received $73 million for this purpose.[41]

Whatever the mix of his motives, Truman responded to Weizmann's congratulatory letter following the November 1948 presidential elections by pointing out how both had been pressing for what each was sure "was right" despite being abandoned by "the so-called realistic experts." "We were both proven to be right," he added, and then concluded by noting how "happy and impressed" he was with Israel's "remarkable progress": "What you have received at the hands of the world has been far less than was your due. But you have made the most of what you have received, and I admire you for it." In view of Moscow's "ruthless betrayal" of every nation that trusted her regarding commitments, he wrote to a concerned Eleanor Roosevelt, he did not believe "that she will fool so canny a people as those in Israel." We should make the new state "our friend," he added, otherwise the U.S. would lose a very strategic position in the Middle East.

The devout Baptist shared with Clifford a strong belief in biblical sources about the Lord's promise to give the Land of Canaan to Abraham and his descendants as "an everlasting holding" (Genesis 17:8), and in the prophecies of Isaiah, Jeremiah, Ezekiel, and Amos concerning the Jewish revival there. When Herzog compared him in 1949 with Persia's King Cyrus for fulfilling the Lord's promise to help the Chosen People return to the Holy Land, or when Ben-Gurion told him in 1961 that he had earned "an immortal place in Jewry history," Truman's eyes filled with tears. He may not have been Cyrus, a title he claimed when visiting the Jewish Theological Seminary with Jacobson in 1953, but the crucial role of this former haberdasher in the rebirth of Jewish sovereignty after two millennia is unquestionable.[42]

On 5 Iyar 5708 in the Hebrew calendar, the arc of history bent to a centuries-old deracinated people, witnessed the resurrection of its national spirit, and reaffirmed Jews' beleaguered trust in their collective destiny. That transformative realization, going beyond a haven from persecution and epitomized in the ambitious—even audacious—revolution wrought by Zionism, had been a very long time in coming. For ages, Jews had intoned "Next Year in Jerusalem!" at the close of Yom Kippur and Passover, never forsaking that dream while filled with memories of longing and lament. Yet Herzl's diary entry on September 3, 1897, that "certainly in fifty years" everyone would perceive that, as a consequence of the movement's first world congress, "in Basle I founded the Jewish State" received its vindication almost to that very date with UNSCOP's majority recommendation for a sovereign Jewish state in Eretz Israel.

The unending fragility of Jewish survival had not come to an end, and independence was secured with a heavy price of blood: 6,000 Palestinian Jews, a full one percent of the population, died in what Israel would later call *Milhemet* (the War of) *HaShihrur* (Liberation), *HaAtsmaut* (Independence), or *HaKomemiyut* (Resurrection). Michael Cohen has averred that "two elements of force majeure" made this a reality: the impact of the Holocaust on American Jewry and the successes of *Tsahal* (an acronym for the Israel Defense Forces) in the armed conflict. Israel would owe the debt of its existence not to the UN resolution but to the force of arms. The latter recalls Weizmann's sage comment after the Balfour Declaration: "Even if all the governments of the world gave us a country it would be a gift of words, but if the Jewish people will go and build Palestine, the Jewish state will become a reality and a fact." To this should be added his argument, which won over Crossman and other influential voices, that, given the substantial number of Arab states, a Jewish commonwealth in partitioned Palestine represented the lesser injustice when weighed against the claim of the country's Arabs to the whole.[43]

The folly of Arab rejectionism cannot be discounted either. With support from neighboring governments, the leaders of Palestine's Arab Higher Committee had turned down the international offer to legitimatize their own state on November 29, 1947—a UN recommendation which the Zionist leadership accepted, and immediately unleashed the civil war. In September 1947, Musa Alami had told the U.S. Embassy's Economic Counselor in London that it would be far better for the United States and the United Kingdom to let the Palestine question "drag on another year or two unsolved" than to take an unjust decision which would throw the Arab world first into internal political turmoil and then progressively into the Soviet camp. Two years later, he candidly declared in the *Middle East Journal* that the Arabs had evacuated their country because they placed their "confidence and hopes," when told that the Arab armies were coming, "that the matter would be settled and everything returned to normal." Yet the resounding military defeat and the tragedy that the number of 300,000–340,000 Palestinian Arabs who had fled their homes prior to the outbreak of the first Arab-Israeli war would swell to nearly 600,000 as the result of the fighting led subsequent Palestinian and Arab discourse to call this "the *nakba*" (catastrophe), claiming that Israel was the main, if not sole, culprit for this result.

Israel soon refused to allow those Arabs who had fled or been expelled to return, fearing destabilization and a militarily subversive fifth column; the Arab states, largely refusing to absorb or properly resettle the refugees in their midst, intimidated or forced even more than that number of Jews to depart their countries. One difference emerged in this respect: three-quarters of these Jewish refugees were quickly absorbed into Israel, where they built new, productive lives.[44]

Rejection meant that Palestine was partitioned through war, with a consequent, tragic harvest. Bunche received the Nobel Peace Prize in 1950 for mediating armistice agreements between Israel and Egypt, Lebanon, Syria, and Jordan (Iraq refused to sign), demarcated by the so-called Green Line, but a tumultuous future lay ahead for Arab and Jew. Jordan formally annexed the West Bank in 1950, a move that the Arab League itself declared illegal and void, and which was recognized only by Great Britain, Iraq, and Pakistan. Since its establishment, the State of Israel has fought eight recognized wars, two Palestinian Arab *intifadas* (uprisings), and a series of armed conflicts in the broader Arab–Israeli conflict. Despite these and ongoing, often lethal, terrorist attacks against Jews living in Israel and abroad, the State of Israel would offer statehood to the Palestinian Arab leadership in 1967, 1979, 2000, and 2005, only to be refused every time.

Peace treaties would be signed with Egypt in 1979 and with Jordan in 1994, but the cries of *jihad* and violent hatred against Israel's legitimacy continue to be heard in the Palestine Liberation Organization's covenant, media, and school textbooks, from the Hamas authority in Gaza, and from the Shia Islamist Hizbollah in Lebanon. Iran, backing Hizbollah militarily and taking over parts of Iraq and Syria, has repeatedly issued threats of nuclear annihilation against Israel. This tenacious commitment to the destruction of the Jewish commonwealth, not the issue of Israeli settlements established beyond the Green Line after the 1967 Six-Day War or borders in general, squanders Arab national energies and has left the conflict between two peoples living in the Middle East unresolved to date. For Rusk, later Secretary of State to Presidents John F. Kennedy and Lyndon B. Johnson who subsequently admitted that State had overestimated the Arabs' military capabilities, in 1948, it has been "the most intractable, unyielding problem of the postwar period."[45]

The struggle for political sovereignty over Palestine until May 14, 1948, given the Arab leadership's firm unwillingness at concession, allowed the Jews no margin for failure. It began in earnest during the 1930s and was delayed because of World War II, and now its culmination was reached with the Mandate's collapse in the three years after V-E Day. The Holocaust, testifying that the inhumanity of man had no finite limit and that the Allied powers chose the role of bystanders while the Jews were almost effaced from the European canvas, drove the *yishuv* to seize the hour. Its uncompromising will found additional confirmation in the survivors' 1946 Passover *Hagada*, prepared in Munich with Klausner's help. Lithuanian-born Yosef Dov Sheinson was speaking for most when declaring in Yiddish for the preface, "*Nito kein shlechter oder guter goles. Yeder goles firt zum untergang*" (There is no such thing as a "bad" or "good" exile. Every exile leads to extinction). *Aliya* to Eretz Israel, garnering the support of Jews worldwide and of many Gentiles, became imperative for the large majority of those yet alive in postwar Europe—British law be damned. The third congress of Liberated Jews in the American zone of Germany resolved in early April 1948 to mobilize all men between 17 and 35 for service in the Hagana.

Twenty-nine-year-old Leonard Bernstein captured Palestinian Jewry's prevalent mood during a first visit one year earlier, writing to beloved mentor Serge Koussevitzky: "There is a strength and devotion in these people that is formidable. They will never let the land be taken from them; they will all die first. And the country is beautiful beyond description." In 1973, Israeli Prime Minister Golda Meir conveyed the same spirit to Joe Biden, then a freshman US Senator (D, Del.) and later the 47th US Vice-President: "We Jews have a secret weapon. We have nowhere else to go."[46]

Reaching the milestone of its seventieth anniversary, the Jewish state of 8.8 million citizens, three-quarters of them Jews, remains the one flourishing democracy in a highly volatile region marked by brutality and dictatorship. Although not fulfilling all the wild dreams of Zionism's thinkers and builders, this high-tech superpower has absorbed more than three million Jews, giving substance to Jeremiah's prophecy of hope (31:17) "Your children shall return to their country." It has brought life to a hitherto sterile landscape, resurrected the ancient Hebrew language, and created a vibrant Jewish culture such as advocated by Ahad Ha'Am (Asher Ginsberg), Herzl's primary ideological opponent.[47] Its Arab citizens, 20 percent of the population, have made considerable progress in varied fields, although more strides forward remain in this respect. Israel has also pioneered in providing medical, agricultural, and other forms of aid to stricken countries around the globe. The price to date for survival against adversaries bent on its very eradication has been high: 23,632 soldiers and security forces have died defending the State of Israel. Still, for one people with a long, tormented history of exile and exclusion in a world without love or redemption, the new commonwealth born in war serves as a testament to Jewish resilience and faith in a better tomorrow.

"There are no frontiers to Jewish hope," exclaimed a survivor aboard the *Exodus 1947* to Ruth Gruber, echoing the coda of the *HaTikva* Zionist anthem's hope of two thousand years "to be a free nation in our land, the land of Zion and Jerusalem." On the night of November 29, 1947, Professor of Archeology Eleazar Lipa Sukenik was working in Jerusalem on a passage from what became known as the Dead Sea Scrolls, which an Arab merchant in Bethlehem had that morning permitted him to examine prior to possibly buying them for the Hebrew University. Just as he was informed of the historic UN vote, the father of Hagana operations chief Yigal Yadin read: "I was driven from my home like a bird from its nest.... I was cast down, but raised up again." The lines, preceded by the phrase "I give thanks to Thee, O Lord," led to that scroll's later being called *The Thanksgiving Hymns*.[48] Hope and gratitude received further reflection in the instance of one woman freed in Bergen-Belsen by a combined British-Canadian military unit on April 15, 1945, when weighing just twenty-eight kilograms who, sixty-six years later, would see her son, Benny Gantz, sworn in as the twentieth Chief of Staff of the Israel Defense Forces.

Antisemitism, contrary to Herzl's prediction that Jew-hatred would disappear as a consequence of the nation reborn, has reawakened energetically in our own day, while perpetual frustration continues to characterize Israel's search for a lasting and meaningful peace with its Arab neighbors. At the same time, ever since the 6–4 vote of the *Minhelet Ha'Am* at the JNF Bauhaus-style house on 11 Zvi Shapira Street in Tel Aviv on May 12, 1948, to reject an American-inspired truce and to declare a state, the passivity which had been the central fact in Jewish political life would be replaced by a sovereign, collective initiative, one even having some control over the flow of events. No longer would Jews cower before the wrath of barbaric massacre, a response decried by Chaim Nahman Bialik, the first bard of Zionist renaissance, in the poem "B'Ir HaHareiga" ("In the City of Slaughter") after the Kishinev pogrom of April 1903. The climactic declaration of national independence two days later was, in Eban's subsequent formulation, "a moment of truth that would move Israel to its ultimate generations."[49] Much struggle and many efforts, despite great odds, had led to that hour. Now that these people had returned to their first anchorage and become reunited with its soil, looking backward to gaze forward, a new journey in the odyssey of Jewish history had begun.

Endnotes

1   Eytan report, May 19, 1948, 93/126/19, ISA; "Palestine Commission," DAG13/3.1.0.1., Box 1, UN Archives; MacCabe to MWM, May 13, 1948, A366/1, CZA; Bernard Wasserstein, *Divided Jerusalem, The Struggle for the Holy City* (New Haven, CT, 2001), 135–141; Ben-Gurion statement, May 15, 1948, S25/1553, CZA. For the last-minute efforts of the International Red Cross's head representative to place the municipal area under his organization's control, see Palestine report to Bevin, May 3, 1948, FO371/68547, PRO.

2   Arab League statement, May 15, 1948, in Moshe Medzini, *Israel's Foreign Relations, Selected Documents, 1947–1949* (Jerusalem, 1976), 135–138; Morris, *1948*, 235; C.L. Sulzberger, *A Long Row of Candles, Memories and Diaries, 1934–1954* (New York, 1969), 398; *New York Herald Tribune*, April 7, 1948; *JTA*, May 16, 1948.

3   Lie, *In the Cause of Peace*, ap. 174; Medzini, *Israel's Foreign Relations*, 140–141; Shertok cable, May 15, 1948, *Security Council Documents, 3rd year, May Supplement 1948* (New York, 1948), 88–89; Report, May 24, 1948, Robison MSS; Molotov to Shertok, May 18, 1948, S25/1559, CZA; *JTA*, May 20, 1948. In a letter to Lovett, Celler made the same point as Lie about Arab aggression. Celler to Lovett, Apr. 10, 1948, Box 23, Emanuel Celler MSS, Library of Congress, Washington, D.C.

4   *Palestine Termination of the Mandate 15th May, 1948* (London, 1948).

5   Attlee to Brodetsky, March 20, 1948, Palestine Committee, Board of Deputies MSS; *JTA*, May 12, 1948; *Palestine Post*, May 13, 1948.

6   Proclamation, May 15, 1948, 41.0/124/31G, ISA; Amost Ben Vered, "The Last Days of the Mandate," *Palestine Post*, May 10, 1951; Wasson to Marshall, May 2, 1948, Rusk-3, SD; Ruffer to Zaslani, May 4, 1948, S25/1559, CZA; MacMillan remarks, May 17, 1948, 999/14/1; ISA; *Illustrated London News*, July 10, 1948. For the Agency's agreement with the British to secure part of the Haifa port by the end of April, see Salomon report, May 2, 1948, 931/7-P, ISA.

7   *JTA*, May 17, 1948; *For the Record, The Memoirs of Eva, Marchioness of Reading* (London, 1972), 188–189, copy in AJ/171, Anglo-Jewish Association Archives, Mocatta Library, London; *JDC Digest*, 7:4 (June 1948): 3–5. It does not appear coincidental that Morgenthau publicized excerpts from his 1943–1944 diaries, lambasting the unwillingness of State and Whitehall to move rapidly to save Hitler's primary victims in World War II, not long before the crucial GA vote on Palestine's political future. "The Morgenthau Diaries, VI—The Refugee Run Around," *Collier's*, November 1, 1947. Citing this article, Wise called on the world's governments to implement the UNSCOP majority report and to open the doors of Palestine to Europe's Jews. Wise statement, October 24, 1947, C3/2038, CZA,

8   Bevin-Sulzberger-Mathews interview, May 24, 1948, Palestine and Zionism-2 file, Sulzberger MSS. For Byrnes's later recollection, C. L. Sulzberger, "Memories: Ethnic Stew," *New York Times*, December 28, 1977. He ascribed the bi-partisan U.S. support for increased Jewish immigration to Palestine to the two major parties "competing for the votes of Jewish citizens." Byrnes address, June 19, 1959. Byrnes MSS.

9   Cunningham to Creech Jones, June 18, 1948, Creech Jones MSS; Creech Jones to FO, May 2, 1948, FO371/68548, PRO; Memo, May 14, 1948, RG25, series A-12, vol. 2093, file AR35/1, pt. 6, PAC; Harold Nicolson, *Diaries and Letters, 1945–1962*, ed. N. Nicolson (London, 1968), 139; Graves Diary, October 1947, C14/32-1, Board of Deputies MSS.

10 McCormick notes, May 22, 1948 (?), Churchill files, Sulzberger MSS; *Duff Cooper Diaries*, 466. Chief Justice Fitzgerald's private sentiments on HMG's retreat, leaving "the plate on the fire to boil over," resembled Graves's indictment. Fitzgerald to MacMichael, November 8, 1947, MacMichael MSS.

11 Truman to Crum, May 15, 1948, Box 776, HSTL; Buxton to Ben-Horin, August 15, 1947, A300/16, CZA; Hutcheson to Phillips, March 12, 1947; Hutcheson to members, April 29, 1947; both in Phillips MSS; Magnes to Mann, April 12, 1948, 21/9, James Marshall MSS, AJA; Ross memo, April 23, 1948, Rusk-2, Palestine, SD; Magnes memos, May 2, 1948, P3/162, CAHJP; *Dissenter in Zion*, 494–497; C.L. Sulzberger memo, May 6, 1948, Palestine and Zionism-2, Sulzberger MSS; April 26, 1948 meeting, M68-68, 1948/4, American Council for Judaism MSS, University of Wisconsin Library, Madison.

12 Truman to Weizmann, May 15, 1948; Truman to Thurman, May 17, 1948; both in OF 204-D, Misc.: State of Israel, HSTL; *FRUS, 1948*, vol. 5, part 2, 1031; Truman to Alfange, May 18, 1948, PSF, Foreign Affairs, Palestine 1948–1952, Box 161, HSTL.

13 Report, May 31, 1948, Robison MSS; Ginsburg to Silver, June 5, 1948, file 7/1, Silver MSS; Sumner Welles, "Recognition of Israel," *Washington Post*, June 29, 1948; Cohen, *Truman and Israel*, Chap. 13; JCS memo, June 21, 1946, CCS 092Palestine, Sec. 2, RG218, NA; Forrestal to National Security Council, Aug. 19, 1948, PSF 194, HSTL; Carry David Stanger, "A Haunting Legacy: The Assassination of Count Bernadotte," *Middle East Journal* 42:2 (Spring 1988): 260–272.The Joint Chiefs of Staff went so far as to recommend the withdrawal of U.S. consular personnel from Palestine "when and if justified by the situation." Memo, n.d., CCS 092 Palestine (6-3-46), Sec. 5, RG 218, NA.

14 Richard H.S. Crossman, "The Roots of Policy," *Zionist Review*, July 9, 1948, 9–10; Crossman to Attlee, September 3, 1948, Crossman MSS; Laski to Frankfurter, Dec. 2, 1948, Box 75, Frankfurter MSS; Churchill speech, Dec. 10, 1948, *Parliamentary Debates, House of Commons*, vol. 459: cols. 715–716. For a similar Crossman-Attlee exchange regarding the Anglo-American Inquiry report, showing the Prime Minister's fixed mind on the Palestine conundrum, see Norman Rose, "*A Senseless, Squalid War*," *Voices from Palestine 1890s-1948* (London, 2009), 101.

15 Cohen, *Truman and Israel*, chap. 14; Stone notes on Truman's speech of October 28, 1948, Box 2, Dewey Stone MSS; Lash, *Eleanor, The Years Alone*, 135–136; Donovan, *Conflict and Crisis*, chaps. 42–43. When Stone promised the President after May that he would raise the funds needed for the election campaign, Truman replied: "Those damned British are not going to push me around and lead me by the nose." "Role in the Making of Two United States Presidents," Box 2, Stone MSS. For Feinberg, see 1885/3 and 5-P, ISA.

16 Cohen, *Truman and Israel*, 260–274; January 26, 1949, *Parliamentary Debates, House of Commons*, vol. 460: cols. 928–948, 1053–1061; James G. McDonald, *My Mission in Israel, 1948–1951* (New York, 1951), chap. 1. Czechoslovakia proved crucial to the establishment of the Jewish state and was its major arms supplier, providing almost 35,000 rifles, pistols, machine guns, mortars, and bombs, as well as 25 Avia S-199 fighter jets, to the fledgling Israel Defense Forces. Anna Aronheim, "Hugo Marom, One of IAF's Founders, dies at 89," *Jerusalem Post*, January 8, 2018. For some of the Czech purchase bills to the Agency's Ueberall, listed there as an Ethiopian government delegate in Paris to purchase exclusively for the Imperial Ethiopian Army, see 93/523/21, ISA.

17 W. E. (Eytan) to Myerson, May 7, 1948, S25/9215, CZA; *Jerusalem Post*, May 22, 1981; Arthur Lourie interview with the author, June 29, 1972. Eban eventually had "Israel" recognized in the Security Council discussion through a stratagem approved by Gromyko, with the Russian's colleague Dmitri Manuilsky of the Ukraine, as the next president of the Council, inviting "the representative of

Israel" to take his seat at the table. Cadogan led the voices in dissent, but there were only six votes (seven were needed) for the challenge. Jamal Husseini walked out, saying that he would not return so long as a representative called "Israel" sat where Eban sat. For the next twenty-five years, until the UN recognized the Palestine Liberation Organization, Palestine's Arabs were not recognized at the highest international agency. Abba Eban, *Personal Witness: Israel Through My Eyes* (New York, 1992), 172–173.

18 W.E. (Eytan) to Myerson, May 7, 1948, S25/9215, CZA; *Jerusalem Post*, May 22, 1981; Yigal Lossin, *Pillar of Fire, The Rebirth of Israel –A Visual History*, trans. Z. Ofer (Jerusalem, 1983); McDonald, *My Mission in Israel*, 22–28; Jon Kimche and David Kimche, *Both Sides of the Hill: Britain and the Palestine War* (London, 1960), 196–198; A/PV 207, May 11, 1949, GA; Daniel Mandel, *H. V. Evatt and the Establishment of Israel, The Undercover Zionist* (London, 2004), 143–148; *Palestine Post*, February 13, 1949; W. Keith Pattison, "The Delayed British Recognition of Israel," *Middle East Journal* 37:3 (Summer 1983): 412–428. For an earlier Evatt statement supporting the Jewish National Home, see March 16, 1946 dinner, S25/7524, CZA.

19 Greer Fay Cashman, "The First Steps of Statehood," *Jerusalem Post*, April 23, 2007; Herzog to London *Times*, February 27, 1947, S25/7161, CZA. In the opinion of former UNRRA chief in Germany General Frederick Morgan, who wished to get the survivors out of Europe (not necessarily to Palestine), "pure common sense" dictated that Jewry as a religious, rather than national, distinction "must continue to be so" unless and until all Jews lived in the new Jewish state to be created in Palestine or become nationals thereof, "which all must admit is absurd." Morgan to Holtzman, December 19, 1947, 6/12, Fanny E. Holtzman MSS, AJA.

20 Anita Shapira, *Land and Power: The Zionist Resort to Force, 1881–1948*, trans. W. Templer (New York, 1992); Sharett, *B'Sha'ar HaUmot*, 238; Yael Zerubavel, "Numerical Commemoration and the Challenges of Collective Remembrance in Israel," *History and Memory* 26:1 (Spring-Summer 2014), 5–38; Ruth Corman, *Unexpected Israel* (Jerusalem, 2016), 158–161; Uriel Bachrach, *The Power of Knowledge, Hemed: The Israeli Science Corps* (Tel Aviv, 2015). For the early thoughts of Ben-Gurion and Shertok on the meaning of a Jewish state, see JAEJ, February 27, 1946, CZA.

21 Minutes of meeting, May 8, 1948, Z6/4/15, CZA; *The Letters of Martin Buber, A Life of Dialogue*, ed. N.N. Glatzer and P. Mendes-Flohr, trans. R. and C. Winston and H. Zohn (New York, 1991), 529; Dan Omer, *B'Ikvot Amud HaEsh* (Tel Aviv, 1981), 171; Katzki to Whiting, March 9, 1946, Box 66,483, UNRRA files, UN Archives; Rice report, March 1, 1946, JDC Archives; Joe Boxenbaum

interview with the author, August 10, 1976; Al Robison interview, February 16, 1977, Ben-Gurion Research Institute, Sdeh Boker; Al Robison MSS, AJHS; Rich Cohen, *The Fish That Ate the Whale: The Life and Times of America's Banana King* (New York, 2012), chap. 17; Nahum Bernstein interview with the author, Mar. 24, 1977; Anthony David, *The Sky is the Limit: Al Schwimmer, The Founder of Israel Aircraft Industries* (Tel Aviv, 2008), 60–95; Simon Rifkind interview with the author, July 25, 1974; Silver to Gurfein, December 18, 1947, 93.03/93/10, ISA; Tom Tugend, "Jerusalem Monument to Honor 1948 Volunteers," *Jerusalem Post*, December 11, 2017. *Mahal* was an acronym for the Hebrew *Mitnadvei Hutz La'Aretz* (Volunteers from Overseas).

22 Teddy Kollek with Amos Kollek, *For Jerusalem: A Life by Teddy Kollek* (Tel Aviv, 1978), 237; Robert Lacy, *Little Man, Meyer Lansky and the Gangster Life* (New York, 1991), 202–203; "A Message to Israel," May 27, 1948, Presbyterian Historical Association Archives, Philadelphia; Buxton to Byrnes, November 30, 1948, Byrnes MSS; Buxton to Ben-Horin, April 22, 1947, A300/16, CZA; Lash, *Eleanor: The Years Alone*, 136–137; January 26, 1949, *Parliamentary Debates, House of Commons*, 460:46, col. 954.

23 *Palestine Post*, February 19, 1946; Epstein to Stern, June 17, 1947, L35/3465; Shertok to Buxton, March 28, 1946, A245/505/2; both in CZA; La Guardia-Attlee interview, September 5, 1946, FO371/57769, PRO; Central Committees to UNSCOP Chairman, July 22, 1947, Box 8, UNSCOP MSS, UN Archives; Kenneth Harris, *Attlee* (London, 1982), 397; Aviva Halamish, "Illegal Immigration: Values, Myth and Reality," *Studies in Zionism* 9:1 (1988): 47–62; Moshe Pearlman, *Ben Gurion Looks Back* (New York, 1963), 98; *Palestine Post*, September 3, 1947. When Pius XII suggested to Bernstein that most of the Jewish DPs might be settled in the United States, which he thought was best equipped to absorb them, McNarney's advisor on Jewish affairs reminded him of the difficulties of acceptance, and also of the wish of most of them to go to Palestine. Responded the Pope: "Yes, I recognize that as their desire." Bernstein memo, September 11, 1946, Bernstein MSS. At the same time, in reply to a Jewish committee seeking his intercession with the Allies to grant their return to Palestine right after Rome's liberation, he said this: "Palestine's many-sided problems could not be the object of s separate examination or one-sided intervention by the Holy See." Dispatch, May 17, 1946, L35/80, CZA. A few months earlier, Pius had declared that the kibbutzim were "inconsistent with the family which is the foundation of organized society." Memo, June 6, 1946, 93.03/2272/2, ISA.

24 Smuts to delegation, April 14, 1947, 93.03/2268/26, ISA; Fabregat proposal, October 8, 1947, MG30, E77, vol. 2, PAC; *Ad Hoc* Committee, October 8,

1947, S25/5460; *S.A. Jewish Times*, Mar. 4, 1955, in A203/210; both in CZA. Fabregat's son later recalled his father, who has a street named after him in Ramat Gan, reading to him accounts about the Dreyfus Affair and having a broad grasp of Jewish history. *Jerusalem Post*, November 29, 2017.

25 Yaacov Ro'i, "Soviet-Israeli Relations, 1947–1954," in M. Confino and S. Shamir, eds., *The U.S.S.R. and the Middle East* (Jerusalem, 1973), 123–146; Gabriel Gorodetsky, "The Soviet Union's Role in the Creation of the State of Israel," *Journal of Israeli History* 22:1 (Spring 2003): 4–20; Thomas J. Hamilton, "Partition of Palestine," *Foreign Policy Reports* 23:23 (February 15, 1948): 286–295; Sharett letter to the editor, *Jerusalem Post*, July 20, 1961. For an early Arab protest over this linkage at the UN Preparatory Commission of January-February 1946, see Memo, April 3, 1946, C3/1760, CZA.

26 Rose, "A Squalid, Senseless War," 130–131. Eshkol would succeed Kaplan as Israel's Minister of Finance (1955–1963), then become its third Prime Minister until his death in 1969.

27 Memo, June 30, 1948, A246/191, CZA; Karsh, *Palestine Betrayed*, 115, and chaps. 6-9; Ghada Karmi, *A Palestinian Story* (London, 2002), 90–101; Sari Nusseibeh, *A Palestinian Life* (New York, 2007), 44–57; S. Sabag, ed., *B'Einei Oyev, Shlosha Pirsumim Araviyim Al Milhemet HaKomemiyut* (Tel Aviv, 1954); Yoav Gelber, "The Beginnings of the Palestininans' Mass-Flight," www.alisrael. com/1948 new; Yoav Gelber, "Druze and Jews in the War of 1948," *Middle Eastern Studies* 31:2 (1995): 229–252; Benny Morris, "Response to Finkelstein and Masalha, *Journal of Palestine Studies* 21:1 (Autumn 1991), 98–114. For an Israeli offer in July 1949 to take back some refugees, which the Arab states refused, see Benny Morris, *Righteous Victims, A History of the Zionist-Arab Conflict, 1881–1999* (New York, 1999), 258. In Safed, the Hagana made use of "the Davidka" (Little David), a homemade mortar which had first been employed in attacking the Abu Kabir neighborhood of Jaffa on March 13, 1948. Although inaccurate, it made a tremendous noise. The greatest victory attributed to the Davidka was the liberation by Palmah's Yiftah Brigade of the Citadel, a strongpoint in the center of Jaffa, on the night of May 9–10, 1948. A rumor quickly spread through the Arab ranks that the Jews had acquired an atom bomb, and the entire Arab community left that night.

28 Joshua Landis, "Syria and the Palestine War: fighting king Abdullah's 'Greater Syria Plan,'" in E.L. Rogan and A. Shlaim, eds. *The War for Palestine: Rewriting the History of 1948* (Cambridge, 2001), 178–195; Thomas Mayer, "Egypt's 1948 Invasion of Palestine," *Middle Eastern Studies* 22:1 (January 1986): 20–36; Walid Khalidi, "The Arab Perspective," in Louis and Stookey, *The End of the Palestine*

Mandate, 110–126, 131; Ilan Pappe, *The Making of the Arab-Israeli conflict, 1947–1951* (London, 1992), 71–75; Alec S. Kirkbride, *A Crackle of Thorns, Experiences in the Middle East* (London, 1956), 153–159; Bernhard G. Bechhoefer, "Unity and Division in the Arab Opposition to the Palestine Settlement," October 29, 1948, SD; Jewish Agency, *Supplementary Memorandum on Acts of Arab Aggression*, March 13, 1948; Jeffrey Herf, *Nazi Propaganda for the Arab World* (New Haven, CT, 2009), chap. 8. For continued discord within the Arab camp beyond Israel's creation, see Zvi Elpeleg, "Why Was 'Independent Palestine' Never Created in 1948?," *Jerusalem Quarterly* 50 (Spring 1989): 3–22.

29 Karsh, *Palestine Betrayed*, 106; Bevin to Damascus and other Arab capitals, May 6, 1948, FO371/68548, PRO; Rusk, *As I Saw It*, 149–150; WJC report, May 17, 1948, C6/116, CZA. Fifteen years before his autobiography was published, Rusk had related that Feisal expressed anxiety about an additional 25,000 (not 5,000)! Rusk interview with the author, Dec. 29, 1975.

30 Buxton to Ben-Horin, November 24, 1947, A300/16, CZA; Dec. 11, 1947, *Parliamentary Debates, House of Commons*, 445, col. 1223; Louis, "British Imperialism," 22. The British historian Arnold Toynbee strongly opposed the GA recommendation, telling an off-the-record meeting of the Council of Foreign Relations in April 1948 that partition, "the reductio ad absurdum" of applying the principle of "territorial nationality," should be discarded in favor of "a despotic government" over Palestine "by a third party" for "an indefinite time to come." He considered the United States to be the ideal choice, with a full halt to Jewish immigration at "some definite time in the future". Meeting, April 20, 1948, Record of Groups, Box XV-B, Council on Foreign Relations Archives, New York City. In the 1960s, he would call the Jews a "fossil of Syriac civilization" that was "fulfilled" in the advent of Christianity, since their continued survival contradicted his volumes on the rise and fall of civilizations, and he bitterly criticized the State of Israel as an example of the vicious disease of nationalism, bringing Jews to commit atrocities upon Arabs in some sense morally equivalent to the atrocities committed upon them.

31 Herbert Friedman, *Roots of the Future* (Jerusalem, 1999), 114–115; Emanuel Neumann interview with Yehuda Bauer, June 21, 1967, Neumann MSS; Gladwyn Jebb, *The Memoirs of Lord Gladwyn* (New York, 1970), 204; Rose, "A Squalid, Senseless War," 125. Dalton informed the Commons how the U.S. loan helped HMG's economic recovery. Dalton Memo, November 10, 1947, Box 5, Dean Acheson MSS, HSTL. When asked by New York Congressman Arthur Klein about Arab lobbying, Truman insisted that the Jewish effort in this regard was unparalleled, that he had no objection to lobbing by either side,

"but, in neither case, does it affect my decisions on judgment." Truman to Klein, May 5, 1948, OF204, HSTL.

32 Bullock, *Bevin*, 167, 181–182; Wm. Roger Louis, "British Imperialism and the End of the Palestine Mandate," in Louis and Stookey, *The End of the Palestine Mandate*, 6; Lawford to Tory, February 2, 1946, CO733/463/75872/138; Wilkinson memo, September 30, 1947, FO371/61956; May 16, 1945, CAB 95/15; all in PRO; McNeil statement, May 23, 1946, Z4/30617,CZA; P (Jon Kimche) letter, February 1, 1946, S25/8004, CZA. French intelligence reported to Hagana counterparts additional steps taken by Clayton to strengthen Britain's hold in the region. Meir Zamir, "The Secret 1947–1948 War between the British and French Intelligence Over the Birth of the State of Israel," *HaAretz*, September 19, 2004. For France's overall pro-Zionist policy, rooted in hostility for HMG's forcing it out of Syria and Lebanon, see James Barr, *A Line in the Sand* (New York, 2012), chaps. 25–27.

33 Austin to Marshall, April 27, 1948, McClintock-2, SD; Hadara Lazar, *Out of Palestine*, 141–142; Frankfurter Diaries, November 18, 1947.

34 Evatt to Australian Delegation, April 26, 1948, Evatt MSS; Pearson to Robertson, Apr. 21, 1948, MG 26, N1, vol. 64, PAC; Report, April 20, 1948, Robison MSS; Secretariat meeting, April 22, 1948, DAG 1/1.1.3, Box 1, UN Archives; FO to New York, April 22, 1948; Bevin memo, Apr. 28, 1948; both in FO800/487, PRO; Austin to Marshall, April 29, 1948, Rusk-3, SD.

35 Senator to Magnes, May 10, 1948, 350/7, Martin Buber MSS, Jewish National Library, Jerusalem; Robert Kennedy, "Jews Have Fine Fighting Force, Make Up for Lack of Arms with Undying Spirit, Unparalleled Courage," *Boston Post*, June 4, 1948; Barker to Antonius, December 6, 1947, P867/9, ISA; Farran to Leftwich, April 17, 1950, A330/760, CZA; Hurweitz, *The Struggle for Palestine*, 281. Sneh would resign from the Jewish Agency Executive at the end of 1947 on ideological grounds, and join the newly formed Mapam (the merger in the United Workers' Party of HaShomer HaTsa'ir and Ahdut HaAvoda-Poalei Zion) as part of its more extreme laborite left wing. Moshe Sneh, *Aharit K'Reishit*, ed. Y. Tsaban, (Tel Aviv, 1982), 94–104.

36 George Weidenfeld, *Remembering My Good Friends, an Autobiography* (New York, 1994), 202; Samuel Shihor, *The Last Days of Chaim Weizmann*, J. Meltzer, trans. (New York, 1960), 86–91; Shadmi to Shaul (Avigur), August 23, 1966, 80/168/2, HA.

37 Amicam Nachmani, *Great Power Discord in Palestine* (London, 1987), ix; Gurney Diary, Mar. 25, 1948; "Last Days of the Mandate"; both in Gurney MSS; Morris, *1948*, 38. For a private venting of frustration at this time by British officialdom,

see "Now, UNO!" by Trafford Smith, head of the Colonial Office's Palestine section who then served on the British delegation at the UN. I am grateful to Mr. Smith for giving me this poem, the lines of which are to be found in the Appendix.

38 Truman to George, October 17, 1946, OF204 Misc., HSTL.

39 R.H. Farrell, ed., *Dear Bess, The Letters from Harry to Bess Truman, 1910–1959* (New York, 1983), 537; May 16, 1948, Lowenthal diary; Epstein to Welles, September 23, 1946 (attaching Pauley report), L35/97, CZA; Audio MP2002-304, HSTL; Welles to Silver, June 18, 1949, Neuman MSS. For Jacobson's immediate intervention after May 14, 1948, see Box 2140, Eddie Jacobson files, AJA. Goldmann favored postponing the state's declaration for two weeks in order to consult with Arab leaders who favored Jewish sovereignty, but who were "completely isolated," in order "to avoid unnecessary war." Goldmann to Neumann, November 23, 1966, Joseph Schechtman MSS, ZA (now in CZA). A scathing cartoon by Herblock soon after the State Department reversal in March 1948 has an American spokesman at the UN standing on his head while explaining U.S. policy, bewildered delegates looking on, under the caption "We Want to Make Our Position Perfectly Clear." *Washington Post*, April 14, 1948.

40 Hal Lehrman, "What U.S. Support Means," *Commentary* 5 (June 1948): 485–492; Buxton to Ben-Horin, November 24, 1947, A300/16, CZA; Matthew Connelly interview with Jeremy N. Hess, November 30, 1967, HSTL; Mann to Magnes, April 1, 1948, 21/9, Marshall MSS; Linton, "Memories of 1948"; Arthur Krock, *Memoirs: Sixty Years on the Firing Line* (New York, 1968), 214; Frank-Crum interview, July 14, 1949, Gerold Frank MSS; Truman message to B'nai Brith Jacobson Memorial, Tel Aviv, May 22, 1965, A.J. Granoff MSS. (courtesy of Leib Granoff); Granoff–Fuchs interview, April 9, 1969; Oscar Chapman interview with Jerry N. Hess, Apr. 21, 1972; both in HSTL. Nahum Bernstein revealed years later that, arranging for microphones to be planted in the British limousine going daily to Lake Success and in the Hotel McAlpin suite of Fares al-Khoury, he passed on information to Feinberg for Truman's knowledge about uncertain delegations in order "to get these people back in line" prior to the crucial UN vote in November 1947. Bernstein interview with the author, March 24, 1977. The debate up to this point on Truman's motivations can be followed by the order of publication of the following: John Snetsinger, *Truman, the Jewish Vote and the Creation of Israel* (Stanford, 1974); Donovan, *Conflict and Crisis*; Even Wilson, *Decision on Palestine* (Stanford, 1979); Ganin, *Truman, American Jewry and Israel*; Cohen, *Truman and the Jews*; Clifford, *Counsel to the President*; McCullough, *Truman*; Warren Bass, *Support any Friend? Kennedy's Middle East and the Making of the U.S.-Israel Alliance*

(New York, 2003); Michael Ottolenghi, "Harry Truman's Recognition of Israel," *Historical Journal* 47:4 (2004): 963–988; Allis Radosh and Ronald Radosh, *A Safe Haven: Harry S. Truman and the Founding of Israel* (New York, 2009). The first act to ease restrictive American immigration quotas at the time, not passed until June 1948, actually discriminated against East European Jews and favored those who had collaborated with Hitler. Only in 1950, after most of the survivors had migrated to Israel, did a revised bill eliminate the antisemitic features of the earlier Congressional legislation. Leonard Dinnerstein, *America and the Survivors of the Holocaust* (New York, 1982), chaps. 5–9.

41 Monty Noam Penkower, "The Venting of Presidential Spleen: Harry S. Truman's Jewish Problem," *Jewish Quarterly Review* 94:4 (Fall 2004), 622–624; Audio MP2002-304 and 307, both in HSTL; Harry Truman's Favorite Poem, Harry S. Truman Presidential Library & Museum, www.trumanlibrary.org/kids/poem.htm; SC-12465, AJA. Josef Cohn later heard from Crum that Truman remarked to the latter he was sorry that Weizmann at the time had not asked him for $200 million. Cohn memoir, "Report on Dr. Weizmann's Visit to the U.S.A.," WA. For Truman's laudatory remarks about the Jewish state and Weizmann at the 1952 Jewish National Fund dinner to mark the establishment of Kfar Truman in central Israel, see *JTA*, May 28, 1952. Asked by Israel Defense Forces chief of staff Moshe Dayan for some advice, Truman replied: "Don't ever trust those goddam sons of bitches in the State Department." Chaim Herzog, *Living History* (New York, 1996), 126.

42 Radosh and Radosh, *A Safe Haven*, 344–347; Truman to Roosevelt, Sept. 18, 1948, Box 4560, E. Roosevelt MSS. According to the biblical texts of *Ezra* and *Nehemia*, in 538 BCE Cyrus the Great permitted the Jews of Babylon, exiled from Eretz Israel by Nebuchadnezar II after he had destroyed the First Temple in 586 BCE, to return to Jerusalem and build the Temple anew. The very last two sentences in *Chronicles 2*, closing the Hebrew Masoretic text, cite Cyrus's fulfilling of Jeremiah's prophecy of return for "building Him a House in Jerusalem."

43 M. Lowenthal, ed. and trans., *The Diaries of Theodor Herzl* (New York, 1962), 223–234; Cohen, *Truman and Israel*, 280; Radosh and Radosh, *A Safe Haven*, 353. Crossman favored a Jewish state within, ultimately, a Greater Syrian Federation in which the Jews would be regarded as "fellow-members of a single Middle Eastern community." R. H. S. Crossman, "The Case for Partition," *New Statesman and Nation*, September 14, 1946.

44 Eyal Benvenisti, *The International Law of Occupation* (Princeton, NJ, 2004), 108; Hawkins to Marshall, September 27, 1947, 501.BB Palestine/9-2747, SD; Musa Alami, "The Lesson of Palestine," *Middle East Journal* 3:4

(October 1949): 373–405; Karsh, *Palestine Betrayed*, 210, 264–267; Morris, *1948*, 412–415; "The Forgotten Refugees," www.davidproject.org. Lyn Julius, *Uprooted* (London, 2018) claims that more than 850,000 Jews from the Arab countries and North Africa were displaced, some 650,000 settling in Israel. The UN Relief and Works Agency, continuing to maintain that *all* descendants of the Palestinian refugees also qualify for refugee status, lists their current number at more than 5.5 million. Israela Oron, "The Palestinian Refugees," *INSS Insight* 1018, Tel Aviv University, February 18, 2018.

45 Rusk interview with the author, December 29, 1975; Rusk, *As I Saw It*, 153. Israel's wars and other conflicts with her Arab neighbors include the War of Independence (November 1947–July 1949); Reprisal operations (1950s-1960s) in response to *fedayeen* incursions from Syria, Egypt, and Jordan; Suez Crisis (October 1956); Six-Day War (June 1967); War of Attrition (1967–1970); Yom Kippur War (October 1973); Palestinian insurgency in South Lebanon (1971–1982); Lebanon War (1982); South Lebanon conflict (1985–2000); First *Intifada* (1987–1993); Second *Intifada* (2000–2005); Second Lebanon War (summer 2006); Gaza War (December 2008–January 2009); Operation Pillar of Defense (November 2012); Operation Protective Edge (July-Aug. 2014).

46 Penkower, *Palestine in Turmoil*; Penkower, *Decision on Palestine Deferred*; Penkower, *The Jews Were Expendable*; Solly Ganor, "The Fabulous Survivor's Passover Haggadah," *ISRAPUNDIT*, April 20, 2011; Sapir report, May 25, 1948, G-Sh'eirit HaPleita, Box 18/109, YIVO Archives; https://leonardbernstein.com/about/conductor/historic-concerts/beersheba-1948; Michael B. Oren, *Ally: My Journey Across the American-Israeli Divide* (New York, 2015), 135.

47 For the opposing views of Herzl and Ahad Ha'Am as to the *raison d'être* of Zionism, see Monty Noam Penkower, *The Emergence of Zionist Thought* (New York, 1991), chaps. 5–6.

48 Gruber, *Exodus 1947*, 120; Hillel Goldberg, *The Jewish Connection* (New York, 1976), 12.

49 *Minhelet Ha'Am, Ginzakh HaMedina*, May 12, 1948 (Jerusalem, 1978), 37–119; Monty Noam Penkower, "The Kishinev Pogrom of 1903," in Monty Noam Penkower, *Twentieth Century Jews, Forging Identity in the Land of Promise and in the Promised Land* (Brighton, MA, 2010), 1–42; Abba Eban, *My Country, The Story of Modern Israel* (New York, 1972), 23. For the drafting of the Israeli Declaration of Independence, see 999/20/25, 999/6/44, and 41.0/124/23; all in ISA; May 13, 1948, *Minhelet Ha'Am*, 120–130.

Bibliography

Archives

American Council for Judaism Archives, University of Wisconsin Library, Madison, WI.

American Jewish Archives, Cincinnati, OH:

      Files: Anglo-American Committee on Palestine; Billikopf, Jacob; Holtzman, Fanny; Jacobson, Eddie; Marshall, James; SC-2837; SC-6610; SC-11769; SC-12465; SC-14070; SC-3124.

American Jewish Committee Archives, New York City:

      Files: Correspondents files; Foreign Countries—Palestine; Jewish Agency; Palestine—US; Paris—Palestine; Proskauer, Joseph MSS; Steering Committee minutes.

American Jewish Historical Society, Waltham, MA (now in the Center for Jewish History, New York City):

      Files: Stone, Dewey MSS; Hadassah, Box 21; Lipsky, Louis MSS; Robison, Al MSS; Robison, Anne MSS; Wise, Stephen MSS.

American Jewish Joint Distribution Committee Archives, New York City:

      Files: General-Jewish Agency 1945–1946; Germany DPs 1946.

Anglo-Jewish Association Archives, Special Collections, Hartley Library, University of Southampton, Great Britain.

Armour, Norman MSS, Dept. of Rare Book and Manuscript Collections, Seeley G. Mudd Manuscript Library, Princeton University, Princeton, NJ.

Attlee, Clement MSS.; Hull University, England.

Baerwald, Paul MSS, Rare Books and Manuscript Collections, Columbia University, New York City.

Begin, Menahem Archives. Menaham Begin Heritage Center, Jerusalem.

      Files: IR-95; IR-032; IR-060; IR-062; IR-082; IR-085; IR-105; Torczyner, Jacques MSS.

Ben-Gurion, David. Archives, Sdeh Boker, Israel:

Files: Correspondence; Diaries; Memoranda.

Bernstein, Philip MSS, Rochester, New York.

Board of Deputies of British Jews Archives, London:

Files: C14/20-2, C14/29-2, C14/31; C14/32-1; Palestine Committee.

Buber, Martin MSS, National Library of Israel, Jerusalem.

Byrnes, James MSS, Clemson University, Clemson, SC.

Celler, Emanuel MSS, Library of Congress, Washington, D.C.

Central Archives for the History of the Jewish People, Jerusalem:

Files: Klausner, Abraham MSS; Magnes, Judah MSS.

Central Zionist Archives (hereafter CZA), Jerusalem:

Files: Agron, Gershon MSS; "Americans for Hagana"—Israel Speaks; Americans for Hagana Benjamin MSS; Auster, Daniel MSS; Ben-Horin, Eliahu MSS; Ben-Zvi, Yitshak MSS; Bentwich, Norman MSS; Boukstein, Maurice (Moshe) MSS; Eliash, Mordekhai MSS; Elyashar, Eliyahu MSS; Friedenwald, Harry MSS; General Council (Va'ad HaLeumi); Great Britain; Hodess, Jacob MSS; Jewish Agency Executive Jerusalem, Minutes, 1945–1948; Jewish Agency Executive London, Minutes, 1945–1948; Jewish Agency Jerusalem, Political Department; Jewish Agency Office London; Jewish Agency Office Washington, D.C.; Jewish Agency US; Leftwich, Joseph MSS; Locker, Berl MSS; Lisicky, Karel MSS; Montor, Henry MSS; Namier, L. MSS; Office of David Ben-Gurion; Office of Eliezer Kaplan; Office of Nahum Goldman; Office of Yitshak Gruenbaum; Sacher, Harry MSS; Sasson, Eliyahu MSS; Sharett, Moshe MSS; Shultz, Lillie MSS; Wahl, David MSS; World Jewish Congress Geneva; World Jewish Congress Israel; World Jewish Congress London; Yahil, Haim MSS; Yudelevitz, David MSS; Zionist Organization Agricultural Settlement Dept.; Zionist Organization Immigration Dept.

Corrigan, Frank MSS, Franklin D. Roosevelt Presidential Library, Hyde Park, NY.

Council on Foreign Relations Archives, Records of Meetings, New York City.

Creech Jones, Arthur MSS, Rhodes House, University of Oxford, Oxford, England.

Crossman, Richard. Diary and Correspondence. Middle East Centre, St. Anthony's College, Oxford, England.

Cunningham, Alan. Correspondence. Middle East Centre, St. Anthony's College, Oxford, England

Dewey, Thomas MSS, University of Rochester Library, Rochester, New York.

Dulles, John Foster MSS, Rare Books and Special Collections, Seeley G. Mudd Manuscript Library, Princeton University, Princeton, NJ.

Eddy, William MSS, Rare Books and Special Collections, Seeley G. Mudd Manuscript Library, Princeton University, Princeton, NJ.

Eichelberger, Clark MSS, Manuscripts and Archives Division, New York Public Library, New York City.

Eisenhower, Dwight D. MSS, Dwight D. Eisenhower Presidential Library, Abilene, KS.

Evatt, H. V. MSS, Flanders University, Adelaide, Australia.

Fischer, Louis MSS, Rare Books and Special Collections, Seeley G. Mudd Manuscript Library, Princeton University, Princeton, NJ.

Forrestal, James MSS, Rare Books and Special Collections, Seeley G. Mudd Manuscript Library, Princeton University, Princeton, NJ.

Frank, Gerold MSS, Manuscripts and Archives Division, New York Public Library, New York City.

Frank Jerome, Jerome MSS, Sterling Library, Yale University, New Haven, CT.

Frankfurter, Felix MSS, Library of Congress, Washington, D.C.

Gildersleeve, Virginia MSS, Rare Book and Manuscript Library, Butler Library, Columbia University, New York City.

Goldman. Robert MSS, American Jewish Archives, Cincinnati, OH.

Grew, Joseph MSS, Diary, Houghton Library, Harvard University, Cambridge, MA.

Gurney, Henry. Diary, Middle East Center, St. Anthony College, Oxford University, Oxford, England.

Hadassah Archives, New York City.

      Files: National Board minutes; Schoolman, Bertha MSS; US Depts.; Youth Aliya.

Hagana Archives, Tel Aviv.

HaShomer HaTsa'ir Archives, Givat Haviva, Israel.

Harrison, Earl. Diary, RG-10.088, U.S. Holocaust Memorial Museum, Washington, D.C.

Hecht, Reuven MSS, Haifa (courtesy of R. Hecht).

Herzog, Yitshak MSS, Heikhal Shlomo, Jerusalem.

Histadrut Archives, Makhon Lavon, Tel Aviv.

Institute of Jewish Affairs MSS, Special Collections, Hartley Library, University of Southampton, England.

International Committee of the Red Cross Archives, Geneva.

Israel State Archives, Jerusalem.

Jabotinsky Archives, Tel Aviv.

Jewish Welfare Board Archives, New York City.

Kennedy, John F. Presidential Library, Boston:

      Files: Powers, David F. Personal Papers; 1939, Presidential Papers, Office Files, Special Events Through the Years.

Kirchwey, Freda MSS, Radcliffe College, Cambridge, MA.

Klarman, Yosef MSS, Jabotinsky Archives, Tel Aviv.

Klein, Julius MSS, Jewish War Veterans Archives, Washington, D.C.

Krock, Arthur MSS, Rare Books and Special Collections, Seeley G. Mudd Library, Princeton University Library, Princeton, NJ.

Labor Party MSS, Transport House, London.

      Files: International Department; Laski, Harold MSS.

Laski, Harold MSS, Archives, Hull History Centre, Hull University, Hull, England.

Lazaron, Morris MSS, American Council for Judaism Archives, University of Wisconsin Library, Madison, WI.

Lehman, Herbert MSS, Herbert Lehman Collections, Rare Book and Manuscript Library, Butler Library, Columbia University, New York City.

Lerner, Max MSS, Sterling Library, Yale University, New Haven, CT.

Lowenthal, Max. Diary, 1948, Abraham Feinberg MSS, 1885/4–P, Israel State Archives, Jerusalem.

MacMichael, Harold MSS, Middle East Centre, St. Anthony's College, Oxford, England.

Magnes, Judah MSS, National Library of Israel, Jerusalem.

McDonald, James G. MSS, Diary and Correspondence. Herbert H. Lehman Collections, Rare Book and Manuscript Library, Butler Library, Columbia University, New York City.

Manson, Harold MSS, Abba Hillel Silver Archives, The Temple, Cleveland, OH.

Mapai MSS, Beit Berl, Kfar Sabba, Israel.

Morgenthau, Jr., Henry. Diaries and Presidential Diaries, Franklin D. Roosevelt Presidential Library, Hyde Park, New York.

Mowshowitz, David MSS, YIVO Archives, Center for Jewish History, New York City.

National Council of Jewish Women MSS, New York City.

Neumann, Emanuel MSS, New York City (courtesy of Emanuel Neumann).

O'Dwyer, Paul MSS, Special Collections, Jewish Theological Seminary Library, New York City.

Palestine Statehood Committee files, Sterling Library, Yale University, New Haven, CT.

Phillips, William. Diary and Correspondence. Houghton Library, Harvard Library, Harvard University, Cambridge, MA.

Public Archives of Canada. Ottawa, Canada.

Presbyterian Historical Association, Philadelphia, PA.

Public Record Office, Kew, England.
> Files: Cabinet papers: 66; 95; 125; 127; 128; 129; 195; Colonial Office papers: 537; 733; Foreign Office papers: 371; 800; Premier: 4 and 8; War Office: 32.

Maimon, Yehuda Leib MSS, Religious Zionism Archives, Mosad HaRav Kook, Jerusalem.

Rifkind, Simon MSS, New York City (courtesy of Simon Rifkind),

Robison, Anne MSS, (courtesy of Anne Robison, now in the American Jewish Historical Society, Center for Jewish History, New York City).

Roosevelt, Eleanor MSS, Franklin D. Roosevelt Presidential Library, Hyde Park, NY.

Rosenheim, Jacob MSS, Agudath Israel of America Archives, New York City:
> Files: AIWO London 1947; Eretz Israel III; Schenkolewski, M. files.

Rosenman, Samuel MSS, Franklin D. Roosevelt Presidential Library, Hyde Park, NY.

Sayre, Francis MSS, Library of Congress, Washington, D.C.

Schulson, Hyman A. MSS, Manuscripts and Archives Division, New York Public Library, New York City.

Sh'eirit HaPleita MSS, YIVO Archives, Center for Jewish History, New York City.

Silver, Abba Hillel MSS, The Temple, Cleveland, OH.

Simon, Ernst MSS, National Library of Israel, Jerusalem.

Smith, Trafford MSS (courtesy of Trafford Smith, now at the Middle East Centre, St. Anthony's College, Oxford, England).

Stansgate MSS, House of Lords Archives, London.

Stimson, Henry L. Diaries, Sterling Library, Yale University, New Haven, CT.

Sulzberger, Arthur Hays MSS, New York Times Archives (currently in the New York Public Library, New York City):
> Files: Bevin; Churchill; Germany; Palestine and Zionism.

Taft, Robert A. MSS, Library of Congress, Washington, D.C.

Taylor, Myron MSS, Franklin D. Roosevelt Presidential Library, Hyde Park, NY.

Truman, Harry S. Presidential Library, Independence, MO:

> Files: Acheson, Dean MSS; Audio MP2002-55, 304, and 307; Ayers, Eben Diary; Cabinet meeting, January 16, 1948; Clayton, William L. MSS; Clifford, Clark MSS; Confidential File, State Department file, Correspondence File Palestine; Connelly, Matt files; Daniels, Joseph MSS; Diary March 1948; Elsey, George MSS; Grady, Henry MSS, Granoff, A. J. Oral History; Harry S. Truman Post-Presidential Papers, Memoirs File, Diaries; Jacobson, Eddie Diary; OF 39 White House Central Files; OF 204 misc.; OF 204-B; OF 204-D misc., State of Israel; OF 204 Palestine; Palestine-Jewish Immigration; President's Secretary's Files (PSF): 82; 156, 157, 159, 160, 184, 186, 187, 194; PSF Daily Sheets 88; PSF Foreign Affairs, Palestine 1948–1952; PSF General; PSF-GF 117; PSF Palestine 1945–1947; PSF Personal File Eleanor Roosevelt; Senatorial and Vice-Presidential File 71; Ross, Charles MSS; Truman Diary; Truman to Crum, May 15, 1948, Box 776; Truman to Sister, March 21, 1948, Truman Papers Pertaining to Family, Business, and Personal Affairs, Family Correspondence file.

Union of American Hebrew Congregations Archives, New York City.

United Jewish Appeal Archives, New York City.

United Nations Archives, New York City:

> Files: Hoo, Victor MSS; UNRRA; United Nations Special Committee on Palestine; A/AC.21.7; A/PV 207, May 11, 1949, General Assembly; US/A/AC.14/6 and 40.

United States State Department Records, National Archives, Suitland, MD.:

> Files: Anglo-American Committee of Inquiry on Palestine; McClintock, Robert MSS; Policy Planning Staff Studies; Rusk, Dean MSS; 501/BB Palestine; 800.4016, DP; 840.48 Refugees; 890F; 867N.01.

United States Navy and War Department Records National Archives, Suitland, MD:

> Files: Army Staff; Joint Chiefs of Staff U.S.; Navy Department General Records; Office of Strategic Services; War Department General and Special Staffs.

Vandenberg, Arthur H. MSS, Bentley Historical Library, University of Michigan, Ann Arbor.

Wagner, Robert MSS, Georgetown University, Washington, D.C.

War Refugee Board MSS, Franklin D. Roosevelt Presidential Library, Hyde Park, NY.

Weizmann, Chaim. Archives, Rehovot, Israel.

Welles, Sumner MSS, Franklin D. Roosevelt Presidential Library, Hyde Park, NY.

Weltsch, Robert MSS, Leo Baeck Archives, Center for Jewish History, New York City.World Agudath Israel Organization Archives, Jerusalem.

World Jewish Congress Archives, London.

World Jewish Congress Archives, New York City (now at the American Jewish Archives, Cincinnati, OH).

Yale, William MSS, Mugar Memorial Library Special Collections, Boston University, Boston, MA.

Zionist Archives, New York (now at the CZA):

Files: Akzin, Benjamin, confidential files; American Council for Judaism; American Zionist Emergency Council minutes; AZEC Confidential Files; Cabinet Committee CF; Henderson Confidential; Jewish Agency Confidential; Political Files–CF; President's File; Szold, Robert; State Dept.–CF; UN—confidential; UN 1946–1948; Washington office—CF; ZOA Executive minutes.

Books

Abu-Lughod, Ibrahim, ed. *The Transformation of Palestine, Essays on the Origin and Development of the Arab-Israeli Conflict.* Evanston, 1971.

Abzug, Robert H. *Inside the Vicious Heart, Americans and the Liberation of Nazi Concentration Camps.* New York, 1985.

Acheson, Dean. *Present at the Creation: My Years in the State Department.* New York, 1969.

———. *Sketches from Life of Men I Have Known.* London, 1961.

Adler, Frank J. *Roots in a Moving Stream.* Kansas City, MO, 1972.

Agron, Gershon. *Asir HaNe'emanut.* Tel Aviv, 1964.

Ajami, Fouad. *The Dream Palace of the Arabs, A Generation's Odyssey.* New York, 1999 ed.

Alterman, Natan. *HaTur HaShvi'i,* vol. 1. Tel Aviv, 1948.

———. *HaTur HaShvi'i,* vol. 2. Tel Aviv, 1954.

Alpern, Sara. *Freda Kirchwey, A Woman of The Nation.* Cambridge, MA, 1987.

Among the Survivors of the Holocaust, 1945: The Landsberg DP Camp Letters of Major Irving Heymont, United States Army. Cincinnati, 1982.

Andrew, Christopher M. *In Defence of the Realm: The Authorized History of MI5.* London, 2009.

Anglo-American Committee of Inquiry, Report to the United States Government and His Majesty's Government in the United Kingdom. Washington, D.C., 1946.

Atrocities and Other Conditions in Concentration Camps in Germany. Washington, D.C., 1945.

Augustin, Andreas. *The Mena House Treasury: Secrets of a Very Special Hotel.* 2007.

Attlee, Clement. *As it Happened.* Kingswood, 1954.

Avidar, Yosef. *BaDerekh LeTsahal, Zikhronot.* Tel Aviv, 1977 ed.

Avizohar, Meir, ed. *Akhshav O LeOlam Lo,* 2 vols. Beit Berl, 1989.

Avriel, Ehud. *Open the Gates!* New York, 1975.

Azcárate y Florez, Pablo de. *Mission in Palestine, 1948–1952.* Washington, D.C., 1966.

A State is Born, The 14th of May 1948. M. Naor, ed. (Ramat Gan, 1996).

Bachrach, Uriel. *The Power of Knowledge, Hemed: The Israeli Science Corps.* Tel Aviv, 2015.

Bar-Zohar, Michael. *Ben-Gurion, A Biography.* New York, 1978.

Barr, James. *A Line in the Sand, The Anglo-French Struggle for the Middle East.* New York, 2012.

Barros, James. *Trygve Lie and the Cold War.* DeKalb, IL, 1989.

Bashan, Raphael. *Sihot Hulin Shel Weizmann.* Jerusalem, 1963.

Bass, Warren. *Support any Friend? Kennedy's Middle East and the Making of the U.S.—Israel Alliance.* New York, 2003.

Bauer, Yehuda. *Flight and Rescue, Brichah*. New York, 1970.

Begin, Menachem. *The Revolt*. Los Angeles, CA, 1972 ed.Bell, J. Boyer. *Terror Out of Zion*. New York, 1977.

Ben-Dror, Elad. *HaMetavekh, Ralph Bunche V'HaSikhsukh HaAravi-Yisraeli 1947–1949*. Jerusalem, 2012.

Ben-Gurion, David. *Likrat Ketz HaMandat*. Tel Aviv, 1993.

———. *Pa'amei Medina*. Edited by M. Avizohar. Tel Aviv, 1993.

———. *Rebirth and Destiny of Israel*. Edited and translated by M. Nurock. New York, 1954.

———. *Yoman HaMilhama*, vol. 1. Edited by G. Rivlin and E. Oren. Tel Aviv, 1982.

Ben-Tov, Mordekhai. *Yamim Mesaprim, Zikhronot MeiHamei'a HaMakhra'at*. Tel Aviv, 1984.

Bendersky, Joseph W. *The "Jewish Threat," Anti-Semitic Politics of the U.S. Army*. New York, 2000.

Benson, Michael T. *Harry S. Truman and the Founding of Israel*. Westport, CT, 1997.

Bentsar, Eitan, and Boris Kolokolov, eds. *Documents on Israeli-Soviet Relations, 1941–1953*, vol. 1. London, 2000.

Bentwich, Norman and Helen. *Mandate Memories, 1918–1948*. London, 1965.

Benvenisti, Eyal. *The International Law of Occupation*. Princeton, OH, 2004.

Beschloss, Michael R. *The Conquerors: Roosevelt, Truman and the Destruction of Hitler's Germany, 1941–1945*. New York, 2002.

Berkman, Ted. *The Lady and the Law, The Remarkable Life of Fanny Holtzman*. New York 1976.

Berle, Jr., Adolf A. *Navigating the Rapids, 1918–1971*. Edited by B. B. Berle and T. B. Jacobs,. New York, 1973.

Berlin, Isaiah. *Enlightening Letters 1946–1960*. Edited by H. Hardy and J. Holmes. London, 2009.

Bernadotte, Folke. *To Jerusalem*. London, 1951.

Bethell, Nicholas. *The Palestine Triangle: The Struggle for the Holy Land, 1935–1948*. New York, 1979.

Bercuson, David J. *Canada and the Birth of Israel, A Study in Canadian Foreign Policy* (Toronto, 1985).

Bilby, Kenneth W. *New Star in the Near East*. New York, 1951.

Blumenson, Martin. *The Patton Papers, 1940–1945*. New York, 1966 ed.

Bosworth, Patricia. *Anything Your Little Heart Desires*. New York, 1997.

Bogner, Nahum. *Eee HaGeirush, Mahanot HaMa'apilim B'Kafrisin*, 1946-1948 (Tel Aviv, 1991).

Brands, H.W. *Inside the Cold War, Loy Henderson and the Rise of the American Empire 1918–1961*. New York, 1991.

Brendon, Piers. *The Decline and Fall of the British Empire, 1781–1997*. London, 2007.

Brener, Michal. *After the Holocaust, Rebuilding Jewish Lives in Postwar Germany*. Translated by B. Harshav. Princeton, 1997.

Bridgman, Jon. *The End of the Holocaust, The Liberation of the Camps*. London, 1990.

Bronson, Rachel. *Thicker Than Oil: America's Uneasy Partnership with Saudi Arabia*. Oxford, 2006.

Bullock, Alan. *Ernest Bevin, Foreign Secretary, 1945–1951*. Oxford, 1985.

Burton, Philip. *A Captain's Mandate, Palestine: 1946–1948*. London, 1996.

Cadogan, Alexander. *Diaries of Sir Alexander Cadogan, 1938–1945*. Edited by D. Dilks. London, 1971.

Cailingold, Asher. *An Unlikely Heroine, Esther's Calingold's Fight for Jerusalem*. London, 2000.

Carlebach, Azriel. *Va'adat HaHakira HaAnglo-Amerikanit L'Inyanei Eretz-Yisrael*, vol. 1. Tel Aviv, 1946.

Cesarani, David. *Major Farran's Hat, The Untold Story of the Struggle to Establish the Jewish State*. Cambridge, Mass., 2009.

Chandler, Jr., Alfred D., et al., eds. *The Papers of Dwight David Eisenhower, The War Years*, vol. 4. Baltimore, MD, 1970.

Chandler, Jr., Alfred D., and Louis Galambos, eds. *The Papers of Dwight David Eisenhower: Occupation, 1945*, vol. 6. Baltimore, MD, 1978.

Charters, David A. *The British Army and the Jewish Insurgency in Palestine, 1945–1947*. London, 1989.

Childs, J. Rives. *Foreign Service Farewell, My Years in the Near East*. Charlottesville, 1969.

Clifford, Clark, with Richard Holbrook. *Counsel to the President, A Memoir*. New York, 1991.

Clark, Thurston. *By Blood and Fire: The Attack on the King David Hotel*. New York, 1981.

Cohen, Michael. *Palestine and the Great Powers, 1945–1948*. Princeton, 1986.

———. *Truman and Israel*. Berkeley, 1990.

Cohen, Rich. *The Fish That Ate the Whale: The Life and Times of America's Banana King*. New York, 2012.

Collins, Larry, and Dominique Lapierre. *O Jerusalem!* New York, 1972.

Colville, John. The *Fringes of Power, 10 Downing Street Diaries 1939–1955*. New York, 1985.

Congressional Record, 76th Congress. *First session, 1939, vol. 84, pt. 13*.

Cooper, Duff. *The Duff Cooper Diaries*. Edited by J. J. Norwich. London, 2005.

Cordier, AndrewW., and Wilder Foote, eds. *Public Papers of the Secretaries-General of the United Nations, 1, Trygve Lie, 1946–1953*. New York, 1969.

Corman, Ruth. *Unexpected Israel*. Jerusalem, 2016.

Crossman, Richard. *Palestine Mission: A Personal Record*. New York, 1947.

———, and Michael Foot. *A Palestine Munich?* London, 1946.

———, Michael Foot, and Ian Mikardo. *Keep Left*. London, 1947.

Crum, Bartley C. *Behind the Silken Curtain*. New York, 1947.

Dalton, Hugh. *High Time and After, Memoirs 1945–1960*. London, 1962.

David, Anthony. *The Sky is the Limit: Al Schwimmer, The Founder of Israel Aircraft Industries*. Tel Aviv, 2008.

Degani, Nissan. *Exodus Meshaderet* (Tel Aviv, 1994).

Dinnerstein, Leonard. *America and the Survivors of the Holocaust*. New York, 1982.

Dixon, Piers. *Double Diplomat*. London, 1968.

Donovan, Robert J. *Conflict and Crisis*. New York, 1977.

Doran, Michael. *Pan-Arabism Before Nasser, Egyptian Power Politics and the Palestine Question.* New York, 1999.

Eban, Abba. *An Autobiography.* New York, 1977.

————. *My Country, The Story of Modern Israel.* New York, 1972.

————. *Personal Witness: Israel Through My Eyes.* New York, 1992.

Eban, Suzy. *A Sense of Purpose, Recollections.* London, 2008.

Eilat, Eliahu. *HaMa'avak Al HaMedina,* vol. 1. Tel Aviv, 1979.

————. *HaMa'avak Al HaMedina,* vol. 2 Tel Aviv, 1982.

————. *HaMa'avak Al HaMedina,* vol 3. Tel Aviv, 1982.

————. *Yoman San Francisco* (Tel Aviv, 1971).

Elath, Eliahu. *Israel and Elath, The Political Struggle for the Inclusion of Elath in the Jewish State.* London, 1966.

Eliav, Arie L. *The Voyage of the Ulua.* Translated by I. L. Taslitt. New York, 1969.

Eliav, Yaakov. *Mevukash.* Jerusalem, 1983.

Engel, David. *Bein Shihrur L'Briha, Nitsolei HaShoa B'Polin V'HaMa'avak Al Hanhagatam, 1944–1946.* Tel Aviv, 1996.

Eshel, Aryeh. *Shvirat HaGardomim.* Tel Aviv, 1990.

Ettinger, Amos. *Tseniha Iveret* (Tel Aviv, 1986).

Evron, Yosef. *Gidi V'HaMa'arakha L'Pinui HaBritim Meh'Eretz Yisrael.* Jerusalem, 2001.

Evatt, Herbert. The Task of Nations (New York, 1949).

Ferrell, Robert H. ed. *Dear Bess, The Letters from Harry to Bess Truman, 1910–1959.* New York, 1983.

————. *Off the Record, The Private Papers of Harry S. Truman.* New York, 1982 ed.

Foot, Michael. *Aneurin Bevan, A Biography, vol. 2: 1945–1960.* London, 1973.

For the Record, The Memoirs of Eva, Marchioness of Reading. London, 1972.

Foreign Relations of the United States, 1945, General, vol. 2. Washington, D.C., 1967.

————, *1945,* vol. 8. Washington, D.C., 1969.

————, *1946,* vol. 7. Washington, D.C., 1969.

————, *1947,* vol. 5. Washington, D.C., 1971.

————, *1948,* vol. 5, part 2. Washington, D.C., 1976.

Friedman, Herbert. *Roots of the Future.* Jerusalem, 1999.

Friedman, Yehoshua. *MeiHurban L'Tekuma.* Tel Aviv, 1994.

Freundlich, Yehoshua. MeiHurban L'Tekuma (Tel Aviv, 1994).

Hefer, Hayim, and Noga Terkel. *Shurot Shurot.* Tel Aviv, 2008.

Herf, Jeffrey. *Nazi Propaganda for the Arab World.* New Haven, CT, 2009.

Herzog, Chaim. *Living History.* New York, 1996.

Hourani, Cecil. *An Unfinished Odyssey, Lebanon and Beyond.* London, 1984.

Howard, Anthony. *Crossman, The Pursuit of Power.* London, 1990.

Galambos, Louis, et al., eds. *The Papers of Dwight D. Eisenhower,* vol. 7. Baltimore, MD, 1978.

Ganin, Zvi. *Truman, American Jewry, and Israel, 1945–1948.* New York, 1979.

Gavish, Dov. *Ulai Hu Od Yavo.* Carmel, 2013.

Gelber, Yoav. *Jewish-Transjordanian Relations, 1921-1948*. London, 1997.

———. *Komemiyut V'Nakba*. Ohr Yehuda, 2004.

Gefen, Aba. *Unholy Alliance* (Jerusalem, 1973).

Gilad, Zerubabel, ed. *Sefer HaPalmah*, vol. 1. Tel Aviv, 1957.

Gilbert, Martin. *Exile and Return, The Struggle for a Jewish Homeland*. Philadelphia, PA, 1978.

———. *Never Despair, Winston S. Churchill 1945–1965*. London, 1988.

Gildersleeve, Virginia. *Many a Good Crusade*. New York, 1954.

Glatzer, Nahum N., and Paul Mendes-Flohr, eds. *The Letters of Martin Buber, A Life of Dialogue*. Translated by R. and C. Winston and H. Zohn. New York, 1991.

Glick, Edward. *The Triangular Connection: America, Israel, and American Jews*. London, 1981.

Glubb, John B. *A Soldier With the Arabs*. London, 1957.

Glick, Edward B. *Latin America and the Palestine Problem* (New York, 1958).

Goda, Norman J.W. *Surviving Survival: James G. McDonald and the Fate of Holocasut Survivors*. Washington, D.C., 2015.

Golani, Moti. *Tsiyon BaTsiyonut, HaMediniyut HaTsiyonit B'Sh'eilat Yerushalayim 1937–1949*. Tel Aviv, 1992.

Goldman, Nahum. *Sixty Years of Jewish Life*. New York, 1969.

Gorney, Yosef. *Shutfut U'Ma'avak*. Tel Aviv, 1976.

García-Granados, Jorge. *The Birth of Israel, The Drama as I Saw It*. New York, 1948.

Goldberg, Hillel. *The Jewish Connection*. New York, 1976.

Goren, Arthur, ed. *Dissenter in Zion, From the Writings of Judah L. Magnes*. Cambridge, 1982.

Greilsammer, Ilan. *Blum*. Paris, 1996.

Grauel, John S. *Grauel, An Autobiography as told to Eleanor Elfenbein*. Freehold, NJ, 1982.

Graves, Richard M. *Experiment in Anarchy*. London, 1949.

Grobman, Alex. *Rekindling the Flame: American Jewish Chaplains and the Survivors of European Jewry, 1944–1948*. Detroit, 1993.

Gross, Jan T. *Fear: Anti-Semitism in Poland after Auschwitz*. New York, 2006.

Gruber, Ruth. *Destination Palestine*. New York, 1948.

———. *Exodus 1947*. New York, 1948.

———. *Witness*. New York, 2007.

Gruszow, Avner. *Memoirs of an Assassin*, trans. B. Partridge. London, 1959.

Hahn, Peter L. *Caught in the Middle East, U.S. Policy toward the Arab-Israeli Conflict 1945–1961*. Chapel Hill, 2004.

Hadari, Zeev (Venya), and Zeev Tsahor. *Oniyot O Medina*. Tel Aviv, n.d.

HaKongress HaTsiyoni HaKhaf-Bet. Jerusalem, 1947.

Hall, William L. *The Fall and Rise of Israel*. Grand Rapids, 1954.

Halamish, Aviva. *Exodus, HaSippur HaAmiti*. Tel Aviv, 1990.

Hamilton, Robert. W. *Letters from the Middle East by an Occasional Archeologist*. Edinburgh, 1992.

Hammer, Gottlieb. *Good Faith and Credit*. New York, 1985.

Harris, Kenneth. *Attlee*. London, 1982.

Hattis, Susan Lee. *The Bi-National Idea in Palestine during Mandatory Times* (Jerusalem, 1970).

Hearings before the Anglo-American Committee of Inquiry, 6 vols. London, 1946.

Heller, Joseph. *The Birth of Israel, 1945–1949: Ben-Gurion and His Critics.* Gainesville, FL, 2000.

Hennessy, Peter. *Never Again, Britain, 1945–1951.* New York, 1993.

Herf, Jeffrey. *Nazi Propaganda for the Arab World.* New Haven, Conn., 2009.

Hirst, David. *The Gun and the Olive Branch, The Roots of Violence in the Middle East.* New York, 2003.

Hoffman, Bruce. *Anonymous Soldiers: The Struggle for Israel, 1917–1947.* New York, 2015.

Hohenberg, John. *Israel at 50: A Journalist's Perspective.* Syracuse, 1998.

Horowitz, David. *State in the Making.* Translated by J. Meltzer. New York, 1953.

Hourani, Cecil. *An Unfinished Journey, Lebanon and Beyond* (London, 1984).

Howard, Anthony. *Crossman, The Pursuit of Power* (London, 1990).

Hurewitz, Jacob C. *The Struggle for Palestine.* New York, 1950.

Hyman, Abraham S. *The Undefeated.* Jerusalem, 1993.

Ilan, Amitsur. *The Origin of the Arab-Israeli Arms Race.* London, 1996.

Jamali, Mohammed Fadhel. *Inside the Arab Nationalist Struggle.* Edited by J. King. London, 2012.

Jebb, Gladwyn. *The Memoirs of Lord Gladwyn.* New York, 1970.

Jeffery, Keith. *The Secret History of MI6.* New York, 2010.

Jessup, Philip C. *The Birth of Nations.* New York, 1974.

John, Robert, and Sami Hadawi. *The Palestine Diary, 1945–1948*, vol. 2. Beirut, 1970.

Julius, Lyn. *Uprooted.* London, 2018.

Kagan, Benjamin. *The Secret Battle for Israel.* Cleveland, 1966.

Karmi, Ghada. *A Palestinian Story.* London, 2002.

Karsh, Efraim. *Palestine Betrayed.* New Haven, CT, 2010.

Kaufman, Edy, Yoram Shapira, and Joel Barromi. *Israel-Latin American Relations.* New Brunswick, NJ, 1979.

Kedourie, Elie. *The Chatham House Version and Other Middle-Eastern Studies.* New York, 1970.

Keith Jeffery. *MI6, The History of the Secret Intelligence Service, 1909–1949.* London, 2010.

Kennan, George F. *Memoirs, 1925–1950.* New York, 1967.

Khalaf, Issa. *Politics in Palestine: Arab Factionalism and Social Disintegration, 1939–1948.* Albany, NY, 1991.

Khalil, Muhammad, ed., *The Arab states and the Arab League.* Beirut, 1962.

Kimche, Jon. *Seven Fallen Pillars, The Middle East, 1915–1950.* London, 1950.

Kirkbride, Alec S. *A Crackle of Thorns, Experiences in the Middle East.* London, 1956.

Kimche, Jon and Kimche, David. *Both Sides of the Hill, Britain and the Palestine War* (London, 1960).

Kimche, Jon and Kimche, David. *The Secret Roads* (London, 1954).

———. *From the Wings, Amman Memoirs 1947–1951.* London, 1976.

Knohl, Dov, ed. *Gush Etzion B'Milhamto.* Jerusalem, 1954.

Kochavi, Aryeh. *Post-Holocaust Politics: Britain, the United States, and Jewish Refugees, 1945–1948.* Chapel Hill, 2001.

Köhler, Lotte, and Hans Saner, ed. *Hannah Arendt—Karl Jaspers Correspondence 1926–1969.* New York, 1992.

Königseder, Angelika, and Juliane Wetzel. *Waiting for Hope, Jewish DPs in Post-World War II Germany.* Translated by J. A. Broadwin. Evanston, 2001.

Kollek, Teddy, with Amos Kollek. *For Jerusalem: A Life by Teddy Kollek.* Tel Aviv, 1978.

Kolsky, Thomas A. *Jews Against Zionism.* Philadelphia, PA, 1990.

Krock, Arthur. *Memoirs: Sixty Years on the Firing Line.* New York, 1968.

Kurzman, Dan. *Ben-Gurion, Prophet of Fire.* New York, 1983.

———. *Genesis 1948, The First Arab-Israeli War.* New York, 1970 ed.

Lacy, Robert. *Little Man, Meyer Lansky and the Gangster Life.* New York, 1991.

Lane, Arthur Bliss. *I Saw Poland Betrayed.* New York, 1948.

Lapidot, Yehuda. *Al Homotayikh, Zikhronot Lohem Etzel.* Jerusalem, 2004.

Lash, Joseph P. *Eleanor: The Years Alone.* New York, 1972.

Lazar, Hadara. *HaMandatorim: Eretz Yisrael, 1940–1948.* Jerusalem, 1990.

———. *Out of Palestine, The Making of Modern Israel.* New York, 2011.

Lazare, Lucien. *Alexsander Glasberg—Komer Yehudi.* Translated by M. Mazel. Tel Aviv, 1991.

———. *The Mission of Abbé Glasberg.* Translated by L. M. Abrami. Amsterdam, 2016.

Levin, Harry. *Jerusalem Embattled.* London, 1997 ed.

Levin, Meyer. *In Search, An Autobiography.* Paris, 1950.

Levy, Robert. *Ana Pauker, The Rise and Fall of a Jewish Communist.* Berkeley, 2001.

Lie, Trygve. *In the Cause of Peace.* New York, 1954.

Litvinoff, Barnet. *Weizmann, Last of the Patriarchs.* New York, 1976.

Living UJA History: Irving Bernstein. Jerusalem, 1995.

Loewenstein, Sharon R. *Token Refuge: The Story of the Jewish Refugee Shelter at Oswego, 1944–1946.* Bloomington, 1986.

Lohamei Heirut Yisrael, Ketavim, vol. 2. Tel Aviv, 1960.

Lorch, Netanel. *The Edge of the Sword: Israel's War of Independence, 1947–1949.* New York, 1961.

———. *Shiv'a Perakim B'Yahasei Yisrael—Amerika HaIberit.* Jerusalem, 1977.

Lossin, Yigal. *Pillar of Fire: The Birth of Israel. A Visual History.* Translated by Z. Ofer. Jerusalem, 1983.

Louis, Wm. Roger. *The British Empire in the Middle East, 1945–1951: Arab Nationalism, the United States, and Postwar Imperialism.* Oxford, 1984.

Lowdermilk, Walter. *Palestine, Land of Promise.* New York, 1944.

Lowenthal, Marvin, ed. and trans. *The Diaries of Theodor Herzl.* New York, 1962.

MacMillan, Harold. *Tides of Fortune.* New York, 1969.

Mandel, Daniel. *H. V. Evatt and the Establishment of Israel, The Undercover Zionist.* London, 2004.

Mankowitz, Zeev W. *Life Between Memory and Hope: The Survivors of the Holocaust in Occupied Germany*. Cambridge, 2002.

Martin, Kingsley. *Harold Laski (1893–1950), A Biographical Memoir*. New York, 1953.

Mattar, Philip. *The Mufti of Jerusalem: Al-Haj Amin Al-Huseini*. New York, 1988.

Mazuzan, George T. *Warren R. Austin at the UN, 1946–1953*. Kent, OH, 1977.

McCulloh, David. *Truman*. New York, 1992.

McDonald, James G. *My Mission in Israel, 1948–1951*. New York, 1951.

Medzini, Meron, ed. *Israel's Foreign Relations, Selected Documents 1947–1974*. Jerusalem, 1976.

Meir, Golda. *My Life*. New York, 1975.

Memorandum on Trusteeship for Palestine (New York, 1948)

The Memoirs of Field-Marshall The Viscount Montgomery of Alamein. New York, 1958.

Memorandum Submitted to the Anglo-American Committee on Inquiry on Palestine by the Jewish Agency for Palestine. Tel Aviv, 1946.

Millis, Walter, ed., *The Forrestal Diaries*. New York, 1951.

Minhelet Ha'Am, Ginzakh HaMedina. Jerusalem, 1978.

Monroe, Elizabeth. *Britain's Moment in the Middle East, 1914–1956*. London, 1963.

Morgan, Frederick. *Peace and War: A Soldier's Life*. London, 1961.

Morris, Benny. *Righteous Victims, A History of the Zionist-Arab Conflict, 1881–1999*. New York, 1999.

———. *1948, A History of the First Arab-Israeli War*. New Haven, CT, 2008.

Morrison, Herbert. *An Autobiography*. London, 1960.

Nadich, Judah. *Eisenhower and the Jews*. New York, 1953.

Nachmani, Amikam. *Great Power Discord in Palestine, The Anglo-American Committee of Inquiry on Palestine into the Problems of European Jewry and Palestine, 1945–46*. London, 1987.

Namier, Louis B. *Conflicts: Studies in Contemporary History*. London, 1942.

Naor, Mordekhai, ed. *Gush-Etzion MeiReishito Ad TaShah*. Jerusalem, 1986.

Nashashibi, Nasser Eddin. *Jerusalem's Other Voice, Ragheb Nashashibi and Moderation in Palestinian Politics, 1920–1948*. Exeter, 1990.

Neumann, Emanuel. *In the Arena, An Autobiographical Memoir*. New York, 1976.

Newman, Michael. *Harold Laski, A Political Biography*. London, 1993.

Nicolson, Harold. *Diaries and Letters, 1945–1962*. Edited by N. Nicolson. London, 1968.

Nusseibeh, Sari. *Once Upon A Country, A Palestinian Life*. New York, 2007.

O'Connor, Anne-Marie. *The Lady in Gold*. New York, 2012.

Official Records of the General Assembly, 1948, vol. II. New York, 1948.

Official Records of the Second Session of the General Assembly, Supplement no. 11, UNSCOP, Report to the General Assembly, vol. 1. New York, 1947.

Offner, Arold A. *Another Such Victory, President Truman and the Cold War, 1945–1953*. Stanford, 2002.

Ohana, David. *The Origins of Israeli Mythology: Neither Canaanites Nor Crusaders.* Cambridge, 2012.

Official Records of the Second Session of the General Assembly, Supplement no. 11, UNSCOP, Report to the General Assembly, vols. 3-4 (New York, 1947).

Omer, Dan. *B'Ikvot Amud HaEsh* (Tel Aviv, 1981).

Palestine: Statement of Information Relating to Acts of Violence. London, 1946.

Palestine: Termination of the Mandate 15th May, 1948. London, 1948.

Pappe, Ilan. *The Making of the Arab-Israeli Conflict, 1947–1951.* London, 1992.

Parliamentary Debates, House of Commons, 1945–1948.

Parliamentary Debates, House of Lords, 1945–1948.

Pearlman, Moshe. *Ben Gurion Looks Back.* New York, 1963.

Penkower, Monty Noam. *Decision on Palestine Deferred: America, Britain and Wartime Diplomacy, 1939–1945.* London, 2002.

———. *The Emergence of Zionist Thought.* Millwood, NY, 1986.

———. *The Holocaust and Israel Reborn: From Catastrophe to Sovereignty.* Urbana, IL, 1994.

———. *The Jews Were Expendable: Free World Diplomacy and the Holocaust.* Urbana, IL, 1983.

———. *Palestine in Turmoil: The Struggle for Sovereignty, 1933–1939,* vol 1: *Prelude to Revolt, 1933–1936,* and vol. 2: *Retreat from the Mandate, 1937–1939.* New York, 2014.———.

———. *The Swastika's Darkening Shadow, Voices before the Holocaust.* New York, 2018.

———. *Twentieth Century Jews: Forging Identity in the Land of Promise and in the Promised Land.* Boston, MA, 2010.

Peres, Shimon. *Battling for Peace.* Edited by D. Landau. London, 1995.

Peterson, Edward N. *The American Occupation of Germany: Retreat to Victory.* Detroit, MI, 1978.

Pilat, Oliver. *Drew Pearson, An Unauthorized Biography.* New York, 1973.

Pimlott, Ben, ed. *The Political Diary of Hugh Dalton.* London, 1986.

Pinkerfeld, Edna. *Lamed Heh,* 3rd ed. Jerusalem, 1998.

Pinkus, Binyamin, ed. *Yahadut Mizrah Eiropa Bein Shoa L'Tekuma, 1944–1948.* Sdeh Boker, Israel, 1987.

Podet, Allen Howard. *The Success and Failure of the Anglo-American Committee of Inquiry, 1945–1946: Last Chance in Palestine.* Lewiston, ME, 1986.

Pogue, Forrest C. *George C. Marshall, Statesman.* New York, 1987.

Porath, Zipporah. *Letters from Jerusalem 1947–1948.* Jerusalem, 1987.

Prister, Roman. *LeLo Peshara.* Tel Aviv, 1987.

Pta'el, Carmi, ed. *HaKefilim: B'Shlihut Hatsala Aluma.* Tel Aviv, 1990.

Radosh, Allis, and Ronald Radosh. *A Safe Haven: Harry S. Truman and the Founding of Israel.* New York, 2009.

Raphael, Marc Lee. *Abba Hillel Silver, A Profile in American Judaism.* New York, 1989.

Repetur, Berl. *LeLo Heref.* Israel, 1973.

Robinson, Jacob. *Palestine and the United Nations*. Washington, D.C., 1947.

Rogow, Arnold A. *James Forrestal, A Study of Personality, Politics, and Policy*. New York, 1963.

Romulo, Carlos P. *Forty Years, A Third World Soldier at the UN*. New York, 1986.

Rose, Norman A. ed. *Baffy, The Diaries of Blanche Dugdale, 1936–1947*. London, 1973.

———. *Chaim Weizmann, A Biography*. New York, 1986.

———. *"A Senseless, Squalid War," Voices from Palestine 1890s-1948*. London, 2009.

Roshwald, Avriel. *Estranged Bedfellows. Britain and France in the Middle East during the Second World War*. NewYork, 1990.

Rusk, Dean. *As I Saw It*. New York, 1990.

Sabag, Shemuel, ed. *B'Einei Oyev, Shlosha Pirsumim Araviyim Al Milhemet HaKomemiyut*. Tel Aviv, 1954.

Sachar, Abram L. *The Redemption of the Unwanted*. New York, 1983.

al-Sakakini, Halil. *"KaZeh Ani Rabotai!."* Edited by Gideon Shilo. Jerusalem, 1990.

Sasson, Eliyahu. *BaDerekh El HaShalom*. Tel Aviv, 1978.

Schechtman, Joseph B. *The Mufti and the Fuehrer*. New York, 1965.

Schiff, David, and Asher Ben-Natan, eds. *Habricha*. Holon, 1998.

Schwarz, Leo. *The Redeemers: A Saga of the Jews, 1945–1952*. New York, 1953.

Security Council Documents, 3rd year, May Supplement 1948. New York, 1948.

Segev, Shmuel, ed. *MeiAharei HaPargod*. Tel Aviv, 1954.

Sereni, Ada. *Sefinot LeLo Degel* (Tel Aviv, 1975).

Shaltiel, Eli. *Tamid B'Meri: Moshe Sneh, Biografia: 1909–1948* (Tel Aviv, 2000).

Shapira, Anita. *Land and Power: The Zionist Resort to Force, 1881–1948*. Translated by W. Templer. New York, 1992.

Sharef, Zeev. *Three Days*. Translated by J. Meltzer. London, 1962.

Sharett, Moshe. *B'Sha'ar HaUmot*. Tel Aviv, 1964.

———. *Yerahim B'Emek Ayalon*. Edited by P. Ofer. Tel Aviv, 2011.

Sheffer, Gabriel. *Moshe Sharett, Biography of a Political Moderate*. Oxford, 1996.

Shehlah, Menahem. *HaKesher HaYugoslavi*. Tel Aviv, 1994.

Shepherd, Naomi. *Ploughing Sand: British Rule in Palestine, 1917–1948*. New Brunswick, 2000.

Sherman, Ari J. *Mandate Days: British Lives in Palestine, 1918–1948*. New York, 1998.

Shihor, Samuel. *The Last Days of Chaim Weizmann*. Translated by J. Meltzer. New York, 1960.

Shinwell, Emanuel. *I've Lived Through it All*. London, 1973.

Sharett, Moshe. *Ma'asar Im Niyar V'Iparon* (Tel Aviv, 2000).

Skinner, Anthony D., ed. and trans. *Gershom Scholem, A Life in Letters, 1914–1982*. Cambridge, MA, 2002.

Slater, Leonard. *The Pledge*. New York, 1970.

Slutzki, Yehuda. *Sefer Toldot HaHagana*, vol. 3, *MiMa'avak L'Milhama*, part 2. Tel Aviv, 1973.

Snetsinger, John. *Truman, the Jewish Vote and the Creation of Israel*. Stanford, 1974.

Sprinzak, Joseph. *Igrot Yosef Sprinzak*, vol. 2. Translated by Y. Shapira. Tel Aviv, 1969.

Stone, I. F. *Underground to Palestine*. New York, 1946.

Sulzberger, Cyrus L. *A Long Row of Candles, Memoirs and Diaries, 1934–1954*. New York, 1969.

Tal, David. *War in Palestine, 1948: Israeli and Arab Strategy and Diplomacy*. London, 2004.

Tannous, Izzat. *The Palestinians: A Detailed Documented Eyewitness History of Palestine under the British Mandate*. New York, 1988.

Tauber, Eliezer. *Deir Yassin: Sof HaMitos*. Jerusalem, 2017.

Tavin, Eli. *HaHazit HaShniya, HaEtzel B'Artsot Eiropa 1946–1948*. Tel Aviv, 1973.

Tauber, Eliezer. *Personal Policy Making Canada's Role in the Adoption of the Palestine Partition Resolution* (Westport, 2002).

Teveth, Shabtai. *Ben-Gurion, The Burning Ground, 1886–1948*. Boston, MA, 1987.

Thomas, Hugh. *John Strachey*. New York, 1973.

Tov, Moshe. *El Murmullo de Israel, Historial Diplomatico* (Jerusalem, 1983).

Trahtemberg Siederer, Leon. *Participacion del Peru En La Particion De Palestina*. Lima, Peru, 1991.

Trevor, Daphne. *Under the White Paper*. Jerusalem, 1948.

Truman, Harry S. *Memoirs by Harry S. Truman*, vol. 1, *Year of Decision*. New York, 1955.

———. *Memoirs by Harry S. Truman*, vol. 2, *Years of Trial and Hope*. New York, 1965 ed.

———. *Mr. Citizen*. New York, 1960.

———. *Truman Speaks*. New York, 1960.

Truman, Margaret. *Harry S. Truman*. New York, 1973.

Tsahor, Ze'ev. *Hazzan—Tenuat Hayim*. Jerusalem, 1997 ed.

The Jewish Case (Jerusalem, 1947).

The Palestine Problem and Proposals for its Solution (New York, 1947).

Urquhart, Brian. *Ralph Bunche: An American Life*. New York, 1993.

Varon, Benno Weiser. *Professions of a Lucky Jew*. New York, 1992.

Vazeh, Pinhas. *HaMesima—Rekhesh*. Tel Aviv, 1966.

Veitz, Yosef. *Yomanai V'Igrotai LaBanim*, vol. 3. Ramat Gan, 1965.

Wallace, Henry. *The Price of Vision: The Diary of Henry A. Wallace, 1942–1946*. Edited by J. M. Blum. Boston, MA, 1973.

Wasserstein, Bernard. *Divided Jerusalem, The Struggle for the Holy City*. New Haven, CT, 2001.

Wdowinski, David. *And We Were Not Saved*. New York, 1963.

Weidenfeld, George. *Remembering My Good Friends, an Autobiography*. New York, 1994.

Weisgal, Meyer. *So Far, An Autobiography*. New York, 1971.

Weizmann, Chaim. *Trial and Error*. New York, 1949.

Weizmann, Vera. *The Impossible Takes Longer*. London, 1967.

Welles, Sumner. *We Need Not Fail* (Boston, 1948).

Williams, Francis. *A Prime Minister Remembers*. London, 1961.

———. *Ernest Bevin, Portrait of a Great Englishman*. London, 1952.

———. *Twilight of Empire*. New York, 1962 ed.

Wheeler-Bennett, John W. *King George VI, His Life and Reign*. New York, 1958.

Wilson, Charles McMoran. *Churchill, Taken from the Diaries of Lord Moran*. Boston, 1966.

Wilson, Evan. *Decision on Palestine*. Stanford, 1979.

Wilson, R. Dare. *Cordon and Search, With 6th Airborne Division in Palestine*. Nashville, 1984.

Wyman, David. *The Abandonment of the Jews: America and the Holocaust 1941–1945*. New York, 1984.

Yagar, Moshe. *Czechoslovakia HaTsiyonit V'Yisrael, Gilgulei Yahasim Murkavim*. Jerusalem, 1997.

Yakhin, Ezra. *Elnakam, Sipuro Shel Lohem Heirut Yisrael*. Tel Aviv, 1993.

Zurayk, Constantine K. *The Meaning of the Disaster*. Translated by R. B. Winder. Beirut, 1969.

Articles

Abu-Lughod, Ibrahim. "The War of 1948: Disputed Perspectives and Outcomes." *Journal of Palestine Studies* 18, no. 2 (Winter 1989): 119–127.

Aderet, Ofer. "Why the Mysterious Swede Who Drew Up Israel's Map Favored the Jews." *Ha'Aretz*, November 25, 2017.

Alami, Musa. "The Lesson of Palestine." *Middle East Journal*, 3, no. 4 (October 1949): 373–405

Al-Hout, Bayan Neweihid. "The Palestine Political Elite during the Mandate Period." *Journal of Palestine Studies* 9, no.1 (1979): 85–111.

Alsberg, Paul. "The 'Emergency Committee' (Va'adat Hamatzav), October 1947–May 1948: Preparing for Statehood." *Studies in Zionism* 10, no.1 (1989): 49–64.

Alsop, Joseph and Stewart. "The Wriggling President." *Washington Post*, February 27, 1948.

Arendt, Hannah. "To Save the Jewish Homeland: There is Still Time." *Commentary* 5 (May 1948): 398–406.

Arnow, David. "The Holocaust and the Birth of Israel: Reassessing the Causal Relationship." *Journal of Israeli History* 15, no. 3 (1994): 257–281.

Aronheim, Anna. "Hugo Marom, One of IAF's Founders, dies at 89." *Jerusalem Post*, January 8, 2018.

Asa-El, Amotz, "The Thirty Years' War." *Jerusalem Post*, December 1, 2017.

Atsmon, Itamar. "Simanim Shel Tekuma." *Segula* 36 (May 2013): 64–67.

Avidan, Yigal. "L'Khol Ish Yesh Mekhir." *Makor Rishon*, September 27, 2014.

Avraham, Yael (Freund). "Gibor Ba'al Korho." *Makor Rishon, Dyukan*, Sept. 7, 2012, 29–30, 32.

Alterman, Natan. "Magash HaKesef." *Davar*, December 19, 1947.

Bar Natan, Aryeh H. "Av Ketana K'Khaf Ish." *Makor Rishon*, April 27, 2012.

Barker, James. "Monty and the Mandate in Palestine." *History Today* 59, no. 3 (March 2009): 30–34.

Barnett, David, and Efraim Karsh. "Azzam's Genocidal Threat." *Middle East Quarterly* 18, no. 4 (Fall 2011): 85–88.

Bauer, Yehuda. "Reishit Hit'havuto Shel Irgun Sh'eirit HaPleita B'Bevaria," *Yad Vashem Studies* 8 (1970): 117–144.

Ben-Dror, Elad. "The Arab Struggle against Partition: The International Arena of Summer 1947." *Middle Eastern Studies* 43, no. 2 (March 2007): 259–293.

———. "How the United Nations Intended to Implement the Partition Plan: The Handbook Drawn up by the Secretariat for the Members of the United Nations Palestine commission." *Middle Eastern Studies* 43, no. 6 (November 2007): 997–1008.

Ben-Gurion, David. "British Socialists Win Election." *Jewish Observer and Middle East Review*, June 26, 1964, 17–19.

Ben-Gurion, David. "Bevin Explains His Difficulties," *Jewish Observer and Middle East Review*, November 13, 1964, 14-16.

Ben-Gurion, David. "Hagana Prepares for the Invasion," *Jewish Observer and Middle East Review*, April 9, 1965, 20-23.

Ben-Gurion, David. "U.N. Special Committee Divides Palestine Into Three," *Jewish Observer and Middle East Review*, June 4, 1965, 20-22,

———. "Cards on the Table Before Bevin." *Jewish Observer and Middle East Review*, December 25, 1964, 15–16.

———. "First Conflict with Labour Government." *Jewish Observer and Middle East* Review, July 17, 1964, 15–16.

———. "The Only Solution." *New Judea* (May 1945): 107–110.

———. "The Palmach Takes the Offensive." *Jewish Observer and Middle East Review*, September 18, 1964, 14.

Ben-Tsur, Zvi. "The Voyage of the 'Hannah Senesh.'" Palmah Information Center, Tel Aviv.

Ben Vered, Amos. "The Last Days of the Mandate." *Palestine Post*, May 10, 1951.

Bendman, Yona. "Gibush HaTokhnit HaBritit L'Hitpanot MeiEretz Yisrael." In *Milhemet HaAtsmaut*, edited by A. Kadish, vol. 2, 589–647. Tel Aviv, 2004.

Bergman, Elihu, "Unexpected Recognition: Some Observations on the Failure of a Last-Gasp Campaign in the US State Department to Abort a Jewish State." *Modern Judaism* 19 (1999): 133–171.

Bergman, Ronen. "The Scorpion File." *Yediot Aharonot*, *Sheva Yamim* magazine (March 30, 2007): 21–28.

"The British Record on Partition." *The Nation* 166, no. 19, part II (May 8, 1948): 3–30.

Browne, Mallory. "Commons Favors Egypt Evacuation." *New York Times*, May 11, 1946.

Buxton, Frank. "A Report in Retrospect.," *New Palestine* June 20, 1947, 136–138.

Carlebach, Azriel. "HaKongress Roked." *Yediot Aharonot*, November 12, 1947.

Cashman, Greer Fay. "After 66 Years, State finally Grants Official Recognition to Jewish Refugees from Arab Lands." *Jerusalem Post*, December 1, 2014.

———. "The First Steps of Statehood." *Jerusalem Post*, April 23, 2007.

Cohen, Aharon. "Why Was Fauzi Husseini Killed?" *Mishmar*, January 3, 1947.

Cohen, Benjamin V. "The United Nations and Palestine." *New York Herald Tribune*, March 16–17, 1948.

Crossman, Richard H. S. "The Case for Partition." *New Statesman and Nation*, September 14, 1946.

Crossman, R.H.S. "Framework for the Jewish State," *Commentary*, 4 (Nov. 1947), 401-407.

———. "The Role Britain Hopes to Play." *Commentary* 5 (June 1948): 493–497.

———. "The Roots of Policy." *Zionist Review*, July 9, 1948, 9–10.

Cunningham, Alan. "The Last Days of the Mandate." *International Affairs* 24, no. 4 (October 1948): 481–490.

Dicker, Herman. "The U.S. Army and Jewish Displaced Persons." *Chicago Jewish Forum* 19, no. 4 (Summer 1961): 290.

Eban, Abba. "Tragedy and Triumph." In *Chaim Weizmann, A Biography by Several Hands*, edited by M. W. Weisgal and J. Carmichael, 249–313. London, 1962.

Eilat, Eliyahu. "Halakti Al Emdat Truman K'lapei Yisrael..." *Ma'ariv*, October 22, 1971, 15.

Eilat, Eliyahu. "Shmuel Irving Rosenman V'Tafkido Lifnei HaKamat HaMedina." *Molad* 7, no. 37–38 (1976): 448–454.

Elath, Eliahu. "That Year, in Jerusalem." *New York Times*, May 4, 1972.

Elpeleg, Zvi. "Why Was 'Independent Palestine' Never Created in 1948?" *Jerusalem Quarterly* 50 (Spring 1989): 3–22.

Eteli, Amihai. "HaKrav ShehNishkhah." *Ma'ayenei HaYeshua*, April 12, 2008, 16–17, 19.

Fogelman, Shay. "Port in a Storm." *HaAretz*, June 3, 2001.

Friesel, Evyatar. "The Holocaust and the Birth of Israel." *Wiener Library Bulletin* 32, no. 49–50 (1979): 51–60.

Ganor, Solly. "The Fabulous Survivor's Passover Haggadah." *ISRAPUNDIT*, April 20, 2011.

Gelber, Yoav. "Druze and Jews in the War of 1948." *Middle Eastern Studies* 31, no. 2 (1995): 229–252.

———. "Maga'im Diplomatiyim Terem Hitnagdut Tseva'it—HaMasa-U'Matan Bein HaSokhnut HaYehudit L'Mitsrayim V'Yarden (1946–1948)." *Katedra* 35 (1985): 125–162.

———. "Partners and Adversaries: Jewish Survivors of World War II, the Jewish Agency, and Britain." In *Vision and Conflict in the Holy Land*, edited by R. I. Cohen, 274–308. London, 1985.

Genosar, Shlomo. "Milhemet HaOlam U'Tekumat Yisrael." *Davar*, May 5, 1965.

Gilad, Elon. "Israel—Day One: The Story of the Day of Independence." *Ha'Aretz*, May 5, 2014.

Golani, Moti. "Britanya V'Hakhra'at 'Milhemet HaEzrahim' B'Eretz Yisrael: 'Mifneh Haifa,' April 1948." *Tsiyon* 64, no. 4 (1999): 455–494.

Goldman, Danny, and Michael J. K. Walsh. "Stranded in Bogas, Cyprus: The Affair of the Pans, January 1948." *Journal of Cyprus Studies* 15 (2009): 45–46.

Goodman, Giora. "Aharei 57 Shanim: Giluyim B'Farashat HaRetsah." *Ha'Aretz*, April 6, 2008.

Gorodetsky, Gabriel. "The Soviet Union's Role in the Creation of the State of Israel." *Journal of Israeli History* 22, no. 1 (Spring 2003): 4–20.

Haber, Eitan. "HaYeled ShehHeinif Et HaDegel Al Toren Oniyat-HaGeirush." 1964, file 3050/6-G, Israel State Archives, Jerusalem.

Halamish, Aviva. "Illegal Immigration: Values, Myth and Reality." *Studies in Zionism* 9, no. 1 (1988): 47–62.

Hamilton, Thomas J. "Partition of Palestine." *Foreign Policy Reports* 23, no. 23 (February 15, 1948): 286–295.

Haron, Miriam Joyce. "The British Decision to Give the Palestine Question to the UN." *Middle Eastern Studies* 17, no. 2 (1981): 241–248.

Harper, John L. "Friends, Not Allies: George F. Kennan and Charles E. Bohlen." *World Policy Journal* 12, no. 2 (1995): 77–88.

Hecht, Esther. "Media in a War Zone: Stronger Than TNT." *Jewish Herald*, April 3, 1996.

Heller, Joseph. "Roosevelt, Stalin and the Palestine Problem at Yalta." *Wiener Library Bulletin* 30 (1977): 25–35.

Hershco, Tsilla, "France and the Partition Plan: 1947–1948." In *Israel at Sixty: Rethinking the Birth of the Jewish State*, edited by E. Karsh and R. Miller, 161–173. Abingdon, 2009.

Hertzberg, Sidney. "The Month in History." *Commentary* 3 (May 1947): 469.

Ilan, Amitzur. "Messianism and Diploamcy 1945–1948: the Struggle for a Jewish State." *Weiner Library Bulletin* 30, no. 41–42 (1977): 36–46.

Jones, Priscilla Dale. "British Policy Towards German Crimes Against German Jews, 1939–1945." *Leo Baeck Institute Year Book* 36, no. 1 (January, 1991): 339–366.

Joseph, Richard, with Waverley Root. "Why So Many GIs Like the Germans Best." *Reader's Digest* 48 (March 1946): 5–8.

Kalev, Gol. "Aborting Was Not An Option." *Jerusalem Post* Magazine (January 19, 2018): 12–15.

Kennedy, Robert. "Jews Have Fine Fighting Force, Make Up for Lack of Arms with Undying Spirit, Unparalleled Courage." *Boston Post*, June 4, 1948.

Khalidi, Rashid. "The Palestinians and 1948: The Underlying Causes of Failure." In *The War for Palestine: Rewriting the History of 1948*, edited by E. L. Rogan and A. Shlaim, 12–36. Cambridge, 2001.

Khalidi, Walid, "The Arab Perspective." In *The End of the Palestine Mandate*, edited by Wm. R. Louis and R.W. Stookey, 110–136. Austin, 1986.

———. "On Albert Hourani, the Arab Office, and the Anglo-American Committee of 1946." *Journal of Palestine Studies* 35, no. 1 (Autumn 2005): 60–79.

———. "Selected Documents on the 1948 Palestine War." *Journal of Palestine Studies* 27, no. 3 (Spring 1998): 62–72.

Kirchwey, Freda. "America and Israel." *The Nation*, May 22, 1948, 565–566.

Kirchwey, Freda. "United Nations Victory, *Nation*, December 6, 1947, 610-611.

Klich, Ignacio. "Latin America, the United States, and the Birth of Israel: The Case of Somoza's Nicaragua," *Journal of Latin American Studies* 20, no. 2 (November 1988): 389–432.

Klich, Ignacio, "Failure in Argentina: The Jewish Agency's Search for Congressional Backing for Zionist Aims in Palestine (1946)," *JUDAICA LATINOAMERICANA, Estudios Historico-Sociales,* II (Jerusalem, 1993), 245-264.

Kochavi, Ariel Joseph. "Britain and the Jewish Exodus from Poland following the Second World War." *Polin* 7 (1992): 161–175.

———. "British Diplomats and the Jews in Poland, Romania and Hungary During the Communist Takeovers." *East European Quarterly* 20 (January 1995): 449–464.

Kovner, Abba. "Shlihutam Shel HaAharonim." *Yalkut Moreshet* 16 (1973): 35–42.

Kramer, Arold. "Arms for Independence, When the Soviet Bloc Supported Israel." *Wiener Library Bulletin* 22, no. 3 (Summer 1968): 19–23.

"La Spezia." *Davar,* June 9, 1947.

Landis, Joshua. "Syria and the Palestine War: Fighting King Abdullah's 'Greater Syria Plan.'" In *The War for Palestine: Rewriting the History of 1948,* edited by E. L. Rogan and A. Shlaim, 178–195. Cambridge, 2001.

Laski, Harold J. "Britain without Empire." *Nation,* March 29, 1947, 353–356.

Lavsky, Hagit. "The Day After: Bergen-Belsen from Concentration Camp to the Centre of the Jewish Survivors in Germany." *German History* 11, no. 1 (1993): 36–59.

Leff, Laurel. "'Liberated by the Yanks': The Holocaust as an American Story in Postwar News Articles." *Journal of Ecumenical Studies* 42, no. 4 (Fall 2003): 407–430.

Lehrman, Hal. "What U.S. Support Means." *Commentary* 5 (June 1948): 485–492.

Levenberg, Hayim. "Yahasei HaGomlin Bein HaNetsiv HaElyon, Sir Alan Cunningham, L'Vein HaMelekh Abdullah 1945–1948." *Iyunim B'Tekumat Yisrael* 5 (1995): 23–36.

"Line-up on Palestine." The *Nation,* October 25, 1947.

Lippman, Thomas W. "The View from 1947: The CIA and the Partition of Palestine." *Middle East Journal* 61, no. 1 (Winter 2007): 17–28.

Louis, Wm. Roger. "British Imperialism." In *The End of the Palestine Mandate,* edited by Wm. R. Louis and R. W. Stookey, 1–31. Austin, 1986.

Mayer, Thomas. "Arab Unity of Action and the Palestine Question." *Middle Eastern Studies* 22, no. 3 (July 1986): 331–349.

———. "Egypt's 1948 Invasion of Palestine." *Middle Eastern Studies* 22, no. 1 (January 1986): 20–36.

———. "The Military Force of Islam: The Society of the Muslim Brethren and the Palestine Question, 1945–48." in *Zionism and Arabism in Palestine and Israel,* edited by E. Kedourie and S. G. Haim, 100–117. London, 1982.

Mayerberg, Samuel K. "President Truman's Buddy." *Kansas City Jewish Chronicle,* September 21, 1945.

Markovitski, Yaakov. "Kalaniyot B'Sdot Dam: HaDivizya HaShishit HaMuteset B'Eretz Yisrael, 1945-1948," *Katedra* 86 (1998), 99-120.

Mann, Nir. "Wingate Night, Revisited." *Ha'Aretz,* March 27, 2011.

Masalha, Salman. "The 1948 War through Arab Eyes." *Ha'Aretz,* March 10, 2017.

Mauriac, François. "L'inhumanité de l'homme." *Le Figaro*, May 12, 1946.

McDonald, James G. "The Time for Decision is Past," *New Palestine* 33 (March 1943): 5–7.

Medoff, Rafael. "Herbert Hoover's Plan for Palestine: A Forgotten Episode in American Middle East Diplomacy." *American Jewish History* 79 (Summer 1990): 449–476.

Meidad, Yisrael. "Pesah Damim." *Makor Rishon*, Musaf Shabbat, April 4, 2014, 17.

Melamed, David. "HaMukhtarim Ba'u L'Varekh," *Makor Rishon*, Shabbat, October 14, 2016, 14-15.

Mikhman, Dan. "MeiShoa L'Tekuma! MeiShoa L'Tekuma? HaHistoriografia Shel HaKesher HaSibati Bein HaShoa L'Hakamat Medinat Yisrael—Bein Mitos L'Metsiut." *Iyunim B'Tekumat Yisrael* 10 (2000): 234–258.

Miller, Rory. "Sir Edward Spears' Jewish Problem: A Leading Anti-Zionist and His Relationship with Anglo-Jewry, 1945–48." *Journal of Israeli History* 19, no. 1 (Spring 1998): 41–60.

Milstein, Uri. "Al Mishmar HaEmek." *Segula* 36 (May 2013): 20–29.

Monroe, Elizabeth. "Arab states and the Strife in Palestine." *The Scotsman*, January 10, 1948.

"The Morgenthau Diaries, VI—The Refugee Run Around." *Collier's*, November 1, 1947, 22–25.

Morris, Benny. "Before the Kidnappings, There Was a Massacre." *Tablet*, June 25, 2014.

———. "The Historiography of Deir Yassain." *Journal of Israeli History* 24, no. 1 (March 2005): 79–107

"Mohammed Hassanein Heikal: Reflections on a Nation in Crisis, 1948," *Journal of Palestine Studies* 18:1 (Autumn 1988), 112-120.

———. "Response to Finkelstein and Masalha." *Journal of Palestine Studies* 21, no. 1 (Autumn 1991): 98–114.

Naor, Abba. "HaYonim El Aruboteihem." *MiBifnim*, 13, no. 3 (November 1948).

Nashif, Taysir. "Palestine Arab and Jewish Leadership in the Mandate Period." *Journal of Palestine Studies* 6, no. 4 (1977): 113–121.

Neiditch, H. Michael. "United States Consul Thomas C. Wasson and the End of the Palestine Mandate." *Studies in Zionism* 10, no. 1 (1989): 65–85.

Offner, Arnold A. "Research on American-German Relations: A Critical View." In *America and the Germans: An Assessment of a Three-Hundred-Year History*, edited by Joseph McVeigh and Frank Trommler, vol. 2, 168–182. Philadelphia, PA, 1990.

Oren, Michael. "The Diplomatic Struggle for the Negev." *Studies in Zionism* 10, no. 2 (1989): 197–215.

Oron, Israela. "The Palestinian Refugees." *INSS Insight* 1018, Tel Aviv University, February 18, 2018.

Ottolenghi, Michael. "Harry Truman's Recognition of Israel." *Historical Journal* 47, no. 4 (2004): 963–988.

Pattison, W. Keith. "The Delayed British Recognition of Israel." *Middle East Journal* 37, no. 3 (Summer 1983): 412–428.

Pearson, Drew. "Mufti Plots Battle in U.N." *New York Daily Mirror*, September 19, 1947.

Penkower, Monty Noam. "The Dreyfus Affair and Its Echoes." In *"The Highest Form of Wisdom," A Memorial Book in Honor of Professor Saul S. Friedman*, edited by J.C. Friedman and R. D. Miller II, 177–211. New York, 2016.

———. "Honorable Failures against Nazi Germany: McDonald's Letter of Resignation and the Petition in its Support." *Modern Judaism* 30, no. 3 (October 2010): 247–298.

———. "The 1943 Joint Anglo-American Statement on Palestine." In *Essays in American Zionism, Herzl Year Book* 8, edited by M. Urofsky, 212–241. New York, 1978.

———."The Kishinev Pogrom of 1903." In Monty Noam Penkower, *Twentieth Century Jews, Forging Identity in the Land of Promise and in the Promised Land*, 1–42. Boston, MA, 2010.

———. "The Venting of Presidential Spleen: Harry S Truman's Jewish Problem." *Jewish Quarterly Review* 94, no. 4 (Fall 2004): 615–624.

Rein, Ra'anan, "Peron, Argentina, V'HaHatsba'a BaUm Al Halukat Eretz Yisrael." *Gesher* 43, no. 135 (Summer 1997): 73–87.

Philpot, Robert. "As Jews Evacuated from Aden Bloodbath, A Daring Mission to Rescue a Torah Scroll." *The Times of Israel*, December 11, 2017.

Rabinovich, Abraham. "Underground in Italy." *Jerusalem Post* International Edition, July 8, 1995, 18–20.

Reston, James. "Bipartisan Policy on Holy Land Seen." *New York Times*, January 27, 1948.

———. "Palestine Issue Put High in Bronx Wallace Victory." *New York Times*, February 19 and 20, 1948.

Roosevelt, Eleanor. "Crisis for Jews." *New York World-Telegram*, June 22, 1946.

Roosevelt, Kermit. "The Partition of Palestine, A Lesson in Pressure Politics." *Middle East Journal* 2, no. 1 (January 1948): 1–16.

Ro'i, Yaacov. "Soviet-Israeli Relations, 1947–1954." In *The U.S.S.R. and the Middle East*, edited by M. Confino and S. Shamir, 123–146, Jerusalem, 1973.

Rozen, Hanan. "Yahasei Yisrael—Czechoslovakia B'Temurat Haltim." *Gesher* 2–3 (September 1969): 266–283.

Schiff, Mel. "President Truman and the Jewish DPs, 1945–46, The Untold Story." *American Jewish History* 99 (October 2015): 327–352.

Sela, Avraham. "Transjordan, Israel and the 1948 War Myth, Historiography and Reality." *Middle Eastern Studies* 28, no. 4 (October 1992): 623–688.

Sharett, Yaakov. "Moshe Sharett V'Hakhrazat HaMedina." In *Shohar Shalom, Hebeitim U'Mabatim Al Moshe Sharett*, edited by Yaakov and Rina Sharett, (Tel Aviv, 2008), 277–295.

Shultz, Lillie. "Britain's Stake in an Arab Victory." *Nation*, May 29, 1948, 595–598.

———. "The Palestine Fight—an Inside Story." *Nation*, December 20, 1947, 675–678.

Silver, Abba Hillel. "We Need the Jewish State NOW!" *Jewish Spectator* (May 1945): 15–18

"Simpozyon al 'Leil Vingate' B'Veit HaRofeh B'Tel Aviv." *Hed HaHagana* 22 (May 1966): 124–132.

Slonim, Shlomo. "The 1948 American Embargo on Arms to Palestine." *Political Science Quarterly* 94, no. 3 (Fall 1979): 495–514.

Sneh, Moshe. "Min HaMeitsar." *HaAretz*, April 12, 1946.

Stanger, Carry David. "A Haunting Legacy: The Assassination of Count Bernadotte." *Middle East Journal* 42, no. 2 (Spring 1988): 260–272.

Stevens, Lewis M. "The Life and Character of Earl G. Harrison." *University of Pennsylvania Law Review* 104, no. 5 (March 1956): 591–602.

Stone, I. F. "The Morgan Affair in Perspective." *PM*, January 6, 1946.

———. "Warning Against A Sell-Out on Palestine." *PM*, October 19, 1947.

———. "The Word is Murder." *P.M.*, July 21, 1947

Sulzberger, Cyrus L. "Memories: Ethnic Stew." *New York Times*, December 28, 1977.

Tal, David. "The Forgotten War: Jewish-Palestinian Strife in Mandatory Palestine, December 1947–May 1948." *Israel Affairs* 6, no. 3–4 (Spring-Summer 2000): 3–21.

Tenenbaum, Baruch. "A Comforting Sense of Deja-Vu." *Jerusalem Post*, April 25, 2013.

Tokarska-Bakir, Joanna. "Communitas of Violence, The Kielce Pogrom as a Social Drama." *Yad Vashem Studies* 41, no. 1 (Jerusalem, 2013): 23–62.

Tripp, Charles. "Iraq and the 1948 War: Mirror of Iraqi Disorder." In *The War for Palestine: Rewriting the History of 1948*, edited by E. L. Rogan and A. Shlaim, 125–150. Cambridge, 2001.

Tugend, Tom. "Jerusalem Monument to Honor 1948 Volunteers." *Jerusalem Post*, December 11, 2017.

Van Devander, Charles, and James A. Wechsler. "Man in the Saddle; Arabian Style." *New York Post*, January 19 and 21, 1948.

Veiner, Eliyashiv. "Ehad V'Od Shlosh Esrei." *Makor Rishon*, *Deyukan*, June 27, 2014, 30–32, 34.

Venya (Hadari, Zeev). "MeiAhorei HaKela'im Shel Parasha Ahat..." *MiBifnim* 12, no. 2 (August 1948): 290.

Visberg, Ahareleh. "Hayom BaYom HaZeh MaMash." *Yisrael HaYom*, April 15, 2013.

Watts, Richard. "Koestler's Novel of Zionism." *New York Times*, November 3, 1946.

Welles, Sumner. "Elements of Security," *Washington Post*, March 30, 1948.

———. "New Hope for the Jewish People." *The Nation* 160 (1945): 511–513.

———. "Recognition of Israel." *Washington Post*, June 29, 1948.

Werdine, Robert. "The Truth About the Nakba." *Times of Israel*, May 17, 2012.

Welles, Sumner. "Recognition of Israel," *Washington Post,* June 29, 1948

Zahalka, Jamal. "Haluka B'Midron HaGeirush." *HaTsad HaSheini* 11 (February 1998): 16–19.

Zamir, Meir. "Britain's Treachery, France's Revenge." *Ha'Aretz* magazine, February 2, 2008.

———. "Espionage and the Zionist Endeavor." *Jerusalem Post*, November 20, 2008.

———. "The Secret 1947–1948 War between the British and French Intelligence Over the Birth of the State of Israel." *Ha'Aretz*, September 19, 2004.

———. "Uncovered: U.K. Intel Encouraged Arab armies to invade Israel in 1948." *Ha'Aretz*, September 14, 2014.

Zerubavel, Yael. "Numerical Commemoration and the Challenges of Collective Remembrance in Israel." *History and Memory* 26, no. 1 (Spring-Summer 2014): 5–38.

Newspapers

American Hebrew. January 9, 1948.

Baltimore Sun. August 22, 1945.

Chicago Tribune. October 6, 1946; December 2, 1946.

Cincinnati Times-Star. October 18–19, 1948.

Davar. September 3, 1947.

Department of State Bulletin, 1945–1948.

Ha'Aretz. October 28, 1945; March 18, 1947; June 6, 1947; August 10, 1947; September 14, 1947; October 14, 1947; November 30, 1947; July 27, 1950; November 30, 2014.

HaBoker. March 10, 1947; May 19, 1947; January 19, 1948.

Haganah, Jewish Resistance, 1947.

Hagana Reports, 1947.

HaMashkif. December 5, 1946; July 31, 1947; January 18, 1948; February 2, 1948.

HaYom. April 18, 1948.

Houston Chronicle. April 24, 1946; August 9, 1946; March 26, 1948; June 18, 1955.

Illustrated London News. July 10, 1948.

Jerusalem Post. July 9, 2006; October 28, 1996; May 22, 1981; November 29, 2017.

Jewish Agency Digest. 1948.

Jewish Telegraphic Agency. 1945–1948; May 27 and 28, 1952.

Kansas City Times. May 13, 1965.

Kol Ha'Am. August 13, 1947.

London *Jewish Chronicle*. November 13 and 16, 1945.

London *Times*. August 15, 1945; November 14, 1945; May 5, 1946; June 20, 1946; October 7, 1946; September 2, 1947.

Manchester Guardian. July 23, 1946; July 31, 2001.

Mishmar. October 16, 1946. December 17, 1947; January 18, 1948.

New Judea, 1945–1948.

New York Herald Tribune, 1945–1947.

New York Post. December 11, 1945; June 26, 1946; October 22, 25, and 28, 1946; November 4, 12, and 23, 1946; August 7, 1947; March 3, 1948.

New York Times. 1945–1948.

New York World-Telegram. November 19, 1945.

Palcor. 1945–1948.

Palestine Affairs. March 1947.

Palestine Post. 1945–1948.

Palestine Press Review. January 9, 1947.

PM. 1948.

S. A. Jewish Times. March 4, 1955.

The Scotsman. January 5, 1948; March 29, 1948.

Star-Journal and Tribune. February 8, 1948.

Tribune. May 20, 1946.

Washington Post. February 6 and 18, 1946; July 23, 1947; May 6. 1973.

Yediot Aharonot, December 19–20, 1946.

Zionist Review. June 15, 1945; May 3, 1946; June 21, 1946.

ZOA Bulletin. 1945–1948.

Interviews with the author

Akzin, Benjamin. July 2, 1972; August 19, 1976. Avigur, Shaul. August 19, 1976. Beeley, Harold. August 15, 1972. Ben Tov, Mordekhai. August 16, 1976. Berlin, Isaiah. July 1, 1976. Bernstein, Bernard. August 23, 1973.Bernstein, Nahum. March 24, 1977. Bernstein, Philip. June 3, 1974. Boukstein, Maurice. June 8, 1978. Boxenbaum, Joe. August 10, 1976. Broad, Shepherd. November 16, 1977. Butler, Neville. August 13, 1972. Buxton, Frank. July 10, 1979. Celler, Emanuel. June 9, 1975. Cohn, Joseph. June 8, 1976. Comay, Michael. August 15, 1976. De Sola Pool, Tamar. February 19, 1976. Dorr, Goldthwaite. August 22, 1973. Eban, Abba. December 4, 1974. Eilat, Eliyahu. June 14, 1972. Epstein, Judith. April 29, 1976. Farago, Ladislas. June 28 and 30, 1977. Friedman, Herbert. November 10, 1977. Ginsberg, Morris. July 7, 1977. Goldmann, Nahum. March 14, 1974. Goldstein, Israel. June 21, 1972. Goldstein, Melvin. February 23, 1978. Gross, Ernest. May 20, 1976. Gurfein, Murray. June 7, 1979. Halprin, Rose. September 29, 1972. Hammer, Gottlieb. December 6, 1977. Handler, Milton. May 26, 1978. Henderson, Loy. August 5, 1973. Holtzman, Fanny. May 11, 1976. Horowitz, David. June 27, 1972. Jessup, Philip. June 10, 1974. Kenen, Isaiah L. July 29, 1973. Kimche, Jon. June 27, 1976. Klarman, Yosef. March 2, 1978. January 14, 1982. Klausner, Abraham. May 19, 1976. Klotz, Henrietta. March 14, 1977. Kolitz, Zvi. August 25 and 28, 1975. Laub, Morris. August 14, 1973. Lelyveld, Arthur. January 11, 1973. Lerner, Max. May 7, 1979. Linton, Joseph. August 22, 1972. Lourie, Arthur. June 29, 1972. Martin, John. June 10, 1976. Mathieson, William. June 24, 1976. Miller, Irving. May 14, 1978. Monroe, Elizabeth. August 11, 1972. Montor, Henry. June 8 and 15, 1977. Nathan, Robert. August 9, 1973. Nesher, Aryeh. September 1, 1977. Netanyahu, Ben-Zion. November 15, 1973; June 2, 1974. Neumann, Emanuel. September 28, 1972; May 28, 1975. Rifkind, Simon. July 25, 1974. Robinson, Jacob. February 13, 1975; Rosenne, Shabtai, March 3, 1975; Rusk, Dean. December 29, 1975. Shapiro, Harold L. May 4, 1976. Shazar, Zalman. July 11, 1972. Stein, Leonard. August 13, 1972. Stone, I. F. February 1, 1978. Torczyner, Jacques. December 10, 1975. Tov, Moshe. August 17, 1776. Villard, Henry. May 17, 1976. Warburg, Edward M. October 27, 1977. Weisgal, Meyer. July 9, 1972. Yarden, Rachel. June 8, 1972. Yosef, Dov. June 21, 1972. Yuval, Moshe. June 12, 1972.

Miscellaneous

Akzin, Benjamin. "The United Nations and Palestine," September 1948, file A401/9, Central Zionist Archives, Jerusalem.

Aliav, Ruth. Cassettes 455–462. David Ben-Gurion Archives, Sdeh Boker, Israel.

"Anglo-American Competition in the Middle East." June 21, 1948, file 93/65/13, Israel State Archives, Jerusalem.

Aran, Ike. Cassette 50. Beit Lohamei HaGetaot Archives, Israel.

Arvey, Jacob. Letter to Monty Noam Penkower, May 26, 1977. (in the author's possession).

Avigur, Shaul. Interview with Jordan Penkower, December 1, 1977.

Avigur to Slutzky. January 9, 1967, file Avigur-16, Hagana Archives, Tel Aviv.

Avigur, Shaul. Cassettes 338–339. Ben-Gurion Archives, Sdeh Boker, Israel.

Avriel, Ehud. Cassettes 452–453. Ben-Gurion Archives, Sdeh Boker, Israel.

Beeley, Harold. Testimony, July 1978. Beit Lohamei HaGetaot Archives, Israel.

Beeley, Harold. Interview with Nicholas Bethell. February 1, 1967, file P-1784, Israel State Archives, Jerusalem.

Barker, Evelyn. Interview with Nicholas Bethell. July 28, 1976, file P-1784, Israel State Archives, Jerusalem.

Bernhard G. Bechhoefer, "Unity and Division in the Arab Opposition to the Palestine Settlement." October 29, 1948, U.S. State Department records, National Archives, Suitland, MD.

Begin, Menahem. Interview with Nicholas Bethell. December 20, 1978, file P-1784, Israel State Archives, Jerusalem.

Ben-Dror, Elad. "UNSCOP: Reishit Hitarvuto Shel HaUm B'Sikhsukh HaYisraeili-Aravi." Ph.D. dissertation, Bar-Ilan University, 2003.

Brailove, Mathilda. Oral history, April 25, 1975. United Jewish Appeal Archives, New York City.

Cassettes 28 and 30. Beit Lohamei HaGetaot Archives, Israel.

Chapman, Oscar. Interview with Jerry N. Hess, April 21, 1972. Harry S. Truman Presidential Library, Independence, MO.

Cohn, Josef. "Report on Dr. Weizmann's Visit to the U.S.A." Weizmann Archives, Rehovot.

Congressional Record—Appendix, January 30, 1948, A647–649.

Connelly, Matthew. Interview with Jeremy N. Hess, November 30, 1967. Harry S. Truman Presidential Library, Independence, MO.

Creech Jones, Arthur. Testimonies, October 29, 1958, file DS 126/4. Elizabeth Monroe MSS, St. Anthony's College, Oxford, England.

Crum, Bartley. Diary, January 1946. Gerold Frank MSS., Manuscripts and Archives Division, New York Public Library, New York City.

———. Letter to Elizabeth Monroe. October 23, 1961, file DS 126/4. Elizabeth Monroe MSS, St. Anthony's College, Oxford, England.

Cunningham, Alan. Interview with Nicholas Bethell, November 24, 1975, file P-1784, Israel State Archives, Jerusalem.

Dorr, Goldthwaite H. Oral history interview, 1962. Rare Books and Manuscript Library, Butler Library, Columbia University, New York City.

Dorr, Goldthwaite H. Oral history, 1962, Rare Book and Manuscripts, Columbia University, New York City.

Eban, Suzy interview, "November 29, 1947: The Story of a Vote." *Toldot Yisrael*. Jerusalem, 2009.

Eban, Aubrey. "A Credentials Ceremony," April 14, 1998. Harry S. Truman Presidential Library, Independence, Mo.

Economist Intelligent Unit. "Middle East Morass." April 8, 1948.

Elath, Eliahu. *Harry S. Truman—The Man and Statesman*. Jerusalem, 1977.

Eilat, Eliyahu. "Halakti Al Emdat Truman K'Lapei Yisrael...", Ma'ariv, October 22, 1971.

Epstein, Eliyahu memorandum, n.d. "Notes on the Military Strength of the Arab Countries," file 21/35-Het Tsadi, Israel State Archives, Jerusalem.

Etzioni, Amitai. Letter to the Book Review editor. *New York Times*, December 12, 1999.

Ewing, Oscar. Interview with J. R. Fuchs, May 2, 1969. Harry S. Truman Presidential Library, Independence, MO.

Feinberg, Abraham. Interview with Jerry N. Hess, January 21, 1972. Harry S. Truman Presidential Library, Independence, MO.

Feinberg, Abraham. Interview with Richard D. McKinzie, August 23, 1973. Harry S. Truman Presidential Library, Independence, MO.

Fierst, Herbert A. Memoir. U.S. Holocaust Memorial Museum, Washington, D.C., January 1, 1972.

Fligelman, Julius. Letter to Monty Noam Penkower, February 6, 1978 (in the author's possession).

"The Forgotten Refugees." www.davidproject.org.

Forrestal, James. Testimony, January 19, 1948. *Investigation of the National Defense Program*, 25448–25450. Washington, D.C., 1948.

Gelber, Yoav. "The Beginnings of the Palestinians' Mass-Flight." www.alisrael.com/1948_new.

Genosar, Shlomo. "Milhemet HaOlam U'Tekumat Yisrael," *Davar*, May 5, 1965.

Ginsburg–Postal interview, October 20, 1967. Bertha Schoolman MSS, Hadassah Archives, New York City.

Goldmann, Nahum to Neumann, Emanuel, November 23, 1966. Joseph Schechtman MSS, Zionist Archives, New York (now in the Central Zionist Archives, Jerusalem).

Goldwater, Monroe. March 1976, UJA oral history, United Jewish Appeal Archives, New York City.

Grady, Henry. "Adventures in Diplomacy" (an unpublished manuscript). Harry S. Truman Presidential Library, Independence, MO.

Granoff–Fuchs interview, April 9, 1969. Harry S. Truman Presidential Library, Independence, MO.

Gurfein, Murray. Revised Draft, May 2, 1978. Harry S. Truman Research Center (courtesy of Murray Gurfein).

Granoff, A. J. Remarks, May 22, 1965, at the Jacobson Memorial dedication, Tel Aviv (courtesy of A. J. Granoff).

Hammer, Gottlieb. March 17, 1975, UJA oral history, United Jewish Appeal Archives, New York City.

Harry S. Truman and the Recognition of Israel. Harry S. Truman Library Institute for National and International Affairs. Independence, MO, 1998.

Hearings Before the Anglo-American Committee of Inquiry, January 7, 8, 9, 10, and 13, 1946 (typescript). Washington, D.C., 1946.

Henderon, Loy. Interview with Richard D. McKinzie, June 14, 1973. Harry S. Truman Presidential Library, Independence, MO.

Herblock cartoon, "We Want to Make Our Position Perfectly Clear." *Washington Post*, April 14, 1948.

Horowitz, David. Oral history, March 20, 1964. Institue for Contemporary Jewry, Hebrew University, Jerusalem.

Hutschnecker memorandum, May 8, 1973, and De Costa to Hutschnecker, July 7, 1970, file K14a/92, Central Zionist Archives, Jerusalem.

Harry S. *Truman and the Recognition of Israel*. Harry S. Truman Presidential Library, Independence, Mo.

Henderson,Loy. Interview with Allen H. Podet, August 5, 1975, MS 163, 2/4, American Jewish Archives, Cincinnati, Ohio.

"In the Arab Camp" report, April 23, 1947, file S44/484, Central Zionist Archives, Jerusalem.

Jacobson, Gaynor. UJA oral history, June 14, 1977, United Jewish Appeal Archives, New York City.

Jewish Agency. *Supplementary Memorandum on Acts of Arab Aggression*, March 13, 1948.

Kenen, Isaiah L. "Feinberg, Abraham." Essay, February 16, 1973 (courtesy of I. L. Kenen).

Kenen, Isaiah L. June 10, 1977, Oral History Collection, American Jewish Committee Archives, New York City.

Klarman, Yosef. Interview with Ayala Dan-Kaspi, September 8, 1976. Hagana Archives, Tel Aviv.

Klarman, Yosef. Interviews, September 28, 1975; October 5, 1975; Klarman-Dan-Kaspi interview, n.d.; all in file A559/33, Central Zionist Archives, Jerusalem.

Klausner, Abraham. Interview, October 1978. Beit Lohamei HaGetaot Archives, Israel.

Krasno, Jean E. Interview with William Epstein, October 22, 1990. United Nations Archives, New York City.

Laski, Harold J. "A London Letter," July 12, 1946. Box 6, Clement Attlee Archives, University College, Oxford, England.

Laub, Morris. March 11, 1976, UJA oral history, United Jewish Appeal Archives, New York City.

Leith, David. "American Christian Support for a Jewish Palestine." Senior thesis, Princeton University, 1957, Princeton, NJ.

Levinthal, Louis. June 29, 1962, Oral history, Institute of Contemporary Jewry, Hebrew University, Jerusalem.

Lewis, Geoffrey W. Letter to the author, January 16, 1976.

Linton, Joseph I. "Memories of 1948," n.d. (my thanks to Dr. Josef Cohn for a copy).

Meir, Golda. Interview with Nicholas Bethell, May 24, 1977, file P-1784, Israel State Archives, Jerusalem.

Meir, Golda. Interview with Jeff Hodes, June 1965. United Jewish Appeal Archives, New York City.

Memorandum on the Administration of Palestine under the Mandate (Jerusalem, 1947).

"Middle East Morass," file OF39, White House Central Files, Harry S. Truman Presidential Library, Independence, MO.

Montor, Henry. Interview with Menahem Kaufman, April 15, 1976, and May 5, 1977. United Jewish Appeal Archives, New York City.

Morgenthau, Henry, remarks, July 24, 1947. UJA Executive Committee, file MRD-1, 432. United Jewish Appeal Archives, New York City.

Myerson, Goldie. "A Report from Palestine," January 25, 1948, file MRD-1, 37/2, United Jewish Appeal Archives, New York City.

Nadich, Judah. Testimony, October 1978. Beit Lohamei HaGetaot Archives, Israel.

Nash, Phileo. Interviews with Jerry N. Hess, August 19, 1966; October 17, 1966; June 8, 1967. Harry S. Truman Presidential Library, Independence, MO.

Nesher, Aryeh. June 15, 1977, UJA oral history, United Jewish Appeal Archives, New York City.

Neumann, Emanuel. Interview with Yehuda Bauer, June 21, 1967. Emanuel Neumann MSS (courtesy of E. Neumann).

Novikov, Nicolai. Telegram, September 27, 1946. digitalarchive.wilsoncenter.org.

"Palestine Partition and United States Security," February 1948, file Julius Klein-Palestine, Jewish War Veterans Archives, Washington, D.C.

Palmon, Yehoshua. Interview for the Hagana Archives, November 10, 1953, file P28/33, Central Archives for the History of the Jewish People, Jerusalem.

Phillips, William. Oral History interview, July 1951. Rare Book and Manuscripts, Butler Library, Columbia University, New York City.

Proskauer, Joseph. Interview with Jerold Auerbach, January 25, 1961. American Jewish History Oral History Interviews, Weiner Library, London.

Rabinovich, Abraham. "Underground in Italy," *Jerusalem Post* International Edition, July 8, 1995.

Rifkind, Simon. Interview, October 1978. Beit Lohamei HaGetaot Archives, Israel.

Robison, Al. Oral History Interview, February 16, 1977. Cassette 206, Ben-Gurion Research Institute, Sdeh Boker, Israel (courtesy of Al Robison).

Roper, Elmer. *A Survey of American Jewish Opinion on a Jewish State in Palestine*, October 1945. Zionist Archives, New York City (now in the Central Zionist Archives, Jerusalem).

Rothberg, Sam. May 4, 1976. UJA oral history, United Jewish Appeal Archives, New York City.

Sachar, David B. "David Niles and American Policy." Harvard College senior honors thesis, Harvard University, 1959.

Sanders, William. Memoir, August 1975. Harry S. Truman Presidential Library, Independence, MO.

Schwartz, Meir. *MiPort de Bouc Ad Hamburg: 50 Shana Le'Yetsiyat Eiropa 1947—"Exodus"* (1997), courtesy of Prof. Meir Schwartz.

Seligman, Man. Letter to the editor, *New Statesman*, August 4, 1972, 160–161.

Sharett, Moshe. Letter to the editor, *Jerusalem Post*, July 20, 1961.

Signatures on Jewish History, Stone and Levine. Weizmann Institute of Science, in Dewey Stone file, United Jewish Appeal Archives, New York City.

Smith, Trafford. "Last Days of the Palestine Mandate at Lake Success," May 3 and 12, 1948 (courtesy of Trafford Smith, now in Trafford Smith MSS, St. Antony's College, Oxford, England).

Sneh, Moshe. Interview with Yaakov Ro'i, April 7, 1970. Institute for Contemporary Jewry, Hebrew University.

Supplementary Memorandum on Acts of Arab Aggression (New York, 1948).

Toledano, Shmuel. Interview with Efrat Rosenberg, January 23, 2008. Channel 2, Israel TV.

Truman, Harry. Message to B'nai Brith Jacobson Memorial, Tel Aviv, May 22, 1965. A. J. Granoff MSS (courtesy of Leib Granoff).

Sonenborn, Rudolph. Interview with Jef Hodes, March 2, 1975. UJA oral history United Jewish Appeal Archives, New York City.,

Wilkins, Fraser. Interview with Richard D. McKinzie, June 20, 1975. Harrry S. Truman Presidential Library, Independence, MO.

Wilkins—Jessup interview, July 21, 1988. Library of Congress, Washington, D.C.

Windham, Ralph. "Kidnapped Off the Bench," file RG 72.16, 1784/4, Israel State Archives, Jerusalem.

Wright, Edwin. Interview with Richard D. McKinzie, July 26, 1974, with Wright letter, April 3, 1977, appended. Harry S. Truman Presidential Library, Independence, MO.

https://leonardbernstein.com/about/conductor/historic-concerts/beersheba-1948.

www.palyam.org/English/Hahapala/List_of_ships/.

http://www.shapell.org/manuscript/jfk-partition-plan-1948-truman.www.trumanlibrary.org/kids/poem.htm.

"*Yetsiat Eiropa (Exodus)*." Kol Yisrael broadcast, April 5, 1964. Beit Lohamei HaGetaot Archives, Israel.

Appendix

Now, UNO!

—Trafford Smith, 1948

War is lurking –
Ugly and devouring.
UN burking,
Situation souring.
Skies are murking,
USSR lowering –
What shall we do?

Arabs stalling –
Jewry dig their toes in,
Bergson balling,
Reinforcement goes in,
UN crawling
Dare not put its nose in –
I feel so blue!

Truman dithering
Chaos supervening
Silver slithering
Hasn't any meaning
Hopes are withering
On each other leaning –
Now, UNO!

Index

CPSIA information can be obtained
at www.ICGtesting.com
Printed in the USA
BVHW040536011019
559848BV00004B/28/P